D1452563

The Truth About Corporate Planning

International Research into the Practice of Planning

By the Same Author

HUSSEY, D. E.
Introducing Corporate Planning, 2nd Edition
Corporate Planning: Theory and Practice, 2nd Edition

HUSSEY, D. E. & LANGHAM, M. J.
Corporate Planning—The Human Factor

HUSSEY, D. E. & WILSON, L.
Social Responsibility—The Management Problem (Forthcoming)

TAYLOR, B. & HUSSEY, D. E.
The Realities of Planning

Other Titles of Interest

BEALE, J. G.
The Manager and the Environment

DAVIS, S. M.
Managing and Organizing Multinational Corporations

DONALD, A. G.
Management, Information and Systems, 2nd Edition

EILON, S.
Aspects of Management, 2nd Edition
Management Control, 2nd Edition

SASAKI, N.
Management and Industrial Structure in Japan

WILD, R.
Operations Management—A Policy Framework

ZAGER, R. & ROSOW, M. P.
The Innovative Organization: Productivity Programs in Action

A Related Journal

LONG RANGE PLANNING*

The Journal of the Society for Long Range Planning and of the European Planning Federation

Editor: Professor Bernard Taylor, The Administrative Staff College, Greenlands, Henley-on-Thames, Oxon RG9 3AU, England

The leading international journal in the field of long range planning which aims to focus the attention of senior managers, administrators and academics on the concepts and techniques involved in the development and implementation of strategy and plans. It contains authoritative and useful articles describing the approaches to long-term planning as practised by modern management in industry, commerce and government.

  * *Free specimen copy gladly sent on request*

The Truth About Corporate Planning

International Research into the Practice of Planning

Edited by

DAVID E. HUSSEY

Managing Partner, Harbridge House Europe

PERGAMON PRESS

OXFORD · NEW YORK · TORONTO · SYDNEY · PARIS · FRANKFURT

U.K.	Pergamon Press Ltd., Headington Hill Hall, Oxford OX3 0BW, England
U.S.A.	Pergamon Press Inc., Maxwell House, Fairview Park, Elmsford, New York 10523, U.S.A.
CANADA	Pergamon Press Canada Ltd., Suite 104, 150 Consumers Rd., Willowdale, Ontario M2J 1P9, Canada
AUSTRALIA	Pergamon Press (Aust.) Pty. Ltd., P.O. Box 544, Potts Point, N.S.W. 2011, Australia
FRANCE	Pergamon Press SARL, 24 rue des Ecoles, 75240 Paris, Cedex 05, France
FEDERAL REPUBLIC OF GERMANY	Pergamon Press GmbH, Hammerweg 6, D-6242 Kronberg-Taunus, Federal Republic of Germany

First edition 1983

Library of Congress Cataloging in Publication Data
Main entry under title:
The Truth About Corporate Planning.
Includes bibliographical references.
1. Corporate planning—Addresses, essays, lectures.
2. Comparative management—Addresses, essays, lectures.
I. Hussey, D. E. (David E.)
HD30.28.G58   1983   658.4'012   82-22250

British Library Cataloguing in Publication Data
The truth about corporate planning
1. Corporate planning
I. Hussey, David E.
658'4'012

ISBN 0-08-025833-6

Printed in Great Britain by A. Wheaton & Co. Ltd., Exeter

About the Author

David Hussey has had many years experience of corporate planning, as a practitioner in industry from 1964 to 1975, and as a consultant since 1976. He is managing partner of the British branch of a leading international firm of consultants. He is an internationally known authority on corporate planning and is the author of several books on the subject, including *Corporate Planning: Theory and Practice* (Pergamon 1974), which won the John Player Management Author of the Year Award. He was one of the founder members of the Society for Long Range Planning, and serves on the editorial board of *Long Range Planning* to which he contributes a regular feature.

Acknowledgements

All businessmen and practitioners owe a debt to those whose researches have helped to improve the quality of corporate planning. In particular I should like to thank those authors (and publishers) who have allowed their work to be reproduced in this collection.

Each contribution is accredited to the author and original publisher. Author affiliations are those at the time of original publication (as this is interesting to readers of the research). They are not necessarily the current affiliation of authors. Where current affiliations are known to be different they are footnoted.

Contents

x *Contents*

Introduction

Need for Better Strategy

Corporate planning has been with us for a long time. In the U.K. it began to be a key topic in the mid-sixties; in the U.S.A. the birth pangs came a little earlier; in many other countries it took a few years longer for the concept to catch on. By the mid-seventies it had become a world wide phenomena, and had survived its first real storm, the energy crisis of 1973/4. In the 1980s it continues as an essential part of the management process.

Over the 15-year period in which I have been involved in the subject there have been changes of emphasis as corporate planning has felt its way towards maturity. The way in which planning processes are applied now differ from the early days as do the aspects that are considered important. The belief that planning enables one to control one's own destiny has given way to a healthier, and more realistic, concept of managing strategy. The desired result in each case may be improved profits, but in my opinion the limited objectives of the second is more helpful to this end than the evangelism of the first.

A feature of any new slant to management theory or practise is the number of research studies that it spawns. Corporate planning is no exception, and the widespread introduction of planning into organisations had led to numerous questions, the answers to which are, often helpfully but usually incompletely, sought in research programmes of various types. Basic questions give way to more complex ones as the practise becomes more widespread. At first researchers want to know whether organisations have implemented corporate planning processes; a next logical point to uncover is whether planning contributes to profits; others might try to identify ways of making corporate planning more effective. Side by side with this is a stream of research into strategic analysis and decision-making; success or failure with acquisitions; the relationship of strategy and structure; the use of computers in strategic decision-making. Singly, these research studies provide useful seeds from which to grow better planning approaches. Put a number of them together and they offer the reader a great deal more.

Many authors of books on corporate planning draw heavily on the

I

published research. Many do not, either because they lack the necessary academic stringency, or because they are floating personal experiences or ideas which are new. Most readers do not have easy access to the body of research that is available. Research-based articles are published, but only the most enquiring are likely to track all of these down. Often the articles appear in journals which are difficult to locate without the service of a skilled librarian. Drawing linkages between research studies is therefore difficult for anyone but the serious student or academic.

This book begins to remedy this situation, by selecting a number of research-based articles, ordering the collection, and linking common themes with an integrating narrative. In this way the rich vein of research undertaken over a fifteen year period can be mined by anyone with an interest in the subject. The book also tries to advance the study of corporate planning, whether under its new name of "strategic management", or its old name "long range planning", positioning it as what it truly is; an integral part of the management process. If planning contributes to profitability, and research evidence suggests that it does, one possible way might be through the improvement of strategic decision making. That this is needed is demonstrated through a number of major studies. Channon (1973),[1] in a major U.K. study spawned by the Harvard Business School programme of research into strategy and structure, noted a number of strategic failings in much of British Industry; concentration on the soft options of the former Empire, rather than on the richer markets of Europe and the U.S.A.; misdirected research and development; failure to plan new product development; a lower rate of productivity increase than competitor countries; an accent on quality as perceived by production instead of attention to the needs of the market place; an acceptance of the American divisional concepts of organisation that was usually introduced by British compromise (without incentive bonus schemes and without properly setting senior management roles to create a true internal market place to compete for scarce resources).

The Commission of Enquiry into the Engineering Industry (1979)[2] ("Finniston Report"), admittedly with a slightly different focus to its area of study, produced a list of broadly similar failings, except that the statistical evidence supporting the report showed that if anything things had got worse during the 9 years since Channon's fieldwork. The between period had seen the virtual eclipse of a number of traditional British industries, of which the motor-cycle industry is perhaps the most memorable and emotive example.

So the evidence suggests that strategy is a major issue in the U.K., and any processes which contribute to better strategic management are worthy of study. Some might put it stronger. It is essential that ways be found to improve strategic management.

Equally worrying is that the U.S.A., a standard of comparison in both these reports, may itself be flawed. A report by *Business Week* (1980)[3] pointed to many problems similar to those identified in the U.K.; a flattening rate of productivity increase; misdirected research and development; strategic failure by management. There were other factors, too, but enough of a common thread to suggest that the need for better strategy is common to most of the developed world.

If evidence of relative failure points to a need, evidence of relative success may demonstrate the remedy. Japan is a striking example of a country with successful businesses, competing on an international basis and with an intensity that has caused the demise of many European and American industries. There are many factors which contribute to Japanese success: one at least is in the field of national and corporate strategy. This might be summed up as the identification of growth areas where volume production by the most modern, cost-effective methods gives an economic advantage that can be increased as output increases: the learning curve effect. Design and the final products pay close attention to the requirements of the market. The market attack moves area by area, frequently advancing segment by segment, so that optimum volume is achieved with one product before moving to the next. The defensive strategy in the markets attacked is usually a segmental retreat up-market, sacrificing volume in the belief that "they" will never match the needs of the up-market segments. Unfortunately, history has proved that "they" usually do. Obviously there is more to Japanese strategy than this, and as mentioned other factors also contribute to success. But Japanese businesses have demonstrated time and time again that there is a connection between success and good strategic decisions.

An inevitable question is whether planning can benefit strategic decision-making. Much of the research included in this book suggests that it can, but there are also many occasions when the planning process is so applied that the potential benefits do not arise. This too is a subject for this book. Before we consider the research findings, it is useful to give some thoughts to the aims of corporate planning, the nature of the planning process, the evolution of planning thought and some definitions of some of the terms. This last point is in many ways the most difficult since there is no commonly accepted glossary of planning terms, and consequently there are almost as many definitions as there are planning authorities.

The Aims of Corporate Planning

There are many reasons why organisations have turned to corporate planning. To some degree these explain why approaches to planning have gradually changed over time, as it has become apparent that the earlier approaches could be improved to bring results closer in line with expectations. Some of the very early approaches had a missionary fervour which led them to promise more than could be delivered. "Planning the control of corporate destiny" might be a good selling title for a seminar, but rather over-emphasises an aim which is virtually impossible to fulfil.

The basic aim of corporate planning is to improve results over time, so that they are better than otherwise would have been achieved. It seeks to do this by encouraging better strategic decisions and more effective implementation of those decisions, and this is achieved because planning aims to fulfil a number of specific needs.

* *Relation with the environment.* Modern business is affected by changes in the business environment to an ever-increasing degree, and one of the aims of corporate planning is to ensure that this is taken into account during the formulation of corporate strategy. The interface of the business and its environment is continually monitored through a good planning process. It is undoubtedly true that business has always been closely related to the environment in which it operates: it is hardly possible to argue, for example, that the Second World War or the Great Depression left businesses unaffected. Modern business faces a more complex situation, where the rapidity of change has become a critical factor, and the breadth of environmental forces has greatly expanded. At one time most books on corporate planning argued for attention to technical change, and quoted as examples the accelerating pace of developments in areas such as electronics. Technological change is still important, but modern business may be even more affected by social, political and economic factors which now have the power to overwhelm the unthinking businessman.

  The turbulence of the business environment turns forecasting into a lottery. Modern corporate planning serves the traditional purpose of keeping the company aware of its environment, *and* enabling the company to be flexible to outside changes. Policy options, alternative strategies and general increased responsiveness are major purposes of modern planning.

* *Charting a decision path to the future.* The wrong way to see a corporate plan is as a form of blueprint to be followed to the letter. For many years thinking corporate planners have argued that a main purpose of planning is to chart a potential map of the future, highlighting decision paths. Again the emphasis is on built in flexibility rather than a prescriptive course of action. The decision path approach enables the planning process to achieve the next purpose, without putting the company into a straitjacket.

* *Understanding the logical consequences of a course of action.* Major actions should have an effect on the fortunes of the firm. Planning tries to help the company think through these, not only in terms of probable profit

outcomes, but also in terms of their impact on structure, resource requirements, people, and future strategy. The relationship between structure and strategy has provided a fertile field for research, although the answers are still often ignored in practise. Strategic implications of a current decision have been explored through a variety of research and experiential analyses. Kitching[4] has shown through a series of studies in a variety of countries that the post-acquistion strategy needs to be thought out too. Many modern papers focus on techniques of analysis (for example portfolio analysis) and the criteria for success in a business sector. It is becoming increasingly obvious that expansion, whether organically or by acquisition, is dangerous unless the firm has a clear understanding of where this will lead, and knows the requirements for long-term success. The Japanese have repeatedly shown the world that the learning curve effect means that in some sectors of industry only the largest firms can survive.

One purpose of planning is to enable management to understand the overall shape of the decision path they are following: too often the decisions are like slices from a continental sausage and are perceived as flat circles rather than their true shape of a long, curved tube.

* *Co-ordination of the complex.* Another aim of corporate planning is to improve profitability through better co-ordination. In simple or-ganisations this may be a relatively easy task, designed to ensure that different organisational components work together and do the agreed things at the right time. The large multi-national, multi-product company faces extremely complex co-ordination problems of man-agement, resources and activity, and a good planning process will go a long way to solving these.

* *Involvement and participation.* A corporate planning process will assist companies to obtain a higher level of involvement of managers in the development of the organisation. How this involvement is obtained in a relevant way is an important criteria in the design of a planning process. The need for involvement if planning is to succeed is a theme which echoes loudly through much of the research on the criteria for successful planning. As will be seen in later sections of this book, planning frequently fails when line managers are not fully involved.

In theory, corporate planning could also be used as a vehicle to achieve widespread worker participation in an organisation. This was one of the philosophies behind the unsuccessful Planning Agreements initiative of the Labour Government in the U.K. in the mid-seventies. In practise planning is rarely used for this purpose at least in the U.K. and U.S.A., although there are examples of organisations which pass their corporate plan to their senior shop-stewards. (See Dugdale (1978)[5] for the practice of William and Glyn's Bank.)

Planning is frequently used as a method of communication up and down the organisation, and this is often a valuable aim of the planning process. This may be particularly important when an organisation is in a situation of major change, whether of top management or as the result of a crisis. The significance of a change situation causing companies to turn to corporate planning comes through much of the research into why companies have introduced planning.

The Nature of the Planning Process

There has been an evolutionary development of planning philosophies which will be discussed later in this chapter. Apart from the basic differences of philosophy, planning processes also vary in their application because of the differences between organisations: style, structure, geography and product complexity. Experienced planners are well aware of the way in which the generalised concepts are shaped and moulded to the particular needs of individual entities, although neither this aspect nor the evolution of planning figures much in the published research.

Although the fit of the concept to the organisation is a highly important variable, the generalised shape of a planning process has value as a starting-point. It is also the starting-point of much of the research.

Most descriptions of corporate planning systems contain a number of common elements, which are shown in Fig. I.1. Turning the system into a process of management requires a little more thought and is discussed later.

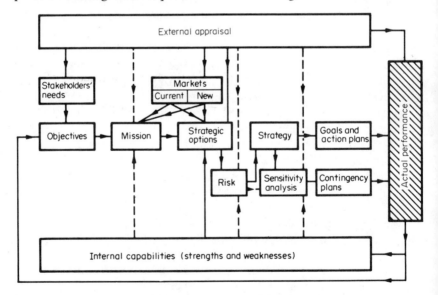

FIG. I.1. *Planning model*

Using Fig. I.1 as a guide, I should like to explore those threads which occur throughout the literature.

* *External appraisal.* One of the major purposes of planning is to relate the organisation to the business environment. The external appraisal is usually positioned as a study of the factors relevant to the business, including forecasts, so that the assessments can be woven into the corporate strategy. Put this way, the implication is that the organisation reacts to the threats and opportunities of the environment, and these words are frequently used to indicate the purpose of the external appraisal. Large organisations may employ a more active strategy, and can modify the environment in which they live: for example, by persuading governments to alter a policy or amend a law. The key nature of the environment has led many organisations to establish top-level external affairs/public affairs functions, whose jobs may include the development of a greater awareness of the environment, the influencing of that environment, and helping the organisation to position itself to respond to it.
* *Internal appraisal.* Another canon of the generalised planning system is that the organisation should know itself. The assessment of strengths and weaknesses, and the relation of these to the threats and opportunities of the external appraisal, provides the interaction which leads to strategic planning. The literature suggests many ways of approaching this task, most of it leading to a concept that has a great deal of face validity: that as far as is relevant plans should be made to correct weaknesses and build on strengths. Certainly a plan which ignores the capability of the organisation must run the risk of failure.

    Between the concepts of the external and internal appraisal are postulated a number of steps essential for the construction of a good plan.
* *Objectives.* A prime plank of many theories of planning is that the organisation should start by defining its objectives. What is it trying to achieve? Schools of thought vary, with some writers arguing that a business has only one real objective which is tied to the profit motive and duties to shareholders. In some books this is suggested as reaching some defined growth in earnings per share, although other profit figures have been postulated. Others argue that in some way the business objective must be to maximise the wealth of shareholders, and therefore should be set in terms of some growth in shareprices.

    There is also some evidence that many organisations do not in practice give much thought to the definition of objectives. Lindblom[6] suggests that it is counterproductive to define objectives, as in many instances agreement can be reached over a strategy by people who

hold conflicting views of the purpose of their organisation.
* *Mission.* Closely allied to the concept of objectives is that of mission. This attempts to answer the question "what business should we be in?". It is possible to develop an argument that this is in fact an answer to the question of which strategic options to choose. This is partly true, in that definition does in fact eliminate some possible courses of action. It can also save a great deal of time, in that definition of mission can cut down the effort put into identifying options which the organisation will never follow.

    Both mission and objectives should be seen as semi-permanent statements of purpose. They should be reviewed periodically, but the probability is that they will outlast several planning cycles. Most planning systems provide for their verification annually.
* *Selection of strategic options.* The heart of the planning system is always a selection from the strategic options available. Most planning systems give this as an overt output of the planning procedure. In defining strategy risk should be taken into account. While this simple step-by-step approach to planning fits the smaller organisation, it hardly does justice to the problems of the complex multi-national. It is for this reason that many complex companies use strategic portfolio analysis at this point in the planning system in order to determine the priorities of their various activities.
* *Sensitivity analysis.* Although the risks of every strategic option should be considered, as far as is possible, during the selection process, it is often useful to subject the whole plan to sensitivity analysis, to identify the overall impact of good and bad factors.
* *Action plans/goals.* The normal planning system will have some means of breaking down the strategic plans into action plans, and typically will relate these to the annual budget. The action planning phase, which will include the definition of goals (milestones which mark progress along the strategic path towards the objectives), is one of the links between planning and control. This is a link which has been explored by research, the general conclusion being that planning will fail if the link is absent.
* *Monitoring and control.* The systems will include the development of monitoring and control mechanisms for various aspects of the plan. Results will feed back to the next planning cycle.

    Most organisations break this general approach into a series of sub-plans. Time horizons may vary between sub-plans, or between the plan or different sectors of the organisation. The optimum length of the planning horizon does not seem to have been the subject of many research studies, although it has (as would be predicted) been found to vary between companies. There are obviously unique characteristics of firm or industry which affect the appropriate length of planning horizon, and the only answer to the question of whether plans should be for 3, 5, 7, 10, or whatever year is to fit the horizons to requirements and characteristics of the business.

Evolution of Planning Thought

Figure I.2 shows one way in which functions and sub-plans can be linked into a process of planning. This follows lines of thinking that began to change around 1975, when many organisations started to put more emphasis on strategy, and less on detailed operational plans. The planning time-horizon of many companies shrank, too, at about this time, as organisations began to be more aware of the discontinuous nature of many of the factors in the business environment.

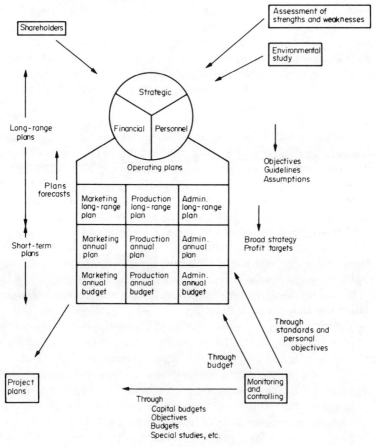

FIG. I.2. *Generalised planning system*

One approach is to divide the planning cycle into three slots: strategic review; corporate plan; annual plan. The first receives the most emphasis, and is a review of strategy against the background of internal and external issues and the expected trends. The analysis and discussion around this phase of the process forces the taking of broad directional decisions at the highest level, before the whole organisation is plunged into detailed plans which may be redundant. After the strategic review phase the steps bear a resemblance to those of Fig. 1.2. The dynamics of fulfilling them change dramatically (reference Hussey[7]).

A second solution which also emerged around the same time is scenario planning. This requires a greater level of sophistication than other forms and, as its name implies, is based on producing plans to respond to scenarios of various "futures" which the company might face. Typically two to three sets of strategic responses will be made, so that effectively the company is producing more than one strategic plan. There is a strong relation between scenario planning and contingency planning: both try to bring a degree of flexibility into management thinking.

Strategic review and scenario planning are latest variants and were not where planning started (nor, probably, will they be where planning finishes). The evolutionary tree goes something like this:

1. *Informal planning.* It would be wrong to claim that in the beginning there was no planning, for thinking managers have always given thought to their organisation's aims and strategic actions. Often the motivation that results from a clear sense of purpose emanating from an entrepreneur that knows that he is doing is as great as anything that can be achieved by formal means. Some of the research studies class the informal planners as "non-planners" in contrast to those who have a more formal approach, but this term should not be taken too literally.

2. *Extended budgeting.* It was logical for organisations with good budgeting systems to seek more perspective to the annual budget. The early solution to this, still used by some organisations, was to extend the budget for a further 2-3 years. The danger of this solution was that it tended to assume that no major changes would occur, and that most present trends and relationships would continue. As a plan, this approach had limited value. Many companies that used it (and some still do) would have considered that they did practise formal planning, and would have been classed with the planners in many research studies. The number of extended budget planners has been declining, and many have switched to a more advanced approach, while others have joined the planners at a more advanced stage in the evolutionary tree.

3. *Participatory approaches.* Early writers on planning followed experts on budgetary control systems in noting that planning was more effective when those who had to implement were involved in the process of planning (or budgeting). This gave rise to a number of approaches, with good and bad elements, the most common of which, bottom-up planning, is still used by many organisations. In its worst form, bottom-up planning can be an empty charade, causing a great deal of activity and paper generation with absolutely no impact on business results.

One common and misguided form of bottom-up planning is like taking a church collection. Everyone is asked to write a plan for his own area. All contributions are dropped in the corporate hat and, after inspection to query the obvious "duds" (the foreign coins of a church collection), are added up and called the corporate plan. "In the meantime, the Board Room carries on making strategic decisions outside the plan, which in time means that the whole system loses credibility and is seen in its true colours as a sham. The 'involvement' is also a sham; it is too narrow to be real and has little or no connection with the way the real decisions are made" (Hussey[8]).

Improvements that try to attain true participation have been tried by a number of organisations. The most common is the structured planning conference, where groups of managers work through a basic planning model, ending up with an action plan. To work, this approach needs a considerable investment in preparation as otherwise it is all too easy to miss out essential analysis.

A more sophisticated approach is to use a carefully designed organisational development approach to strategy, using an OD man as a change agent, and managed in a way that ensures commitment at all levels.

Participation is a key element in successful planning. It is not the only element, as analysis is also critical.

4. *Top-down approaches.* Some organisations have developed planning approaches which involve only a few people at the top of the organisation. Such an approach may be dominated by Operational Research techniques and computerised corporate models. Objectives are set without any participation of those who are expected to achieve them.

5. *Modern stages of evolution.* The most up to date approaches to planning have tried to improve the quality of analysis, to address the problems of uncertainty, and to gain a better blend of participative and analytical approaches. Three sub-systems can be distinguished, although in practise they are likely to be cumulative, in that the last sub-system will usually incorporate elements of the other two.

(a) *Strategic analysis (policy options)*. This type of approach rightly sees the differences of strategic decision-making at various levels of the organisation. It sees the top-level task as one of identifying and deciding between major strategic options, and puts emphasis on careful and well-researched analysis. Strategic portfolio analysis techniques are likely to be used.

(b) *Scenario planning*. The uncertainties in the future led to the use of improved environmental analysis techniques, and eventually to the type of scenario planning technique described earlier.

(c) *Strategic management*. The final evolutionary phase has been the concept of strategic management. Various planning processes may be developed to support this, usually blending behavioural and analytical concepts. One such approach is the strategic review approach already described.

It is important to stress that these various forms of planning, and some hybrid variations, all still exist. Various organisations may be at different points on the evolutionary tree. Even the most recent researchers into planning therefore run the risk that "planning" does not mean the same thing to each of the respondents.

In addition, researches carried out in the 1960s and early 1970s are likely to be on the earlier stages of evolution. In part the more recent stages have come about because of the problems and weaknesses identified in some of the earlier researches.

Definitions of Planning Terms

The lack of a common glossary has already been noted, and the discussion of the evolution of planning shows that even the term "planning system" may in practise mean very different things to different people. The research articles do not always define all the planning terms (and often this is not necessary), but the reader should be aware of potential semantic differences.

1. *Corporate planning*. Early writing tended to use the term *long range planning*, largely because the major new element was looking beyond the short term plan of the annual budget. Thus one of the earliest major pieces of published research (E. Warren[9]) was published as a book *Long Range Planning: The Executive Viewpoint*. Modern writers have accepted that planning should be comprehensive, and should embrace the short and the long term. Corporate planning, or comprehensive business planning, tends to be favoured as a more useful title. Steiner,[10] in a parallel research study to his survey reproduced later in this book, defined "comprehensive corporate planning" as:

"... the systematic and more-or-less formalised effort of a company to establish objectives, policies, and strategies to achieve objectives. ... The degree of formality will vary much.' He stressed that there are an infinite number of possible arrangements for planning, and his study mainly contrasted companies with some form of formal planning approach, with companies with "intuitive" approaches.

Irving,[11] in the thesis on which the article (see Chapter 4) by Taylor and Irving was based, used this definition of corporate planning:

1. The formal process of developing objectives for the corporation and its component parts, evolving alternative strategies to achieve these objectives, and doing this against a background of a systematic appraisal of internal strengths and weaknesses and external environmental changes.

2 The process of translating strategy into detailed operational plans and seeing that these plans are carried out.

Together the Steiner and Irving definitions appear to encapsulate what most writers and practitioners mean by the term corporate planning.

2. *Objectives.* Ackoff[12] provides a useful definition. "Desired states or outcomes are objectives. Goals are objectives that are scheduled for attainment during the period planned for." Ansoff[13] sees objectives as: "... decision rules which enable management to guide and measure the firm's performance towards its purpose." Argenti[14] takes up the concept of purpose, and argues that the real objective of an organisation is its *raison d'être* which is fundamental and un-alterable, and in the case of a company is tied to the concept of profit. Humble[15] takes the meaning of objectives closer to the views of the behaviouralists and links it to a concept of individual tasks and performance standards.

Ansoff[13] adds the concept of "constraints" "... decision rules which exclude certain options from the firm's freedom actions." He distinguishes these from the responsibilities which the firm may voluntarily accept as obligations.

Drucker[16] brings the concept of mission, which "... requires management to decide what business the enterprise is engaged in, and what business it should be engaged in".

It is possible to see the general term "objectives" as having each of these meanings. Many writers divide the term into:

1. Primary objective, or purpose of the firm which is semi-permanent.
2. Mission: what business should the firm be engaged in?

3. Goals: "milestones" derived from strategy and which provide a means of controlling progress towards the primary objectives.
4. Standards of personal performance: related to goals *and* the job of the individual.

But be warned. Some authorities use the term goals to mean the primary objective, and the term objectives to mean goals! In addition others blur the first two meanings I have given.

3. *Strategy.* Strategy may be seen as the major means by which the company tries to achieve its objectives. Kempner[17] provides some useful comments:

Strategy. A proposed action or sequence of actions intended to have a far reaching effect on the company's ability to achieve its objectives. Strategy is often confused with policy and with tactics. Policy decisions are wider than strategic which in turn are wider than tactical decisions. Policy decisions often remain valid for a decade or more. Strategic decisions may remain valid for a period of several months to several years. Tactical decisions usually refer to a period of less than a year: these time-spans can only be an approximate guide. While policy decisions can include the setting of overall company objectives and constraints as well as means, strategic decisions usually refer only to means.

Note that strategy may take on a different meaning according to level in a complex organisation. At head office level strategy may be seen as management of the strategic portfolio in relation to the changing environment, and from this level all activities of divisions may be considered "operational". At the level of the division there will be a major portion of this operational task which is rightly seen as strategic. Similar differences of perception may occur between the division and its own sub-units.

Similarly objectives and strategy may change according to hierarchial perception as part of its strategy Head Office may define the role of each division. This definition is seen by the division as part of its objectives.

4. *Strategic plan.* Hussey[15] states "I see the strategic plan as something which defines the objectives of the organisation and the means by which those objectives are to be attained". Steiner[18] says "Strategic planning is the process of determining the major objectives of an organisation and the policies and strategies that will govern the acquisition, use, and disposition of resources to achieve those objectives". What is strategic depends, as mentioned above, on the hierarchial level in the organisational structure. Apart from an occasional confusion of the strategic task at corporate level with that at subsidiary level, most authorities would accept these definitions.

5. *Operational (operating) plan.* I see these as essentially a sub-set of the total strategic task, and as the plans for an existing area of business.

Denning,[19] another author who has contributed to planning through research and whose work is included in this book, states operating plans to be ". . . the forward planning of existing operations in existing markets with existing customers and facilities".

6. *Environment.* The corporate planner generally uses this term to mean the total business environment in which the firm operates. It therefore embraces economic, political, social, demographic, technological, legal, ecological and infrastructure factors. The term "environmental scanning" is used to mean the process of continually monitoring and analysing information on this environment. "Environmental appraisal" is a study of the corporation in relation to its environment. Sometimes the word "external" is used in place of "environment".

To a scientist the term environment may have a different, although possibly related meaning. A manager in the automative industry will almost invariably perceive the term as relating only to emissions control on engines. There is, therefore, a need to be sure that the wider planning meaning is understood.

7. *Corporate appraisal.* Several terms are used to mean the process of assessing strengths and weaknesses, opportunities and threats within an organisation. Frequently there is a division between "external appraisal" (see "environment" above) and "internal appraisal". The word "audit" is sometimes used to replace "appraisal". Acronyms are also used by some to describe this activity:

SOFT   : (Strength, opportunity, fault, threat).
SWOT   : (Strength, weakness, opportunity, threat).
WOTS-UP   : (Weakness, opportunity, threat, strength, underlying planning).

8. *Strategic management.* A modern term which may be defined as strategic planning plus something. It is the concept of continually *managing* all aspects of the company's strategy and its relationship with the business environment.

Organisation of this Book

The research papers have been divided into four parts:

1. The extent of and reasons for planning.
2. Does corporate planning pay?
3. Criteria for success or failure.
4. Particular aspects of planning (for example, acquisition, use of computers).

To some extent these divisions are artificial and overlap. Some insight into reasons for planning success or failure is provided by some of the papers under the first heading. The connecting editorial narrative attempts to draw attention to items of particular interest.

The editorial introduction to each part also links the selected papers to other research studies which could not be included for various reasons (copyright, length: some findings fill an entire book, or repetition where the research paper was very similar to material selected for this book). The final task of the editorial sections is to draw out common threads from the findings, and to show how one piece of research supports or explains the findings of another.

The papers selected all speak for themselves, and with the exception of the Society for Long Range Planning's Membership survey have not been subject to any editorial changes.

They make fascinating reading, and will add to the skills and knowledge of anyone who is concerned with management and business planning, whether as student, teacher, researcher, or practitioner.

References

1. D. C. Channon (1973) *The Strategy and Structure of British Enterprise*, MacMillan.
2. Comission of Enquiry into the Engineering Industry (1979) *Engineering Our Future*, H.M.S.O.
3. Business Week (1980) *The Reindustrialisation of America*, June 30th, 1980.
4. (a) J. Kitching (1967) Why do mergers miscarry?, *Harvard Business Review*, November–December 1967.
   (b) J. Kitching (1973) *Acquisitions in Europe: Causes of Corporate Successes and Failure*, Business International, Geneva.
5. I. Dugdale (1978) Corporate planning and control systems in William and Glyn's Bank. *Long Range Planning*, October 1978.
6. C. E. Lindblom (1959) The science of muddling through. *Public Administration Review*, Volume 19, Spring 1959.
7. D. E. Hussey (1978) *Corporate Planning in Inflationary Conditions*, Institute of Cost and Management Accountants.
8. D. E. Hussey (1981) *Corporate Planning: An Introduction for Accountants*, Institute of Chartered Accountants in England and Wales.
9. E. K. Warren (1966) *Long Range Planning: Executive Viewpoint*, Prentice Hall.
10. G. Steiner (1972) *Pitfalls in Comprehensive Long Range Planning*, Planning Executives Institute.
11. P. Irving (1970) *Corporate Planning in Practice: A Study of the Development of Organised Planning in Major U.K. Companies*, M.Sc. Dissertation, University of Bradford.
12. R. C. Ackoff (1970) *A Concept of Corporate Planning*, Wiley–Interscience.
13. H. I. Ansoff (1965) *Corporate Strategy*, McGraw Hill.
14. A. J. A. Argenti (1968) *Corporate Planning: A Practical Guide*, Allen & Unwin.
15. D. E. Hussey (1974) *Corporate Planning: Theory and Practice*, Pergamon.
16. P. Druker (1969) *Managing for Results*, Pan.
17. T. Kempner (Editor) (1976) *A Handbook of Management*, Penguin.
18. G. Steiner (1969) *Top Management Planning*, MacMillan.
19. B. W. Denning (1971) *Corporate Planning: Selected Concepts*, McGraw Hill.

PART 1

The Extent of and Reasons for Planning

Introduction to Part 1

Extent of Planning

There has always been a great interest among researchers in the extent to which planning is practised, the reasons for planning, and what is included in corporate planning activity. Among the first researches I have discovered are those of two U.S. organisations: the Stanford Research Institute (SRI) and the Conference Board. Both have extended their interest into all aspects of planning. Unfortunately, the publications of SRI are generally confidential to subscribers and cannot be accessed by most of us. However, SRI have very kindly allowed me to include an article based on a study of planning in a number of U.S. companies (Ringbakk, Chapter 1). Worth mentioning, for those who can get hold of it, is their parallel study of planning in Western Europe (V. Schuller-Gotzburg and Dawson[1]).

One of the early Conference Board Studies led to an article which showed that by 1966, in the U.S.A., over 90 % of manufacturers practised some form of formal planning. (Brown, Sands and Thompson[2]).

In the U.K., one of the first surveys to be published appeared in 1968 (Kempner and Hewkins[3]). The findings of this study, that few British companies had implemented corporate planning while a number of executives rejected it completely, were widely published, although the full report was not publicly available. It was to be expected that planning would not have been widespread across the U.K. at that time, but the almost complete absence observed in this research caused some surprise. Researches published later help explain the Kempner and Hewkins findings. It achieved a sample of only 24 respondents, 3 from finance and insurance and the remainder spread over 13 industrial classifications. At around the same time, Denning and Lehr carried out a survey with 300 respondents, although this was not published until 1971 (Chapters 2 and 3). This larger sample showed that 22 % of companies had a corporate planning system, but that only in 10 standard industrial classifications were more than 25 % of companies engaged in planning. In some industries planning had clearly not started. In others it had clearly taken off. Chemicals and Allied Industries had 52 % of its companies involved in planning. This industry was not represented in the Kempner and Hewkins study.

If it were needed, further endorsement of the Denning and Lehr findings comes from the Society for Long Range Planning's survey (Chapter 5). This showed that about 25 % of its 385 respondents had introduced corporate planning in 1968 or earlier, and that the date of introduction varied greatly by industry. For example, the median year of introduction for Banking, Insurance and Finance was 1971, with very few having any involvement before 1967. For the data as a whole, the median year for introducing corporate planning was 1970 (although for some industries it was as early as 1968). The last year of the Society data was 1973, and by this time some 86 % of the respondents practised corporate planning.

These two surveys give a very good picture of the growing popularity of planning in the U.K.

Eppink, Keuning and de Jong (Chapter 7) studied planning in Holland, and believe from their findings that the state of formal planning lagged the U.K. by about 5 years. Their small sample of 20 revealed that 85 % were planning by 1974, but that for 80 % planning was only introduced after the 1970s. It would be unwise to generalise too far from this finding, although other aspects of the study are useful.

Kono (Chapter 6) compares planning in Japan with that in the U.S.A. and found 77 % of Japanese companies and 85 % of U.S. companies had a long range plan in 1975.

Csath (Chapter 12) provides a study of strategic planning in Hungary, suggesting that some aspects of management at least are common throughout the world. There is thus clear evidence that planning is widely practised internationally. Is there any evidence to suggest that the findings apply to business regardless of its size? Chapter 10 shows the results of a survey by Bhatty which examined medium-sized companies in the U.K. during 1978. His sample of 26 suggested that only 46 % of medium sized companies practised planning and that for most it was an activity begun in the 1970s. It would be unwise to speculate whether this finding could be extended beyond the sample.

Some insight into strategic planning in small business in the U.S.A. is provided by Unni in Chapter 11.

Reasons for Planning

There is some interesting evidence that points to the reasons why companies practise corporate planning. Taylor and Irving (Chapter 4), in a study of a number of companies which applied corporate planning, found that the stimulus was often a major change. Only 18 % of their sample identified no specific trigger. By for the biggest stimulus was some top management change (36%), but among the other causes listed were exposure to outside influences, technological developments, merger, or reaction to a critical situation.

Denning and Lehr (Chapter 3) found that the rate of technological change was a major factor in the introduction of planning. Ringbakk (Chapter 1) mentions that companies often do not make the adjustments needed to introduce planning "except under crisis conditions".

The SRI[4] study, on which Ringbakk's article was based, listed a number of externally caused reasons for organised planning: dynamics of the environment and changing business conditions, increased competitive pressures, market changes and technological development. Internal reasons included the increased size of the organisation.

Size and capital intensity were also found to be important in the Denning and Lehr survey.

The limited evidence of the Eppink, Keuning and de Jong survey (Chapter 7) suggest that the two most important reasons for planning were "top management advocacy" and "recommendations of management consultants". However, presumably these were the trigger, but not the real cause.

Kono (Chapter 6) gives the high growth of the Japanese economy, technological innovation and short product life cycles, severe competition between corporations, and National Economic plans on the most important background reasons behind the high incidence of corporate planning in Japan.

The Nature of Corporate Planning

With the evidence suggesting that crisis and change are direct causes of the introduction of corporate planning it is surprising to find that, in the U.K. at least, as many as 34% of organisations do not formally forecast events outside the organisation, while some 75% have no contingency plans (Society for Long Range Planning survey, Chapter 5). This issue will be referred to again in Part 4.

The Society's survey lists some of the activities undertaken under the umbrella of corporate planning. What was perhaps the most surprising was the comparatively small proportion of respondents who formally attempted organisation, manpower or diversification planning.

Deficiencies from the ideal were also observed by Ringbakk in his U.S. survey (Chapter 1), who noted "great variations in the completeness and quality of plans". Taylor and Irving also observed that there were great deficiencies in the planning efforts of a high proportion of the companies they surveyed. These deficiencies are perhaps one reason for the theme of chief executive dissatisfaction that runs through so many of the surveys, from the earliest studies to the study by Bhatty (Chapter 10) which is one of the most recent in terms of time. This theme will be returned to in Part 3, which will look at the research evidence which shows how planning can be improved.

Gouy (Chapter 8) provides insight into the way strategic decisions are made in large European companies. He shows, for example, that the marketing function is likely to exercise relatively more influence on strategic decision making than in France, where finance is seen as more significant. He also reveals that computers play little part in *strategic* decision-making in Europe. Although Gouy's overall sample of 47 firms is significant, the breakdowns by country are less so. Some of the industry samples are very small indeed and the findings should be interpreted carefully.

Read together, the surveys selected in this part provide a great deal of information on the scope of corporate plans, and the length of the planning horizon. Five years is the most common planning horizon, although press articles have suggested a recent tendency to reduce the horizon. Whether the 3-year horizon found by Bhatty is an endorsement of this tendency, or is applicable only to the medium-sized companies he surveyed is a matter of pure speculation.

The Corporate Planner

Some aspects of the top management/planner relationship have been investigated more thoroughly by research into the success or failure of corporate planning, and will be returned to later. Ringbakk (Chapter 1) found that 4 out of every 10 of his respondents cited the problem of gaining top management support for planning Taylor and Irving (Chapter 4) stressed the need for personal involvement of the chief executive: they found, however, that 26 % of their respondents had planners who did not report to the chief executive. The Society for Long Range Planning (Chapter 5) found from their large sample that 48 % of corporate planners did not report to the chief executive, while 52 % did.

The most comprehensive background information on the qualifications and experience of the corporate planner in the U.K. is provided by the Society's survey, although Taylor and Irving (U.K.) and Eppink, Keuning and de Jong (Holland) provide interesting information from their studies. From the Society's findings we know that some 83 % of planners have a university degree and 82 % belong to a professional body in addition to the Society for Long Range Planning. Management (23 %) is the most popular professional body, followed by accountancy (17 %). The most common degree specialisations are economics (21 %) and engineering or science

(26 %). Some three-quarters of those responsible for the planning function are likely to be between 31 and 50 years of age, and the typical planner is likely to be over 36. He is likely to have had less than 5 year's experience of corporate planning. As approximately two-thirds of planners are appointed from within the organisation, the planner's experience with that organisation is likely to be longer than his experience with planning.

Has the lack of experience of corporate planners (which of course was inevitable in the earlier years) and the tendency to recruit from within been a contributory factor in the lack of satisfaction of a high number of respondents of many of these surveys? It is reasonable to assume that this may be the case. There is limited evidence that consultants are not as widely used as they might be to make up for these deficiencies. In the U.S.A. one survey (Brown and O'Connor[5]) suggests that only 27 % of companies used consultants to help introduce corporate planning: in Europe one would expect this figure to be lower and Gouy's survey suggests that only 2 of his 47 respondent companies used consultants for planning work. The research findings suggest that corporate planning, although widely used, is perhaps not quite as easy to do well as might be thought. Consequently, although there is evidence of success, which will be discussed in Part 2, there is also evidence that many aspects require careful attention if planning is to work. The factors which contribute to success or failure are the subject of Part 3.

Factors which Influence the Planning Process

Al Bazzaz and Grinyer (Chapter 9) provide a bridge between this section of the book and Part 3, in concentrating on identifying the factors which influence the breadth of planning responsibilities, the nature of contributions to the process and those which create difficulties within the process. Finally, the authors examine the factors which influence changes required in the process. They found considerable variability within their sample of 48 U.K. companies (the survey date was 1974), although on the whole the state of the art was very much as described by other researchers. They felt that the uncertain environment after 1974 was leading to a greater dissatisfaction with formal systems.

This dissatisfaction is possibly one of the causes in the greater emphasis on strategy that is now found in planning processes and which appear more definitively in the study by Gluck, Kaufman and Walleck (see Part 3, Chapter 23).

References

1. V. V. Schuller-Gotzburg and R. W. Dawson (1971) *Organised Planning in 50 West European Companies*, Stanford Research Institute.

2. J. K. Brown, S. S. Sands and G. C. Thompson (1969) Long range planning in the U.S.A.—NICB, *Long Range Planning*, March 1969.
3. T. Kempner and J. W. M. Hewkins (1968) *Is Corporate Planning Necessary?*, British Institute of Management.
4. K. A. Ringbakk and R. W. Dawson (1968) *Organised Planning in 40 Major U.S. Corporations*, Stanford Research Institute.
5. J. K. Brown and R. O'Connor (1974) *Planning and the Corporate Planning Director*, Conference Board, U.S.A. (Report 627).

Further Research References

6. J. C. Higgins and R. Finn (1977) The organisation and practice of corporate planning in the U.K., *Long Range Planning*, August 1977.
7. J. W. Gotcher (1977) Strategic planning in European multinationals, *Long Range Planning*, October 1977.
8. S. J. Bazzaz and P. J. Grinyer (1981) Corporate planning in the U.K.: The state of the art in the 70's, *Strategic Management Journal*, Volume 2.
9. J. Stoppard and T. Kono (1981) *Long Range Planning Practices of Japanese and U.K. Companies*, unpublished analysis of a mail survey.

1

Organized Planning in Major U.S. Companies

K. A. RINGBAKK

Organized Corporate Long-Range planning is neither as well accepted nor as well practiced as suggested by the literature on the subject. Although much planning is done, the effort is often sporadic, it is lacking in co-ordination, and it is less formalized and sophisticated than much of the literature suggests. Neither corporate nor division managers have fully accepted organized planning as part of their responsibility. Without the wholehearted support of line executives, the planning in many cases has been more in words than deeds. It therefore is appropriate to evaluate current corporate planning practices in terms *how* advanced and how formalized is this management function. Looked at empirically, the conclusion is that organized corporate planning is still in its early evolutionary stages. Although substantial advances have been made from the era of no formal planning, there still are substantial improvements ahead and there are major developments to be made before its true potentials are realized.

These general conclusions and the detailed presentation that follows are the result of a large-scale study begun in 1967. This study was carried out under the auspices of Stanford Research Institute and was completed while the author was on the faculty of The Graduate School of Business at The University of Wisconsin, Madison. The objective of the study was to determine how leading United States corporations formally plan for the future and to ascertain the characteristics of the *best* and most *advanced current* planning practices and philosophies. The focus of the study was on organized corporate planning in firms that have some experience with such planning. In selecting companies to be interviewed, efforts were made to select those that were known to have formalized their planning. The

This article was originally published in *Long Range Planning*, Volume 2, No. 2, December 1969. Much of the material it contains is the copyright of the Stanford Research Institute, with whose permission the article is reproduced.

sample was also selected to include companies that represented industries with different technologies, different markets, and different geographic locations. To make it possible for our researcher to do all the interviewing, the number of companies included in the sample was limited to forty. In these forty leading corporations, the author personally interviewed the corporate planning executives. In about one quarter of the companies two planning executives or corporate executives participated in the interview.

Nearly all of the forty corporations studied have widely diversified product lines. They serve different markets, ranging from 100 per cent military and government to 100 per cent consumer goods. Most of the companies are active in international business. In terms of corporate structure, 90 per cent are multidivisional and decentralized.

It should be noted that this sample is not a random sample. Statistical inferences about organized corporate practices in big business in general are thus not warranted. However, since efforts were made to include those companies that were supposedly doing the *best* job in planning, it can reasonably be assumed that *business firms in general are doing less* than the companies surveyed. This justifiable inferences are thus related to the fact that business in general more likely is doing a much lesser job in their planning. This is important to keep in mind when evaluating the findings.

It has long been accepted that corporate long-range planning is an integral part of management's work and responsibility[1]. Many writers have further argued that managers in practice *do* what the textbooks say they should do; i.e. it is suggested in the literature that corporate planning is practiced extensively and well. A note of interpretation should be inserted to qualify this. In most surveys undertaken to ascertain the extent and format of long-range planning practices, mailed questionnaires have been used to collect the necessary data. This is, of course, a very blunt research instrument and the opportunity to go into depth or probe is virtually nonexistent. Since corporate long-range planning is such a nebulous and amorphous subject, one may rightly question the validity of inferences and conclusions drawn after using mail surveys only to collect data on this aspect of managerial activities. Thus, there may have been an overstatement of facts, overlooking of inadequacies, and over-emphasis of data validity—particularly when the response rates have been low. And because of the use of inadequate research tools and correspondingly weak data on which the conclusions are based, many of the findings may not adequately portray reality.

Having observed the dichotomy implied in the early recognition of the paramount importance of planning (e.g.: Henri Fayol; see the reading list at the end of the article) and the recent wave of interest in the subject as reflected in a proliferation of articles, books, speeches, seminars and management conferences on the subject, a study was designed to determine what the state of the art actually is. Specifically, the objective of the study was to determine how leading United States corporations formally plan for the future and to ascertain the characteristics of best current planning practices and philosophies.

For the purpose of this study, the following definition was adopted:

Corporate planning is the formalized process of developing objectives for the corporation and its subparts as well as developing and evaluating alternative courses of action, doing this on the basis of a systematic evaluation of external threats and opportunities and internal audit of strengths and weaknesses.

Several interpretative points about this definition are in order.

1. *Planning is a process.* As such it should be undertaken at different management levels in an organization. The process should be a continuous one since the dynamics of business require more or less continuous changes in business behaviour. The process can deal with different levels of problems and is essentially the same regardless of organizational or management characteristics.

2. *The process is the most fundamental and the plans are the outputs of the process.* As such the plans are not to be treated, synonymously with planning although they may adequately reflect the planning process. The plans of necessity are developed at given points in time and lack the capacity of continuous adaptation as environmental changes make adjustments necessary. This means that the continuous planning process may require or infrequent outputs of formal plans, the frequency depending on the rate of changed realized by the firm and flexibility in the plans.

3. *The greater the complexity of the decision-making, due to the dynamics of business and company size and inflexibility, the more likely it is that a formal planning system will be required where different management groups perform parts of the process.* When referring to planning in terms of a system, the concern is with who is responsible for carrying out which tasks in the planning process, who is responsible for generating the various inputs such as forecasts, premises, and assumptions, and what procedures have been set up to perform the planning process.

4. *Corporate planning covers different time horizons.* The formal planning system must therefore be designed to permit the necessary flexibility to make adaptive change possible. To deal with the different levels of problems and to permit the interaction and co-operations among different management groups, the planning system must be designed to meet the unique needs of the organization. This means that no one universal planning system can be developed which can be applied equally well to different organizations.

Stated differently it can be said that corporate planning is pre-action analysis and decision-making in the face of uncertainty, as related to the allocation of the firm's scarce resources.

Figure 1.1 illustrates basic steps and activities considered in this study. This model suggests there are certain properties and inputs which can be considered necessary conditions for effective planning to take place. These for research purposes can be translated into hypotheses to be subjected for testing. For the purpose of this discussion it will suffice to identify the most important of these conditions and ascertain to what degree they were found in the companies studied.

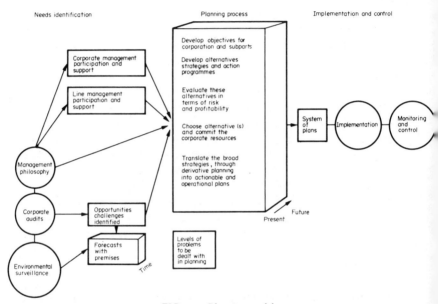

FIG. 1.1 *Planning model*

1. *There must be management support for corporate planning.* This support should take the form of active participation and must be present at the corporate as well as operating levels. It can be argued that this is the most fundamental condition which must be met since staff planners alone cannot do the planning. It has been pointed out that planning and doing are two parts of the same job. Of necessity the doer must be the planner and lack of support for planning means that the doer will go on with his tasks without proper attention to the future implications as well as significant inter-relationships between activities when making his decisions. Because of the paramount importance of such management support and because of the

surprising responses regarding these, the findings and implications of the response are discussed in some detail.

2. *One can argue in favour of developing comprehensive planning documents that cover all aspects of the firm's activities in an integrated.manner.* Such documents serve the purposes of fostering consensus as well as communications, they ensure clarification of unresolved conflicts, and they help the executive identify major issues that must be dealt with. As such, the plans can be treated as a measure of the quantity and quality of planning done.

3. *Data inputs required in the planning effort should be developed in a systematic, explicit fashion.* These inputs can be classified as internal and external. The internal data inputs will usually be developed on the basis of the financial and accounting data commonly available as a function of past business activities. Ideally they should be developed on the basis of corporate audits so that all strengths and weaknesses are identified. External data should be developed through environmental surveillance in order to understand what the threats and opportunities in the environment are. These inputs should be made explicit so that they can be communicated throughout the corporation and the assumptions and premises developed should be set forth in writing.

4. *These objectives for the corporation and its subparts should be formalized and they should be comprehensive enough to cover the major factors affecting corporate success.* Without specifying all the properties of the model in detail, the reader from the following discussion of the findings and the corresponding interpretations will be able to judge the relevancy of the conclusions drawn. More detailed but implicit part of the model are also brought out in the discussion of the significance of the various findings.

Organized corporate planning is not as well accepted or as well practised as commonly assumed. A major reason for that is that in many cases neither corporate nor division managers have fully accepted formal planning for more than the budgeting period as part of their responsibility. This was found in several ways to be a major problem in current corporate planning practices. It is seen in Table 1.1 where the corporate executive in charge of planning was commenting on the most crucial problem realized in his company's planning efforts.

More than half the respondents, 53 per cent, cited their major problem as that of getting operating managers to accept planning as part of their job and to do the planning for their area of responsibility. One vice-president said that the single most important problems faced in his organization was to "sell line personnel on the value of planning as a tool for day-to-day operations".

TABLE 1.1. *Most crucial problems faced in corporate planning*

Type of problem	Percentage[a]
Getting operating management's acceptance of and participation in planning	53
Getting corporate management's support for the planning function	39
Need to improve forecasting and the quality of the informational inputs	36
Inadequate thinking in terms of the future and understanding of those factors of importance to long-term success	36
Lack of realism and conciseness in the plans due to lack of analytical thinking	36

[a] The percentage is based on the frequency with which these problems were cited. All statistical information is based on this planning study.

Another executive was rather blunt when he said: "The key problem is to change the very conservative operations thinking in some influential spots in management. To get this change has led to one of the nastiest, dirtiest political problems I have faced in planning. It is a very difficult issue."

From the same table of findings can be seen that about four in ten of the survey companies pointed to *the problem of getting top management's support for corporate planning*. Together, the acceptance of planning by operation management and corporate management constitute the most frequent and the most serious problems in planning. One newly appointed planning vice-president who previously had been in charge of one of his corporation's many divisions referred to the major problem as an "educational process". He suggested that "the real problem is to make the department and division heads prepared for the planning job". Another planning executive, working for a corporation that has one of the most sophisticated planning systems encountered, commented: "The biggest problem is management's eternal desire to slip back on intuition at all levels. There is the seemingly inherent quality of not wanting to change and as the intuitive approaches have been successful in the past, there is a natural desire to continue to do the same. In addition to that problem, which is *the* major one, we have the basic difficulty inherent in evaluating the futurity of actions and decisions. Also, it is difficult to determine where the limits are; namely, what *can* we really do?" Still another executive simply suggested: "It is the ubiquitous problem of the planner—getting support at all levels in the corporation".

Tied in with these facts, it can be seen when analyzing the responses that *there is said to be a lack of realism and conciseness in the plans, and there is inadequate thinking in terms of the long-run implications* of present decisions as well as the need to make present decisions in order to attain objectives in the future. These problems were each cited by 36 per cent of the participants. Also related to management's attitude towards planning is the apparently inadequate thinking done in certain functional areas such as finance and in manpower planning. One respondent said that his management is "least able to plan effectively for major capital facilities". The inadequacy of planning inputs and the need for improving the forecasting techniques were listed by 36 per cent of the companies. In some cases where the company was heavily dependent on government in one way or other, it was found that a major problem was that of predicting the actions taken by government agencies. One company particularly sensitive in this respect had found that their major problem was "the uncertainty of actions by political bodies. It is easier to predict our competitors' actions". These findings clearly suggest that management has been unwilling to accept formal planning to the extent one might expect. This has affected the way in which planning tasks are being performed, the small amount of effort that is being expended on planning for the future relative to short-term performance, and it has affected the quality of the planning in the future will determine whether formal corporate planning gains in importance or whether it remains relatively ineffective.

When considering the reasons underlying these problems, it becomes apparent that they may not be subject to immediate or easy solution. Consider the most frequently cited unwillingness of operating people to accept and participate in planning. The operating manager is likely to perceive as a dichotomous choice the improvement of short-run profits by concentrating on current operations and the spending of more time on planning. Knowing that his performance in the past has been measured by short-run operating results, the operating manager naturally is inclined to concentrate his efforts here. In addition, he knows the *doing* part better than planning and given the human tendency to avoid the new and different, the operating manager is likely to choose and concentrate on current operations. Also, since promotions are likely to come to the capable operating manager, he knows that short-run performance is relatively more important than the long-run performance as a criterion for a new position. [1] One may hypothesize that a parallel exists in the case of the chief executive. He most likely reached his position because he was an exceptionally good operating manager. Those qualities may not be ideal for the top management position, but they undoubtedly are the ones that propel him to the top. Changing from an emphasis on operations to planning requires a re-orientation many top executives are not able to make. The combined effort of line management being judged on the basis of operating effectiveness and top management being steeped in operational tradition makes it difficult for staff planners in the corporation to get the participation in and attention to planning which it deserves and requires for success. Often corporations do not make the adjustments except under crisis conditions.[2]

Formal Planning Documents

Of the 40 companies surveyed, only 28 had corporate planning documents that covered all aspects of operations in an integrated manner, that were comprehensive in terms of subject matter, and that covered a period of three years or more. Such planning documents, we will refer to them as corporate plans, are usually developed jointly by corporate management and division management, and with the assistance of planning staff. The other 12 companies all had plans that were *less* comprehensive and less complete. Of these 12 companies, 3 had plans that were developed by their divisions but were not consolidated into a corporate document; 2 had what amounted to mere projections or forecasts for which the necessary objectives and supporting action programmes were lacking; and the remaining 7 had traditional budgets which generally are developed for control purposes. This information is presented in Table 1.2

TABLE 1.2. *Broadest planning documents available in writing*[a]

Scope of plans	Number	Percentage
Companies having:		
Complete corporate plans[b]	28	70
Companies having:		
Functional and divisional plans only as their most comprehensive planning documents[c]	3	7
Companies having:		
Forecasts and projections only as their most comprehensive planning documents[d]	2	5
Companies having:		
Traditional budgets only as their most comprehensive planning documents[e]	7	18
Total	40	100

[a] Since each company commonly has several planning documents in writing, only the most complete and comprehensive one available in each company has been included here.

[b] The 28 companies that have corporate plans usually have all the other types of planning documents too, whereas the remaining 12 companies have progressively less complete and comprehensive plans.

[c] Refers to plans developed at the divisional level and where there are no or only minor inputs from the corporate level.

[d] Refers to mere projections, usually about environmental factors or sales, where objectives or action programmes have not been developed for the time period in question.

[e] Refers to budgets generally developed as short-run control documents.

Although 70 per cent of the companies had corporate plans, it was found that there are great variations in the completeness and the quality of these plans. It is thus fair to say that a number of these companies, despite their having corporate plans, still did not have the type of planning documents that could be rated on par with what the best companies have. It thus was found to be substantial quality differences in the plans. It is important to note that of the 40 corporations surveyed, only a handful of these were judged to be doing an excellent corporate planning job.[3] Looked at differently, 30 per cent of the companies did not have comprehensive plans for all parts of their operations for time periods exceeding the traditional budgeting period. The significance of this becomes apparent when considering the obvious differences between the corporate plans and all other plans. Two dimensions of planning are dealt with in corporate plans. First is the task of integrating and coordinating the operations of several autonomous or semi-autonomous divisions to ensure that different parts of the corporation are not working at a cross-purpose. The search for synergistic effects is fraught with difficulties of which only some reach the printed page. Most remain tucked away in corporate files; then from a conversation or publication viewpoint are kept obscure.[4]

Second, corporate planning should concern itself with the more strategic problems associated with defining objectives and developing the corresponding courses of action required to realize these objectives. The written planning documents can be used as a measure of quantity and quality of planning undertaken. Some planning authorities have gone so far as to say that "if you cannot write it down, then you have not thought it through".[5] Looked at this way, it can be concluded that the planning in a very large proportion of the corporations surveyed leaves much to be desired. Only a few companies can be said to be doing a complete planning job. The findings show that many of the companies are not doing very comprehensive planning for the corporation as a whole and that some are not planning ahead for more than traditional budgeting periods.

Based on best company practices, the following synthesis is possible. In its most complete form, a corporate plan contains an outline of the broad objectives for the corporation as well as subordinate objectives for each of the divisions; a study of environmental factors such as market changes and trends, competitive developments, technological change, and general economic factors that may affect the outcome, of the planned actions; an audit of company resources to indicate relative strengths and weaknesses; a set of assumptions and premises about those factors that will determine company success; and a set of strategies and action programmes required to realize the various objectives in view of the company's position relative to external threats and opportunities.

By relating the comprehensiveness of the plans to the planning time

TABLE 1.3. *Time horizons for the broadest planning documents*

Scope of plans	Time horizon in years					
	1	3	5	6	10	Total
Complete corporate plans		2	18	1	7	28
Functional and divisional plans only		1	2			3
Forecasts and projections only					2	2
Traditional-type budgets only	5	1	1			7
Total	5	4	21	1	9	40

horizon, greater insight is gained. This is done in Table 1.3 where the planning horizons used for the various planning documents are added to the basic information in Table 1.2.

Table 1.3 is largely self-explanatory. Suffice it to say that the more comprehensive the planning effort, the further ahead companies tend to plan. The five year planning horizon is most common, used by 21 companies. Five companies were found to have planning documents covering only one year into the future. The data thus suggest that there are substantial variations among companies in terms of how comprehensively they plan and the time period for which they plan.

Despite differences among companies, it is possible to generalise about the most comprehensive long-range plans. The following points therefore represent a synthesis of what the better long-range plans contain. As such it reflects management's thinking and the nature of the planning job done by these companies.

1. *There is a heavy financial emphasis in long-range plans.* All planned actions are translated into financial terms and formats such as balance sheets, profit and loss statements, and cash-flow projections for each of the years the plan covers. The financial data are translated into ratios such as return on investment, earnings per share, and return on assets employed.

2. *Corporate plans generally contain but one strategy alternative.* Courses of actions to be followed in the case of changes in important parameters are not usually included. This does not mean that such alternatives have not been considered, but management appears disinclined to develop more than one major strategy. Respondents pointed out that this is an area needing improvement.

3. *Company strengths and weaknesses relative to external opportunities and threats are evaluated.* The extent to which this is done varies widely. This study did not attempt to determine the quality of the different facets of planning. However, it may be noted that few companies have been able to integrate systematic surveillance of the environment with a management

information system. This is an indication of inadequacy in matching a firm's capabilities with environmental requirements.

4. *Corporate plans also usually contain a set of premises and assumptions, but these are not set forth in detail.* Neither are probabilities attributed to the possible outcomes. Only two of the respondents said they used the concept of probability in their planning and both had introduced the concept for the first time in 1967.

Risk is not explicitly estimated in most corporate plans and risk analysis for different ventures and projects is only done informally. Point estimates are nearly always used when considering the likely outcomes of different courses of action. In some of the companies having computer facilities and programs respondents felt that risk analysis and probability estimates would soon be included in the long-range plans.

5. *Evaluation of diversification through mergers and acquisitions in part of many corporate plans*, reflecting management's concern with corporate growth. In some companies, the corporate planning department had been charged with the responsibility of conducting diversification studies and even engaging in preliminary negotiations.

6. *The typical corporate plan in most instances contains a set of objectives*, usually in terms of growth in the financial dimensions referred to above. While nearly all companies have financial objectives, only some have broader objectives dealing with fundamentals such as products to make and markets to serve.

Some long-range plans amount to nothing more than the sum of divisional plans. In extreme cases it was found that the division plans are not even integrated into a single document. Although such practice represents the exception, it is interesting to observe the reasons for the practice. One respondent felt there is a danger that the planning documents become the focus of attention whereas the emphasis should be on the planning process. This respondent argued that there is a tendency to "over-adhere" to plans once they have been developed, resulting in loss of flexibility.

Another respondent felt that the environmental changes his company was experiencing were so substantial that it was not meaningful to integrate division plans into a master document. In a third case it was learned that no standard planning format had been developed. The reasoning in this corporation was that a format developed at headquarters tended to induce division managers to think along the same lines as the one who developed the format. The format might lead an operating manager to attempt to outguess corporate management and produce plans accordingly. This respondent felt that to foster creativity and innovation in the divisions, the only requirement should be the use of a standard accounting system for the corporation to permit financial comparisons.

To illustrate the divergence in practices, the formal plans developed by two corporations will be described.

In example number one a strategic plan and a budget are prepared annually. The strategic plans covers five years and this horizon was chosen, according to the respondent, because it was a convenient number. The company have found that it is able to quantify relatively accurately for two years into the future. Beyond three years it was found that things become so unpredictable that it is unwise to be specific, and qualitative planning therefore becomes necessary. In the strategic plan the emphasis is on broad trends and environmental changes rather than detailed projections. In this company, the budget is derived after the strategic plan has been approved so that the short-range plan conforms to the long-range planning. In commenting on this practice the respondent pointed out that,

> We want our plans to reflect management's thinking, not specific numbers *per se*. It is more important to identify the issues and opportunities management must deal with. I think much current planning goes wrong because the people get trapped in the 'numbers game' when writing the plan.

In example number two the following planning documents were in writing:

1. *Five-year plan.* This document, according to the respondent, was primarily financial in orientation and, although the same type of plan had been developed for more than a decade in this company, it still was no more than extended budgeting. This respondent pointed out that a number of financial performance measures constituted the major portion of this document. Originally, performance of various parts of the corporation was merely extrapolated into the future, but in recent years attention also has given to new business developments. The five-year plan includes profit and loss statements with derivative information about space needs, the capital needs and uses, personnel needs, and cash flows.

2. *Programme plans.* Such documents were not developed on a regular basis but only as needed. One example would be the development and introduction of major new products requiring co-operation between two or more divisions. The programme plan was used for broad programmes having varying time horizons that depended on the characteristics of the programme. The respondent said this type of plan represented a "top-down" view in which major trends were emphasized and in which major tasks that must be performed were considered.

3. *Strategic recommendations.* General problems affecting large segments of the corporations were dealt within these documents. Such plans had no set time horizon and were developed by task forces or groups of top executives with the aid of the corporate staff. Such recommendations were used as guides in important decision-making. An example would be one

recently developed on foreign competition in terms of what developments were to be expected in the years to come and how the threats presented by foreign competition could be dealt with.

This respondent held that there is an hierarchical relationship among these sets of planning documents. This management has chosen a relatively informal approach to planning in order to maintain flexibility. The actual preparation of plans is by top management. The respondent felt that, despite the need for some financial projections, the five-year plan of dubious value because of the rapid rate of change the company is experiencing.

In sum, there are substantial divergencies among companies as to the completeness and apparent quality of their plans. Some companies had developed very comprehensive documents that truly reflected a comprehensive planning job. Others were found not to have what the respondents would consider useful documents. In the words of one executive, "The plan is nothing but a beautiful document, placed on a shelf once completed, and never used."

Management's Planning Role

Management at both the corporate and divisional levels *participate* considerably less in planning than one might expect. Since planning is the means by which future performance can be affected and determined, it is surprising to find top management playing a relatively small role in the *preparation* of plans. This is shown in Fig. 1.2. The task of initially preparing a long-range plan is usually a responsibility of the management assisted by

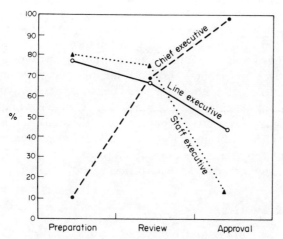

FIG. 1.2. *Participants in corporate long range planning*

staff planners. Only one in ten of the chief executives were reported to participate in the original development of the plans. After a plan has been drafted, the chief executive plays a more active role. In 70 per cent of the cases the chief executive was participating in the review—meaning that in 30 per cent of the cases he was not. Approval of the plans is mainly the function of the chief executive, but where he has not participated in the preparatory or review stages, his approval is likely to be of a "rubber stamp" nature. In addition to inadequate participation in the preparing and reviewing of plans, top management was also said to spend less time on planning than might be expected. These findings combined suggest what may be the most serious problem standing in the way of effective corporate planning. It is hard to see how planning can acquire a true status in an organization unless it elicits the time and interest of the man in the organization who has the ultimate responsibility for it.

The following example illustrates the extreme of what can happen when top management does not believe in corporate planning. The case was encountered in a corporation with 1966 sales in excess of one billion dollars. This corporation had experienced substantial fluctuations in sales in two of its divisions during preceding few years and its earnings were low. The respondent explained that corporate planning had been introduced in 1963 by a president who retired two years later. He was replaced by an executive who had come up through finance and saw little benefit to be derived from corporate planning. According to the respondent, the president was only interested in financial budgeting and therefore made planning a controllership function. The respondent stated that his corporation had never had a strong central management. Consequently, objectives and performance requirements had not been developed at headquarters. The division managers had extensive autonomy and received little central direction. As an example of management's philosophy, the respondent explained that one of the two top men was a "free-wheeling" type who tended to act on impulse and did not want to use a systematic approach to decision-making. This had resulted in going into new ventures foreign to the firm, while little effort had been made to improve operations where the pay-off potential had not been realized. Not surprisingly, in view of the top management's orientation, the decision had been made, immediately prior to the interview, to dissolve the planning department as of the end of the year. This example illustrates the importance of top management support for corporate planning.

Corporate Objectives

Many of the corporations interviewed do not have well defined or clearly defined objectives. From Table 1.4 can be seen that 9 per cent of the

TABLE 1.4. *Major corporate objectives*[a]

Nature of objectives	Percentage
I Not developed or agreed upon	9
II Companies having objectives in financial terms only	28
Primarily in terms of:	
Earnings per share	11
Return on investment	9
Combination of financial measures	6
Return on assets employed	3
III Companies having objectives in broader terms than financial only	63
Primarily in terms of:	
Growth in market share, sales, and profitability	63
Diversity and broad areas of business interest	34
Future, or long-range, position and reorientation of company	14
Technological leadership	11
Social responsibility	11
Performance relative to competitors	9
Increased brand identity and corporate image	9
Raw materials development	6

[a] The respondents were asked: "What are your key company objectives?" and "How did you arrive at these objectives?"

TABLE 1.5. *Inputs and techniques used in developing the plans*

Nature of inputs and techniques	Percentage
Financial statements	100
Budgets and accounting analysis	97
Break-even analysis	79
Correlation and trends analysis	79
Statistical inference and analysis	66
Operations research	48
Mathematical models and simulation	45
Linear programming	28
Input−output analysis	24
Game theory	14

respondents did not have any formal corporate objectives, 28 per cent had objectives in financial terms only, for a total of 37 per cent. The remaining 63 per cent had developed corporate objectives that were more comprehensive. These broader objectives generally were dealing with what business the firm was aiming at, performance in various dimensions relative to competition, and financial performance criteria for both the corporation as a whole and for each of the divisions.

In several of the companies written objectives did not exist prior to the introduction of formal planning. A corporate planning department usually sets about to change this situation at once, but this may not be easily accomplished. [6]

An example of this was found in a large corporation that in recent years has been concerned primarily with survival. A few years ago a set of objectives was developed by the corporate planning department in co-operation with the president, but they had not been officially adopted since company policy could not be adopted until accepted by the divisions. Some of the division managers had refused to endorse the proposed objectives with the result that the company had unofficial objectives which were operationally meaningless. The respondent further stated they were "church and country" type of objectives that were not specific enough to give the company direction.

Two companies provide examples of the sets of objectives several companies were found to have. One respondent listed the following corporate objectives:

1. Growth in sales at a predetermined rate.
2. Steady growth in annual profits.
3. Increased market penetration with our present customers.
4. Move into new important markets that hold a promise for additional growth in profits.
5. Provide an excellent environment for managers and employees.
6. Maintain excellent research and development capabilities.

In the second company these objectives were in writing:

1. Predetermined gains in annual earnings of 8 to 10 per cent.
2. Overall growth in return on investment in excess of 10 per cent.
3. Favourable market performance relative to competition.
4. Creation of a viable, enduring corporation.
5. Improved relative performance in our international operations.
6. Diversification in a manner such that there will be continued compatibility in products and technology.

An intriguing question that arises in this connection is what objectives are appropriate for different planning categories. It may well be that different objectives are needed for strategic planning and for budgeting. Possibly, the performance criteria used for operations planning may not be the right ones for extended budgeting or for strategic planning. [7]

The manner in which objectives are defined depends on the nature of management. As might be expected, in companies dominated by a strong chief executive, the objectives generally will reflect his thinking and philosophy. One such chief executive reportedly sat down one Sunday and wrote a set of objectives by hand based on his own ideas of what the company should be. These objectives were communicated to the subordinate management levels and became the basis for much of their planning.

Another chief executive, the founder of the company, wanted to make his company one of the major corporations in the United States and this was to be accomplished through mergers and acquisitions. Although his objectives have not been put on paper, they have been communicated to subordinate executives through memos, speeches and discussions.

One good example of the role the planning department can play in the development of company objectives was found in a corporation where formal planning was introduced in 1965. The company had failed to grow with the rest of its industry and its management had been very conservative and cautious towards expansion. One of the first things the head of the planning department felt needed to be done was to determine the basic company philosophy. Internal search did not provide an answer since no objectives had been developed. This led to a larger internal study which lasted 15 months. The purpose of the study was to evaluate the company's standing in all of its markets in order to appraise the company's future. Its relative position was determined by a study carried out under the name of a "marketing audit" because of the implications that might result if the true nature of the study had been known. Early in the study, the planning department proposed a set of objectives but when these were being too readily accepted by top management, the vice-president of planning demurred. He wanted the objectives to become something the top executives evolved, so a task force of eight executives was organized to develop objectives. The president participated actively with the task force throughout the period and with the planning department personnel who served as a staff for the task force. The task force required each company division to write a report on its objectives and directions. These were integrated into one document outlining fourteen objectives agreed upon by key company executives. The document covered important questions such as: What business are we in? What do we want to be in? What growth do we want for the various parts of the company? What performance do we want in profitability and size? The planning executive was happy with the result because he felt the objectives were significant and attainable, primarily because they had been developed by the decision-makers.

Inputs and Techniques Used

For planning to be meaningful and adequate a number of assumptions, premises, and general planning inputs must be developed. These inputs permit the assessment of corporate capabilities relative to external threats and opportunities. Table 1.5 provides additional insight into the substance of corporate planning as practiced among leading U.S. corporations. Every respondent reported using financial statements as one input in updating and revising of plans. 97 per cent also used information from budgets and accounting analyses in developing plans, while 79 per cent used break-even analysis. As for techniques to handle and manipulate the information, 79 per cent used correlation and trend analysis, while 66 per cent used statistical inference and analysis. Less than half the respondents, 48 per cent, said they employed operations research in their planning.

The least used techniques were input-output analysis, used by 24 per cent, and game theory, used by 14 per cent of the companies.

Many of the respondents commented on the prospective use of input–output analysis and expressed interest in employing such analysis to better identify new market opportunities. The significance of these findings to the broader aspects of planning, however, is that inputs and techniques are being used that imply a fairly high degree of analytical sophistication on the part of the line executive doing the planning. That this may not be a valid assumption is suggested by the fact that management has not been able to harness the computer for sophisticated use.

Some of the respondents alluded to the inherent danger in emphasizing advanced quantitative, and sometimes esoteric, new techniques, since the use of these techniques may become an end in itself. There is the danger that the use of such tools becomes equated with planning and that the operating manager fails to reason through the fundamentals of the planning process so as to understand the basic relationships that underlie success or failure. When discussing future changes anticipated in the practice and acceptance of corporate planning in the latter part of this chapter, more will be said about the use of computer and other new analytical techniques in planning.

Premises and Assumptions

In Table 1.6 another important aspect of planning—assumptions and premises is dealt with. In 72 per cent of the cases, planning assumptions and premises are developed at both corporate and divisional levels. Assumptions developed at the corporate level are the ones that pertain to the firms as a whole or affect the operation of two or more divisions. These assumptions are made under the promptings of the corporate planning department and deal both with external factors such as changes in the economy, political factors, and market trends, and with internal objectives for various business areas, cash availability, capital limitations, priorities for investments, markets to the developed, and direction of research and development. Divisions, in turn, are responsible for assumptions that pertain to their own operations. Examples of these are assumptions about

TABLE 1.6. *Formal development of planning premises and assumptions*

Scope of premises and assumptions	Percentage
Developed for the firm as a whole at corporate headquarters, and on a divisional basis of operating management[a]	72
Developed by divisions only[b]	19
Corporation highly centralized and all planning done at headquarters[c]	8

[a] The assumptions developed at corporate headquarters are generally those that pertain to the operations of the firm as a whole or that affect several divisions. The divisions are responsible for those relevant to their specific activities.

[b] In some of the highly decentralized companies or where central direction appeared to be lacking, the divisions were responsible for developing all the relevant assumptions and premises.

[c] The major decision-making was made by corporate management.

demand for product lines, competitive position, technological change, and costs. In 19 per cent of the companies, no assumptions are developed at the corporate level. The full responsibility for developing whatever assumptions are required lies with the divisions and these assumptions are reviewed as part of the plans before approval by corporate management. It should be stressed that not all companies require planning assumptions to be spelled out in detail; many are not even made explicit or stated. This means that an evaluation of the quality of the assumptions and the conclusions based on the assumptions cannot be made. Also, in only two of the companies responding to this question was it found that probability estimates are associated with the planning assumptions. One reason given for this was a lack of familiarity with probability theory. As the quality of planning improves and more of the crucial aspects are made explicit, one may expect to find more application of probability theory to planning. In the remaining 8 per cent of the cases, it was found that the organization was highly centralized and that all the major planning was done at the corporate level.

The broader significance of these findings to planning is that companies appear to be doing a less than adequate job in developing the planning assumptions that underlie many of the action programmes developed. This means that the choice of strategies is unduly restricted. The fact that not all assumptions are stated explicitly and in writing, and that the great majority of companies are not assigning probabilities to the likely outcome of the variables about which assumptions are made, suggests that there is room for considerable improvement at this stage of the planning process. Another implication of this finding is that since only point estimates are used in making planning assumptions, relative risks associated with the various courses of action is difficult to assess.

Table 1.7 deals with a related matter: the extent to which the planning assumptions are communicated throughout the firm. In 49 per cent of the

TABLE 1.7. *Distribution of planning premises and assumptions*

Mode of distribution	Percentage
The premises and assumptions are communicated throughout the firm[a]	43
No communication of premises and assumptions throughout the firm[b]	49
Communication not necessary[c]	8

[a] Such communication may be done formally as in cases where the premises and assumptions are written up and distributed.

[b] Because of lack of similarity between divisional activities or because of apparent lack of central direction, no distribution was attempted.

[c] In three centralized companies there was no need for such distribution since the major planning was done at headquarters.

companies no attempt was made to communicate throughout the firm. This means that the assumptions developed in a given division were not made available to the management of other divisions. The rationale for this lack of interdivisional communication of assumptions was generally found to be that the markets served and the operations of divisions themselves were thought to be so different that no benefit would be derived from such an exchange. Those assumptions developed at the corporate level typically are communicated to the operating levels through the planning instructions that are developed annually. They are also communicated informally through the assistance the corporate planning department provides in the development of the divisional plans. It should be apparent that there may be little or no interaction among divisions in their planning efforts. Neither the basis for the planning, such as planning premises or assumptions, nor the plans themselves are exchanged among divisions on a systematic basis in the majority of the firms. This fact places even more burden on top management in the review and acceptance of division plans requiring awareness of conflicting interests and activities on the part of different divisions. It further means that synergistic effects, so desirable according to current literature, may be foregone.[8]

Use of Accounting Data

Another major planning input considered was accounting data and the findings on the use of these are presented in Table 1.8. Eighteen of the 34 companies responding to this question held that the accounting data developed for financial reporting were not adequate for planning purposes. Of the comments made regarding the inadequacy the most frequently mentioned related to the way the data are collected and organized. One half of these respondents found accounting data inadequate because they are "history-oriented" and collected with the custodial responsibility in mind.

Because of this orientation they are of limited use in planning for the future. In line with this argument, several companies reported that they found the information generated by the accounting system inapplicable for strategic planning. From the findings and related comments, it may be concluded that more forward looking and externally orientated information is required for corporate planning. Some planning departments have attempted to supplement traditional accounting data by developing management information systems with planning needs in mind, and others have attempted to modify or alter their accounting systems to this end. The latter effort has generally failed, but the former is still being pursued in some companies.

Table 1.8 also shows that 16, or 47 per cent, of the companies found accounting data adequate for planning. The general observations made by these respondents that their accounting systems had been modified and integrated into broader management information systems which provided useful information; that the deficiencies in accounting data were recognized but that some of the data could be used, particularly when converted into ratios and other broad measures; and that for much of planning the concern was with conceptual issues and problems for which financial data could not be expected and were not needed. It can be said that there is a strong financial orientation in the planning inputs used. Data generated for

TABLE 1.8. *Use of accounting data for planning*

Question: "For Planning Purposes, do you find the Accounting Data developed for Financial Reporting adequate?"

YES	47 per cent
NO	53 per cent

Comments from the companies answering in the negative

Nature of comment	Percentage
The data are not collected on a business-like basis and are broken down in wrong way	50
The information is not appropriate for strategic planning	39
Accounting data are history-oriented while future-oriented data are needed in planning	33
The data are inadequate and new financial thinking needed	33
Other[a]	16

[a] One respondent pointed out that since the accounting data are only single point deterministic probabilities, there is no accounting for what may happen if projections made from them are wrong; one respondent found the accounting data inappropriate for monitoring and control of planned performance; the third respondent in this category flatly stated that in his company's planning "we do not even use accounting data".

financial reporting and through accounting analyses are used extensively, particularly for the type of planning referred to as extended budgeting. Such planning is characterized by use of the approaches to planning found in traditional budgeting, except that a longer planning horizon is used, there is more extrapolation and projection of past performance, and much concern with co-ordinating and integrating the interdependent activities of a multidivisional organization. Where financial data have been generated and organized with decision-making in mind, the use of such data is both logical and meaningful.

It should be noted, however, that for strategic planning, where the concern is with the relationship between a firm's product offerings and the markets to be cultivated, information different from that generated by the traditional accounting system is required. Here one expects to find considerable emphasis on environmental analysis for strategic planning.

In summary, much of the data generated for financial reporting constitutes an important input for the planning of some firms. Therefore, attention should be given to the management information needs when designing the reporting system and the accounting system should be modified to generate information useful for planning. In addition, supplementary information must be collected systematically about environmental factors important to decision-making. Since this information is of a different nature from custodial accounting information, it would logically be collected by a different department such as the corporate planning department or by division staffs. When considering what planning assumptions are developed, how they are developed and distributed, it can be concluded that many firms are doing less than might be expected. This is evident from the absence of defined assumptions underlying the plans, the use of point estimates instead of a range of probabilities, and the lack of interaction among divisions in the development of the assumptions and plans. In relating these conclusions to some of the earlier findings, some explanations can be found. Corporate planning is new; many firms do not have sufficient experience with it to have eliminated the problems associated with changing the orientation from short-term budgeting to comprehensive corporate planning and for all relevant time periods: much of what passes for planning is merely an extension of traditional budgeting, with the addition of some variables due to the extended planning horizon; and management at all levels is devoting too small a proportion of its time to planning.

Because of the importance of data inputs in planning and because of the lacking experience and sophistication in areas such as environmental surveillance, it may be desirable to pursue this issue of data in planning in still greater depth.

In order to use highly structured techniques and the computer in planning, it is necessary to quantify. But in order to quantify, it is necessary to define and this is an area in need of refinement and emphasis. The data used so far are primarily generated by traditional accounting systems organized with the custodial responsibility in mind. A number of respondents contended that present accounting data were inadequate for strategic planning and they consequently have spent considerable time and effort on supplementing these data with managerially oriented inputs and information. The respondents who were unhappy with accounting data for planning purposes have often been frustrated in their attempts to change the accounting system. They argue that the accountants have failed to understand the nature of planning. One respondent pointed out that his department had fought a continuous battle with company accountants for years over what inputs were to be generated by the accountants for planning purposes. He concluded that "the accounting people are only interested in cost tallies. They do not recognize profit opportunities. Despite many tries, we have not even been able to get a relevant breakdown of expenses." Another respondent, who, like the one above, works in a corporation that has developed a moderately complex set of mathematical models and uses the computer extensively—pointed out that the accounting data in many cases reflect arbitrary policy decisions.

> There is a lack of objectivity in the accounting system. If you, for instance, have a conservative management deciding on how to keep the books, straight-line depreciation will be used. The single-point deterministic probability associated with the accounting data is a further factor making it less than ideal for planning purposes.

Accounting data are used to varying degrees in planning. It is most appropriate for operational planning, least appropriate for strategic planning, and of intermediate value for extended budgeting.

Several companies have found the use of ratios and indexes more useful than raw accounting data in their planning. Said one respondent:

> The detailed accounting data are too cumbersome to use. We need a "quick and dirty" approach and have therefore developed various ratios instead. We have put these on the computer and when varying the parameters, we get a fairly good idea of the implications.

Another respondent was even more vocal in commenting on the accounting data:

> It is terrible, it is late, and it is not aggregated in any way. It is mere data and it needs to be converted into information that is useful for decision-making. Our information are the same as management's information needs. Planning does not have special needs. We simply want good management information but from accounting so far we have not been able to get any of that.

Based on the above observations it can be said that there are inadequacies and deficiencies in many of the planning practices studied. The respondents

TABLE 1.9. *Additional improvements needed in the corporate planning effort effort*

Nature of improvements needed	Percentage
More conceptual thinking about the future to get a more strategic perspective instead of current financial emphasis	43
Better integration of the planning effort throughout the corporation	35
Improvements in environmental analysis, particularly in advanced forecasting	35
More proficiency in the use of computer, advanced techniques, and tools to improve the handling of data	27
Better communications between the executive officers and operating managers	22
More and better planning at the divisional level	16
Better implementation of changes already begun	16
Greater acceptance of planning	16
More probing reviews before the plans are accepted	14
More diversification and venture studies	11
More realistic plans and a longer range perspective needed	11
Make the planning process a more continuous and rhythmic one	11
Better understanding of planning in terms of what it can do and cannot do	11
Improved financial planning	8
Simplification of the planning tasks	5

TABLE 1.10. *Major changes expected in planning in the next decade*[a]

Nature of change	Percentage
Better understanding of planning and thereby greater acceptance and practice at all levels	71
Increased use of sophisticated techniques and methods[b]	52
More and better environmental analysis	21
Improved quality of informational inputs and use of more relevant data[c]	21
More mechanization of the planning process making the planning tasks easier	18
More complete analysis of the significant relationships important for success	12
The acceptance of planning as a major function on par with marketing and finance	12
More planning will be done in medium-sized and small companies	6
There will be a new class of managers trained in planning	6

[a] The respondents were asked: "What major changes do you expect in the practice and acceptance of planning in the next decade both in your company and in general?"
[b] Most of this development was seen in conjunction with new computer uses and electronic data processing.
[c] Some respondents expect more data on a real-time basis; some expect specialized data services will become available.

in most cases were fully aware not only of the shortcomings but also what specific solutions were required to improve their performance. Many of these improvements and changes have been realized so far while additional ones were felt needed. From Tables 1.9 and 1.10 can be seen what the respondents held to be important changes both from the viewpoint of their companies in particular and business in general.

Changes Required

Without summarizing all the points, the following general comments can be made:

1. *The most significant change in terms of the future success of corporate planning is related to management's acceptance of the function.* So far there has been some resistance to formal planning on the part of both corporate and operating managers as seen in the proportion of time spent on planning and in their participation in the planning process. Respondents generally are optimistic, however, and expect that increased experience will bring about greater acceptance by management of planning as a part of their job that cannot be delegated to staff.

With increased experience, management will better understand the nature of corporate planning, what it can and cannot do, and how it can be used without losing corporate flexibility. As more is learned about the function, it may become possible to simplify parts of the process and to place more emphasis on those aspects which are most fundamental to corporate success. One example would be reduced concern with format and detail, and greater emphasis on content and fundamental relationships such as the product-market mix. Also, with additional experience, misapplication of analytical techniques is likely to diminish. This does not mean that the computer and mathematical techniques will be discarded, but that they will be used more selectively for planning problems where their use is appropriate.

2. *Many respondents anticipate new uses of electronic equipment and analytical tools in the future.* The computer and newly developed management information systems will make more and better information available when needed. This will enable management to use information more systematically in decision-making. Where models can be developed, the computer will be used for testing alternative courses of action. This means that more strategies can be developed and evaluated easier and faster than has been possible. Similarly, many respondents felt that parts of the planning process will be mechanized as more analytical tools are perfected. As some of the time-consuming and tedious parts of planning are made faster and simpler, increased use of the computer may contribute to greater acceptance of planning in the firm. This will also permit greater emphasis

on the planning process instead of the planning documents. This should also lead to a decreased financial emphasis in planning and more emphasis on strategic planning problems.

3. *Some respondents foresee a broader role for the corporate planning department in the years to come.* They think the departments will become responsible for such matters as environmental surveillance, identification of new opportunities and product needs, economic analysis, as well as market research for the corporation. This could be a case of "empire-building" and not all respondents felt the same way about this development, as can be seen by the comments of one respondent:

> Where planning has developed as a separate function, away from the operations of the firm, it will fail of its own futility. So far it has been fashionable for the chief executive to brag about the fact that his company has a corporate planning department headed by a vice-president, and using all kinds of sophisticated tools and techniques.
>
> But then, some day in the future, as sufficiently many planning failures have been realized, it may well become fashionable for the chief executive to take the opposite stand, and, while at his country club, boast that, "we finally saw the light and fired those 'so and so's' costing us over 400,000 dollars a year".
>
> That is a sad ending since it will happen not because of planning being an inadequate tool, but because it has not been used right. The task of planning is an inseparable part of the executive's job, but it, unfortunately is human to emphasise those tasks we are good at. So, the top executive tends to delegate the planning responsibility to his staff while he himself goes on empahsizing those things that made him good line executive. But planning cannot be entirely delegated, only parts of it can. The ultimate responsibility for planning must lie with the line manager. My job, as a vice-president of corporate planning, is to get the line manager to do the planning. I can see the future of this function as hinging on the ability of the planning staff to get the line manager to accept more of what is really his job in the first place.

Another respondent pointed to certain changes that he expected, which he thought would be to the good.

> First, we recently have realized a greater use of the computer both for the storage and manipulation of data, and for the testing of alternative strategies. Second, some of the myths about planning will be disspelled and planning will become a staff function on the same basis as e.g. marketing. Third, there will be a class of managers trained in planning and like the economists, they will have their own set of techniques and tools. Finally, by means of the data availability and the additional use of electronic data processing equipment, the study of the relationship between the firm and its environment will be simplified and improved. These will all lead to higher quality planning.

The conclusions regarding the future changes in planning indicate that they will largely be determined by management's willingness to continue to support the function, by operating managers' ability to do the planning for their area of responsibility without sacrificing short-run efficiency, and by developments that will facilitate the mechanics of the planning process. The human problem may be the most difficult to deal with and the change here is not likely to come about easily or rapidly.

Two observations made in connection with the need for organized corporate planning imply that the function must grow in stature. In words of one respondent:

> It is unthinkable not to plan. Our business is very complex and we have tremendous amounts at stake. Because of the human desire to maintain the *status quo* and perpetuate the past, it would be unthinkable to let things get out of control. So we start by requiring all managers to plan.

Another respondent stated:

> If members of management . . . could think through a problem and all its ramifications, as well as evaluating the opportunities, and match the resources accordingly, then formal planning would not be necessary. But when the process is so complex that it becomes too much for the human mind, then in order to have control over the business, a formalized corporate planning system must be set up to properly identify the problems and to decide rationally on the allocation of the corporation's resources.

Synthesis and Conclusions

Based on the many findings and insights gained in the course of this study, the following observations can be made.

1. Organized corporate long-range planning appears to be in its early stages of evolution and has not gained as high a stature or recognition in the business organization as has been commonly assumed.
2. Most corporate planning today has a strong financial orientation despite the inability to adequately project the behaviour of the factors underlying the financial results. Most of the planning done resembles what is done in traditional budgeting.
3. Of the changes taking place, the most significant relate to the increased acceptance of organized corporate planning by corporate and division management and the greater use of planning inputs and techniques that will improve the quality of the planning job. This will all result in planning gaining in stature and thus becoming a more integral part of management's activities in the future.
4. There is considerable divergence in planning practices as evidenced by differences in the formal plans developed. While some companies have very complete and comprehensive plans, others have nothing more than traditional budgets extending one year into the future.
5. Most planning is characterized by undue quantitative and financial concern. This often represents a meaningless numerical exercise since the major factors *causing* sales and growth often are not considered in any detail—while the anticipated results are.
6. Companies plan ahead for varying time periods. The majority plan ahead for five years while a small number use ten years as their

planning horizon. A lengthening of planning horizons is expected by the survey companies.

7. The reasons organized corporate planning has become important stem from changes in such enviornmental factors as demand, competition, technological developments, and the role of government. Since these factors are likely to be even more dynamic in the future, the importance of planning will grow correspondingly.

8. The foremost objective of organized corporate planning is the improvement of management's performance by making managers analyze in a systematic manner all the interacting variables making up the total corporate system before making decisions.

9. Along with this objective and the general developments envisioned, it is expected that progress will be made in the generation of informational inputs about internal and external factors. Such improvements are seen as likely because of the improvements in the use of analytical techniques and the computer in planning.

10. And related to these changes, it is expected that some of the planning tasks will be mechanized—freeing executive time for those problems that are susceptible to change through planning and adaptation.

A Further Reading List

(a) Henri Fayol, *General and Industrial Management*, Sir Isaac Pitman and Sons Ltd., London, 1949. This is the classical treatment of the management functions first presented by Fayol as a paper titled "Administration Industrielle et Generale" presented to the Congress of the Societe de l' Industrie Minerale in 1908. Main contributors to the management literature who have followed this universalist approach are W. Robinson, L. Urwick, J. Mooney, Alvin Brown; a bestseller among management textbooks following the same approach is Harold Koontz and Cyril O'Donnell, *Principles of Management*, McGraw-Hill Book Co., New York. In the Third Edition of this text, see particularly pages 69—93.

(b) Brian W. Scott, *Long-Range Planning in American Industry*, American Management Association, Inc., New York, 1964, pp. 52—55.

(c) Paul E. Holder, *et al., Top-Management Organization and Control,* Stanford University Press, Stanford University, 1941, pp. 4—5.

(d) Edward H. Hampel, *Top Management Planning*, Harper and Brothers Publishers, New York, 1945, p. 10.

(e) *Idem.*, p. 406.

(f) "Calling the shots on 19—". *Business Week*, September 20, 1952, p. 84.

(g) "Plan tomorrow's profits", *Nations Business*, August 1958, p. 29.

(h) George A. Steiner, *Top Management Planning*, The Macmillan Company, New York, 1969, p. 15.

(i) *Idem.*, p. 15.

(j) Martin R. Kaiden, "Planning for tomorrow: How large industrial companies plan for the future", unpublished Master's thesis, Graduate School of Business, New York University, New York, 1967, p. 26.

(k) James K. Brown *et al.*, "The status of long-range planning", *The Conference Board Record*, September 1966, p. 17.

(l) *Idem.*, p. 17.

References

1. ´For an excellent discussion of some of these problems, see E. Kirby Warren, *Long Range Planning: The Executive Viewpoint*, Prentice-Hall Inc., Englewood Cliffs, N.J. 1965, particularly chapter 5.
2. For a discussion along these lines, see the new classic article by Theordore Levitt, "Marketing myopia" in *Harvard Business Review*, July-August, 1960, pp. 45 — 56.
3. This has been supported by some other students of planning. See "Long-range planning: Seance or science", *Sales Management* , January 15, 1969, pp, 31 — 34. Quote: "Andrall Pearson, a McKinsey & Co. director, appeared to sum up the opinion of most planning theorists when he told SM (Sales Management) that only one in five industrial companies make the grade in planning, 'and that's a generous figure' said Pearson. who rates consumer companies slightly higher". pp, 31 — 32.
4. An example of this problem is Allied Chemical's experience. "As late as the 1950's, . . . , communication was so poor and planning so rudimentary (at Allied) that three separate divisions built three different phtalic anhydride plants." See "How Allied Chemical breaks with its past", *Business Week*, April 5, 1969, pp. 80 — 84.
5. See John T. Hickey, "Guidelines to successful future planning", in *Financial Executive*, November 1966, pp. 32 — 40. Quoting from p. 36: "Writing down the details of the plans and the assumptions made in developing the plan is vital to its success. Writing down all aspects of the plan provides a checklist which the planners may use to determine that they have given careful consideration to each aspect of the plans development. Writing things down also provides well defined and carefully considered information about the organization's projected future."
6. For an interesting discussion of problems related to this, see Bruce Payne, "Corporate planning: All dressed up and no place to go", *Management Review*, Vol. 52, No. 4, April 1963, pp. 40 — 50.
7. For a discussion of objectives, see Charles H. Granger, "The hierarchy of objectives", *Harvard Business Review*, Vol. 42, No. 3, May-June 1964, pp. 63 — 74, and Robert N. Anthony, "The trouble with profit maximization", *Harvard Business Review*, Vol. 38, No. 6, November-December 1960, pp. 126 — 134.
8. For a discussion pertaining to`synergistic effects, see H. Igor Ansoff, *Corporate Strategy*, McGraw-Hill Book Co., New York, 1965, particularly chapters 2 and 3.

2

The Extent and Nature of
Corporate Long Range Planning in
the U.K.: Part 1

B. W. DENNING AND M. E. LEHR

There is ample evidence that the interest of businessmen in corporate long range planning has recently risen rapidly. It appears, however, that there is some confusion about what is meant by the term, and definitive knowledge of the subject is limited. The knowledge as reflected in the literature can broadly be classified into three areas:

1. Techniques of analysis and forecasting suitable for decision making with long term implications. [1]
2. Analysis of individual steps necessary in developing plans. [2]
3. Research into the particular practices and experience of individual companies. [3]

Most of the good written work in this field is American, but from the point of view of the manager, much of it seems to suffer from a lack of clarity about the real purposes of different forms of long range planning and the different requirements that these various forms impose.

Definition of Terms

In the research which will be described in this and subsequent articles, a specific definition of corporate long range planning has been made. This

---

This article was originally published in the *Journal of Management Studies*, Volume 8, No. 2, May 1971.

[1] See, for example, Merrett, A. J., and Sykes, A., *Finance and Analysis of Capital Projects*, London: Longmans, 1965.
[2] See, for example, Ansoff, H. I., *Corporate Strategy*, New York: McGraw-Hill, 1965.
[3] See, for example, Steiner, G., *Managerial Long Range Planning*, New York: McGraw-Hill, 1963.

definition can best be explained through the use of diagrams illustrating a pattern of development which has occurred in many companies.[4]

(a) Operational Planning

At any moment of time a company will be planning its current operations. These can be defined as the manufacture of its current products, the sale of those products in existing markets and the deployment of the labour force and executive organization necessary to develop, manufacture and sell its current product or service range from its present facilities. Forward planning of these activities may be carried out on a one, three, five or ten year basis but planning the continuation and development of current products in existing markets with present facilities is a particular type of planning which can draw heavily on past data and accumulated experience. This type of planning is arbitrarily defined as 'operational planning' and is illustrated in Fig. 2.1 where the left hand rough shape represents the company at a present moment of time along various relevant dimensions of market share, profitability, size etc. The right-hand circle represents the projection forward.

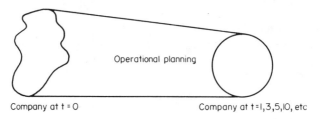

Company at t = 0   Company at t = 1,3,5,10, etc

FIG. 2.1.   Operational planning

Two points are worth noting about this diagram. First, the total size etc. of the forward projection is shown as being smaller than the present. This is not always the case but increasingly it is so within the tight definition of operational planning above. The most dramatic examples of this phenomenon occur in industries susceptible to rapid technological advance such as the pharmaceutical and electronics industries.

Secondly, the information derived from planning operations forward for say five years frequently provides essential data for strategic appraisal and it is for this reason that one aspect of an effective corporate planning

[4] See, for example, Learned, Aguilar and Valtz, *European Problems in General Management*, Irwin, 1963. Cases: "Compagnie Electro Mécanique", "KLM Royal Dutch Airlines". "Distillers Chemicals and Plastics Ltd." Case developed at the London Business School; Steiner, G., *op. cit.*

process is the preparation of detailed forward plans by operating units over five or ten years, of which the first year is essentially the annual budget.

(b) Project Planning

In addition to its existing products, markets and facilities, any company will also have a number of projects in varying stages of development. A project is widely defined and would include a new product, a new factory, the introduction of a new computer system, the entry into a new market, an intended joint venture or acquisition, or a new equity or debt financing. Project planning in this research is defined as planning any addition to or modification of existing operations capable of separate assessment, analysis and control. In some industries, such as construction or shipbuilding, the majority of company activities may consist of projects.

Project planning is defined in this way partly for clarity of exposition and partly because the planning of a project calls for different and identifiable approaches and techniques. Project assessment, approval and control call for a special data base, specific forecasting techniques, detailed technical estimates, financial evaluation, critical path planning and PERT control. Joint ventures and acquisitions call for specialized search activities, assessment techniques and financial, analytical and negotiating skills. Thus, as a form of planning, project planning can and should be viewed differently from the planning of existing activities.

Bearing in mind that any company at a moment of time will have projects in various stages of planning and execution, this form of planning can be shown diagrammatically (Fig. 2.2), as the next stage in the development of corporate planning. If operational plans and project plans are brought together, then by combining the results of these planned activities is is possible to obtain a projection of the company at a future point of time.

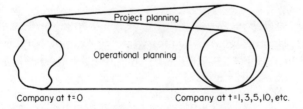

Company at t=0   Company at t=1,3,5,10, etc.

FIG. 2.2. *Operational and project planning,*

(c) Strategic Planning

The third type of planning is strategic planning. In practice, the recognition of the need for strategic planning frequently arises through a critical appraisal of the combined results of operational plans and project plans. These combined results offer a picture of the company at some point of time in the future. Implicitly or explicitly, the directors and top management of a company normally have an idea of the desired future shape and size of the firm. If this is explicit in terms of goals in key areas[5] then comparison between goals and planned results becomes quickly apparent. More frequently where goals are not formally articulated, the planned results may show an unsatisfactory element in one or more obvious dimensions such as profitability or market share and these discrepancies form the strategic gap. Diagrammatically, this position is shown in Fig. 2.3.

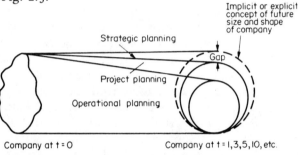

FIG. 2.3

If such a gap can be identified it can trigger a formal or informal process of strategic planning. But strategic planning demands different conceptual approaches and different types of forecasting, analysis and decision to operational or project planning. It requires the examination of the firm as a whole in relation to its environment and determination of the future posture of the company, especially its product market posture. It may require the examination of new protential areas of activity, the consideration of potential acquisitions, or even merger with another company.

The inter-relationship of operational, project and strategic planning

These different types of planning have been carefully defined partly to make a classification which is relevant to business, but also because the types of planning have different purposes, require different information and value inputs, require different analytical and planning techniques, produce different outputs and have different degrees of uncertainty. Thus, a focus for analysis is developed which can offer fruitful results in the development of a more systematic approach to the subject of corporate planning.

[5] Drucker, P., *The Practice of Management*, New York: Harper and Row, 1954; Chapter 7. Denning, B. W., "The integration of business studies at the conceptual level", *Journal of Management Studies,* Vol. 5, No. 1, February 1968.

Nevertheless, the different types of planning are clearly interrelated. For example:

1. New decisions emerging from strategic planning will often give rise to projects to implement the strategy.
2. Project planning and operational planning will be comparatively ineffective unless a framework of goals, policies and criteria for evaluation have been developed as a result of strategic planning.
3. The integration of projects into operations requires planning.
4. New projects may become a major part of the operations of a particular unit.
5. Frequently, the most important strategic decision will be to increase substantially the effectiveness of present operations, rather than more dramatic new moves. Under these circumstances, operational planning becomes the key method of implementing strategy.

Thus, despite the classification made, it would be misleading to imagine that these forms of planning can or should exist in isolated compartments.

The new element in corporate planning

There has recently been a great deal of interest in corporate long range planning as if it were something new. Yet this is highly questionable. Companies have had strategies, companies have planned projects and companies have planned operations over long or short term periods for many years. It certainly is true that a more systematic, analytical approach is now being taken to all three types of planning, especially strategic planning.

However, one significantly new element is the attempt to develop formal, systematic, integrated planning systems incorporating strategic planning, project planning and operational planning; and it is the discussion of the issues involved in developing more effective processes to produce better overall plans and action which seems vitally to concern the practising manager.

This can be suggested diagrammatically by a small addition to Fig. 2.4.

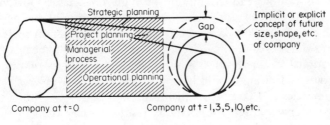

FIG. 2.4

The Present Research

Bearing this pattern of development in mind, it was decided to investigate the extent to which long range planning for the company as a whole had been introduced into British companies. A company doing long range planning was arbitrarily defined as one which was doing *formal, systematic planning for the company as a whole*, on a *continuous basis* over a period of *three years ahead or more*. This activity would be viewed as a managerial process over time.

Implicit in this approach are some important underlying hypotheses. The first of these is that a new managerial process with its inevitable expense, effort and attitudinal disruption will only be introduced if the top management believes that it is likely to produce greater effectiveness or efficiency. Many companies have historically operated successfully without such systems and many more continue to do so. Thus, there is a critical assumption that the introduction of an expensive and time-consuming process such as long range planning is a managerial response to particular business circumstances or managerial problems with which existing systems were unable to cope effectively.

It is hypothesized that the critical circumstances under which the introduction of such a process becomes justified are conditions of high financial risk or opportunity implying a critical strategic need, or a condition of great organizational complexity implying a critical co-ordinative need. Key parameters within these broad categories which were hypothesized are as follows:

Financial risk or opportunity	Degree of capital intensity Rate of technological growth Growth and variability of turnover/profit
Complexity	Size Type of organization structure Degree of vertical integration

If the assumption that formal systematic long range planning is a managerial response to conditions of high financial opportunity/risk and/or organizational complexity is correct, it should be possible to establish degrees of correlation between the introduction of such systems and the parameters quoted. Such correlation would tend to be related to the organizational characteristics above. Thus, it would be expected that longer range planning would have been adopted to a greater extent by some industries and companies than others.

This first article offers some tabular results of the extent of corporate long range planning processes in the United Kingdom in 1967. A second article will relate the existence of long range planning processes to ratings of the parameters noted earlier and to combinations of these parameters. Broadly, however, the introduction of long range planning processes shows the highest correlation with size and organizational complexity, second highest with the rate of technological change, third highest with the degree of capital intensity and little correlation with the variability of profits. Correlation with the degree of vertical integration was not found possible since no simple practical system of measuring or assessing the extent of vertical integration could be devised.

The second hypothesis is concerned with the examination of long range planning as a process over time. Any process can be analysed as a system with inputs, activities or transformations, and outputs. The activities and transformations must be organized and a major problem in developing a long range planning system is the allocation of responsibility for the necessary work. The assumption is made that if the basic needs for which long range planning was introduced were different in different companies, then quite different processes should exist. Further work will analyse the different organizational pattern in companies where the institution of long range planning appears primarily as a response to the different needs. Certainly there is evidence that different patterns of organization of the process correspond with the different managerial needs, strategic or co-ordinative, for which a company appears to have introduced long range planning. [6] In companies with complex organizations in business circumstances of great strategic risk or opportunity, organization of the activity reflects the dual needs.

The final hypothesis concerns the results achieved by companies with long range planning systems. If the arguments concerning the reasons for long range planning are valid, there is no *prima facie* reason why companies with long range planning systems should necessarily show better results than companies without such systems. [7] There is, however, a slight presumption that over a period of time the results of companies with long range planning systems should be better than the results of companies of the same size in the same industry without such systems. This presumption must, however, be very slight, since the quality of decisions made during the planning processes, the efficiency of execution of those decisions, and environmental factors which may be peculiar to a particular company are likely to outweigh the effects of a particular system. It is

[6] Denning, B. W., "Organizing the corporate planning functions", *Long Range Planning,* June 1969.

[7] This would be borne out by Professor T. Kempner in his survey of planning practices in British companies. While the anticipated connection between results and planning is not made explicit there is little evidence to suggest that there is any necessary connection. *Is Corporate Planning Really Necessary?*, BIM pamphlet, December 1968.

hoped to offer a comparative analysis of the business results of companies which have and have not undertaken long range planning.

Method of research

A questionnaire (Appendix III) was pre-tested by personal interview with three companies of markedly different characteristics which had introduced long range planning at different times in order to see whether the questionnaire was answerable without undue misunderstanding. One reason for this was that the questionnaire was so designed that if a company was carrying out formal systematic long range planning, it would take less than thirty minutes to complete, but if not, then the questionnaire would be virtually impossible to answer. In June 1967 the questionnaire was mailed to the chief-executive of each of the top 300 industrial and commercial companies in *The Times* list of 1966. Financial companies and nationalized industries were excluded because both types of concern have important special factors. In certain cases, follow up information was obtained by interview, by telephone, by discussion with a company executive or by scanning newspaper and journal articles. Finally, a supplementary short questionnaire consisting only of questions (1a), (b) and (c) was sent to fifty companies who had not completed the original questionnaire. The questionnaire was directly addressed to executives known to be in a position where they would be involved in any long range planning system.

Descriptive results

Tables of results are given in Appendixes I and II at the end of this article.

Appendix I shows that 75 per cent of companies replied in some form to the first questionnaire. The reasons for non-completion have been classified and in most cases where the classification is "in process of change of system", the company specifically stated that it was in the process of examining its approach to more systematic long range planning. Ninety-eight companies (33 per cent) completed the initial questionnaire and a further thirty-seven companies its successor. Application of the definition of long range planning to all the companies completing either question-naire indicated that sixty were not planning systematically up to three years ahead, and seventy-five had a planning system as defined.

Using the Standard Industrial Classification, it was only in the following industries that 25 per cent of the top 300 companies definitely carried out long range planning. These are:

Chemical and Allied Industries
Mechanical Engineering
Electrical Engineering

Vehicles
Other Metal Goods
Textiles
Paper, Printing and Publishing (all paper companies)
Other manufacturing (glass, rubber)
Construction
Conglomerate Holding Companies

Dates of introduction

Appendix II isolates two key factors, the date of introduction of long range planning and the time period over which the system operates.
On a cumulative basis the following results appear:

		Companies introducing during period
Companies doing LRP before end 1960	21	
		13
by end 1962	34	
		16
by end 1964	50	
		25
by mid 1967	75	

Of the 21 companies starting long range planning by 1960,
  5 were chemical companies
  4 were mechanical engineering companies

Time span

On a cumulative basis the following time spans were noted:

Companies planning out to 10 years or more	12
Companies planning out to 6 years or more	15
Companies planning out to 5 years or more	59
Companies planning out to 4 years or more	63
Companies planning out to 3 years or more	75

Of those companies planning ahead 6 years or more,
  6 are in the chemical industry
  2 are in the construction industry.

Virtually every company with a long range planning system adopted the rolling plan concept and this pattern seems essential if flexibility is to be retained in the face of uncertainty. The most popular time horizon for continuous planning is five years. This seems to represent a balance between the ability to make reasonable forecasts and the costs of operating the system. Only in chemicals and construction companies was ten years a frequent time span. This probably reflects the long term project thinking necessary in these industries.

Individual responsible for long range planning

(Based on initial questionnaire only).

The following table concerning the background of the executive responsible for long range planning is of interest. It would not be appropriate to describe all these individuals as corporate planners, since some companies maintain a systematic process without a separate corporate planning department.

Functional background	All companies	Companies with 5 years' experience of long range planning
Finance and Accounting	12	5
Economics	8	4
Technical	10	4
Law	2	1
General Management	17	8
Not identifiable	16	7
	65	29

These figures lend some support to the thesis that the initial thrust for long range planning tends to arise from the finance group in a company and that the role of chief accountant or finance director is initially often combined with that of a long range planner. They also support the contention advanced in an interview with the corporate planner of one company with over twenty years' experience of long range planning that the critical quality in a corporate planner is a general management capability.[8]

Foreign affiliation

A final point of interest concerns the extent to which British subsidiaries of foreign corporations have taken the lead in developing long range planning. These figures emerge in Table 2.1.

---

[8] It is interesting to find this view supported by Professor Kirby Warren in his book, *Long Range Planning. The Executive Viewpoint*, New York: Prentice Hall, Chapter 3.

TABLE 2.1

Date of introduction of planning	Independent British public companies	Wholly or partly owned subsidiaries of foreign companies
By end 1960	14	7
end 1960—end 1962	9	4
end 1962—end 1964	16	—
end 1964—mid 1967	25	—
Total planning	54	11
Total in sample	282	18
% Planning	23%	61%

Observations

The results tabled in this article can be viewed as being statistically weak. Although 78 per cent of companies answered the request for information in some way, only 33 per cent completed the first questionnaire. This low proportion of full responses needs to be viewed in the light of three factors.

(a) The design of the questionnaire, which was simple to complete if long range planning, as defined, was being carried out, and virtually impossible to complete if it was not.

(b) The general knowledge of the degree to which long range planning exists available to the writers through other professional sources.

(c) The original assumption about companies which replied only to the second questionnaire, where of the thirty-seven replies only eight had long range planning systems, and of these, four were already suspected of having them through other sources of knowledge. Thus it is considered that the conclusions which can be drawn from the figures are less suspect than would be the case on a bare statistical assessment.

It is reasonably clear that a small percentage of British companies had introduced long range planning by the summer of 1967. Bearing in mind the fact that the questionnaire was sent to the top 300 companies in *The Times* list and that long range planning is clearly associated with size and organizational complexity, it is reasonable to assume that a lesser proportion of smaller companies had introduced long range planning by that time.

It should be borne in mind that there is no underlying presumption that all companies should have a long range planning system, nor at this stage has any judgement been made of the quality of long range planning or of the process itself. Indeed the argument is very different. The argument is first that certain companies in particular business circumstances require a system but that it may not be justified for other companies in different circumstances; and secondly that observation of the different types of process may lead to some criteria for judgment about the efficacy of the process as developed in any one company. Until such criteria have been developed, it would be inappropriate to make any judgement of quality.

Appendix I

The extent of corporate long range planning in the United Kingdom Overall analysis of responses

		Initial Questionnaire								Supplementary questionnaire			Totals	
		Companies completing		Replying but not completing reason for no answer					No reply					
Standard Industrial Classification		No. of companies to whom questionnaire sent	Have planning system	Have no planning system	In process of change of system	Pressure of other business	Other specific reasons given	No reason		Have planning system	Have no planning system	No reply	Have planning system	Have no planning system or no information
I	Agriculture, Forestry, Fishing	2	1	—	—	—	—	—	—	1	—	—	1	1
II	Mining and Quarrying	1	—	—	—	—	—	—	—	1	—	—	—	1
III	Food, Drink, Tobacco	47	5	5	6	7	4	8	12	3	9	3	8	39
IV	Chemicals and Allied Industries	23	12	3	3	1	1	1	2	1	2	—	13	10
V	Metal Manufacture	17	1	2	4	1	2	1	6	—	4	2	1	16
VIa	Mechanical Engineering	43	11	7	2	6	5	2	10	1	2	1	12	31
VIb	Electrical Engineering	19	8	—	1	1	2	2	5	—	—	1	8	11
VII	Shipbuilding and Marine Engineering	6	—	—	—	1	1	2	2	—	—	—	—	6
VIII	Vehicles	11	3	1	—	1	3	2	1	1	1	1	4	7
IX	Other Metal Goods	5	2	—	1	—	—	1	1	—	1	—	2	3
X	Textiles	8	2	—	—	2	—	2	2	1	1	1	3	5
XI	Leather Goods and Fur	—	—	—	—	—	—	—	—	—	—	—	—	—
XII	Clothing and Footwear	2	—	—	1	—	—	—	1	—	—	—	—	2
XIII	Bricks, Pottery, Glass, Cement	15	3	6	1	3	—	—	2	—	1	1	3	12
XIV	Timber and Furniture	1	—	—	—	1	—	—	—	—	1	—	—	1
XV	Paper, Printing and Publishing	14	4	3	2	1	—	—	4	—	—	2	4	10
XVI	Other Manufacturing	8	3	—	—	1	1	—	3	—	—	1	3	5
XVII	Construction	5	3	—	—	—	2	—	—	—	—	—	3	2
XVIII	Gas, Electricity and Water	—	—	—	—	—	—	—	—	—	—	—	—	—
XIX	Transport and Communication	15	1	—	1	—	4	2	7	—	1	—	1	14
XX	Distributive Trades	20	—	—	4	1	6	4	5	1	3	—	1	19
XXI	Insurance, Banking and Finance	—	—	—	—	—	—	—	—	—	—	—	—	—
XXII	Professional and Scientific Services	—	—	—	—	—	—	—	—	—	—	—	—	—
XXIII	Miscellaneous Services	14	2	1	1	2	2	1	5	—	2	—	2	12
XXIV	Conglomerate Holding Companies	24	6	3	1	1	6	2	5	—	1	—	6	18
	Total	300	67	31	28	30	39	30	75	8	29	13	75	225

Appendix II

The extent of corporate long range planning in the United Kingdom
Companies with long range planning—dates of introduction—time span

Standard Industrial Classification	No. of cos. asked	No. of cos. completing	No. of cos. with LRP	Date of introduction	Time span
Agriculture, Forestry and Fishing	2	1	1	1965—1	3 years—1
Mining and Quarrying	1	—	—	N.A.	N.A.
Food, Drink & Tobacco	47	22	8	1950—1	
				1962—1	5 years—5
				1963—1	4 years—1
				1965—3	3 years—2
				1966—2	
Chemicals	23	18	13	pre 1939—1	
				1947—2	10 years—4
				1950—1	8 years—1
				1952—1	6 years—1
				1962—2	5 years—6
				1964—2	3 years—1
				1965—1	
				1966—3	
Metal Manufacture	17	3	1	5 yr. plan 1950	10 years.
				10 yr. plan 1962	
Mechanical Engineering	43	21	12	1955—2	
				1958—1	
				1960—1	10 years—1
				1961—1	5 years—9
				1962—2	4 years—1
				1963—2	3 years—1
				1965—1	
				1966—2	
Electrical Engineering	19	8	8	1955—1	
				1959—1	7 years—1
				1962—4	5 years—6
				1964—1	4 years—1
				1966—1	
Shipbuilding and Marine Engineering	6	—	—	—	—
Vehicles	11	6	4	1949—1	
				1952—1	5 years—4
				1961—1	
				1963—1	
Other Metal Goods	5	3	2	1956—1	5 years—2
				1964—1	

Companies with long range planning—Dates of introduction—time span   *(contd.)*

Standard Industrial Classification	No. of cos. asked	No. of cos. completing	No. of cos. with LRP	Date of introduction	Time span
Textiles	8	4	3	1961—1 1962—1 1963—1	 10 years—1 5 years—2
Leather Goods and Fur	—	—	—	—	—
Clothing and Footwear	2	—	—	—	—
Bricks, Pottery, Glass, Cement	15	10	3	1957—1 1965—1 1966—1	10 years—1 5 years—1 3 years—1
Timber and Furniture	—	—	—	—	—
Paper, Printing and Publishing	14	7	4	1960—1 1964—1 1965—1 1967—1	 5–15 yrs—1 5 years—2 3 years—1
Other manufacturing	8	3	3	1966—3	10 years—1 5 years—2
Construction	5	3	3	1956—1 1963—1 1964—1	3–15 yrs—1 3–10 yrs—1 5 years—1
Gas, Electricity and Water	—	—	—	—	—
Transport and Communication	15	2	1	1964—1	4 years—1
Distributive Trades	20	4	1	pre-1958	5 years—1
Miscellaneous Services	14	5	2	1957—1 1967—1	3 years—2
Conglomerate Holding Companies	24	10	6	1963—1 1964—2 1965—1 1966—2	 5 years—3 3 years—3

Appendix III

Questionnaire on Long Range Planning
Confidential

Name and position of respondent:
Name of organization:
Number of operating divisions or sub-groups:
Number of employees:
Approximate annual sales: Less than £5 million
        £5–£20 million
        £20–£50 million
        £50–£100 million
        Over £100 million
Main products:

---

1. Does your company have a formal planning sequence?   Yes/No*
   If so,
   (a) Over what time period does it operate?
   (b) When was this plan introduced?
   (c) Do you regard this sequence as 'long range planning'?
                   Yes/No*

2. Does your company have one department which deals exclusively
   with this planning sequence?   Yes/No*
   If so,
   (a) How many management level staff are there in the department?
   (b) Are there specialized sub-departments within the department?
                   Yes/No*
   If so, what are they?

3. Who is responsible for this planning sequence?

4. To whom does he report?

5. From what sort of background does he come?
   (e.g. economics, engineering).

6. Is there a division in responsibility between 'operational' and
   'strategic' planning?   Yes/No*
   If so, could you explain briefly:

7. Below is a list of functions that are sometimes held to be part of long
   range planning. Could you please indicate the extent to which the
   planning department (or long range department if one exists) in your

---

* Delete where necessary.

company is responsible for these functions? If there are other functions for which your planning department has some responsibility could you please add these to the list?

	Responsibility for intiation	Responsibility for co-ordination	Responsibility for detailed work	No responsibility
Economic Forecasting				
Technological Forecasting				
Establishment of Assumptions about the future				
Economic Analysis of markets				
Sales Forecasting				
Estimation of product life cycles				
Determination of Corporate goals				
Appraisal of top management's attitudes				
Examination of company's strengths and weaknesses				
Evaluation of top management's proposals				
Determination of markets in which to operate				
Development of new products				
Market development				
Manpower projections				
Capital budgeting				
Preparation of investment proposals				
Planning new facilities				
Integration of divisional plans				

8. Would you be prepared to give further information on a confidential basis to research staff of the London Business School about your planning systems? Yes/No*

* Delete where necessary.

3

The Extent and Nature of Corporate Long Range Planning in the U.K.: Part 2

B. W. DENNING AND M. E. LEHR

Introduction

In an earlier article a broad description with tabular results was given of some research into British corporate long range planning practice.[1] A careful definition of long range planning was given and a hypothesis about reasons for its introduction was advanced. This article examines the relationship between the incidence of long range planning systems and certain key parameters of financial opportunity/risk and complexity.

The Definition of Planning Companies

"Planning" companies were defined as those companies which answered yes to the question "Does your company have a formal planning sequence?" and who stated that this sequence covered a time period of at least 3 years. The remaining companies were classed as "Other than Planning", including as a subset those companies that positively identified themselves as "Non-planning" by answering the first question in the negative.

The Key Parameters

If the introduction of formal long range planning is, in fact, a managerial response to critical strategic or co-ordinative needs, one would expect evidence to that effect in the observed pattern of incidence. Vital strategic needs exist in situations of high financial risk or opportunity, whereas co-

---

This article was originally published in the *Journal of Management Studies*, Volume 9, No. 1, February 1972.

[1] Denning, B. W. and Lehr, M. E., The extent and nature of Corporate Long Range Planning in the U.K., *Journal of Management Studies*.

ordinative needs increase with the complexity of organizations. The following key parameters were selected for the analysis:

Financial Risk/Opportunity—Rate of technological change
　　　　　　　　　　　　—Degree of capital intensity
　　　　　　　　　　　　—Growth and variability of turn-
　　　　　　　　　　　　　over/profits
　　　　　Complexity—Size
　　　　　　　　　　—Type of organization structure
　　　　　　　　　　Degree of vertical integration

The construction of satisfactory objective measures of these variables is difficult, but once done, analysis can proceed using standard statistical techniques. In fact meaningful measures, described later, were constructed for all the above variables except the degree of vertical integration.

Financial Risk and Opportunity

1. Rate of Technological Change

Although any assessment of the rate of technological change will be qualitative, judgements by independent experts have some degree of objectivity. Accordingly, six independent experts in universities, government departments and consultancy firms were asked to rate each company on a five-point scale, ranging from 1 (very slow) to 5 (very rapid). The mean of the six ratings for each company was used as the basic measure of rate of technological change. See Appendix I for comparison and examination of the statistical implications.

Table 3.1 gives the mean composite ratings and standard deviation for the three basic categories from which it is apparent that the difference in means between "planning" and "other than planning" companies is high relative to the standard deviation. When tested against the normal distribution, the probability of the means differing by as much as 0.5 with sample sizes of 76 and 224 is less than 1 in 1000. These figures offer some evidence that "planning" companies tend to have a higher rate of technological change than the remainder. The same conclusion emerges from a study of the

TABLE 3.1. *Comparison of Composite Technological Change Ratings by Category of Company*

	Planning	Other than planning	Non-planning
Mean composite rating	3.14	2.63	2.71
Standard deviation	0.45	0.32	0.30
No. in sample	76	224	42

individual ratings (Table 3.2), although the degree of variation is higher. This is significant evidence that there was an adequate degree of objectivity in the ratings used.

These figures demonstrate that the rate of technological change and the introduction of long range planning are connected, a view strengthened by the more detailed breakdowns given in Table 3.3 and Fig. 3.1, where a

TABLE 3.2. *Mean Technological Change Ratings by Expert and Category of Company*

	Planning		Other than planning		Non-planning	
Expert	Mean	Standard deviation	Mean	Standard deviation	Mean	Standard deviation
1	2.24	0.65	2.01	0.54	1.98	0.50
2	3.36	0.70	2.83	0.86	2.76	0.94
3	3.01	1.13	2.44	1.01	2.60	0.62
4	3.18	1.10	2.37	0.91	2.67	0.75
5	3.21	0.63	2.62	0.58	2.71	0.49
6	3.87	0.85	3.50	0.86	3.57	1.01
No. in sample	76		224		42	

TABLE 3.3. *Incidence of Long Range Planning by Rate of Technological Changes*

Composite rating	Total companies	Planning companies	Planning companies as % of total
1.00 — 1.25	0	0	—
1.25 — 1.50	2	0	0.0
1.50 — 1.75	10	1	10.0
1.75 — 2.00	23	2	8.7
2.00 — 2.25	26	2	7.7
2.25 — 2.50	65	10	15.4
2.50 — 2.75	37	5	13.5
2.75 — 3.00	55	20	36.4
3.00 — 3.25	24	9	37.5
3.25 — 3.50	26	8	30.8
3.50 — 3.75	6	4	66.7
3.75 — 4.00	13	6	46.2
4.00 — 4.25	8	4	50.0
4.25 — 4.50	3	3	100.0
4.50 — 4.75	2	2	100.0
4.75 — 5.00	0	0	—
Total	300	76	25.3

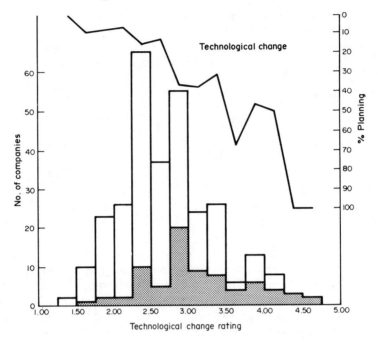

FIG. 3.1

strong correlation between the rate of technological change and the existence of formal long range planning is evident. Thus we may view rate of technological change as a progressive stimulus towards the introduction of formal long range planning.

2. Degree of Capital Intensity

There are many possible measures of capital intensity. Since space does not allow a full treatment of the arguments for any one measure, it will merely be noted that given the objectives of the research, the measure of capital intensity required needed to isolate the higher risk assets. This led us to choose as a measure of capital, fixed assets at cost less land and buildings since those include the majority of single purpose assets, normally those of the highest risk. Accordingly, the measure of capital intensity is fixed assets at cost excluding land and building per employee.[2]

[2] Capital intensities calculated in this fashion may still give rise to considerable anomalies, e.g. because assets data may include overseas subsidiaries whilst the number of employees relates to the U.K. only. Such anomalies were corrected where possible by comparison with capital intensities, turnover per employee, etc., of other companies in the same industry.

There is a clear tendency for planning companies to have a higher capital intensity than those without planning systems (Table 3.4).

TABLE 3.4. *Comparison of Capital Intensities by Category of Company*

Fixed assets at cost (less land and buildings) per employee	Planning	Other than planning	Non-planning
Mean capital intensity	3023	2367	2145
Standard deviation	2554.9×10^4	255.0×10^4	388.8×10^4
No. in sample	76	224	42

However, the difference in means is not a significant measure in this case, for the distribution of capital intensity is highly skew—a few companies have very high capital intensities—nor is the standard deviation a meaningful statistic. Nevertheless, Table 3.5 and Fig. 3.2 suggest a relationship between capital intensity and long range planning, although it is less impressive than with rate of technological change. In part this may result from the choice of measure, for as noted earlier, we cannot be certain that the fixed assets and employees figures refer to the same establishments, and the effect of inflation upon fixed asset valuation may be important. Nevertheless, the comparatively low incidence of planning among even highly capital intensive firms suggests that capital intensity is less critical than the rate of technological change.

TABLE 3.5. *Incidence of Long Range Planning by Capital Intensity*

Fixed assets at cost (less land and buildings) per employee		Number in class	Number of planning companies in class	Percentage of planning companies in class
Above	Not above			
0	505	30	3	10.0
505	700	30	5	16.7
700	852	30	6	20.0
852	1055	30	7	23.3
1055	1209	30	7	23.3
1209	1375	30	8	26.7
1375	1585	30	7	23.3
1585	2120	30	10	33.3
2120	4130	30	11	36.7
4130	30000	30	12	40.0
Total		300	76	25.3

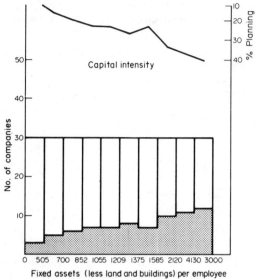

FIG. 3.2

3. Growth and Variability of Turnover/Profits

Turnover figures over 10 years were not sufficiently broadly available to draw any conclusions relating to this variable. However, profit figures gross of depreciation are available for most firms over 10 years, and these were employed for the analysis of growth and variability. Profits net of depreciation would have the disadvantage that their variability is critically dependent upon capital intensity, an undesirable characteristic if variables are to be as nearly independent as possible.

Growth and variability are very closely related parameters. The degree of variability in profits is entirely dependent upon the secular trend about which these are assumed to vary. For this analysis an exponential curve was fitted to the profits data by least-square methods and this was used to observe deviation of actual profits from this curve.[3]

---

[3] Thus, if we know profits (P) for years $1 - 10$, we can fit the curve:

$$P_t^* = P_0(1 + g)^t$$

to the data

where

P_t = actual profits in year t,
P_0 = predicted profits in year o,
P_t^* = predicted profits in year t,
g = growth rate of profits.

A summary analysis of growth and variability of gross profits is given in Table 3.6, and in neither case is the difference in means significant with respect to the standard deviation:[4] Thus, there is little to suggest that variability of growth and profits, as measured, help to explain the existence or non-existence of corporate planning. The detailed breakdowns of Tables 3.7 and 3.8 (Figs 3.3 and 3.4) confirm this. There is much variation

TABLE 3.6. *Comparison of Growth Rate and Variability of Gross Profits by Category of Company*

	Planning	Other than planning	Non-planning
Mean growth rate (%)	11.29	8.66	9.47
Standard deviation	128.22	116.40	169.91
No. in sample	71.	216.	41.
Mean variability (%)	13.79	13.77	15.91
	111.51	147.03	299.04
	71.	216.	41.

TABLE 3.7. *Incidence of Planning by Growth Rate of Gross Profit*

Growth rate % Above	Not above	Number in class	Number of planning companies in class	Percentage planning in class
−35.0	−1.4	32	4	12.5
−1.4	3.2	27	7	25.9
3.2	5.2	28	7	25.0
5.2	6.5	31	6	19.4
6.5	8.6	31	10	32.3
8.6	10.0	29	8	27.6
10.0	12.0	25	5	20.0
12.0	14.9	27	6	22.2
14.9	21.6	31	10	32.3
21.6	70.0	26	8	30.8
Total		287	71	24.7

The growth (g) fitted by this method is the geometric growth rate and the corresponding measure of variability is the mean percentage absolute deviation, which can be expressed mathematically as:

$$\frac{1}{10} \sum_{r=1}^{t=10} \frac{|P_t - P_t^*|}{P_t^*} \times 100.$$

[4] There were thirteen firms for which insufficient data are available to calculate accurate measures of the growth rate and variability of gross profits.

TABLE 3.8. *Incidence of Planning by Variability of Gross Profits*

Variability		Number in class	Number of planning companies in class	Percentage planning in class
Above	Not above			
0	4.4	33	5	15.2
4.4	5.5	25	10	40.0
5.5	7.6	29	6	20.7
7.6	9.0	27	7	25.9
9.0	10.6	29	8	27.6
10.6	12.1	27	6	22.2
12.1	14.9	29	7	24.1
14.9	18.1	28	6	21.4
18.1	26.0	28	6	21.4
26.0	75.0	32	10	31.3
		287	71	24.7

in the incidence of planning from class to class but no discernible pattern to it.

It should not be overlooked, however, that both of the measures have serious deficiencies. First, they do not distinguish internal expansion from growth by merger, and these two forms of growth have markedly different

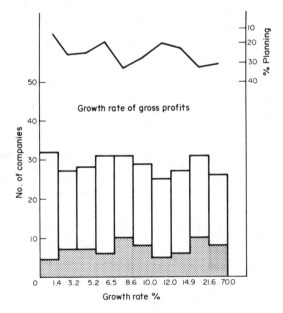

FIG. 3.3

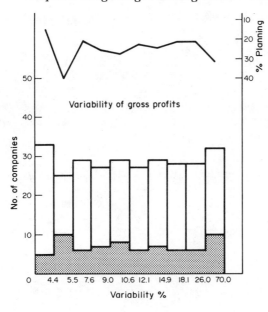

FIG. 3.4

effects upon an organization. Secondly, merger growth completely violates the assumption of smooth exponential growth, producing an unduly high measured variability. There is no way out of this dilemma, for nearly all the 300 companies are affected. But if we eliminate those companies where merger effects predominate (Table 3.9), there is no improvement in the degree of explanation, confirming our view that growth and variability barely influence the incidence of corporate long range planning.

TABLE 3.9. *Adjusted Growth Rate and Variability of Gross Profits by Category of Company*

	Planning	Other than planning	Non-planning
Mean growth rate (%)	10.52	8.72	8.30
Standard deviation	135.37	103.62	155.37
No. in sample	47	176	24
Mean variability (%)	9.35	11.36	13.36
Standard deviation	83.26	97.11	201.76
No. in sample	47	176	24

Complexity

4. Size

Size of company is an elusive concept. Four possible measures were examined—fixed assets at cost, fixed assets at cost (excluding land and buildings), turnover, and number of employees. Comparative means and standard deviations for these four measures by category are given in Table 3.10.

TABLE 3.10. *Comparison of Measure of Size by Category of Company*

	Planning	Other than planning	Non-planning
Fixed Assets (at cost)			
Mean	101,364	42,695	41,545
Standard deviation	$33,644 \times 10^6$	2495×10^6	2114×10^6
No. in sample	76	224	42
Fixed Assets (at cost) *excl. Land and Buildings*			
Mean	94,743	33,474	31,269
Standard deviation	$21,730 \times 10^6$	2137×10^6	2100×10^6
No. in sample	76	224	42
Turnover			
Mean	178,585	74,990	101,092
Standard deviation	$82,534 \times 10^6$	1119×10^6	$24,200 \times 10^6$
No. in sample	76	224	42
No. of employees			
Mean	33,955	15,753	19,153
Standard deviation	1984×10^6	284×10^6	496×10^6
No. in sample	76	224	42

Table 3.10 displays what one would intuitively expect, that larger companies are more likely to plan formally; but it cannot be said that any one dimension of size is clearly superior to the others. The separation between the means of the planning and other than planning categories is high whatever measure is chosen, and a highly skew distribution prevents the standard deviation from providing useful information.

The breakdown for each variable shows (Fig. 3.5) that fixed assets excluding land and buildings is the best single explanatory variable and Table 3.11 and Fig. 3.6 demonstrate that size is an extremely important parameter, the incidence of planning in the largest companies being as high as 67 per cent.

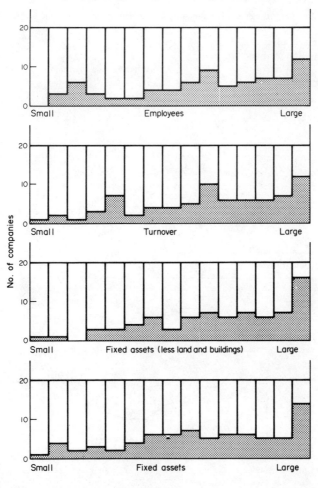

FIG. 3.5

5. *Organization Structure*

Organization structure is a different type of parameter susceptible to classification rather than measurement with a spectrum of organization structure that makes it difficult, for example, to distinguish functional from divisional structures. However, great subtlety of classification seemed inappropriate and the companies were allocated to one of seven categories as follows:

1. Single-plant functional.
2. Multi-plant functional.

TABLE 3.11. *Incidence of Planning by Fixed Assets at Cost (less Land and Building)*

Fixed assets at cost (less land and building) £m		Number in class	Number of planning companies in class	Percentage planning in class
Above	Not above			
0.0	4.8	30	1	3.3
4.8	6.9	30	1	3.3
6.9	8.9	30	5	16.7
8.6	11.2	30	5	16.7
11.2	14.6	30	7	23.3
14.6	19.2	30	8	26.7
19.2	23.5	30	10	33.3
23.5	34.0	30	10	33.3
34.0	75.2	30	9	30.0
75.2	1740.0	30	20	66.7
Total		300	76	25.3

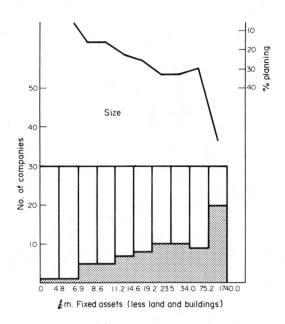

FIG. 3.6

3. Multi-plant divisional (not more than one foreign manufacturing subsidiary).
4. Multi-plant divisional (two to five foreign manufacturing subsidiaries).
5. Multi-national (more than five foreign manufacturing subsidiaries).
6. Subsidiary of foreign multi-national.
7. Conglomerate.

Categories 1−5 are in ascending order of complexity, but the last two are somewhat different, with no necessary increase in complexity between 5 per cent and 6 per cent. The conglomerate companies were classified into a separate group since they have co-ordinative needs of a distinctive type.

Organization structure appears to play a considerable part in determining the strength of the pressure towards the introduction of formal long range planning (Table 3.12 and Fig. 3.7). The average length of time that long range planning had been in existence at the date of the questionnaire is also given in Table 3.12. It strikingly confirms the conclusions drawn from pattern of incidence data. Not only is corporate planning more frequently found in the more complex organizations, but it will have been introduced at *a much earlier date.*[5]

Furthermore, the pioneering role of overseas-owned companies is clearly displayed, well over half of those in our sample being engaged in corporate long range planning. Another interesting conclusion is that the co-ordinative needs peculiar to conglomerate companies do not result in a greater tendency towards the introduction of long range planning.

TABLE 3.12. *Incidence and Average Length of Long Range Planning by Organization and Type*

Type of organization	All companies	Planning companies	Planning as % of total	Average Length of existence (yr)	Standard deviation
1	—	—	—	—	—
2	9	1	11.1	18.0	0
3	87	9	10.3	4.4	11.1
4	78	19	24.4	3.7	2.6
5	85	30	35.3	7.0	38.1
6	17	11	64.7	12.6	29.1
7	24	6	25.0	3.3	1.2
Total	300	76	25.3		

[5] The single planning company in group 2, something of an anomaly, is a product of government influence. It is therefore a special case.

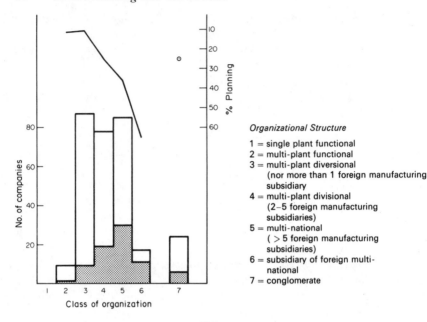

FIG. 3.7

6. Vertical Integration

Differences in vertical integration are not susceptible to the analytical approach so far used. We discovered no simple method which would enable us to assign values to this parameter; nor did we feel ourselves able to make even rough groupings. Given sufficient data on input and output a scale might be constructed and this could be a further research step. However, we are left only with an unsupported view, arguable from first principles, that there is greater complexity where successive operations must be closely integrated internally than when all materials and components can be obtained externally and all sales are to outside customers.

The Problem of Independence

The type of analysis so far carried out assumes the independence of the variables in two quite different ways: first, it assumes that the variables themselves are independent of one another, and second, that their effects upon the incidence of long range planning are independent. There is no *a priori* reason to think that either of these is true.

First, the variables we have employed cannot reasonably be considered independent. For example, there is clearly some relationship between size and organization structure. Even where there is no causal relationship, however, it may happen that variables are linked because of the industry structure of this particular sample. High technological change and capital intensity, for example, are both characteristics of the petro-chemical industry. Although in our sample this is balanced by the much less capital-intensive electronics sector which also has a high rate of technological change, relationships of this kind may well lead to erroneous conclusions, if the effects of variables are evaluated independently.

Similarly, the second assumption cannot be sustained. We would not expect a high rate of technological change alone to prompt the introduction of sophisticated procedures in comparatively small one-product companies. Different environmental factors clearly act together in prompting a company to introduce formal long range planning. The nature of the relationship may be very complex—the effects of some combinations of variables may be additive, some may be independent, whilst others may exhibit a threshold effect.

A Multivariate Approach

If the probability of a company being in the category "planning" is constant over time, then the statistical technique of discriminant analysis may be employed. This seeks to establish that linear function of the independent variables that best explains the separation of the sample into two groups. The value of the function for any firm will then indicate the likelihood of that firm being found in the category planning.

For our sample the linear function that gave the best separation between the two categories was:

$$Z = 2.49 \text{ TEC} + .56 \text{ CAP} + .90 \text{ GRS} - .07 \text{ DEV}$$
$$+ 1.83 \text{ EMP} + 1.17 \text{ FAC} - .86 \text{ SAL} + 1.47 \text{ ORG}$$

where

TEC is technological change rating,
CAP is capital intensity (at cost less land and buildings),
GRS is squared deviation of growth rate of gross profits from mean growth rate of sample,
DEV is variability of profits,
EMP is number of employees,
FAC is fixed assets at cost, less land and buildings,
SAL is turnover,
ORG is organization structure.*

Since each variable has been divided by its standard deviation the coefficients broadly indicate the relative importance of the different parameters. However, the negative coefficient of SAL indicates the presence of non-linearities which qualify any conclusions: this coefficient becomes positive when other size variables are withdrawn from the model. Thus the three size variables must be considered together. If only one size variable is included, number of employees gives the best separation, contrary to the conclusions of the earlier unvariate analysis.

The relative values of the coefficients of the other variables are, however, comparatively stable and their values are significant. Only in the case of growth rates did a transformation increase the explanatory power of the variable.

The mean values of Z for the two categories planning and other than planning, were 22.31 and 17.80 respectively. This means that if the value of Z for a particular company was more than halfway between 17.80 and 22.31 we would expect to find it in the category planning. On this basis we can test the efficiency of our discriminant function by examining how many companies it misclassifies. The figures are given in Table 3.13. Clearly the predictive efficiency of this approach is not great since only 78 per cent of non-planning companies and 58 per cent of planning companies are correctly classified.

TABLE 3.13

		No of companies classified in group		
		Planning	Non-planning	Total
No. of companies in group	Planning	44	32	76
	Non-planning	49	175	224
	Total	93	207	300

This result, however, highlights one important characteristic of our problem: there is no presumption that companies will automatically be planning formally because they are in situations of high risk or complexity. They may react to such situations by introducing formal planning systems; but they may not. Furthermore, a static analysis can only deal with the situation at a point in time and cannot take into account the possibility that a company will introduce planning in the future.

A major characteristic required of our function is that most planning companies will show high values and that few low-valued companies will be planning. The discriminant function we have obtained does in fact exhibit this characteristic. Of the companies with the 100 lowest values only 6 are planning companies, whilst no fewer than 36 of the planning companies, almost half, are found within the 60 highest values, 18 of them within the 29 highest values. Considering the limitations of both data and model, this must be considered significant evidence in support of the underlying hypothesis.

A Dynamic Multivariate Approach

The probability function of a company becoming engaged in long range planning does not remain constant over time. The situation is dynamic. There is a steady increase in this probability for all companies over time, as literature proliferates and knowledge spreads. This may or may not be desirable but it is an observed fact. Secondly, the process is dynamic in that we should be concerned with the *change* for the non-planning to the planning category, rather than the existence or non-existence of a planning system at a point in time.[6]

It has not proved possible to construct a model which is theoretically sound and for which the parameters can be estimated from our data. However, it is possible to demonstrate by the use of a regression model weighted by date of introduction that one could considerably improve upon the explanatory power of the discriminant function arrived at earlier.

However, the purpose of this research is not predictive, in the sense that we are not attempting to establish threshold conditions under which corporate planning should be introduced. Rather we are examining sets of conditions and needs which may have led managers to introduce corporate planning before it became fashionable, and the differences in types of process as a response to the needs. Thus, the marginal improvements in ability to predict by a more sophisticated model, while of academic interest, have little relevance to the problems with which we are concerned.

Conclusions

This article has briefly explained the methods and presented the results obtained in the exploration of the hypothesis that the introduction of formal systematic corporate long range planning is a managerial response to two separate sets of needs—strategic or co-ordinative. Examination of certain critical dimensions of strategic need indicated a strong positive relationship between the introduction of long range planning and a high rate of technological change, a positive and strong relationship with capital intensity, and a slight tendency for planning to exist where growth is either above or below average. Strong relationships also exist between the

---

[6] There is, of course, the possibility that a company may in time abandon a planning system that has been introduced if it becomes inappropriate, but the presumption is that a system will tend to be retained once it has been established.

introduction of long range planning and both the size of company and the complexity of its organization structure. The third element of complexity, degree of vertical integration, could not be explored. Multi-variate analysis strongly supported the tentative conclusions drawn from a variable by variable study.

It had been anticipated that complexity would be an important element in the introduction of long range planning, but its equal position with strategic factors was unexpected, and lends support to the view that the nature and design of the planning process may be critical in obtaining an effective response to management's needs.

Secondly, the findings lend support to the view advanced in the earlier article, that if long range planning is introduced to meet different managerial needs, it is appropriate that the organization of the process should be different in companies with different key parameters. We are currently examining aspects of the planning processes in the companies which responded positively to our questionnaire against the different variables and within this framework, hope to provide some normative approaches to the organizing of corporate planning.

Appendix

Distribution of Technological Change Rating by Expert

	No. of companies given rating:					Total companies	Mean rating	Standard deviation
Expert	1	2	3	4	5			
1	70	147	76	7	—	300	2.07	0.58
2	20	59	143	64	14	300	2.96	0.87
3	46	103	82	56	13	300	2.58	1.10
4	43	107	101	32	17	300	2.58	1.08
5	8	115	117	57	3	300	2.77	0.66
6	1	35	106	100	58	300	3.60	0.88

Although considerable variation is seen both in the mean ratings and in the dispersion of individual ratings about the means, the *comparative* ratings accorded to different companies displayed a high degree of uniformity. Because of this consistency, the mean of the six individual ratings was used as a composite measure of the rate of technological change for each company. As had been hoped, the distribution of this variable was very close to the normal distribution, a quality looked for in a satisfactory measure of the rate of technological change. Standard statistical tests were, therefore, appropriate for the analysis of the date.

4

Organized Planning in Major U.K. Companies

B. TAYLOR AND P. IRVING *

During recent years, increasing attention has been paid to Corporate Long Range Planning in U.K. business and academic circles. Prior to 1962, the phrases "Corporate Planning" or "Long Range Planning" were virtually unknown on the British Management scene, whereas today many managers are becoming increasingly familiar with their use, even though they may not fully appreciate their implications.[1]

Although planning existed in some British companies prior to 1962, it was certainly not accorded the attention it is today. In the short space of 9 years, a major revolution has occurred in management thinking which is evidenced by the numerous articles, seminars, courses and conferences on Corporate Long Range Planning.

Despite all the publicity, relatively little is known about organized corporate planning in British companies. According to the Kempner— Hewkin survey published in 1968:

> Whatever may be said, few companies have implemented corporate planning which is the acid test of acceptance. A number of executives reject it completely, either verbally or by their actions. Others pay lip service to it for a variety of reasons, the foremost of which is perhaps a lack of comprehension of what corporate planning is really about.

While not disputing these findings which relate to companies in general, one might question whether they apply to firms that have some experience of corporate planning.

To find the answer, one must look at the American experience and in particular, at the work of K. A. Ringbakk, who in 1967 undertook a study of organized corporate planning in major U.S. companies.

Ringbakk states:

> Organized corporate long range planning is neither as well accepted nor as well practiced as suggested by the literature on the subject. Although much planning is

This article was originally published in *Long Range Planning*, Volume 3, No. 4, June 1971.
* University of Bradford Management Centre. Prof. Taylor is now with the Administrative Staff College, Henley-on-Thames.

done, the effort is often sporadic, it is lacking in co-ordination and it is less formalized and sophisticated than much of the literature suggests.[2]

These findings indicate that in both Britain and America, organized corporate planning is not as well developed as the publicity suggests and although this might be expected in Britain, one might question why so little progress has been made in America where the emphasis on organized planning started in the immediate post-war era.

If one examines the planning literature, it is apparent that relatively little is known of the reasons why a subject of such generally accepted importance has seen so little effective development in practice. Furthermore, the general lack of progress cannot be explained solely on the grounds of ineffective management, as many otherwise highly effective organizations have encountered difficulty in getting on with the work of planning.[3]

Research Method

Against this background it was decided to undertake a study to determine:

1. Whether the findings of Ringbakk and Kempner—Hewkin relating to the present state of development of corporate planning in Britain and America are supported by the experience of major British companies with some experience of corporate planning.
2. Why leading British companies are developing corporate planning.
3. What major factors have affected its development in these companies.
4. To draw from the findings some conclusions about the future development of corporate planning and the benefits to be obtained from it.

It was considered that the only way to tackle the research was to talk to appropriate personnel responsible for the development of planning in each company, but it was recognized that if interviews had been confined only to corporate planning executives, there were considerable dangers of bias. In order to counter this and at the same time, broaden the base of the research, a senior line manager and the chief executive or a senior board member was interviewed in about one third of the sample.

While the dangers of personal bias by planning executives are inherent in a study of this nature, subsequent interviews with other interested parties indicated no evidence of distortion.

The fieldwork took place between May and December 1969, and in total, over 120 hours were spent in interviews.

Choice of Companies

The companies selected were drawn from 16 industrial classifications and nearly all of them supply diverse products to many different markets. About half of the companies operate internationally and in size, their annual turnovers range from £16 m to over £1,000 m.

An indication of the experience of these companies is given by the year in which steps were first taken by them to establish corporate planning.

Date	Percentage
1968	3
1967	19
1966	8
1965	16
1964	16
1963	11
1962	19
No response	8
	100

While acknowledging that this sample is not random, it is broadly based in terms of industrial classification and size. It is however, deliberately biased towards major U.K. companies with some experience of corporate planning in an effort to shed new light on this relatively new and complex business concept.

Corporate Planning Defined

For the purpose of this study, corporate planning is defined in two parts:

1. The formal process of developing objectives for the corporation and its component parts, evolving alternative strategies to achieve these objectives and doing this against a background of a systematic appraisal of internal strengths and weaknesses and external environmental changes.
2. The process of translating strategy into detailed operational plans and seeing that these plans are carried out.

The Literature

The literature on planning suggests that the development of organized corporate planning is a complex and difficult task, as evidenced by the general lack of progress in both Britain and the United States.[4] For it to develop at all, there must be an awareness of the need for change and a willingness on the part of corporate management to deal with chance on a continuing and co-ordinated basis. Not all companies recognize the need for change, nor do they deal with it in the manner suggested above and therefore in such companies, planning is unlikely to make much progress.

Given that this particular difficulty will not apply to all companies, the development of organized planning seems to depend to a large extent, on the ability of the planner to involve the chief executive, the top management team and line management in the planning process, and get them to accept it as a meaningful and worthwhile exercise which merits a great deal of serious attention. In this task, he will be impeded by a variety of problems, many of them political or psychological in nature. He will have to contend with misconceptions, distorted communications and the natural reluctance of people working under considerable pressure to sit down and think about the problems of the future. A great deal depends upon the planner himself and upon his ability to anticipate the problems and frustrations which he will inevitably encounter.

The Findings

The Significance of Management Style

Table 4.1 shows the composition of companies in the sample. Of the 27 companies, 22 had separate formal planning functions, 4 had no formal planning and 1 had planning organized and controlled as part of the finance function. The 4 companies without formal planning were extremely interesting in that 1 had tried to introduce planning and failed, and in 2 of the other 3, the respondents identified a need for a more formal approach to planning, but felt it was incompatible with their existing management style. Thus, 3 of the 4 companies without formal planning had been

TABLE 4.1. *The Planning Function*

	Number of companies	Percentage
Companies with a separate formal planning function	22	82
Companies in which planning is organized and controlled as part of the finance function	1	4
Companies having no formal planning[a]	4	14
	27	100

[a] Of the 4 companies with no formal planning function, 1 had tried to introduce planning and failed, while 2 had a management style which was incompatible with a formal approach to planning.

prevented from translating a felt need into meaningful practice and their experiences are worth examining to find out why this was so.

"Management Style" is the characteristic way a company operates its business. It is "the way we do things around here". Though it is difficult to summarize the concept of style for a number of companies the management style of a particular company is easily observable.[5]

A comparison of management styles in companies with and without separate planning functions indicates a close degree of correlation, which suggests that the development of a formal approach to planning is significantly affected by the particular management style.

One planner explained his situation as follows:

> Each operating company differs—some are active—some are content to jog along. This is a reflection of the type of Board we have. If you are to have effective corporate planning, you must have effective discipline in the Board. Effective discipline means continuing attention to the matter in hand. Most Boards operate in an *ad hoc* manner— they get enthusiastic but fail to follow things through. Most non-executive directors are not prepared to give continued disciplined attention; they want to be consulted one afternoon a month.

A further comment on this subject was offered by a planner in an organization which, prior to the introduction of planning, had been dominated by non-executive directors. He said:

> Prior to the introduction of planning, the company was run by a lot of Scottish Chartered Accountants, whose idea of strategy was to go round at night switching off the lights.

In another organization, the whole style and direction of the company was dictated by the dominant personality of the Chairman, who "likes to do everything for himself" and has established his own information and communication systems. His approach was essentially informal and he was continually examining company strengths and weaknesses. All strategic decisions were taken by three main directors and the company's development was governed by the extent to which threats or opportunities were anticipated by the Policy Executive and acted upon. This example confirms the findings of Kempner and Hewkins who observed that the entrepreneur who has built his business from next to nothing and still dominates it as chief executive, invariably has little time or taste for formal planning processes.[6]

From the analysis one can draw the following tentative conclusions. Corporate planning is both a philosophy and a style of management based on a continuing systematic analysis of the company and its environment. It requires a certain disciplined approach which may be imcompatible with company tradition and top management philosophy and, therefore, its universal application is unrealistic. Any attempt to introduce a formal approach to planning in an organization with an informal management style is likely to fail unless it is accompanied by a dramatic re-orientation of top management philosophy. At best, it would probably be ignored in the decision-making process and as a result would be completely ineffective. At worst, it may be looked on by the organization as evidence of creeping bureaucracy and treated accordingly. Perhaps these conclusions can best be summarized by Erwin von Allem, who said:

> Ultimately, the question reduces to the unchanging character of human behaviour, without changing a management it is not really safe to assume that significant changes can be made in the action pattern of the company.[7]

Planning Needs

> I couldn't run the Company without a management planning system. The only way of controlling it is through management by exception. The old fashioned budgeting systems are absolutely worthless—the difference between management planning and budgeting is action. The biggest change is a change in attitude—the difference between saying that's what we expect to happen and that's what we are going to make happen.

This was the reply of a main board director of a large international group, when asked "Why was it decided to introduce corporate planning in your company?"

As shown in Table 4.2, within the majority of companies participating in the study, planning is generally considered to be necessary for a variety of reasons, although emphasis on its importance differs. In some situations, senior executives see planning as a control system, in others, it is seen as a means of keeping ahead of changing market trends. Some managers view planning as a disciplined thought process, others see it as a means of changing direction. As the General Manager of a Consumer Products Division of a large organization commented:

> I feel planning is essential—without it, you don't know where you are going, it makes you look at a field in the widest possible sense, and consider alternatives. It makes you appreciate that there is change and the need to plan ahead to meet it. When you are in a fast moving environment, unless you can predict market trends, you will be continually behind.

A main Board Director of a textile group said:

> If you have a long range plan, you have to take a much closer look at the organization to highlight its strengths and weaknesses. It makes a managing director sit down and say "where do I want to be in 3 or 5 years' time?" It's a thought provoking process—once you've been provoked into thought, benefits must inevitably follow.

The Deputy Chairman of the same group said:

> We've been growing very rapidly as a group, therefore tidy setting down of objectives has been God's gift to us. We now realise how essential it is—we could have saved ourselves a lot of time and trouble had we had it before.

TABLE 4.2. *The Need:*[a] *Why was it Decided to Introduce Corporate Planning in Your Company?*

Number of need	Percentage
Need to weld together a number of companies carrying on different activities under different styles of management	4
Need to protect established interests against the threat of change	5
Need to respond to rapid environmental changes or a critical situation	14
Need for systematic growth and a unified sense of direction	5
Need to broaden base by acquisition	4
Need for better control system particularly in relation to capital investment	4
Need for systematic exploitation of growth opportunities	4
Need for more effective use of resources	9
Need to fill gaps in organization or co-ordinate overall activities following decentralization	14
Need to grow rapidly	5
Need to maintain initiative by anticipating new situations rather than reaching to them	9
The lead time required for major changes in direction	4
No specified need	19
	100

[a] In some cases planning functions are created in response to a combination of the above needs. Where this has occurred, the major need only is indicated above.

The Chairman of the U.K. Division of a multi-national company said:

I think it is impossible to operate without planning, principally because the size of investment means that you can't afford mistakes and also because of the lead time required to acquire, install and put into operation equipment. If we don't plan in advance, it takes at least 2 years to change direction, and we may miss opportunities—if you don't plan you cannot operate.

A General Manager in the Chemical Industry said:

The business and its component parts are all pointing in the same direction. Everyone knows what we are trying to achieve. Only by the process of planning can you really sort out what your objectives should be and apply analytical questioning to those objectives. It is inherently a control system—the chances of success are increased by the planning approach because you've done your homework. It's a way of living rather than a technique.

A Senior Line Manager of a National Building Contractor observed:

We couldn't exist without it—our resources would be over stretched or underutilized. You can't use your resources effectively without planning. It gives a target that must be worked to and indicates the implications of not meeting target. It motivates people all the way down the lines—one is always striving to improve on existing performance.

These comments illustrate that planning is seen differently in different situations but in each situation if planning is to develop at all, it must satisfy a need. The starting point for the development of planning, is, therefore, awareness of a need and prescription of the planning concept as the most effective way to satisfy it.

In many cases the need arises as a result of a company's historical background and environmental conditions. Let us consider some typical examples.

To Defend the Company Against a Threat

Competition

This company for many years dominated the U.K. market for a certain product. It was essentially a one-product company although some diversification into other fields had occurred. Until the late 1950's, the company had had no serious competition, and the successful entry of a competitor in the early 1960's posed a threat to its dominant market position. This resulted in a radical change of attitude and the awareness of a need for a defensive strategy to counter the threat which had developed. The result was the creation of a planning group whose initial assignment was to formulate a group defensive strategy.

Take over

In two companies, planning was viewed partly as a defensive weapon to preserve independence against possible takeovers. Both these companies were relatively small with a turnover less than £50 m. and both felt vulnerable to takeover following the Finance Act 1967, and its provisions concerning disclosure of information. In one of the companies, a specific function of the planning department was to watch for possible takeover bids and formulate defensive strategies.

To Respond Rapidly to a Crisis

In 1962, an International Oil Company was showing a poor return on investment. It was losing market share, was short of crude oil, and had been in a serious situation as a result of the first Suez crisis. The company was clearly in trouble and top management became aware of the need for a fundamental re-appraisal of its activities. In response to this situation, a group planning department was formed whose first task was to formulate a group strategy which contained a recommendation that planning should be a continuous process permeating through the organization from top to bottom.

A Textile Company was operating in a rapidly changing environment. There were evident changes in the market. Existing competitors were investing heavily and new competitors were entering the market from allied industries. The management realized that the company needed to change direction rapidly in response to the changing market and the competitive situation and estimated that the decisions they were taking should have been taken at least 4 years previously. In response to this situation, a planning function was formed to carry out urgent studies of the future size and structure of the industry, and the company's position in it.

To Weld Together a Number of Companies

An organization marketing consumer goods consisted of a number of separate marketing and manufacturing companies supplying products to the household services and home appliance market. The manufacturing companies sold to the marketing companies, who in turn marketed the products. This arrangement was obviously unsatisfactory, and resulted in a merger of the marketing companies followed about 2 years later by a further merger with the manufacturing companies. These mergers brought several problems, one of which was to co-ordinate the activities of a number of separate companies on different sites with different styles of management.

In some cases, as a result of changes taking place in an industry, growth is necessary for survival. In a number of old established industries, particularly those suffering from over capacity, the trend is towards larger units as companies integrate both horizontally and vertically to protect markets and raw material supplies and secure economies of scale. Often the choice is between growth to a dominant industry position or loss of independence and this realization can result in a will to grow rapidly. In the early stages of growth acquisitions may be made in an *ad hoc* manner, but as the organization gets bigger there is a realization that its various segments can no longer operate in isolation, nor can large investments in new equipment continue to be made on an *ad hoc* basis. This results in a growing awareness of a need for greater co-ordination, a unified sense of direction and future growth which is planned and systematic. As a main board director of one such group said:

> Once you decentralize and get general managers running their own business, they want to know where the group is going. They say—This is fine, but where are we going in total—how do each of our divisions function as a corporate whole?

It is interesting to note that in this case, pressure for a greater sense of direction came from within the organization resulting in a climate conducive to the development of planning.

The Will in a Company to Grow Rapidly

One Mining Investment company has experienced extremely rapid growth over the past 15 years and operates by locating new mineral sources and developing mines. Having located an ore-body, it obtains a forward contract for a large proportion of the output of the mine at a given price for a further period of time. This contract is then used as collateral for securing loans which are used to finance the investment needed to develop the mine. As a result of this method of operation, the company has no marketing or cash flow problems, and manpower problems are overcome by appointing local staff. The size of a typical project is large and can be as high as $100 m. The method of operation is a direct result of the will of the company to grow rapidly and necessitates constant location of new mineral sources and their development. The need to plan is inherent in the nature of the business, and is necessitated by the lead time between locating an ore-body and developing a mine (typically 8 years) and the problem of controlling enormous capital project and accurately forecasting forward world metal prices.

Perhaps one of the more interesting reasons for adoption of the planning philosophy was given by the Chief Executive of a national building contractor:

> What one tries to do is force people to think. It is a discipline imposed from above which is necessary because of the specialist backgrounds of those people who are now general managers. I put the number one criteria as—does it help the general manager of any operating company to do his job better? The real pay-off is in improved management performance overall. I make no apology for pursuing this kind of philosophy—my justification is that I think this is the right pattern of management for the future.

Each of the situations described above is different and each demonstrates the varying needs that planning fulfills. There are many different needs and, therefore, many different forms of planning. It follows that planning is not homogeneous, but varies with each situation.

Although each situation differs, a common pattern emerges. Many of these companies operate in highly competitive environments and some face increased international competition. Others have experienced extremely rapid growth resulting in problems of co-ordination and an awareness that their various segments can no longer operate in isolation. Increasingly, they are subject to internal pressures from a new and younger generation of managers, better informed and educated than ever before. At the same time, relationships between superiors and subordinates are changing; autocracy is in decline, and there is a growing trend towards a participative style of management.

One further point emerges, most of the companies described above have experienced rapid internal or external change. Existing methods of dealing with change have been inadequate and in many cases, inability to cope becomes a matter of survival. Having tasted change and felt its impact, there is an awareness of the need to be better prepared in the future and thus a new approach to the problem of change is required.

The Stimulus for Planning

The starting point for the development of planning is awareness of a need and prescription of the planning concept as the most effective way of satisfying it. However, in many cases, it is apparent that need awareness "won't make planning happen" and therefore it is necessary to distinguish between the need for planning and the event which provides the stimulus for its introduction. As Ansoff observes:

> Unlike operating and administrative decisions, strategic decisions are not self-regenerative. Attention to strategy is either assured on a continual basis through special organizational arrangements or it remains dormant until triggered off by some major event inside or outside the firm.[9]

Planning needs and stimuli may, or may not, be the same and in some cases the need may have been apparent for some time before some event results in action taken to translate it into meaningful practice. In others, the need and the event may be one and the same as, for example, where planning is introduced in response to a critical situation.

As shown in Table 4.3, the most common event providing the impetus for establishment or reshaping of a planning function is a change of leadership. *In 36 per cent of the sample, action had been taken following main*

TABLE 4.3. *The Stimulus: Did any Major Event Provide the Stimulus for its Introduction or Reshaping?*

Nature of event	Percentage
Change of chief executive or main board directors	36
Exposure to external influences[a]	18
Technological developments[b]	9
Merger	5
Reaction to critical situation	14
No specific event	18
	100

[a] There are of course numerous external influences, e.g., recommendations from consultants, informal discussions between group chairman or exposure to the wide variety of courses and literature on planning.

[b] An excellent example of technological developments providing the stimulus for reshaping a planning function is contained in R. A. Long's paper "*Planning in British Railways*".

board changes. This, perhaps, is not surprising, following new appointments, a change of direction is to be expected; planning is a tool created to help the chief executive and board to analyse alternative policies systematically and make a careful choice and control performance against an agreed programme.

In view of the amount of "noise" generated by planning and the proliferation of articles, seminars, courses and conferences on the subject, it is not surprising that in 18 per cent of the sample, the decision to establish a planning function in response to a particular situation was as a result of an external influence.

In 9 per cent of the sample, technological developments were influential in the introduction of planning. In one company, technological developments indicated new growth opportunities and resulted in the need to choose from alternatives in a formal way. However, in this context it is important to distinguish between innovations of product and innovations in the use of electronic equipment and analytical tools for planning. As yet, it is too early to say that increasing penetration of quantitative analysis allied to the electronic computer has made a significant impact on planning in major U.K. companies. However, the findings here represent but the "tip of the iceberg" as a great deal of development work is being carried on, which, as yet, has had no significant impact.

In 19 per cent of the companies visited, the need for planning and the event which provided the stimulus for its development were the same—for example, where planning was introduced as a result of a merger or in response to a critical situation. Although at first glance the low proportion of companies in this situation tends to refute the view that companies in trouble are more likely to develop planning. One cannot discount this completely. Since a large proportion of companies introduced planning following board changes, the implication in some cases could be that these changes occurred because of unsatisfactory performance. Support for this view is offered by von Allmen who observes:

> The launching of a major effort into corporate planning is often the signal of a panic reaction to impending serious problems which are already in so advanced a stage that only some outside miracle could successfully intervene. [10]

In 18 per cent of the sample, there was no specific event having any impact on the development of planning. In most of these cases, planning evolved over a period of time, and developed as a result of changes in attitude and thinking within the organization.

The Importance of "Climate"

"There is a tide in the affairs of men which taken at the flood leads on to fortune." This is how the Planner of a large industrial company expressed the significance of pressures within an organization and their impact on planning efforts. The concept of "climate" is difficult to define but in this sense it means the existence of attitudes within the organization which may or may not be conducive to the development of planning. To understand fully the significance of attitude, it is necessary to examine the sort of approach which the planning philosophy requires, and compare this with traditional attitudes which may be found in a large number of middle and senior managers today.

Briefly, *the planning philosophy is a philosophy of change, with emphasis on the future rather than the present and a logical rather than intuitive approach to decision making. It places little value on company tradition and openly questions the adequacy of conventional approaches to the problems of the future.* In particular, it questions historical methods of resource allocation, whether of capital or revenue, and refutes the assumption that any function or segment of an organization is automatically entitled to the same share of resources in the future as it had in the past. Thus, the philosophy advocates a look at things from first principles, questions, assumptions, ideas, methods of approach and company tradition, which may have existed for many years. Moreover, it requires a more flexible mental approach; individual managers are required to become more business oriented and less parochial. In many cases they are being asked to think fundamentally for the first time and to question established approaches and conventions which hitherto had been considered sacred.

Not surprisingly, the above requirements contrast vividly with mental attitudes found in a large number of senior and middle managers in British industry today. Many of these managers started their working lives in the 1930's, when the emphasis was on security and a job for life with one organization. In many cases, they have had little opportunity of formal business education or exposure to influences outside their industry and naturally their approach is largely conditioned by their environment and experience. In addition, many have functional or specialist viewpoints. Furthermore, many have been schooled by autocratic managements and brought up to believe that company policy is sacred and not to be questioned.

As shown in Table 4.4, in one third of the sample, organizational climate was said to be a significant factor influencing the acceptance of a formal approach to planning. Of the 9 companies affected, 7 had a climate conductive to the development of planning and 2 had a climate which was not conductive to its development. To understand fully the significance of this and the reasons which underlie it, it is necessary to examine their attitudes to change and the underlying factors which shaped these attitudes.

Table 4.4 shows that the 7 companies which has a favourable climate towards planning had all recently undergone radical change, or had been

TABLE 4.4. *Company Climate*

	Number of companies	Percentage
Companies with climate conductive to the development of planning[a]	7	26
Companies with climate not conductive to the development of planning[b]	2	7
Companies in which climate had no significant impact on the development of planning	18	67
	27	100

[a] Of the 7 companies with a climate conducive to the development of planning, 2 had experienced recently declining profits, 1 felt susceptible to take-over following the disclosure provision of the Companies Act, 1967, 1 had undergone rapid continuous change in response to technological developments and changing market conditions, 1 had emerged from a Monopolies Commission enquiry with new leadership, 1 had had its dominant market position threatened by the entry of a competitor and 1 had undergone severe pruning in the interests of survival.

[b] Of the 2 companies with a climate not conducive to the development of planning, 1 had experienced a previous planning failure and 1 was traditionally in-bred, and had not had to contend with radical change.

affected by events resulting in an expectancy of change. This suggests that there is some correlation between attitudes to planning and attitudes to change and that the climate towards planning will tend to be favourable in those organizations where change is accepted as a normal or desirable process.[11]

The following two contrasting examples illustrate the point: A computer company which had experienced extremely rapid growth, was operating in a fast moving environment and had learned to adapt itself to continuous change in response to technological developments and changing market conditions. Such was the pace of change, that it was accepted as a completely normal and desirable process and planning was welcomed as a means of dealing with change in a systematic manner.

An engineering company, old and well established, inbred, with a high proportion of long service employees and a 40 per cent share of the U.K. market for a particular product. After the war, the company had been in a sellers' market, which during recent years had changed. Despite the changing market, the company management was conservative. It had followed the same paths for a number of years and had not had to contend with radical change. Over these years, certain traditions had developed; divisions had established a certain amount of jealously guarded autonomy, there was little personal responsibility and there were no sanctions for poor performance. As the corporate planner

commented, "generally speaking, no one gets sacked for poor performance, rather they are moved sideways".

In the second company, the planner encountered tremendous communication and attitudinal problems, which were directly related to the
company environment.

A major difficulty is that the organizational climate in any company is
completely intangible and, although easily recognizable, will tend to be
changed materially only be major events. Such events are not every day
affairs and many managers who are now struggling to develop planning
against an adverse company climate might do well to consider whether or
not they are wasting their time.

Political Implications

We must also recognize that because planning deals with decision-
making at the highest levels, it has certain political implications which
cannot be ignored. These arise partly from the nature of the process, partly
from the individual company situation and partly from the interaction of
personalities in pursuit of personal and corporate goals.

Table 4.5 shows the extent to which "internal politics" threatened or

TABLE 4.5. *Company Politics: Were Any Internal Political Problems Encountered?*
How Were These Overcome?

Nature of political problem	Number of companies	Percentage
Demarcation problems in the sense that planning embraced Activities traditionally carried out by other functions	3	11
Disputes over control of functions or staff vital to the success of planning	1	4
Seizure of planning by a board member in pursuit of a personal objective	1	4
Fear of planning on the grounds that it poses a threat to established spheres of influence or was likely to expose personal weaknesses	2	7
Planning controlled by a function, e.g. marketing and consequently viewed as a functional rather than corporate activity	1	4
The existence of a main board member with the title, director of planning, or equivalent, who in theory but not in practice was in charge of planning	1	4
No political problems	18	66
	27	100

impeded the development of planning. In one third of the sample, companies' planners experienced political difficulties in establishing corporate planning and although the nature of the problem varied considerably, the result (unless it was solved) was inevitably the same. A discredited planning function viewed by the rest of the organization with a certain amount of cynicism and suspicion.

In 11 per cent of the sample, political demarcation problems occurred, in the sense that planning embraced activities traditionally carried out by other functions. Some typical comments were:

> When you inject a new operation which is going to take over functions previously carried out by other people, you need to do a hard sell.

> The essence of planning is to ensure that what one is doing is clearly understood through the company.

> If people understand what it is all about, they will agree more readily.

Although weak or distorted communications can result in demarcation problems, these will occur anyway if any function feels that the introduction of planning threatens its traditional role. This can be particularly dangerous in the case of the finance function, who may wonder how corporate planning will fit in with the company's annual budgeting system. These fears were voiced by the deputy chairman of an international company who spoke of "a certain resentment in the treasurer's department, who felt that their traditional role was being usurped". To a lesser extent, this may also apply to marketing function, particularly if the distinction between marketing planning and corporate planning is not clearly made.

Sometimes the planner recognizes a potential political problem and takes steps to avoid it, for example:

> The planner in one organization had a close personal relationship with the chairman. He was invited by the chairman to join the organization to carry out acquisition and diversification studies and, recognizing the shortcomings of the existing budgeting methods, he made proposals for the development of corporate planning. Realizing that the creation of a separate planning function might be interpreted by the finance function as a threat to its traditional role and, keeping in mind the importance of the role of the financial staff in planning, he deliberately cultivated their support "because all planning ends with finance". He did this by deliberately involving the finance function in formulating group objectives and drafting procedures and timetables.

A closely allied problem is dispute over control of functions or staff vital to the success of planning. This occurred in one situation where the planner had little option but to stand firm and insist he was given control of the necessary resources. To do so and at the same time avoid creating a dangerous political situation, required an unusual combination of courage and diplomacy as shown in the following example:

A major problem facing the planner was the size and complexity of the task, which could only be tackled effectively using mathematical techniques and operations research personnel. Unfortunately, there were three separate O.R. groups within the organization, each of which had been created and was controlled by a different board member.

Each of the teams was engaged in a separate study in a different part of the organization which presented problems for their withdrawal and full time secondment to planning. Although there was a separate need for planning, the creation of a planning function caused a great deal of resentment. It was viewed with a certain amount of suspicion and, in order to overcome this, two steering groups were formed which preserved vested interests. Working groups were created which reported to the steering group and they visited parts of the organization, seeking advice and ensuring participation in local investigations.

In both of these cases, political problems were overcome by preserving interests in participation. Unfortunately, not all political problems are so easily solved nor do they all arise because planning threatens existing interests.

A most dangerous political situation occurs where a Board member views planning as a political weapon and siezes control of it to further his own ends. This happened in a number of companies participating in the study—with unfortunate repercussions.

A difficult situation may arise where planning is viewed as a personal threat, either to an existing sphere of influence or on the grounds that it may expose poor management performance or personal weaknesses.

Consider the following example:

A major problem was the attitude of a board member who felt that planning would expose his weaknesses. This created a potentially dangerous situation because, of the other board members, two were uncommitted, and the chairman was not deeply involved. The situation was saved by the appointment of a new commercial director, who had been directing planning in his previous company and who proved to be an invaluable ally in influencing attitudes at board level.

A number of respondents stressed the importance of sensitivity to the atmosphere and politics within an organization, and the need to be seen to be independent. Others saw as a key task, the job of smoothing political difficulties by keeping in constant touch with the operating company chairmen. One planner specifically referred to the need "to introduce planning by stealth".

In view of the highly political nature of the activity, it is perhaps not surprising that the introduction of corporate planning has resulted in certain cases in top level casualties. In at least two organizations, the chairman left under pressure from the other board members because he was unable to accept the planning philosophy.

As one respondent commented:

> The two men who were leading us into chaos left the organization; they were constitutionally unable to take a long term view. If you've got people who react rather than anticipate, this is what happens.

It is interesting to note that two-thirds of planners in the sample experienced no political difficulties and one might ask whether there was any significant difference in approach between the companies and those who experienced such difficulties. Although each situation differed, three things were especially noticeable. First, the importance attached to communications in removing fear and suspicion and promoting a greater understanding of the benefits of planning. Second, the particular care taken at the outset to preserve existing interests in participation and, third, strong leadership and involvement by the chief executive. Not only did this indicate the importance of planning to the rest of the organization, but also it prevented other powerful personalities from taking advantage of the situation.

The Planner

A number of definitions of the planner's role were offered by respondents, but running through them all was the common theme that *planning is a line job*. The role of the planner therefore is not to do the planning, but to design, sell and direct the planning effort. Let us consider some typical definitions:

> He has got to do more than just the sums. He must be a coordinator; line management must do the planning. He must also think about where the division should be going in terms of growth, strategy, e.g. for years 2 and upwards. He must consult people and act as a catalyst—challenge their ideas. You end up with something which is the joint product of consultations and brainstorming. He must also sell his ideas to the people who matter.
>
> He is a co-ordinator responsible for initiating, collecting and collating divisional plans; also responsible for continual revision of long range plans and looking into new activities. He advises on the scope, techniques and timetable of planning, plus integration of the long term and short term plan. He achieves leadership by persuasion; he monitors all progress towards meeting the plan.

These comments are particularly interesting because they identify a number of major functions of the planner. His job consists of designing the planning system, selling his ideas to the Chief Executive and Board, building up personal contacts and relationships throughout the organization and, through these, persuading and educating line management to embrace the planning philosophy. He must help the operating managers to plan and, at the same time, challenge their ideas. Finally, he must coordinate the total planning activities within the organization on a continuous basis, monitor all progress towards the achievement of plans and he must continually be looking and thinking ahead in terms of the future purpose and direction of the organization.

> The job of the planner is to make sure that the ideas come from the chaps who have to implement them. Everything that happens is the result of operating management; they must believe that what they do is their idea.

Background

Table 4.6a shows the basic discipline or training of the 27 professional planners. Although at first sight planners appear to be drawn from a wide variety of backgrounds, closer examination reveals that two groups predominate. Thirty-four per cent of planners have an economics or finance background and a further 33 per cent have backgrounds so diverse and experience so varied that it is impossible to group them other than very loosely. Apart from these two groups, planners are drawn from what

TABLE 4.6a. *The Planner's Background:[a] What is the Background and Training of the Executive in Charge of Planning in your Company?*

Basic discipline or training	Total	Percentage[5] internal appointment	External appointment
Economics	16	—	16
Finance	18	18	—
Marketing	11	3	8
Technical	7	7	—
Research	4	—	4
Others[b]	33	29	4
No response	11	—	—
	100	57	32

[a] The "planner" in this context, is the "professional" in charge of the practical development of planning in the organization. In some companies there is, in addition, a board member for planning who may have other responsibilities, e.g. Corporate Development, Overseas Companies, Government and International Liaison, who represents planning on the board, but is not involved in detail. All reference to the "planner" in this and subsequent tables refer to the former.

[b] The backgrounds of planners falling into this category are extremely varied and their experience broadly based. Most of these have had both staff and line experience in a number of different functions for periods from between 2 and 10 years.

might be termed "general management" i.e. a variety of functional backgrounds combined, in most cases, with extremely varied experience.

The predominance of these two groups is extremely interesting, particularly when related to whether they were internally or externally appointed. Although overall there is a definite reference for internal appointments (with 57 per cent of planners being appointed internally and 32 per cent being appointed externally), it is especially significant that all planners with an accounting background and 29 per cent out of 33 per cent of the miscellaneous group were internal appointments.

To some extent the predominance of accounting background is a reflection of the evolution of planning from budgeting, but this is not the whole story. In a small number of companies planning was organized and controlled by the accounting function for a variety of reasons of which perhaps the most obvious was confusion about the nature of the activity and the language used to express it.

Equally significant is the large percentage of internal appointments from the miscellaneous group. The backgrounds of planners falling into this category are extremely varied and their experience broadly based. Most of them had had both staff and line experience in a number of different functions for periods from between 2 and 10 years. Their existence is a clear indication of the importance attached to familiarity with the organization, breadth of experience and personal relationships established over a number of years.

As shown in Table 4.6a, all planners with an economics background were external appointments, some of whom were on their second planning appointment. This suggests the emergence of a group of professional planners comprised predominantly of economists who, presumably because of their familiarity with environmental analysis, are thought to be well suited to the particular challenge of planning. Although a basic knowledge of economics is useful, to assume that any one discipline equips a man to face the political, intellectual and human problems of the planner shows a complete misunderstanding of the nature of the job.

In a small number of companies, the approach to planning was directly influenced by the planner's basic discipline or training. For example, a computer specialist tended to concentrate on model building, a marketing man was heavily biased towards marketing strategy and a finance man created little more than an extended budgeting system. In each of these cases, the emphasis on functional specialism indicates that the wrong man was selected. The original discipline of the planner is unimportant; his background, general outlook and way of thinking is vital.

It is perhaps interesting to note that a number of respondents expressed considerable reservations about the appointment of accountants as planners. These reservations stemmed from fear of over-concentration on figures combined with doubts about the ability of accountants to adjust their mental processes from control situations to the problems of change and uncertainty. The following comments were typical:

> Previously, when we had a straight commercial man, the figures tended to take charge and sight was lost of the action that had to be taken to achieve the figures,

or

> Accountants tend to be rather narrow in their approach to planning—they tend to look at the figures without looking behind the figures,

or

> Accountants are more used to control situations than forward situations; they are used to black and white, they are not used to dealing with uncertainty.

These comments support the view of E. Kirby Warren, who points out that the major reason for selecting the controller stems from the misconception that since all plans are eventually translated into financial terms, the controller is the logical choice; but that because the talents and attitudes of the controller are almost opposite to those required in a director of long range planning, placing the planning function under the average controller will assure its sterility.[12]

Perhaps the most interesting comment on this subject was offered by a main board director of an international group who felt that it was psychologically disastrous to place planning under the control of finance; he said:

> Our first efforts at running planning were put under the control of finance and this nearly killed them. All the instructions were drafted by finance and at the last minute we held them back. We knew that if the instructions were sent out by finance everyone would think it a finance function and this would spell disaster to it psychologically.

It is apparent that the planner has a definite advantage if he is appointed internally and is well known and respected throughout the organization. He brings to the job the status, prestige, intimate knowledge of the business and goodwill which he has built up over his period in the company. As one planner commented:

> Had the planner been appointed from outside, his chances of success would have been greatly diminished. The planner draws on a bank of goodwill built up over his period in the company.

A number of respondents emphasized that, in order to be accepted by line management on equal terms, the planner must have demonstrated success in a line management job. As one main board director put it:

> He must be respected and trusted throughout the organization. One of the most difficult things is to get this respect, and trust, unless he has run his own sweet shop.

In a number of companies where external appointments had been made, remarkable progress had been achieved in a relatively short time and in considering the relative merits and de-merits, it must be remembered that an outsider will be considered to be independent and may also bring to the organization valuable planning expertise combined with an objective approach. Perhaps the relative arguments for an against can best be summed up by the following comments:

A senior line manager:

> The argument for an external appointment is "independence"; on the other hand, an internal appointment knows the background, the people and has a head start over the outsider.

A Deputy Chairman:

> We took a ready made type; if you do not have the right sort of expertise, you have to buy it.

Bearing in mind the above comments, perhaps the ideal choice for the executive in charge of planning is an ex-general manager who is known and respected throughout the organization. Such a man is likely to have broad horizons, breadth of experience, familiarity with the organization, be acceptable to line management and have a degree of maturity and a certain status which is so necessary if people are to accept his ideas. The value of this sort of background is enormous and its significance is illustrated by the observation made by one ex-general manager: "At one time or another, approximately 30 per cent of group senior management have worked for me."

Personality

The importance of personality was stressed by virtually all respondents. As one main board director said:

> It is extraordinary how personality overshadows everything on paper. If you do not get the right man with the right contacts it will fail. If you have the right people the right system will follow.

Or as the Chairman of a paper company said:

> He must be able to draw things out of people, be accepted by them and persuade people to accept his ideas and not only use their ideas. He must be quite a diplomat.

These comments illustrate very clearly the personality characteristics required of a planner and their relevance to the problems he will face.

Status

Table 4.6b shows the status of planners as measured by their salary range and reporting relationship. Sixty-seven per cent of the planners were

TABLE 4.6b. *Planner's Salary: What is
his Level of Remuneration?*

Salary range	Percentage
Under £3000	—
£3000—4000	4
£4000—5000	11
£5000 of over	67
No response	18
	100

earning over £5000 per annum and from comments made by many of the respondents, it is obvious that this figure is conservative.[13]

Although in general terms salary is an indication of the status of planning, in a number of specific cases it had nothing at all to do with it. In at least half a dozen companies the planner was personally invited by the chairman or the chief executive to take up the appointment. As one planner commented:

> Salary probably didn't have much to do with the status of planning—it was rather a personal appointment in a way.

An alternative method of assessing the status of planners is to examine their reporting relationship. One could argue that unless the planner reports directly to the Chief executive, he is unlikely to have sufficient standing within the organization. This opinion was voiced by a main board director of a large international group, who said:

> He must report directly to the chief executive—who else can he report to? If he reports to finance, he is dead and buried before he starts. If he is going to be at the right level to run this thing he must be responsible to the chief executive. If you make him responsible to another director, people can always go over his head.

It is perhaps useful to keep this comment in mind when considering what happens in practice as shown in Table 4.6c. This table shows that of the 23 companies with formal planning departments, 16, or 70 per cent of planners reported directly to the chief executive or an "inner policy body" meaning that 30 per cent did not.

It is worth noting that in all four companies where the planner reported to an individual other than the chief executive the planning function was largely ineffective.

These findings combined suggest that although planners in general enjoy fairly high status, as measured by remuneration, this in itself is of little value if the function has neither the political independence nor standing which accrue from a direct relationship with the chief executive. Clearly the

TABLE 4.6c. *Planner's Reporting Relationship: Does he Report Directly to the Chief Executive?*

Reporting relationship[6]	Number of companies	Percentage
Companies in which the planner reports directly to the chief executive or an "inner policy body"	16	59
Companies in which the planner reports to an individual other than the chief executive	7	26
No response	4	15
	27[a]	100

[a] Of the 27 "professional" planners, only 4 were board members. All 4 were responsible for another function in addition to planning, their titles being as follows:
Director of Corporate Planning and Marketing.
Director of Finance and Economic Co-ordination.
Financial Director.
Head of Group Planning (including Accounting and Financial Evaluation).

problem is not to pay planners more money, but rather to get some chief executives to take a more active interest in something which is their responsibility anyway. One final word on the question of status was offered by the chief executive of a national building contractor, who observed that:

> It's more important that the planner has ability to make a contribution rather than status. If a person has what it takes the function will create its own status.

Board Involvement in Planning

"The Board thought they could buy six yards of corporate planning." This is how the planner of a large organization described the methods of his board to planning. It implies a degree of misunderstanding about the nature of the process and the essential requirements for its development.

Within the sample companies, boardroom attitudes to planning varied considerably. In some companies there was complete commitment. For example:

> We take it very seriously; we have chairman's meetings solely on long range planning bringing in the divisional managing directors as required. I must stress that at group board level, we are continually involved.

> Planning is a tremendous amount of work, it's not something that can be done superficially. If you try to do it superficially, you may as well not bother. As far as I am concerned, it is either a meaningful working document, or it is wastepaper.

> The board consists mainly of executive directors: as a board, there was wholehearted approval for setting up the planning organization.

In others there were considerable reservations partly because of age and resistance to change, but also because of the inability of some members to grasp the philosophy:

> Acceptance almost split into age groups; some of the older ones were a bit imperialistic about it and took the attitude—"I don't want anyone running my side of the business".

> A major problem stemmed from an intellectual incapacity of some people to grasp the philosophy".

Table 4.7 shows the nature and extent of board involvement in planning. In those companies without formalized planning, the emphasis is largely on financial projections supplemented in certain cases by *ad hoc* strategic studies. These are primarily viewed as the responsibility on the financial director with rather less involvement of other board members. Only one of these companies has corporate objectives and these are expressed solely in financial terms. In those companies with formal planning departments, board involvement is far less than one might expect. By far the most common form of involvement is the establishment of a

TABLE 4.7. *Board Involvement: What is the Nature of Board Involvement in Planning Efforts?*

Nature of involvement	Number of companies	Percentage
A. *Companies with formal planning departments*		
Representation on a central planning committee	9	41
Agreement of corporate and divisional objectives[a]	15	68
Involvement in procedures, documentation, guidelines[b]	6	27
Receipt and consideration of plan[c]	20	91
Participate in regular progress reviews	9	41
Organize conferences to consider future policy	5	23
Little or no involvement	3	14

B. *Companies without formal planning departments*
In the 4 companies without a formal planning department, planning consisted largely of financial projections supplemented in certain cases by *ad hoc* strategic studies.

[a] In only 15 of the 22 companies with formal planning departments had corporate objectives been agreed by the board. In the remaining 7 companies, 1 company had operating targets only, 2 companies had no formal objectives but certain objectives were 'understood', 2 companies had no formal objectives and planning consisted of a series of *ad hoc* strategic studies, 1 company was at present developing objectives and 1 organization had objectives which had been assumed for the purpose of the planning exercise, but not ratified by the board.
[b] In 4 of these companies, involvement occurred through representation on a central planning committee.
[c] In 5 companies, representatives of the board received plans personally either through representation on a planning committee, or by personal visits.

committee, usually consisting of the chief executive and senior directors, to undertake a wide variety of activities concerned with planning. This method was used by 41 per cent of the sample, meaning that in 59 per cent of the sample, involvement either did not take place, or took place in some other way.

The activities of central planning committees vary considerably as do their descriptions. In most cases, their main function is to act as an inner policy body and approach all proposals which affect the future direction of the organization, including the corporate plan. In some companies, committees take decisions on everything from setting objectives to agreeing procedures; in others they receive and consider plans and recommend acceptance or rejection to the full board. Although details vary from company to company, these committees perform three very important functions:

(a) They involve the "decision takers" in the planning process and thereby ensure that there is no separation between planning and decision making.
(b) By preserving interests in participation they ensure the political *status quo.*
(c) By involving the chairman and senior directors, they provide visible evidence of the importance attached to planning and so encourage the rest of the organization to accord it high status and attention.

Only 68 per cent of companies with formal planning departments had corporate objectives agreed by the board. In most of these companies written objectives did not exist prior to the introduction of formal planning, a situation which most planning departments set out to remedy at once. Boards generally do not become involved in detailed agreement of procedures, documentation, and guide lines relating to plan preparation. This sort of involvement occurred in only 27 per cent of the sample mainly as a result of board representation on a central planning committee. In virtually all companies, boards receive and consider plans. All too often this is a mere formality and offers little opportunity for probing in depth. In only 41 per cent of companies did the board participate in regular progress reviews against the plan, as distinct from budget reviews which were reviews of figures only. Only 5 companies, or 23 per cent of those with formal planning organized conferences to consider future policy.

Participation

In 3 companies there was little or no board involvement, with the result that in these organizations planning was rather ineffective.

The following example illustrates what can happen when top management pays little attention to planning. The case was encountered in an international company with a multi-million pound turnover.

This company has had a central planning function for at least 5 years. At the outset its role was not clearly defined which caused certain political difficulties and meant that the sort of organization required was obscure. Despite the existence of a planning function, there are no long term corporate objectives and no corporate plan based on an assessment of alternative strategies. Major strategic decisions are taken not necessarily as a result of a strategic plan, partly because the industry itself may be subject to international political pressures. The main contribution to the planning function consists of producing a strategic review which is updated every second year, and produced for an 8-year period. The time scale is historical and not based on the lead time required to make changes in direction. The strategic review contains an analysis of future market demand together with details of existing constraints, current and future problems, and certain financial statistics. The review is submitted to the group board who, after acceptance, circulate it to certain board members and head of departments.

All planning which gives rise to any action is done in the divisions themselves the tendency being to project the existing pattern of growth on a historical basis. The head of the planning function reports to a board member (not the chief executive) in the same way that all departments report to a board member. The chief executive does not appear to be involved in any way in strategic planning, and the future direction of the group is largely based on approval of major capital investments which are sanctioned by the board. Although the planning function has been involved in acquisition studies, this appears to be more because of the type of staff available than an awareness of their connection with planning.

Here the absence of board involvement has resulted in a most ineffective planning function. It is ignored in the decision-making process and its standing within the organization is low. Failure to clearly define its role at the outset resulted in certain organizational and political difficulties which further lowered its standing.

These findings suggest what may be a most serious problem standing in the way of effective corporate planning. Despite the verbal protestations quoted earlier, It is apparent that board involvement in planning is more a matter of words than deeds. The underlying reasons for this are many and varied, but foremost is the inability of some board members to grasp the concept; and the lack of understanding among others of the nature of the process or the essential requirements for its development. Indeed, in some companies this is a major problem; and it is difficult to see how planning can acquire the sort of status and support it needs if certain board members do not fully understand it.

Chief Executive's Involvement in Planning

Without exception, all respondents including senior line managers and board members stressed that without the active support and involvement of the chief executive, corporate planning could never get off the ground. Although from company to company there were differences of emphasis, the overall conclusions were the same. The following comment is typical:

> You can set up a planning system anywhere, but if you don't have the inspiration from the top you will find your plan is a washout. The inspiration comes from the chief executive all the way down the line; it is the personal qualities of leadership which makes the plan capable of being produced by the system.

Table 4.8a shows the nature and extent of the chief executive's involvement in planning. In view of the importance of involvement as indicated by the above verbatim comments, it is surprising to note that in only 67 per cent of the sample was the chief executive said to be personally involved; meaning that in 33 per cent of the sample he was not personally

TABLE 4.8a. *The Chief Executive: What is the Nature of the Involvement of your Chief Executive in Planning Efforts?*

Nature of involvement	Number of companies	Percentage
Personal involvement in strategic planning and future organization plans[a]	18	67
Personal communication of corporate objectives for the benefit of divisional and lower levels of management	11	41
Involvement in examination of divisional plans[b]	13	48
Involvement in regular progress reviews against plan	13	48
In his general approach ensures that the importance of planning is communicated throughout the organization	17	63
Actively helps and supports planning efforts in other ways[c]	4	15

[a] Involvement in strategic planning is largely a matter of degree and varies considerably from company to company. It is therefore not possible to generalize about the nature of the involvement except to say that in this context it means more than saying "yes, I think it's a good idea".

[b] In this context involvement in examination of divisional plans can take place either through representation on a planning committee or personally. However, it is fair to say that the former is more common than the latter.

[c] See detailed commentary.

TABLE 4.8b. *The Chief Executive: Do you Consider He Could Have Given more Help or Support?*

Degree of involvement	Number of companies	Percentage
Companies who consider *more* help or support could have been given[a]	7	26
Companies who consider *no more* help or support could have been given	16	60
No response	4	14
	27	100

[a] An analysis of comments received from those respondents who consider the chief executive should have given more support is as follows:

One respondent said, "The main difficulty is that the chairman himself does not understand the concept and benefits of planning".

One respondent felt that support was needed from the top—"To commission studies to enable objectives to be formulated, organizational issues determined, and planning responsibilities clarified".

Four respondents felt the need for more personal involvement. As one of them commented. "He should have been involved more in the thought processes in the early stages. He should have given more time and allowed presentations to go further down the Group".

One respondent who obviously felt the need for more personal involvement rationalized its absence by saying, "It's not his way to hammer in a rigid formal system".

involved. Chief executives generally do not become personally involved in communicating corporate objectives for the benefit of divisional and lower levels of management. This type of involvement occurred in only 41 per cent of the sample companies. In less than half the sample (48 per cent) was the chief executive involved in examination of divisional plans. In only 48 per cent of the sample, was the chief executive involved in regular progress reviews against the plan. In only 63 per cent of the sample was the chief executive said to ensure that the importance of planning was communicated through the organization. In 15 per cent of the sample, respondents indicated that the chief executive actively helped and supported planning efforts in other ways. These findings combined suggest that planning is neither as well accepted nor supported as one might expect. In slightly less than half the companies could chief executives be said to participate fully in the planning process, although 67 per cent were involved to a lesser degree. *Undoubtedly the most surprising finding is that 33 per cent of chief executives were said not to be personally involved in strategic planning.*[14] These findings are supported by those of Ringbakk, who found that less than 1 in 10 of chief executives were reported to participate in the original development of plans.[15] They are also confirmed in Table 4.8b which shows that 26 per cent of respondents considered that the chief executive should have given more help or support.

It is perhaps appropriate to point out that not all companies suffer from these problems. Indeed, in a number of company's chief executives provide the required inspiration and leadership as evidenced by the following comments:

> He is the motive force in planning; he brought in McKinsey and established operational planning and he also set up strategic planning. He views planning as a style of management.

> He set up the Planning Group and appointed the planning manager; he looks on it as a direct extension of his own office.

> We certainly shouldn't succeed without the support of the managing director. He chaired planning conferences and made brilliant speeches; he really is quite a remarkable man.

Where such inspiration flowed from the chief executive, it was very noticeable that little difficulty was experienced in the introduction of planning or in its subsequent development. Unfortunately this degree of commitment is the exception rather than the rule, as not all chief executives embrace the philosophy or provide the same degree of support.

As certain planners said:

> The main difficulty is that the chief executive does not understand what planning is all about.

> One of the major problems is the philosophy of the chief executive, which is "planning is a good thing, but I leave it to the deputy general manager".

> He has been chief executive for less than a year, so our experience is limited. However, he hasn't been involved so far because of short-term fire-fighting, and his immediate problem is to get costs down in the short-term.

These findings, together with the many observations and comments received from respondents suggest that there are three major factors which underlie lack of chief executive involvement in planning.[16]

These are:

1. Misunderstanding about the nature of the process and the essential requirements for its development.
2. Inability to change from an emphasis on operations to planning.
3. Difficulty in adjusting mental attitudes to the requirements of the planning philosophy.

One further point on this subject; because the chief executive has such a profound effect on the development of planning, if he is actively against it, it has no hope of success. As one respondent commented cynically:

> If you have the active resistance of the chief executive you may as well give up and concentrate your energies on getting rid of him instead.

Method of Introduction

It is no surprise to find that virtually all respondents stressed the importance of the method of introduction. It affords the opportunity to remove misconceptions and fears, promote a clear understanding of the concept and obtain tentative acceptance by the organization. While the need to sell the concept was generally accepted, there were considerable differences of opinion as to how this should be done.

Planners made the following points:

> A series of formal meetings were held at which the chief executive and chairman did most of the talking. The first meeting was an introductory meeting to explain the concept and introduce the planner. The second meeting was to inform managers as to the procedure—what was required, and how it would be worked. It was absolutely essential to show publicly that the chairman and chief executive were behind it.

> People should be involved and know what planning is all about. We showed them the problem and invited them to participate in setting group objectives and formulating strategy. The presentation was followed by personal contact with each divisional managing director to show by example what planning was and indicate the difference between operational and strategic planning.

While accepting the need to sell the concept, many respondents disagreed with a formal presentation as the best method of doing this. There were numerous reasons for this. One respondent felt that a formal presentation could have been misconstrued by the divisions and interpreted by them as a lecture on how to run their businesses. He said:

> A formal presentation could have done harm, i.e. those head office so and so's lecturing the divisions on how to run their businesses. There was no formal presentation but much personal contact in an informal way with managers. It was sold to de-centralized management by telling them that capital would be available as long as it was justified and intentions clearly stated.

Comments such as this supported the findings shown in Table 4.9 in which approximately 60 per cent of companies did not hold formal presentations for either board members or senior managers. Instead, the majority of these companies relied on informal lobbying. It is interesting to note that although only 30 per cent of respondents held formal presentations, a further 15 per cent felt that such presentations were desirable. These were mainly companies who had experienced difficulties as a result of inadequate communications and lack of understanding which usually stemmed from board misconceptions.

A number of respondents referred to the need to "educate" management on planning theory and philosophy. There are numerous ways this may be done, but perhaps one of the most effective was used by the top management of a large divisionalized organization who made the managing director of each subsidiary responsible for selling the philosophy

TABLE 4.9. *Method of Introduction: When Introducing Planning to the Organization, was there any sort of Formal Presentation on the Concept and Benefits?*

	Number of companies	Percentage
(a) *For the 10 most influential individuals*		
Yes	8	30
No	16	59
No response	3	11
	27	100
(b) *For major functional officers and middle management*		
Yes	7	26
No	17	63
No response	3	11
	27	100
(c) *Respondents views of desirability of a formal presentation*		
Essential	6	30
Desirable	8	15
Inessential	4	22
No comment	9	33
	27	100

to his company. By doing so, they ensured that each managing director acquired the necessary understanding and that planning became a "personal" philosophy in each subsidiary. Consequently little difficulty was experienced with either the status of planning or the degree of attention it received.

Bearing in mind the above comments, certain factors clearly emerge as being essential to any attempt to introduce corporate planning.

1. The chief executive must be visibly and actively involved. It is essential that he fully understands and accepts the philosophy and provides the inspiration for his subordinates.
2. Regardless of the approach adopted, it must be supported by personal contact. Since the planner works through and with people he depends on their co-operation for his success. He therefore cannot afford to have any misunderstanding or misconceptions concerning his role and must start at the outset to build up good relationships and remove fears that may be held.
3. As many people as possible must be involved in the early stages. No

one must feel that they are deliberately excluded. Particular care must be taken to emphasize that corporate planning is not the exclusive province of the board.

4. The importance of communications cannot be over-emphasized. If people do not fully understand the concepts and the benefits, they can hardly be expected to give it the sort of time and attention required to get it established.

Perhaps this can be summed up in the words of one general manager when explaining how planning was introduced into his company. He said: "We carried out an exercise in seduction."

Line Management Motivation in Planning

"The planner's job is to see that planning is done and that it happens; line management do the planning." This comment by the planner of a well-known marketing company illustrates the importance of the planner's ability to convince line management to accept planning as part of their job and to undertake it for their area of responsibility. This is certainly no easy task for a variety of reasons and according to Ringbakk's survey, is a major problem; being cited as such by 53 per cent of his respondents.[17] Bearing in mind the size of this response, one could argue that if planning is to make any progress at all there must be a better understanding of how line management can be motivated towards it.

As shown in Table 4.10, there are four major determinants of line management motivation in planning. These account in total for 70 per cent of total responses with five other factors accounting for the balance.

Thirty per cent of all respondents stressed the importance of involvement in cultivating line management acceptance and emphasized that if plans are prepared in isolation, resistance will be met. Some typical comments illustrating this are set out below:

> Personal involvement brings personal commitment. The more people that are involved the greater the chance of success. If plans are prepared in isolation, resistance will be met.

> It is essential that if you are doing corporate planning you must have contact with the operating companies. You cannot do planning in some sort of think tank.

> Pre-planning days—I was the only man thinking about the future—the people down the line were thinking only about the present. When planning was introduced it got them out of the run of day to day activities, and involvement in the future was exciting to them. In addition, they were directly concerned with the long term well being of the division.

> People like to think that the business they work for knows where it is going. They like to work in a controlled atmosphere, i.e. that objectives are stated and plans formulated. I think you should keep people involved as far as possible. You must tell

TABLE 4.10. *Line Management: Whats in your Opinion, is the Greatest Incentive to Line Management for Good Planning Performance?*

Nature of incentive	Percentage[b]
Involvement: Line management must feel that planning is theirs and meaningful to them. It must help them to do their jobs better and thus make their lives easier	30
Company Pride: That as a result of planning their company develops a reasonable sense of direction and is successful	22
Achievement: It provides a mechanism for achievement of clear goals either corporate or personal	14
The awareness that top people in the company consider planning to be a senior and important part of management	13
A conviction that the business cannot operate successfully without planning	8
Judgement on the basis of performance in the medium term as well as in the short term	5
A proper understanding of what planning is all about	3
That future capital expenditure allocations should be linked to performance	3
Fear: The knowledge that poor planning will result in sanctions	2
	100

[a] This question was asked of all the respondents interviewed, including senior line manager and board members. There was no significant difference between the response given by planners and the response given by line managers and board members.
[b] The percentage is based on the frequency with which these incentives were cited.

people what you are doing in a total business sense. People are intelligent; they like to know; they want to know. Planning allows people to perform their jobs more satisfactorily; they can allocate resources to the best advantage; they can be more professional.

After involvement, the most frequently cited incentive was "company pride" defined by one main Board director as "to work for a company which is going places". Twenty-two per cent of all respondents mentioned this factor, and the two separate requirements which are necessary for its development. These are, first, that the company develops a reasonable sense of direction and, second, that as a result of planning, it is successful.

Although the development of a clear sense of direction will provide a temporary boost to morale, if morale is to be permanently sustained, then the organization must be successful. This, of course, is obvious; one can hardly imagine morale being sustained for very long in any organization that is going down hill, no matter how clear its sense of direction. This was confirmed by the planner of an Animal Food Group who said:

> The true motivation is that the company is successful as a result of planning. A good planning job will not be appreciated if the company is not doing well.

Fourteen per cent of respondents saw in planning a mechanism for fulfilment of aspirations and a means of encouraging people to continually strive for improvement. As the planner of a marketing company commented:

> Achievement—they want to work for a successful company in which they themselves are successful—achievement of clear goals, either corporate or personal.

The significance of these comments is perhaps clarified if considered in relation to the size and complexity of the sample companies, most of which had an annual turnover in excess of £100 m. Inevitably in organizations of this size, individuals may feel that they are mere "cogs in a wheel" unable to make a significant contribution in relation to the whole.

Thirteen per cent of respondents felt that a key motivator was "an awareness that top people in the company consider planning to be a serious and important part of management". This merely confirms previous comments on the importance of chief executive's involvement and the effect this has on the degree of commitment from his subordinates.

It is perhaps worth noting that sanctions are not the answer for bad planning. Although "fear" was mentioned as a motivator by one respondent, this was in a company in which planning had failed. One could argue that the planner may have had more success, had he realized that few companies succeed by the sanctions they impose.

These findings, together with the comments received, clearly indicated that planning cannot be imposed or injected; it will only work if line management want it to work. For it to stand any chance of acceptance, it must heavily involve line management and be relevant to their problems. Involvement in itself, however, will not necessarily lead to acceptance. Unless planning produces a definite pay off in terms of improved performance of facilitating the job of management, or providing some inner satisfaction or achievement, then it will be rejected as being of little value.

Conclusions

At the start of this study it was stated that the aims were to determine:

1. What is the present state of development of planning in major British companies with some experience of corporate planning.
2. Why leading British companies are developing corporate planning.
3. What major factors have affected its development in these companies.
4. To draw from the findings some conclusions about the future development of corporate planning and the benefits to be obtained from it.

The conclusions set out below should be considered in the light of these aims.

Before stating the conclusions it is perhaps appropriate to point out that the emphasis of this study was towards a qualitative analysis of planning practices in a small number of leading British companies, rather than towards a quantitative study of organized planning in British companies in general. In view of the emphasis and the limited time available, the number of companies in the sample was limited to 27 and as a result, there must be some reservations about the general application of the conclusions to be drawn from the findings. Most of the sample companies were large (the smallest had an annual turnover of £16 m) and almost by definition they have tended to be more progressive companies who are pioneering development in this area. This is not to say that many of the findings and conclusions may not apply to smaller, or less progressive companies, rather it means that in drawing any general conclusions from the findings, the emphasis of the study must be borne in mind, and due caution exercised.

However, many of the findings are supported by results of other studies of corporate planning in leading companies.[18]

Based on the many findings and insights gained in this study, the following observations can be made:

The State of the Art

Corporate Planning in major U.K. companies is neither as well developed nor as fully accepted as one might expect. Less than half the sample companies were found to have complete corporate plans and a further 22 per cent had functional or divisional plans only, with little or no input from the corporate level. In a number of companies there was a heavy bias towards financial projections where objectives or action programmes had not been developed for the time period in question. In others, "planning" consisted of little more than extended budgeting.

Since an effort was made to select those companies who were thought to have made substantial progress in the development of corporate planning, one may conclude that industry in general is doing much less.

These findings therefore support those of Ringbakk and Kempner— Hewkins concerning the present state of development of corporate planning in Britain and America.

Why Companies are Developing Corporate Planning

In the majority of companies, the starting point for the development of corporate planning is an awareness of the planning concept and its application to current needs. Since the emphasis is on satisfying current needs, the phrase "long range planning" is rather misleading. Although the view taken may be long term, the emphasis is on the short term with the long term in mind, and indeed most of the planning effort in major U.K. companies is directed to this end.

Because planning presents new possibilities for dealing with change, it is seen differently by different people and may be required to satisfy a wide variety of needs. It follows that planning is not homogeneous, it varies with each situation.

Although each situation differs, a number of common factors emerge in those companies most convinced of the need for corporate planning. Many have experienced rapid internal or external change. Existing methods of dealing with change have been inadequate and in many cases inability to cope becomes a matter of survival. Others are operating in an increasingly competitive environment. Lower tariffs mean increased international competition and in many cases growth is necessary for survival. The trend is therefore towards larger units as companies integrate both vertically and horizontally to protect markets and raw material supplies.

Yet growth brings its own problems; as the organization gets bigger, its various segments can no longer operate in isolation nor can new investments be made on an *ad hoc* basis. Growth through diversification can result in rapid changes in the balance of activities which gives rise to a need for greater co-ordination and a unified sense of direction.

At the same time, relationships between people and authority are changing. Autocracy is in decline and there is a growing trend towards a more participative style of management. Furthermore, a better informed and educated generation of managers is emerging who increasingly are exerting pressures for a more professional management approach.

Major Factors Affecting the Present State of Development

In view of the recent growth of interest and the changes mentioned above, it is somewhat paradoxical that progress to date has been so poor. The reasons for this are extremely complex, and vary considerably from company to company, however, from the evidence which has emerged some general conclusions can be drawn.

Because Corporate Planning is both a philosophy and a style of management, it requires a certain disciplined approach which may be incompatible with existing company traditions or top management philosophy. Any attempt to introduce a formal approach to planning in an organization with an informal management style is likely to fail unless it is accompanied by a dramatic re-orientation of top management philosophy. It follows that the universal application of corporate planning is unrealistic; it must be compatible with the existing or proposed management style.

For Corporate Planning to develop at all, a certain mental flexibility is required to question assumptions, ideas, methods of approach and traditions, which may have existed for many years. Whilst some companies, particularly those whose situation results in an acceptance, desire, or expectation of change appear to have developed the required degree of mental flexibility, others experience considerable difficulty in adjusting and this can be a major barrier to acceptance.

Corporate Planning is a highly sensitive political activity whilst the political dangers should not be overstated (they affected the development of planning in one third of the sample), they need not occur provided certain precautionary measures are taken. The most important of these is strong leadership and involvement by the chief executive which effectively will prevent other powerful personalities from taking advantage of the situation.

Despite verbal protestations to the contrary, it is apparent that board involvement in planning is more a matter of words than deeds. The underlying reasons for this are extremely complex, but foremost is the inability of some board members to grasp the concept, the lack of understanding among others of the nature of the processor the essential requirements for its development. In those companies with little or no board involvement, the planning function was most ineffective. The consequent separation between the centre of power and the centre of planning meant that planning was ignored in the decision making process and its standing within the organization was low.

The unanimous view is that without the active support of the chief executive, no corporate planning system can be successfully introduced. Bearing this in mind, it is interesting to consider what happens in practice. In slightly less than half the companies could chief executives be said to fully participate in the planning process, although 67 per cent were involved to a lesser degree. In approximately one-third of the same, chief executives were said not to be personally involved in any way in strategic planning and one is forced to conclude that planning in these companies is not taken seriously.

Many chief executives find it difficult to accept the need for corporate planning. In some cases chief executives are in their sixties and this can be a major factor conditioning their attitude to planning; partly because what happens in 5 years time will not affect them anyway, but also because as they come to the end of their career some of them may become less flexible and more resistant to change.

In the initial stages of development, the planning function derives its status and hence the degree of attention it receives from the standing of the individual who is placed in charge. Although planners in general enjoy a fairly high status as measured by remuneration, this in itself is of little value if the functions has neither the political independence nor standing which accrue from reporting directly to the chief executive. While status is important to the development of planning in the short run, in the longer term, it is not critically important. Planning will stand or fall on the contribution it can make to the success of line management.

The personal attributes of the planner are one of the most important determinants of the development of planning in any organization. People with the required personal qualities are difficult to find, and therefore expensive and either of these factors can result in lower calibre appointments.

While the method of introduction is important in the initial stages of development it is not important in the long term.

Because planning is both a philosophy and a style of management, it will inevitably run counter to the personal philosophy and personal style of many individuals. For example, the logical and systematic approach required may in fact be directly opposed to the natural behaviour of the "opportunist" who essentially manages by flair and intuition.

There is considerable confusion in line management over the concepts of planning, budgeting and forecasting. This was the major area of difficulty encountered by over 50 per cent of planning executives who felt that it impeded the development of planning in a variety of ways. Among various adverse effects which stemmed from this was a tendency by line management to produce figures, not plans, pre-occupation with day to day affairs at the expense of the future and difficulty in convincing line management to take planning seriously for their area of responsibility.

Future Developments

As a result of the changes mentioned earlier in these conclusions and the rapid increase in the pace of change, the growth of interest in corporate planning is likely to increase substantially over the next 10 years. The extent of its future development however, will depend largely on the efficacy or otherwise with which existing barriers can be removed.

Perhaps the key factor likely to retard the development of corporate planning in the future, is that it is a definite style of management which is unlikely to appeal to all managers of all companies in all situations. While there is likely to be growing acceptance in the larger complex organizations, there will always be some people who, while paying lip service to the concept, are unable to adopt it as a management style.

As the pace of change accelerates, more and more companies will be forced to adopt it in the interests of survival. Many of today's managers who started their working lives in the 1930's will retire and their place will be taken by a new generation of managers trained and educated in a vastly different environment to that of their predecessors. The result will be a new approach to the problems of change and a greater willingness to treat them in a systematic and co-ordinated fashion.

There appears to be a growing trend towards a more participative style of management. The new generation of managers increasingly will be encouraged to think more broadly and develop the sort of mental flexibility planning requires.

Since corporate planning is "new", preliminary misunderstandings are to be expected. With the passage of time and the wider development of business education inside and outside the company, this problem may gradually diminish, removing with it one of the major reasons for lack of involvement at all levels of management.

Many of the most successful chief executives who at present rely primarily on entrepreneurial flair are approaching the age of retirement. Their places will be taken by executives who have had more training in modern management techniques. The changes in management approach may be reflected in improved standards of planning.

Planning has evolved partly as a result of growing awareness of the inadequacy of existing budgeting systems and a trend towards the use of more sophisticated management techniques. While the impact of the use of electronic equipment and analytical tools has not yet been great, many companies are devoting increasing attention to their use. Increasingly, in the future, the use of the computer and quantitative techniques will be major influences in the development of planning.

Planning provides a mechanism for the fulfilment of aspirations, it is therefore more likely to be accepted in large complex organizations where the problems of continually sustaining motivation may be formidable.

The successful development of planning in the long term depends on its acceptance by line management. It cannot be imposed or injected and will only work if line management want it to work. For it to stand any chance of acceptance, it must heavily involve the operating managers and be relevant to their problems. Involvement in itself however will not necessarily lead to acceptance. Unless planning produces a definite pay-off in terms of improved performance, in facilitating the job of management, or providing some inner satisfaction of achievement, then it will be rejected as being of little value.

The Benefits of Planning

While any assessment of planning benefits must be largely subjective, it is perhaps worth noting that virtually all respondents were enthusiastic about the benefits to be derived. Although many found it difficult to say "by planning we have achieved this" there were several instances where corrective action had been taken in response to a changing situation. It is, of course, impossible to list all the benefits claimed, but for the purpose of illustration, a selection are listed below.

Many companies felt they were tending to get better value for their capital investment, and were making fewer mistakes.

A number of respondents felt that planning indicated problems before they occurred.

Many felt that planning had resulted in a dramatic change of interest, and attitude, throughout their organizations. One claimed that it had revitalized the interest of senior managers in the future of the company.

Some saw planning as a discipline which continually points out that there is change and the need to plan ahead to meet it. One executive referred to "an awareness forward that enables us to anticipate changing market conditions".

Many companies have been forced to rethink the nature of their business and set more specific long term objectives. In some organizations for the first time there has been a co-ordinated unified effort to achieve predetermined objectives. The result has been improved morale and more efficient use of resources.

Perhaps the most significant benefit claimed was that planning enables departmental managers to have a much clearer understanding of the whole operation. It was said to have resulted in broader horizons and a change in attitude from parochialism to business orientation.

As one general manager said, "There is no sacred ground, if everyone understands the objectives, they are better placed to criticize the approach".

This list is not comprehensive, nor can it be at the present stage of development. In many companies, corporate planning is in its infancy and the potential benefits are just beginning to emerge. With improved standards of planning and greater experience in application further benefits will be identified which at present are unknown. Perhaps the above can best be summarized by the following comment made by a divisional general manager:

"The value is in the process rather than the result. When you drop a stone into a pond, there is no knowing how far the ripples will extend."

Acknowledgement

This article is based on an M.Sc. dissertation submitted by Peter Irving, at the University of Bradford Management Centre in May 1970.

References

1. J. W. M. Hewkin and T. Kempner, Is corporate planning necessary, *BIM Information Summary*, 134, p. 36 (Dec. 1968).

2. K. A. Ringbakk, *Organized Planning in Major U.S. Companies—A Survey*, Stanford Research Institute, p. 1 (1969).
3. R. Mainer, *The Impact of Strategic Planning on Executive Behaviour*, Boston Consulting Group (1965).
4. See:
   J. W. M. Hewkin and T. Kempner, Is corporate planning necessary, *BIM Information Summary*, 134, p. 35 (Dec. 1968).
   H. E. Wrapp, Organization for Long Range Planning, *Harvard Business Review*, p. 37 (Jan/Feb. 1967).
   R. Mainer, *The Impact of Strategic Planning on Executive Behaviour*, Boston Consulting Group (1965).
   C. O. Rossotti, *Two Concepts of Long Range Planning*, Boston Consulting Group (1970).
   E. K. Warren, *Long Range Planning, The Executive Viewpoint*, Prentice Hall, New Jersey (1966).
   K. A. Ringbakk, *Organized Planning in Major U.S. Companies: A Survey*, Stanford Research Institute, p. 13, 25 (1969).
5. Research Report to the Public Opinion Index for Industry: *Long Range Planning for Growth*, Opinion Research Corporation, p. 15 (1965).
6. J. W. M. Hewkin and T. Kempner, Is corporate planning necessary, *BIM Information Summary*, 134, p. 35 (Dec. 1968).
7. E. von Allmen, Setting up corporate planning, *Long Range Planning*, Vol. 2, No. 1 (1969).
8. R. A. Long, Planning in British Railways, *Long Range Planning*, Vol. 2, No. 2 (1969).
9. H. I. Ansoff, *Corporate Strategy, An Analytical Approach to Business Policy for Growth and Expansion*, McGraw-Hill, New York and London, p. 123 (1965).
10. E. von Allmen, Setting up corporate planning, *Long Range Planning*, Vol. 2, No. 1 (1969).
11. See: R. M. Worcester on "Resistance to change" in: Managing change, *Long Range Planning*, Vol. 3, No. 2 (1970).
12. E. K. Warren, *Long Range Planning, The Executive Viewpoint*, Prentice Hall, New Jersey, p. 45 (1966).
13. A. Presanis, *Corporate Planning in Industry*, Business Publications Ltd., London (1970).
14. G. A. Steiner, Top management's role in planning, *Long Range Planning*, Vol. 1, No. 4 (1969).
15. K. A. Ringbakk, *Organized Planning in Major U.S. Companies: A Survey*, Stanford Research Institute p. 25 (1969).
16. For an excellent discussion of these problems, see E. K. Warren, *Long Range Planning, The Executive Viewpoint*, Prentice Hall, New Jersey, p. 36 (1966) and K. A. Ringbakk, *Organized Planning in Major U.S. Companies': A Survey*, Stanford Research Institute, p. 15 (1969).
17. K. A. Ringbakk, *Organized Planning in Major U.S. Companies: A Survey*, Stanford Research Institute, p. 13 (1969).
18. Long Range Planning in the U.S.A.—N.I.C.B. Survey, *Long Range Planning*, Vol. 1, No. 3 (1969).

5

Society for Long Range Planning: Organisation and Membership Survey: March 1974

EDITED VERSION OF A SURVEY BY P. KNOWLSON

In March 1974 Peter Knowlson undertook a membership survey for the Society for Long Range Planning. This was published by the Society in the form of a series of tables with narrative explanation, and the majority of this report is reproduced here. The only omission is a series of data on remuneration of planners, which is of an ephemoral nature.

The Society for Long Range Planning was, at that time, the only U.K. association for people with a constructive interest in corporate planning. Its membership included corporate planners from most major U.K. organisations, although there was also an unquantifiable number of practitioners who were not Society members.

Returns of questionnaires were very high, 73 % for the part 1 questionnaire which sought data on an individual basis and 63 % for the part 2 questionnaire which asked for information about the organisation. To a very large extent, this sample size might be expected to overcome the problem of bias, although there is no information on the non-respondents which would allow the degree of bias to be assessed.

One third, and relatively small, factor which should be considered is that the Society has a small minority of its members outside the U.K. These were not separated from the U.K. respondents in the analysis (which was designed to meet the Society's own needs).

These three qualifications accepted, the report still provides fascinating information from a much larger population than that on which most other research studies have been based; 613 individuals and 385 organisations responded, and the size of this population gives considerable confidence in the validity of most of the findings.

What is of particular value is the insight which the survey provides of the

---

The survey was published by the Society for Long Range Planning in December 1974.

job of the corporate planner, and the experience, qualifications and skills he is likely to have. It also shows the extent to which different planning activities are carried out in organisations, and what is interesting here is the number of omissions by companies which claim to practise planning.

I personally found fascinating the information analysed by industry on the year of introduction of planning (although I doubt that the pre-1963 planners are talking about the same thing). This fairly large sample aids interpretation of many of the earlier pieces of research.

Membership Survey—March 1974
Report by Peter Knowlson

1. Introduction

During 1973 the Executive Committee of the Society for Long Range Planning decided that it would be helpful if they obtained a more detailed picture of the membership of the Society and the organisations for which they work. A pilot questionnaire was designed and tested on the Executive and this led to a revised questionnaire which was sent out to all members in March 1974.

Since a number of organisations were corporate members and several organisations were represented by more than one individual member, the questionnaire was divided into two parts:

Part 1 (requesting information about members) was sent to all members (i.e. both individual members and those nominated by corporate members to receive Society mailings).

Part 2 (which requested information about the organisations employing members) was sent to one person in each of the organisations represented by the membership.

2. Response

Table 5.1 shows that a high proportion of the membership returned questionnaires about themselves (73 %) and 63 % of members returned a questionnaire about their organisation; 357 of the 613 members returning questionnaires were responsible for corporate planning within their organisation.

3. Acknowledgements

The Executive would like to record its appreciation of the hard work done by the staff of the Society (Pat Skitmore, Sandy Temple and Miss

TABLE 5.1. *Number of Questionnaire sent out and Response*

Category	Part 1—member questionnaires			Part 2—organisation questionnaires		
	Number sent out	Number returned	% Replying	Number sent out	Number returned	% Replying
Individual members	680	468	70	520	312	60
Employees of 49 corporate members	160	145	81	85[b]	73[b]	86
Total	840	613[a] members	73	605	385 organisations	63

[a] 357 of these (58% of those replying) were responsible for corporate planning.
[b] Several corporate members returned separate questionnaires for organisations which formed part of their organisation.

Dauris) in preparing the questionnaire and reply envelopes, mailing them to members, and chasing up those who had not replied. It is also deeply indebted to David Potts and John Hunt of ICI Runcorn who devised and handled the computer programme for processing the replies in such a way that we received the analysis printed in tabular form.

We also fully appreciate the contribution of all those members who completed the questionnaires.

TABLE 5.2. *Type and size of organisations employing SLRP members*

Type of employer	Replies in group	% of replies	1–199 employees	200–499 employees	500–4999 employees	5000–24,999 employees	25,000 or over employees
Self-employed	11	2	1			1	
Industrial or Commercial Co.	468	76	51	33	141	147	96
Nationalised Industry	56	9	5		6	16	29
Central-Government	13	2	1	1	1	2	8
Local Government (inc. schools)	3	0.5	1				
University or College of Tech.	18	3	10	1	7	2	
Statutory authority	9	1	3	1	2	2	1
Other	35	6	12	9	9	5	
Grand total	613	100	84 (14%)	45 (7%)	166 (26%)	175 (29%)	134 (22%)

TABLE 5.3. *Main activity and annual turnover of organisations—Individual members*

Main activity of organisation	Replies in group	% of all replies	Less than £1m	£1m–£10m	£11m–£50m	£51m–£200m	Over £200m
Mining or Quarrying (not coal)	9	1		1	1	4	3
Food, Drink or Tobacco	37	6	2	2	11	12	12
Chemicals or Pharmaceuticals	36	6	7	7	9	12	8
Oil, Coal, Gas or Electricity	19	3	1	1	1	5	12
Metals & Metal Manufacture	24	4	1	1	2	11	9
Mechanical Engineering	24	4		5	10	5	4
Electrical Eng. & Electronics	28	5	1	5	3	8	11
Motor Vehicles, Aircraft, Ships	17	3	1	1	8	5	2
Textiles, Fibres or Footwear	8	1		3	5		
Other Manufacturing Industry	57	9	2	11	10	24	10
Construction	18	3	1	3	1	11	2
Transport (inc. Post Office)	19	3		1	6	5	7
Retailing and Distributive	14	2		2	7	2	3
Banking, Insurance, Finance	41	7	3	8	6	4	20
Consultancy	54	9	28	19	6		1
Research	8	1	6	2			
Education and Training	20	3	9	5	5		1
Central Govt. Administration	2			1			1
Representative Org./Govt. Agency	5	1	1	4			1
Other Non-manufacture Industry	28	5		6	8	5	8
Grand total	468	76	53 (9%)	88 (14%)	99 (16%)	113 (18%)	115 (19%)

TABLE 5.4. *Main activity of organisation and annual turnover—blue Questionnaires returned by corporate nominees*

Main activity of organisation	Replies in group	% of corporate member replies	Less than £1 m	£1 m–£10 m	£11 m– 50 m	£51 m–£200 m	Over £200 m
Mining or Quarrying (not coal)	1	1					1
Food, Drink or Tobacco	7	10			1	2	4
Chemicals or Pharmaceuticals	8	11		1	1	3	3
Oil, Coal, Gas or Electricity	2	2					2
Metals & Metal manufacture	4	5		1	1	1	1
Mechanical Engineering	5	6			1	4	
Electrical Eng. & Electronics	2	2				1	1
Motor Vehicles, Aircraft, Ships	1	1				1	
Textiles, Fibres or Footwear	1	1				1	
Other Manufacturing Industry	10	14		3	3	2	2
Construction	5	7			2	2	1
Transport (inc. Post Office)	2	2					2
Retailing and Distributive	4	5		1		1	2
Banking, Insurance, Finance	9	12			1		8
Consultancy	3	4	2	1			
Research	1	1					1
Education and Training	1	1	1				
Central Govt. Administration	1	1					1
Representative Org./Govt. Agency	4	5	1		3		
Other Non-manufacture Industry	2	2				2	
Grand total	73	100	4 (5 %)	7 (10 %)	13 (18 %)	20 (27 %)	29 (40 %)

TABLE 5.5. Age, status and reporting relationships of SLRP members

Age group	Replies in group	Response for C.P.	%	Status					Reports to				
				Chief exe-cutive	Dep. chief exec.	Director	Head of dept.	Other	Chief exe-cutive	Dep. chief exec.	Director	Head of dept.	Other
$< = 25$	2	1	50				1	1	1		1		3
26–30	50	24	48	1		3	22	24	19	3	14	11	9
31–35	119	71	60	7	7	11	45	49	37	7	38	28	16
36–40	113	62	55	6	3	24	47	33	45	7	28	17	21
41–45	125	76	61	15	4	24	49	33	55	8	29	12	18
46–50	103	70	68	10	5	25	39	24	46	9	22	8	10
51–55	61	35	57	8		20	20	13	24	6	15	6	4
56–60	35	18	51	3	1	5	15	11	18	2	7	4	1
61–65	5	1				1	3	1	3		1		
Total	613	357	58	50	20	113	241	189	248	42	155	86	82

TABLE 5.6. *Role of Departments of Members*

Role of department	Replies in group	Percentage of total
Coordinate the preparation	341	55
Contribute to part	144	23
Assist by collecting data	54	9
Take no formal part	74	12
Grand total	613	100

TABLE 5.7. *Status and Reporting Relationship of Corporate Planners*

Status of member	Replies in group	% of corporate planners	Chief executive	Dep. chief executive	Director	Head of department	Other
				Reporting to			
Chief Executive	44	12	9				35
Deputy Chief Executive	18	5	17				1
Director	79	22	65	6	3		5
Head of Department	154	43	68	18	56	7	6
Other	62	17	26	4	9	17	6
Grand total	357	100	185(52%)	28(8%)	68(19%)	24(7%)	52(15%)

TABLE 5.8. *Nature of Employer and Status of Members*

Type of employer	Replies in group	Respons. for C.P.	% of those involved in C.P.	Chief executive	Dep. chief excutive	Director	Head of department	Other
				Status				
Self-employed	11	6	50	3		1		7
Industrial or Commercial Co.	468	286	61	43	16	93	188	128
Nationalised Industry	56	33	59	2	2	8	29	15
Central Government	13	5	39			1	6	6
Local Government (inc. schools)	3	2	67			2		1
University or College of Tech.	18	3	17	1	1	1	2	13
Statutory authority	9	6	67		1	3	2	3
Other	35	16	46	1		4	14	16
Grand total	613	357	60	50	20	113	241	189

TABLE 5.9. *Titles of members of SLRP*

	Those responsible for corporate planning	Those not responsible for corporate planning	Total	
			Number	% of all replies
Chairman	7ª	3	10	1.5
President	1		1	
Chief Executive	5		5	1
Managing Director	32	6	38	6
Deputy Managing Director	3		3	0.5
Vice-President	2		2	0.5
Partner	2	3	5	1
Director	73	32	95	15
Total Board Level	125	44	159	26

ª Include three who are also Managing Director and one who is also Chief Executive.

TABLE 5.10. *Titles including Corporate Planning or recognisable equivalent those responsible for Corporate Planning*

Those responsible for Corporate Planning:

Controller Corporate Planning	1	Long Range Planning Manager	3
Co-ordinator Strategy and Finance	1	Manager Corporate Planning and	
Corporate Planner	3	Financial Control	1
Corporate Planning Co-ordinator	2	Manager Corporate Planning	5
Corporate Planning Director	1	Manager Corporate Strategy	1
Corporate Planning Executive	1	Manager Long Range Planning	5
Corporate Planning Manager	12	Manager Long Term Planning	1
Corporate Planning Officer	3	Manager Plans Co-ordination	1
Director of Corporate Planning	9	Manager Corporate Planning	1
Director Long Range Planning	1	Managing Director Corporate	
Director Strategic Planning	1	Strategy	1
Forecast and Planning Manager	1	Manager Corporate Planning and	
Group Corporate Planner	5	Management Services	1
Group Corporate Planning Director	1	Planning Co-ordinator	2
Group Strategic Planner	1	Senior Corporate Planner	2
Head of Corporate Planning	9	Staff Member Long Range Planning	1
Head of Planning and Forecasting	1	Strategic Planning Executive	1
Head of Strategic Planning	2	Strategic Planning Manager	1
Long Range Planner	1	Vice-President Corporate Planning	1
Long Range Planning Executive	1		

Fifty-six had Corporate Planning in their title, 30 had closely related titles. A further 35 had Planning in their titles, e.g. Planning Manager (15), Group Planner (9), Head of Planning (6).

A total of 171 had Planning in their titles.

TABLE 5.11. Age and whether members have university degree or equivalent, and type of degree

Age group	Replies in group	No degree	Arts	Econo-mics	Engineering science inc. maths.	Social science	Medical	Business school	Other
< = 25	2	1				2		1	
26—30	50	3	3	14	13	2		9	6
31—35	119	9	10	22	27	2		32	17
36—40	113	17	9	27	26	4		6	24
41—45	125	27	14	18	38	3		7	18
46—50	103	23	4	30	27	1		7	11
51—55	61	14	1	13	17			4	12
56—60	35	8	4	4	10	1		3	5
61—65	5	2		1	1				1
Grand total	613	104 (17%)	45 (7%)	129 (21%)	159 (26%)	13 (2%)		69 (11%)	94 (15%)

TABLE 5.12. *Age and membership of professional body or society*

Age group	Replies in group	% of all replies	Statistics	Finance accountancy	Operational research	Law	Scientific	Management	Other
< = 25	2	100		1				1	
26—30	37	74	2	6	8	1	3	8	9
31—35	93	78	8	20	11		5	22	27
36—40	89	79	2	31	8	1	8	19	20
41—45	105	84	6	18	7	1	15	30	28
46—50	82	82	7	16	5	1	13	27	13
51—55	55	90	3	8	2	1	7	21	13
56—60	32	92	4	5	1	1	9	10	2
61—65	4	80	32				2	1	2
Grand total	499	82	32 (5%)*	105 (17%)*	42 (7%)*	6 (1%)*	62 (10%)*	139 (23%)*	113 (19%)*

* Of total returning questionnaires.

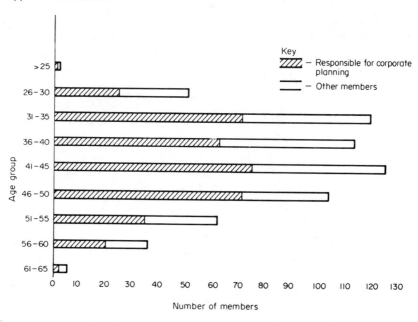

FIG. 5.1. *Number of members, by age group.*

TABLE 5.13. *Age and number of years involved in corporate planning—planners only*

Involvement corp. planning	Replies in group	% of total in group	25	26–30	31–35	36–40	41–45	46–50	51–55	56–60	61–65	65
Nil	3	1				1	1	1				
Under 3 years	59	16	1	11	15	16	6	9	1			
3–5 years	131	37		9	31	24	35	18	8	6		
6–10 years	123	34		4	23	19	26	28	18	5		
11–15 years	33	9			2	2	7	11	7	4		
16–20 years	4	1					1	2		1		
21–25 years	3	1						1	1	1		
26–30 years	1									1		
Grand total	357	100	1	24	71	62	76	70	35	18		

TABLE 5.14. *Age and number of years involved in corporate planning—all replies*

Involvement in corp. planning	Replies in group	% of total in group	25	26–30	31–35	36–40	41–45	46–50	51–55	56–60	61–65	65
Nil	21	3.5		4	3	3	4	4	1	1	1	
Under 3 years	92	15	2	21	21	22	13	11	1	1		
3–5 years	217	35.5		19	54	44	49	26	13	10	2	
6–10 years	212	34.5		6	37	39	46	38	32	12	2	
11–15 years	58	9.5			4	5	11	20	12	6		
16–20 years	7	1					2	2	1	2		
21–25 years	4	0.5						2	1	1		
26–30 years	1									1		
30–35 years	1									1		
Grand total	613	100	2	50	119	113	125	103	61	35	5	

TABLE 5.15. *Age and the number of different organisations which corporate planners have been concerned with corporate planning*

Age group	Replies in group	Number of organisations					Appointed to present post	
		None	One	Two	Three	Four or more	From within	From outside
< = 25	1		1				1	1
26–30	24	2	9	6	7	2	9	15
31–35	71	3	32	21	13	4	40	31
36–40	62	4	30	21	3	7	41	20
41–45	76	3	39	15	12	7	53	21
46–50	70	1	31	20	11	1	43	27
51–55	35		23	8	3		25	9
56–60	18		11	2	2	3	14	4
Grand total	357	13	176	93	51	24	226	127

TABLE 5.16. *Annual turnover and use of corporate planning*

Annual turnover of organisation	Replies in group	Status of corporate plan							
		Prepare a corporate plan	%	Employ a corp. planner	%	Incorporated in larger plan	%	At highest level in organisation	%
Less than £1 m	40	28	70	7	17	11	39	17	61
£1 m–£10 m	77	62	81	36	47	25	40	37	60
£11 m–£50 m	84	74	88	56	67	27	36	47	64
£51 m–£200 m	96	89	93	72	75	29	33	60	67
£200 m & Over	88	77	87	66	75	16	21	61	79
Total	385	330	86	237	62	108	33	222	67

TABLE 5.17. *Size of company and use of corporate planning*

Number of employees	Replies in group	Status of corporate plan							
		Prepare a corporate plan	%	Employ a corp. planner	%	Incorporated in larger plan	%	At highest level in organisation	%
Self-employed	3	2	67			1	50	1	50
1–199	59	42	71	13	22	16	38	26	62
200–499	30	26	87	15	50	9	35	17	65
500–4999	126	106	84	77	61	43	41	63	49
5000–24,999	107	101	94	84	78	30	30	71	70
Over 25,000	60	53	88	48	80	9	17	44	83
Total	385	330	86	237	62	108	33	222	67

Table 5.18. Activity of organisation and use of corporate planning

Main activity of organisation	Replies in group	Prepare a corporate plan	%	Employ a corp. planner	%	Status of corporate plan			
						Incorporated in larger plan	%	At highest level in organisation	%
Mining or quarrying (not coal)	5	4	80	3	60	1	20	3	60
Food, Drink or Tobacco	30	29	97	25	83	11	38	18	62
Chemicals or Pharmaceuticals	35	31	89	26	74	7	23	24	77
Oil, Coal, Gas or Electricity	10	10	100	10	100	4	40	6	60
Metals & Metal Manufacture	17	16	94	11	65	5	31	11	69
Mechanical Engineering	22	20	91	13	59	4	20	16	80
Electrical Eng & Electronics	17	15	88	12	71	7	47	8	53
Motor vehicles, aircraft, ships	13	10	77	10	77	3	30	7	70
Textiles, Fibres or Footwear	8	7	87	5	62	2	29	5	71
Other Manufacturing Industry	51	46	90	36	71	19	41	27	49
Construction	20	16	80	8	40	6	37	10	62
Transport (inc. Post Office)	16	16	100	13	81	4	25	12	75
Retailing and Distributive Trades	13	8	62	4	31	1	12	7	88
Banking, Insurance, Finance	39	35	90	27	69	12	34	23	66
Consultancy	36	26	72	8	22	10	38	16	62
Research	6	2	33					2	100
Education and Training	12	11	92	4	33	6	55	5	45
Central Govt. Administration	3	1	33	1	33			1	33
Representative Org./Govt. Agency	9	8	89	5	55	2	25	6	75
Other non-manufacture industry	23	19	83	16	70	4	21	15	79
Grand total	385	330	86	237	62	108	33	222	67

TABLE 5.19. *Activity of organisation and when corporate planning was introduced*

Main activity of organisation	Replies in group	Number with corp. planning %	Year of introduction Before 1963	1963–1964	1965–1966	1967	1968	1969	1970	1971	1972	1973
Mining or quarrying (not coal)	5	4	80							2			
Food, Drink or Tobacco	30	29	97	2		2	1	3	6	4	3	2	7
Chemicals or Pharmaceuticals	35	31	89		3	3	3	5	2	2	6	7	2
Oil, Coal, Gas or Electricity	10	10	100			2	1	1	2	1			
Metals & Metal Manufacture	17	16	88	1		3	1	5	1	1	5	3	
Mechanical Engineering	22	20	91	1	1	1	1	4	3	3	2	2	3
Electrical Eng. & Electronics	17	15	88	5	1		1	2	2	2	1		1
Motor vehicles, Aircraft, Ships	13	10	77	2		1	1	1	3	3			1
Textiles, Fibres or Footwear	8	7	87			1		1		1	2	2	
Other Manufacturing Industry	51	46	90	2	2	5	2	7	5	10	6	4	
Construction	20	16	80	1	2		3		2		7	1	
Transport (inc.													

TABLE 5.19 (cont.)

Main activity of organisation	Replies in group	Number with corp. planning %	Year of introduction									
			Before 1963	1963– 1964	1965– 1966	1967	1968	1969	1970	1971	1972	1973
Post Office)	16	16	100	1	1	2			|5|	1	3	1	2
Retailing and Distributive Trades	13	8	62	1				2		|1|	1	1	4
Banking, Insurance, Finance	39	35	90	1	1		1	4	4	5	|4|	8	8
Consultancy	36	26	72	1		2	3	6	|1|	4	4	1	3
Research	6	2	33							1	1		
Education and Training	12	11	92	1		1		1	1	|3|	2		1
Central Govt. Administration	3	1	33								|1|		
Representative Org./ Govt. Agency	9	8	89	1					2		|4|		1
Other non-manu- facture industry	23	19	83	1		1	2	1	1	2	|2|	4	5
Grand total	385	330	86	21	12	25	19	43	40	|46|	55	34	43

Note: ‖ = Median year of introduction.

TABLE 5.20. Turnover and extent of different planning activities with an organisation

PART I

Annual turnover	Replies in group	Setting & reviewing objectives			Forecasting events inside organisation			Forecasting events outside organisation			Proposing/ selecting strategies			Organisation planning		
		F.	L.	N.C.	F.	L.	N.C.	F.	L.	N.C.	F.	L.	N.C.	F.	L.	N.C.
Less than £1m	40	23	13	1	8	25	4	15	19	3	22	13	2	12	19	6
£1m–£10m	77	49	25	2	31	39	6	49	23	4	41	29	6	39	30	7
£11m–£50m	84	54	26	3	35	43	5	55	27	1	46	35	2	34	42	7
£51m–£200m	96	68	27	1	58	34	4	71	18	7	60	34	2	43	38	15
£200m & over	88	66	20	1	63	23	1	66	17	4	67	19	1	46	37	4
Grand total	385	260	111	8	195	164	20	256	104	19	236	130	13	174	166	39
of which Industrial or commercial companies	305	211	88	4	155	134	14	208	80	15	185	112	6	138	135	30
Nationalised industry	26	19	6	1	15	9	2	18	8	—	19	5	2	12	11	3

TABLE 5.20 (cont.)

PART 2

Annual turn-over	Financial planning			Manpower planning			Diversification planning			Divestment planning			Contingency planning			Eval./Review perf. v plans		
	F.	I.	N.C.	F.	I.	N.C.	F.	I.	N.C.	F.	I.	N.C.	F.	I.	N.C.	F.	I.	N.C.
Less than £1m	27	8	2	19	15	3	6	18	13	2	6	29	6	19	12	23	8	6
£1m–£10m	65	10	1	37	32	7	22	35	19	8	28	40	15	43	18	56	18	2
£11m–£50m	70	12	1	41	34	8	30	34	19	23	29	31	20	43	20	62	18	3
£51m–£200m	88	7		49	33	14	37	50	9	23	52	21	21	53	22	77	16	3
£200m & over	80	7	1	58	24	5	42	31	14	28	31	28	33	39	15	64	18	5
Grand total	330	44	5	204	138	37	137	168	74	84	146	149	95	197	87	282	78	19
of which Industrial or commercial companies	261	39	3	159	114	30	116	144	43	72	126	105	71	167	65	227	64	12
Nationalised industry	25	5	1	19	6	1	5	10	11	7	6	13	12	7	7	20	5	1

Key: F = Formal and Regular Procedures Exist.
       I. = Informal Consideration Given.
       N.C. = Note Considered.

6

Long Range Planning—Japan–U.S.A.—A Comparative Study

T. KONO*

Introduction

Much of the literature on the analysis of Japanese management system in comparison to American or European management practices place stress on such characteristics as lifetime employment, promotion and wage increase by length of service, group decision with bottom-up approach, ambiguous responsibility of individuals, and company-wide union. These analyses are more concerned with operational decisions, motivation and leadership. This paper is more concerned with *strategic decisions* such as those likely to be related to long range planning.

This analysis is based on (a) visits to more than 30 companies in the U.S. and to a number of companies in Japan, (b) mail questionnaire surveys in both countries, (c) published materials in both countries. Research of the practices of American corporation was conducted during one year stay as Fulbright Visiting Scholar at the Graduate School of Management, UCLA from 1974 through 1975.

Different environments call for different combinations of strategy, structure and decision making, and if there is a good fit between these types of subsystems, different combination will bring about the same good performance. This paper will try to apply a contingency approach to the analysis of long range planning in the two countries (Kast and Rosenzweig, 1973).

The Spread of Long Range Planning and Reasons for Planning

In both countries, long range planning has high diffusion. In the U.S., more than 80 per cent of large corporations have some kind of long range

This article was originally published in *Long Range Planning*, Volume 9, No. 5, October 1976.

* The author is Professor of Business Administration, Gakushuin University, Japan.

TABLE 6.1. Spread of Long Range Plans

Does your company have a long range plan?	U.S. (per cent)	Japan				
		(per cent)	(per cent)	(per cent)	(per cent)	(per cent)
(1) Yes	85	77	78	80	84	91
(2) No	11	3	6	9	5	1
(3) Under preparation	4	16	16	11	11	7
(4) In the past we had it, but now under consideration	0	3	—	—	—	—
If yes, is it formal or informal?						
(5) Formal and written	74	75	76	78	78	88
(6) Written, but not formally approved	22	21	24	22	18	7
(Year of survey)	1975	1975	1963	1965	1967	1970
(Number of companies responded)	27	74	324	372	321	175

(1) All surveys were conducted by questionnaires by mail.
(2) For survey of 1975, see Appendix.

plans, the same is true in Japan (see Table 6.1). These figures are much higher than in Europe. Table 6.1 shows the long term trend in Japan, there is a trend of increasing spread, but in 1975 there is a slight downturn because of uncertainties caused by oil problems. There are several reasons for this high spread in Japan. (a) A high rate of growth of economy and new opportunity as a result of technological innovation resulted in short life cycle of products, which necessitated innovation. (b) Severe competition between corporations gave rise to the need of rational strategic decision making, which could be attained by long range planning system. (c) National economic plans were announced frequently which stimulated long range planning.

Then there are internal reasons (a) group decision making is popular in Japan, and long range planning could be a means of group contributions to decisions. (b) The attitude of management is innovative; thus they had a positive attitude toward long range strategy.

In the United States, technological innovation, competition, and the desire of top management to make rational decision may be the background reasons for there being a higher spread than is the case in Europe.

From this background comes the direct reasons for planning. Table 6.2 shows the reasons which are considered as important.

High growth, technological innovation and serve competition necessitate the examination of the basic problems of companies. Long lead time

TABLE 6.2. *Reasons for Long Range Planning*

	U.S. (per cent)	Japan (per cent)
(1) To examine basic problems of the company	39	82*
(2) To make decisions based on long range forecasting	52	53
(3) To take action at an early stage considering lead time	30	31
(4) To improve short range planning such as budgeting	17	13
(5) To make strategic plan by collecting the ideas of the whole organization	17	21
(6) To improve communication throughout the organization	13	20
(7) To coordinate the individual projects, such as projects for new products and projects for expansion	13	25
(8) For better allocation of resources	65	38*
(9) To clarify goals and policies of the company	44	89*
(10) To assure unified opinion among top executives	9	25
(11) To educate departmental managers	0	6

(1) Percentage is number of companies checked for these items.
(2) For survey method, see Appendix.
(3) * Indicates significant differences of percentage (level of risk of significance, less than 5 per cent).

necessitates taking decisions long before the real need to fill the future gaps with respect to goals appears.

In order to cope with competition, rational decisions are required to have competitive power, so the formal process of strategic decision is desirable, and goals and policies of the company should be made clear.

Apart from these similarities of reasons for having long range plans, there are differences.

For American corporations the integration of the strategies of poly-centralized divisions are one of the important reasons for long range planning. Table 6.2 shows that the better allocation of resources is the most important reason. In contrast, in Japan, top management and the planning department play the most important role to make strategic decision, so long range planning is used to improve the decision at the top. Table 6.2 shows that, to examine basic problems, to clarify goals and policies are of higher importance for these reasons.

These differences may arise from the difference of the organizational structure, that is, American corporations are more diversified in product strategy and more divisionalized in organization.

Planning Process in the Organization

The planning process in the organization may be classified into three types: "Bottom-up", "Top-down" and "Interactive". This relates to where the basic idea is presented, where the plan is reviewed and where the plan is decided.

The bottom-up approach usually results in the corporate planning department being small; the information collection is mostly done by operating units; and goals of the divisions, strategies of the divisions, plans by products, functional plans, etc., are all initiated by operating units. This is a decentralized planning process. The planning department initiates only the format, and coordinate the planning activities of operating units. It should be noted, however, that even in bottom-up process, some key strategies are prepared at the corporate level. They are acquisitions and new product development which does not belong to any existing division.

In case of top-down approach, basic information, goals of each department, key strategies are decided at the corporate level, and they are given to operating units as a guideline. The operating units then build the "tactical plan". In this approach the planning department is stronger, and plays a more important role. Operating units have less authority to decide the strategy.

The interactive process is a compromise between the above two. In this approach the ideas are formulated by interaction between top manage-ment, the planning department and operating units. The planning department will collect environmental information and will submit strategic issues to the top. The top management will decide the goals and broad direction. Then by vertical interaction, strategies are formulated. In addition, there is a vertical division of labour. Some strategies such as acquisitions, joint ventures and new projects which are not assignable to departments are studied by corporate planning department or by corporate development department, and are implemented at corporate level. Operating units will then follow the guidelines given from the top, and build strategy specific to the division and build operational plan.

If there is a two plan system, long range strategic plans are worked out largely at corporate level, while medium range plans are developed by operating units.

In the United States, there is a greater tendency to plan using the bottom-up process. My field research suggested, for example that about two-thirds of the companies in any population have a bottom-up process, while one-third used an interactive approach. The top-down process was not noted in the company. According to the questionnaire survey, as Table 6.3 shows, the plan is prepared in many cases by operating units, and is reviewed by planning department, staff department and through meetings of the chief executive officer with heads of divisions and departments. The final decision is taken mostly by chief executive officers and boards of directors.

Table 6.4 is a general description of planning method, and it shows that about half of the companies use bottom-up approach (No. 1 item and No. 4 item).

In case of Japanese corporations, as the Table 6.3 shows, the planning department takes more initiative, it is reviewed by management commit-tee, and final decision is taken by a management committee and the president who is a chief executive officer. Table 6.4 shows that two-thirds are by interactive process (item 3).

What is the reason for this difference? (a) The environment of American corporations is more stable than that of Japanese corporations, thus there is less need of innovation, thus bottom-up approach will suffice. (b) American corporations are more diversified and more multi-national management oriented. (c) American corporations are more decentralized. Decentralization comes partly from stable environment, diversification and multi-national activity, but there are some other reasons.

As a philosophy of management, American corporations are more division oriented (Steiner, 1975) and more decentralized. Long range planning is used for integrating the strategy of divisions, and also for control purpose of division managers. The long range plan is a commit-ment of the managers of the divisions.

Japanese corporations are more centralized. There are many papers

TABLE 6.3. *Planning Process in the Organization*
(Which department prepares, reviews and finally decides the long range plan)

	Preparing		Reviewing		Final Decision	
	U.S. (per cent)	Japan (per cent)	U.S. (per cent)	Japan (per cent)	U.S. (per cent)	Japan (per cent)
(1) Planning department	39	86*	57	7*	9	4
(2) Division or line department	87	39*	22	11	13	0
(3) Corporate staff department	30	35	70	12*	4	0
(4) Special committees	4	4	13	11	4	2
(5) Task force (or Project team)	9	9	4	2	0	0
(6) Committee for long range planning	0	7	13	11	4	0
(7) Meeting of chief executive officer and department (devision) executives	0	2	61	14*	26	2
(8) Management committee by full-time executives	0	0	22	63*	22	52*
(9) Chief executive officer	0	2	39	4	61	40*
(10) A committee of board of directors	0	0	4	0	4	0
(11) Board of directors	0	0	9	5	35	9*

* For methods of survey, see Appendix.

TABLE 6.4. *Decentralization of Planning Projects*
(How is the initiation or preparation, not the decision, decentralized)

	U.S. (per cent)	Japan (per cent)
(1) Decentralized to operating units (divisions)	39	14*
(2) Centralized by corporate planning department	9	14
(3) Prepared chiefly by corporate planning department with the participation of operating units	13	51*
(4) Prepared chiefly by operating units with participation of corporate planning department	44	23*

* For method of survey, see Appendix.

describing that the Japanese style of decisions are bottom-up and group decision oriented (for example, Johnson and Ouchi, 1974). According to my survey, this generalization does not hold. The strategic decision making process is not bottom-up, it is rather top-down or interactive process. The reason for this is due to the faster change of environment, which necessitated Japanese corporations using a top-down innovation approach.

The top management is a group body and innovation oriented. In addition to these facts, Japanese corporations are less diversified and have less spread of divisionalization. They used the acquisition approach to a less extent as an entry strategy, which is another reason for centralized organization.

For operational decision, the situation is different. Operational policy is decided by staff department, and ideas are submitted from the middle, and group decisions are used. Decision as an application of the policy, or the working decision is also done by group which is often termed "Ringi".

In the United States, operational policy may be decided by participation of many departments, but working decisions are made by responsible individuals. This system may come from social setting which is more individualistic than group oriented.

Recently there is a change of strategic decision among American corporations. During and after the oil problem, the U.S. economy experienced unprecedented uncertainty, and also a considerable depression. This suggested the need to change strategy. When the bottom-up approach is used and when every department intends to grow simultaneously, efficient use of limited strategic resources are not assured. Like General Electric, many corporations started to concentrate basic strategies, after evaluating each product by growth potential of the industry, and by competitive ability of the corporation. The corporate planning department will help decide which products should have priority to resource allocation, and which product should be cut down or sold to other organizations. Thus the uncertainty of environment is changing the bottom-up process of American corporations.

System of Plan

1 Time Horizon and the Two Plan System

Time horizon of planning depends on three factors. Lead time from idea to implementation, how long the results of a decision stays in the organization, or how long a decision binds the organization, and predictability of the future.

The time horizon of the U.S. corporations are longer than the Japanese corporations, as Table 6.5 shows. In Japan, 3 and 5 years are the most frequent, while in the United States, 5 years are predominant. The reason for this difference may be that the environment for Japanese corporations is less certain, and harder to predict. Consequently the time horizon is shorter.

In the United States the time horizon is usually single, while in Japan two plans with different time horizons are becoming popular. As Table 6.5 shows, about 30 per cent of the companies surveyed have medium range plan in addition to long range plan.

In the ideal case, long range plan stresses the strategy of corporations, it decides the area of business and new directions to enter. It is more narrative than quantitative, more conceptual than financially oriented. It lists major projects and states priorities. It is mostly worked out at the corporate level.

On the other hand, medium range plan covers 2 or 3 years, it is more quantitative and stresses the allocation of resources. Detailed schedule of projects, and planning by products and capital investments, financial plans are important items. It is mostly worked out by operating units.

The merits of two plan systems are as follows. (a) Emphasis on strategic issues becomes possible by separating strategic plan from quantitative plan. (b) More trust of long range planning by shortening the quantitative plan is possible. Financial plans beyond 3 years are not very meaningful because of uncertainty. Thus, economy of information processing, by better allocation of processing cost to strategic issues, can be attained.

In the United States many companies have strategy plans, plans by products, plus functional plans. For example, in the case of the Pfizer Corporation, their strategy plan has no time horizon, it is a decision on business area, while the "3 year operational plan" is more financially oriented. In the case of the Northrop Corporation growth strategy is decided first, this includes new business, new products, joint ventures and acquisitions, and this strategy is followed by plans by product and by functional plans.

TABLE 6.5. *Time Horizon*

	Long range plan		Medium range plan (if you have two plans)	
Time span	U.S. (per cent)	Japan (per cent)	U.S. (per cent)	Japan (per cent)
(A) Time span				
(1) Over 10 years	4	2		
(2) 10–7 years	9	4		
(3) 5 or 6 years	74	56*		
(4) 4 years	4	2		
(5) 3 years	9	32*	4	20 ⎫ 30*
(6) 2 years		5	9	10 ⎭
(B) Quantitative plans for each year				
(7) Target year only	13	20	4	0
(8) Numbers for each year	78	80	9	28

(1) If the company has two comprehensive long range plans with different time horizon, the plan with shorter time horizon is called medium range plan.

(2) For method of survey, see Appendix.

These cases indicate that though the time horizons of both plans are the same, corporations in both countries are going to have two plan system, in the sense that important projects are stressed separately from quantitative plans.

2 Four Types of Long Range Planning by Character

By character the long range planning systems may be divided into four types: (a) forecasting type, (b) goal-setting type without details, (c) individual problem solving, but not comprehensive, (d) systems approach type.

The forecasting type contains only the analysis of future performance of the particular corporation, to the effect that the future problems and gaps are identified. In this sense, this type may be called a problem-finding type, which aims to gauge the gap between the desired level of goals and projected performance if the new strategy is not introduced and present policy is maintained. The solution to fill the gap is planned in a short range plan or outside the comprehensive plan, and this has serious drawbacks. In Japan this type is decreasing, and in the U.S. it is rare.

The goal setting type has goals and policies which the corporation desires to achieve stated in the plan, but detailed plans are lacking, they are planned at divisional level or in short range plan.

In Japan this type of planning is popular among medium and small businesses, and there is a similar tendency in the United States, but the frequency is much lower. In the United States there is a tendency to write a plan and to have more documentation, while in Japan, management likes to have less documentation because of good communication between top management and middle management through daily activities.

In this type, goals and policies have effects of giving stimulus to the divisions, but innovative strategy is difficult to work out.

Individual problem solving type without comprehensive planning is rare in both countries.

The fourth type which might be called "systems approach" includes all of the above three types. It analyses the future gaps of the corporation, aims to develop strategies and programmes to fill the gaps, and after assuring that the gaps are filled by new strategies, establishes achievable goals. This is an ideal type of planning.

The decision making process follows from broad policy to a detailed programme, this is one of the concepts of the systems approach. The structure of the total system is overviewed firstly and then sub-systems are designed. Moving from broad strategy to detailed projects, from long range strategy to medium range is typical of this process.

In Japan, the major strategies are developed at the corporate level. It is assumed that the corporate planning department has sufficient ability to look for new strategies, or to mobilize the other staff department and operating units in presenting the ideas of new strategies. Top management will review the new strategies with the corporate planning department. By this interactive process, innovative strategies can be located and developed.

In case of American corporations, the goals are assigned to each division, the gaps of each division are identified and the solutions to fill the gaps are worked out by each division. This is a bottom-up approach, and also a systems approach.

3 Quantitative or Project Emphasis

Long range plan may be very quantitative or have a project emphasis. A project emphasis means that the most important 5−10 issues will be selected, and the solution of these selected issues will be the core of long range plans.

The issues will be both the opportunities and means to avoid the risk. For example, new product development projects, foreign investment to manufacture a product, projects for vertical integration, and important capital investment or acquisition projects. Those projects which have considerable impact on the performance of corporations are selected, and resources for research and development are concentrated on their important issues.

These issues are looked for all the year around, not only during a period of long range planning.

In the comprehensive planning process, priorities are given, schedules are set, and resources are allocated to the projects. These resource allocations are consolidated in the functional plans.

Planning which does not have a project emphasis includes such planning approaches as follows:

Too many problems or problems of every departments are analysed.
Only quantitative plans (e.g., long range sales, production, resource plans and financial plans) are stressed.

Nonetheless, there are a number of merits of a project emphasis.

It is easier to implement, because a limited number of projects are selected, and efforts are focused on these projects.

It is more effective planning, because causal variables are tackled. Financial planning are rather end-results variables of strategic decisions, so if there are only financial plans, then the planning of key factors of financial results are lacking.

According to my survey, the majority of planning in the U.S. has a project emphasis (Table 6.6), while in Japan about 50 per cent has a project

TABLE 6.6. *Characteristics of the Long Range (and Medium Range) Plan*

	U.S. (per cent)	Japan (per cent)
A. (1) Forecast only	22	14
(2) Clarifying goals, without details	13	16
(3) Individual problem solving, not comprehensive	4	0
(4) Comprehensive, including all of the above	61	68
(5) Others (describe)		
B. (1) Mostly quantitative 17	46*	
(2) Emphasis on projects and also quantitative consolidation	65	51
(3) Long range project only		7

* For method of survey, see Appendix.

emphasis, and there is an increasing trend towards it. It is my opinion that the more emphasis is placed on projects, the more advanced the planning system and the greater probability of success.

The quantitative nature of planning of many Japanese corporations is one of the problems. This survey shows that it is perceived as a problem by many corporate planners. This feature may come from high growth environment, and from lower level of diversification, because in these situations number can be an important aspect of planning.

4 Components of Long Range Plan

A typical model on components of long range plan is illustrated by Table 6.7.

The components are essentially the same in both countries; as Table 6.8 shows. There are more similarities than differences.

Acquisition is considered as important strategy in the U.S. (No. 9), while it is seldom used in Japan, rather internal new product development is considered as important (No. 8).

There is more stress on new market development in the U.S. (No. 11), while there is more stress on new products development in Japan, because the market area is wider in the United States.

Manpower planning (No. 22) and education planning (No. 23) are considered more important in Japan. Life time employment is common in Japanese corporations, once a man is employed he will stay for his lifetime, so manpower has to be planned carefully. In the U.S. lay-off is easy, so there is less emphasis on manpower planning.

Contingency plans have surprisingly high frequency in the U.S.

TABLE 6.7. *Typical model of components of plan*

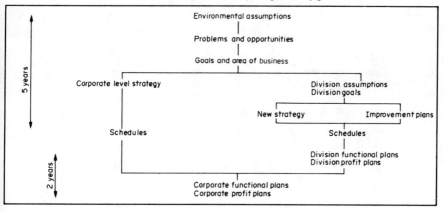

(1) Functional plan includes marketing, production, research and development, capital investment, personnel.
(2) In case where the company is not divisionalized, "division" should be replaced by "product".

Contingency plans mean that there are plural plans preparing for the situations which are different from the assumed standard on most probable situations, upon which the standard plan is based.

In Japan, this approach is used less frequently, perhaps because of the different level of sophistication.

5 Uncertainty and Long Range Planning

The difficulty of forecasting the future environment and future results of actions taken is the most serious problem in long range planning. Yet companies have to make large investments for both research and facilities now, based on long term anticipation, because the lead time is long.

Decision under uncertainty suggest several alternatives. Arranged by the degree of uncertainty, the following can be listed.

(a) Improvement of information collection and method of forecasting. Three points forecasting.
(b) Revision of plan.
(c) Sequential decision.
(d) Monitoring system.
(e) Contingency plan.
(f) Diversification of products and markets.
(g) Strengthening the resisting power.

Table 6.8. *Components of Long Range Plan*

	U.S. (per cent)	Japan (per cent)
(1) Environment forecasting	48	74
(2) Analysis of the company strength and weakness	48	58
(3) Forecasting the future of own company under present policy	48	42
(4) Problems and opportunities of the company	65	40
(5) Mission and objectives of the company as a whole	52 ⎫	95
(6) Goals and policies of long range plan	48 ⎭	
(7) Diversification	39	30
(8) Internal new products development	35	53*
(9) Company acquisition	39	2*
(10) Research and development	35	37
(11) New Market development	57	26*
(12) Multi-national management	13	23
(13) Strengthening the marketing competitive power	30	37
(14) Cost reduction plan	35	53*
(15) Computerization plan	17	25
(16) Others	4	
(17) Sales plan (marketing plan)	74	67
(18) Production plan	35	67
(19) Capital investment	78	90
(20) Investment subsidiaries	35	39
(21) Material plan	17	26
(22) Manpower plan	52	86*
(23) Education and management development	13	23*
(24) Employee welfare	9	12
(25) Planning of organization	26	26
(26) Estimated profit and loss statement	87	70
(27) Estimated flow of funds	83	72
(28) Estimated balance sheet	78	49
(29) Assignment of responsibility	22	25
(30) Schedule of programme	35	—
(31) Unsolved problems	22	25
(32) Contingency plans for adverse situations	57	4*

* For research method, see Appendix.

Three points forecasting

This is to predict the sales or profit within a range, and usually maximum, probable and minimum are used as the three points. One Japanese film company takes into consideration optimistic and pessimistic cases for total national sales, share of the imports and the share of its own company. Two levels of three factors make 12 combinations, but they are reduced to three points. The most probable case is standard assumption which is used for the standard quantitative plan. One American aerospace company uses probability of success in bidding. The back logs and the expected repeat orders constitute the minimum, new projects are multiplied by the probability of success, and the sum of this amount plus the minimum make the probable sales. This is the basis of the comprehensive plan. New projects multiplied by optimistic probabilities constitute optimistic sales.

The merits of range forecasting are various. The planner can recognize the real meaning of the expected value of estimation. This is to prevent the planner from building the comprehensive plan on too pessimistic or too optimistic assumptions. Secondly, the causes of minimum values are identified beforehand, thus it becomes possible to have early warning systems or to have contingency plans which attempt to prevent performance falling below the expected average.

About one-third of Japanese companies use range forecasting, but their comprehensive plans are based on the most probable assumptions. How many American corporations are using range forecasting is not clear, but according to my field research, a large number of companies are using this method.

Revision of plan. A majority of companies in both countries update the plan every year, adding another year. This is important, because assumptions on the environment change. However, about 40 per cent of Japanese corporations have a fixed term approach (as we see in Table 6.9).

TABLE 6.9. *Updating of Plans*

	U.S. (per cent)	Japan (per cent)
(1) Revised yearly adding another year	78	56
(2) Term is fixed, and the plan is revised every year	0	11 ⎫
(3) Term is fixed and the plan is revised as occasion demands	13	11 ⎪ 44*
(4) Term and plan are revised as occasion demands	4	18 ⎬
(5) Term and plan are fixed	4	4 ⎭
(6) Important project plans are revised independent of the long range plan	22	20

* For the method of survey, see Appendix.

The reasons for this difference arise from several factors. The long range plan is considered more as a goal by Japanese corporations since it is developed by a centralized process, and it is easier to understand the target if the term is fixed. Secondly, in the U.S. the long range plan is used for controlling divisions, so the plan has to be as close to the reality as possible, so the plan has to be revised every year or even more frequently.

Sequential decision. This means (a) to make partial commitment, collect information through it, and then make larger commitment. For example, a new product is sold in a small city as an experiment, and if successful the launch is expanded to a large scale. This means also (b) to make a flexible decision first and wait until more accurate information is available, then make detailed decisions later.

The two-time span plan is an example of the latter approach, and this is used more often in Japan as Table 6.5 shows.

In long range strategy, new directions are decided, and important projects are agreed upon, in medium range plan a quantitative detailed plan is formulated, so policy decisions are taken for long-term horizon.

Project emphasis rather than quantitative plan is related to sequential decisions. If a plan is too quantitative this usually results in too rigid decisions.

Monitoring system. This is an early warning system. A Japanese company manufactures educational materials for schools, and the key factor of the new direction of change is a new decision of the Ministry of Education, so the company tries to monitor the discussions of the Ministry. To a pharmaceutical company the change of regulation on medical insurance has a tremendous impact on the demand, so this factor is monitored. This monitoring system is frequently used by Japanese corporations.

Contingency plans. This is a recent development, and half the American companies surveyed have contingency plans, while Japanese corporations seldom have them. An American oil company has contingency plans for such key factors as an oil embargo by oil producing companies, change of regulation on sulphur contents of oil, unsuccessful issue of a new bond. Another aerospace company has contingency plans for the failure of bidding for a large number of new fighter planes. The process of contingency planning is as follows: (a) Identifying key environmental factors of performance. Both the size of impact and the probability of occurrence are measurements to select the key factors. (b) Building the standard plan based on the most probable assumption. This is a comprehensive plan. (c) Selecting several key assumptions other than the most probable situation for each product, and building the contingency plan on coloured papers. This contingency plan is not integrated into comprehensive plan. Not only the worst case, but also chance situations are taken as assumptions. A contingency plan is not a detailed plan, but it prescribes who should do what, in what case, and what is expected as the result of that action. (d) Monitoring event is selected, and trigger point is stated clearly.

Contingency plans have several advantages. The company can take quick action in preparation for adverse situation, and for chance events as well. The company can take better action because it is planned when enough time is available. It increases the usefulness of long range planning and decrease the distrust of planning. It does not result in too much complexity of planning because the contingency plan is not integrated into comprehensive plan.

The reasons for more diffusion of contingency plan in the U.S. have already been analysed, and probably the most important reason is that long long range planning in the U.S. is used for a declared commitment of division managers, and it is used for control of divisions by head office, and rewards are related with the accomplishment of plan, so the plan has to be realistic.

6 Follow up and Implementation

Follow up of the plan is important to assure implementation and to obtain information for revision.

Follow up consists of reviewing projects and reviewing of quantitative parts of the plan. In both areas, the U.S. corporations are doing better than Japanese corporations, as Table 6.10 shows. In the majority of American corporations, project plans are reviewed several times a year. About half of them review the quantitative parts of long range planning several times a year, while Japanese corporations review the plan through the budget period.

Progress and performance are closely related to some kind of economic rewards such as bonus or stock option in the U.S., as Table 6.10 shows. It is also important to note that not only the implementation but also the quality of planning is frequently reflected in rewards in the U.S.

This system applies to a large number of personnel above the manager level.

Many companies use some form of management by objective system (MBO) and this system is based on long range planning, and the evaluation of the performance of MBO is reflected in the bonus which is paid.

But the situation is quite different in Japan, they are seldom related to economic rewards (as Table 6.10 shows).

What are the effects of reward system connected with long range planning in the United States? The long range plans have to be agreed fully by the operating units, so this encourages the bottom-up approach.

In Japan, it can be a top-down approach, thus one of the results is the difference of organizational process of planning.

Another effect is that the plan has to be realistic, so the plan is updated more frequently, and contingency plans have to be worked out.

TABLE 6.10. *Follow Up and Rewards for Implementation*

	U.S. (per cent)	Japan (per cent)
A. Follow-up of projects		
(1) No	9	28
(2) Several times in a year	65	26*
(3) Once a year	22	19
Others		9
B. Follow-up of quantitative parts of plan is actual performance against quantitative parts of long range plan reviewed by head office?		
(4) No	26	74*
(5) Once a year	22	35
(6) Several times a year	48	
(7) Performance against budget is reviewed	17	60*
(8) Performance against other short range plan is reviewed	9	7
(9) No follow up at all	0	9
C. Is progress and performance related to some kind of economic reward of managers (bonus or stock option).		
(10) Not at all	30	65*
(11) To some extent	48	26*
(12) To a great extent	22	0*

* For method of survey, see Appendix.

It affects the extent of implementation, and plans are thus better implemented in the U.S.

What are the reasons of this difference of reward system?

The United States is a functional society (or multiple society), and corporations are considered as economic organizations. Participants are more concerned with economic rewards, and they request quick feedback from their contribution, otherwise they will leave and go to another organization.

In Japan, the loyalty of the employee to the organization is high and they will work for it for their lifetime, so the evaluation of employee tends to be done by the accumulation of long-term performance. Performance on long range planning is not ignored in evaluation, but it is reflected in future promotion, or future pay increases along with the other performance.

However, evaluation by efforts towards long-term effects, not by short-term effects, is becoming more important in Japan, so there is a growing concern to relate some rewards to the quality of planning and also to the accomplishment of the plan.

Implementation means that, (a) the long range plan has detailed action programmes, is incorporated into annual budgets and has the necessary allocation of resources, (b) the plan is put into action.

There are some doubts that plans in Japanese corporations are not implemented well. During the oil problems, the assumptions of plans deviated drastically from the facts. This resulted in dramatic change in implementation. In 1970 survey, 43 per cent of companies said that long range plans were completely implemented, but in 1975 survey the figure dropped to 11 per cent. Instead, companies with partial implementation increased from 48 per cent to 64 per cent. But it should be emphasized that in majority of cases, the long range plan was implemented to some extent, though there is a difference in the extent by company.

It may be true to say that long range plans in the U.S. are more accepted and more widely implemented.

There are three reasons for this difference.

One is the volatility of environment, the Japanese economy and society is changing, at a faster rate and contingency plans were still to be tried in the future.

Another is the difference in the extent of participation. In Japan, we observed that there is less participation by the operating units, so if the plan is to be implemented by the operating units, then there is a problem. However, the long range plan is supposed to be strategic, and it is devised by the strategic department. For development of the project, a project term is used more frequently, as it is for implementing the plan. This frequent use of project team may alleviate the defects of less participation, but perhaps it is also the cause of dissatisfaction in the operating units concerned.

Lastly the reward system concerning long range planning is different. As has been argued in Japan, the economic reward system is not related to long range planning.

Conclusion

In the U.S., long range planning is used for integrating the strategies of divisions and to control the divisions. The planning process is more a bottom-up or guide-line and build-up approach.

In Japan, long range planning is used for improving the strategic decision by top management, so the planning process is more a centralized interactive process.

Project emphasis rather than quantitative plan is common characteristics in both countries, but American corporations are more advanced in this respect. Many Japanese corporations mention that project emphasis is the key success factor of planning.

To cope with uncertainty, American corporations update their plans every year or even over shorter interval, and adopt contingency plans.

To the same end, Japanese corporations use two time horizon plans which are composed of long range strategy and a medium range plan. This system is closely rated with systems approach.

With respect to follow-up and implementation, American corporations use more closely controlled follow-up, while long range planning is used for evaluation of managers of divisions, with the quality of plans and accomplishments being reflected in the economic rewards.

Japanese corporations are less inclined to follow up the long range plan itself, but it is considered as important to implement it through budget and also through the project plan. Project teams are quite frequently used.

The contingency theory maintains that different approaches can have the same result if there is a good fit between the sub-systems, the findings of this paper confirm this theory.

References

Furukawa, E. (ed.) (1973) *Growth of Japanese Corporations, an Empirical Analysis.*
Holden, Fish and Smith (1941) *Top Management Organization and Control.*
Johnson, R. and Ouchi, W. (1974) Made in America under Japanese Management, *Harvard Business Review,* September—October.
Kast, F. and Rosenzweig, J. (1973) *Contingency Views of Organization and Management.*
Kono, T. (1968) *Analysis of Corporate Growth.*
Kono, T. (1971) *Business Policy.*
Kono, T. (1975) *Analysis of Long-range Planning.*
Kono, T. (ed.), (1972) *Cases of Long-range Planning II.*
Kono, T. (1974) *Analysis of Corporate Strategy.*
Koontz, H. (1967) *The Board of Directors and Effective Management.*
Nakane, C. (1966) *Human Relations in the Vertical Society.*
Ringbakk, K. A. (1975) Corporate Planning in Major Japanese Enterprises (Discussion Paper).
Steiner, G. (1969) *Top Management Planning.*
Steiner, G. (1975) Pitfalls in Multi-national Long-range planning, *Long Range Planning,* April.
The Conference Board (1972) *Planning and the Chief Executive.*
The Conference Board (1974) *Planning and the Corporate Planning Director.*

Appendix

Method of Survey

(1) Date of visits in the U.S.: From August 1974 through 1975.
(2) Date of mail survey: In the U.S., questionnaires were sent out in May 1975 to 152 companies in the southern California area, to which 26 companies responded (response ratio 17 per cent), and 23 companies with long range plans were analysed.

In Japan, questionnaires were sent out in November 1975 by mail to 536 companies, to which 74 companies responded (response ratio 13.8 per cent), and 57 companies with long range plans were analysed.

(3) Distribution of companies by industry:

| | Mail Survey | | | | |
| | U.S. | | Japan | | |
	Companies Responded	Companies with long range plan	Companies responded	Companies with long range plan	Visits in the U.S.
(1) Mining and Construction	3	3	4	3	4
(2) Food and Fisheries	1	1	3	2	2
(3) Fibre, Pulp and Paper			8	6	
(4) Chemicals	1		12	8	2
(5) Petroleum, Rubber, Soil and Stone	2	2	6	5	4
(6) Iron, Steel and Nonferrous Metals			10	8	
(7) Machinery			5	4	1
(8) Electrical Applicances and Precision Machine	5	5	11	11	6
(9) Transportation Equipment and Machinery	3	3	7	3	3
(10) Finance and Insurance	5	4	2	2	4
(11) Commerce, Service, Real Estate, Communication, Warehousing and Transportation	5	4	3	2	7
(12) Electricity and Gas	1	1	3	3	
Total	26	23	74	57	33

(4) Distribution of companies by assets (U.S.) or sales (Japan) is as follows:

| | Mail Survey | | | | |
| | U.S. | | Japan | | |
	Companies responded	Companies with long range plan	Companes responded	Companies with long range plan	Visits in the U.S.
Over $10,000 million	1	1	0	0	1
$9999−$1000 million	10	9	12	10	15
$999−$333 million	5	5	15	10	9
$332−100 million	5	5	23	19	3
$99−33 million			17	12	1
$32−10 million	5	3	6	5	2
Under $10 million			1	1	2
	26	23	74	57	33

(5) Co-operation: To conduct mail surveys, the author could have the co-operation of Los Angeles Chapter, Planning Executive Institute, Los Angeles in the U.S. and Management Centre in Tokyo, Japan.

7

Corporate Planning in the Netherlands

D. J. EPPINK, D. KEUNING AND K. DE JONG *

Introduction

One of the reasons that led the authors to conduct an investigation into the practice of corporate planning in the Netherlands is the lack of empirical material about this phenomenon and about the problems encountered by corporate planners in the planning process. Another reason for this project was found in students' requests for instruction in planning techniques used in practice. The last—but not the least—reason was to find out in how far there was a discrepancy between planning theory and planning practice.

In the planning literature a number of implicit assumptions are made, e.g. formal planning is an accepted mode, management culture permits the use of techniques of increasing sophistication in the planning process and, finally, techniques play a major part in formal strategic planning. The question might be raised whether these assumptions are correct. The published results of investigations in other countries suggest that these assumptions are not entirely realistic.[1] We wanted to concentrate on the Dutch situation. To achieve this we had to get an overall picture of the practices in the Netherlands. The authors finally had to adopt a moderately structured "vacuum-cleaner approach".

The pilot study was mainly focused on the use of planning techniques. As our point of departure we chose two schemes from Ansoff's book *Corporate Strategy*.

- Checklist for competitive and competence profile.
- Outline for industry analysis.[2]

We elaborated these schemes by generating very detailed questions that we thought a firm should ask itself when using them. We supposed these

This article was originally published in *Long Range Planning*, Volume 9, No. 5, October 1976.
* The authors are all at the Free University, Amsterdam.

questions would be answered in a structured way by using techniques. More specifically we had the impression that corporate planners would be able to answer our questionnaire by pointing out the techniques they or other people in the firm used in trying to answer these questions.

We distributed this questionnaire among corporate planners of two big Dutch companies that had already introduced formal corporate planning systems some years ago. During the interviews these planners told us that they did not apply this approach to strategic problems. In both instances the respondents felt that the technique approach was far too comprehensive and that it distracted the attention from the real problems they encountered in their daily work. Their impression was that this would apply to the majority of their colleagues in other firms. Their comments corroborated our initial intuitive hesitation concerning the importance of techniques in the strategic planning process.

This result made it necessary to opt for another approach that had a wider scope and was less rigid. Problems in the planning process and problems encountered by the planners had to be stressed when it was our aim to gain insight into the practice of corporate planning. The final research design had to be much more exploratory in nature. To this end we drew up a questionnaire divided into five parts:

- General information.
- The corporate planner.
- The corporate planner in the firm.
- The firm in its industry.
- Techniques. [3]

The same two corporate planners who participated in the pilot-study reviewed the new questionnaire and observed that this new version was much more viable and that it would give more relevant information than the first.

This new questionnaire was used in interviewing corporate planners in 20 big Dutch companies. Each interview took approximately 2 to 4 hours. The people we interviewed all held top positions in their companies. They were either line managers, to whom the task of corporate planning was assigned, or staff specialists assisting line managers in this area. Some of the line managers were members of the top-management team, the others had positions directly below top management. The majority of the respondents, however, were staff specialists. The authors realize that this may have led to some bias in the responses. In view of the observations made by Taylor and Irving stating that " . . . the dangers of personal bias by planning executives are inherent in a study of this nature . . ." but that " . . . subsequent interviews with other interested parties indicated no evidence of distortion",[4] we felt confident that our findings would give a true enough picture of reality.

The main criterion for the selection of these companies was the membership of the "Vereniging voor Strategische Beleidsvorming", the Dutch branch of the Society for Long Range Planning. Some firms that did not meet this criterion, were accepted when we knew that they had a formal strategic planning system. In order to avoid a clash with another research project we did not interview planners in Philips, Unilever, Shell, AKZO and Estel.

The firms that co-operated in this study were active in a variety of industries. As can be seen in Table 7.1 the majority of the companies belong—based on 1973 sales figures—to the 200 largest Dutch firms. Of four firms the turnover figures were not available either because they were part of a larger concern, or because the turnover was not given as the firm regarded it as irrelevant information (this was a financial institution).

TABLE 7.1. *Turnover of the Companies Investigated*

1973 turnover in D.fl. × 1 min.	Number of interviewed firms in the class	Total number of Dutch firms in the class
200—499	4	104
500—999	4	52
1000—1999	5	27
2000—4999	2	9
5000—>	1	6
Unknown	(4)	
	16 (20)	198

Source: Annual reports and *Financial Dagblad*, 12 September 1974.

In order to be able to relate certain findings to characteristics of the firms we made a classification along two dimensions. The first was a distinction between firms in a growth and in a consolidation stage. Criteria used in this connection were the growth in turnover and/or investments, diversification and internationalization. We also took into consideration the reply to a question in the questionnaire. The second criterion was the classification scheme used by Channon:

- *Single product.* Firm grew by expansion of one product line so that at least 95 per cent of sales lay within this single product area.
- *Dominant product.* Firm grew primarily by expansion of one main product line but which in addition had added secondary product lines making up to 30 per cent or less of the total sales volume.
- *Related product.* Firm grew by expansion by entering related markets, by the use of a related technology, by related vertical activities or by a

combination of these, so that no one-product line accounted for 70 per cent of the total corporate sales.

● *Unrelated product.* Firm grew by expansion into new markets and new technologies unrelated to the original product-market scope so that no one line accounted for 70 per cent of the total corporate sales.[5]

Table 7.2 shows the classification of the firms investigated along these two dimensions.

TABLE 7.2. *Classification of the Companies Investigated*

	Single product	Dominant product	Related product	Unrelated product
Stage				
Consolidation	7	3	1	2	1
Growth	13	2	1	6	4
	20	5	2	8	5

Findings

Year of Introduction of Formal Corporate Planning

Table 7.3 shows that in 80 per cent of the companies formal corporate planning was introduced in the beginning of the 1970s. This finding is in line with those of Steiner and Schoelhammer who noted that: "For a majority of the firms comprehensive and systematic long range planning is still in an evolutionary phase."[6]

TABLE 7.3. *Year of Introduction of Formal Corporate Planning*

Year of Introduction	Number of companies
1962	1
1967	1
1968	1
1969	1
1970	4
1971	4
1972	3
1973	1
1974	1
No corporate planning department	(3)
	17 (20)

We have the impression that in Holland the start of formal corporate planning has shown a time-lag of about 5 years, compared with that of the U.S.A. or the U.K.[7]

This clear-cut picture deserves further comments. In the above table three firms are included that have no planning department at corporate level; it is remarkable that these three firms are all highly diversified. This does not mean that there is no planning at all. One of the three companies used to have a corporrte planning department until 1967. In view of the problems the firm encountered at the time and at the advice of external consultants this department was discontinued. The responsibility for business planning[8] was then delegated to the divisions. The top management in this company regards portfolio management, cash management and cash planning as their responsibility. This also goes for the other two, also diversified, companies, which did not mention portfolio management explicitly. In all these three companies the concern-controller was actively involved in these activities at corporate level. These three companies all had a management style—characterized by a bottom-up approach—which was rather different from the two other diversified companies in the sample that had a corporate planning department.

In three companies formal corporate planning was started after a taskforce or a committee had done preliminary work in this field. The time-lag between the activities of these committees (started about 1965) and the start of formal corporate planning (about 1970) was approximately 5 years.

Reasons for Starting Corporate Planning

A wide variety of reasons led to the decision to start formal corporate planning as can be seen in Table 7.4. A number of the reasons mentioned correlate with findings published by Ringbakk, Taylor and Irving.[9] Several firms mentioned two or more reasons. A number of them find their root causes in *external threats* such as decreasing markets, change in external regulations, increasing uncertainty, etc. In the early planning literature corporate planning is generally viewed as intrinsically good, but the responses gave us the impression that it is often only introduced after the situation had deteriorated and after the management saw corporate planning as one of the possible ways out of the situation.

Decreasing profitability was mentioned in six cases. In general one is inclined to think in terms of net profit in this respect. An analysis of available annual reports showed that in many cases a decrease of the ROI over a number of years preceded the start of formal corporate planning. This phenomenon was not mentioned in any of the cases. One might conclude that a drop in net profit is regarded as more dramatic than a drop in ROI.

TABLE 7.4. *Reasons for Starting Formal Corporate Planning*

Reasons mentioned	Frequency of answer
Advocacy by top management	9
Recommendation of management consultants	8
Bottom-up pushing because of absence of clear objectives, goals and policies	7
Decreasing profitability	6
Mergers and their consequences	4
Changing external regulations	2
Change in organizational structure	2
Increasing size of the company	2
Search for diversification	2
Decreasing market share	1
Surplus of financial resources	1
Increasing uncertainty	1
Need for internationalization	1
Increase in number of specialisms in the company	1
Increasing profitability	1
Very large market share	1
Need for systematic information processing in view of future diversification	1

On the face of it, the number of times that advocacy by top management of corporate planning was mentioned seems encouraging for later success. When taking into account, however, problems as "planning-mindedness" of the firm and "formulation objectives" this kind of optimism is unwarranted, as we will show later in this article.

Management consultants can be involved in the introduction of corporate planning in two ways. In eight firms a consultant advocated corporate planning. In five out of these eight cases he was asked to design and to implement a planning system. The other three firms followed his advice but worked out their own system.

In four cases corporate planning was started after important merger or acquisition activities and in two cases after a change from a functional organization structure to a divisional structure. In all these cases corporate planning was expected to provide a major contribution to facilitating co-ordination.[10]

How Corporate Planning is Done

Corporate planning is done in two distinct ways:

- By a *staff department* linked to one of the managing directors.
- By a group of line managers from different levels and disciplines assisted by one or two planning specialists in a *planning committee*.

Table 7.5 shows that the "staff planning" mode is used almost twice as much as the "committee" mode. Closer analysis shows that the "committee" mode was in all cases chosen in 1970 or later. When looking at the firms that started corporate planning in 1970 or later one will note that the two modes are used in equal distribution. In general, the "committee" is chosen for expected higher motivation and involvement in the planning process of people at all levels in the organization. In this way one hopes to counteract the *idée fixe* that planning is an unnatural activity that limits the flexibility and freedom of action. When relating the organizational form in which planning is done, to the problems a planner has to tackle, more specifically the problem of planning-mindedness, this expectation of top management is unwarranted. Planning-mindedness of the organization is mentioned as a problem in 70 per cent of the firms with a planning committee, whereas the same problem is mentioned "only" by 55 per cent of the companies with a staff planning department. An *a priori* preference for the committee mode cannot be supported on the basis of the data.

TABLE 7.5. *Year of Introduction of Formal Corporate Planning and Organizational Form of Planning Effort*

Year of introduction	Number of companies	Planning committee	Staff department
1970 and later	13	6	7
Before 1970	4	—	4
No formal corporate planning	3[a]	—	—
Total	20	6	11[b]

[a] In these three cases no corporate planning department was in existence. However, concern controllers and/or the department of economic affairs at corporate level are very much involved in the decision-making and allocation of resources.

[b] Of the 11 companies where corporate planning was done by staff people, seven had a separate planning department directly linked to a member of the board. In the four others corporate planning was done by the controller's department, the department of economic affairs or the marketing department.

Size of Planning Department and Background of Corporate Planners

The size of the planning department is generally very small as can be seen in Table 7.6. The average number is three specialists in the staff planning mode and one or two in the committee planning mode.

In the 17 firms that had a corporate planning department in either of the two modes, a total of 42 planning specialists were employed. In Table 7.7 we summarize the background of these specialists.

TABLE 7.6. *Size of Planning Staff and Organization*

Size in number of planning specialists	Staff department	Planning committee
1	3	4
2	4	1
3	—	1
4	1	—
5	1	—
6	1	—
7	1	—
Total number	11	6
Total number of planning specialists	33	9

TABLE 7.7. *Background of Corporate Planners*

Background of corporate planner	Number of specialists	
	Staff department	Planning Committee
Finance/accounting	14	5
Marketing	5	1
Technical	4	3
R & D	1	—
Macro-economics	2	—
OR, econometrics, statistics	6	—
Law	1	—
Total	33	9

It is remarkable that the background of the relative majority of the planning specialists lies in the accounting and finance area. This picture is similar to the one found by Taylor and Irving in the U.K.[11] It may be accounted for by a need for a systematization in the information gathering and in the management of the firm, but in our opinion this does not necessarily imply that effectiveness is an automatic consequence of such a systematization.[12] For the survival of the firm additional capabilities are required. In this respect it is remarkable that the marketing input expressed in the number of specialists employed in planning departments is rather low. This may well cause the innovative potential as required in the entrepreneurial support mode (see later in this article) not to be fully exploited.

The six mathematically orientated specialists are found in three firms: one of those employed three of them, one firm had two and the last firm one. The other disciplines mentioned in Table 7.7 are more evenly spread over the companies.

The finance and accounting background of the Dutch planners manifests itself among other things in the techniques the planners use. We will deal with techniques employed in the planning process later in this article.

When relating the size of the planning department to the background of the specialists employed one will observe that it is the smaller departments in particular that are filled with finance and accounting specialists. In the larger staff departments one finds a greater variety of disciplines represented

In the majority of the Dutch firms the planner is an internal appointee; in 85 per cent of the cases the planner had been employed in another position in the same firm before becoming a planner. This finding differs from the data presented by Taylor and Irving which showed that about 60 per cent were internal and 30 per cent external appointees, with 10 per cent unknown. [13]

Our data firmly corroborate the often stated view that in order to have satisfactory results in corporate planning it is vital to have an intimate knowledge of the industry and the firm. The question may be raised whether this is a self-fulfilling prophecy or not, as the statement could also mean that planning is not regarded as a profession with a philosophy and an approach of its own, which can be used in different settings. It might well be the case that corporate planning specialists would be more easily interchangeable, if corporate planning is indeed looked upon as a professional activity by managers and also by planners themselves.

Problems Corporate Planners Work On

Corporate planners are working on a wide variety of problems. In Table 7.8 we give a survey of the problems mentioned and the frequency with which a specific problem was set forth. Furthermore we split up the frequency between firms in a consolidation and in a growth stage. In Table 7.9 we added another dimension: single product, dominant product, related and unrelated, but only for the fourteen problems that were mentioned most frequently.

When analysing the problems it becomes clear that quite a number of them can be related to the dynamics of the environment. One can think of problems such as inflation, the energy crisis, the emergence of new competition, technological breakthroughs, etc.

Inflation apparently has a great impact on firms in the consolidation phase. Looking more closely at Table 7.9 one will see that three out of the four in the growth-unrelated class mention this problem, whereas only one out of six firms in the growth-related class mention inflation as a problem.

TABLE 7.8. *Problems Corporate Planners Work On*

Problems of corporate planners	Frequency of answers	Consolidation stage 7 companies	Growth stage 13 companies
Planning-mindedness of the organization	13 ×	4 ×	9 ×
Formulation of objectives	12 ×	5 ×	7 ×
Inflation	11 ×	6 ×	5 ×
Designing and modifying the planning system	9 ×	1 ×	8 ×
Diversification and internationalization	9 ×	5 ×	4 ×
Cash planning, resource allocation, cash flow	8 ×	2 ×	6 ×
Change in governmental regulation and political situation	8 ×	3 ×	5 ×
Collecting external information	7 ×	3 ×	4 ×
Energy crisis, scarcity of raw materials	6 ×	4 ×	2 ×
Decreasing profitability	5 ×	4 ×	1 ×
Co-ordination problems: (long term— short term; interfunctional and inter- division)	5 ×	1 ×	4 ×
Assessment of strategic profile	3 ×	—	3 ×
Assessment of growth vector	3 ×	1 ×	2 ×
Problems of scale	3 ×	1 ×	2 ×
New competition and product-break- through	2 ×	2 ×	—
Control of stocks	2 ×	2 ×	—
Change in distribution pattern	2 ×	2 ×	—
Sensitivity to the business-cycle	2 ×	1 ×	1 ×
Contingency planning	1 ×	—	1 ×
Building factories abroad	1 ×	1 ×	—
Reorganizing unprofitable subsidiaries	1 ×	1 ×	—
Assisting in crisis situations	1 ×	—	1 ×
New corporate identity	1 ×	1 ×	—
Acceptance of corporate planning department	1 ×	—	1 ×
Consequences of acquisitions	1 ×	—	1 ×
Corporate values and norms	1 ×	—	1 ×
Location investigation	1 ×	—	1 ×

For this discrepancy we have not been able to find a satisfactory answer. Channon found a similar difference in performance between related and unrelated firms in the service industry. The related firms all had a higher score on such performance measures as growth in earnings per share, growth in assets per share and return before and after income tax.[14] One possible explanation for this phenomenon is that related firms are in a much better position to realize synergistic possibilities than unrelated firms.

The energy crisis and the raw material shortage in general are mostly indicated as problems in single product firms in a consolidation phase. It is remarkable that planners in five out of seven firms in the consolidation phase mention diversification and internationalization as a problem they work on. Are these growth directions an answer to the external threats perceived by consolidating firms?

Designing and modifying the planning system as well as financial and organizational co-ordination problems appear most often in growing firms. Cash planning, resource allocation and cash-flow control are seen as problems in both the growth-related and growth-unrelated categories. Organizational co-ordination problems such as exist between divisions and geographical areas are almost exclusively found in firms in the growth-related class. In the unrelated class these kinds of problems are less obvious since the only ties between the divisions are financial links via top management.

Above we have referred to the dynamics of the environment. Because of the present turbulence and the attention devoted to it in the planning literature one would have expected to find a number of instances where the preparation of *contingency plans* was a problem the planner should be working on. This was found only in one case. This is the more surprising, as the research was started about 1 year after the oil crisis of 1973. The contingency plan we found was of a rather general nature and not designed to tackle the consequences of *specific* threats. The above problems can be related to the type and organization structure of the company or the stage of development. The problems of *planning-mindedness* and of *formulation of objectives* are of a much more general nature. The problem or a lack of planning-mindedness—found in 6 per cent of the firms—is tackled via different strategies. In some cases there was a large-scale educational effort aimed at acquainting people in the organization with the planning philosophy and at training them in the use of various simple planning techniques. Another strategy we found was that corporate planners support managers at different levels in their day-to-day decision-making in exchange for their co-operation in corporate planning. This approach seems effective, but one should bear in mind that it is a rather time-consuming method. Therefore it seems useful to place the operational problems of the managers in a longer term perspective. In doing this the manager gets acquainted with corporate planning. Complementary to the above two strategies is the one in which the planner shows that he is not just a deskworker who issues forms to be filled out, but that he is prepared and even anxious to leave his desk and get out into the "field". He needs to build up the image of a living person and not the one of some obscure functionary. These three strategies are used to make lower levels in the organization planning-minded, but they do not satisfy the need to make

TABLE 7.9. *Problems of Corporate*

Number of companies	5	C:3 G:2	2

Problems of corporate planners	Frequency of answer	Single product	Consolidation growth	Dominant product
Planning-mindedness of the organization	13 ×	4 ×	C:2 G:2	1 ×
Formulation of objectives	12 ×	3 ×	C:2 G:1	—
Inflation	11 ×	3 ×	C:2 G:1	1 ×
Diversification + internationalization	9 ×	2 ×	C:2 G:—	1 ×
Designing and modifying the system	9 ×	1 ×	C:— G:1	—
Cash planning, resource allocation, cash flow	8 ×	—	—	1 ×
Change in governmental regulation	8 ×	3 ×	C:2 G:1	2 ×
Collecting external information	7 ×	4 ×	C:3 G:1	1 ×
Energy crisis, scarcity of raw materials	6 ×	4 ×	C:3 G:1	—
Decreasing profitability	5 ×	1 ×	C:1 G:—	1 ×
Co-ordination problems (inter-divisional/functional)	5 ×	—	—	1 ×
Assessment of strategic profile	3 ×	—	—	—
Assessment of growth sector	3 ×	1 ×	C:1 G:—	—
Problems of scale	3 ×	1 ×	C:— G:1	—

top management planning-minded. Corporate planners in three firms judged this necessary; in at least two of these cases top management had advocated corporate planning!

In six of the seven cases where bottom-up pushing was mentioned as one of the reasons leading to the start of corporate planning there was a notable lack of planning-mindedness. In four of these six firms where the committee planning mode was operative we still found a lack of planning-mindedness in spite of the higher motivation expected of this form.

Planners per Class of Companies

C:1		C:2		C:1	20 C:7
G:1	8	G:6	5	G:4	G:13

Consolidation Growth	Related product	Consolidation growth	Unrelated product	Consolidation growth	Total consolidation growth
C:— G:1	4 ×	C:1 G:3	4 ×	C:1 G:3	C:4 G:9
—	6 ×	C:2 G:4	3 ×	C:1 G:2	C:5 G:7
C:1 G:—	3 ×	C:2 G:1	4 ×	C:1 G:3	C:6 G:5
C:1 G:—	4 ×	C:1 G:3	2 ×	C:1 G:1	C:5 G:4
—	5 ×	C:— G:5	3 ×	C:1 G:2	C:1 G:8
C:1 G:—	4 ×	C:— G:4	3 ×	C:1 G:2	C:2 G:6
C:1 G:1	2 ×	C:— G:2	1 ×	C:— G:1	C:3 G:5
C:— G:1	2 ×	C:— G:2	—	—	C:3 G:4
—	2 ×	C:1 G:1	—	—	C:4 G:2
C:1 G:—	3 ×	C:2 G:1	—	—	C:4 G:1
C:— G:1	4 ×	C:1 G:3	—	—	C:1 G:4
—	3 ×	C:— G:3	—	—	C:— G:3
—	1 ×	C:— G:1	1 ×	C:— G:1	C:1 G:2
—	1 ×	C:1 G:—	1 ×	C:— G:1	C:1 G:2

As far as the formulation of objectives is concerned we found two extremes. In one firm the president needed less than 1 hour to set the objectives for his very sizeable firm, whereas in the other company it took several years of discussion. From the interviews we got the impression that the personality of the president and the style of management in general are of crucial importance here.

In view of the problems of lack of planning-mindedness and formulation of objectives (symptoms of resistance to planning?) a remark made by one of the respondents may be significant:

> In general, planning is a very unnatural activity. For the great majority of people working in organizations this seems to be even more the case when they have to work on long range and corporate planning. They have the impression that planning limits their flexibility and they are afraid that long term commitments limit their future freedom of action.

This remark is not only applicable to lower levels in the organization but may be even more so to top management.

The Corporate Planner in the Firm

Corporate planners assign different weights to the various aspects of their job. We asked them to score on a 5-point scale to what extent they thought the following aspects to be important:

- *Stimulating*: selling the planning system to the organization.
- *Motivating*: keeping the planning idea alive.
- *Co-ordinating*: planning process; between divisions; between functions.
- *Initiating*: making plans on one's own initiative.
- *Evaluating*: judging past performances and plans for the future.

An analysis of the scores showed that the corporate planner regards his co-ordinating role as the most important; with slightly lower scores the evaluating, stimulating and motivating roles followed in descending scale of importance. Initiating is regarded as the least important, which is in accordance with the often expressed view that line managers must plan and must take the decisions. The corporate planner regards his role as a supporting though not a passive one. The corporate planner has to be active because of the fact that line managers tend to give priority to operational problems and in some cases even do not want to think about strategic problems.

The co-ordinating role and the advisory aspect of the work of the corporate planner is even more striking when one observes the frequency with which task-forces or *ad hoc* committees were formed to tackle problems in the planning process. In 17 of the 20 companies such groups were active in trying to "solve" problems such as:

- Future societal developments.
- Designing and improving the planning system.
- Restructuring the company.
- Acquisitions.
- Consequences of mergers.

The corporate planners very often had a co-ordinating function in these committees, but they did not solve the problems themselves.

It is clear that the corporate planner's job is mainly of an advisory nature. Only in four cases he was assigned the responsibility for the execution of specific projects after management had taken the decision to start the project. The fact that corporate planners have only an advisory job does not mean that they do not have any functional authority. In the majority of the firms they can give directions as to the planning procedures, the timing of the planning process, the forms to be filled out, etc. In his advisory function the planner supports top management as well as managers at lower levels in the firm. In only three cases the corporate planner had executive authority, but this was because he was a high position line manager.

Top Management and the Planning Process

One of the reasons leading to the introduction of corporate planning is its advocacy by top management (see Table 7.4). In this respect it is important to gain insight into the "depth of commitment" of top management in the planning process. We also wanted to find out to what extent there was a discrepancy between the ideal situation—as seen by the corporate planner—and the existing situation and the causes of this gap.[15]

To this end we asked the corporate planner to indicate on a seven-point scale how strong the involvement in the planning process of the president or another member of the top management should be. The result is shown in Fig. 7.1.

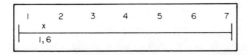

FIG. 7.1. *Ideal top management involvement in the planning process as seen by corporate planners.*

The average score was 1, 6 with a very small deviation from this point. This means that corporate planners think that top management involvement should be strong to very strong. As regards the question of how much time should be spent on planning either in the general sense or in discussions with the corporate planning department, corporate planners thought that approximately 40 per cent of top management's time should be devoted to strategic planning issues. Here the deviation was much larger: the answers varied between a 20 per cent low to an 80 per cent high. The ideal situation was not reached in almost half of the cases. In 9 out of 20 companies there was a discrepancy in the eyes of the corporate planner, yet in 4 out of these 9 cases corporate planning was introduced because of top management's advocacy. In a way this confirms the view that "it seems to be difficult to make many top executives really planning-conscious".[16]

The difference between the two situations was accounted for by the following factors in the nine cases cited:

- Top management is too much involved in operations (4 ×).[17]
- Lack of motivation of top management (3 ×).
- Lack of time, not further specified (1 ×).
- Too many representative obligations (1 ×).

In the nine companies where there was a lack of top management involvement we found that seven mentioned planning-mindedness and six formulating objectives as problems. This is a high correlation, if not a causal relation.

Top management involvement in the planning process seems to be very important, but it cannot be labelled as the one and only reason for success. In firms where the ideal situation existed (11 companies) planning-mindedness and formulation objectives were both mentioned in six firms. Apparently it is necessary to create "a climate in the company which is congenial and not resistant to planning"[18] even if top management leaves nothing to be desired. The question then arises who should create this climate and how it should be created if top management cannot provide it. Must this be done by the corporate planner?

Planning Procedures

As can be seen in Table 7.10 companies have rather different planning horizons. Planning horizons between the magic numbers 5 to 10 years

TABLE   7.10. *Length   of   Planning Horizon*

Planning horizon	Number of companies
3 years	5
4 years	2
5 years	7
10—> years	3
Unknown	(3)
	17(20)

seem to be unpopular or unpractical. In view of the environmental uncertainty there seems to be a tendency to shorten the planning horizon.[19]

One of our questions was aimed at getting information on some aspects of the formal planning system (FPS). In nine cases we were given planning documents; in ten cases we had to rely on an oral account of the FPS; in one company we were not able to get a clear picture of the FPS.

Concerning the nature of the FPS it is useful to make a distinction between *extrapolative* and *normative* planning. Normative planning—to be characterized as an outside-in approach—is strongly externally orientated. This kind of approach to planning was found in ten companies. Analyses of strengths and weaknesses, threats and opportunities, environmental surveillance, mission analysis are components of the FPS here. In nine companies we found a FPS that was very much of an extrapolative kind—to be characterized as an inside-out approach. In these instances the planning system was very often developed from the budgeting system in which no formal normative step was built in. Forecasts were often made on the basis of historical data: the future can be explained by the past.

In a number of firms that practised extrapolative planning the respondents made comments that indicated that they did not wish the extrapolative nature to be permanent; the interviews gave us the impression that the extrapolative approach had to be regarded as an intermediate, but necessary step to be taken.

Concerning the problem of the lack of planning-mindedness the extrapolative start can be very practical. It starts with a situation that is known to everybody in the company and which is rather concrete. The risk of people judging the planning effort to be too theoretical and too impractical is minimized in this way. Starting planning in this way gives rise to a new danger of ignoring to a large degree the importance of the environment. If one is aware of this danger at least some compensatory measures can be taken. In the last section of this article we propose a step-by-step approach for the introduction of formal corporate planning that is based on these two approaches.

Techniques

"Assuming that new quantitative techniques are not as useful as advertised" is one of the least important pitfalls that Steiner and Schoellhammer found in their recently published research.[20] This correlates with our finding that corporate planners gave the impression of not finding techniques of very great importance in their job. Two comments may illustrate this point:

"Techniques simplify the problem too much."

"Every idea starts either with a dream of something new, or with some dissatisfaction with the existing situation. Techniques are very often used to prove one is right."

As can be seen in Table 7.11 techniques in the finance and accounting area are used most frequently, whereas advanced forecasting and other techniques are used much less. This is probably due to the background of the Dutch planners, who are very often trained in the field of finance and/or of accounting.

TABLE 7.11. *Techniques Used in the Planning Process*

Techniques	Frequency	Techniques	Frequency
● **Investment Selection Methods**		**Forecasting** (*cont.*)	
(1) Pay-back Period	14 ×	(31) Profit Improvement Planning	10 ×
(2) DCF: Internal Rate of Return	12 ×	(32) Queuing Theory	2 ×
(3) DCF: Net Present Value Method	14 ×	(33) Risk Analysis	10 ×
		(34) Sensitivity Analysis	13 ×
● **Financial Ratios**[a]		(35) Utility Theory	2 ×
(4) Liquidity Ratios	18 ×	(36) Regression and Correlation Analysis	14 ×
(5) Leverage Ratios	12 ×	(37) Incremental Analysis	6 ×
(6) Activity Ratios	25 ×	(38) Multiple Regression and Correlation Analysis	9 ×
(7) Profitability Ratios	27 ×	(39) Random Sampling	7 ×
(8) Dupont Analysis (ROI)	11 ×	(40) Sampling Theory	4 ×
		(41) Bayesian Statistics	1 ×
● **Forecasting Techniques and Miscellaneous**		(42) Dynamic Programming	1 ×
(9) Delphi Method	5 ×	(43) Industrial Dynamics	1 ×
(10) Panel Consensus	9 ×	(44) Linear Programming	9 ×
(11) Visionary Forecast	12 ×	(45) Markov processes	3 ×
(12) Historical Analogy	10 ×	(46) Monte Carlo Simulation	4 ×
(13) Moving Average	14 ×	(47) Non-Linear Programming	2 ×
(14) Exponential Smoothing	10 ×	(48) Numerical Taxonomy	3 ×
(15) Box-Jenkins Method	4 ×	(49) Technological forecasting	6 ×
(16) X-11	9 ×	(50) S-curves	8 ×
(17) Trend Projection	11 ×	(51) Envelope Curves	4 ×
(18) Econometric Model	9 ×	(52) Learning curves	7 ×
(19) Input–Output Model	3 ×	(53) Morphological Analysis	1 ×
(20) Diffusion Index	3 ×	(54) Scenario's	6 ×
(21) Leading Indicator	4 ×	(55) Impact Analysis	1 ×
(22) Life Cycle Analysis	8 ×	(56) Relevance Tree	1 ×
(23) Brainstorming	12 ×	(57) Contextual Mapping	1 ×
(24) PERT	14 ×	(58) Normex Reconciliation	—
(25) Break-even Analysis	14 ×	(59) SOON Charting	—
(26) Business Game	6 ×	(60) Technical Mission Analysis (TMA)	—
(27) Contribution Analysis	13 ×	(61) Strength/Weaknesses Analysis	6 ×[b]
(28) Cost-Benefit Analysis	10 ×		
(29) Decision Tree	7 ×		
(30) Heuristics	5 ×		

[a] Financial Ratios covered 4 Liquidity, 2 Leverage, 4 Activity, and 4 Profitability Ratios.
[b] We started explicit asking for this technique only after the 10 interview.

Concluding Remarks

At the end of this article it may be useful to state some of the conclusions and propositions stemming from this research project.

● In the Netherlands corporate planning was—in general—introduced in the early 1970s, often after the company had gone through a period of growth. The clearance of the "debris" after such a period of unplanned growth then appears to be an intermediate but necessary stage before further growth is possible. Corporate planners play a very active, but difficult role in this process.

● Our research suggests two modes in which the planner can support line management in the planning process. The first is a support function in the *planning system mode*, the second is a support function in the *entrepreneurial mode*. In the planning system mode the corporate planner is generally internally oriented; he is engaged in designing the FPS, collecting data, the internal co-ordination and preparation of operational plans. In the entrepreneurial mode the corporate planner is more externally oriented: he is primarily engaged in a search for threats and opportunities, discontinuities, evaluation of new business ventures, contingency planning and the preparation of strategic plans. These two modes require different skills of the corporate planner. In the planning system mode the emphasis is more on financial, accounting and technical skills, whereas in the entrepreneurial mode it is more on commercial and innovative skills. Both modes require—in addition—interpersonal, diplomatic and political skills.

● Corporate planners often appear to be identified with the support function in the entrepreneurial mode. Strategy making is perceived as externally oriented. However, the data show quite clearly that many corporate planners are working in the planning system mode. They are mainly concerned with internal problems, having to design the planning system, and thus have very little, if any, time left to work on really strategic issues. In this respect we observed a gap between expectation and reality of the work of the corporate planner. The background of the Dutch corporate planner seems to provide the basis for working on the problems at hand. However, training in finance and accounting is based on the belief in the economic man doctrine. This doctrine leaves no room for irrational behaviour. Yet, this kind of behaviour *is* found in companies. The internal problems the planners have to tackle are mainly of this kind. *Resistance to planning* cannot be explained rationally and logically, but it *is there*. In this connection the following remarks are heard more often than not:

"Planning is an unnatural activity."

"Planning limits freedom of action and flexibility."

These two remarks already warrant the assertion that corporate planners face an *identity crisis*. This idea of an identity crisis is even more prominent when the dilemma between the entrepreneurial mode and the planning system mode is stressed by the increasing turbulence and the discontinuities in the environment.

- The awareness of this dilemma implies that the introduction of corporate planning will require a step-by-step approach. To overcome resistance to planning and to avoid undesirable boomerang effects, corporate planners should bear this step-by-step approach in mind.

Our research suggests the following profile of such a successful planner, especially when he is introducing formal corporate planning, but also afterwards:

Corporate planners help line managers in improving their day-to-day operational decision making, but they realize very well that the responsibility for decision making is in the hands of line managers. Respecting this responsibility of the line managers is a prerequisite for corporate planning to have a good start.

A precondition for this is that line managers personally know the corporate planner and are aware that the corporate planner is more than a functionary issuing documents and forms to be filled out. A corporate planner therefore is much more than a desk worker. He is a living person in the organization and has an open eye for current problems, but he always tries to see and to present them in an overall—longer term, strategic—perspective, in order to make the line managers aware of possible discontinuities.

In exchange for such a support corporate planners hope to gain the co-operation of line management for corporate strategy-making and strategy-planning.

Only when the stage is reached where planning is a second nature so that planning is no longer regarded as too theoretical and too impractical, i.e. where operational planning is self-supporting in a perspective of strategic planning, corporate planners move from the planning-system mode into the stage of the entrepreneurial mode where strategic planning issues can get great attention.

A corporate planner thus has the difficult task to find out where the margins are for moving on in such a stage model for the survival of his company.

Corporate planners then have the challenging task of stimulating and vitalizing the company as far as planning is concerned. This is only possible if top management is actively involved in the planning process. Top management should at least back corporate planners in their educational task, not by precepts but by examples.

References

1. See, e.g., P. H. Grinyer and D. Norburn, Strategic planning in 21 U.K. companies, *Long Range Planning*, August (1974); B. Taylor and P. Irving, Organized planning in major U.K. companies, *Long Range Planning*, June (1971); G. A. Steiner and H. Schoellhammer, Pitfalls in multi-national long range planning, *Long Range Planning*, April (1975); K. A. Ringbakk, Organized planning in major U.S. companies, *Long Range Planning*, No. 1 (1969).
2. H. I. Ansoff, *Corporate Strategy*, pp. 90−91 and p. 126, Pelican Books, Harmondsworth (1968).
3. See for detailed questionnaire D. Keuning, D. J. Eppink and K. de Jong, *Practice of Corporate Planning in the Netherlands: an investigation of 20 companies*, Vrije Universiteit Amsterdam, Economic Faculty, Research Memorandum No. 32, September (1975).
4. *Op. cit.*, p. 10.
5. D. F. Channon, *The Strategy and Structure of British Enterprise*, pp. 12−13, MacMillan, London (1973).
6. *Op. cit.*, p. 10.
7. G. A. Steiner and H. Schoellhammer, *op. cit.*, p. 10; B. Taylor and P. Irving, *op. cit.*, p. 11.
8. R. F. Vancil and P. Lorange, Strategic planning in diversified companies, *Harvard Business Review*, p. 82, January−February (1975).
9. B. Taylor and P. Irving, *op. cit.*, p. 12; K. A. Ringbakk, *op. cit.*, pp. 13−14.
10. For an elaboration of this view we refer to: M. Athreya, Planning as integration, in: J. W. Lorsch and P. R. Lawrence (eds.), *Studies in Organization Design*, pp. 168−186, Irwin−Dorsey, Homewood (1970).
11. *Op. cit.*, p. 17.
12. See also B. Taylor and P. Irving, *op. cit.*, p. 18, where they treat the role of the controller in the planning process.
13. *Op. cit.*, p. 17.
14. D. F. Channon, *The Strategy, Structure and Financial Performance of the Service Industries*. Working Paper Manchester Business School, 1975, Table 4.
15. G. A. Steiner and H. Schoellhammer, *op. cit.*, p. 5.
16. G. A. Steiner and H. Schoellhammer, *op. cit.*, p. 5.
17. See also G. A. Steiner and H. Schoellhammer, *op. cit.*, pp. 4 and 5.
18. G. A. Steiner and H. Schoellhammer, *op. cit.*, pp. 4 and 5.
19. Planners Kijken Minder Ver, *FEM*, 17 September (1975); X. Gilbert and E. Langaard, *La Planification Reactive*, Paper presented at the Seminar on Recent Researches on Planning and Control, Aix-en-Provence, June (1975).
20. *Op. cit.*, pp. 6 and 7.

8

Strategic Decision-making in
Large European Firms

M. GOUY*

The lead that the American theoreticians had in the field of business administration provided us with management tools which were mainly based on research undertaken in the U.S.

We therefore know very little about the way European managers select strategies, although the interest shown by the numerous firms which agreed to take part in this survey shows that it is not a problem to underestimate.

This article outlines the results of research made in Great Britain, Germany and France which focused on the main aspects of strategic decision making in large firms.

Information was collected during interviews with 55 top-managers among which were 22 Presidents or Chief-Executives and 15 Planning Directors. Forty-seven firms were visited (16 in Great Britain, 13 in West Germany and 18 in France) covering 11 different fields of activity: Food and tobacco, Electrical and mechanical engineering, Chemicals, Textile, Oil refining and petro-chemicals, Iron and steel, Cosmetics, Vehicles, Computers and Packaging.

Their annual turnover ranged from 26 to 7800 millions U.S. $ and the number of employees from 1000 to more than 50,000. Fourteen of the companies belong therefore to the 500 leading firms in the world.

Corporate objectives and their development, strategic information, decision processes and techniques utilized were successively investigated in order to compare the methods used in the three countries and the different types of companies.

The analysis brings to light only minor differences due to the geographical origin, and tends to prove that the nationality has little to do

This article was originally published in *Long Range Planning*, Volume II, No. 3, June 1978.
* Deputy Trade Commissioner Le Consiller Commercial, P.O. Box 407, Dacca 2, Bangladesh.

with the way strategic decision are taken. On the contrary strong correlations appear between the processes used in selecting strategies and the different types of firms which were defined according to size and activity.

Facts about Strategic Decision-taking in Europe

The Objectives

The corporate objectives are always set at the highest level of the hierarchy, i.e. the "Direction Générale", the "Vorstand" and the "Board of Directors" but very little is said about the role of the "conseil d'administration" or the powerful "Aufsichtrat".

Is this due to the fact that these centres of decision exert little influence on the business administration or is it a deliberate will to ignore them?

Most of the interviewees suggested that objectives do not adequately perform the role of co-ordination and incitement which they are supposed to play. The main indicators of Finance and Marketing are of major importance in the objectives which were discussed during the interviews. There is little need to emphasize the fact that profitability is one of the main goals in all the firms of the sample. Nevertheless, according to the results which are summarized in Table 8.2, it seems essential to British companies. Objectives related to human relations are more often mentioned in Great Britain and France than in Germany where social conflicts are less frequent.

The lack of enthusiasm of the German firms which appeared in numerous interviews can be traced to the little interest taken in the objective of expansion in comparison with the French results. Nevertheless one should not stress too much a phenomenon which could simply be due to an excess of pessimism in Germany or optimism in France. . . .

Finally, the importance given to diversification by British firms probably reflects the hesitations of an economy facing multiple difficulties.

The Information

The results show that the strategic decision is essentially based upon internal sources of information. Nearly all the firms visited have their own

TABLE 8.1. *The objectives are not clear enough*

	Great Britain	Germany	France	Total
Sufficient definition	3	5	8	16
Non-optimal definition	4	5	2	11
Insufficient definition	3	2	3	8
No answer	6	1	5	12

TABLE 8.2. *Company objectives*

	Great Britain	Germany	France	Total
Base	16	13	18	47
Profitability	16	9	9	34
Social relations	7	2	7	16
Market share	5	4	6	15
Expansion	3	2	9	14
Diversification	6	4	2	11
Shareholder's interest	2	5	1	8
Client's interest	3	3	1	7
Export	3	—	2	5
Market volume	4	—	—	4
Image	3	1	—	4
Stability	2	1	1	4
Reduction of losses	1	3	—	4
Optimization of production	—	2	2	4
Reduction of costs	—	1	2	3
Financial independence	—	1	1	2

marketing department which provides them with information on the environement or the market fluctuations.

In strategic matters, contacts with customers or competitors are scarce and only a few French companies attempt a direct collaboration with competitors in order to gather data on the environment or the future of their industry. In the two other countries, these direct contacts are not disclosed and might not exist. Another external channel of information, the press, is said to play very little role in high level decisions.

It appears that the main items of information used in a strategic decision come from both the Marketing and Finance departments. The item "market size" which was neglected in the objectives regains importance as well as "information on new products" and "R & D": Sixty-eight per cent of the European managers who took part in this survey admit that they are not entirely satisfied with the information system used in their company. According to them, the quality and rapidity of the flow of information should be improved.

The Decision-making Process

It appears very clearly that both Finance and Marketing functions exert a strong influence on strategic decision taking. However, some national differences are worth noticing (see Table 8.4).

English firms emphasize to a considerable degree the role of the Marketing Department, whereas Finance takes the lead in France and is one step behind Production in Germany.

TABLE 8.3. *Major items of information used in strategic decisions*

	Great Britain	Germany	France	Total
Base	16	13	18	47
Profitability	8	10	16	34
Market share	9	9	15	33
Market size	8	9	12	29
R and D	8	6	11	25
Personnel	6	6	9	21
Goverment policy	5	6	10	21
Social and economic climate	6	9	5	20
Costs and resources	7	5	5	17
Capacity and production costs	5	2	6	13
Turnover	2	2	6	10
Technological changes	1	2	2	5

TABLE 8.4. *Influence exerted on strategic decision*

	Great Britain	Germany	France	Total
Marketing	10	5	3	18
Finance	4	3	9	16
Production	4	4	2	10
Sales	1	2	3	6
Personnel	2	—	—	2
Planning	1	—	2	3
R & D	2	—	1	3
Equal influence	—	5	4	9

Furthermore, German managers insist on the balance of influence existing between the various functions, which is not the case in Great Britain. The process of decision making is initiated by a "Bottom-up" movement in France much more often than in the two other countries and it seems that the hierarchy is used in a more dynamic way in France (see Fig. 8.1).

Five types of decision-making processes are mainly used in the firms visited. They are classified from 1 to 5 (i.e. centralized to decentralized) and composed of six steps: (a) the initiation of the process; (b) the "green light" for survey; (c) the survey; (d) – (e) the evaluation of the results; and (f) the decision.

This classification shows little difference between the countries and only confirms that the average French firm uses a slightly more decentralized

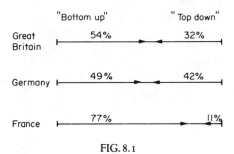

FIG. 8.1

process. The mean type is 2.9 in Great Britain, 3 in Germany and 3.4 in France.

The analysis gives better results when the type of firm is considered (see Fig. 8.2). The sample is then divided into "Mother" companies, Subsidiaries, Nationalized or Multinational firms and the average types are as follows: "Mother" companies 3.8; Subsidiaries 3.2; Multinational 2.3; Nationalized 2.2.

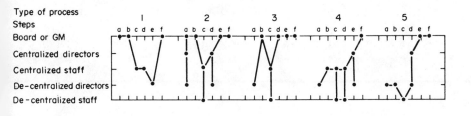

FIG. 8.2

The conclusion is that the type of decision-making process is directly related to the level of dependence of the firm:

Type 1: Strict control used in multinationals;
Type 2: Adaptable to small firms or large companies being reorganized;
Type 3: Often used by independent firms with a complex organization;
Type 4: Used in near subsidiaries; and
Type 5: Only used by independent firms.

It appears that in the three countries the review of strategy is undertaken annually. The results differ very slightly in Germany where the review is less frequent but one should note that 25 per cent of the British firms have an undetermined frequency of review against 15 per cent in Germany and 5 per cent in France. However, nearly all the interviewees seem satisfied by the frequency and flexibility of their review of strategy as shown in Table 8.5.

TABLE 8.5. *Flexibility of the review of strategy*

	Great Britain	Germany	France	Total
Adequate flexibility	8	9	12	30
Little flexibility	6	3	2	11
No flexibility	1	—	1	2
No answer	1	1	2	4

The Tools of Decision-making

Although the computer is used in almost all the visited firms, it is said to be of very little help in the choice of a strategy (see Table 8.6). Simulation programs have been adapted to various management problems even if they often focus only on Finance and Marketing (see Table 8.7). Nevertheless,

TABLE 8.6. *The use of computers*

	Great Britain	Germany	France	Total
For general problems				
Yes	15	13	17	45
No	1	—	1	2
For strategic problems				
Yes	3	4	7	14
No	12	9	10	31

TABLE 8.7. *Field of utilization of simulation models*

	Great Britain	Germany	France	Total
Finance	4	4	8	16
Marketing	4	4	8	16
Production	1	5	5	11
Corporate models	5	1	4	10
Planning	2	4	3	9

they are said to be unreliable and not accurate enough to answer the requirements of the top-management (see Table 8.8).

TABLE 8.8. *Drawbacks of the simulation models*

	Great Britain	Germany	France	Total
Lack of efficiency	2	2	6	10
Lack of usefulness	4	4	1	9
Difficult modelization	2	2	2	6
Lack of flexibility	—	1	3	4
Unprofitability	1	2	—	3

Furthermore, European firms seldom call on consultants for strategic matters (see Table 8.9). These are used in many fields, but organization is the area where they are considered as the most helpful (see Table 8.10). The German firms tend to use the know-how of consultants in production whereas the English firms reach a good balance between the various functions. Besides, it is worth noting that nearly 50 per cent of the French firms rely on consultancy to solve their problems of organization.

TABLE 8.9. *Use of consultants*

	Great Britain	Germany	France	Total
Used	4	2	4	10
Seldom used	7	9	7	23
Not used	4	2	5	11

TABLE 8.10. *Area of use of consultants*

	Great Britain	Germany	France	Total
Organization	5	3	8	16
Marketing	5	1	5	11
Finance	6	—	2	8
Production	3	5	—	8
Personnel	3	—	1	4
Planning	1	1	—	2

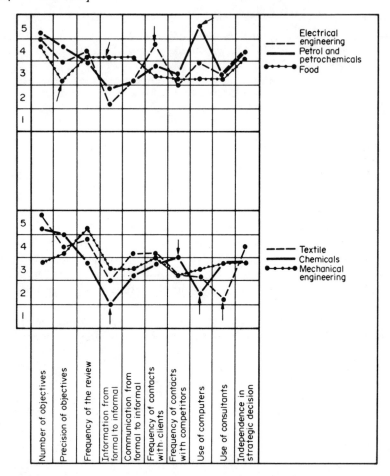

FIG. 8.3. *Electrical Engineering:* 5/4/4.5/2.2/3.2/4.8/3/4/3.5/4.5/; *Petrol and Petro-chemicals:* ———5.2/4.8/4/2.8/3.2/3.8/3.5/5.5/3.5/4.5; *Food:* 4.8/3.2/4.2/4.2/4.2/ 3.5/3.2/3.2/3.2/4.2/; *Textile:* 5.8/4.5/4.8/3/4.2/4.2/3.2/3.2/2.2/4.5/; *Chemicals:* 5.2/5/3.8/2/3.2/3.8/4/2.5/3.8/3.8/; *Mechanical Engineering:* 3.8/4.2/5.2/3.5/ 3.5/4/3.2/3.5/3.8/3.8/

Analysis and Typology

The firms which are the base for this survey are different in many ways. However, three elements can differentiate them easily; their size, their type as well as their activity.

The purpose of the second part of this paper is to investigate the relationships existing between these elements and the factors which characterize a strategic decision making process.

Various methods can be used in this respect and the analysis of arithmetical means can give good results as shown in Fig. 8.3.

Here, each of the 47 firms is evaluated according to 10 variables. The scale of this evaluation is from 1 to 5 which enables the calculation of the mean of each sector of industry whose sample is large enough to be representative.

The following characteristics appear then clearly on the graph: The Food Industry is the sector where the objectives are the less precise. It nevertheless has a very informal system of information and is considerably different from the Chemical sector as far as this variable is concerned.

The firms of the Electrical Engineering sector seem to have more contacts with clients than in any other sector. The frequency of contacts with competitors is very similar in all groups of companies with the exception of the Chemical Industry. Computers are very often used in the Oil Industry and the Textile sector seem to have little confidence in consultants.

The Factorial Analysis

In addition to the study of arithmetical means, the factorial analysis has been chosen for two reasons: the computerization of this analysis allows the study of a complex phenomenon (composed in this case of 11 variables) as well as a clear graphical representation.

One must put the stress on the fact that this method results from the choice of factors which represent only part of the phenomenon. In the present case 32.7 per cent of the phenomenon is explained by the combination of factor 1 (20.1 per cent) and Factor 2 (12.6 per cent). (A third factor would have increased the precision by approximately 10 per cent but the graphical representation would then have been tri-dimensional).

The analysis by means of two factors leads to the following representation (see Fig. 8.4) which gives the relative importance and position of the variables and will, from now on, be used as reference.

Each vector represents one variable and is characterized by its orientation and length. The longer the vector, the more reliable the variable. This is for instance the case with variables 1, 5, 6, 7, 10. The other piece of information which is given by this graph concerns the correlations existing between the different variables. In the sample, variables 5 and 6 are strongly correlated as well as 4 and 5. (Given the difference in length of their respective vectors, variables 4 and 11 show a lesser correlation, the former with 5 and 6, the latter with 8 and 9.)

Whenever two vectors show opposite orientations, they are said to be anti-correlated (see variables 10 or 11).

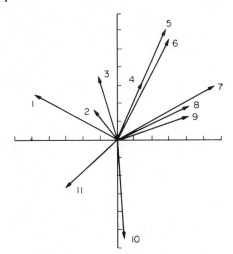

FIG. 8.4. 1: independence of process; 2: frequence of review; 3: meeting with competitors; 4: use of consultants; 5: complexity of the organization; 6: meeting with clients; 7: use of computers; 8: number of objectives; 9: precision of objections; 10: informal information; 11: informal communication.

Typology

This representation results from the compilation and analysis of the data gathered in the firms of the sample. Each of them has therefore a specific position on the graph but, although it is quite possible, the 47 company names hidden behind the dots will not be disclosed. They will only be differentiated by the items "Size", "Diversification", "flexibility" and "Area of activity", the name of the firm bringing no other valuable information whatsoever.

Size. The sample has been divided in three groups according to the number of employees (less than 9000, from 9000 to 50,000, more than 50,000). The distribution of the dots in each of the three groups is clear and self explanatory. Relatively small firms tend to concentrate in the area of variables 10 and 11. Middle size companies are located in the areas 1, 2 and 3 stressing the flexibility in the decision making process as well as a clear definition of objectives (areas 7 and 8).

Some still have an informal strategic decision-making but they are a minority (area 11).

As far as the large groups are concerned, the concentration occurs in areas 5 and 6 where the methods used are essentially formal.

Diversification. The analysis applies this time to diversification and gives similar results (see Fig. 8.5): The more diversified the activities of the firm are, the more formal is the strategic decision-making process.

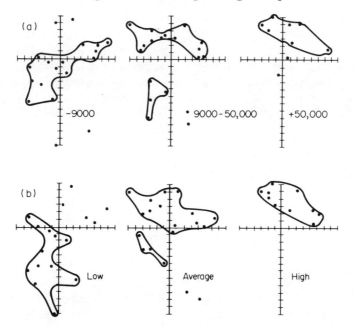

FIG.8.5. *Points—Size:* -9000: $3/4/7/14/16/19/20/22/23/24/25/29/30/31/33/36/43/$
$44/47$; $9000-50,000$: $2/6/8/10/11/12/17/18/26/27/32/34/35/37/38/39/40/42/45/$;
$+5000$: $1/5/9/13/15/21/28/41/46/$.
Diversification—low: $7/11/12/14/16/20/22/30/31/32/35/36/40/42/43/44/47/$;
average: $3/4/6/10/13/17/18/19/21/24/25/27/29/33/34/37/38/39/46/$;
high: $1/2/5/8/9/15/23/26/28/41/45/$.

Co-ordinates of points in Figs. 7.5, 7.6 and 7.7

Point	Abscissa	Ordinate	Point	Abscissa	Ordinate	Point	Abscissa	Ordinate
1	−1	+2.1	17	−2	+1	33	+2.2	−5
2	−0.5	+1.7	18	−0.7	+1.5	34	+2	+0.2
3	+2.5	0	19	+0.2	−0.2	35	−1.5	−2.7
4	−2	−1.5	20	−2.2	−3	36	−1.3	−1.7
5	+1.2	+2.5	21	+3.2	+0.7	37	−0.5	−2.2
6	−3	+2.5	22	+3.5	+1.2	38	−1.5	−1.5
7	−0.7	−0.2	23	+2.7	+1	39	−1.5	+1.3
8	−1	+2.3	24	−2.2	−0.5	40	+0.2	+1.5
9	−0.7	+3	25	−0.2	+2.5	41	+0.7	+1.2
10	−1.5	+2	26	+2.3	+1.3	42	+1.2	−3.6
11	+2	+0.7	27	+1.2	−4.5	43	−1.5	0
12	−2.3	+0.7	28	−0.2	−1	44	−0.2	−6
13	+0.5	+2.5	29	+1.7	+1	45	+2.2	+0.2
14	−0.2	−0.6	30	+1	+2.7	46	+0.4	+0.1
15	−1.5	+2.5	31	+0.5	−1	47	+2.6	+0.5
16	−0.5	−2.7	32	−1.7	−4			

Type of industry. The sample is in this case divided into two groups, namely heavy and light industry. In the heavy industry group are gathered companies whose activity requires large investments and which therefore are not as flexible as firms dealing with light industry (Oil, Iron and Steel, Chemicals, as opposed to Food and Tobacco or Mechanical Engineering). The results cannot be clearer (see Fig. 8.6), heavy industry concentrating in areas 1–9 (formal process) when light industry takes position in areas 10 and 11.

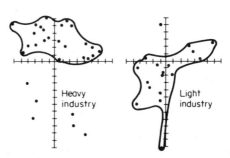

FIG. 8.6. *Points—Heavy industry:* 1/2/4/5/6/8/9/10/12/13/21/23/26/27/30/32/34/ 35/39/40/41/42/45/46/47/; *Light industry:* 3/7/11/14/15/16/17/18/19/20/22/24/ 25/28/29/31/36/37/38/43/44/.

Sector of industry. When the size of the sample is large enough (around 10 firms for each group), the factorial analysis can be used to differentiate the various sectors of industry.

Among the four which are studied here (Food and Tobacco—8 firms, Electrical Engineering and Electronics—10 firms, Mechanical Engineering—11 firms, Oil Petrochemical and Chemical Industry—9 firms) two show a clear concentration. Facing a strategic decision, firms of the Food Industry seem indeed to adopt similar methods or attitudes (see Fig. 8.7). These are much less formal than those adopted by the companies regrouped in the Electrical Engineering and Electronics Industry.

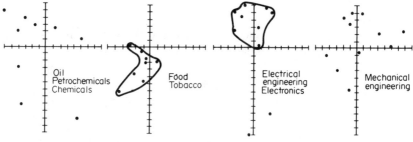

FIG.   8.7. *Food:*   7/14/20/28/31/36/37/43/;   *Electrical   Engineering:* 5/8/915/27/30/39/40/44/46/; *Mechanical Engineering:* 1/2/3/13/16/19/22/24/25/29/38/; *Oil petrol and petro-chemicals:* 4/6/10/17/18/32/33/41/47/.

Not all sectors show such a homogeneity and the firms represented in the Mechanical Engineering or the Oil, Chemical and Petrochemical Industry are very much scattered on the graph.

Main Implications

To summarize the main findings of the survey, the strategic decision making process as seen in 47 European firms is still to be improved.

Clearly, decision-making in general and strategic decision making in particular is not easy, but improvements have to be achieved at least in the following fields:

(a) A better communication of corporate objectives and global strategy should allow every decision-maker to feel more concerned with strategic thinking.

(b) The organization of work should ensure that more time and resources are devoted to creativity so that operational thinking should not be the main pre-occupation of the decision-makers.

To go further in global recommendations would be too vague and unhelpful. The study tends to prove that all firms do not and cannot react in the same way when faced with strategic problems because of their difference in size, activity or flexibility. This is the reason why it is necessary, particularly at the stage of recommendation to adopt different approaches:

(a) *Medium size firms*

(1) Adapted to the size of the firms, the strategic decision-making process should be flexible.

(2) The system of information should be simple and efficient.

(3) Although personal contacts can improve the atmosphere and in so doing the quality of communication, the need for rigour should not be underestimated.

(b) *Large firms*

(1) The major objective should be known to every decision maker and play a role of co-ordination.

(2) The process of strategic decision-making should be clearly defined, and structurized, so that no overlapping or conflict of responsibility can hamper the decision.

(3) Strategic thinking and creativity should be established, possibly within the frame of a "strategic evaluation" department.

(4) The improvement of the information system should be considered as a priority and should justify important investments (MIS for instance).

(c) *Diversified activities*
   (1) Reviews of strategy should be decentralized.
   (2) Each division should take part in the definition of the objectives.
   (3) A "strategic evaluation" department should constantly assist the top management in reviewing strategies and balancing common interest with divisional interest.

(d) *Less diversified activities*
   (1) The "main factors for success" should be defined.
   (2) The information system should be derived from the study of the "main factors for success" and focus on a permanent monitoring of environmental changes.
   (3) The choice between alternatives being more risky than in diversified firms, risk evaluation technique should be used as well as simulation models which find their best field of application there.

(e) *Heavy industry*
   (1) This type of industry which is characterized by heavy and long term investments as well as a considerable inertia must put the emphasis on the quality of decision making rather than its rapidity.
   (2) Simulation, quantification of variables should be used to a large extent.
   (3) Decision should not be based on intuition but on carefully selected criteria.
   (4) Decision-makers should have a perfect knowledge of the limits of their tools of decision making.
   (5) The information should be carefully checked, filtered and analysed. Here again, the quality is more important than the rapidity.

(f) *Light industry*
   (1) This type of industry has to react quickly to numerous and important modifications of its environment and its system of review must be extremely flexible.
   (2) The process of decision-making must be suited to a high frequency of use.
   (3) The information must be gathered quickly but synthetized and filtered efficiently to avoic confusion.
   (4) Every possible aid (computerization for example) must be used in a constant care for rapidity.

Acknowledgement

The author would like to acknowledge the help of all the persons who took part in the conception and realization of this survey, in particular Mr Jeff Wooller, Technical Editor (London), and Mr Hans Pokorny, Consultant (Düsseldorf).

9
How Planning Works in Practice— A Survey of 48 U.K. Companies

S. AL-BAZZAZ * AND P. M. GRINYER[†]

Surveys at the turn of the decade suggested that adoption of corporate planning in the United Kingdom, West Germany and France was later than in the U.S.A.[1-6] Moreover, corporate planning was in no country as sophisticated and "advanced" as one would imagine from the literature. Subsequent surveys concentrated on the pay off, contributions, pitfalls and problems encountered.[7-13] Within the U.K., verbatim accounts of problems and benefits of corporate planning were given by both Hewkins and Kempner[1] and Irving,[14] although they gave only examples and no quantitative indication of relative importance.

The Companies Surveyed

Companies in the sample were drawn from two sources. First, 11 companies represented on the Organization Study Group of the Long Range Planning Society in London collaborated. Second, 37 companies were drawn at random from those with head offices located in the South East of England and listed in the European Directory of Economic & Corporate Planning (1974). Checks to determine if there were significant differences between these two sub-samples suggested none, and all 48 companies were, therefore, grouped into one main sample.

The frames from which the samples were drawn inevitably influenced the characteristics of the companies in the survey. By design, only companies with an active involvement in strategic planning were included. The companies were large (see Table 9.1), from 19 industries including both service and manufacturing, had their major plants or operations, on

This article was originally in *Long Range Planning*, Volume 13, No. 4, August 1980.
* S. Al-Bazzaz is at the Kingston Regional Management Centre.
† P. H. Grinyer, Professor of Economics at the University of St. Andrews, St. Andrews, Scotland KY 16 9 AL.

TABLE 9.1. *Characteristics of the sample*

(1) Industries included: Chemicals, building and construction, food.and beverage, data processing, banking, transportation, petroleum, printing and publishing, insurance, gaseous products, steel, tobacco, automotive accessories, paints, engineering, unrelated activities

(2) Size:	Variable	Range	Mid point of median category
	Sales (annual)	£5m to over £2000m	£150m
	Net capital employed	£1m to over £2000m	£150m
	Net profit before tax	under £1m to £500m	£12.5m
	Wages (annual)	under £1m to £500m	£17.5m
	No. employees	under 1000 (two companies) to over 300,000	£7500m
	No. of sites	1 to over 2000	15

(3) Dispersion of sites

Per cent with all of 3 most important sites in U.K.	54.2
Per cent with at least 1 of 3 most important sites in U.K.	64.6
Per cent with all of 3 most important sites overseas	35.4

(4) Hierarchical status of company

Status	Per cent of sample
Parent (including 3 nationalized industries representing 6.3 per cent of the total sample)	56.25
Division	20.8
Subsidiary	22.9

(5) Charter

	Per cent of sample
Service company only	25.0
Manufacturing company only	43.1
Manufacturing with service operations	31.9

(6) Organizational structure

	Per cent of sample
Functional	39.6
Divisional product	31.3
Divisional geographic	8.4
Divisional geographic and product	20.7

the whole, concentrated in the United Kingdom, but with a large minority operating major plants overseas, ranged from functional to highly divisionalized structures, and from marketing predominantly a single product line to highly diversified undertakings.

Problems of Operationalization

The questions dealing with difficulties and contributions were open-ended to allow full expression by the interviewees. Answers were then classified and tabulated. By this means tables of seven main types of contributions, six types of difficulties, seven types of required changes and nine types of planners' responsibilities were compiled. The subjective nature of the process was recognized and other data collected were used to check the resulting classification.

Functions of Corporate Planners

Over 80 per cent of the respondents identified no more than four areas of responsibilities and no more than 8 per cent more than four. The responsibilities cited are shown in Table 9.2. Apart from the 46 per cent of companies in which corporate planners perceived themselves as giving advice and making proposals and the 29 per cent in which special projects were undertaken, the emphasis was on the design and operation of the planning process, including forecasting, evaluation, communicating and collating information and control.

TABLE 9.2. *Extent of prevalence of each type of responsibility*

Type	Percentage
1—Design and administration of plans and initiation of planning process	58
2—Proposals, advice and recommendations	46
3—Analysis and evaluation	44
4—Coliation and co-ordination of plans	38
5—Monitoring and control	35
6—Ad hoc work and special projects	29
7—Information, data, reporting and communication	27
8—Assumptions and forecasting	23
9—Development of planning concepts and function training	17

As may be seen from Table 9.3, the perceived responsibilities of corporate planners varied between the hierarchical level of the organization they served, those in parent companies tending to have more wide-

TABLE 9.3

Corporate planners' responsibility category	Parent		Subsidiary		Significance of difference
	No	Percentage	No.	Percentage	
Propose and advise	15	55	4	36	Highly significant
Analysis and evaluation	12	44	4	36	Significant
Collation and co-ordination	12	44	4	36	Significant
Special projects	8	29	4	36	Not significant
Information and reporting	7	25	1	9	Highly significant
Assumptions and forecasts	6	22	2	18	Not significant
Control	11	40	3	27	Significant
Development of planning	4	14	1	9	Not significant

Significance levels:
"Highly significant" denotes a probability of less than 1 in 100 that the difference could have occurred by chance.
"Significant" denotes a probability of less than 5 in 100 that the difference could have occurred by chance.
"Not significant" denotes a probability of more than 5 in 100 that the difference could have occurred by chance.

ranging functions than those in subsidiaries. Corporate planners in the former tended to have the responsibilities to propose and advise, provide information and report, analyse and evaluate, collate, co-ordinate and control with significantly greater frequency. However, differences relating to special projects, assumptions and forecasts and the development of planning were not significant. These results are consistent, with Lorange and Vancil's[15] suggestion that, in large companies, one of the main planning tasks is co-ordination of the plans, but there are clearly other responsibilities of equal significance.

The responsibility for actually writing the plans covering the various areas of business activity rested with line management in 85.4 per cent of companies and with the corporate planning function in only 14.6 per cent, a difference so large that there was a probability of less than 1 in 1000 that it was due to the chance of sample selection alone. Our findings confirmed, then, those of Hewkins and Kempner[1] and of Taylor and Irving[5] on the planner's role and the responsibility of operational management in the planning exercise.

Contribution of Corporate Planning Systems

Contributions claimed by corporate planners interviewed were analysed into seven categories.

Some 83 per cent of the sample quoted contributions from four or less categories. None thought that improvements were made in all the seven. Table 9.4 shows the contributions and their relative frequencies. Under each head, but particularly in the area of profit and growth, the strength of the contribution thought to have been made inevitably varied, but the open ended answers obtained did not permit its measurement. This is clear from the examples of verbatim answers.

TABLE 9.4. *Extent of mention of each type of contribution*

	Per cent of respondents
Perceived improvement in: Type	
1—Awareness of problems, strengths and weaknesses	85.4
2—Profits and growth	47.9
3—Information and communication	39.6
4—Systematic resource allocation	35.4
5—Co-ordination and control	29.2
6—Morale and industrial relations	16.7
7—Quantification	4.2

(i)   Yes, I am convinced of it (contribution). If we did not have plans, we would not be nearly as profitable as we are and would never achieve objectives. . . . without planning, we would be lost. I think it most certainly contributes to profits.

(ii) I do really believe it has improved our financial position, that is, the company moved from loss three years ago to profit for the last two years.

(iii) I think it has contributed to profits but I can't quantify it. For example, planning led to raw material substitution to get profit improvement through cost reduction.

(iv) I would like to think that it contributed to profits, growth, etc., but I cannot quantify.

The order of contributions in Table 9.4 is very similar to that found by Greiner *et al.*[16,7] However, improvements in information and communication were seen to be more important in the U.S. study. In addition, no direct mention was made of profits or growth in the Harvard study, although 56 per cent of Greiner *et al.*'s respondents said planning had a "High Impact on Operating Performance". Given the difference in methodology, and the precise categories of contributions used, however, the findings of the two studies are perhaps surprisingly consistent. For instance our results provide support for Greiner *et al.*'s statement that formal planning makes "educational" and analytical contributions by "helping managers to discipline their thinking, achieve a clearer focus on specific goals . . . ". This role of planning was further illustrated by the fact that within the virtually 50 per cent of companies with such documents, planning manuals were used not only to provide an extensive description of the planning system, but also to develop a wider understanding of the role of corporate planning and its underlying concepts.

Difficulties in Planning Systems

All the interviewees had encountered major difficulties but only 19 per cent more than two. The most frequently mentioned difficulties were related to the interface with line departments. Table 9.5 shows that this was alluded to by two in every five corporate planners. Some thought the difficulty inevitable because of their staff or advisory role. Others thought it resulted from insufficiently clear lines of authority and responsibility. One third of planners experienced difficulties with respect to data collection and communication, complaining of inability to obtain necessary information, uncertainty of its delivery and unreliability on the one hand and excessive quantification by technically-qualified staff on the other. Difficulties in obtaining information were inevitably linked with general attitudes to corporate planning, and style of management, within a number of companies, i.e. to the "culture" of the company. This was unfavourable to corporate planning in nearly a third of the companies. No doubt the proportion would have been much higher if companies without corporate planning had been included in the sample. This resistance and, possibly, misunderstanding of corporate planning may have stemmed, in part, from its potential threat to existing vested interests. It was encouraging, however, that only one in eight corporate planners thought that lack of trust of new techniques and other attitudes of top management impeded planning. Resistance to corporate planning was obviously concentrated below the chief executive.

TABLE 9.5. *Types of difficulties in formal corporate planning systems*

Type	Per cent of respondents
1—Departmental interface	41.7
2—Data and communications	33.3
3—'Culture'	29.2
4—Forecasting	27.1
5—Time and timeliness	16.7
6—Top management attitudes	12.5

Difficulties in forecasting were mentioned by 13 respondents. Unpredictability of government policy and of public expenditure where companies were major suppliers to the state were given as causes. In general, it was suggested that the pace and number of sources of change in the environment were increasing, making long range prediction more difficult and less valuable and, perhaps, requiring bigger and faster systems to evaluate the possible effects of an event. There were indications, therefore, of increased environmental turbulence. Forecasting and planning problems in general were compounded by use of different time scales within sub-units of the company within a number of companies. In others necessary data were not available at early enough times to permit orderly forecasting and evaluation.

Weaknesses of Planning Systems

Forty-four per cent of the respondents expressed satisfaction with their planning system. Some saw no reason to change a system they had designed themselves. Others believed that evolutionary change was occurring anyway and, therefore, no interference was necessary. A third group suggested that it was too early in the system's development to suggest change.

In contrast, over half the respondents thought improvement necessary. The changes thought to be required were not the same in number or in kind. One-third of the total sample, and three-quarters of those desiring change, thought that only one weakness needed removal but a further ninth gave two. The required changes mentioned are tabulated in Table 9.6. Perhaps predictably, the majority of respondents wanting change wished to have greater formality, documentation, co-ordination or control. Others reflected the problems already identified, and quoted by early researchers too, by calling for a change in attitudes towards planning within their companies. Only 8 per cent of the respondents wanted more time, however. A small minority of planners, even as early as 1974, had perceived that their systems had become too formal. The fact that the percentage was as low as 6.3 no doubt reflected the relatively short lives of

TABLE 9.6. *Types of changes required in formal corporate planning systems*

	Percentage of respondents
More formality	12.5
More quantification and details	12.5
More co-ordination and control	12.5
Changed attitudes and more influence for planning	12.5
Need more time	8.3
Less formality and less sophisticated systems	6.3

many of the corporate planning systems, for Lorange and Vancil[17] detected that formality of planning was tightened in the early years of a system, became less necessary once the discipline of planning was widely accepted by line management, and was then reduced as it appeared increasingly burdensome and unnecessary. Among our sample, too, the cry for greater informality was from companies with a longer experience of corporate planning.

In general, the results on difficulties and required changes, which also indicate areas of dissatisfaction, are largely consistent with those of Vancil, Ringbakk, Steiner and Schollhammer,[10, 12, 18] all of whom suggested that top management's support is critically important, that line management involvement in planning is essential, but that a lack of sympathy and understanding of planning concepts militates against these conditions in many companies.

Interrelationships Between Responsibilities, Contributions, Difficulties and Changes Required

Statistical analysis showed that the numbers of responsibilities, contributions, and difficulties perceived by corporate planners in the 48 companies were significantly, positively correlated, i.e. vary together. Similarly, the number of changes required in the planning system and difficulties encountered were positively correlated, as might have been expected.

There are a number of possible explanations. The correlations may reflect real associations between the numbers of responsibilities, contributions, difficulties, and required changes. However, because the questions were open-ended the apparent relationships may merely reflect the fact that some respondents were more articulate than others, giving a fuller account of just every aspect.

One way of seeking to determine whether the correlations reflect more than differences in loquacity of the interviewees was to examine relationships between individual responsibilities, contributions, difficulties, and required changes and total numbers cited in the other categories. Not only is it inherently interesting to know, for instance, the tasks associated with a greater number of perceived difficulties, any relationships found can be examined to determine whether they are reasonable. If found to be so, the case for suggesting that the positive correlations between numbers of responsibilities, contributions and difficulties, for instance, reflect real associations is greatly improved.

To this end, statistical analysis was undertaken, results being presented in Table 9.7 and in Fig. 9.1. The relationships suggested by the analysis seem

TABLE 9.7. *Correlations between individual items and total numbers of responsibilities, contributions, difficulties and changes required*

Changes required	No. of responsibilities	No. of contributions	No. of difficulties	No. of required changes
(1) More formality	NS	NS	NS	0.41^a
(2) More quantification and details	NS	NS	NS	0.41^a
(3) More co-ordination and control	0.26^a	NS	0.22^b	0.33^a
(4) Need time	-0.21^b	NS	0.26^a	0.38^a
(5) Need more money	NS	NS	NS	0.24^a
(6) Changed attitudes and influence	NS	NS	NS	0.27^a
(7) Less formality and more simplicity	NS	0.24^a	0.19^b	0.30^a
Responsibilities				
(8) Production of plans	0.22^b	NS	NS	NS
(9) Propose and advise	0.37^a	0.24^a	0.22^b	-0.15^d
(10) Analyse and evaluate	0.49^a	NS	NS	NS
(11) Collate and co-ordinate	0.29^a	NS	0.14^d	0.31^a
(12) Special projects	0.42^a	NS	-0.13^d	NS
(13) Infn. and reporting	0.15^d	0.13^d	NS	NS
(14) Assumptions and forecasts	0.39^a	NS	NS	0.31^a
(15) Control	0.20^c	NS	0.23^a	NS
(16) Devt. of planning	0.30^a	0.23^b	0.17^c	NS
Contributions to				

TABLE 9.7. (cont.)

responsibilities	No. of contributions	No. of difficulties	No. of required changes	No. of Changes required
(17) Awareness and analysis	NS	0.19^b	0.27^a	0.17^c
(18) Profit and growth	NS	0.61^a	0.24^a	0.14^d
(19) Systematic resource allocation	NS	0.46^a	NS	NS
(20) Co-ordination and control	NS	0.35^a	0.28^a	NS
(21) Quantification	0.21^b	NS	-0.16^c	NS
(22) Infn. and communication	NS	0.52^a	0.19^c	0.17^c
(23) Morale and ind. relations	0.24^a	0.46^a	NS	NS
Difficulties of				
(24) Data and communications	NS	0.14^d	0.21^b	NS
(25) Culture	0.18^c	NS	0.43^a	NS
(26) Deptal interface	NS	0.20^c	0.42^a	0.17^c
(27) Timeliness	-0.18^c	NS	0.33^a	0.24^a
(28) Forecasting	0.18^c	0.31^a	0.30^a	NS
(29) Top mgt	NS	NS	0.14^d	0.14^d

[a] Denotes very highly statistically significant, i.e. a chance of less than 1 in 1000 of the result being due to chance alone.
[b] Denotes highly statistically significant, i.e. a chance of less than 1 in 100 of the results being due to chance alone.
[c] Denotes statistically significant, i.e. a chance of less than 5 in 100 of the results being due to chance alone.
[d] Denotes strongly suggested, i.e. a chance of less than 1 in 10 of the results being due to chance alone.
NS Denotes not statistically significant.
The coefficients shown are Kendall's tau.

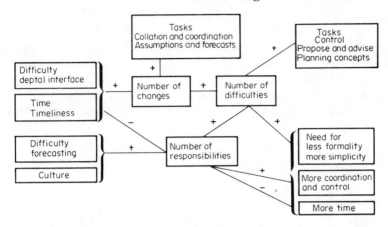

FIG. 9.1. *Relationships between responsibilities, contributions, difficulties and cheques required.*

to make sense. Corporate planners assuming the more active roles of proposing, advising, controlling and inducing their colleagues to accept planning concepts tended to encounter more difficulties. Where more difficulties were perceived by corporate planners some wanted more co-ordination and control, others more time, and yet a third group wished to back out of an apparently overly formal and complex system. Those who chose the first response seemed to have more responsibilities. In turn, those with more responsibilities tended to identify difficulties with forecasting, which might be resolved by more co-ordination, and management "culture". Somewhat paradoxically, however, it was those with fewer responsibilites who tended to both complain of lack of time and demand more time.

Relationships with the number of desired changes are also intuitively reasonable. Where corporate planners were conscious of difficulties in obtaining data in a timely manner, of having enough time to carry out their responsibilities adequately, and of obtaining good working relationships with line departments, they tended to suggest more changes in their planning process. High numbers of such changes were, in turn, associated with the tasks of co-ordination, collation, setting planning assumptions, and producing forecasts which might well generate precisely such difficulties.

Again, it was precisely where corporate planners assumed more active roles, taking the tasks of proposing and advising as well as developing planning upon themselves, that they believed their contributions to be greater. Thus the positive correlation between the numbers of difficulties and contributions, which seem to make no immediate sense, could well be due to both the problems and contributions such influence seeking corporate planners create, i.e. the apparent statistical relationship between them is a reflection of a common dependence on a more active corporate planning role.

Thus the additional statistical analysis strengthens the case for believing that the relationships between total numbers of responsibilities, contributions, difficulties, and required changes reflect real association within the companies in the sample.

Relationships with the Planning Process and its Context

Although research to which earlier reference has been made investigated benefits and pitfalls of corporate planning, there is a conspicuous absence of systematic analysis of the relationships between each of tasks, contributions, difficulties and changes required and the context of the planning process. Vancil[18] did suggest that success is heavily dependent on the formality of the company as a whole, as well as the status of the chief planner. Ringbakk, Steiner and Schollhammer[10, 12] and much of the prescriptive literature have also stressed the importance of the corporate planner's reporting level. With a quite different emphasis, Thune and House[9] suggested that corporate planning pays particularly in industries with faster rates of change, but did not use measures of the rate of technological change, for instance. A thorough analysis of the relationship between perceptions on responsibilities, contributions, difficulties and required changes on the one hand and major characteristics of the planning system, company, technology, and its market environment on the other remains to be done. To meet this need, statistical analysis was undertaken using the data collected by Al-Bazzaz[19] and results are reported in Table 9.8. Full descriptions of the scales may be found in Grinyer and Al-Bazzaz[20] but for the purpose of this article they be taken as largely self-explanatory. Where this is not so their meaning is clear from the text.

Factors Influencing the Breadth of Corporate Planning Responsibilities

No causal relationships may be inferred from these correlations for the direction of causality can only be hypothesized and significant associations may be due to common dependence on other variables. None the less, by drawing on experience it is possible to suggest a causal model which would explain the statistically significant relationships. This is done in Fig. 9.2. Detailed analysis of the design of the planning process and its context,[20] shows that the former is strongly related to the size of the company, age of

TABLE 9.8

	No. of responsibilities	No. of contributions	No. of difficulties	No. of changes required
(1) Co. charter	NS	-0.25^a	-0.22^c	NS
(2) Co. status	NS	0.17^c	0.37^a	NS
(3) Structure	0.14^d	0.20^b	0.28^a	NS
(4) Strategy	NS	-0.22^c	NS	NS
(5) Vertical span of control	NS	NS	0.20^c	0.18^c
(6) Lateral span of control	-0.14^d	NS	0.19^c	NS
(7) Number of sites	0.24^a	NS	0.20^c	-0.15^d
(8) Geographic dispersion	NS	NS	0.23^b	NS
(9) Country of ownership	NS	NS	-0.23^b	NS
(10) Dependence on suppliers	0.29^a	NS	-0.18^c	NS
(11) Dependence on 10 largest customers	NS	NS	NS	NS
(12) Dependence on parent's products/services	-0.41^a	-0.29^c	-0.42^a	-0.36^b
(13) Per cent of sales to 5 largest customers	-0.39^a	-0.24^c	-0.31^b	NS
(14) Per cent of sales to general public	0.18^c	0.17^c	NS	NS
(15) Per cent of sales to wholesalers/agents	NS	NS	NS	0.21^c
(16) Per cent of sales to ind. users/govt.	NS	NS	NS	-0.17^d
(17) Per cent of sales to retailers	NS	NS	NS	0.15^d
(18) Ranking in 1st market	NS	NS	NS	NS
(19) Ranking in 3rd market	NS	0.22^c	0.27^b	NS
(20) Share in 1st market	NS	-0.16^d	NS	NS
(21) Share in 2nd market	NS	NS	NS	NS
(22) Share in 3rd market	NS	-0.17^d	NS	NS
(23) Past market turbulence	NS	NS	NS	NS
(24) Future market turbulence	NS	NS	NS	NS
(25) Production concentration	0.23^c	0.18^c	NS	NS
(26) Investment gestation period	0.23^b	NS	NS	NS
(27) Technical inflexibility	0.25^b	NS	NS	-0.16^d
(28) Need for product innovation	0.15^d	NS	-0.16^c	NS

TABLE 9.8. (cont.)

(29) Rate of technological change	NS	NS	NS	NS
(30) Planning specialism	0.18[c]	NS	0.14[d]	−0.28[a]
(31) Age of formal planning system	0.23[b]	NS	NS	−0.28[a]
(32) Formal post of chief planner	NS	−0.21[c]	−0.20[c]	−0.19[c]
(33) Number of planning staff	NS	NS	NS	NS
(34) Meetings attended	0.16[c]	0.26[a]	0.20[c]	0.21[c]
(35) Frequency of board meetings attendance	NS	0.21[c]	NS	NS
(36) Frequency of group planning meetings attendance	0.23[c]	0.25[a]	0.48[a]	0.19[c]
(37) Frequency of capital budgeting meetings attendance	NS	NS	0.38[a]	NS
(38) Frequency of divisional/functional planning meetings attendance	0.34[a]	NS	NS	0.10[c]
(39) Number of types of planning documents used	NS	NS	NS	NS
(40) Number of written plans used	NS	0.26[a]	0.21[b]	0.35[a]
(41) Number of forecasting techniques used	0.31[a]	0.24[a]	NS	0.15[d]
(42) Number of evaluative techniques used	0.26[a]	NS	NS	NS
(43) Rate of return percentage in 1973	NS	NS	NS	−0.18[c]
(44) Net capital employed 1969	NS	NS	NS	0.25[c]
(45) Net capital employed 1970	NS	NS	0.15[d]	0.30[a]
(46) Net capital employed 1971	0.22[c]	NS	NS	0.16[d]
(47) Net capital employed 1972	0.23[b]	NS	0.14[d]	NS
(48) Net capital employed 1973	NS	NS	0.17[c]	NS
(49) Turnover 1969	0.23[b]	NS	NS	0.29[a]

(50) Turnover 1970	0.26[b]	NS	NS	0.24[c]
(51) Turnover 1971	0.26[a]	NS	NS	0.20[c]
(52) Turnover 1972	0.24[a]	NS	NS	NS
(53) Turnover 1973	0.25[a]	NS	NS	NS
(54) Net profit before tax 1969	NS	NS	NS	NS
(55) Net profit before tax 1970	NS	NS	0.15[d]	NS
(56) Net profit before tax 1971	0.15[d]	NS	NS	−0.18[c]
(57) Net profit before tax 1972	0.14[d]	NS	NS	−0.16[c]
(58) Net profit before tax 1973	NS	NS	NS	−0.29[a]
(59) Number of employees 1969	0.24[c]	NS	NS	NS
(60) Number of employees 1970	NS	NS	NS	NS
(61) Number of employees 1971	NS	NS	NS	NS
(62) Number of employees 1972	NS	NS	NS	NS
(63) Number of employees 1973	0.20[c]	NS	NS	NS
(64) Wages 1969	0.18[d]	NS	0.26[d]	NS
(65) Wages 1970	NS	NS	NS	NS
(66) Wages 1971	NS	NS	0.19[d]	NS
(67) Wages 1972	0.22[c]	NS	NS	NS
(68) Wages 1973	0.26[a]	NS	NS	NS
(69) Planning committee	NS	NS	−0.13[d]	NS

The coefficients shown are Kendall's tau.
[a] Denotes a chance of less than 1 in a 1000 that the result is due to chance.
[b] Denotes a chance of less than 1 in 100 that the result could have been due to chance.
[c] Denotes a chance of less than 5 in 100 that the result could be due to chance.
[d] Denotes strongly suggested but not staticsally significant.

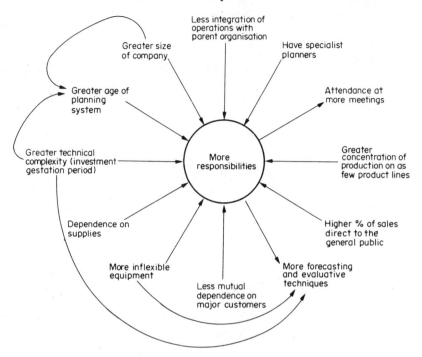

FIG. 9.2. *Factors influencing the breadth of corporate planning responsibilities.*

the planning process, and technical inflexibility and complexity, these technical characteristics being, for instance, highly significantly linked to the number of forecasting and evaluative techniques used. It is consequently no surprise that these very factors are related to the number of tasks assumed by corporate planners. Large companies have greater problems of co-ordination and control, particularly where involved in diverse businesses (see Grinyer and Spender[21] for an analysis of such problems), and respond more slowly to environmental threats and opportunities due to more extended chains of communication and greater bureaucracy (Grinyer[22] refers to research which has shown the relationship between company size and bureaucracy). Under these circumstances, the needs met by corporate planning may be wider, and the number of responsibilities of the corporate planner correspondingly greater.

The relationships with technical factors make equal sense. Where the investment gestation period is long, a characteristic usually associated with complex, special purpose, and expensive plant, the investment decision can be justified only in terms of forecast conditions several years at least ahead. Not only forecasts but also careful evaluation of alternatives are important, for major investment decisions on new plant create substantial hostages to fortune, as illustrated by the history of overcapacity in the chemical industry in the last decade. Risk cannot be avoided by careful forecasting and analysis, but it may be reduced, and even where this is not so a sense of greater security may be induced. Where plant involved is not only large, complex and expensive but also highly inflexible, i.e. special purpose, and production is concentrated on a narrow band of products, the risks attendant on investment are obviously increased because the range of possible future conditions in which its operations would be profitable are by definition restricted. Lack of alternative supplies of raw materials or bought in parts (dependence on suppliers) increases the risk inherent in such investment. It is scarcely surprising therefore that planners have wider responsibilities, and use more forecasting and evaluative techniques in discharging them, in companies with long investment gestation periods, less flexible production equipment, and a greater dependence on existing suppliers.

From Table 9.7 and Fig. 9.2 it may be seen that planners tend to assume more responsibilities as the corporate planning process becomes more mature. This may signify growing acceptance, and wider participation by planners in the decision making process, but could also be due to other factors on which both the age of the process and the number of responsibilities are both dependent. For instance, size of the company and inflexibility of its production technology may account for both, for they are positively correlated with the age of the planning process too.[20]

The remaining factors bearing on the number of responsibilities of the planner are dependent on parent organizations for goods and services, on the one hand, and on major customers (in terms of their share of total sales), on the other. Dependence on parents for goods suggests integration into the logistic flows of a larger enterprise, which is vertically integrated, with the corollary that major decisions relating to the business may be taken at a much higher hierarchical level. Not only this, the dependence on the parent gives a higher degree of security, buffering the company from at least one part of a potentially hostile environment. Perhaps strangely, the same is probably true of heavy dependence on major customers among our sample, for reasons analysed more fully by Grinyer, Al-Bazzaz and Yasai[23] and Grinyer and Al-Bazzaz.[20] Stripped of the statistical analysis, the argument is quite simple, but accords well with both our own and others' personal experience. The companies in the sample were very large, those heavily dependent on their major customers also tended to have high market shares, and hence the dependence was mutual. Rather than being subject to buffeting at the whim of major customers, these companies had a relationship which economists have called bilateral monopoly,[24] in which each party has considerable bargaining power. Whilst theorists like

Coddington see this inducing competition between the parties for the best terms, a condition which can be observed in some cases, a frequent situation among large companies is collaboration to achieve a mutually advantageous outcome. This is a situation described by Rhenman,[25] on the basis of his Swedish research, as "joint optimization and joint consultation". New products are designed in consultation with, and to meet the needs of, the major industrial customers who also provide forecasts of future requirements and even tentative delivery schedules. Under these circumstances, the supplier is buffered from the uncertainties of the final market place by his major customers, who bear the managerial burden of responding to market fluctuations and threats. It follows, then, that dependence on major customers, just as much as upon parent organizations, reduces the need for, and so the width of responsibilities of, corporate planning.

Factors Influencing Extent of Contributions

Factors influencing the extent of contributions of the planning process, i.e. the number of types of contributions claimed by the interviewee within the company, are illustrated in Fig. 9.3. In this case the direction of causality can scarcely be in doubt since the contributions are by definition those of operating the planning process within the context of the company and its

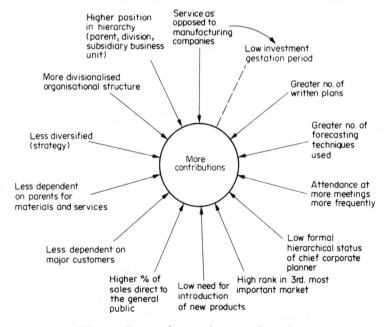

FIG. 9.3. *Factors influencing the extent of contributors.*

environment. Hence the independent variables may be analysed into three categories, the planning process, company characteristics, and the market environment.

Four aspects of the planning process seem to be related to the extent of its contributions. It is perhaps scarcely surprising that the number of areas of the business for which there were written plans, the number of forecasting techniques used, and attendance at more meetings more frequently led to wider contributions. Contributions are clearly related to the extent of involvement and effort to some extent at least. What did surprise us was that the extent of claimed contributions tended to be negatively related to the status of the most senior planner. This reverses the orthodox, normative, views to which reference has already been made. Although it could be argued that, strictly, there is no contradiction because earlier literature related to "success" or "pitfalls" (conditions leading to lack of success), whilst our focus here is upon breadth or extent of contributions, the prescriptive implications are quite contrary. Considerable caution must be used, however, for the size of the coefficients were so small that the status of planners could account for no more than 4 per cent of the variability in contributions. Moreover, low status of planners was also associated with recognition of more difficulties and need for more changes in the process, to which we turn later. None the less, it is quite possible that there is a tendency for planners reporting to line executives to become more fully integrated into the operational planning process, and so to contribute more fully than if located at more elevated levels. If this is so, however, the tendency is weak, and should not be allowed to dominate other considerations.

Surprisingly, size and technology, the main influences on the number of responsibilities of corporate planners suggested by the statistical analysis, had no significant relationship with the number of contributions (with the apparent exception of the investment gestation period). Company characteristics found to be associated with this number were charter (service, manufacturing, or both), hierarchical status of the organization (parent, division, or subsidiary business unit), the divisionalization of the organization structure, and the extent of diversification (strategy). Only the first of these four causes surprise. We had expected that, because of their greater logistic complexity and technological factors discussed in the last section, manufacturing companies would be perceived to have obtained wider contributions.

This was especially so in view of the fact that manufacturing companies tended to be more diversified.[19] An explanation may be in the different roles that corporate planners play in service and manufacturing companies. In the former, corporate planners were more involved in generating proposals and control, but senior and line management tended to initiate reviews of plans and evaluate alternatives more frequently. An impression is given, therefore, of corporate planners taking a more creative and influential a role within a collaborative approach to planning within the service companies as opposed to manufacturing ones. If this is so wider contributions might be expected from corporate planning. Given that service companies tended to have low investment gestation periods the greater number of contributions cited by them would explain the otherwise inexplicable association between the latter two.

Status of the organization, divisionalization of organizational structure, and diversification of product lines may all be seen to be related to difficulties of communication, of understanding the constituent businesses, and of co-ordination. Because of its functions of co-ordination and control,[20] corporate planning could be expected to meet a substantial need in parent companies, with long vertical chains of command. However, in diversified companies planners tended to emphasize control rather than participation in proposal generation and evaluation[20] which could explain their lower number of reported contributions.

Among the environmental factors, those that bear upon contributions of corporate planning are largely the same as those related to responsibilities, in particular dependence on a parent and major customers. The greater security that such dependence is assumed to induce may equally be expected to limit the contributions that corporate planning can make. Since dependence on major customers tends to be negatively correlated with the percentage of total sales direct to the general public, which necessarily involves sales to many customers, this second factor's relationship with contributions may be seen as another expression of the same theme. Two environmental factors remain. First, where the company has a high rank, i.e. a lower share, in its third most important market the contributions of corporate planning were seen to be wider. Share or rank in the first and second markets have no significant relationship with contributions, however, possibly because most of the sample had strong positions in those but in their third markets the spread of market shares and ranks was wider.

There may well be greater scope for an effective contribution from planning where the market rank is relatively high, in that greater penetration can often be achieved without attracting retaliation from market leaders, which would suggest that this could be an important factor. Less explicable is the tendency for *more* contributions to be claimed where the need for introduction of new products was thought to be low. No intuitively reasonable explanation occurs to us. The apparent relationship is probably attributable largely to the fact that service companies perceived both more contributions from corporate planning and less need for introduction of new products.[20]

Factors Creating Difficulties

The number of types of difficulty recognized by corporate planners can also be reasonably regarded as dependent on the planning process, the company, and its environmental linkages. Results of the statistical analysis suggest then the causal model illustrated in Fig. 9.4.

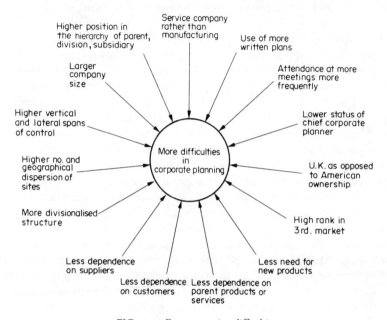

FIG. 9.4. *Factors creating difficulties.*

Similarities with Fig. 9.3 are immediately apparent. Greater involvement by planners, in terms of attendance at more meetings more often and use of more written plans, is seen to generate more difficulties as well as more contributions. Passive planners, with little involvement, may be expected to avoid many difficulties! Low status of the chief planner also leads to difficulties, as suggested in earlier literature, and noted above.

Again, the company characteristics associated with contributions seem to be largely related to difficulties, too. Size of company, higher vertical and lateral spans of control, divisional structures, higher status of the company in the group hierarchy (where appropriate), and the number and dispersion of sites all, it has been argued, contribute to greater difficulties of communication, co-ordination and control, and of rapid response to environmental changes. They consequently influence both the responsibilities and contributions of corporate planning. Yet the argument has been in terms of the difficulties they generate and which corporate planning may help to overcome. These very difficulties must be confronted by the corporate planners themselves and are therefore likely to be reflected in their statements on this score.

These arguments have already been rehearsed, the difference being one of emphasis or slant, but this is not so where the new company characteristic, country of ownership, is concerned. From Table 9.8 it may be seen that this factor bears significantly only on difficulties but that in this case there is a probability of less than 1 in a 100 of the result occurring by chance. Hence although country of ownership accounts for only about 5 per cent of the total variation in the number of difficulties it is still a significant factor. Given that the scale runs from U.K. (low) through continental Europe to U.S.A. (high), the analysis suggests a clear tendency for companies with American parents to perceive less difficulties in corporate planning. This could well be a cultural phenomenon. North American companies tend to employ more business graduates, espouse management techniques more quickly and ardently, and adopted corporate planning earlier and more enthusiastically than those in the U.K. By means of exchanges of personnel, visits, and implantation by the parent of formal planning systems within the subsidiaries as one level of a hierarchical process of co-ordination and control, it is very likely that the American culture permeates the U.K. subsidiaries which are consequently more favourably orientated towards corporate planning than their U.K. owned counterparts. Again, the fact that corporate planners in service companies perceived more difficulties than those in manufacturing ones may be in part a matter of culture, but it is more likely to be related to the more active role they tend to play and the reactions and problems this generates.

Environmental factors too follow the now familiar pattern. Mutual dependence on customers, and now suppliers, buffers the company against environmental turbulence and so reduces the difficulties of corporate planning, as well as the tasks and contributions of the planners. Again the rather paradoxical relationship between need for new product innovation and difficulties of planning may be attributed to a common dependence on organization charter (i.e. whether or not the company is involved in manufacturing).

Factor Influencing Changes Required in the Planning Process

As with contributions and difficulties, it is assumed that the desire for changes in the planning system is created by its features, the company characteristics, and environmental linkages. Given this assumption, we may derive the causal model illustrated in Fig. 9.5 from the statistical correlations in Table 9.8, always with the proviso that some of the

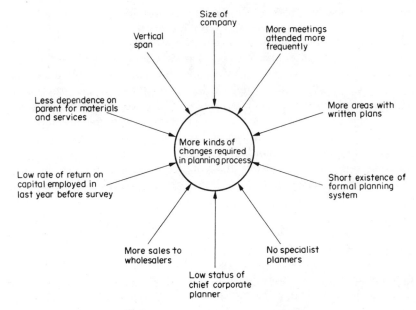

FIG. 9.5. *Factors influencing changes required in the planning process.*

relationships might possibly be due to common dependence on other factors.

Because of the number of types of changes desired in the planning process is a measure of dissatisfaction, like the number of perceived difficulties, one would expect similar factors to bear upon it. Indeed, it could be argued that the proposal changes is a response to difficulties. This expectation is largely confirmed. More types of changes are suggested where corporate planners are more fully involved, in terms of both attendance at meetings and the number of areas with written plans, where the status of the chief corporate planner is low, the size of the company is high, the vertical span of control is great, there is less dependence on the parent for materials and services, and there are more sales to wholesalers (and hence less to government and industrial users with whom there is a relationship of mutual dependence).

New factors entering Fig. 9.5 also make considerable intuitive sense. Where the planning system is relatively young, in our sample at the time of the survey frequently under 2 or 3 years old, many difficulties had still to be ironed out. On the other hand, as suggested in the earlier descriptive section on required changes, others with newly designed systems were unwilling to contemplate changes before they had been given a chance to work. It is quite possible that the relationship found was, then, largely dependent on the large number of relatively new systems within the sample. In addition, since the statistical methods used assumed a one directional relationship, and involved data collected at one point in time as opposed to over a longer period within a smaller sample of companies, they cannot illuminate the possibility of a cyclical pattern of dissatisfaction and change. As indicated earlier Lorange and Vancil[17] suggest that increasingly formal procedures and tight planning discipline are often rejected once line managers have acquired the habit of planning and as irritation with the bureaucratic aspects of the system grows. We would hypothesize that when the formal planning systems are dismantled, an erosion of the planning discipline created among line managers by their operation will commence. In time the very needs for systematically addressing strategic issues, co-ordinating and controlling within the corporate whole which led to the initial adoption of formal systems will reappear. An appropriate response may then be a greater formality of corporate planning. If this speculation is right, rather than an increasing satisfaction with a planning system as it matures, one will be confronted by a cyclical pattern of change, satisfied implementation, perception of weaknesses and mounting dissatisfaction, leading to further change. At the centre of this cycle will be fluctuating emphasis on centralization as opposed to decentralization of decision making within the corporate body, on formalized as opposed to informal methods, and on systematic as opposed to more judgmental decision making.

Concluding Points

From the descriptive and statistical results presented here a number of general points emerge clearly. At the time of the survey, in 1974, there was considerable variability within the sample of 48 large U.K. companies in terms of the responsibilities, contributions, difficulties, and changes required of corporate planning. Yet on the whole the descriptive findings are consistent with those of earlier researchers despite differences in time and national location of their studies. Since 1974, we perceived a swing towards greater dissatisfaction with formal systems as the environment became uncertain in the economic crisis of 1974–1975 and more informality in strategic decision taking, a trend which could well be beneficial.[26] In time, however, we suspect that this may be reversed as problems created begin to outweigh advantages.

Having said this, clearly the role, contributions, difficulties, and dissatisfactions expressed as required changes were related to the planning process itself and the status of the corporate planner. Greater involvement, in terms for instance of more written plans, more meetings attended, and more forecasting techniques used, led to both wider contributions and difficulties. If the cyclical model hypothesized in the last section is correct, this relationship with the extent of involvement could lead to a cyclical pattern of greater and less involvement of corporate planners as designers and operators of formal systems.

Company characteristics also bear strongly upon the extent of each of responsibilities, contributions, difficulties and required changes. Size of company, organizational shape, charter, degree of diversification and country of ownership all enter into the pattern of influence. Similarly, technology has a very strong bearing on the responsibilities of planners in particular. All of these influences are nested in a wider pattern related to dependence on parents, suppliers and customers as well as place in the market. Taken together, these factors can be seen as creating needs that shape the responsibilities and so the extent of contributions of corporate planners, but at the same time confront the corporate planners with difficulties. The very forces which drive a company to set up a corporate planning system may undermine it so leading to the cyclical pattern hypothesized in the last section.

The better the design of a corporate planning system matches the needs of the situation which stimulates its creation, i.e. the better it meets the situational needs, the less intense these difficulties should be compared with its contributions and the longer it should survive before the adverse effects it inevitably creates mount to an insupportable level. As Lorange and Vancil[17] suggest, experiences of the 1960s in the U.S.A. left planners wiser if more cautious, and we can reasonably assume that where a large number of companies respond to given contingencies with specific characteristics of the process this may well reflect a learning process. A contingency approach to the design of corporate planning systems is clearly required, as suggested by Lorange and Vancil.[17] Interested readers will find an account of such an approach in Grinyer and Al-Bazzaz.[20]

References

1. J. M. W. Hewkins and T. Kempner, Is corporate planning necessary?, *British Institute of Management*, London (1968).
2. K. B. Brown *et al.*, Long range planning in the U.S.A.—National Industrial Conference Board survey, *Long Range Planning*, **1** (3) (1969).
3. W. H. Strigel, Planning in West German industry, *Long Range Planning*, **3** (1) (1970).
4. H. Schollhammer, Corporate planning in France, *Journal of Management Studies*, **7** (1) (1970).
5. B. Taylor and R. Irving, Organised planning in major U.K. companies, *Long Range Planning*, **3** (1) (1976).
6. K. A. Ringbakk, Organised planning in major U.S. companies—A survey, Stanford Research Institute (1969).
7. F. J. Aguilar, R. C. Howell and R. F. Vancil, *Formal Planning Systems 1970: A Progress Report and Prospectus*, Harvard University Press (1970).

8. H. I. Ansoff, J. Avner, R. G. Brandenberg, F. E. Portner and R. Radosevitch, Does planning pay? The effect of planning on success of acquisitions in American firms, *Long Range Planning*, **3** (2), December (1975).
9. S. S. Thune and R. J. House, Where long range planning pays off, *Business Horizons*, August (1970).
10. K. A. Ringbakk, Why planning fails, *European Business*, Spring (1971).
11. D. M. Herold, Long range planning and organizational performance—a cross-validation study, *Academy of Management Journal*, March (1972).
12. G. A. Steiner and H. Schollhammer, Pitfalls in comprehensive long range planning: a comparative multinational survey, *Long Range Planning* (1973).
13. J. C. Camillus, Evaluating the benefits of formal planning systems, *Long Range Planning*, **8** (3), June (1976).
14. P. Irving, Corporate planning in practice: a study of the development of organised planning in major U.K. companies, M.Sc. dissertation, Bradford University (1970).
15. P. Lorange and R. F. Vancil, How to design a strategic plan-system, *Harvard Business Review*, September/October (1976).
16. L. E. Greiner, *Integrating Formal Planning into Organizations*, Aguilar *et al.*, *op cit.*
17. P. Lorange and R. F. Vancil, *Strategic Planning Systems*, Prentice-Hall, Englewood Cliffs (1977).
18. R. F. Vancil, See Vancil's contribution to Aguilar *et al.*, *op cit.* (1970).
19. S. J. Al-Bazzaz, Contextual variables and corporate planning in 48 U.K. companies, Ph.D. Thesis, CUBS (1977).
20. P. H. Grinyer and S. Al-Bazzaz, Corporate planning in 48 U.K. companies: a contingency model, Working Paper of the City University Business School, London (1979).
21. P. H. Grinyer and J. C. Spender, *Turnaround: Recipes for Managerial Success*, Associated Business Press, London (1979).
22. P. H. Grinyer, Organizational structure: The Aston Programmes I, II and III, *Long Range Planning*, **11**, 89–92, December (1978).
23. P. H. Grinyer, S. Al-Bazzaz and Ardekani Yasai, Strategy, structure, the environment and financial performance in 48 U.K. companies, Working Paper of the City University Business School (1978). Accepted for publication in the *Academy of Management Journal*.
24. A. Coddington, *Theories of the Bargaining Process*, George Allen and Unwin, London (1968).
25. E. Rhenman, *Organisation Theory for Long Range Planning*, Wiley, London (1973).
26. P. H. Grinyer and D. Norburn, Planning for existing markets—perceptions of executives and financial performance, *Journal of the Royal Statistical Society*, Series A, **B8** (1) (1975).

10

Corporate Planning in Medium-sized Companies in the U.K.

E. F. BHATTY

Introduction

Corporate planning, which consists of specifying the desired future of an organization as well as the means of achieving it,[1] emerged as a distinct management function in the immediate post-war years. And today, as Taylor[2] has noted, "the practice of corporate planning is . . . established on a worldwide basis and it continues to grow rapidly."

A substantial body of literature exists on both the philosophy and the theory of corporate planning. In addition, a considerable amount of research has been directed by both academics as well as consultants at investigating actual practice.[3]

However, the major portion of this research has centred on analysis of corporate planning practice in large companies and the industrial giants. A less substantial and more recent body of work has concerned itself with corporate planning in small businesses.

Between the industrial giants and the small businesses lie the medium-sized companies, and these have received little attention in the research and teaching of corporate planning. As a result, the practice of corporate planning in medium-sized companies, both in regard to its nature and extent, has remained largely uninvestigated.[4]

This study attempts a preliminary exploration of the area in the U.K. context.

Twenty-six companies participated in the survey. The information was collected by means of a questionnaire, with follow-up by mail and telephone. The method of research is set out in greater detail in the Appendix.

This article was originally published in *Long Range Planning*, Volume 14, No. 1, February 1981.

The author is a Doctoral Candidate in Management, University of Aston Management Centre. Building, Gosta Green, Birmingham.

Characteristics of the Companies

The range of business activities of the responding companies is shown in Table 10.1.

TABLE 10.1. *Business activities of responding companies*

Nature of business activity	Number of companies	Per cent of companies
Food manufacture	3	75.0
Textiles	4	18.2
Footwear, apparel, textile goods	1	9.1
Wood, cork except furniture	1	50.0
Paper-making, pulp, board	1	20.0
Printing, publishing	2	66,7
Leather, fur	1	50.0
Rubber, plastics	2	15.5
Chemicals	6	85.7
Non-metalic mineral manufacture	2	15.4
Basic metal industries	6	37.5
Metal products	5	17.2
Electrical, electronics	6	37.5
Transport equipment	2	13.3
Specialized manufacturing	4	23.5
Machinery and equipment	11	31.4
Building and construction	4	57.1
Business, professional services	1	33.3

Note: Total of companies exceeds 26 as 69 per cent of the companies operate across more than one product group.

As can be seen, the companies participating in the study operate in industries with widely diverse technologies and across many different markets. The responding companies, thus, represent corporate planning across a broad spectrum of interests, diverse approaches, and varying degrees of competition.

Their annual turnover ranges between £9 m and £160 m, the average turnover being £54 m. The number of people employed by the companies ranges between 1800 and 4999, the average employment being 3244 people. Less than one-third (31 per cent) of the companies produced only one product; the rest were multi-product firms.

Findings

The study was designed to investigate eight major areas of interest: (1) the extent of corporate planning in medium-sized companies, (2) the system of corporate planning, (3) corporate objectives, (4) inputs into the corporate plans, (5) formalization of the corporate planning function, (6) the planning horizon, (7) control of corporate plans, and (8) chief executive assessment of corporate planning as practised in their companies. The findings in each of these areas are presented below.

Extent of Corporate Planning

Ninety-six per cent of the companies responding to the survey reported that they prepare corporate plans. Clearly, corporate planning is well-established among medium-sized companies, a result which complements the conclusions of other researchers who have reported widespread acceptance of corporate planning in small companies,[5] as well as large business organizations in the U.K.,[6] U.S.A.,[7] Japan[8] and Europe.[9]

The possibility of this high positive response being the result of sample bias was investigated via the analysis of non-response, and the results of the investigation are reported in the Appendix. In view of the findings, and also because of the general acceptance of corporate planning,[10] it can be concluded that the high positive response can be taken to be largely representative of actual practice in medium-sized companies.

An essential prerequisite for undertaking any form of integrated corporate planning is the establishment of a separate corporate planning department.

As Table 10.2 shows, less than half (46 per cent) of the companies reported that they have a separate planning department. As the Table also shows, the impetus to the establishment of separate planning departments came about in the mid-1960s. However, as can be seen, the establishment of a planning department is essentially a 1970s phenomena, some 60 per cent of them being set up after 1970.

TABLE 10.2. *Year planning department set up*

Year planning department established	Number of companies	Per cent of companies
Before 1950	1	8
1951−1955	—	—
1956−1960	1[a]	8
1961−1965	—	—
1966−1970	3	25
1971−1975	5	42
1976 onwards	2	17

[a] Enlarged and more coordinated department set up in 1978.

The size of the planning departments shows a considerable variation in size. Thirty-six per cent of the companies had a staff of 2−3 employees, 27 per cent had 6 employees, and 18 per cent had between 8 and 10 employees in their planning department. The typical strength of the planning department was 5 employees. No association could be established between the strength of the planning department and the size of the company. However, it was noted that planning departments established before 1970 were some 36 per cent larger than the planning departments set up after 1970.

As Table 10.3 shows, the corporate planning department reported, in the main, to the chief executive. However, in one-quarter of the companies it reported, not to the chief executive, but to a functional director—either finance, commercial or engineering. The board was not involved in a direct reporting relationship with the planning department.

TABLE 10.3. *Position to which planning department reports*

Position to which planning department reports	Number of companies	Per cent of companies
Board of Directors	1	8
Chief executive	8	67
Other directors	3	25

Summary. We see, thus, that though corporate planning is widespread among medium-sized companies, less than half of them have set up separate planning departments. These were established mainly after 1970, and are small in size. The majority of them report to the chief executive.

System of Corporate Planning

The literature stresses the overriding responsibility of the chief executive for corporate planning in the organization.[11]

Although this was borne out by Table 10.4, the evidence in favour of the chief executive is not nearly as definite as envisaged in the literature. In only 39 per cent of the companies was the chief executive directly responsible for the preparation of the corporate plan; in the majority of companies, therefore, he was only associated with the process.

A group of senior executives jointly were responsible for the preparation of the corporate plan in another 35 per cent of the companies, and in such cases, the task of co-ordination was most often undertaken by the finance function.

The contribution of the planning department itself in the preparation of the corporate plans was largely confined to that of prov ding inputs into the planning process. In only 15 per cent of the companies was the planning department itself responsible for preparing the corporate plans.

TABLE 10.4. *Preparation of corporate plans*

Person(s) responsible for preparation of corporate plans	Number of companies	Per cent of companies
Board of Directors	1	4
Chief executive	10	39
Senior executives	9	35
Management Planning Committee	2	8
Planning department	4	15

Note: Percentage total exceeds 100 because of rounding.

Table 10.4 also shows that the involvement of the Management Planning Committee and the Board of Directors in the preparation of the corporate plans is minimal.

On the other hand, as Table 10.5 shows, the board was largely responsible for the approval of corporate plans, this being so in just over half (54 per cent) of the companies. As can also be seen, the role of the chief executive in the approval of corporate plans was not inconsiderable. The role of management planning committees in both the preparation and the approval of corporate plans is minimal. [12]

TABLE 10.5. *Approval of corporate plans*

Person(s) responsible for approving of corporate plans	Number of companies	Per cent of companies
Board of Directors	14	54
Chief executive	10	39
Management Planning Committee	2	8

Note: Percentage total exceeds 100 because of rounding.

Tables 10.4 and 10.5 taken together reveal a broad and general hierarchical relationship between the participants in the process of preparation and approval of corporate plans. Corporate plans prepared by the planning department are generally approved by either the Management Planning Committee or the chief executive; plans prepared by the Management Planning Committee or a group of senior executives are usually approved by the chief executive; and plans prepared by the chief executives are always approved by the board.

Line management contribution to the planning process, like that of the planning department, is largely indirect. In fact, although all the companies reported some degree of line management involvement in the preparation of the corporate plans, this involvement varied widely. Some 54 per cent of the companies reported this to be considerable; another 35 per cent stated that it was restricted to providing selective inputs only; while 11 per cent reported little line management involvement in the process of preparing the corporate plans. In only 12 per cent of the companies was line management given the direct responsibility for preparing the corporate plans.

An observably strong association was noted between line management involvement in the development of corporate plans and the spread of a company's product activity: companies which operated across a larger number of product groups reported a greater degree of line management involvement. Also, companies which had not set up separate planning departments reported considerable line management involvement in the development of their corporate plans.

The necessity of the chief executive spending a large proportion of his time in planning the future of the company is generally accepted in the literature.[13] However, as Table 10.6 shows, this is not borne out in practice.

TABLE 10.6. *Time spent by chief executive on corporate planning*

Per cent 7	Number of companies	Per cent of companies
1−10	13	52
11−20	3	12
21−30	2	8
31−40	4	16
41−50	3	12

Note: Only 25 of the 26 companies answered this question.

Half the chief executives of medium-sized companies spend less than 10 per cent of their time on corporate planning. Clearly, chief executives do not consider the future to be more important than the present.[14]

Both Steiner[15] and Eppink *et al.*[16] have suggested that ideally chief executives should spend up to 40 per cent of their time on corporate planning. In medium-sized companies we find that, in fact, only 14 per cent of the chief executives do so.

Inevitably, the very small amount of time devoted to corporate planning must reflect in the quality of the final plan.

Summary. Though chief executives of medium-sized companies are largely responsible for the preparation of the corporate plans, the majority of them spend less than 10 per cent of their time on it. The planning department functions largely to provide inputs into the corporate plan. And in companies which do not have a separate planning department, line management contribution to the plan preparation process is reported to be considerable. Approval of the plans is, however, largely the prerogative of the board.

Corporate Objectives

As can be seen from Table 10.7, the board was directly responsible for setting the corporate objectives in nearly half (46 per cent) of the companies, and together with the chief executive and the Management Committee in another 42 per cent of the companies. The influence of the board in determining the corporate objectives of medium-sized companies is thus seen to be predominant.

TABLE 10.7. *Person(s) determining the corporate objectives*

Person(s) responsible for determining the corporate objectives	Number of companies	Per cent of companies
Board of Directors	11	46
Chief executive	1	4
Board and chief executive	9	38
Board, chief executive and Management Planning Committee	1	4
Objectives implicit and unwritten	2	8

Note: Only 24 of the 26 companies answered this question.

The role of the board in setting these objectives varies, however, with the size of the company. In the smaller companies, and in companies which did not have a separate planning department, the objectives were developed by the board largely without consultation with other company executives. In the larger companies, on the other hand, the objectives are established through a process of bilateral negotiation between the board and the chief executive.

In the majority (92 per cent) of companies these objectives are explicit and are set down in writing. Only two of the companies reported that their objectives were implicit and unwritten. "They are understood", stated one of the companies.

By far the greater proportion of the companies do not have one, single, overriding objective. Some 80 per cent of the companies developed a set of multiple objectives, ranging from 2 objectives in some 46 per cent of the companies to 4/5 objectives in the case of another 13 per cent of the companies. (Two companies, in fact, stated that they each had $1\frac{1}{2}$ pages of formal objectives.)

Table 10.8 summarizes the key corporate objectives of medium-sized companies. As can be seen, the majority of companies put profitability as their prime objective,[17] with marketing running a close second. A few of the companies also develop people-oriented objectives, but it is evident that concern for people is slight.

TABLE 10.8. *Key corporate objectives in medium-sized companies*

Key corporate objectives	Number of companies reporting
Profitability	13
Sales and marketing	12
ROCE	10
Growth	7
EPS/Dividends	3
Employee relations	3
Management development	2
Cash flow	2
Cost control	1

Note 1: Two of the 26 companies did not want to disclose their corporate objectives. Both companies employed in excess of 4000 people, had a turnover of around £5m, and had substantial interests in chemicals.

Note 1: Table incorporates multiple replies.

In general, financial objectives tend to predominate over other objectives. And despite the current emphasis on societal responsibilities of business and the satisfaction of stakeholder interests, none of the companies reported any social objectives.

An observably strong association was noted between the size of the company and the quality of its objectives. The larger companies, and these tended to have planning departments, generally developed objectives in financial terms. The smaller companies, and these tended not to have a separate planning department, placed greater emphasis on marketing objectives.

Summary   We see, thus, that the development of corporate objectives is largely the prerogative of the board in medium-sized companies. Multiple rather than single objectives tend to be the rule. The larger companies develop financial objectives, while the smaller companies mostly develop marketing objectives. However, none of the companies develop any social objectives at all.

Inputs into the Corporate Plans

The objectives a company develops are, as Hussey[18] puts it, "only precursors to strategic action"—namely, the drawing up of the corporate plan. The essential elements are well-known:[19] an assessment of threats and opportunities perceived in the external environment in which the company operates and over which it has little or no control; an appraisal of the company's internal strengths and weaknesses; and finally, the identification and analysis of strategic alternatives.

Table 10.9 summarizes the extent to which these elements are considered, and taken into account, by the medium-sized companies while developing their corporate plans.

TABLE 10.9. *Inputs into the corporate plans*

Major inputs in a corporate plan	Companies taking account of specific elements in their corporate plans	
	Number	Per cent
Environmental analysis		
Political developments	20	77
Economic trends	24	92
Social trends	20	77
Corporate appraisal		
Company strengths and weaknesses	24	92
Life cycles of current products	22	85
Product-market analysis		
Technical advances in the industry	25	96
Future markets	25	96
Future competition	25	96
Future customer requirements	26	100
New products to be developed	25	96
Strategic analysis		
Analysis of alternative opportunities	25	96
Evaluation of new areas of investment	23	89

As can be seen, the extent to which medium-sized companies undertake an analysis and appraisal of the different inputs that go into a corporate plan varies quite considerably.

Relatively little weight appears to be given to environmental analysis: only 77 per cent of the companies report that they undertake an analysis of political developments and social trends. Apparently, the chief executives of medium-sized companies do not believe that the socio-political environment can much affect their business in the future.

Many of the chief executives see more clearly, however, the impact of movements in the economy on the future of their business operation, and some 92 per cent of them report that they do consider the impact of economic trends on their business while drawing up their corporate plans.

The position of medium-sized companies in regard to the second major input into the corporate plans—namely, an appraisal of corporate strengths and weaknesses—is somewhat less clear, perhaps even a little ambiguous. Ninety-two per cent of the companies reported that they undertook a corporate appraisal while drawing up their corporate plans. However, when asked about a specific element of the appraisal—namely, the life cycles of their current product portfolio—only 85 per cent of the companies reported that they took this into account while drawing up their corporate plans.

The analysis thus far tends to suggest that chief executives of medium-sized companies attach relatively little importance to environmental analysis and corporate appraisal while developing their corporate plans.

In marked contrast, however, product-market factors are perceived to be extremely important in relation to the future of the business. In a remarkable degree of unanimity, all (100 per cent) of the companies stated that they took account of future customer requirements in drawing up their corporate plans. In addition virtually all (96 per cent) of them also reported that they took technical advances in their industry into account while drawing up their corporate plans, and an equal number reported that they undertook special studies to identify future markets, the nature of future competition, and the kind of new products to be developed.

Clearly, from the considerable attention and analysis that product-market factors get, one can conclude that chief executives of medium-sized companies consider competitors and competition—and not so much any external threat or internal weakness—as representing the more immediate, and potentially more damaging, threat to the long-term prospects of their business.[20]

The development of information inputs is, however, only part of the corporate planning process. The analysis and evaluation of this information is equally important. It leads to the generation of several strategic alternatives, and the choosing of one of them.

From Table 10.9 we can see that the majority (96 per cent) of companies not only undertake an analysis of future problems and an assessment of alternative opportunities, but that many (89 per cent) of them undertake an evaluation of new areas of investment as well.

It would appear, therefore, that the development of alternative strategies is fairly common in medium-sized companies. However, it is suggested that this response be treated with some caution, for two reasons.

First, as this study did not attempt to determine the quality of corporate planning in medium-sized companies, it is difficult to decide from the responses whether, in fact, any strategic analysis is being done. And, secondly, the literature [21] reports, with a remarkable degree of unanimity, that strategic analysis is the major area of neglect in actual practice. The situation, it is felt, is unlikely to be different in medium-sized companies.

One can only conclude, therefore, that the majority of medium-sized companies do evaluate alternative courses of action before committing their company to one of them. However, it is contended, in view of the evidence from actual practice, that these alternatives will not be strategic but extrapolative, developed informally rather than systematically, and evaluated intuitively rather than mathematically.

Summary. We see, thus, that the corporate plan as developed by medium-sized companies is extensive in coverage, but lacking in intensity and depth in several areas. Clearly, it is not the well-balanced and integrated system envisaged in the literature.[22] In actual practice we find that the chief executives of medium-sized companies place greater emphasis on product-market factors [23]—the "harder" and more tangible [24] aspects of corporate planning, than on the "softer" and less tangible elements to be found in the company's external and internal environment.

Formalization of the Corporate Planning Function

Formalization is essential to any systematic and logical approach to corporate planning. The importance of formal procedures and written communications in the preparation of the corporate plan is widely stressed in the literature.[25] Stages of the planning procedure are scheduled, and progress controlled through a time-table.

Table 10.10 shows that the corporate planning function exhibits a high degree of formalization. Between 89 and 96 per cent of the companies use written documents and formal meetings in the development of information for, and the preparation of, their corporate plans. In 89 per cent of the

TABLE 10.10. *Formalization of the corporate planning process*

Nature of formalization	Number of companies	Per cent of companies
Written documents	25	96
Formal meetings	23	89
Informal meetings	22	85
Time-tabling of plan preparation	23	89

companies the stages of the plan are scheduled in advance, and the preparation of the plan controlled through a time-table.

Table 10.10 also shows that the information used in the preparation of corporate plans is generated through multiple channels; exclusive reliance is not placed on any one, single channel or information generation.

Formal channels tend to be used more often than informal channels in the generation of information used in the preparation of the plans. Nevertheless, as can be seen, the companies also make extensive use of informal meetings to generate the information relevant to corporate planning. Clearly, despite the frequent use of formal channels, companies do not allow their previous informal channels of information generation to completely die out.[26]

Summary. We see, thus, that the corporate planning process in medium-sized companies is largely formal, using multiple channels for information generation. However, despite the formalization, medium-sized companies continue to make extensive use of informal channels to generate the information required for corporate planning.

The Planning Horizon

Table 10.11 shows that when it comes to planning ahead, the medium-sized companies view the future essentially over three distinct time periods: 1 year ahead, 3 years ahead and 5 years ahead.

TABLE 10.11. *Planning horizon in medium-sized companies*

Time horizon of planning	Number of companies	Per cent of companies
1 year	7	28
3 years	12	48
5 years	6	24

As the Table shows, the most popular planning horizon for medium-sized companies is 3 years, with nearly half (48 per cent) the companies preparing their plans over that time period.

Another 28 per cent of the companies planned only 1 year ahead. These were the smaller companies, and most of them did not have a planning department. This possibly limited their access to information necessary to corporate planning, and in such a situation, clearly, a rather short time horizon is more appropriate than one which is longer.

Only 24 per cent of the medium-sized companies planned over the longest time horizon of 5 years. All these companies resorted to a system of three-tier planning—a 1-year operational plan, a 3-year intermediate plan, and a 5-year long-range plan. The notable characteristic of this three-tier planning system is that plans till the intermediate time horizon are worked out in depth and detail; thereafter they are largely qualitative.

The majority (88 per cent) of companies prepared their plans annually, but not all the companies planned ahead equally in the functional areas.

As Table 10.12 shows, the time period of planning varies from function to function in medium-sized companies.

TABLE 10.12. *The planning horizon in specific functional areas*

Specific functional area	Per cent of companies planning		
	Up to 1 year ahead	Up to 3 years ahead	Up to 5 years ahead
Engineering	12	64	24
Finance	12	48	40
Marketing	24	44	32
Materials	28	48	24
Organization	16	52	32
Personnel	24	44	32
Production	32	48	20
R & D	13	52	35
Technical	13	54	33

Note: Two companies reported that they did not do any planning ahead at all in the Research & Development area, and one company reported that it did not plan ahead in the Technical area.

If we designate planning up to 1 year ahead as short-term planning, planning up to 3 years ahead as medium-term planning, and planning up to 5 years ahead as long-term planning, we see that the majority (88 per cent) of medium-sized companies are oriented towards long-term planning in the area of finance only.

In the area of product development, most (87 per cent) of the companies undertake only medium to long-term planning, while in the product manufacturing area the emphasis of many (80 per cent) of the companies is clearly on short to medium-term planning.

It is interesting also to note that at a time when the literature[27] is increasingly emphasizing the importance of long-term resources planning, three-quarters of the medium-sized companies undertake only short to medium-term planning in the area.

In the area of product development, most (87 per cent) the time horizons is distributed more evenly. Nearly half (44 per cent) the companies planned essentially for the medium-term, and of the rest almost equal numbers planned ahead for the short-term (24 per cent) as for the long-term (32 per cent).

Summary. We see, therefore, that while the most popular planning horizon is 3 years, small but significant numbers of companies plan for longer and shorter periods ahead. In the functional areas, too, the time period of planning varies, with long-term planning being done in the area of finance only, and essentially short-term planning being undertaken in the increasingly critical area of materials and resources.

Control of Corporate Plans

The rewards of corporate planning are realized only when plans are implemented. To facilitate this, corporate plans are broken down into specific, manageable, time-constrained action programmes. Control is exercised both by reviewing the progress of these programmes, and on the basis of a regular revision of the overall plan itself.

Eighty-five per cent of the companies break the plan down into specific action programmes for the achievement of plan targets. Review of these programmes, as can be seen from Table 10.13, is usually done in two stages: a monthly review of actual performance against programme, and then a final, comprehensive annual review which is used as the basis for revising the corporate plan. The general basis for control of the corporate plan is, thus, the monthly review and the annual revision.

TABLE 10.13. *Review and revision of corporate plans*

Frequency of review and revision	Number of companies undertaking	
	Review	Revision
When necessary	—	4
Continually	3	1
Monthly	7	1
Quarterly	4	2
Half-yearly	3	3
Annually	8	16
Not done at all	2	3

Note: Table incorporates multiple replies.

However, while there is a large measure of consensus about an annual revision among medium-sized companies, the pattern for the review of the plan is not nearly so definite. Monthly and annual reviews are by far the most popular, though some 30 per cent of the companies favour the quarterly and half-yearly review.

It is important also to note that 10 per cent of the medium-sized companies do not undertake any sort of review at all.

Also, though a few companies report that they review their plans "continually", and revise them "when necessary", in general, the majority of medium-sized companies favour a fixed time period for both the review and the revision.

Despite reviews and revisions, however, the best of plans cannot anticipate unexpected adverse circumstances. To meet such circumstances it is necessary to draw up contingency plans.

Nearly two-thirds (65 per cent) of the companies reported that they prepare contingency plans. The companies which did not prepare contingency plans were generally the smaller companies, and these, as noted in the previous section, tended to have a rather short planning horizon.

Summary. We see, thus, that medium-sized companies have a fairly comprehensive system for controlling the corporate plan. The general basis for control is the monthly review and the annual revision. In addition, the majority of companies also report that they prepare contingency plans to meet unexpected adverse circumstances.

Chief Executive Assessment of Corporate Planning

It is now generally agreed[28] that corporate planning does lead to improvement in corporate performance, and this constitutes a major reason for its widespread acceptance by companies of all sizes.

But are chief executives satisfied with corporate planning as practised in their companies? Are there any disadvantages of corporate planning? What changes would they want to see made in order to make corporate planning more effective?

These questions evoked responses which should prove to be of interest to teachers, researchers and consultants in the field.

As Table 10.14 shows, just over half (54 per cent) of the chief executives reported that they were satisfied with corporate planning as practised in their organizations.

TABLE 10.14. *Chief executive assessment of corporate planning*

Chief executive assessment	Number of companies	Per cent of companies
Expressed satisfaction	14	54
Expressed qualified satisfaction	4	15
Expressed dissatisfaction	8	31

Fifteen per cent of the chief executives expressed only qualified satisfaction with corporate planning as practised in their organizations, while another 31 per cent of the chief executives expressed dissatisfaction.

We thus see that there is a substantial body of chief executives who are dissatisfied with corporate planning.

The likely cause(s) for their dissatisfaction were also investigated: chief executives were asked, if in their view, corporate planning has any disadvantages. The results are summarized in Table 10.15.

TABLE 10.15. *Disadvantages of corporate planning*

Disadvantages of corporate planning	Number of companies
Inhibits flexibility and adaptability	7
Plans turn out to be inaccurate	5
Very time consuming and complex	5
Becomes a master rather than a tool	2
Diverts attention from daily operations	2

Note 1: Only 16 of the 26 chief executives answered this question.
Note 2: Table incorporates multiple replies.

Nearly three-quarters (73 per cent) of the chief executives stated that corporate planning had disadvantages. As can be seen from Table 10.15, this dissatisfaction centred round three areas. First, chief executives see planning as inhibiting both the corporate flexibility of response and its rapid adaptability to a changing environment. Secondly, chief executives see corporate planning as a very complex and time consuming exercise. And thirdly, chief executives express dissatisfaction with corporate planning because the plans turn out to be inaccurate.

The fact that the disadvantages cited by chief executives of medium-sized companies in the U.K. are substantially similar to the ones reported by Higgins and Finn[29] in the context of major U.K. companies shows that the concept of corporate planning as put forward by the academics—the teachers, researchers and consultants in the area—does not quite easily translate into actual practice.

Chief executives were, therefore, asked to indicate the changes that they would like to see made to make corporate planning more effective. The response, however, was surprising.

Sixteen of the twenty-six, or nearly two-thirds (62 per cent) of the chief executives, made no reply at all: 2 of them, in fact, returned the questionnaire with this particular question left unanswered, while the remaining 14 took shelter behind the reply that they were satisfied with corporate planning as practised in their companies.

Among the 10 chief executives who did reply to this question there was no broad, overall agreement as to the changes they would like to see made to make corporate planning more effective.

As Table 10.16 shows, their prescriptions were wide-ranging, contradictory, and diverse—and singularly few in number!

TABLE 10.16. *Changes to make corporate planning more effective*

Changes to make corporate planning more effective	Number of companies
More in depth analysis of inputs	3
Speeding up of the planning process	3
Better understanding of the planning process	2
More defined role for the chief executive	2
More emphasis on people, not numbers	1
Spend more time on corporate planning	1

Note 1: Only 10 of the 26 chief executives answered this question.
Note 2: Table incorporates multiple replies.

The diversity of replies reflects, of course, the particular difficulties of individual companies. But their paucity, from a normally vocal group, reflects perhaps a lack of full understanding of the concept and the use of corporate planning.

Summary. We see, thus, that nearly half the chief executives are quite explicit in expressing their dissatisfaction with corporate planning, and nearly three-quarters of them feel that corporate planning has disadvantages. Taken together, one can only conclude that there is a substantial measure of dissatisfaction with corporate planning among chief executives of medium-sized companies. Surprisingly, however, chief executives appear to be largely unable to suggest changes that would make corporate planning more effective.

Conclusion

Corporate planning as practised in medium-sized companies is not the well-balanced and integrated system envisaged in the literature: it is essentially one-dimensional in nature, focusing as it does on mainly the economic aspects of strategy formulation; it only inadequately addresses the strategic problem of adapting the organization to its environment; it fails to consider alternative futures; and it limits not only current flexibility in medium-sized companies, but inhibits also their developing the potential for future growth.

Practical Implications

Clearly, corporate planning in medium-sized companies needs to be improved considerably. The results and findings of the study point to a number of areas in which action can be taken to effect this improvement. In some of the areas new initiatives are called for, but in the main the need is for existing practice to be revised in line with recent research findings mainly through *joint* action by academics and chief executives.

Implications for the Chief Executive

The study suggests, firstly, a deeper commitment by the chief executive to corporate planning; secondly, a decentralization of the corporate planning process in medium-sized companies; and thirdly, a better understanding by the chief executive of the concept of corporate planning.

A deeper commitment on the part of the chief executive to corporate planning is clearly a prime necessity in order to improve corporate planning practice in medium-sized companies. The fact that half the chief executives spend less than 10 per cent of their time on corporate planning reflects not only their lack of commitment to, but possibly their lack of comprehension of, the nature of corporate planning. These two states are, in fact, inter-related: unless there is a larger commitment there does not exist the basis for greater understanding, while a lack of comprehension inhibits any deeper commitment. The initiative needed to break out of this vicious circle must come, clearly, from the chief executive himself. However, it is apparent that the assistance of the academic would do much to help the chief executive appreciate the necessity for making such a commitment.

Together with a deeper commitment, however, decentralization of the corporate planning process is also necessary. It is evident from the data that corporate planning in medium-sized companies is largely a top-down process, with the planning function concentrated mainly at the chief executive level. Inevitably, this centralized approach to corporate planning, together with the small amount of time spent on it, must have consequences that reflect in the quality of the plan.

In this context, it is interesting to note that Vancil[30] has reported greater accuracy in corporate planning in companies where there is (a) a greater commitment by the chief executive to, and (b) a larger association of diverse groups in, the preparation and development of the plan.

In addition to a deeper commitment and a decentralization of the corporate planning process, a third and vital step required in improving corporate planning process in medium-sized companies is the development of a better appreciation and understanding by chief executives of the concept of corporate planning itself. This is easier said than done. Chief executives tend to use corporate planning almost exclusively as a *technique* for improving productivity and profits. Few apply social tests to the programmes developed to determine the effect of these programmes on, and the acceptability of these programmes to, the people within the organization. Even fewer are aware of the dysfunctional effects of corporate planning on employee motivation and morale, and through this on corporate performance.

This narrow perspective, this view of the corporate planning process as a system for preparing plans—rather than as a framework for organizational analysis and decision making, which it is—is a result as much of the training of the chief executive and the reward system which directs his actions towards maximizing short-term profits, as it is of the failure of academics to persuade the chief executive that corporate planning is a philosophy of change and not a battery of techniques;[31] that organizational effectiveness and not corporate performance must be the goal of corporate planning; and that, in the final analysis, the corporate plan must represent a balance between the needs of the organization and the needs of its members.

Clearly, such misconceptions will have to be removed, and such misuse will need to be corrected, before corporate planning practice in medium-sized companies can be improved. This is the task facing academics and the business schools.

Implication for the Academics and the Business Schools

Misconceptions can be removed and misuse can be corrected largely through a re-orientation of chief executive attitudes towards the longer run: this is the first task facing the academics. However, it is becoming apparent that the existing system of corporate planning with its emphasis on economic factors mainly is a far from satisfactory system: it does not take account of behavioural variables on which corporate performance so critically depends. The development of an integrated system of corporate planning, one which incorporates *both* behavioural and economic variables, is, therefore, the second task facing the academics. The operational applicability of such an integrated system has, however, to be demonstrated. Experience with the existing system of corporate planning shows that chief executives find it both complex and time consuming. The third task before the academics, therefore, is the development of newer approaches to corporate planning so that the integrated system will not only be operationally applicable, but also conceptually acceptable to the chief executive.

The hardest task of all is, clearly, the re-orientation of chief executive attitudes from their present preoccupation with short-term profits towards a focusing of attention on longer-term organizational objectives. It is, however, the prime task facing academics, and a start can be made by:

(a) proving to the chief executives in real and concrete terms that they may, in fact, be purchasing short-term profitability for their companies at the expense of its longer-term ability to survive and grow,[32]

(b) convincing chief executives of the benefits of altering the pay and wages systems so as to recognize, reward and reinforce strategic decision making which alone can ensure the growth and survival of the organization in the long run, and

(c) re-designing business school curricula so as to place a somewhat diminished emphasis on technical skills and the specialist approach they engender, and a correspondingly greater stress on the development of conceptual skills and the holistic approach which will increasingly be required to monitor and cope with changes in the environment in a positive and purposeful way.

Together with the re-orientation of chief executive attitudes towards the future must proceed efforts towards the development of an integrated system of corporate planning which would take account of *both* economic and behavioural variables.

The existing system of corporate planning suffers from two major disadvantages, one theoretical and the other practical. The theoretical disadvantage is that the existing system of corporate planning emphasizes largely the economic aspects of strategy formulation;[33] its practical disadvantage is that chief executives find it operationally both complex and time consuming. If, now, behavioural variables are added to this already complex and time consuming system, one can only expect that the integrated system of corporate would become even more so. This, clearly, is a step in the wrong direction.

Despite this, the necessity of incorporating behavioural variables into the corporate planning system is vital. It derives from the fact that organizations, being inescapably social as well as economic systems, cannot expect to survive and grow through an emphasis on one or other of its dual aspects.[34] An undue emphasis on profits, as is favoured by many organizations today, may, in fact, operate to the detriment of morale in the organization in the long run. Such a policy will quite clearly adversely affect the organization's ability to survive and grow.

It is in this context that the development of an integrated system of corporate planning is proposed. Such an integrated system would eliminate the existing lop-sided emphasis on economic factors alone, and bring balance to it by emphasizing equally the need for profits by the organization, and the needs of the members of the organization.

Beyond the design of such an integrated system of corporate planning, however, lies the question of its operational acceptability. The third task facing academics, therefore, is the development of newer approaches to corporate planning which would make it more acceptable to the chief executive. The essence of these newer approaches would be the development of simpler, less comprehensive systems of corporate planning that exist at present.

One of these approaches could fruitfully be developed out of the practice currently being used by American companies: that of undertaking detailed planning not for the total company itself, but for a few selected, major projects only.[35] Such an approach would clearly be attractive to chief executives, and has the added advantage of being made operational fairly quickly.

A more rigorous approach, and one that will require extensive development and refinement through academic-chief executive co-operation, would be the development of a contingency approach to corporate planning. Once again, not all the aspects of a business or all the variables impinging upon its performance would be reviewed in detail by the chief executive, but only those specific circumstances and conditions, both economic and behavioural, upon which the future growth and survival of the company is, at that time, contingent.[36]

The essence of the contingency approach is that there is no one, best way of carrying out corporate planning:[37] that it is the degree of change and complexity in an organization's task environment which determines the style and structure of its corporate planning system, as well as its content. In organizations faced with relatively stable task environments, for example, a fairly standardized and routinized system of corporate planning would be suitable. In an unpredictable and changing task environment, on the other hand, a more flexible system of corporate planning would clearly be more appropriate.

Such an approach in practice would challenge the chief executive to think analytically and with a broader perspective than is possible under the existing system of corporate planning, and allow him to continuously consider completely new opportunities: a factor which would increase the flexibility of the organization. Such an approach would also serve to convince the chief executive that corporate planning is a dynamic, ongoing process rather than an annual event.

Since at present contingency theory is not sufficiently developed to offer detailed prescriptions for managing any particular set of contingencies, the area offers a rich field for exploration by students at business schools, teachers, researchers, consultants—and the thoughtful practitioner.

Acknowledgment

The author would like to acknowledge the advice and assistance of Mr. A. J. Bennett and Ms. Rosemary N. Scott.

References

1. Russell L. Ackoff, *A Concept of Corporate Planning*, p. 1, Wiley-Interscience, New York (1970).
2. Bernard Taylor, The concept and use of corporate planning, in *Corporate Strategy and Planning*, Bernard Taylor and John R. Sparks (Eds.), p. 3, Heinemann, London (1977).
3. Both theory and practice are comprehensively covered by *A European Bibliography of Corporate Planning 1961 – 1971* which was issued as a supplement to *Long Range Planning* of June (1972). An update was issued as a supplement to *Long Range Planning* of August (1978). The trans-Atlantic view is well-served by the references listed in George A. Steiner, *Top Management Planning*, pp. 733 – 770, Macmillan, New York (1969).
4. During the literature search only one survey study was located: J. Bacon, *Planning and Forecasting in the Smaller Company*, Conference Board, New York (1971). No comparable studies investigating British experience were found.
5. Jeffrey C. Shuman, Corporate planning in small companies—a survey, *Long Range Planning*, pp. 81– 90, October (1975).
6. J. W. M. Hewkin and Thomas Kempner, *Is Corporate Planning Necessary? A Survey of Planning Practices in British Companies*, British Institute of Management (1968); B. W. Denning and M. E. Lehr, The extent and nature of corporate long range planning in the United Kingdom—Part 1. *The Journal of Management Studies*, pp. 145 – 161, May (1971) and Part II, *The Journal of Management Studies*, pp. 1 – 18, February (1972); Bernard Taylor and Peter Irving, Organized planning in major U.K. companies, *Long Range Planning*, pp. 10 – 26, June (1971); Peter H. Grinyer and David Norburn, Strategic planning in 21 U.K. companies, *Long Range Planning*, pp. 80 – 88. August (1974); J. C. Higgins and R. Finn, The organization and practice of corporate planning in the U.K., *Long Range Planning*, pp. 88 – 92, August (1977).
7. Stanford Research Institute, *Planning Research Highlights*, SRI, Melno, California (1963); James K. Brown, Saul S. Sands and G. Clark Thompson, Long range planning in the U.S.A.—NICB survey, *Long Range Planning*, pp. 45 – 51, March (1969); K. A. Ringbakk, Organised planning in major U.S. companies, *Long Range Planning*, pp. 46 – 58, December (1969); Robert M. Worcester, Planning for growth in leading U.S. companies, *Long Range Planning*, pp. 8 – 14, March (1970); Ronald J. Kudla, Elements of effective corporate planning, *Long Range Planning*, pp. 82 – 93, August (1976); Harold W. Henry, Formal planning in major U.S. corporations, *Long Range Planning*, pp. 40 – 45, October (1977).
8. Japan Movement Association, *Long Range Business Planning in Japan*, Japan Management Association, Tokyo (1966); Toyohiro Kono, Long range planning— Japan – U.S.A.—a comparative study, *Long Range Planning*, pp. 61 – 71, October (1976).
9. H. J. Worms, How does German industry plan? *European Business*, pp. 20 – 30, February (1967), Hans Schoellhammer, Corporate planning in France, *European Business*, pp. 22 – 31, July (1969); D. Jan Eppink, Doede Keuning and Klaas de Jong, Corporate planning in the Netherlands, *Long Range Planning*, pp. 30 – 41, October (1976); Armin Topfer, Corporate planning and control in German industry, *Long Range Planning*, pp. 59 – 68, February (1978). See also, Michel Gouy, Strategic decision making in large European firms, *Long Range Planning*, pp. 41 – 48, June (1978).
10. See, for example, George A. Steiner, *Top Management Planning*, pp. 14 – 15, Macmillan, New York (1969) and Bernard Taylor, New dimensions in corporate planning, *Long Range Planning*, pp. 80 – 106, December (1976).
11. See, for example, Myles L. Mace, The president and corporate planning, *Harvard Business Review*, pp. 49 – 62, January – February (1965); James K. Brown, Saul S. Sands and G. Clark Thompson, Long range planning in the U.S.A.—NICB survey, *Long*

Range Planning, p. 49, March (1969); George A. Steiner, The critical role of top management in long-range planning, *Financial Executive*, July (1966); Basil W. Denning, Top management and long-range planning in Basil W. Denning (editor), *Corporate Planning: Selected Concepts*, pp. 52–59, McGraw-Hill, London (1971); Bernard Taylor and Peter Irving, Organized planning in major U.K. companies, *Long Range Planning*, pp. 20–22, June (1971); Ronald J. Kudla, Elements of effective corporate planning, *Long Range Planning*, p. 87, August (1976).

12. In large companies, by contrast, the role of such committee is quite important. See, James K. Brown, Saul S. Sands and G. Clark Thompson, Long Range planning in the U.S.A.—NICB survey, *Long Range Planning*, pp. 47–49, March (1969), and Bernard Taylor and Peter Irving, Organized planning in major U.K. companies, *Long Range Planning*, pp. 19–22, June (1971).

13. See, for example, Myles L. Mace, The president and corporate planning, *Harvard Business Review*, p. 56, January–February (1965); K. A. Ringbakk, Organized planning in major U.S. companies, *Long Range Planning*, pp. 49, 51, December (1969); Ronald J. Kudla, Elements of effective corporate planning, *Long Range Planning*, p. 91, August (1976); D. Jan Eppink, Doede Keuning and Klaas de Jong, Corporate planning in the Netherlands, *Long Range Planning*, p. 38, October (1976).

14. E. Kirby Warren, *Long-Range Planning: The Executive Viewpoint*, p. 59, Prentice-Hall, Englewood Cliffs, New Jersey (1966).

15. George A. Steiner, *Top Management Planning*, Charts 1–3 on p. 26, Macmillan, New York (1969).

16. D. Jan Eppink, Doede Keuning and Klaas de Jong, Corporate planning in the Netherlands, *Long Range Planning*, p. 38, October (1976).

17. This finding confirms the sustained and single-minded emphasis on profitability among firms of all sizes. See, for example, George W. England, Personal value systems of American managers, *Journal of the Academy of Management*, pp. 53–68, March (1967), Peter H. Grinyer and David Norburn, Strategic planning in 21 U.K. companies, *Long Range Planning*, p. 82, August (1974), David Norburn and Peter H. Grinyer, Directors without direction, *Journal of General Management*, 1 (2), 42, (1974), and Michel Gouy, Strategic decision making in large European firms, *Long Range Planning*, p. 42, June (1978) in the context of large companies, and Jeffrey C. Shuman, Corporate planning in small companies—a survey, *Long Range Planning*, p. 90, October (1975) in the context of small business firms.

18. D. E. Hussey, *Corporate Planning Theory and Practice*, p. 114, Pergamon Press, Oxford (1974).

19. Bernard Taylor, Managing the process of corporate development, in *Corporate Strategy and Planning*, Bernard Taylor and John R. Sparkes (Eds.) p. 162, Heinemann, London (1977).

20. David I. Cleland and William R. King, Competitive business intelligence systems, *Business Horizons*, 18, 19–28 (1975).

21. See, for example, K. A. Ringbakk, Organized planning in major U.S. companies, *Long Range Planning*, pp. 50, 53, December (1969); Roland J. Kudla, Elements of effective corporate planning, *Long Range Planning*, pp. 92–93, August (1976); Bernard Taylor, Corporate planning and organizational change, in *Corporate Strategy and Planning*, Bernard Taylor and John R. Sparkes (Eds.), p. 219, Heinemann, London (1977).

22. Bernard Taylor (please see reference 21 above), in fact, in a more general context, makes the point that 'researchers who look for the total system are doomed to disappointment'.

23. Bernard Taylor, The concept and use of corporate planning, in *Corporate Strategy and Planning*, Bernard Taylor and John R. Sparkes (Eds.), p. 8, Heinemann, London (1977).

260   E. F. Bhatty

24. Harold W. Henry, Formal planning in major U.S. corporations, *Long Range Planning*, p. 43, October (1977).
25. See, for example, Basil W. Denning, *Corporate Planning: Selected Concepts*, p. 2, McGraw-Hill, London (1971); Peter H. Grinyer and David Norburn, Strategic planning in 21 U.K. companies, *Long Range Planning*, p. 80, August (1974); D. E. Hussey, *Corporate Planning Theory and Practice*, p. 7, Pergamon Press, Oxford (1974); Bernard Taylor, The concept and use of corporate planning in *Corporate Strategy and Planning*, Bernard Taylor and John R. Sparkes (Eds.), p. 8, Heinemann, London (1977).
26. Francis Joseph Aguilar, *Scanning the Business Environment*, Macmillan, New York (1967).
27. Bernard Taylor, Strategic planning for resources, in *Corporate Strategy and Planning*, Bernard Taylor and John R. Sparkes (Eds.), pp. 237–256, Heinemann, London (1977), and the references listed.
28. Bernard Taylor, The concept and use of corporate planning, in *Corporate Strategy and Planning*, Bernard Taylor and John R. Sparkes (Eds.), p. 8, Heinemann, London (1977). See also the studies by Stanley S. Thune and Robert J. House, Where long range planning pays off, *Business Horizons*, August (1970); H. Igor Ansoff, Jay Avner, Richard G Brandenburg. Fred E. Portner and Raymond Radosevich, Does planning pay? The effect of planning on success of acquisitions in American firms, *Long Range Planning*, pp. 2–7, December (1970); B. W. Denning and M. E. Lehr, The extent and nature of corporate long range planning in the United Kingdom—Part 1. *The Journal of Management Studies*, pp. 145–161, May (1971); David M. Herold, Long range planning and organizational performance: a cross validation study, *Academy of Management Journal*, pp. 91–102, March (1972); Peter H. Grinyer and David Norburn, Strategic planning in 21 U.K. companies, *Long Range Planning*, pp. 80–88, August (1974).
29. J. C. Higgins and R. Finn, The organization and practice of corporate planning in the U.K., *Long Range Planning*, p. 92, August (1977).
30. Richard F. Vancil, The accuracy of long-range planning, *Harvard Business Review*, pp. 98–101, September–October (1970).
31. Bernard Taylor, Corporate planning and organizational change, in *Corporate Strategy and Planning*, Bernard Taylor and John R. Sparkes (Eds.), p. 297, Heinemann, London (1977).
32. See the discussion on "organizational effectiveness" in Edgar H. Schein, *Organizational Psychology*, Prentice-Hall, Englewood Cliffs, New Jersey (1970). See also the article by Warren G. Bennis, Toward, a "truly" scientific management: the concept of organizational health, *General Systems Yearbook*, **7**, 269–282, New York (1962).
33. Bernard Taylor, Strategies for planning, *Long Range Planning*, p. 29, August (1975).
34. Alvar Elbing, *Behavioural Decisions in Organisations*, Chapter 2, Scott, Foresman, Glenview, Illinois (1978).
35. Toyohiro Kono, Long range planning—Japan–U.S.A.—a comparative study, *Long Range Planning*, p. 66, October (1976).
36. John W. Newstrom, William E. Reif and Robert M. Monczka (Eds.) *A Contingency Approach to Management: Readings*, p. xiv, McGraw-Hill, New York (1975).
37. Don Hellriegel and John W. Slocum, Jr., *Management: Contingency Approaches*, p. 246, Addison-Wesley, Reading, Massachusetts (1978).

Appendix: Method of Survey

This paper is based on a study conducted between July and August 1978 in part fulfilment of the requirements for the degree of Master in Industrial

Administration (now re-titled as Master in Business Administration) at the University of Aston in Birmingham.

Owing to the limitations of time and finance, the data presented in this study was collected by means of a questionnaire only. Ideally, a combination of research methods would be more suitable for a study of this kind: questionnaires supplemented with in-depth interviews, and a participant—observer role in carefully selected organizations.

The questionnaire was developed along the lines of an inverted funnel, which allows a gradual broadening of the scope of the inquiry from very specific towards more and more general questions. It was pre-tested in a pilot study at the Management Centre, and then addressed to the chief executives of 100 medium-sized manufacturing companies. For the purposes of this study, a medium-sized company was defined as one employing between 2000—4999 people.

Because the study was restricted to manufacturing companies, de-terministic sampling was chosen as the appropriate sampling technique. The CBI/Kompass Register—U.K. 1977 was chosen as the sampling frame.

The 100 companies to whom the questionnaires were sent were located in the "industrial heartland" of the U.K.—the area encompassed by Lancashire and Yorkshire in the north, Lincolnshire in the east, the West Midlands in the south, and Salop, Cheshire and Merseyside in the west. Follow-up was done by telephone and letter.

The mailed questionnaire produced a total of 50 replies (questionnaires + letters). However, only 26 of the 29 questionnaires returned were fully usable. This 26 per cent response rate, on which the conclusions of the study are based, is broadly in line with the response rates achieved by other studies in the area and which also used the mailed questionnaire as their main method of inquiry.

Non-response was also investigated, and the reasons for non-participation are presented in Table 10.17.

TABLE 10.17. *Reasons for not participating in the survey*

Reason for non-participation	Number of companies	Per cent of total
Pressure of work	11	52
Send survey to parent company	3	14
No corporate planning system	2	10
Chief executive away on tour	1	5
Questionnaire not received	1	5
Do not participate in such surveys	1	5
No reason given	2	10

Note: Percentage total exceeds 100 because of rounding.

As can be seen, only 10 per cent of the companies investigated did not participate in the survey because they did not undertake any corporate planning. This response, following accepted convention in survey investigations, can be taken to be largely representative of all non-respondents. We can, therefore, reasonably conclude that the majority of medium-sized companies do undertake corporate planning, but for the various seasons listed in Table 10.17, did not participate in the survey.

Future researchers in the area should note the significant 52 per cent of chief executives who cited "pressure of work" as their reason for not participating in the study.

For the purposes of analysing the results the companies were ranked by a combined index of employment and turnover, and divided into two groups for purposes of making comparisons: the smaller and the larger companies.

Manual methods of data analysis were used, not only because of the large qualitative content of the data received, but also because of the limited number of responses to the survey.

It needs to be emphasized, however, that the conclusions of the study are based on a small proportion of the population. Also, as this was only an exploratory study, the findings are tentative, and need to be tested on a much large scale using a combination of research instruments.

11
The Role of Strategic Planning in Small Businesses

V. K. UNNI

Strategy and Success

Stangner in his study of top executives reported that wherever strategic planning was implemented by a top management committee, the organization produced a higher profit as a percentage of capital.[1] The Steiner study identified strategic factors governing success in particular industries.[2] Thune and House observed the results of matched pairs of companies in the food, drug, machinery, petroleum and chemical industries. They found that the firms which had formal strategic planning significantly outperformed their own past results.[3] The Eastlack and McDonald study on strategic planning by chief executive officers,[4] the Igor Ansoff study of strategic decisions on mergers and acquisitions,[5] the Herold study of companies in drug and chemical industries,[6] the Guth study of strategic factors responsible for the growth of larger firms,[7] the Schoeffler *et al.* report on large corporations[8] have all shown that firms with strategic planning can really outperform the non planners. In addition, these studies also suggest that:

(a) the chief executive officers who involved themselves in strategic planning headed the fastest growing organizations; and
(b) the results of strategic planning were visible in terms of all financial and sales measures such as return on equity, return on investment, asset growth, sales growth, and others.

The above findings definitely suggest the benefits of strategic planning, but the following add to management interest in the area:

(a) the conditions of most businesses change so fast that strategic

This article was originally published in *Long Range Planning*, Volume 14, No. 4, August 1981.

Note: Dr. Unni is now Associate Professor of Marketing at Illinois State University. At the time of publication he was with North Carolina Art University.

planning is the only way to anticipate future problems and opportunities; [9]

(b) strategic planning provides all employees with clear goals and directions to the future of the organization; and

(c) a standard can be established against which future performance can be compared.

Taking the relationship of strategy and success as given, this article considers the need to develop strategic planning for small businesses. It summarizes the findings of a survey of strategy in small businesses.

Small Business Strategy

Although there is research evidence to support the fact that strategic planning should, and does, pay off in successful operations, not much attention is paid by small businessmen. Therefore, the importance of strategic planning to the success of the small business cannot be over-emphasized. Since the entrepreneur is more involved with day-to-day operation problems, about which there is an urgency, he may not give enough conscious time and effort to the endeavor of strategic planning. Many changes that slip up on and surprise management are the type that can be detected only through an analytical approach to strategy. [10]

The process of strategic planning requires no more than applied common sense which most small businessmen have. They simply assume that it is useless to state their objectives formally which are self-evident. The nature of small business, in that the owner/manager has to function in several different capacities on different levels of the organization, leaves management with no real time for planning. [11] This is true in many respects, since the small business firms do not have an abundance of managerial talent as do large corporations. The average "fire fighting" businessman consequently perceives long-range planning as an esoteric activity which can be successfully undertaken only by highly trained intellectual giants which are available only within large organizations. [12]

There are few small business owners/managers who have done very well without a well-planned strategy because of their personal drive and sheer momentum. All small businessmen even "lucky" ones, need the right kind of imagination to foresee the future with some degree of accuracy. In that case, the strategy for small business is as much an art as it is a science. [13] There is the necessity to develop this art of strategy formulation in small business especially because many sophisticated concepts do not find places in small business.

There are only a few research studies or models about the framework of small business strategy planning applicable to small entrepreneurial operation. The Hastings study of 106 small manufacturers in Minnesota revealed the extent of planning and forecasting among small manufacturers, the responsibility for setting objectives, the areas considered in planning, and the data used in forecasting.[14] The Najjar study of planning in small manufacturing companies in Ohio concluded that top management planning is related to perceived benefits to the company.[15]

Though an exact planning procedure is difficult to specify, Wheelwright in his findings from a research program on strategy at the Stanford Business School specified important steps before any strategic planning procedure can be selected.[16] Stanford has analyzed a simple strategic planning model which may be also applied in small business.[17] The model showed the interaction of objectives, resources, and environment where time was considered both as a point and a span. John and Lindberg identified critical factors responsible for the survival and growth of small business.[18]

Strategic planning in itself is no guarantee of success in small business, but research studies indicate how the direction, goal, and ultimate destiny of the organization can be shaped by developing a proper strategy. Accepting the importance of strategic planning one might expect that such a procedure plays an important role in small businesses. The following is an analysis of a survey of planning in small businesses in a major metropolitan area of North Carolina.

Method

Sample

The sample for the study was taken from the Directory of Manufacturers published by the local Chamber of Commerce and from a list of minority small businesses published by an affiliate of the Office of Minority Business Enterprise and the U.S. Department of Commerce. A randomly selected sample of 80 minority and 80 non-minority small businesses was asked to participate in this project. Only those small businesses that were in existence for at least 2 years were selected, assuming these firms reasonably have had occasion to use strategic planning during that time. Only 62 minority and 58 non-minority small businesses responses were useable for the study.

The small business entrepreneurs operated many kinds of business fields, and the businesses were arbitrarily classified as follows to provide a framework for discussion. The fields of small businesses are very similar to the fields of businesses in general. The majority of small firms (both minority and non-minority) in the sample size were in retailing followed by the service industries, as shown in Table 11.1.

TABLE 11.1 *Sample size*

	Minority (n = 62)	Non-minority (n = 58)
Contract construction	2	1
Finance, insurance, real estate	1	1
Manufacturing	3	4
Retailing	32	39
Service industries	18	11
Transportation, communication	4	1
Wholesaling	2	1

Procedure

A Likert-type questionnaire was used for the study. The first part of the questionnaire sought company characteristics, such as the type of owner-ship, experience and educational background of owner, number of employees, owner's age and average working hours per week. The second part of the questionnaire focused on strategic planning by identifying the extent to which the business made plans, how far it met requirements of a plan and the problem it had in planning.

Though confidentiality of responses was assured, the pretesting of the questionnaire revealed an unwillingness of small businessmen to specify their profit and sales over the last few years. Consequently only their overall satisfaction or dissatisfaction was reflected in the questionnaire.

The three primary research hypotheses in this study are:

(1) among small business owners, the proportion who make use of overall planning in their businesses is the same for both minority and non-minority;

(2) all observed characteristics, such as the type of ownership, number of employees, average working hours per week, age of the firm, owner's experience, owner's age and educational background, were related to their planning efforts;

(3) since sales and profit growth could be considered as indicators of business success, those small business owners with satisfactory profit (profit growth) were also satisfied with sales (sales growth).

Results

All the respondents agreed that a good strategy greatly increases the likelihood of success in business, but their response did not reflect the extent to which they actually make use of planning. Further the survey result also indicated that the proportion who make use of overall planning was not the same for both minority and non-minority businessmen (Table 11.2).

TABLE 11.2. *Planning activities among minority and non-minority small business owners*

Planning activities	Calculated chi-square[a]
Planning (overall)	7.60[b]
Planning (sales)	0.26
Planning (purchase)	2.10
Planning (advertising and sales promotion)	6.30
Planning (manpower)	2.37

[a] 1 degree of freedom.
[b] Significant at 0.05 level.

Those who planned the business as a whole were only 10 per cent among minority and about 40 per cent among non-minority owners. Planning for advertising and sales promotion was relatively limited in both cases, 4 per cent of minority and about 22 per cent of non-minority sample. Since the majority of respondents were in business only for the last 2 years, an explanation could be that they were all interested in getting established and learn rather promoting their business. Planning was extensively used in the area of sales, 81 and 85 per cent among minority and non-minority businessmen respectively. Though improving sales ranked high in all planning activities, it was paradoxical that relatively less effort was limited to advertising and sales promotion. Since there was a difference among minority and non-minority small businessmen in the overall use of planning, several personal characteristics were compared to different aspects of strategic planning.

Among the minority small businesses, characteristics such as the type of ownership, number of employees, the average working hours per week, age of the firm, and experience of owner were not related to the extent to which they make use of planning and meeting the requirements of a good plan. But the owner's age and educational background seems to be related to their making use of plans. Among the minority respondents, 62 per cent were high school graduates, 24 per cent were college graduates, and 14 per cent were high school dropouts. Those engaged in strategic planning were found to be typically college educated and in the age group of 31–35.

Among the non-minority small businessmen, characteristics such as the number of employees, owner's age, and average working hours per week were not related to their planning efforts. But the type of ownership of business, age of the firm, owner's experience, and educational background were related to planning aspects. Those with franchise businesses, college education, previous related experience and older firms seem to make an effort in using strategic planning. Thus, the second hypothesis for the study could be only partially accepted (Table 11.3).

The intercorrelations between company characteristics also showed that older firms have more experienced managers; owners with high educational qualifications (3 per cent had graduate degrees) were involved in relatively new businesses; and management of recently started small businesses were found to be spending more time per week than managers of older firms. Among the types of ownership, non-minority franchise owners and minority family-owned businessmen seem to have higher education.

Regarding the third hypothesis, among minority small businesses only 5 per cent were extremely satisfied and 6 per cent extremely dissatisfied with profit levels and the percentages for non-minority were 10 and 2 per cent respectively. Fifty four per cent of minority respondents and 71 per cent of non-minority owners were satisfied with their present profit levels. An analysis of those satisfied owners revealed that they were not satisfied with sales growth. Within the same population, 93 per cent minority and 89 per cent non-minority were dissatisfied with sales growth. The study indicates that those small businessmen satisfied with profit tend to be dissatisfied with sales growth.

As shown in Table 11.4, there was no correlation between company characteristics and business success. Other analyses revealed that among the respondents, the maximum number of employees was 68 in minority small business (janitorial service) and 42 in non-minority furniture businesses (furniture manufacturing is North Carolina's second most important manufacturing industry). The oldest firm in the study was a 56-year-old minority owned funeral service and the youngest was a 2-year-old ice cream stand owned by non-minority. Among the total respondents, about 83 per cent agreed that their main reason for going into small business was to make money while 6 per cent stated a desire for independence, to set one's working place. Only about 2 per cent of total respondents were in small businesses with a primary objective to serve the community and none went into business because of an inability to get salaried employment.

Discussion and Implications

The causes and cures of small business failures have been studied and discussed in the literature.[19] On the other hand, comparatively little information is available concerning successful small businesses. The present study of successful small businessmen indicate that they fail, cope and learn

TABLE 11.3. *Correlations[a] between company characteristics and strategic planning among minority and non-minority small businesses*

Company characteristics	Strategic planning					
	Extent to which company makes plans		Meeting requirements of plans		Limitations in planning	
	Minority ($n = 62$)	Non-minority ($n = 58$)	Minority ($n = 62$)	Non-minority ($n = 58$)	Minority ($n = 62$)	Non-minority ($n = 58$)
Nature of ownership	0.03	0.27[b]	0.04	0.24[b]	0.06	0.21[b]
Number of employees	0.04	0.05	0.03	0.02	-0.01	-0.03
Owner's age	0.26[b]	0.01	0.27[b]	0.03	0.08	0.06
Average working hours per week	0.02	0.04	0.05	0.06	-0.01	0.02
Age of the company	0.07	0.31	0.03	0.29[b]	0.02	0.08
Experience of the owner	0.05	0.36[b]	0.04	0.42	0.01	0.09
Educational background	0.25[b]	0.42[b]	0.31[b]	0.36[b]	0.05	0.04

[a] Pearson product moment correlation coefficient.
[b] Significant at the 0.05 level.

270   *V. K. Unni*

TABLE 11.4. *Correlations*[a] *between company characteristics and business success criteria*

Company characteristics	Business success criteria			
	Profit satisfaction		Sales growth satisfaction	
	Minority ($n = 62$)	Non-minority ($n = 58$)	Minority ($n = 62$)	Non-minority ($n = 58$)
Nature of ownership	−0.14	−0.09	−0.10	−0.06
Number of employees	−0.08	−0.07	−0.08	−0.12
Owner's age	−0.06	−0.02	−0.13	−0.08
Average working hours per week	−0.07	−0.11	−0.09	−0.06
Age of the company	−0.05	−0.04	−0.07	−0.05
Experience of the owner	−0.04	−0.06	−0.09	−0.04
Educational background	−0.08	−0.09	−0.06	−0.02

[a] Pearson product moment correlation coefficient.

in the struggle for survival. Judgment, experience and intuition seems to play a very important role in determining success that any well-structured technique of strategic planning. This is in conformity with Gilmore's study where the old, size-up approach was emphasized.[20]

Among the barriers to planning, lack of planning knowledge is the most serious obstacle and this suggests that more exposure to strategic planning is a must for small businessmen, The need for more programs in such an area is obvious. The central objective for entering into small business to make money. This conforms with Stegall's findings[21] and it is not paradoxical to say that only those businessmen that profit will make any lasting contributions to society.

The survival of small businesses under study indicate that their growth strategies made them to continue in business. Though no attempt in this study was made to find the need structure of small business owners, other studies have found that growth strategies result from power needs of managers.[22] The mania for growth was very visible in the present study when the respondents expressed their earnest desires to increase sales. Peter Drucker has mentioned that high growth companies may be faced with identity crisis[23] and Worchester has indicated that growth requires a particular management style.[24] Obviously, there is room for a number of studies to delineate the nature and characteristics regarding managerial styles of small businessmen. The successful minority small business under study did not differ from their non-minority counterparts with regard to the characteristics which make for success and this is in conformity with the findings of Hornaday and Aboud.[25]

Infact, at no time and in no place has the climate for new small business been so good. It appears that regardless of minority or non-minority, policies and strategies that will make the firm survive are the same and efforts should be made to improve the planning knowledge of this vital sector of our economy.

Acknowledgement

.The result of this study was first presented at the Annual Meeting of the Academy of Management, Houston, Texas, in March 1979.

References

1. Ross Stangner, Corporate decision making, *Journal of Applied Psychology*, **53**, 1–13 (1969).
2. George A. Steiner, *Strategic Factors in Business Success*, Financial Executives Research Foundation, New York.
3. Stanley Thune and Robert House, Where long range planning pays off, *Business Horizons*, **13**, 81–87 (1970).
4. Joseph Eastlack, Jr. and Phillip McDonald, CEO's role in corporate growth, *Harvard Business Review*, **48**, 150–163 (1970).
5. Igor H. Ansoff, Richard G. Brandenburg, Fred E. Portner and Raymond Radosevich, *Acquisition Behaviour of U.S. Manufacturing Firms, 1964–1965*, Vanderbilt University Press, Nashville, TN (1971).
6. David Herold, Long range planning and organizational performance: a cross validation study, *Academy of Management Review*, March (1972).
7. William D. Guth, The growth and profitability of the firm: a managerial explanation, *Journal of Business Policy*, **2** (1972).
8. Sidney Schoeffler, Robert Buzzell and Donald Heany, Impact of strategic planning on profit performance, *Harvard Business Review*, **52**, 137–145 (1974).
9. William F. Glueck, *Business Policy: Strategic Formation and Management Action*, McGraw-Hill, New York (1976).
10. N. H. Broom and Justin G. Longnecker, *Small Business Management*, South-Western Publishing Co., Cincinnati (1979).
11. John V. Petrof, Peter S. Carusone and John E. McDavid, *Small Business Management: Concepts and Techniques for Improving Decisions*, McGraw-Hill, New York (1972).
12. A. M. Forbes, Long range planning for the small firm, *Long Range Planning*, **7**, 43–47 (1974).
13. Donald P. Stegall, Lawrence L. Steinmetz and John B. Line, *Managing the Small Business*, Irwin, Homewood, Ill. (1976).
14. Delbert C. Hastings, *The Place of Forecasting in Basic Planning for Small Business*, Small Business Administration, Washington DC (1961).
15. M. Naggar, *Planning in Small Manufacturing Companies: an Empirical Study*, Doctoral dissertation, Ohio State University (1966).
16. Steven C. Wheelwright, Strategic planning in the small business, *Business Horizons*, **14**, 51–58 (1971).
17. Melvin J. Stanford, *New Enterprise Management*, Brigham Young University Press, Provo, Utah (1975).
18. Theodore Chon and Roy A. Lindberg, *Survival and Growth: Management Strategies for the Small Firm*, AMACOM, New York (1974).

19. John Frank, Why business fails: a report from SOCRE, *Interaction*, **10** (1984); Eric J. Fredland and Claire E. Morris, A cross section analysis of small business failure, *American Journal of Small Business*, **1** (1976); Kamal E. Said and Keith Hughley, Managerial problems of the small firm, *Journal of Small Business Management*, **15** (1977).

20. Frank F. Gilmore, Formulating strategy in smaller companies, *Harvard Business Review*, **49**, 71–81 (1971).

21. Stegall *et al.*; *Ibid.*

22. F. Troughton, Growth and organization in business: their roots in nature, *Management International Review* (1970).

23. Peter Drucker, *Management*, Harper & Row, New York (1974).

24. Robert Worchester, Planning for growth in leading U.S. firms, *Long Range Planning*, **3**, (1970).

25. John A. Hornaday and John Aboud, Characteristics of successful entrepreneurs, *Personnel Psychology*, **24** (1971).

12

Strategic Planning in Hungarian Industry

M. CSATH

"Keeping mistakes secret, is equal to enlarging them"
Illyés Gyula (1902–)

Planning has a rather long history in Hungary.

It started in the late fifties with the national plans which were broken down in detail to the companies, and which imposed production and sales tasks and the level of resources.

The companies had no other rights to decide about their activity than to combine the materials, machines and people with the tasks given from outside. On the one hand, this was good and was the only possibility at the time. The power was absolutely centralized at the top and the decisions were made at the top. There were new worker-managers everywhere in the industry, who generally did not have enough knowledge about how to manage a company. On the other hand, there were demands for everything and ample human resources to employ everywhere. At the same time there was a strong aspiration to industralize the country, which manifested itself in enormous investments in the iron and steel industries. These decisions were political ones and the national plans reflected them clearly.

This economic policy and the centralized planning in close connection with it resulted in a rather fast economic growth which brought big structural changes in the economy and in industry. However, the growth often went together with a waste of resource, especially with the human resources. At the same time the very low level of achievement both for the companies and for the individuals caused a permanent bargaining about the possibilities and the tasks.

Neither the companies nor the individuals wanted to admit their

---

This article was especially written by Professor Csath, who is with the Department of Industries, Budapest, for this book.

capabilities to produce more or better, because this behaviour made it possible for them to fulfil the plans easily.

This form of making the economy operate could not become a long-term solution. The first problems presented themselves when the resources began to become exhausted. During this same period the Hungarian economy has become more and more open.

The products, the technologies, the structure of production and naturally the productivity and efficiency of production had to be compared with those of the developed countries.

The comparison proved that there was a big need to change the controlling system of the economy, especially the planning and regulatory system. The main direction of the change seemed to be to delegate more responsibility to lower levels, especially to the company level.

The new economic system came into operation on the first of January 1968.

The directives of the reform declared that:

— The methods of national and company planning must be improved, scientific management must be incorporated into the planning process, especially the use of mathematics and the computer sciences.
— The national plans need not be broken down to the company level. Indirect controlling systems (interest in profit-making, taxation and credit policy) motivate to fulfil the national plans.
— The companies had to make their own plans taking into account the demands of the market, the available resources and the national plans.
— The managers were to be responsible for their plans and did need not have to account for their achievement to the Ministries or the National Planning Office.
— The companies, the managers and individuals must have more opportunity for risk-taking and share the results of it.

The economic reform, as is evident from its declaration, wanted to combine the centralized, planned controlling of the national economy with the active role of the market, and the material stimulation of companies and individuals.

On the first of January 1973 the Planning Act came into force. In terms of this law plans must be made only on the national and corporate level. This was a big change, as the Act excluded several ministries from the planning process. But this has caused a rather confused situation: the ministries have survived the reform, but their tasks have not been clearly defined, especially those closely connected with planning.

It was said in the Act that:

— the companies should make their plans on the basis of the information

about the national plans, economic regulation, market conditions, and their own resources and knowledge;
— the President of the National Planning Office, in line with the competent Ministers and leaders of the nation-wide authorities would issue methodological guides for helping the company planning. But the companies could choose whether to take these guides into account.

What important assumptions were included in the Planning Act?
I think that at the least the following ones were assumed:

— there will be a modern, up-to-date nation-wide planning system, which is not very detailed, but gives quick information about the government's long- medium- and short-term objectives;
— the economic regulating system will follow the changes in the world economy as much and as quickly as is necessary to keep pace with the development trends of the world;
— the regulating system will be consistent and give free scope to entrepreneurship;
— direct intervention into company life will come to an end, or at least will be very much limited;
— there will be changes in the management of the companies in favour of good, well-trained, risk-taking managers.

But what really has happened? Without going into the details I want to remark on two important factors:

— although the attitude of planning has really changed a lot (and this must be regarded as a good achievement), methods of planning have not improved quickly enough;
— lack of definition of the role of the several authorities and especially the ministries of the industrial branches has caused problems. Ministries have intervened in companies to influence the decisions, thereby sharing unnecessarily responsibility between the company managers and the authorities.

The reason for these problems was that the decisions were not decentralized enough and very little has been done to modernize the organization of the controlling authorities, especially the ministries, or for that of the planning information system.

Along with this process something new has been born: the changes brought by the new waves of the economic policy have created a new circle of managers. They have their own opinion about the future of the companies, for which they are responsible. They have not spent their time asking the ministries what to do in their companies. These managers have changed their attitude toward the authorities. They wanted to be the initiators, and they have started to influence the central ideas.

These were also the managers who have got down to the strategic planning work. Some of them, especially those responsible for smaller companies, began with some informal type of strategic planning, without any kind of systematic, regular documentation. Others have chosen another way, that of composing several routines of formal planning methods into a complex, integrated, unified and comprehensive strategic plan. This latter circle of managers has been rather limited but contained some eminent large enterprise managers. But despite their strategic plans they had to make the regular 5- and 1-year plans in harmony with the national planning system, which has developed little in methods, or content.

Before speaking more about this strategic planning practice, let me make a short comparison between official planning and plans, and strategic planning and plans. I have chosen, perhaps a little arbitrarily, some features of planning and I try to compare the same features in both planning practices (Table 12.1).

Naturally few comparisons are perfect. Official planning methods have improved recently to a certain extent and there are very few examples of this ideal strategic planning activity in industry.

However, the main features of official planning and the problems behind them cause companies difficulties in becoming competitive and adaptive.

This is a critical problem in those companies where there is nothing but official planning. These companies more and more fall into an unexpected situation and need the help of the authorities. But the authorities want, and are able, to help them less and less.

The radically changing environment, the strengthening pressure of the competition, the necessary adaption for survival together with the changing behaviour of the central controlling authorities all tend to force the companies to find better management methods, in particular, flexible planning methods. These must be the methods of corporate strategy-making, or strategic planning.

Results of Strategic Planning in Hungary

I could not avoid a short historical review of planning practice in Hungary. I think it is useful to illustrate the development, and at the same time, to demonstrate the present state of art in strategic planning. But while I describe the results of strategic planning one has to remember that this planning is still co-existing with the so-called official planning. Let me give an example. The first company which started strategic planning in Hungary is big and in the rubber industry.

TABLE 12.1

Features	Official planning	Strategic planning
1. Time horizon	5 or 1 year	depending on the characteristics of the company, it can be 5 to 15–20 years
2. Organizing the planning process	periodical	continuous
3. Information base	mostly from the past, and collected just before the planning cycle	partly from the past, but mostly from the future gained by forecasting. Data collection is continuous and the information base is up-dated regularly.
4. Philosophy of planning	satisficing	adaptive
5. Content of the plans	separated chapters of plans: plans for production, sales the necessary manpower, investments, profit, social expenditure, organizing of the jobs, etc.	complex, comprehensive unified strategic actions incorporating the whole process from marketing through R&D, production and to sales
6. Detailing	it has enormous amount of numerical and verbal details	as detailed as it is necessary for decision-making
7. Manipulation of uncertainty	based on one-point, that is deterministic estimates	it takes the uncertainty, and therefore the risk, of strategic actions into account
8. Method	nothing special; simple further planning, generally the continuation of the past tendencies	search for the breaking points in the future tendencies, evaluating the possible actions for the case of several scenarios into the future
9. Purpose of planning	to fulfil the plan, to achieve the set of the plan objectives	to help the adaptation of the company in the changing environment
10. Usage of the plan	with the passage of time the plan loses its immediacy, and at the end of the planning period its only usage can be the explanation of why it has not been fulfilled	it is the means by which top managers manage, control, organize and stimulate the processes and the people. It is a philosophy shared by managers at every level in the company

This company has initiated the best strategic planning system so far. But what are they doing in planning? There is a strategic planning department in the company which reports directly to the general top manager. There are very good specialists in this department: economists, engineers, mathematicians, sociologists and even psychologists. They continuously look for new opportunities, and think about possible innovation and its timing. They also use many specialists from outside the company. These specialists, among them foreign experts, help the company to anticipate future events, especially the technical progress of the business. The planning team is eager to know the place of the company in the world market, to compare systematically their results with those of the competition.

At the same time there is another planning department in the company, which belongs to the economics manager. This department is responsible for making the 5- and 1-year plans, on the basis of information from the national plan. They complete the forms which have to be sent to the industrial authority, the Industrial Ministry, giving information about the company's aims. This parallel planning is not a good solution, but this situation has evolved from the difficult circumstances in which the companies operate in Hungary today. They still have to inform their supervisory authority, which from the first of January 1981 is the Industrial Ministry, about their plans, aims and ideas in every 1 and every 5 years.

But these plans are really not appropriate for steering the companies on today's stormy seas. Some companies have already found a better way to improve their performance. They make strategy for the future. But they are forced to do this through a duplicate planning effort.

Other companies are trying to improve the official planning methods. Some do nothing other than explain why the plans could not have been fulfilled. These companies work on a short-term, day-to-day basis.

Let me enter a little more deeply into the details of strategic planning practice in industry. In the first place it is interesting to show how the companies think about fundamental features, content and meaning of strategic planning. The majority of those who are practising strategic planning agree that strategic planning

— must be a complex, integrated, comprehensive activity which deals with the future survival of the company;
— must be therefore based especially on the information which can be collected about the future;
— has to deal with those areas of activities which have significant effects on the future;
— must be done continuously, that is the objectives and goals, and the strategic actions have to be up-dated with changes in circumstances;

—must be the responsibility of the top management.

Simultaneously there are managers who find it sufficient to concentrate mostly on the technical, technological side of the future. Their strategies contain general ideas about the development of products and technologies, and the investments necessary for these purposes. Apart from the fact that these strategies are not complex, and do not take seriously into account many important factors (such as the future financial or human resources), they are not sufficiently market-oriented. These managers trust in technical progress for a secure future for the company. They say that this is the more certain factor of the future, and all the other economic factors, market demand and prices, production costs, financial and human resources, are unforecastable and therefore are not worth bothering with.

There are interesting examples of the fate of companies having such kind of strategy.

Some of them have been lucky to find a way of product and technology development which is well accepted by the market, that is, which makes profitable production and sale possible. But there are other companies which have made big investments, poured out money into developments the results of which have soon proved to be unreliable. These companies cause great trouble for the economy, because they generally, sooner or later, need some kind of subsidy.

There are passionate debates on the information basis, and the available methods for gaining information about the future. This is an acute problem which is partly caused by the formal planning system.

As the national planning system is a cyclical one, it demands and gives out general information periodically, that is annually and the fifth year. This on the one side means that there is an organized, regulated information exchange between the two, the national and company planning level, just before making the national 5 and 1 year plans.

On the other side there is the problem of the longer view of the future. As the national plans cover 5 years at the most, all the companies who need a longer strategic-planning horizon feel the lack of appropriate central information. This problem is closely connected with the shortening of the national planning period. As the planning activity at the national level is a cyclical, periodical one, the maximum time span which actually can be covered is 5 years.

But after a year there is only a 4-year view, and in the fourth year of the planning cycle there is only one more year of the national plan. As the national plans contain decisions about the future economic policy, growth rate, investment possibilities, etc., and even about the future of some branches of the economy, this often results in uncertainty for the companies closely affected by these decisions.

The arguments of those few companies critically influenced by central decisions have to be accepted. They are more limited in making their own strategy, especially for more than 5 years. But at the same time there are really very few companies in the country whose total activity would be determined by central decisions. I think that the central decisions must be regarded as external conditions, as external opportunities or threats for the company, and they must be brought into the corporate strategy in this manner.

This is a point where I need to emphasize the importance of the personality, knowledge and ability of the top managers. I am convinced about the importance of managerial behaviour in this respect. If the top managers are initiators, real entrepreneurs, and they are interested enough they do make strategies which take into account the possible central steps. Even more importantly, they try to influence the central decisions on the basis of that more detailed and in-depth knowledge and ideas which can be only generated and known on the company level.

There are many managers who share this point of view. These are the new, well-trained and risk-taking top managers, mentioned earlier, who lead in the processes of strategic planning. They must be increasingly strengthened by the state behaviour. The regulating system should operate in such a way that only this kind of managerial attitude will be accepted. Waiting for central directions, and when results are obtained, asking for central help, cannot be an acceptable managerial style.

But besides this very difficult problem (which involves the decision process, the planning and regulating system, the controlling of managerial and company performance and the selection of the managers), there is a methodological problem. This should be easy to solve once the other issues are settled. The methodological problem is a lack of comprehensive knowledge about the various forecasting methods and techniques, and especially those for investigating an uncertain future. These methods are not widely used even in those companies where there is a good strategic-planning practice. Even today, the most commonly used forecasting methods are trend extrapolation, time-series analysis and regression analysis. There are a few examples of econometric modelling but these are mostly theoretical attempts made in research institutes and universities, and not in real company situations.

The application of various judgemental approaches have recently started to arouse the strategy-makers' interest. There are already some practical examples of the use of the Delphi technique and cross-impact analysis for forecasting possible futures. There is still no practical usage of scenario-writing techniques in industry.

The usage of all these techniques understandably did not become interesting and urgent for companies until they themselves felt the effects of uncertainties caused by the rapid changes in the world economy. But this was too late. Companies have to be measured on the basis of how they can adapt to the uncertainties and unexpected surprises.

Once having been pushed into such situations, managers will be eager to find the best available management methods, and among them the most useful forecasting techniques. This highlights another aspect of the problem, the availability of good specialists. We do not yet have sufficient of them, as university education for a long period has not given primary importance to strategic-planning methods. But there is a definite change in this area, and therefore more and more young specialists are emerging from the universities well armed with all the necessary knowledge. They must be well used and allowed to work.

This brings us to the third important aspect on which there is debate in Hungary. This is the involvement of the top managers in the planning process. There are managers who have a firm conviction that they should make strategy alone and for just themselves, or possibly with, and for, just a narrow management band. They mostly have strategies which are neither clearly defined, nor documented, and generally not well founded or validated. These strategies sometimes exist only in the heads of the managers. The ideas in these strategies are very often autocratic and divorced from reality.

There is another type of the manager who thinks that the most detailed strategy is the best. They generally pursue the planning department to make more and more calculations often "l'art pour l'art". The majority of the calculations deal with the past and try hard to extrapolate the future on every aspect of the company. These strategies are very similar in content and method, to the earlier practice of formal planning.

Another typical feature of this kind of strategic planning can be that the involvement of top management in the planning process becomes very formal. It is confined to asking for more and more numbers, which is rarely enough to generate ideas and innovations in the company. Creative thought should be initiated, managed and stimulated by top management.

At last let me mention those managers who, in my opinion, have chosen the best way to be involved in the planning process. Their opinion is that the strategic planning process must be a democratic one. They involve everyone from inside the company, whose knowledge they rely on, and many good specialists from outside, too. They are at the same time very active in the planning process, especially in developing objectives and shaping and selecting strategic actions. They are generally managers of the innovative type, searching for new opportunities for the company. They generally keep the planning process moving, continuously asking for relevant information, proposals and ideas. They use the more sophisticated methods for generating more alternatives and to evaluate their possible future effects. They do not forget that their strategy can be implemented only if they can have it accepted by the collective and the macro and mezzo environment. This is on the one side the question of democracy and involvement of the people, and on the other side a necessary conciliation process with the environment; buyers, suppliers, co-operators, and the diverse authorities.

I have tried to give a picture about the reality of the strategic planning behaviour of the Hungarian managers. Let me explore further on a cross-section of planning practice itself.

In doing this I will mostly write about the practice of the best companies. At this point let me mention the name of that top manager, who, many years ago, developed a strategic planning system for his company. The name of this manager is Horvath Laszlo. He wrote a book on this experience with the title: *The long range plan of a company.** It was issued in 1973 by the Economic and Law Publishing House in Budapest. This was the first practical book about strategic planning in Hungary. His book, and previous and subsequent articles, have had a great influence on strategic-planning practice. Those companies who are most effective in strategic planning have followed in his path and have used his ideas and practical approaches to strategic planning. They have tried to find the best methods to fit the unique characteristics of their companies. Unfortunately this is at present only a small portion of all industrial companies.

I would estimate it can be only 5 – 10 per cent of the whole. The other two types of strategic planning attitude I have mentioned come to about another 15 – 20 per cent. Altogether 20 – 30 per cent of the industrial companies have some kind of strategic-type planning practice, together with the official planning. The remainder have some version of the official planning.

Let me return to the practice of the best companies. Firstly their strategic plans are complex and integrated, focus on questions of vital importance and are initiated and managed by top management.

They consist of three main parts:

— the objectives and goal system,
— the analysis of resources and means,
— strategic actions.

Strategic planning starts with the determination of the objectives, purposes and goals. These are closely connected to the main principles of the companies, which are:

* In Hungarian: *Horváth László: A vállalat távlati terve. Közgazdasági és Jogi Könyvkiado,* Budapest, 1973.

—harmonizing or adjusting,
—survival,
—development,
—risk,
—humanity,
—democracy.

Harmonizing means that the company's interests must be in tune with that of the society. The interest of a company is not allowed to violate rules of morality, and must take into account objectives for the development of society.

The principle of survival requires no explanation.

Development is one step further than simple survival. It is the aspirations for maintaining the quality of life in the company, strengthening the company and, where justified, growing.

Risk refers to the situation of competition, in which the companies have to live and struggle. It is evident that risks have to be taken if a company is to win.

The principles of humanity and democracy are concerned with peoples' life in the company. In the long run the company's activity must be for the benefit of employees of the company. This means dealing with social situations, increases of income, developing personal abilities and skills involving training and retraining, allowing wide participation in management.

On the basis of these basic principles a hierarchy of objectives, purposes and goals is usually determined. The main groups of the objectives are:

—harmonising with the objectives of the national economy;
—solvency, effectiveness, and profit-making, market development and development of technical and economic potential;
—having good specialists.

The main difference between those objectives and general principles is that the objectives are quantified and definitive. They are the ends which the company seeks to achieve through its strategic actions. Such kinds of quantitatively expressed objectives can be, for example:

—profit (throughout the planning horizon),
—the proportion of profit available for investment, and for employees,
—market share,
—proportion of new products,
—performance standards.

Objective systems thus contain several groups of objectives, of varying importance and time horizon, which makes it possible to build up a hierarchy of objectives.

This is only a very broad picture of strategic objectives. These always occur in the strategies, but vary considerably with each company.

The second common feature of the strategies is the analysis of resources and means. This has to be explained more broadly. It means a deep and honest appreciation of the company's capabilities in the areas of:

— marketing,
— production,
— R & D,
— finance,
— machinery,
— manpower,
— organization,
— management,
— information systems.

This appreciation aims at finding the opportunities and limitations which will effect the achievement of objectives.

The third major part of the strategies is the identification of strategic actions. The most common types of actions cover:

— R & D,
— production and marketing,
— investment actions,
— training and retraining.

In most cases the actions are considered in all aspects and interrelationships, and for the whole life cycle.

In some cases described the options usually include R & D actions or investment. Alternative actions are rarely fully worked out. Their purpose is to prepare the company for unanticipated future changes, and help it to shorten its reaction time. At present this is the usual practice of only a few companies do strategic planning. This failure can cause serious adaptation problems in the sometimes rapidly changing conditions.

There is one very interesting trend in planning the timing of actions. This is caused through the rapidity of change, uncertainty, and the increasing scarcity of resources.

Timing deals with the ordering of the various actions sequentially in parallel in terms of time. The techniques used are generally some kind of a heuristic approach. Some companies using mathematical methods to improve the reliability of planning are trying to apply simulation technique for timing.

To sum up, I think that this group of companies are ahead in strategy-making. More typically objective formulation is the strongest and the elaboration of actions, especially sensibility analysis, in the weakest point of strategic planning practice.

No company applies contingency planning in Hungary at all.

I have already mentioned briefly the application of mathematical methods and computers in planning. Let me elaborate.

It is a weak area in every type of planning. At the end of the sixties there was a great boom in these methods. Most companies, but generally on the Ministries' initiatives, started to use linear programming methods as the basis of their 5-year plans. I was that time in the "Industrial Economics, System Design and Computing Institute" of one of the Ministries and had the chance of constructing eight such linear programming models. But this enthusiasm has cooled off rather rapidly, because of the many constraints of the method. But unfortunately companies have tended to swing to the other extreme. As they were disappointed in linear programming they have rejected all mathematical methods. I undertook a research study 4 years ago to obtain practical knowledge about the methods used in planning. Thirty companies in different areas were interviewed. I found two who used mathematical approaches in planning. One used a linear programming model for optimizing resource utilization, the other a simple simulation model which was used for comparing possible future production, sales and investment actions on the basis of changes in the market. The model also covered possible changes in the regulating system, that is proportions of profit shared between the company and the state. The company has found this model, which was started by me 6 years ago, interesting and useful, and therefore uses it regularly if some basic data or condition supposed has changed or if there has emerged any good idea worth checking as a "what if" possibility. They have asked to change the model twice when significant structural changes have happened in the regulating system that means the model has to be reformulated.

The programme was written by a mathematician for an ICL System 4 computer, in FORTRAN. I wrote about this modelling in a publication issued in 1980 with the title: *Methods for preparing strategic decisions.**

The simulation method has not been widely used although there are a few examples, as I have mentioned for the timing strategic actions.

Over all I have to acknowledge that in strategic planning there are very few applications of mathematical methods. Only the already mentioned qualitative and quantitative forecasting techniques are used. This is mostly because of lack of knowledge. There are not too many people in Hungary who are familiar with up-to-date mathematical methods which can be used in planning. There are also computer and software problems. A further

---

* The Hungarian title was: Csath Magdolna: A stratégiai terv-döntések elökészitésének módszerei. KG INFORMATIK, Budapest, 1980.

problem is the general lack of special information systems for planning.

Even the best strategic planning practices suffer from these deficiencies. Let me turn to a very much debated point of strategic planning, the time horizon.

There is a permanent discussion about the time horizon of strategic planning.

There are managers who say that because of the fast changing of inside and outside circumstances it is impossible to plan for a longer period than 5 years.

Others state that the company can only plan for the same period of time for which the national plans are drawn up. They say they need the information of the national plans for company planning. However, those who want to keep firm control of the company's future think differently. Firstly, their basic principle is that their only chance to take precautions against threats or to take advantage of the opportunities of the future is if they think about it in advance, and for as long ahead as it is necessary. These managers take into consideration the behaviour of the government, plans and the regulating systems, and all other factors which can change and therefore can cause problems or give good possibilities for the company's activity.

Let me give an example of taking the regulating system into account. The company I have already mentioned which uses simulation techniques for planning has built this factor as a stochastic one into the model. They use there a triangular distribution to characterize changes of the regulating system. They assign three values on the basis of their past experiences and the present and possible future national economic situation. The highest, which is the pessimistic value, shows that maximum portion of the company's profit, which can be due as tax: the lowest value shows that minimum taxation rate which can be envisaged to provide the most optimistic estimate of profit remaining in the company. The first value can be estimated in the first place on the basis of the problems of the economy and the contribution of the company to solving them.

The second value can be given on the basis of the probable future economic policy, the possible degree of centralization of incomes, the welfare programmes, the stimulation of the economy, etc. Between these two extreme values the company determines a so-called realistic value with the help of known tendencies, leaving out the possibility of big changes in state behaviour, and in the regulating system. After doing this the company uses the model to investigate the different strategic actions against the future possibilities. They take similar action with market possibilities and other elements.

The managers who want to be prepared for future changes and do not want to restrict their ideas about the future because of the national plans choose a different time horizon for their strategic planning. The time horizon is generally settled between 5 and 15–20 years. There are typical features of the companies which are used when deciding the planning horizon. They have not the same importance everywhere, but they are generally taken into consideration in every company. These typical features are the following:

— life cycle of the products,
— the obsoletion cycle of the technologies,
— the obsoletion time of the crafts and professions,
— the age of the machinery and equipment,
— the average length of service of the people in the company,
— the role in the market; leader or follower,
— the position in innovation,
— the whole lifetime of the main strategic actions.

When using these factors to determine the planning horizon that put the weight on those 8 which are for some reason especially important. There is another fact worth mentioning. The timing of strategic actions can modify the planning horizon. The maximum time span of the parellal and sequentially scheduled actions is also an important factor.

Naturally the fixing of a given planning horizon does not mean that every activity has to be elaborated in the same detail.

There are dominant strategic actions and objectives which must more carefully elaborated over a longer period.

In practice companies in the machine-building, chemical and pharmaceutical industries have a planning horizon at about 10 years. Companies in light industry have a 5- to 6-year planning horizon and those in the metallurgical, ship-building, motor-train or rubber industry have a 10- to 20-year planning horizon.

How should I summarize my observations and opinions about strategic planning in Hungary? It is a rather new practice here and not at all widespread in application.

The application and the methods used, vary with the capabilities of the managers. However, the competitive situation and the independence of the company are also relevant factors. The more stormy the competition the company has to weather, and the more it has to solve its problems without help, the more probable it is that it will be interested in making strategy.

The methods have to be improved, especially in respect of the use of mathematical methods and computers in the planning process.

Good books are needed, both in translation and of Hungarian authorship.*

It is very important to develop, both technically and in content, the information base of planning. This means the necessity of developing information systems for planning on the one hand, and the use of the more sophisticated forecasting and appraisal methods, on the other hand.

It would help the strategic planning activity of the companies a lot, if the national planning system moved faster towards a strategic concept with less detail, more action-orientation. It should look further into the future for the most important areas and should be continuous process, having a revolving approach so that the length of planning horizon is constant. This activity has already started at the national level. The sixth 5-year plan which started in 1981 has already been made less detailed and more flexible. But I think we have only taken the first steps towards an up-to-date dual level planning system. At this point I should mention the problem of controlling the 5- and 1-year plans of the companies, and the role of the Ministries in this process. I should like to remind readers of the organization problem mentioned previously, that is, that the modernization of the organization of the central decision-making authorities did not take place in 1968. As a continuation of the reform, the three great industrial Ministries—the Metallurgical and Machine-building, the Light and the Heavy Industrial Ministries—were merged with a reduced number of staff from 1st January 1982 with the name Industrial Ministry.

The new Ministry still has not really found its place in the national planning system. It deals, for example, with the reviewing of the companies' plans in the industry and with comparing their total numbers with the same ones in the national plans. This is naturally not the broken-down numbers of the national plan on the company level, but the inversion of it, that is, the building up of some of the values in the national plan from the companies' numbers. Supposing that the companies' plans are correct, it can only be a snapshot of the ideas in the industry, which will perhaps change in the future. This is that side of the planning activity which asks for urgent change.

But there is another new side of the planning activity which was started soon after the foundation of the new Ministry. This is long-range planning for several industrial branches, and is a shared activity with the National Planning Office.

At the same time the Ministry has started a widespread educational

* The first comprehensive book on strategy-making will probably come out in 1983 with the title: Strategy making: theory and practice. (The authors: László Horváth and (Magdolna Csath.) David E. Hussey's well-known and widely translated book, *Introducing Corporate Planning* will soon be published in Hungarian. Both books will be edited by the Hungarian Economic and Law Publishing House, Budapest.

programme for those companies who are not yet dealing with strategic planning.

The Economic and Planning Department of the Ministry has organized a series of lectures given by theoreticians and top managers experienced in the practice of strategic planning. In addition it has made available a guide to strategic planning and a list of the accessible literature on strategy-making for the companies.

This initiative will possibly help the companies to understand the importance of strategy-making and to start them looking for the best way to establish their own strategic-planning methods.

The development of planning methods has begun at both levels, but there is still very much to do, including the tidying-up of the planning activity in the Industrial and remaining other Ministries of Branches of the economy. In addition to the development of the planning system and methods, it is very important to have a regulating system which is able to respond rapidly to changes in the environment.

It has to be consistently normative and has to let those companies with best performances to develop. This is an essential condition for making managers interested in strategy formulation.

The short history of strategic planning in Hungary has already proved that the companies who had a sound strategy, were more easily able to adopt themselves to the changing environment, including the regulating system and state behaviour.

They seldom or never need help from the authorities. They have been able to develop better, and have rather good products, more up-to-date technologies and better specialists. This demonstrates a direction which is worth while supporting and stimulating. This improves chances of success for the companies, and ultimately helps the whole economy to adapt more quickly to the rapid changes everywhere.

This was very nicely expressed by a distinguished economist of Hungary, Gábor Havas, who has written in one of his articles that "Minor 'tactics' are suitable only for gaining time, but real economic improvement can only be reached through comprehensive strategies."

And finally, let me cite the great Hungarian reigning prince Gábor Bethlen who, in the seventeenth century, gave a very pregnant manifestation of strategic thinking when he said, that: "Policy must be made for a hundred years ahead. It should never be forgotten that the big stone thrown into a well by one madman cannot be extracted by a hundred clever people."

Appendix

The article is based on the following research studies and other materials:

Research Studies and Lectures:

1. A research on the fifth 5-year planning practice of the industrial companies based on interviews with planning specialists and top managers.
It was done in 1977. About thirty companies were involved into the research. (110 pp.)
2. A research on the sixth 5-year planning practice of the industrial companies based on answers given to a question-list in connection with the planning problems.
It has just been finished at the beginning of 1982. (60 pp.)
3. Several lectures on strategic planning for managers in the Management Education Centres in Budapest, and lecture-notes given to the listeners.
4. A study based on reviewing twenty-five strategies from the chemical industry area. It was made in 1980. (121 pp.)
5. Proposals on improvement of the strategic planning methods for the chemical companies. A study for the Ministry of Heavy Industry. It was done in 1980. (113 pp.)
6. A study based on reviewing forty-seven strategies from several areas of the industry. It has just been finished at the beginning of 1982.

Articles

1. Contradictions of planning in the industrial branches. *The Observer*, Budapest, 29 Mar. 1978. (1 p.)
2. About the medium-term planning problems on the basis of the fifth five year planning in the industry. *Economic Review*, Budapest, 6   1978.
3. The methods of making decisions based on strategic planning. KG INFORMATIK (which was the publishing authority of the Machine-building and Metallurgical Ministry). It was issued in 1980. (63 pp.)
4. Strategic planning in the companies. *The Observer*, 28 may 1980. (2 pp.)
5. Simulation methods in Corporate planning (together with Dezsö Karácsony, who is an economical manager of a telecommunication company). *The Observer*, 4 Feb. 1981. (2 p).

PART 2

Does Corporate Planning Pay?

Introduction to Part 2

Until the 1970s there was little hard evidence that corporate planning was an economically viable activity: in other words, that it does pay. True, there was plenty of individual testimony of the case history type, which provided considerable insight into many other aspects of planning. But evidence from the minority of organisations prepared to make public, coherent statements in an objective way is hardly sufficient to prove that the majority would benefit.

Some early surveys included opinion from respondents on the benefits of planning. Tayor and Irving (Chapter 4) quote a number of these. But again this is indicative, rather than definitive evidence. Most surveys, as will have already been seen, include some statistical evidence on the depth of satisfaction or dissatisfaction chief executives felt over their planning efforts. This makes good supporting evidence, but does not by itself prove that corporate planning pays off.

In 1970 the position changed, and three major research studies were published which provided proof of the value of corporate planning.

Thune and House (Chapter 13) analysed the results of certain U.S. companies up to 1965, using matched pairs of "planning" and "non-planning" companies. The results were further analysed so that each "planning" company's performance after the introduction of planning was compared with its pre-planning performance. For the first time, clear evidence was produced which demonstrated that planning, in general, did lead to an improvement in results.

Herold[1] extended and validated part of the Thune and House study, although it was only possible to do this for five of the eighteen matched pairs of companies used in the original work. All of these five were in the drug and chemical industries. Herold concluded that companies in those industries which engaged in corporate planning significantly out-performed companies that did not.

Both of these companies had a relatively small sample size, although that for the Thune and House study is large enough to allow one to feel some confidence in it.

Vancil (Chapter 14) published some findings on the accuracy of long

293

range planning, based on a "data bank" provided by sixty planning companies. This study showed how accuracy could be increased through attention to the design of the process (these findings are relevant to Part 3 of this book). Having indicated that accuracy was attainable, the author questioned whether it was desirable. Too much emphasis on accuracy could lead to self-fulfilling prophecies, which stifles creative thinking and the willingness to take risks.

The third research landmark which appeared in 1970 was the publication of a study of the success of acquisitions in American firms by Ansoff, Avner, Brandenburg, Portner and Radosevich. This had a much larger sample base of ninety-three usable responses, and provided the first "quantitative and statistically significant proof that acquisition planning pays". On the basis of the financial criteria in the study "planners" both out-performed and performed more predictably than "non-planners". (Other aspects of acquisition behaviour are included in the work by Kitching Part 4, Chapter 29.)

Yet another study was published in 1975. Malik and Karger (Chapter 16), using a sample of thirty-eight companies in three industries and comparing "planners" and "non-planners", again proved that planning pays.

The final study selected for this part (Bowman, Chapter 17) used a very different research technique. This analysed the annual reports of eight-two American companies in the food-processing industry. The more successful companies were found to show "strategy and a concern for strategy" through their annual reports. Unsuccessful companies complained about the effect of weather and government controls, were less clear about their plans and strategies, and tended to be less willing to change.

This research study is fun to read, and suggests that those who know where they are going have more chance of getting there. The cynic might be foreveen for suggesting that what it also shows is the alacrity with which managers claim credit for all good results and find excuses for bad ones!

All of this body of research is American based, and I know of no parallel studies from other countries. It seems reasonable that the findings should be equally valid in other countries. There is perhaps one caution. In the U.K. we do not always introduce new approaches in the appropriate way, and it may well be that fewer British companies would achieve benefits from planning than is the case in the U.S.A. Channon[2] found that British companies did not apply the American divisional management concept as effectively as the Americans did, and this was one reason for the lower performance in the U.K. Would a similar conclusion hold good for corporate planning? I have no evidence, and can only suggest that the matter is worth pondering.

References

1. D. M. Herold (1972) Long range planning and organisational performance: A cross validation study, *Academy of Management Journal*, March 1972.
2. D. F. Channon (1973) *The Strategy and Structure of British Enterprise*, MacMillan.

13

Where Long Range Planning Pays Off: Findings of a survey of formal, informal planners

S. S. THUNE AND R. J. HOUSE

This article reports the results of a study of the changes in economic performance associated with formal long-range planning in U.S. firms with annual sales of $75 million or more. To determine whether changes in performance are associated with long-range planning it is necessary to make two comparisons: *first*, the performances of a group of companies over two equal periods of time before and after they initiated planning, and, *second*, the performances, during a comparable period of time, of companies that use formal planning with a group of comparable companies that do not. Further, it is necessary to discount any differences found in the above comparisons that may have resulted from such factors as inertia prior to the initiation of long-range planning, historical factors such as patent advantages, or historically superior managerial performance.

In order to make the above comparisons, a sample of thirty-six firms representing six industrial groups was carefully selected from ninety-two companies that responded to a questionnaire submitted by the authors.[1] The purpose of the questionnaire was to identify those companies actively engaged in formal long-range planning. Responding companies were classified as formal planners if their questionnaire responses indicated that

This article was originally published in *Business Horizons*, XIII: 81–87 (1970), August 1970.

Copyright 1970, by the Foundation for the School of Business at Indiana University. Reprinted by permission.

Mr. Thune is corporate planning manager for the Givaudan Corp.; Mr. House is an associate professor of management, the Bernard M. Baruch College of The City University of New York, and a member of Dunnuck, Folton & Associates, management consultants.

[1] All firms in nine industries with sales of $75 million for 1965 were sent the questionnaire. Of the 145 firms contacted, 92 responded.

they determined corporate strategy and goals for at least three years ahead, and if they established specific action programs, projects, and procedures for achieving the goals. Companies that did not meet these requirements were classified as informal planners.

Table 13.1 presents a breakdown of the respondents by planning approach and industry. From the ninety-two responding companies, seventeen formal and nineteen informal planners were selected in a manner permitting reasonable comparisons over at least seven years. Table 13.2 describes these companies by industry, and by sales of the base-line date, that is, the date they initiated formal planning. As the table shows, the pairs of firms (formal–informal) are well matched.

TABLE 13.1. *Summary of Questionnaire Response*

Industry	Number mailed	Companies responding	Formal planners	Informal planners
Drug	14	8	6	2
Food	21	9	6	3
Chemical	22	19	16	3
Steel	16	7	4	3
Oil	22	17	14	3
Machinery	14	8	3	5
Communications	4	3	2	1
Electronics	23	16	16	0
Aircraft	9	5	4	1
Total	145	92	71	21

Company Performances

The performances of formal and informal planners were computed over periods of seven to fifteen years, depending on their industry. In some industries (steel, for example) it was possible to make comparisons over a period as long as eleven years because of the early date at which long-range planning was introduced in that industry. The specific periods studied varied by industry as follows: drugs, 1960–65; food, 1958–65; chemicals, 1958–65; steel, 1955–65 oil, 1959–65; and machinery, 1959–65.

The performances of the companies were then analyzed in terms of five economic measures: sales, stock prices, earnings per common share, return on common equity, and return on total capital employed.[2] A statistical analysis comparing all formal versus informal planners during the above periods (see Fig 13.1) shows that the planners significantly outperformed

[2] All indexes are adjusted for changes in the number of common shares outstanding. Changes in accounting procedures were taken into account in the calculations and analysis.

TABLE 13.2. *Composition of sample**

Industry group			Sales as of base line data		
		Formal planners		Informal planners	
Drug	A	180	A'	160	
	B	200	B'	200	
	C	220	C'	270	
	Ave.	*200*	Ave.	*210*	
Chemical	A	105	A'	160	
	B	115	B'	175	
	C	225	C'	235	
	Ave.	*143*	Ave.	*190*	
Machinery	A	110	A'	155	
	B	160	B'	160	
	C	180	C'	200	
	Ave.	*150*	Ave.	*173*	
Oil	A	370	A'	310	
	B	1,200	B'	560	
	C	1,760	C'	1,100	
			D'	775	
	Ave.	*1,110*	·Ave.	*686*	
Food	A	350	A'	300	
	B	500	B'	315	
			C'	415	
	Ave.	*425*	Ave.	*380*	
Steel	A	75	A'	100	
	B	700	B'	110	
	C	1,100	C'	710	
	Ave.	*625*	Ave.	*307*	

* A and A', B and B', . . . = matched pairs.

the informal planners on three of the five measures: earnings per share (44 percent), earnings on common equity (38 percent), and earnings on total capital employed (32 percent). Because these results are statistically significant, average data can be used for comparison.[3] Although the results for average sales and stock price appreciation were also substantially greater for the planners, a company-by-company comparison showed that these averages were greatly influenced by a single company. The average data, therefore, could not be used.

A second way to analyze the data is to compare the performance of the formal planners from the time they initiated planning through 1965 with

[3] The statistical method used was a two-way analysis of variance, using industrial grouping and formal planners versus informal planners as the independent variables, and changes in sales, stock prices, earnings on common equity, earnings per share, and earnings on total capital as the dependent variables. Five analyses of variance were computed, one for each measure of economic performance.

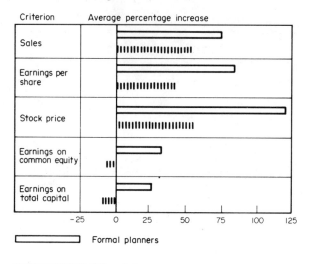

FIG. 13.1. *Performances of formal and informal planners during planning period.*

their own performance over an equal period of time prior to the start of formal planning. Figure 13.2 presents such a comparison for five of the six industries based on data available for that period of time. (The steel companies were omitted because the preplanning period for this industry was atypical; the eleven-year period prior to 1955, the year in which the companies initiated formal long-range planning, would have required consideration of performance during World War II.)

Here again, we find a remarkable association between economic performance and long-range planning; planners outperformed themselves on all three available measures of economic performance. The increases are impressive: 38 percent in sales, 64 percent in earnings per share, and 56 percent in stock price appreciation. Data on earnings on common equity and total capital are not available for the preplanning period.

Although the preceding comparisons make an impressive case for long-range planning, they could have resulted from other factors: generally superior management, an early product monopoly position, or some other earlier advantage that resulted in continuing superior performance. To determine whether such forces did, indeed, account for our findings, the performance of the informal planners was compared to the performance of the formal planners during a period of time *prior* to the data formal planning was adopted. The length of time over which this comparison was made was equal to the period during which formal and informal planners were compared in Figs. 13.1 and 13.2. This comparison showed no significant difference between the two types of planners.

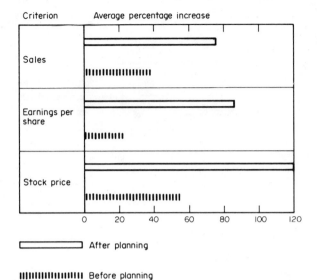

FIG. 13.2. *Performances of companies before and after formal planning. Data used for five industries. Steel was excluded because the preplanning period for this industry was a typical. Data on earnings on common equity and total capital were not available for the preplanning period.*

Thus, the first major conclusion of the study is quite clear: formal planners, from the time they initiated long-range planning through 1965, significantly outperformed informal planners with respect to earnings per share, earnings on common equity, and earnings on total capital employed. Furthermore, these companies outperformed their own records based on an equal period of time before they began formal planning. Finally, informal planners did not surpass formal planners on any of the measures of economic performance after long-range planning was introduced.

Industry-by-industry Comparisons

The second phase of the study consisted of an industry-by-industry analysis. In this phase, the informal planners were compared to the formal planners within each industry; their performance during the planning period was compared with their own performance during an equal period of time prior to the adoption of formal plans. Figure 13.3 presents comparisons of the average changes in economic performance for both types of planners, by industry, during the planning period.

The long-range planning firms in the drug, chemical, and machinery industries consistently outperformed the informal planners on all five

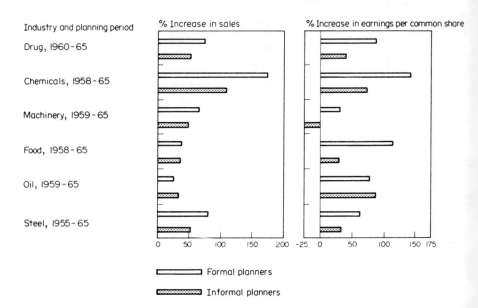

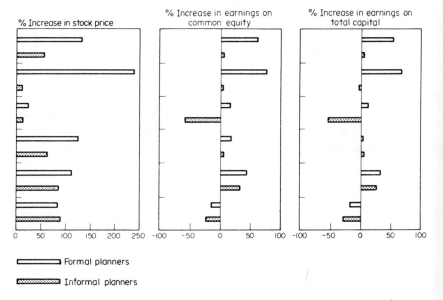

FIG. 13.3. *Performances for formal and informal planners during planning period.*

criteria of business success. It can also be seen that the planners in the food industry did better with respect to earnings per common share, stock price appreciation, and earnings on common equity; were approximately equal to informal planners with respect to sales increases; and were slightly lower with respect to earnings on total capital.

However, from 1950 through 1957, prior to the adoption of formal planning by the food industry, the planners performed slightly better than the informal planners in all categories. This earlier advantage suggests that their higher performance after the initiation of long-range planning may well be a result of their performance during the previous planning period. Thus, these findings should be discounted since no clear association can be established between economic performance in the food industry and long-range planning.

The same phenomenon occurred prior to the adoption of formal planning in the oil industry; for the period from 1952 through 1958, companies that began formal planning in 1959 outperformed informal planners in all five measures of economic performance. Thus, the slightly superior economic performance of the planners in the oil industry during the planning period is not only associated with the initiation of long-range planning but also with earlier competitive performance. With respect to the steel industry, no comparisons were possible for an equal period prior to the adoption of long-range planning because of the early date at which planning was initiated in this industry.

Why Industrial Differences?

It is clear that companies that initiated formalized long-range planning in the drug, chemical, and machinery industries have significant competitive advantages over those that did not, beginning with the time they started planning through 1965. These findings raise the question as to why formal long-range planning is more closely associated with economic performance in certain industries. For example, we might ask why the food, oil, and steel companies did not enjoy the same economic advantages after initiating planning, even though their preplanning performance had been better than that of the informal planners.

Several factors may account for these findings. First, political or governmental factors may have a bearing on firm performance; for example, the production and distribution of oil are known to be highly dependent on international political forces and of steel on defense plans. However, we find this explanation does not hold in the food industry where production and distribution are not related to such factors.

Another factor that may account for industry differences concerning the association between planning and performance may be the size of the companies within the industry. To test this possibility, correlations were computed between the sales of the company as of the initiation of planning and changes in the five indexes of business success. As can be seen from Table 13.3 consistent negative correlations were found between sales and economic performance for the long-range planners; the opposite was found for informal planners. Thus, among the informal planners the rich got richer; among the formal planners, the poor got richer.

TABLE 13.3. *Correlations Between Sales at Beginning of Planning Period and Changes in Measures of Economic Performance*

Increase	Formal planners	Informal planners
Sales	−.404	.278
Earnings per share	−.301	.204
Stock price	−.210	.081
Earnings on total capital	−.302	.326
Earnings on common equity	−.296	.427

Differences in the performance of planners from industry to industry might also be attributed to the degree of competitiveness in the market place. All three industries in which formal planners had the least impressive results operate in markets characterized by a lower rate of technological innovation and new product introduction. On the face of it, this appears to be a plausible explanation. One indication of technological innovation within an industry is the amount of expenditure for research and development. Table 13.4 presents data on R&D expenditures in the six

TABLE 13.4. *R&D Funds in Manufacturing Companies (as % of net sales, 1960—65)*

Industry	1960	1961	1962	1963	1964	1965
Food and kindred products	0.4	0.4	0.4	0.4	0.4	0.4
Chemicals and allied products	4.5	4.3	4.2	4.3	4.5	4.2
Industrial chemicals	5.7	5.2	4.9	5.1	5.0	4.6
Drugs and medicines	4.6	4.3	4.3	4.7	5.9	5.9
Petroleum refining and extraction	1.0	1.0	1.0	1.0	1.2	1.2
Primary metals	0.8	0.8	0.8	0.8	0.8	0.8
Primary ferrous products	0.6	0.7	0.6	0.7	0.7	0.7
Machinery	4.7	4.2	4.0	4.2	4.3	4.1

Source: *Basic Research, Applied Research and Development in Industry, 1962 and 1965* (Survey of Science Resources Series; National Science Foundation, NSF 65—68).

industries studied from 1960 to 1965. It is clear that the advantages associated with formal long-range planning are primarily concentrated in the more rapidly changing industries, and that positive economic performance and formal planning are most strongly related among the medium-size companies in the rapidly changing markets.

In this study, companies that engage in formal long-range planning, when considered as a group, have historically outperformed a comparable group of informal planners. Further, it was found that the successful economic results associated with long-range planning tend to take place in the rapidly changing industries and among the companies of medium size. These findings are consistent with what we would expect intuitively; it would be expected that changes in managerial practices in smaller firms are less likely to be offset by inertia and more likely to exert leverage.

However, it would probably be naive to conclude that formal planning is the sole cause of the successful performance of the firms studied. It is more likely that these companies are using other analytically oriented and modern management practices in other decision areas as well. For example, we have speculated that firms engaged in formal planning also use more sophisticated methods for organization design and analysis; managerial selection, development, and compensation; and administrative control. Thus, it is most likely that formal planning is a characteristic of a well-managed firm rather than the single cause of successful economic performance.

Although the data make an impressive case for long-range planning by firms in the medium-size, rapidly changing category, the results should be considered suggestive rather than conclusive. Because serious efforts were made to isolate critical variables by matching companies by size and industry, the sample was necessarily small, and the matched groups were still less than perfectly comparable.

14

The Accuracy of Long Range Planning

R. F. VANCIL

How accurate is corporate planning? What factors affect that accuracy? Is accuracy even desirable?

Formal long-range planning—perhaps the most significant new management development to emerge in the 1960's—has now been around long enough to permit us to begin to answer these questions. In this brief article I shall make a start.

As part of an ongoing program of research and instruction in formal planning systems at the Harvard Business School, corporate planners from some 60 companies participated during the last academic year in the creation of a "data bank" of detailed information about planning practices.

For several months these persons—whose companies constitute a broad cross section of U.S. business, though the sample is biased in that it represents only those companies involved in formal long-range planning—supplied answers to more than a thousand questions. So the bank is rich in the scope of its data, though its depositors are relatively few.

To obtain answers to one set of questions, we asked the planners to dig out copies of the plans prepared in previous years and report their contents. The number of respondents here was small, reflecting the laboriousness of the task the turnover of planning personnel, the inability to find old documents, and the simple fact that some companies have not been doing

Reprinted by permission of the *Harvard Business Review* "The accuracy of long range planning by Richard F. Vancil (September–October 1970). Copyright © 1970 by the President and Fellows of Harvard College; all rights reserved.

Author's note: A comprehensive report of the methodology used and the findings from the survey from which this report is drawn was presented at the third annual Workshop for Planning Executives, held at the Harvard Business School in May 1970. Copies of the proceedings document, *Formal Planning Systems—1970*, can be ordered from the Intercollegiate Case Clearing House, Soldiers Field, Boston, Mass. 02163. That document also acknowledges the substantial contributions which many of my students and faculty colleagues have made to this project.

long range planning very long. Nonetheless, the data from their replies present a fascinating first look at how accurate the planning has been in these companies. One item, sales volume, is shown in *Exhibit I*.

Most companies' long-range plans are for five years ahead, so those prepared in 1964 were the first attempts to forecast 1969 sales revenue. For the 16 companies which reported their 1964 plans, the revenue planned for 1969 turned out to be only 84 % of the volume actually generated in 1969.

As the graph shows, the average accuracy improved progressively as the year under consideration approached—which, of course, is not surprising. The 1969 revenues which 39 companies indicated they set in 1968 amounted, on average, to 99 % of the actual volume. Another measure of the increasing accuracy of shorter term forecasting is reflected in the dispersion of the planned revenue/actual revenue ratio; the standard deviation from the mean was 27.8 percentage points in 1964 and only 7.5 percentage points in 1968.

The plans turned out to be consistently conservative. This can be attributed to at least two factors:

1. Most acquisitions are unplannable events, at least in terms of size and timing. Thus, if 1969 sales revenues included the contribution of recently acquired companies, the plans of earlier years should not be evaluated in terms of subsequent actual results. Unfortunately, we were unable to isolate such instances in our data, so all I can say with certainty is that acquisitions cause a downward bias in the ratios in *Exhibit I*.

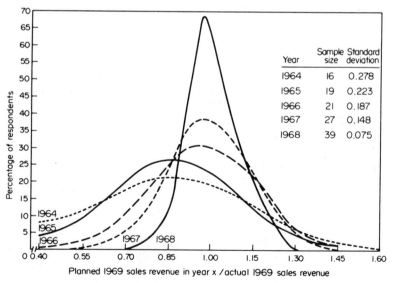

Year	Sample size	Standard deviation
1964	16	0.278
1965	19	0.223
1966	21	0.187
1967	27	0.148
1968	39	0.075

Planned 1969 sales revenue in year x /actual 1969 sales revenue

FIG. 14.1. *Accuracy of companies' planned 1964–1968. Planned 1969 sales revenue in year x/Actual 1969 sales revenue*

2. Inflation also tends to make plans appear conservative in retrospect, at least to the extent that plans are prepared in terms of then-current price levels. Using the composite Industrial Price Index to adjust all figures to 1969 dollars has the effect shown in *Exhibit II*.

Exhibit II. *Accuracy of companies' planned 1969 revenues, 1964—1968, adjusted for inflation via Industrial Price Index*

Year plan was prepared	Mean ratio of planned/actual 1969 revenue		Industrial Price Index (1957—1959 = 100)
	Raw data	Price adjusted	
1964	.841	.937	101.2
1965	.849	.933	102.5
1966	.951	1.024	104.7
1967	.972	1.030	106.3
1968	.986	1.020	109.0
1969			est. 112.7

The price-adjusted figures may be a better measure of the accuracy of planning than the raw data. While plans are expressed in financial terms, they are executed in physical action such as plant construction. So the conservatism of the 1964 and 1965 plans is not as great as it first appears.

On the other hand, the slight optimism in 1966—1968 may not be due entirely to the expansionist psychology of those times; as the rate of inflation increased in the late 1960's, corporate planners may have incorporated its expected effects into their forecasts. In that event, the price adjustments for those years in *Exhibit II* would be redundant.

What Affects Accuracy?

Having large amounts of data on file for each of the participating companies, we were able to search for the causes of accuracy in a variety of dimensions. One subset of these dimensions, which we call "situational factors," describes the corporate situation in which long-range planning is being done. Another is "system design features," describing various aspects of the formal planning system used by each company.

Situational Factors

To our surprise, the situational factors do not provide much explanation of why corporations differ in their ability to plan accurately. We have found no significant correlations between planning accuracy and such factors as capital intensity, organization structure, rate of return on investment, or the impact of technological change on product obsolescence. In one sense, this finding is encouraging because it seems to indicate that the achievement of accuracy is not significantly constrained by the nature of the business.

There are a few company characteristics, however, which do appear to correlate with planning accuracy. The main findings are:

In terms of planning "bias" (the tendency of plans to be consistently high or low), companies with a low rate of profit growth were inclined to be relatively more optimistic than high-growth companies.

In terms of absolute "accuracy" (ignoring whether the planning deviation is higher or lower than actual), companies with a high rate of profit growth were very accurate in forecasting for one or two years ahead relative to other companies, but not so accurate for the fourth or fifth year out.

Large companies do more accurate planning than smaller ones, and accuracy is lower among companies in highly competitive industries.

System Design Features

The survey provides the first proof that the techniques used for formal planning do affect the accuracy of the resulting plans. The main findings are:

Accuracy is greater in those companies which asserted that an important purpose of planning is "to provide a frame of reference for the operating budget."

The old cliché that "the top executive must be involved in planning" apparently has a pay-off in terms of accuracy; the greater his involvement, the more accurate the plans tend to be.

On the other hand, the familiar "top-down versus bottom-up" dichotomy of the way goals and objectives are set showed a surprising result. The more "top-down" the process, the more likely the plans will be inaccurate (either too high or too low). To put it another way, when subordinates have helped set their own goals, they tend to deliver what they promised.

Rigorous discipline in "linking" the plan to the budget, either by permitting no variation or requiring a complete explanation of any change, helps to improve accuracy.

Optimistic plans tend to be supported with more detailed financial documentation than are pessimistic plans.

Is Accuracy Desirable?

While these findings indicate that accuracy in long-range planning is attainable if the right techniques are used, this does not necessarily mean that it is desirable. There are no positive correlations in our data between planning accuracy and the respondents' opinions about the overall effectiveness of their planning systems.

Another cliché of the planning trade is: "The value of planning lies in the *process* of creating plans, not in the plan itself." If that is true, accuracy should not be viewed as an end in itself.

Pushing the desire for accuracy to an extreme, through a combination of devices such as top-down goal setting and tight linkage, may produce only a self-fulfilling prophecy. Creative thinking and willingness to take business risks may be stifled. One wonders whether the apparently accurate plans in such a situation are the effect of a good planning system or the cause of below-optimum performance.

My summary appraisal of these data is that the planning is reasonably accurate, particularly in the near term, and more accurate in the long term than has been supposed.

How a company carries on its long-range planning depends on the kind of enterprise it is and what use it wants to make of the results of its planning. Taking steps to improve accuracy may be effective, but only at the potential loss of some of the "mind-stretching" benefits that could result from a less disciplined approach.

15

Does Planning Pay?
The Effect of Planning on
Success of Acquisition
in American Firms

H. I. ANSOFF, J. AVNER, R. G. BRANDENBURG,
F. E. PORTNER AND R. RADOSEVICH *

Both practitioners and researchers of management have shown increasing concern about the effects of corporate planning on the performance of the firm. The costs of planning are very tangible and often sizeable, particularly if top management is providing the involvement and support required by an active planning process. The benefits, however, are much less tangible. Many top managers, when faced with the rapid change of the last several decades and the uncertainties of the long-range future, have wondered if corporate level planning of the major thrusts of the firm does pay off.

The purpose of this paper is to present evidence which suggests that corporate level planning has indeed been strongly related to the past successful performance of large American firms. The data to support this conclusion came from a larger study which was designed to test the effectiveness of corporate mergers and acquisitions as a means of growth.

The Study

The study was designed to investigate the relationships between performance and methods of growth for a large sample of U.S. manufacturing firms during the 20 year period from 1947–1966. The sample was subdivided into firms which used acquisitions as the primary

* Vanderbilt University, Graduate School of Management.
This article was originally published in *Long Range Planning*, Volume 3, No. 2, December 1970.

vehicle for growth and those which grew through internal development. For those firms that grew by acquiring, some characteristics of behaviour in the planning, search, evaluation and integration processes were examined to determine their relationship to the performance of the firm. These characteristics, such as the degree and type of planning, were investigated by using an extensive questionnaire.

The behavioural characteristics were next related to the results. These were evaluated in two ways:

(1) A subjective evaluation by management provided in responses to the questionnaire, and

(2) a quantitative evaluation based on standard financial data furnished by the Standard and Poor Compustat Tapes.

In structuring both the questionnaire and the financial performance analyses, we sought to compare the pre-acquisition and post-acquisition behaviour. That is, we tried to define the performances of firms before they entered merger and acquisition programmes and to compare these to the post-programme performances. We then correlated typical patterns of acquisition behaviour with the changes in performance to determine whether particular types of behaviour are likely to be associated with success.

In selecting firms for this comparison, we required an acquisition-free period which was sufficiently long to establish representative performance measures both before and after the programme. Thus every programme that was studied had a period of at least 4 years without acquisitions, a period in which acquisitions occurred with no more than 1 year elapsing between two successive acquisitions, and a minimum post-acquisition period of 2 years. This definition reduced the total number of manufacturing firms listed on the Compustat tapes to 412 firms with acceptable programmes. As we experimented with the time length of pre- and post-acquisition periods, we discovered that other sets of parameters greatly reduced the number of acceptable firms. Therefore, our study was confined to the 412 firms. While this approach gave us very important insights in acquisition behaviour, it has two limitations. First, longer pre- and post-acquisition periods would have been desirable to provide more representative performance measures. Secondly, those firms which have been continually engaged in acquisition activities (typically, the conglomerates) constitute a disproportionately small number in our sample.

The Questionnaire

The questionnaire was divided into two sections—the first sought subjective descriptions of the acquisition activity and the second requested objective information from company records. We asked that the first part be completed by someone who was directly involved in the acquisition programme. We suggested that the second part be completed by a staff analyst. Both the cover letter and the questionnaire were personalized by referring to the names and dates of acquisitions in order to identify the programme under investigation for the respondent. Wherever possible, the questionnaires were mailed directly to executives who had previous association with the investigators. For most questions, checklists of alternative answers were presented in order to minimize the time required of the respondent. We felt that the possible disadvantage of restricting the range of answers was more than offset by the increased probability of response and the ease of coding the data.

To test the validity of the data, several checks for consistency were built into the questionnaire. Inconsistencies were noted in only 2 per cent of the responses. There was also little evidence of post decision rationalization which would invalidate the analysis. Many respondents quite frankly expressed dissatisfaction with their acquisition process upon being assured that their replies would be treated as highly confidential.

From the mailing of 412 questionnaires, we received 93 usable replies—a response rate of 22.6 per cent. These 93 firms had acquired 299 other firms during the acquisition programmes under investigation; however, over 66 per cent of the acquiring firms accomplished only one or two acquisitions. This paper deals with the section of the questionnaire which studied two different types of acquisition planning behaviour. The first type determines whether, and when, the firm should seek acquisitions. Such planning typically includes an explicit statement and ranking of corporate objectives. This type of planning may also identify certain acquisition strategies. In planning literature, this type of planning is commonly described as "strategic".

The second is operational planning of the mechanism for acquiring, given that the firm has already decided that it is going to acquire and has specified the objectives of the acquisition programme. This type of planning is evidenced by establishing procedures for searching for candidates, standards for their evaluation, and allocation of specific budgets in support of the acquisition activity.[2,3]

The Objective Measures of a Firm's Performance

The study used twenty-one different measures of performance on thirteen separate variables. For most variables, the performance was measured in more than one way to minimize the effects of bias from any one type of measure. Table 15.1 shows the performance variables used, the

TABLE 15.1. *Performance Variables and Associated Types of Measures*

Variable	Type measures* I	II	III
Sales	X	X	
Earnings	X	X	
Earnings/Share	X	X	
Total Assets	X	X	
Earnings/Equity	X	X	
Dividents/Share		X	
Stock Price (Adjusted)		X	X
Debt/Equity		X	X
Common Equity		X	X
Earnings/Total Equity		X	X
P/E Ratio (Adjusted)			X
Payout (Dividends/Earnings)			X
Price/Equity Ratio			X
Total	5	10	6

*I. Average of Annual Percentage Change

$$100 \frac{1}{n} \sum_{t=1}^{n} \frac{X_t - X_{t-1}}{X_{t-1}} \quad \text{where} \quad \begin{array}{l} n = \text{number of years in period.} \\ X_t = \text{value of variable in } t^{th} \text{ year of period.} \end{array}$$

II. Average Percentage Change Over Period

$$\frac{100}{n} \frac{(X_n - X_1)}{(X_1)}$$

III. Average Value Over period

$$\frac{1}{n} \sum_{t \times 1}^{n} X_t$$

types of measures associated with each variable, and the equations for each type of measure.

Two types of change measures were used to measure growth rate differentials in order to minimize inherent distortion of any single measure. The Type-I measure was the mean of the yearly rates of change over the period. This measure tends to exhibit an upward bias for widely fluctuating variables. The Type-II measure incorporates only the values of the variable in the first and last year of the period and, consequently, can be significantly distorted by a single anomalous value. Comparison of the two types of measures facilitates the recognition of irregular performance values. One type of measure, the Type-III, was used to determine the simple average value of a variable over the measurement period. This type of measure is most amenable to analysis if such performance variables as price/earnings and debt/equity ratios are used.

The computer programme which was written for the analysis of financial data incorporated restrictions on values of performance variables to assure that no one extraordinary value could significantly distort the results. Definitions of each variable are given in the Standard and Poor's Compustat Tapes Manual. They are generally consistent with common interpretations of the terminology used in business practice. For example, "earnings" means income after all operating and non-operating income but before extraordinary income as listed in company annual reports.

The Results of the Study

The Diversity of Planning Practices

One part of the questionnaire analysis was concerned with the variability in the planning behaviour of firms. The questionnaire singled out eight characteristics of managerial behaviour during acquisition activity. Four of the characteristics described the process of systematically establishing plans, and four described the systematic execution of plans such as, search for opportunities, evaluation and integration of acquisitions into the parent firm.

The results of the questionnaire analysis revealed a distinct polarization of the respondents into distinct groups whom we called, respectively, "planners" and "non-planners". The planners, who exhibited at least six of the eight systematic characteristics, comprised 27.7 per cent of the sample. The non-planners, whose descriptions of their planning processes revealed three or fewer of the characteristics, comprised 58.5 per cent of the sample.

Interestingly, a majority of the firms which engaged in comprehensive formal planning were also systematic in execution of their plans. Formal planners were defined as firms that exhibited at least three of the four planning characteristics. Systematic executors of plans were defined analogously. Using these definitions, 60 per cent of the formal planners were also systematic executors of their plans.*

Planners v. Non-planners—a comparison of performance

An interesting result of the study is a lack of correlation between subjective and objective measures of success. Where the measures of

---

* This result is at variance with evidence supported by a recent S.R.I. study [see reference (3)], that execution does not always follow planning. A possible explanation of our result may lie in the fact that, unlike typical corporate planning efforts, acquisition planning is confined to a small top level management group. This group is not under external pressure to plan from higher level managers and when it does plan, it plans its own activities.

successful performance are the preceptions of top management, the results of the study are inconclusive. Where success is measured by objective financial performance before and after acquisition programmes, the results are surprisingly conclusive.

Subjective Measures

The results shown in Fig. 15.1 are typical of the inconclusive evidence, when the subjective perceptions of top management are used as the measures of success. The table divides the sample into four sub-samples:

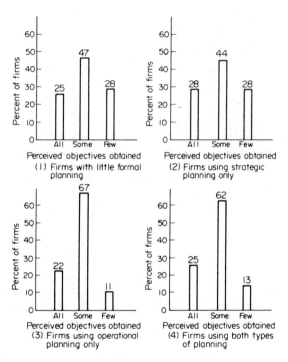

FIG. 15.1. *The perceived achievement of objectives for different degrees of Planning.*

1. Firms with little formal planning
2. Firms using strategic planning only
3. Firms using operational planning only
4. Firms using both types of planning.

The graph for each of these subsamples shows the percentage of firms within that subsample whose executives reported either all, some, or few of the objectives accomplished for the acquisition programme. Examination of the table shows that managers of firms which planned, claimed, on the average, a lower incidence of failure (few objectives obtained).

There appear to be two explanations why perceived achievements show little difference between planners and non-planners. First, the firms that did not plan had no explicit statements of expectations and, hence, could more readily adjust their aspirations *ex post facto*. Secondly, a number of non-planning firms (particularly those seeking vertical acquisitions) achieved success without careful planning and analysis, because their acquisitions were relatively small firms whose operations were already well known to them through previously existing supplier or customer relationships.

Objective Measures

Much more conclusive and significant results are obtained when the objective measures are used.

Table 15.2 presents a summary of the statistical tests which compared some values of the objective performance variables for firms that did extensive planning to the values for those firms that did little planning. The Roman numerals in parentheses after each performance measure indicates the type of measure used, as was defined in Table 15.2. Looking at the first performance measure as an example, the difference between the average annual sales change (Type-I measure) in the post-acquisition period and the average annual sales change in the pre-acquisition period was calculated for all planners and for all non-planners. The median value of the distribution of these changes (differences) was a 2.16 per cent increase for the firms with extensive planning and a 4.52 per cent *decrease* for firms that did little planning. The level of statistical significance of the difference in median values for these two groups is 0.005. With the exception of the total assets growth rate change for strategic planning, *the firms that exhibited extensive planning of their acquisition programmes significantly outperformed the firms that did little formal planning*. The measures on which the planners most notably out-performed the non-planners are the sales growth rate, the earnings growth rate, the earnings/share growth rate and the earnings/common equity growth rate.

Because of the distinct dichotomy of planning practices which was previously mentioned, we were able to analyze the objective data in another manner to validate the above results. Objective financial data were available for twenty-two of the twenty-six firms that exhibited at least six of the eight characteristics of formal planning and systematic use of plans. The performance of these twenty-two firms (Group I) were compared to the performance of forty firms (Group II) that exhibited no more than four of the eight characteristics.

The results of this analysis not only supported the superior average

TACP-K*

TABLE 15.2. *Medium Values of Performance Measures for Planners and non-planners*

Performance measure	Strategic planning			Operational planning		
	Extensive planning	Minor planning	Confidence level of difference[a]	Extensive planning	Minor planning	Confidence level of difference[a]
Sales Growth Rate Change (I)	2.16	−4.52	0.995	1.75	−2.86	0.90
Sales Growth Rate Change (II)	1.70	−6.08	0.95	1.70	−3.74	0.90
Earnings Growth Rate Change (I)	13.55	0.50	0.995	8.73	1.10	0.90
Earnings Growth Rate Change (II)	11.91	3.46	0.90	8.09	1.30	0.80
Earnings/Share Growth Rate Change (I)	13.71	−0.73	0.995	8.91	0.67	0.90
Earnings/Share Growth Rate Change (II)	11.87	3.17	0.95	9.89	6.26	0.80
Total Assets Growth Rate Change (I)	−0.43	−1.55	0.60	−1.55	−1.44	0.90
Total Assets Growth Rate Change (II)	−1.29	−1.90	0.50	−1.87	−1.68	0.50
Earnings/Common Equity Growth Rate Change (I)	13.58	3.09	0.99	8.94	5.04	0.80
Earnings/Common Equity Growth Rate Change (II)	11.38	1.80	0.975	9.68	4.86	0.80
Total Equity Growth Rate Change (II)	−1.61	−3.64	0.80	−1.61	−3.64	0.60
Earnings/Total Capitals Growth Rate Change (II)	9.52	5.99	0.90	9.39	5.99	0.80

[a] Using the Wilcoxon signed Rank and H Tests.

performance of the planners but also revealed that the planners performed more consistently.

Table 15.3 shows median values of the distributions of differences in the average post-acquisition and the average pre-acquisition performances for the two groups. The 22 firms in Group I showed a smaller change in performance in only two of the 13 variables for which there was a statistically significant difference between the groups. Furthermore, in one of these variables (the payout ratio) it is possible to justify either a high or low value as being consistent with good management. The other variable (the price/earnings ratio) is a performance measure for which management has less direct control. The values in the table therefore reflect a substantial advantage in performance improvement for those firms in Group I. Again the measures on which the planners most notably out-performed the non-planners were sales growth rate, earnings growth rate, earnings/share growth rate and earnings/common equity growth rate.

TABLE 15.3. *Median Values of Changes in Pre- and Post-acquisition Performance Measures for Firms in Group I and Group II*

Performance variable	Value of test statistic	Median group I	Median group II
Sales Growth I	2.50[a]	2.25	2.06
Earnings Growth I	3.25	14.08	2.26
Earnings/Share Growth I	3.32[a]	13.71	2.22
Total Assets Growth I	−0.39	0.19	1.34
Earnings/Common Equity Growth I	2.47[a]	14.00	3.98
Sales Growth II	2.82[a]	2.64	−6.08
Earnings Growth II	3.00[a]	17.51	0.05
Earnings/Share Growth II	3.35	16.70	−1.24
Total Assets Growth II	0.43	−1.00	−2.55
Earnings/Common Equity Growth II	3.11[a]	12.08	3.43
Payout Ratio Growth II	−0.06	5.21	−3.14
Total Equity Growth II	1.96[a]	−0.86	−5.50
Earnings/Total Capital Growth II	2.88[a]	10.97	4.47
Stock Price Growth II (adjusted)	1.82[a]	−0.03	7.33
Debt/Equity Growth II	−0.23	−2.11	−0.33
Price Earnings Ratio III	−2.19[a]	−0.28	0.98
Debt/Equity Ratio III	1.36	0.00	−0.06
Payout Ratio III	−2.30	−0.04	0.06
Price Equity Ratio III	−0.59	0.18	0.52
Total Equity III	−0.73	23.49	31.52
Earnings/Total Equity III	1.61	−0.01	−0.03

[a] Indicates significant difference at the 0.05 level (95 % confidence level).

The firms with systematic planning and execution not only performed significantly better on the average but also were more predictable in their performances. This is shown in Table 15.4. When the variances of the distributions of the performance variables are used as measures for predictability of performance, the firms in Group I are more predictable on every measure except one. There is greater variability in the performance across firms in Group II for every pre- and post-acquisition performance difference except for the rate of sales growth. The variability in the performances of firms in Group II, as measured by the standard deviation of the distribution of performances, is more than twice as great as the comparable measure for the firms in Group I for the earnings, earnings/share, earnings/common equity and earnings/total capital growth rate changes.

TABLE 15.4. *Comparison of Means and Deviations of Performance Measures for Firms in Group I and Group II*

	Means		Standard deviations	
	Group I	Group II	Group I	Group II
Sales Growth Rate Change I	2.75	−0.63	12.62	9.25
Earnings Growth Rate Change I	13.14	10.86	31.62	45.13
Earnings/Share Growth Rate Change I	12.83	9.98	32.44	44.01
Total Assets Growth Rate Change I	−0.64	0.57	6.42	8.54
Earnings/Common Equity Growth Rate Change I	11.39	10.52	28.63	40.21
Sales Growth Rate Change II	−0.82	−11.28	17.91	24.60
Earnings Growth Rate Change II	13.61	2.03	32.33	72.10
Earnings/Share Growth Rate Change II	14.01	1.79	30.28	68.06
Total Assets Growth Rate Change II	5.16	−8.93	13.05	25.68
Earnings/Common Equity Growth Rate Change II	12.28	8.45	21.68	54.63
Payout Ratio Growth Rate Change II	−3.34	−3.80	14.96	27.77
Total Equity Growth Rate Change II	−1.22	−7.61	7.86	15.33
Earnings/Total Capital Growth Rate Change II	12.80	7.15	24.47	19.05
Adjusted Stock Price Growth Rate Change II	7.77	−10.42	32.53	45.21
Debt/Equity Growth Rate Change II	−6.00	−1.85	16.79	18.86
Price/Earnings Ratio Change III	−0.16	2.07	2.29	5.54
Debt/Equity Ratio Change III	0.00	−0.10	0.17	0.27
Payout Ratio Change III	−0.02	0.15	0.14	0.60
Price/Equity Ratio Change III	0.70	0.80	0.91	0.94
Total Equity Change III	58.91	67.77	95.65	127.34
Earnings/Total Equity Ratio Change III	−0.02	−0.03	0.04	0.04

The frequency histograms of the performance measures provide some insight about the different sources of variability between the two groups. The histograms of the earnings growth rate changes for the two groups (shown in Figure 15.2) are typical of the distributions for most of the measures. These distributions support the conclusions derived from the subjective measures; that is, the planners achieved their higher average performance and lower variability primarily by avoiding failure. Several of the non-planners had performances that surpassed the best performance in the group of planners, but a much higher percentage of the non-planners had very poor performances.

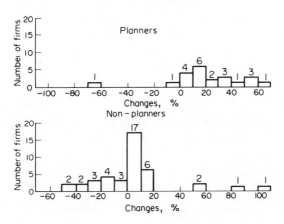

FIG. 15.2. *Frequency histogram of the distribution of earning growth rate changes for planners and non-planners.*

Summary of Findings

The following are the principal findings of the study:

(1) Firms which engage in acquisition activity tend to take one of two distinctive approaches to acquisition planning. The first is an unplanned opportunistic approach and the other, a systematic planned approach. If a firm fails to plan any phase of the programme, it is likely to forego planning altogether. If a firm does plan a phase, it is likely to make a complete strategic and operating plan.

(2) Firms which do plan tend to use these plans and to exhibit deliberate and systematic acquisition behaviour.

(3) Although subjective evaluation of results by management does not differ greatly between planners and non-planners, objective financial measurements show a substantial difference.

(4) On virtually all relevant financial criteria, the planners in our sample significantly outperformed the non-planners.

(5) Not only did the planners do better on the average, they performed more predictably than nonplanners. Thus, planners appear to have narrowed the uncertainty in the outcomes of acquisition behaviour.

(6) To the best of our knowledge, this study has offered the first quantitative and statistically significant proof that acquisition planning pays.*

Acknowledgements

The study was performed at Carnegie-Mellon University under a grant from the McKinsey Foundation. The authors would like to express their sincere gratitude to the Foundation for their patience in giving them complete freedom to pursue this study over a period of 2 years, unhampered by demands of progress reporting. We would also like to thank the large number of American business firms which have taken the trouble to reply to our lengthy questionnaires and to those firms, and individuals, who explained to us the circumstances which prevented them from responding.

References

1. H. I. Ansoff, J. L. Avner, R. G. Brandenburg, F. E. Portner and H. R. Radosevich, *A Study of Acquisition Behaviour of U.S. Manufacturing Firms During the Period 1946–1965*, to be published.

2. H. I. Ansoff, *Corporate Strategy*, McGraw Hill, New York (1965).

3. H. I. Ansoff, *Evolution of Corporate Planning* Stanford Research Institute (September 1967).

4. Robert J. House and Stanley Thune, *Where Long Range Planning Pays Off*, The Bernard M. Baruch College, to be published.

---

*A more recent study [see reference (4)] has offered a quantitative proof that firms with long range planning also outperform firms which do not do long range planning.

16

Does Long Range Planning Improve Company Performance?

Z. A. MALIK AND D. W. KARGER

Managers are beset by specialists pleading for the value of the techniques that are their *raison d'être*. Promises of results flow like streamlets in a spring thaw. Often, however, the facts do not support the promises. Is this the case with long-range planning?

Some might consider such a question ridiculous since planning has long been a recognized and accepted element of the management process. But recent experience—the debacle many companies experienced during the 1974−75 recession—has caused some managers to question whether the cost of long-range planning is justified by the benefits. Perhaps a review of the experience of a group of companies that has engaged in formal planning and of a group that has not, will be instructive.

Planners vs. nonplanners

A broad survey—in terms both of the number of industries and of the variables examined—was undertaken by the authors to compare the results obtained by Formal Integrated Long-Range Planners (FILRAP) with those of informal planners. (The FILRAP planners had to use the major planning steps summarized in box above to qualify.) FILRAP planners and a comparable group of non-FILRAP planners—loosely categorized as informal planners—were identified through the use of a questionnaire, the responses to which indicated the type and degree of planning engaged in by the company. The questionnaire, which a CEO could answer in a few minutes, was mailed to 273 companies with annual sales of about $50 to $500 million drawn from six industries. The firms were an unbiased selection from *Moody's Industrial Manual and Value Line Investment Survey*. The covering letter defined the objective of the research, promised

The Major Steps in the Integrated Formal Planning Process

1. Identify the planning manager and coordinator.
2. Identify and educate the planners and inform them of their objectives. The planners are the major department heads of the organization, including divisional and plant executives. Ultimately, the planning effort involves all members of management.
3. Distribute to each planner data indicating where the organization has been, how it arrived at its present state, what its present thrust appears to be, and so forth so that all planners will have the same view of the organization. The data should include an approximately ten-year (past) financial and market history and a definition of the strengths and weaknesses of the firm in every functional area, including facilities and ⁻ manpower.
4. Define for the planners the future horizon and what is expected in between— economic, industrial, legal, sociological, and technological. Take into account all product lines, all countries in which you have or expect to have operations, and all geographic areas of consequence.
5. Select a planning site away from the office so the planners can concentrate on planning. (Many companies have the planning director chair planning meetings.)
6. Set down the planning steps, which may vary from company to company depending on whether there are divisions, multiple product line, widely scattered plants, and so forth.
7. Define the present businesses the company is in and possible future business directions. Define products, markets, and other boundaries of operation.
8. Obtain the strategic objectives of the firm from its senior management. Important tactical objectives should be set forth by top management. The planners must identify opportunities and design ways to take advantage of them. These objectives are the basis for the company's five-year plan.
9. Prepare in detail the first year of the five-year plan including capital and expense budgets; cash flow projections; product, market, manpower, production, and other important short-term plans.
10. Operate as planned and measure performance against the plan.

anonymity, indicated that public financial data would be used in an effort to determine if there was a difference in business results between FILRAP and non-FILRAP planners, and promised respondents a report of the findings. Enough replies were received to enable an analysis to be made for three industry groups, if chemical and drugs were combined.

No. of companies providing usable data

	Planners	Nonplanners
Chemicals and drugs	5	5
Electronics	7	8
Machinery	7	6

Not enough responses were obtained from apparel and food companies for a meaningful analysis to be made.

Performance was measured over the 1964–1973 period. While some pertinent financial data were obtained from SEC-10K reports and annual reports, almost all needed data were available in convenient form in *Value Line Investment Survey* data sheets. The annual financial measures used were: (1) sales volume, (2) sales per share, (3) cash flow per share, (4) earnings per share, (5) book value per share, (6) net income, (7) rate earned on capital,(8) rate earned on net worth, (9) operating margin, (10) percent of dividends to income, (11) capital spending per share, (12) stock price (average), and (13) price/earnings ratio (average).

Arithmetic means were calculated for each of the measures, by year, for each firm over the ten-year period and the planners were compared with the nonplanners for each industry group.

What did we learn?

Data for the electronics industry are presented in Table 16.1. The companies in this industry evidenced the greatest differences between

TABLE 16.1. *Comparison of Results Obtained by Planners and Nonplanners: Selected Electronics Companies*

	Planners (N = 7)		Nonplanners (N = 8)	
Index	Range	Mean	Range	Mean
Annual Rates of Change	(%)	(%)	(%)	(%)
1. Sales volume[a]	9.9−42.5	22.6	−1.0−11.9	9.0
2. Sales/share[b]	6.5−16.5	12.3	−3.0−8.5	5.9
3. Cash flow/share[b]	8.0−14.0	10.4	−12.5−11.5	1.9
4. Earnings/share[b]	9.0−14.5	12.2	−13.5−13.5	1.1
5. Book value/share[b]	4.0−13.0	8.4	−4.5−9.5	3.4
6. Net income (cum)[c]	135.0−667.0	265.0	−67.0−308.0	52.0
Mean Annual Rates[d]	(%)	(%)	(%)	(%)
7. Earnings/capital	6.9−16.5	11.3	4.8−15.1	8.2
8. Earnings/net worth	6.3−16.5	12.2	4.3−15.6	8.8
9. Operating margin	6.9−17.7	12.6	4.9−14.5	10.0
10. Dividend/net income	5.0−58.0	35.0	37.0−62.0	47.0
Mean Values/Year[e]	($)	($)	($)	($)
11. Capital spending/share	1.00−5.35	2.02	.50−2.17	.98
12. Stock price	18.00−50.00	28.00	9.00−39.00	23.00
13. P/E ratio	12−38	23.00	13.00−64.00	27.00

Key: (a) Mean of simple annual rate of change over period 1963–1973. (Calculated by author.)
(b) Compounded annual rate of change over the period. (Source: *Value Line Survey*)
(c) Cumulative percentage change during the period. (Calculated by author.)
(d) Mean of annual rates for the period. (Calculated by author.)
(e) Mean of annual values for the period. (Calculated by author.)

TABLE 16.2. *Comparison of Results Obtained by Planners and Nonplanners:*
Selected Electronics, Machinery, and Chemical/Drug Companies
(Percent by which mean results of planners exceeded mean results of
nonplanners.)

Index	Electronics	Machinery	Chemical and drugs
Annual Rates of Change	(%)	(%)	(%)
1. Sales volume[a]	151	127	45
2. Sales/share[b]	108	68	32
3. Cash flow/share[b]	447	151	32
4. Earnings/share[b]	1009	321	64
5. Book value/share[b]	147	186	52
6. Net income[c]	410	[292:1]	65
Mean Annual Rates[d]			
7. Earnings/capital	38	48	11
8. Earnings/net worth	39	86	13
9. Operating margin	26	55	32
10. Dividend/net income	−26	−12	−9
Mean Values/Year[e]			
11. Capital spending/share	106	−14	−38
12. Stock price	23	−15	0
13. P/E ratio	−13	13	22

Key: (a) Mean of simple annual rate of change over period 1963−1973 (Calculated by author.)
(b) Compounded annual rate of change over the period (Source: *Value Line Survey*.)
(c) Mean of annual rates for the period (Calculated by author.)
(d) Cumulative percentage change during the period (Calculated by author.)
(e) Mean of annual values for the period (Calculated by author.)

planner and nonplanners. However, an examination of Table 16.2, which summarizes the differences for the three industries analyzed, clearly shows that the differences in performance for planners vs. nonplanners in all industry groups are large. (And while the data are not shown here, the one apparel company that engaged in formal planning did far better than the five nonplanning apparel companies.) In general, the differences in performance on the first nine measures were statistically significant, that is, these could not be attributed to chance factors. The results for measures 10 through 13 are mixed.

So, the answer to the question of whether long-range planning is more promises than results seems clear: more results. Hard data suggest long-range planning pays. And since studies by others have produced similar results, the weight of evidence is mounting rapidly. Companies engaged in long-range planning are using a management tool that has demonstrated its worth.

17

Strategy and the Weather*

E. H. BOWMAN

Introduction

It is the purpose of this article to contrast the attitudes and behavior of less successful companies with more successful companies. The food-processing industry was chosen for this comparison purpose. What then can be said about less successful companies?

Food-processing companies that are less successful complain about the weather. They also complain most vigorously about government price controls. They talk less about the coming changes in their environment, about their product/market *portfolio*, and about where they are going. They are less inclined to change their organizations and are more inclined to engage in franchising. They engage less in joint ventures in foreign countries. They are less clear in their plans to cope with the energy crisis, and also to respond to the world-wide protein demand. They engage more in acquisitions and divestments and less in international activities. Finally, they are less concerned with corporate social responsibility.

At a more abstract level, they plan less, cope with their environment more awkwardly, and do not concentrate on value added. All of these characteristics differentiate them from more successful companies in their own industry.

How is it possible to make all of these declarative statements? The answer is to read their annual reports.

Reprinted from "Strategy and the Weather" by E. H. Bowman, The Ohio State University *Sloan Management Review*, Volume 17, No. 2, pp. 49–62, by permission of the publisher. Copyright 1976 by the Sloan Management Review. All rights reserved.

* The author wishes to thank the Sloan School of Management, M.I.T. for research support from its Irving Wilson Fund for Management Education and Research (established by the Alcoa Foundation); and The Ohio State University for support from the Graduate School research funds. Also thanked is the collaborator on an earlier phase of this research, Professor Mason Haire.

The Data Base

In order to make this study, and another related to it, the food-processing industry was chosen as a broadly based industry which included many companies. *Moody's Industrial Manual*, 1973, was used as a source of company names in the industry.

Five subgroups were listed under food-processing: Cereal and Grain, Fishery Products, Miscellaneous Products, Vegetables and Fruits, and Vegetable Oil Products. The total list of company names was 217, with about 50 multiple counts of the same names (because of the subgroups), about 25 foreign companies which were excluded, five companies for which addresses were unavailable, and about 35 companies which had less than half of their business in the food industries (e.g. ITT, RCA, SCM) which were also excluded. The annual reports for the remaining companies were solicited (about 100 net) and 82 have been received and processed.

Methodology, 1

The methodology employed in the study was a particular kind of content analysis, combined with a determination of average return on investment (Return on Equity, ROE) over a five-year period. The ROE figures were determined from *Standard and Poor's* and *Moody's* manuals.

In a study which focused on corporate social responsibility, all eighty-two annual reports were read and line-by-line discussion of corporate social responsibility was coded.[1] The two authors of this earlier study cross-checked each other for consistent coding. The methodology was to count the line-by-line discussion of corporate social responsibility as a percentage of total annual report discussion of all topics, and use this percentage as a surrogate for the level or intensity of actual activities. Discussions of international activities, and acquisition and divestment activities were similarly coded. The more widely ranging activities referred to in the declarative statements at the beginning of this article were handled somewhat differently and will be described later.

The first organizing scheme then scaled the eighty-two annual reports along the variables of interest, such as corporate social responsibility, and then determined the ROE which corresponded to the segmentation along these scales.

The Two Tests of Validity

Both theoretical and empirical checks of this "research instrument" are warranted. The annual report is like a projective test and it is as well an

---

[1] See Bowman, E. H. and Haire, M., A strategic posture toward corporate social responsibility, *California Management Review*, Winter 1975.

"unobtrusive measure" for this purpose. The company and the chief executive officer can address virtually any set of issues they wish. Secondly, the annual report is written essentially to the *shareholder*, and one should not expect unusual puffery on issues like corporate social responsibility, or even international activities.

The first empirical test of annual report discussion as a research instrument involved a search for a list of companies independently arrived at as outstanding in their corporate social responsibility activities. Milton Moskowitz, editor of *Business and Society*, had provided such a list in *The New York Times*, February 11, 1973. It included fourteen companies as being outstandingly responsible firms. Our first test chose fourteen other companies to supply as matched pairs for comparison purposes. Each of these fourteen matched pair companies of this second set was chosen from the same industry as the corresponding Moskowitz company, of approximately the same size, and randomly selected where alternatives were available.

The test hypothesis of course was that the outstandingly responsible companies discussed issues of corporate social responsibility more in their annual reports on a line-by-line coding basis than did the neutrally chosen matched pair companies. They did. The average for the first group was a 4.80 percent discussion, and of the second group was a 1.74 percent discussion, a statistically significant difference (binomial pair-wise comparison, at the .017 level of confidence).

The second, independent, and completely different, test of the annual report discussion as a reliable measure of activity rate was in the area of international activities. Similarly to the line-by-line coding of corporate social responsibility discussion, a coding on international activity discussion was made from the annual reports to determine the percentage of the total discussion devoted to this topic. For the forty (of the eighty-two) companies which are listed on The New York Stock Exchange, *Standard and Poor's* provides detailed reports including in most cases the percentage of the company's business generated by international activities. The rank order of company international percentage for both lists (i.e., annual reports discussion coding and *Standard and Poor's* percentage of international business) could then be compared. This comparison of the two lists, both ranked from high to low in activity rate, offers an additional test of annual report line-by-line coding. Using the Spearman Rank Order Correlation Coefficient, the list orders were significantly similar (coefficient of .64, level of significance of .001).

Both of these tests then, using standard statistical methodology, suggest that the annual report discussion, line-by-line, is a reasonable surrogate for real activity.

The Whole Sample

At the end of this article's second paragraph it is stated that less successful companies "engage more in acquisitions and divestments and less in international activities. Finally, they are less concerned with corporate social responsibility." From the whole sample of eighty-two corporate annual reports, using a line-by-line coding of discussions as a surrogate of activity and each company's five-year average return on investment, it is possible to prepare the following table:

Return on Equity

Annual Report % discussion	Acquisitions & divestments	International	Corporate social responsibility
High rate	8.9 %	12.9 %	14.7 %
Low rate	12.8 %	8.0 %	10.2 %

Within the table is listed the median ROE of those companies within the category. Though all the companies are included, the category segments are not all the same size because they depended in part on the activity measure. In each case the difference in ROE is approximately 50 % higher for the more successful companies.

This article, which focuses on the less successful companies, does not stress the behavior of the most successful companies. In the earlier paper dealing essentially with corporate social responsibility it was demonstrated (and statistically significant at the level of .02) that those companies which manifested a middle-level or average amount of corporate social responsibility activities were on the average the most profitable companies with a median ROE for the five years of 16.1 %. A second group of companies with the most activity in corporate social responsibility had a median ROE of 12.3 %. And as reported here, the third group with the least activity in corporate social responsibility had a median ROE of 10.2 %. This article focuses on this last third and lumps the first two groups together.

Some speculation may be permitted on these three activities—corporate social responsibility, international, and acquisitions and divestments. It is maintained here that those companies which evidence least activities in corporate social responsibility (compared to their industry peers) are least sensitive to important factors and changes in their environment, and behave least proactively regarding these many constituency groups. They sense, anticipate, adapt, negotiate, and cope least adequately.

With respect to international activities, it may be that those with least to offer the marketplace go less far geographically. Another way to express this same idea is to note that an activity that is special to the company, that shows a rather unique capacity or talent, will probably imbed more of what the economist refers to as value added. The more useful activity a corporation devotes to the material it purchases, the more likely it offers, or appears to offer, something which other companies cannot offer, and the more sensible it is to carry on these activities internationally. This also offers the possibility of some particular economies of scale. It offers a wider selection of investment opportunities and business development possibilities.

The greater activity in acquisitions and divestments may more clearly be a result than a cause of less commercial success. Here also our more extensive survey of all eighty-two companies reveals that a middle-level of such activities is associated with the most successful companies, with either end of the spectrum being occupied by the less profitable firms. The *least* successful, however, are those whose activities approach the peripatetic and frenetic, and have a relatively high rate of acquisitions and divestments.

Methodology, II

In order to have a picture of how the corporations in the food-processing industry view their strategy, a number of the annual reports were once again reviewed for the purpose of abstracting some actual comments. The eighty-two annual reports were first divided into quartiles by five-year return on equity (ROE). The top quartile and the bottom quartile were chosen for investigation. Next, from each of these sets of twenty (or twenty-one) annual reports, the five reports with the most pages were chosen for detailed review.[2]

It turned out that all of these ten companies were relatively large, with nine out of ten in the top half of the total eighty-two companies according to size (i.e., size of company apparently correlates with length of report), and all ten are listed on The New York Stock Exchange. The median ROE (for the five years) for the top quartile five was 17.1%, and for the bottom quartile five was 5.9%—a rather large difference.

To reiterate, the organizing scheme here was a segmentation according to ROE. A group of companies which were least successful was to be compared to a group of companies which were most successful. Actual comments in their annual reports on various topics were to be the basis for the comparison. The statistician might be willing to call this a poor-man's discriminant analysis.

A word of caution is warranted because this methodology permitting

---

[2] The reports with the most pages were chosen in order to get the most material (with the least amount of noise) for review. The author was also subjected to time constraints which prevented him from reviewing all of the annual reports.

most of the introductory declarative statements is not for the most part statistically sound. The sample is small (though fair), and the instrument is blunt. In part due to these caveats, it is necessary to draw more heavily on theory and intellectual speculation—this is not an uncommon substitute at the margin, theory for sound empirical data. At the extreme the substitution is complete—all theory and no data, not a very attractive scheme.

The Differentiating Content

Clearly annual reports talk about many things. Profit (or loss), sales volume, products, and facilities would be high on the list. It is the purpose here to highlight the differentiating content; that is, the nature of the discussion which is different between the low-profit companies and the high-profit companies.

All quotes about a given topic were copied from all ten reports. Though no brief is offered for statistical proof, the copying was straightforward. The interpretation is speculative. The declarative statements at the beginning of this article will now be taken in their first order.

1. "Food-processing companies that are less successful complain about the weather"

There were many (seven) different comments mentioning unfavorable weather conditions in the low-quartile companies and *no* mention in the high-quartile companies (and it should be repeated that the ROE figure which separates the company quartiles is an average for *five* years).

> "The (Name) Division shares industry concern this year over the severe and unusual weather that punished major growing areas and is causing some disruption in crop yields." (4th Quartile)
> " . . . continued wet weather during the last season delayed harvesting and caused increased raw-product expense due to the need for additional drying." (4th Quartile)
> "The primary earlier factor contributing to the poor results was the adverse weather condition experienced in the states of Arkansas and Mississippi where the Company's plants are located." (4th Quartile)
> "Unusually heavy rainfalls in Central Arizona and in the Salinas Valley caused the loss of a large part of the Arizona spring lettuce crop, and inhibited planting of Salinas Valley lettuce during the winter months." (4th Quartile)
> " . . . Group showed a decline in earnings due principally to the effects of a severe blowdown suffered in the (Honduras) Division." (4th Quartile)

The thesis could be advanced that companies with less satisfactory results complain. More likely, it is that their basic business puts them in a situation which is more vulnerable to the occasional and persistent vagaries of the weather (and that their complaints are justified). If the business is a "commodity" business, with little "value added," there will be little margin or flexibility to cope with supply difficulties.

2. "They complained most vigorously about price controls"

Again, of course, one thesis would be that the companies currently less successful by commercial standard (for five years) would use this as an excuse this year (of price controls) in their annual reports. A less obvious thesis perhaps is that they are less successful because they are more "commodity-oriented" than their more successful sisters. These latter appear to have higher value-added products and the associated development, packaging, convenience, and advertising that goes with it. Note also that only the fourth-quartile companies mentioned nondelivery and temporary withdrawal from markets—none of the first-quartile companies mentioned this. Only a few of the actual remarks will be reproduced here (and there may be bias in the selection). The first set is from the fourth-quartile companies and the second set from the first-quartile.

> "The price-freeze announced June 13 of this year was most disruptive. It became necessary from time to time to curtail or suspend operations at both vegetable oil refineries of the (Name) Division and temporarily stop selling certain items. Current phase IV regulations concerning edible vegetable oil products are still adversely affecting operations at these refineries. . . . It appears that the phase IV Price Control Program will restrict the right of the Company to raise prices except to the amount of increased costs; however, complete publication of these regulations for the food industry has not yet been made. . . . Your company has been and continues to operate under stringent Federal price controls. These controls, though politically expedient, have not reflected economic fact." (4th Quartile)

> "The well-publicized problems of food processors under the 'Freeze,' largely continued during the early stages of 'Phase IV,' penalized this Division. To avoid selling at below cost under the ill-conceived, counter productive regulations, numerous sale and purchase contracts were cancelled, and production was substantially curtailed. . . . The negative effect of the 'Freeze' and 'Phase IV' on pre-tax profits for this Division is estimated at approximately $2 million, about equally divided between the two fiscal years." (4th Quartile)

> ". . . due to the Federal Government's unreasonable illogical interpretation of 'ceiling prices' as applied to the products of this Division . . . losses were incurred on inventories and future sales commitments. . . . " (4th Quartile)

The next quotes all come from the first-quartile companies—the most profitable. While they are not enthusiastic, they give the flavor of a different group.

> "In 1973 sales and earnings of (Name) reached record levels for the 18th consecutive year. Worldwide sales advanced 13 % and earning 11 % above the record levels of 1972. It is a pleasure to report this accomplishment as it was achieved in a particularly difficult period of price controls, soaring commodity prices, rampant inflation, increasing interest rates, material and energy shortages, fluctuating currencies and

tension in international affairs." (1st Quartile) (It may be that the current management are geniuses—it may also be that the corporate stragegy had been carefully selected over an extended period of time.)

"An increasing amount of restrictive legislation and regulation, at all levels of government, is proving difficult, but we are taking steps to respond positively." (1st Quartile)

"The gradual pass-through of rising costs permitted in Phase IV seems reasonable to us when viewed as a transitional step toward the goals of de-control, which we have advocated and still prefer. Despite problems associated with the Economic Stabilization Act, we are confident we will be able to achieve our programmed objectives in fiscal 1974." (1st Quartile)

"We have conscientiously complied with the controls and regulations imposed by each of the various phases of the economic stabilization programs. . . . While we are in agreement with the general intent of the government's economic control effort, which is to curb inflation and bring balance to the economy, we firmly believe that the economy would be better served by the absence of controls and we look forward to the early removal of these regulations." (1st Quartile)

"With respect to the utilization of energy and commodity resources, inhibiting governmental controls exist throughout the world. Temporary restraints such as the 'freeze' in the U.S. . . . may be useful or even necessary to spur public interest and reaction. However, controls, as they continue, become self-perpetuating, complicated, ineffective and then damaging as they lead to imbalance in the economy. We believe the free market system is in the best long range interests of the general public, our customers, and (Name), and provides the best mechanism to achieve the fair and equitable use of resources." (1st Quartile)

3. "They talk less about the coming changes in their environment, about product/market portfolio, and about where they are going"

Where it is difficult to adequately convey the quantitative sense of this differentiating characteristic, there were virtually to real discussions of such important issues in the fourth-quartile annual reports. The first-quartile companies were replete with them. Something like twenty to twenty-five different copied quotes were available to choose from. A sample is offered here. Considering the concept that an annual report might be thought of for our purposes as a "projective test," it is obvious that these ideas are at the "front of their minds."

"(Name)'s domestic food activities are taking advantage of the increasing rates of change in eating patterns; the continuing desire for convenience in preparation, service and cleanup; the growing interest in variety and the satisfaction of individual consumer tastes; and the growing interest in nutrition and value. . . . The trend away from three formal meals to a much more disintegrated pattern of family eating is providing opportunities in several different areas. . . . The snacking phenomenon continues to grow as snacking is now the most frequent eating occasion, and product opportunities in this category continue."(1st Quartile)

"We also believe environmental trends are favorable to the future of our consumer non-food areas and specialty chemicals and worldwide markets for our products. Our success will be assured if we can continue to identify the changing desires and needs of consumers and develop the products and services that provide them with good quality and value." (1st Quartile)

"The year 1973 was a difficult one for the imported table wine trade. Higher prices coupled with unfavorable exchange rates resulted in substantial price increases of table wines from the traditional areas of Europe. Nevertheless, imported table wines continued to grow at a faster rate than their domestic counterparts. The wine explosion in this country continues unabated and the outlook for accelerated growth of imported table wines has been considerably enhanced by the strengthening of the dollar." (1st Quartile)

"We continue to recognize that the feed business is essentially local, but one which benefits from the strengths of a national organization. We also recognize the need to serve a more sophisticated group of livestock and poultry producers whose requirements are becoming more complex." (1st Quartile)

"(Name) is engaged in three principal lines of business. The first line of business consists of consumer packaged foods, beverages and related products sold to consumers under advertised brands. . . . The second line of business consists of food and related products which we manufacture and/or sell to food service establishments such as restaurants, hotels, armed forces installations, hospitals and other institutions, and to the baking industry. . . . Thirdly, (Name) manufactures and sells products to industrial customers." (1st Quartile)

"The broad dimensions and deep strengths of our North American grocery business—the 'heart-land' of this company and its largest single contributor to sales and profits—make it the obvious source of the funds we will need in the future to broaden both our product lines and business base." (1st Quartile)

"The New U.S. grocery products of fiscal 1973, and others still in early development stages, are regarded as the forebears of new product families which (Name) anticipate will be created in increasing numbers as each division applies its research and development capabilities to the new Strategic Business Units and adopts technological advances which are generated by the scientists in Corporate Research." (1st Quartile)

"Although heaviest emphasis will be on internal growth efforts, the company will also alert to additional promising areas; it may be expected to enter selected new fields and develop new opportunities. For example, in recognition of the growing movement toward a service economy—and to capitalize on the rising sophistication, educational interest and affluence of consumers—the company is currently conducting probes in consumer service areas." (1st Quartile)

"The preponderance of the Consumer Products (capital expenditure) budget will be expended for the expansion of pet food production capacity. . . . The Agricultural Products and International budgets include significant funds for construction and expansion of feed production facilities. In New Venture Management our industrial and food protein production capacities and our mushroom production facilities will be significantly expanded." (1st Quartile)

"Over the past decade, a program of wide diversification and the acquisition of new lines of products have greatly altered (Name)'s make-up today. The Company is actively and profitably engaged in many different types of businesses. They range from foods to pharmaceuticals, from toys to shower curtains; each major line includes the potential for growth essential to (Name)'s future. Trademarks and brand-name products are the basis for our business." (1st Quartile)

"In the past 10 years, (Name) has undergone a major reshaping, moving from an agricultural commodity to a consumer oriented company. The present strategy continues the plan formulated in 1965 of: (1) maximizing the profit growth of continuing business by expanding market share, broadening existing product lines and entering new product areas that offer substantial growth potential; (2) building significant new businesses that take advantage of changing consumer life styles and expected increases in disposable income world wide." (1st Quartile)

One of the few quotations from a fourth-quartile company which even comes close to all of the above, which are only a sample, is the following:

> "On June 13, 1973, the Company announced that it was withdrawing from cotton merchandising in the United States. This withdrawal, to be carried out on an orderly basis over the months ahead, will eliminate the possibility of losses such as those incurred in the year just ended, and will free up substantial working capital for other use. Through the years, U.S. cotton merchandising activities have obviously been profitable, but the wide fluctuations in earnings and the lack of future opportunities for large profits caused the company to restructure the merchandising activity in 1969 to avoid major, unhedged market positions and finally, this year, to withdraw. . . . The original economic foundation of the Company beginning in 1904 was provided by profits from cotton merchandising. In subsequent years, expansion into a wide range of interlocking, related activities was built on this financial base." (4th Quartile) (This is close to the old saw of "the exception which proves the rule.")

4. "They also are less inclined to change their organizations. . . . "

As the product/market strategy of the corporation develops and changes, perhaps responding to changes in the environment, organization forms can be seen as a means for increasing the efficiency of the decisions and the operations. For the relatively mature corporation, organization means reorganization. First-quartile companies seem to mention such changes more often (seven times) than the fourth-quartile companies (one or two times). This at least connotes the possibility of stagnation and perhaps missed opportunities. A sample of the first-quartile and all of the fourth quartile are presented.

> "During 1973 this division was reorganized into two separate operating units—a Food Service Division and an Industrial Division. The reorganization primarily involved changes to reduce distribution costs, to obtain deeper market penetration and to keep pace with customer requirements." (1st Quartile)
>
> "We restructured (Name) domestic grocery business around specific consumer markets. The key to this change is the organizational concept of the Strategic Business Unit, a grouping of products naturally related by their position on the consumer's menu rather than for reasons of technology, history, or method of distribution. We foresee significant efficiencies in this new structure for the management of our established businesses in the United States." (1st Quartile)
>
> "In fulfillment of its commitment to remain responsive to consumers, (Name) established a Consumer Affairs Center in fiscal 1973. The Center functions as a clearinghouse for information from both inside and outside the company on the satisfaction our products provide customers—in the areas of nutrition, safety, packaging, product performance, and consumer information. As new consumer-oriented issues begin to emerge, the Consumer Affairs Center helps to develop corporate positions and policies." (1st Quartile)

The fourth-quartile companies' mention of organization changes are numerically fewer, and also seem a bit less innovative.

"(Name) is placing greater emphasis on overseas (Name) seed sales and technological service and has recently formed the (Name) Export Company. (Name) is presently testing new proprietary hybrid (Name) seed in many foreign countries." (4th Quartile)

"The staff of the Corporate Development Department has been augmented to enhance its new product development capabilities." (4th Quartile)

5. " . . . *more inclined to engage in franchising"*

While many of the companies in the food-processing industry have been moving into the "fast-food business," the more profitable companies seem to do it essentially on a "wholely-owned" basis, while the least profitable seem to do it on a franchise basis.

This of course can be a result of lack of profitability and therefore financial resources, rather than a cause. Franchising is mentioned five times by the least profitable companies, and only once by the most profitable. Only this once-mentioned is included here.

"Despite intense competition in the fast-food business and substantial cost pressures, (Name) turned in a modest profit for the year. (Name)'s operations are being concentrated in key franchise areas. The pruning of unsatisfactory units, for which provision was made in the previous year, is well under way." (1st Quartile)

6. *"They engage less in joint ventures in foreign countries"*

While it might be anticipated that successful companies, which by definition here means profitable companies, would have the financial resources to start most or all of their foreign ventures alone (compared to the opposite case for less successful companies), this is not the case. Four cases are noted from the first-quartile companies, and only one from the less successful companies. Several of the first, and the one latter, are presented.

"Negotiations toward formation of a joint venture in Japan with a major Japanese food firm were undertaken as a means of strengthening management in that country." (1st Quartile)

"A new joint venture yeast plant in Jamaica is now supplying fresh and dry yeast to the Caribbean Free Trade Area group of countries. . . . (Name) is a fifty-one percent subsidiary of (Name) and is owned jointly with (Name) of The Netherlands." (1st Quartile)

" . . . (Name) has entered into agreements with the Government of Japan and the (Japanese) Company to use an enzyme process developed in Japan for increasing (productivity). Final U.S. Food and Drug Administration approval for use of the enzyme in the process is anticipated in the near future. (Name) is making a sizable investment in its (Name) Montana factory to adapt and test the Japanese technology." (4th Quartile)

7. "*They are less clear in their plans to cope with the energy crisis . . .*"

The energy crisis, especially during the petroleum embargo, but also during the natural gas shortages, has affected many companies in the food-processing industry, and several of the companies mention it. The less successful companies do not mention their plans to cope with it, while several of the most successful companies do. An example follows:

> "The Company is fully aware of the urgent necessity to find and adopt stringent conservation measures throughout its operations. Like other large manufacturers, (Name) uses energy in many forms and spends in excess of $9 million annually for its energy requirements. . . . Perhaps the most critical form of energy in (Name)'s operation is natural gas. . . . (Name) is able to substitute propane gas for natural gas and we have installed stand-by propane units at several of our bakeries. We hope to add similar units at other plants if they are needed." (1st Quartile)

It's one thing to wring your hands over adversity; it's quite another to take explicit steps to cope with it and buffer yourself from it. This is perhaps not an indication of strategy, but it is a difference in style.

8. "*They are less clear in their plans . . . to respond to the world-wide protein demand*"

It is clearly not certain how the world will cope with this demand. Many of the problems involved are political. It is potentially both a great need and a real market opportunity. New processes and products may help meet this need. Here again, though the evidence is less robust than with some of the other issues, there is an apparent difference between the least successful five companies and the most successful five companies. One of the former and three of the latter mention it. The first and one of the other three are provided here.

> "As a major agriproducts company, (Name) is moving in new directions to meet the coming worldwide demand for food, particularly nutritive, high protein foods such as beef, soybeans, peanuts, rice and others." (4th Quartile)
>
> "The increasing awareness and concern over mounting worldwide protein shortage, particularly in the developing nations, have spurred considerable research into the creation of new sources of protein foods. (Name) has been among the major food companies engaged in a research and development program to meet world requirements for vital proteins. Much of our research has been centered on 'textured' vegetable proteins made from soybeans. In the past year the U.S. market for textured vegetable protein for human consumption has more than doubled. Industry sources project that this market will grow from its current estimated 100 million pounds to over 2.5 billion pounds by 1985. Our research staff has developed a broad technology for textured vegetable proteins, which is readily adaptable for use in a wide variety of foods containing beef, poultry or fish. In 1972 (Name) established the Protein Foods Division to develop, manufacture, and market world-wide this new line of textured vegetable proteins trade marked (Name)." (1st Quartile)

While it is of course folly to over-generalize from a single two-fold comparison, there appears to be an enormous difference in these quotations (and the fourth-quartile quote is the *only* one available from the sample). The first-quartile quote (the second presented) is illustrative of this whole article. It implies analysis of some depth, market/volume projections, product and process development (note value-added), product use, brand name, organization structure—all in this one cameo—*planning, responding proactively to the environment, and focus on value-added.*

The Generalizations

From the survey of annual reports (and report discussion as a reasonable surrogate for reality is substantiated by two independent tests), a number of differences seem apparent between less successful and more successful companies. Strategy and a concern for strategy may be seen as underlying these differences.

In the continuing stream of decisions, essentially by top management, about what kind of a company it will choose to be and how it will fit into its environment in a constructive way, the basic strategy of the company is vital. Strategy includes the choice of environmental domains, which are essentially product/markets, the determination of the nature of the interactions with these domains, and the internal adjustments suggested by these first two choices.[3] This strategy is ideally a sensible integration of the goals of the firm, the nature and competence of the firm, and the perceived opportunities and risks in the environment.

The successful company, and here we have something close to a tautology, chooses its strategy with some care. Strategic analysis can be thought of as a *continual search for rent*, where rent is to be interpreted in the economic meaning of returns to a unique place.

These returns, which are essentially in addition to the basic cost of capital, normally come from "value added." This unique place, and these returns, are usually found by research and development, new process development, new product development, brand names, reputation, service, and advertising. In a few cases it may come from synergy, or a fortunate combination of characteristics. Commanding market share of a particular market segment can be a result of this value added.

In conclusion, what is so fundamental about strategy and the weather? It is an interesting signal. The insight presented here, if any, is that the more successful companies essentially place themselves in a favorable niche in their environment, and buffer themselves from the more unpredictable and less controllable aspects of it. They frequently do this by focusing on value added. And such focus require both analysis and planning.

[3] See Bowman, E. H., Epistemology, corporate strategy, and academe, *Sloan Management Review*, Winter 1974, pp. 35–50.

PART 3:

Criteria for Success or Failure

Introduction to Part 3

It would be unfair to suggest that only those papers which I have chosen to include in this part deal with the success or failure of corporate planning, and readers will have already noticed a concern with these issues, particularly in Ringbakk (Chapter 1), Taylor and Irving (Chapter 4), and Bhatty (Chapter 10). Taylor and Irving in particular draw attention to corporate climate and the internal political problems of planning, and to the important role of top management.

Two of the earliest works appeared in book form. Scott[1] distilled a useful textbook from his studies of planning practise in various U.S. companies. This would not quite have fitted the requirements of the collection in this part of this book since it is a manual of good practise, rather than a study of relative success or failure. The book is still worth reading, although out of date.

The second study, by Warren,[2] is not dated and in my opinion is essential reading for anyone who is involved in even the smallest way with corporate planning. This book was something of a landmark and has influenced many writers and researchers, as well as a fair number of practitioners. It was based on a study of planning practise in fifteen major U.S. corporations and critically evaluates and improves the state of the art.

Warren drew attention to various confusions and misconceptions that frequently surround corporate planning. He identified three major "roadblocks" to the success of planning: an overwhelming concentration on short-term issues connected with pressure for present profits; backgrounds and personalities of many chief executives and operating personnel; backgrounds and personalities of many staff planners. He lists four tests which line managers use to judge the seriousness of any new planning initiative:

—Who is selected as planning director and how does top management treat him?
—What sort of backing does the chief executive give to longer-term proposals?
—What is top management's response to good and poor planning effort?
—How does corporate planning affect individual rewards?

Warren also stressed the importance of a measurement and control approach that was appropriate to corporate planning, and noted many deficiencies in (what was then) current practice.

Much of what he published in 1966 still emerges in the studies that have been made since. Although many additional points have been made by later researchers, there is continual reinforcement and elaboration of his basic themes. We know from the researches published in Part 1 of this book that a significant proportion of top management is less than satisfied with their corporate planning activity, and that this feeling appears to have no geographical boundaries. Yet if researchers continue to identify the same basic mistakes this suggests that either something in the psychological make-up of chief executives prevents them from taking good advice, or that they are ignorant of it. I suspect the latter, drawing my conclusions from the natural tendancy to appoint corporate planners from within the organisation observed in Part 1, the lack of significant planning experience of many in this function, and the failure of many to seek external advice from those who do know.

Although many of the attributes of planning success or failure repeat themselves, there is also an evolutionary aspect to planning. This is particularly apparent from the research studies which appear in Chapters 21 and 23.

Ringbakk's study of U.S. companies appeared earlier in this book. Another research-based paper of his has been chosen to open this part (Chapter 18). From studies of over 350 companies in Europe and the U.S.A. he deduced ten major reasons why planning sometimes fails:

—Failure to integrate corporate planning into the firm's total management system.
—Lack of understanding of the different dimensions of planning.
—Failure to gain the involvement of management at various levels in the organisation.
—The planning task delegated to staff who *do* the planning.
—Failure to understand that plans as developed will have to change.
—Trying to move too wide to quickly when introducing planning.
—Failure of management to operate through the plan.
—Confusion of financial extrapolation and projection with planning.
—Failure to obtain the necessary information needed for planning.
—Failure to see the overall picture of planning and putting too much effort on petty detail.

At about the same time as this article was published (1971) Steiner[3] was completing a landmark study of the pitfalls in planning. He found from his sample of 215 U.S. companies that there was a considerable degree of satisfaction with planning: only 24% claimed to be dissatisfied. He used a checklist of fifty planning pitfalls, and ranked these according to the degree of significance attached to them by his respondents. The top ten are listed below. It is significant that every company that reported falling into one of the top ten also reported dissatisfaction with its planning effort.

These findings were later incorporated with those of an international study by Steiner and Schollhammer (Chapter 20). Although there were some differences in specific countries, world wide the same top ten pitfalls were identified as the most significant (the order of these were not the same as in the U.S. study). The world wide top ten pitfalls, in priority order, were:

1. Assumption by top management that planning can be delegated to a planner.
2. Current problems taking all top management time at the expense of longer-term issues.
3. Failure to develop company goals.
4. Failure to create the right climate for planning.
5. Failure of top management to carry out reviews of plans prepared by divisional and departmental heads.
6. Lack of involvement of line personnel in the planning process.
7. Treating planning as something separate from the management process.
8. Top management's lack of understanding of planning.
9. Having the corporate planner at too low a level in the hierarchy.
10. Failure to use plans as standards for measuring management performance.

For good measure, the remaining forty pitfalls are also listed in Steiner and Schollhammer's paper.

Grinyer and Norborn (Chapter 19) published a study of strategic planning in twentyone U.K. companies (chronologically this fell between the U.S. and the international "pitfall studies" mentioned above. They found that nineteen of these appeared to be practising some form of formal strategic planning. However despite this, they found confusion over objectives, ambiguities over decision-making responsibility, and surprisingly little consideration of longer-term environmental influences in the review of alternative strategies. Their findings stress the political nature of strategic decision-taking.

The political and behavioural aspects of major strategic decisions also emerged in a book by Quinn.[4] This was based on in-depth studies in nine major companies. He found that major strategies emerge from a process of "logical incrementalism". They did not suddenly emerge from power interplays, nor from a single massive decision matrix. Instead the most effective strategies tended to come step by step from an interactive process

". . . in which the organisation probes the future, experiments, and learns from a series of partial (incremental) commitments rather than through global formulations of total strategies". Quinn's book is concerned with ways of managing this process of logical incrementalism.

Martin's study, Chapter 20, is based on a 7-year programme of continuous research into good planning practice, initially a major research programme over the period 1973—75. A review of the findings is made annually to monitor any changes, and at the time of publication of Martin's article three such reviews had been held. He identifies many problems in planning processes and found major difficulties in half of the sample of 100 U.K. companies. These had some relationships to problems found by other researchers, my main reason for selecting his article was his common-sense approach. The major problem he identifies are: getting line managers to plan; support from top management, inadequate thinking about the future, poor business understanding by managers, lack of realism and the need for better forecasting. He identifies the need to train many managers involved in planning (a need which generally goes unheeded by top management). It is interesting that this training need is also emphasised in the next study selected for this book.

Chapter 21 is a paper by Henry (1977) who surveyed twenty-nine major U.S. corporations. One of his most interesting findings was that most of the companies in his sample had redesigned their planning system in the 1970s. This is perhaps not as surprising a finding as Henry suggests, and supports the evolutionary nature of planning which has already been referred to. Henry's study again emphasised the, by now familiar, factors which contribute to planning failure, the main surprise here being that 11 years after Warren's[2] study managements are still making the same mistakes. Some additional problems were identified, particularly around the interaction of corporate planning department with the rest of the organising and around failures to train managers so that they understand corporate planning.

The last article I have chosen for this part (Chapter 23) is a study by Gluck, Kaufman and Walleck. This produces a definitive view of the evolutionary nature of planning (although their classifications are a little different from my observations which appear in the introduction to this book). They postulate four phases in the evolution of strategic planning:

1. Basic financial planning, seeking better operational control, aiming to meet budgets.
2. Forecast-based planning, seeking more effective planning for growth and trying to *predict* the future.
3. Externally oriented planning, seeking increased responsiveness to markets and competition, trying to think strategically.

4. Strategic management, seeking to management all resources to create competitive advantage and trying to "create the future".

Their findings were based on a sample of 120 companies. The importance of them to this part of the book is to leave the thought that although they all share common planning pitfalls, many of the factors that affect planning success or failure in a phase IV company would be very different from those in a phase I company.

References

1. B. W. Scott (1962) *Long Range Planning in American Industry*, American Management Association.
2. E. K. Warren (1966) *Long Range Planning: The Executive Viewpoint*, Prentice-Hall.
3. G. Steiner (1972) *Pitfalls in Comprehensive Long Range Planning*, Planning Executives Institute.
4. J. B. Quinn (1980) *Strategies for Change*, Irwin.

18
Why Planning Fails

K. A. RINGBAKK

What happens when a company decides to undertake serious corporate planning? Very often, top executives see the need for a formal planning system, but when the system is actually put into practice, it fails to function the way it was intended to.

Ento International is a typical example. Involved in the basic processing industry with the majority of its output being sold to the aluminum and steel industries, Ento exported over 70 % of its output to customers located in a dozen countries. For most of its life, the company had enjoyed a seller's market and had concentrated on production and expansion of capacity. In recent years, however, Ento had seen new processes introduced in the steel industry make the demand for its output grow at a limited rate; developments in the aluminum industry were rumored to be taking place which would largely reduce the need for Ento's materials. The board of management therefore decided long-range planning would offer the necessary panacea.

Their first step was to create a planning department. This department was given responsibility to develop the necessary plans and was to report to the executive vice-president. The vice-president called in a well-known consulting firm to help get the planning effort on its feet. During the first year, the department worked closely with the consultant to develop Ento's first long-range plan.

As their work progressed, they were able, using the procedures and forms provided by the consulting firm, to issue a planning manual to all the managers in the operating divisions. The planning manuals basically outlined the steps an individual division would have to go through in order to come up with its own ten-year plan. The planning department also issued a set of detailed forms to be filled in each year by each of the company's profit centers. In addition, the planning department developed its own mathematical model of Ento which permitted very interesting sensitivity analyses and alternative evaluation exercises. The consulting

---

This article was originally published in *European Business*, Spring 1971.

firm's European Area manager and the planning director wrote two articles about Ento's advances in the use of management science techniques in planning. They were proud to be able to demonstrate how they used the computer and various optimizing techniques to enable management to make a more rational choice between alternatives.

Planning—An Esoteric but Meaningless Exercise?

However, after two years, the planning system had failed to clear up some of Ento's major problems: Ento did not have an improved sales or profit picture, the strategic plan had not been successfully developed, and there was frustration throughout the organization about the complex forms and procedures which the central planners required all departments to complete in September, October, and November of each year.

What had gone wrong? All along the path of establishing its planning system, Ento had made several unfortunate strategic choices.

For one thing, the management had created a central staff planning department instead of putting the responsibility with the line management. As Ento's management learned later, planning and doing are part of the same job, and when the top executives are not personally engaged in the process, it can be doomed from the start.

In fact, interviews with operating management showed that they considered planning as an esoteric exercise, a once-a-year activity concerned with the generation of not too meaningful documents. The result was that each division went through crash programs to produce a plan that it felt top management was not concerned with.

How true this was can be measured by the plan itself—presented to management in an attractive green leather cover with the title in glittering gold letters—or the general lack of comprehension and interest on the part of the top executives when the planning department presented them with mathematical models and explanations of its techniques. The material had been too technical and sophisticated, and line management came away aloof, perceiving the techniques more as a toy than an operating tool. In overhauling the planning system, management came to realize that the complicated and subtle techniques were only one part of the planning process. Before they could be used effectively, management had to take care of simpler, more basic tasks, like carrying on a corporate audit to analyze the company's strengths and weaknesses or improving its marketing inputs. Their strategic plans could not be developed without being based on their unique strengths.

Is this case exceptional or caricatural? Unhappily not. The results of a wide survey of decision-making and planning practices in over 350 European or American corporations carried out by the author show the contrary. This investigation also included over 65 companies which participated by means of in-depth interviews giving a very detailed insight into their planning practice.

The other part of our research is based on a detailed questionnaire containing 32 pre-structured and open-ended questions covering the most important aspects of planning and decision-making philosophy and practices. Many companies, in addition to filling in this questionnaire, sent us supplementary information such as planning manuals, copies of their planning documents, statements of corporate objectives, annual reports, etc. The 286 participating companies thus form the sample the main characteristics of which are described below.

But what do we mean by planning? In its entirety, it is a field that reaches into five dimensions—Philosophy, Inputs, Process, Outputs, and System— which I lump together under the acronym PIPOS (see Fig. 18.1). Let us describe very briefly what is meant.

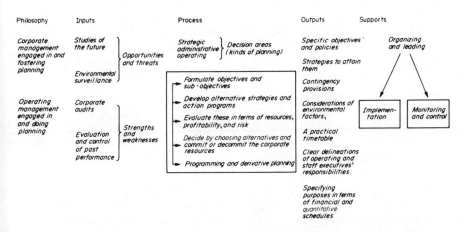

FIG. 18.1. *The five simple elements of planning.*

Planning as a *philosophy* grows out of the overall management philosophy of the firm. If the general management style is based on last-minute decisions, hastily arrived at by intuition, planning will not fit in. It results naturally when management uses sound analyses—which make clear the major relationships in a decision—before choosing a path of action or committing resources. Generally these analyses (of the significant elements of the environment and the firm) are arrived at through scientific management principles. In brief, planning is not only a tool but a management style as well.

Another characteristic of planning as a philosophy is future orientation on the part of the decision-makers. One company studied in a ten-year span had made a complete turn-around in terms of market surveys and products made. The chief executive officer explained how its assessing likely future developments had enabled his company to chart a course which had higher pay-off potential and a lower level of risk. In 1959 more than 90 % of its sales were derived from agricultural products. By 1970 a complete turn-around had occurred in which less than 10 % of its sales came from such agricultural products. Here management, looking ahead, identified the need for getting into a new business. But the overall management philosophy stretches into other areas as well.

Both corporate and operating managers must be actively engaged in the planning for their areas of responsibility, and broad participation in planning is solicited from throughout the company.

As regards "inputs," the alert planning executive must monitor market trends, customer behavior and demand, competition, government as a customer as well as a regulator and a political force, channels of distribution, and those interest groups and institutions outside the firm with a bearing on the firms' actions and success.

He will often scrutinize changing value systems, technological developments, the impact of decreasing leisure time, increasing corporate social conscience, and the increasing role of multinational corporations. Said one planning officer about their "advanced conceptual planning":

> An interesting development with advanced conceptual planning was that managers looking 15 to 20 years into the future had fun doing it and learned something about their future. This all resulted in much better *five-year plans* from each of these divisions. Even though it is costly and time-consuming, it has made division executives see the five-year plans in a different perspective.

Corporate audits are inputs needed to relate the firm to the environment. Designed to assess the firm's capabilities and general competitive strengths as well as weaknesses, such audits give management a profile of all areas of operations so that strategies can be built on strengths and not on weaknesses.

Evaluation of past performance is also a necessary input for decisions regarding future actions.

The Rush to do Long-range Planning

But the "process" of planning may be the most important dimension, and it must be adapted for a particular time period and for the area of decision-making, be it strategic, administrative, or operating. Often these decision areas are chosen according to a function such as marketing, production, finance, management development, or research and development.

In the rush to do long-range planning, however, many firms often forget that it is more important to decide on the kind of planning to be done in terms of decision areas than to come out with a bright new five-year plan.

The process can be set in motion for a period of one, two, or five years, but will quickly be grounded if the planners are unclear about the necessary attention to be devoted to strategic versus administrative problems.

Given the increased tendency towards decentralized organization and greater participation in decision-making, it becomes clear that each manager must be responsible for the planning of his area of responsibility. Part of the process or whole subprocesses should therefore be carried out at each management level.

Most of the executives interviewed explained that the problem lies in having sufficiently general objectives to apply to the firm's overall direction, all the while remaining specific enough to be significant. "Even though on the surface our objectives may seem simple and meaningless," commented one corporate planner who summed up the problem, "they still represent a careful consideration and evaluation of the future. Of course, I doubt whether we will be any more satisfied with our current objectives and statements ten years from now than we are today. These statements must be dynamic and change with the changing nature of business—only the purposes will remain fixed."

From this process there must emerge a plan, in written form, for experience has shown that "if you cannot write it down, you have not thought it through."

The outputs (listed on Fig. 18.1) will no doubt vary with each company. Pressure occurs for executive time and attention in such areas as inventories, profits, or marketing. Nowadays, the market is often the most important factor to consider in planning.

The head of the corporate planning department of an American automobile company has this to say:

> It is necessary to develop the plans according to the (above) format covering environment, objectives, and strategies. This must be done for 1) the total division, 2) business subgroups, and 3) functional subgroups. For us, we have realized that money is earned in the market, ergo, this has become the most important subgroup in planning.

The last element of the PIPOS dimension is planning as a "system". Once the plan has been made, measures must be taken to insure that the tasks planned are carried out, that executive involvement with the plan is clearly outlined, and that the different dimensions of planning are well linked to the management system itself.

And, like any system, it must be conceived of as part of the regular, orderly way of managing. The outputs must be adaptable to any major changes that occur within or without the firm.

However, understanding planning does not mean immediate successful application. Of the firms interviewed in our survey, each one reported minor or major difficulties in one area or another. Through a compilation of these areas, we have arrived at ten reasons why planning fails.

Corporate Planning not Integrated into Total Management System

Corporate planning has not been integrated into the firm's total management system.

To be meaningful, corporate planning must be related to the total process of managing. A company with a total managing system considers market needs to then determine product design. This in turn establishes the firm's product offering from which follow the resource needs and the organization of the resources. Based on this, production will take place followed by distribution of the product which is paralleled by marketing communications. This may then satisfy the market needs.

The problems arise when corporate planning is not properly fitted into this management system. If planning is a process—a process of preparing for action, that is—it must mesh with the processes of organizing, leading, and controlling.

The effort managers devote to planning is determined by the importance they attach to planning as a means of managing. (Naturally, the type of planning—strategic, administrative or operating—will vary with each manager's needs.) The lack of understanding of benefits of planning, confidence, participation, resource allocation for planning, use of plans by executives and control of what was planned seem to be an impediment to the effectiveness of planning systems in many companies.

When asked whether executives should spend more time on their corporate planning effort, the companies replied: *yes,* 79.4 %, *no,* 17.5 %, n.a., 3.1 %.

In the comments on this question, only 15 companies stated explicitly that their executives spent an adequate portion of their time on planning.

An equally difficult area occurs in companies in which managers plan but do not act. In one U.S. conglomerate, a top manager explained, "Broadly seen, planning is managing. It is one of line management's key functions. Without understanding this, one often develops paper plans only. And corporate planning is nothing but a paper tiger."

A *second reason* for the failure of planning is *lack of understanding of the different dimensions of planning.* To recall our acronym, PIPOS, planning must be based on "philosophy," "inputs," "process," "outputs" and "system". Often one of these dimensions is neglected for others. Inputs may be poorly assembled or incomplete. Or planning may be insufficiently

TABLE 18.1

The answers to the question "What would you list as the most crucial problems you face in your planning?" are very often related to "human" problems in planning.

	Number of firms
Recognize need for planning as opposed to current operations; to overcome resistance against planning	33
Confidence in and support of planning	8
Commitment to, and interest and participation in planning	44
Understanding of planning, availability of know-how on planning	23
Getting the right people for planning, allocation of time and money for planning	23

conceived of as a process; the planners may not review the plans often enough or make the plans adaptable to changes in the environment.

Missing links in the planning process and consequently in the output of this process often occur in many companies. The data in Table 18.2 were generated in response to the question:

The weakest point in the planning process of many companies is the generating of alternative strategies, their evaluation, the selection of the best ones, and the subsequent inclusion of several alternatives in their plan. The phenomenon that in most cases the plans are "one-alternative plans" suggests that their value and application are to a certain extent dubious.

In one large company in the survey, the planning dimensions were

TABLE 18.2

"The following represent elements that may be part of a company plan. For each of these elements, please indicate what is presently being done in your company."

	Now include in our plan	
	Number of firms	Percentage
Broad overall objectives	207	72.4
Specific sub-objectives	184	64.3
Outline of actions required to reach objectives	173	60.5
Alternative courses of actions, alternative strategy	76	26.6
Identification of responsibilities for various planning tasks	153	53.5
Programming for implementation of planning tasks (action programs)	125	43.7
Check points for control of what was planned	126	44.1
Companies with written plans	240	84.0

poorly understood and insufficient resources had been committed to the planning department. The plans were theoretically formed by the company's 26 subsidiaries, to be then reviewed at headquarters. From there, a synthesis was to occur forming divisional plans and, based on these, the corporate plan. The planning department, however, consisted of only two people plus a secretary. It could not do all the work expected of it. The subsidiaries suffered when trying to make up their own plans for they rarely had the benefit of the planning department's activities.

The corporation finally realized that planning was not just a tool or technique, but a way of managerial living. Courses were organized to teach division managers how to approach planning and to explain its many facets and the involvement necessary for it.

The first two reasons related to the lack of understanding of corporate planning have been and still are the biggest stumbling blocks to successful corporate planning systems. However, these are not all. Other reasons also often stand in the way of better planning.

All of Management must be Involved

Management at different levels in the organization has not properly engaged in or contributed to the planning activities is the third reason. In many companies lip service has been paid to planning. Although management at the top has in words recognized the importance and desirability of formal planning, the necessary action and involvement have not resulted. In many cases top management has embraced planning as a panacea to all corporate ills. There has been a "faddish" acceptance of planning but the appropriate steps to ensure its success have not been taken. The general tendency has been to set up a formal planning staff to whom planning has been delegated. Since planning is such an integral part of managing, it must be the ultimate responsibility of line management. Planning attempted by staff has been doomed to failure.

A further problem at the top level has been managers who expect immediate results from planning. With greater and greater short-run orientation, the emphasis shifts to producing tangible results within one or two years. Since planning, however, is concerned with the futurity of current decisions—with implications for four or five years ahead—this ends up putting the horse before the cart.

When it comes to operating management, the horse is of a different color. Their first and foremost responsibility is, of course, current operations. The concern has been more with the next quarter than with the next year or beyond.

In our survey we ran into companies where operating management refused to accept planning beyond the budgeting period. In many cases, the major point of conflict was operating management's refusal to accept a set of objectives developed at headquarters.

In other cases, the refusal stems from a deeper psychological problem. People tend to avoid the uncertain and the foreign. Change represents uncertainty and is very often perceived as a threat. The tendency therefore is to stick to the same known methods used successfully in the past. Very often planning is equated with "the management of change." To convince reluctant managers to perceive change as opportunities rather than threats becomes a necessary task when introducing widespread corporate planning.

In one U.S. corporation that recently began formal planning, top management found that it took more than a heavy concern with planning or a large investment in planning efforts at the executive level. Only after three years had top management and operating management arrived at the same outlook towards planning—as an activity that they believed in and were willing to rely upon. And even after the three years, management still feels the need to inculcate their operating managers with this approach to managing.

Obviously the blame for failure cannot be put on either the consultants or the managements of the firms. Both client and consultant share the responsibility for developing a system which is appropriate for the task at hand.

However, when companies decide to establish a formal planning system, they often get carried away. They wish to have each and every aspect of planning completed the first time through the planning cycle. The result is that they attempt too much at one time. They get either bogged down in too much detail, or hung up on the lack of formal objectives, the inadequacy of their input information, and a general haziness about how planning should be done throughout the organization. Disillusionment and frustration come hard on the heels of this first planning attempt.

It is better to start primitively, using a crude system, than not to be able to start at all. The simple planning system which is correct will be much more efficient than an elaborate and sophisticated one which is not. It is also much easier to expand the elementary than to change the complex.

An obvious corollary is the importance of developing the system for the people who will be using it. How many times do managements fail to realize that it is easier to adapt systems than it is to change people?

Fascination with tools and techniques can provide other problems in this area. Instead of creating a detailed idea of what the management system should look like, of which people should be where, managers often go straightaway towards the refinements, the sophisticated techniques. They must not become the ends rather than the means.

The Planning Department should not Plan

The responsibility for planning is often wrongly vested solely in a planning department. Planning and doing are two parts of the same job. As such, planning is line management's responsibility and cannot be delegated to a staff. If staff can assist in the planning jobs, it can never replace line management in creating the basic planning skeleton.

However, many firms set up a special planning department. In the companies surveyed, no fewer than 68 executives stated that the planning department *does* most of the planning and develops the plans for various areas of operation.

(Out of this number, 19 executives stated that the planning department should develop objectives, strategies, and policies; 16 executives stated that the planning department develops the total corporate plan, and about 25 executives even said that their planning department develops plans for functional areas such as marketing, production, R & D, personnel, and finance. Instead of acting as a catalyst and coordinator, the planning department is doing the job which should logically be done by the functional and operating departments.)

To prove their usefulness, the planning departments set to work developing highly elaborate plans. Says one executive interviewed, "They developed the plans which are leather-bound and have gold letters on them. These are then put on corporate bookshelves for all to see but nobody to use."

A vicious circle can then arise. Line management abdicates its responsibility in face of a special "planning department." The plans developed by the department are removed from the reality of operations and are either too complicated or irrelevant. Line management then criticizes the plans as being "Ivory Tower" and refuses to use them. The planning ends up meaningless and in vain.

In many companies, management expects that the plans as developed will be realized. But planning must be a continuous, dynamic process, reflecting changes taking place particularly outside the firm. A given plan is static. Reflecting the premises and assumptions, the forecasts, and the general inputs available at the time it was developed, the plan may be out of date fairly rapidly after development.

The typical attitude for the corporations having mastered the planning approach to managing was the following voiced by one chief executive:

> One cannot check long-range planning by its coming to pass. There will be many changes before we get to a predetermined point in the future. Plans will change and we need to have flexibility in planning. It is ludicrous to do five-year planning every five years. Instead, we need to plan every year. The plan is only an indicator that this is what a company should be doing, that this is the direction it should be going in.

A good manager should be measured as much on his ability to deviate from a plan as on his ability to fulfill it.

The sixth reason is often that *in starting formal planning too much is attempted at once.* Many companies in both Europe and the United States launch themselves whole-heartedly into their planning systems. Often bought from outside consultant organizations, the systems are elaborate and complex. Most of the time, too elaborate and too complex, lacking adaptations to the unique aspects of the corporation, they end up being totally useless.

How typical is the example of one of the Norwegian firms in our survey! Made up of various autonomous profit centers, the corporation felt itself too complex to develop a planning system from scratch. It therefore turned to an international consulting firm. They devised a formal planning system which for the first three years failed to give management what it wanted. In the words of one top executive, "The system exists and functions well, but does not produce what we want it to." It took a long while for the company's management to modify the system to fit their peculiarities and requirements.

Another common complaint came from one Swiss manager whose corporation has extensive international operations. They too had called in a consultant who actively participated in the development of the planning system and the first set of plans. Each activity and function had a set of formal objectives, sub-objectives and action programs. "They're complete," said the manager, "but there are so many plans we can't keep track of them." They ended up by "deformalizing" the system, replacing it with a more primitive and elementary one.

What is relevant is first the development of a right plan. When significant and unforeseen changes take place, the existing plan may no longer be the right one. It is then necessary to develop the new plan. This again stresses the importance of making the planning process a continuous one.

Management often Disregards the Plan

Management fails to operate by the plan: this is the seventh reason for failure.

As long as the plan developed is the best plan available and appears right under the circumstances, the plan should be used. In cases where planning as an overall management philosophy has not been fully absorbed, the tendency is to engage in short but hectic periods of plan development to meet certain corporate requirements. After much pain, long hours, and much frustration, a plan is finally put together and submitted. At that point the tendency frequently is for executives to mutter, "Thank God *that's* over! Now we can get back to business again!"

One company pointed out that developing plans must make managers think and resolve the different problems they will be encountering in their operations. Furthermore, although over a long period of time the plan may end up being out of date, there must be sufficient stability so that corporate resources can be committed. One of the qualities of good management will be the ability to adhere to the plan even when the going gets tough.

That extrapolation and financial projections are confused with planning is another planning pitfall. To the extent that the future will be the same as the past, only more so, one can extrapolate past actions and results into the future and argue that this is what will happen. However, when the future differs in significant respects, such extrapolative thinking becomes inadequate. In areas of technology, competition, international business, and the like, the changes taking place are of such a fundamental nature that a new approach to planning may indeed be required.

Much planning today can be described as extended budgeting. In the average firm this has meant planning starting with today and going five years into the future. The concern has largely been with the financial and quantitative results with which one is concerned in one-year budgeting. However, the underlying causal factors which determine the financial results often have not been adequately covered. More fundamental qualitative thinking is required. What appears to be needed most urgently is "strategic planning."

Planning falls into two categories: action planning and strategic planning. *Action planning* relates to the planning which starts with today and goes into the future as far as possible or necessary. Action planning is built around current products and current markets and the momentum the firm has as of today. This type of planning takes into consideration both the products and markets which are in development and which will begin to yield commercial results in the time period being planned for. An example is the inclusion of revenue and profit expected from a product which will be introduced one year from the moment when the planning is done.

Strategic planning, on the other hand, is characterized by great freedom since resources have not been committed. Here management makes decisions regarding new products, new markets, or a combination of new products and new markets. It is such strategic planning which will command more and more of management's attention in the 1970s.

Planning with the Wrong Information

Inadequate inputs used in the planning could be the ninth reason for failure.

Much of the information readily available in the corporation is not suitable for the planning. The information generally generated is control-oriented and has not been developed for decision-making purposes. The information needed in planning usually requires a substantial alteration of the company's management information system. For strategic decision-making where the concern is with relating the firm to the environment, environmental surveillance is required. In reality, previous little environmental surveillance takes place.

Also, the internal data commonly generated in the firm tend to be inadequate for planning purposes. While it is often recognized that management represents the company's scarcest resource, there are few management audits undertaken to determine the breadth and depth of the management team. For example, in most Norwegian corporations management is strong when it comes to technology and engineering, but marketing and commercial expertise are lacking. What is needed are corporate audits looking at the whole set of assets that the firm boasts.

These needs are only just now being discovered. When asked about environmental studies and management audits, barely more than half the companies admitted to including them in their plans. Table 18.3 is fairly indicative.

TABLE 18.3

Question: "The following represents elements that may be part of a company plan. For each of these elements please indicate what actually is being done in your company."

	Companies which include them in their plan	
	Number	Percentage
Study of environment	149	52.1
Company strengths and weaknesses	149	52.1
Assumptions about future:		
— Competitive actions	143	50.0
— Inflation	137	47.9
— Market—trends and changes	206	72.0
— Technological change	165	57.7

Many executives have commented on the inadequacy of accounting data in their planning. The data are history-oriented and collected with the custodial responsibility of accounting in mind. To be meaningful, planning requires inputs from across the functional boundaries of the firm. In reality, this is not taking place (see Table 18.4).

Most firms report that information and other inputs are produced unevenly both for the short run (one year ahead) and for three years ahead.

TABLE 18.4

Question: "Which of the following groups regularly prepare written inputs which are used in your planning?"

	For one year ahead Number	For three years ahead Number
Accounting	243 (85.0 %)	122 (42.7 %)
Engineering	175 (61.2 %)	155 (40.2 %)
Finance	235 (82.2 %)	162 (56.6 %)
Legal	51 (17.8 %)	34 (11.9 %)
Market research	182 (63.6 %)	137 (47.9 %)
Marketing	220 (76.9 %)	154 (53.8 %)
Personnel and industrial relations	162 (56.6 %)	91 (31.8 %)
Planning	185 (64.7 %)	155 (54.2 %)
Public relations	78 (27.3 %)	27 (9.4 %)
Research & development	191 (66.8 %)	132 (48.3 %)
Sales	234 (81.8 %)	149 (52.1) %
Top management	162 (56.6 %)	137 (47.9) %

Although 84 % of the respondents have written corporate plans, only 76.5 % do total long-range planning for a period of three years or more. What usually happens is that the following hitches occur:

1. The accounting and finance departments are the most prolific providers of inputs in the short run, causing a *budgeting bias* among the firms surveyed.
2. Finance also ends up being the most important for the period three years ahead. The planning then has an inadequate base. If finance is an auxiliary function, its activity logically follows and is based on the primary functions of production and marketing. Most firms need a relatively greater input from sales, marketing, marketing research, and research and development.
3. Taking the reciprocal of the percentages, one must conclude that a surprisingly large proportion of firms do *not* get the necessary inputs from top management ($100 \% - 47.9 = 52.1 \%$), engineering ($100 \% - 40.2 = 59.8 \%$), marketing ($100 \% - 53.8 = 46.2 \%$) or personnel ($100 \% - 31.8 = 62.2 \%$).

Without such inputs one may question whether the planning done can be anything more than of an extrapolative kind.

Too Much Emphasis on only One Aspect of Planning

Many companies fail to see the overall picture of planning. They get hung up on little details. A major fault is focusing too much attention on formulation of company objectives. Most companies try to set objectives. In fact, 99.3 % of the companies surveyed felt they needed objectives. However, only 86.7% believe these objectives should be in writing, and only 34.6% thought that written objectives exist in other firms.

In other words, planning generally needs objectives, but can sometimes do without complete, written statements if this means stifling the planning effort.

Sometimes planning can be done without formal written statements— especially if this means a shot in the arm for other areas of the planning effort. A portion of the executives replied that they do without a set of objectives for the following reasons:

— It reduces creativity and innovation or causes inflexibility.
— Executive refusal to accept the responsibility that the formal objectives dictate.
— Objectives expressed as a statement are so over-simplified as to be useless.
— Real objectives are personal objectives of top management, determined by the way they are rewarded.
— It would require useful thinking on a difficult subject, something which not everybody is prepared to do.
— Management feels that everybody knows the objectives anyway.
— Planning per se is not formalized.

Obviously, there is no binding rule. Each company will have to decide for itself whether or not it needs written objectives.

Moreover, the essential point lies elsewhere. As our survey has shown, planning is a complicated and delicate matter. Each of the ten reasons for failure can emerge closely interwined with another.

19
Strategic Planning in 21 U.K. Companies

P. H. GRINYER AND D. NORBURN

Introduction

During the last twenty-one years there has been a growing advocacy of systematic, formal, rational approaches to corporate planning by both academics and consultants.[1] These approaches vary in detail but share a number of common features. First they are formal. Procedures used in the planning process are prescribed and often documented. Stages of the planning process are often scheduled and progress is controlled against the resulting time-table. Consequently, second, responsibility for taking strategic decisions is clearly defined, and assumed to be generally recognized by senior executives.[2] Third, corporate objectives are made explicit and provide an integrating, directive force throughout the organization. They so become the apex of a hierarchy of objectives.[3] In addition, they are yard-sticks against which performance may be measured and alternative strategies judged.[1] Fourth, the environment of the company is monitored to both signal the need for a review of strategy,[4] and provide information as a basis for choice between alternative strategies.[1]

Evidence suggests that a large number of companies in the USA and UK have now adopted such formal approaches to corporate planning.[5]

This article was originally published in *Long Range Planning*, Volume 7, No. 4, August 1974.

Note: Dr. Grinyer is now Esmee Fairbairn Professor of Economics (Finance and Investment) at St. Andrews University.

[1] See in particular Ansoff (1965) and Gilmore and Bradenburg (1962). A review is given in Grinyer (1971).

[2] Early advocates of clear role definition in strategic planning include Selznick (1948) and Simon (1960). There have been many since.

[3] See Emery (1969), Simmons (1968) and Grinyer (1972) for example.

[4] See Aguilar (1967) for an outstanding account of how this is done in a number of American companies.

[5] Early studies by Hewkin and Kempner (1968), Ringbakk (1969), Strigel (1970), Schollhammer (1970) and Irving (1970) suggested that formal planning was neither as widespread nor sophisticated as the literature suggested. However, publications by Wagle

However, there is little evidence to show how formal planning actually affects strategic decision taking, or that it pays in terms of financial performance.[6]

To learn more about the way in which UK companies make strategic decisions in practice, and how this is related to financial performance, 91 directors in 21 different companies were interviewed. In most of the companies interviewees included the Managing Director, Marketing Director, Financial Director and Production Director. The companies were drawn from the glass, oil, chemical, scientific instrument, engineering, metal working, building, and leisure industries. Their sizes ranged from annual turnover of less than £5 million to over £25 million. Multiple interviews were conducted in each company to make sure that results were not distorted by unusual individual perceptions and to permit measurement of the extent of agreement between directors on each of the points covered. A test was then applied to determine whether the level of agreement could be due to chance alone. For instance, in most cases there was less than a 5% probability that two-thirds or more of the executives would agree by chance only, and hence this level of agreement was taken in such cases to signal that the answer given was correct. This we have called the "consensus" answer.[7]

Use of this approach provided information on strategic planning in each of the 21 UK companies. Objectives, who was responsible for setting them, and who most strongly influenced this choice were established. Responsibility for initiating and for taking decisions affecting market penetration and product range was determined. Means by which relevant information was acquired by directors interviewed were identified. The specific items of information received and used both to signal the need for review and in the review itself were found. In addition, by comparing answers given by individuals with "consensus" answers, the level of agreement between board members on each of the above was measured.[7]

These were then related to financial performance. A number of measures of financial performance· were considered and all found to be strongly positively correlated. Hence, a single measure, return on net assets, was used. To allow for differences between the trading environments of the companies, the performance of each company was compared with the mean return on net assets for companies in its own trading environment, or

---

and Jenkins (1971) and Ringbakk (1972) now suggest wider adoption. Our own study suggested very wide adoption.

   [6] The studies published to date are those of Thune and House (1970), Herold (1972), Ansoff et alia (1970) and Denning and Lehr (1972). These all used mailed questionnaires, which means that the samples might have been self-selected and biased.

   [7] A fuller account of choice of the sample frame, selection of the sample, and characteristics of the company may be found in Norburn (1972) and Grinyer and Norburn (1973). These also give details of the research methodology.

competitive segment. The resulting differences were standardized to allow for differences in volatility of these segments.[7] The resulting figures were averaged over five years[8] to allow for variations in performance between years.

The analysis this permitted revealed some relationships of practical significance. They suggest that some, but not all, aspects of planning pay. We turn to the question of which in subsequent sections.

How the 21 Companies Plan Strategy

Formality

Each of the 91 executives was asked to select the appropriate description for the strategy planning process from a list of four. In 15 of the companies, the "consensus" answer was that the planning process involved pre-ordained flows of information, which were discussed at scheduled management meetings as a matter of routine. Executives interviewed in four of the companies were unable to reach consensus.[9] However, further detailed examination of the information flows used indicated formality, i.e. use of preordained, written flows, in each case. Only two companies showed agreement that pre-ordained flows of information and scheduled meetings were not used: in these detailed examination of information flows confirmed the informality of the process.

So in the 21 companies 19 appeared to be using some form of formal corporate planning. This suggests that there has been a substantial growth of formal strategic planning over the last three or four years.[5]

Objective Setting

Executives interviewed were asked who assumed responsibility for setting objectives and who most strongly influenced their choice. They were also asked what changes they would make to the existing situation.

Only four of the 21 companies failed to achieve consensus on the identity of the objective setter. Twelve companies agreed that the chief executive, the Managing Director, was responsible. Four companies agreed that corporate objectives were a board responsibility. In one company, a subsidiary of a holding company, there was consensus that the Chairman, as the voice of the parent, set objectives. Not one of the 91 executives interviewed wished to change the status quo.

The findings so confirm that corporate objectives are the responsibility

[8] Exponential smoothing was used with a heavy weight on the last year.
[9] I.e. the test on consensus, when applied showed that there was more than 5% probability if the level of agreement being due to chance.

of the chief executive, or alternatively the Board, and that this is thought proper by the top management team.

However, he is strongly influenced in his choice by the Marketing function, which may be seen from Table 19.1 to be the dominant influence in 18 of the 21 companies. Finance is surprisingly weak in its influence, as are Production and Technical functions, each having strong influence in only nine companies. Moreover, whilst there was agreement in four more companies that Finance should be more influential, and in three that Production should be, it would appear that the major influence of Marketing was accepted as desirable.

TABLE 19.1. *Functions Agreed to Exert Strong Influence Over Objectives*

Function	No. of companies where exerts strong influence	No. of companies where agreed that should exert strong influence
Chairman[a]	5	5
Managing Director[a]	3	3
Marketing	18	18
Financial	9	13
Production	9	12
Personnel	1	1
Technical	9	9
Others	4	4

[a] In companies where he was not agreed (by "consensus") to be responsible for setting objectives. The function was taken to exert a strong influence in the company when a sufficient number of interviewees identified it to satisfy the "consensus" test, i.e. to ensure that there was less than 5 % probability that the answer was due to chance. The number of companies which thought that a function should exert influence was determined similarly.

In view of the importance of financial objectives, see below the heavy dominance of the Marketing function is surprising.

Objectives

What objectives did the companies have and what did they think desirable? Answers are summarized in Table 19.2.

Financial performance was clearly thought to be of over-riding importance. Executives in 19 of the 21 companies agreed that profitability was an objective although this figure masks differences of opinion over an appropriate measure. No more than three companies could agree on any other objective.

The small number of objectives agreed by each company is implicit in Table 19.2. Eleven of the companies could agree on only one objective,

TABLE 19.2. *Company Objectives*

Objective	Existing		Desired	
	Stated[a]	Consensus[b]	Stated	Consensus
Liquidity	6	1	17	6
Profitability	21	19	21	21
Coverage	2	0	5	1
Leverage	1	0	3	0
Volume	4	0	16	7
Penetration	15	3	18	9
Product development	14	3	19	10
Market development	13	2	20	14
Diversification	3	1	14	4
Pricing	2	0	14	3
Customer service	7	0	14	8
Capacity utilization	4	0	17	7
Steady production	1	0	15	2
Production costs	3	0	19	11
Industrial relations	7	1	14	6
Company image	9	1	18	6
Community responsibility	4	1	6	0
Corporate productivity	7	0	18	6
Others	10	3	3	1

[a] "Stated" gives the number of companies in which at least one interviewee stated the objective.
[b] "Consensus" shows the number of companies in which the level of agreement was such that the "consensus" test was satisfied, i.e. there was less than 5 % probability that the result could have been due to chance.

profitability, six had two, one had three and two had four. Executives in one company couldn't agree on a single objective. By comparing the number of companies in which an objective was stated, by at least one executive, with the number in which there was agreement on this point it becomes apparent that the main reason for this low number was *differences* between executives on what the objectives were rather than a common, agreed perception of a low number.[10] This suggests an alarming level of disagreement over corporate purpose among the top management team in the 21 UK companies.

Yet there would appear to be a general desire for a greater definition of the corporate purpose among executives. Table 19.2 shows that interviewees would prefer more objectives. More marketing and production objectives, in particular, were thought desirable. One wonders why, given this consensus among top managers on a need for more objectives, they haven't been adopted.

[10] The median number of objectives stated by at least one individual in the company was six compared with the median of one for those agreed.

This confusion over objectives is particularly surprising in view of the apparently wide adoption of formal planning processes. It may reflect the difficulty experienced in many companies in setting explicit, unambiguous objectives. Alternatively, it might suggest that, even although such explicit objectives exist (as in quite a few of the companies visited), they are not taken seriously by the directors who ultimately have responsibility for making decisions. The decision makers continue to work with their own personal sets of objectives. These two possible explanations may, of course, be related. Whether the explicit objectives arrived at by the formal planning process do not, due to difficulties of adequately identifying objectives, reflect the personal value systems of directors with decision making power, it is less likely that they will be recognized by these decision makers.

Strategic Decision Taking

Executives interviewed were each asked who was responsible for initiating a review and for the final decision on action for each of nine types of decision. Of these six related to greater market penetration (pricing, distribution, costs, advertising and promotion) while three were longer term 'and concerned the product range (product improvement, product drop, and product introduction). The interviewees were also asked who strongly influenced these decisions.

Analysis of the answers showed that the chief executive dominates all these fields of decision taking. In view of the marketing orientation of the decisions, it was no surprise to find that there was wide mention of the Marketing function, and that it clearly exerted a strong influence over all nine decisions. Surprisingly, though, the Finance and Production functions were seen to have virtually no influence, except that Finance had responsibility in seven companies for initiating reviews on costs.

However, although the general picture to emerge is clear, there were considerable disagreements within companies.

In one company, the executives interviewed could not agree about responsibility for a single decision, and there was agreement on all nine in only one company. Table 19.3 shows the number of companies, out of the total of 21, which agreed on responsibility for between zero and nine of the decisions. The average (median) number of decisions on which there was agreement on the decision makers was the same for both initiation of the review and final action, i.e. six. Table 19.3 also indicates that, as was to be expected, there was even more disagreement about who influenced the decisions.

Over all of the companies, and all of the possible decision making roles, we found that 52% were disputed. Moreover, of the disputed identities,

TABLE 19.3. *No. of companies which could agree on the decisions*

	Decision-makers		Decision influencers	
No. of decisions agreed[a]	Initiation	Action	Initiation	Action
0	1	1	2	3
1	0	1	3	1
2	1	1	4	5
3	1	2	3	6
4	0	2	5	3
5	7	3	1	0
6	2	3	0	2
7	4	3	3	0
8	4	3	0	0
9	1	2	0	0
Medians	6	6	3	3

[a] By consensus test: i.e. where level of agreement is unlikely (i.e. has a probability of less than 5 %) to be due to chance.

83 % concerned managerial functional responsibility. Disagreement on decision making roles within the 21 companies is, therefore, of alarming proportions. The apparent confusion, like that over objectives, casts grave doubts on the adequacy of the avowedly formal planning processes in the companies.

Means of Obtaining Relevant Information

As already indicated, monitoring the environment, and collection of data relevant to strategic decisions, is central to most corporate planning processes. Interviewees were therefore asked how information relevant to stragetic decisions was obtained. Consensus answers for the 21 companies are summarized in Table 19.4.

The findings underline the prevalence of formal data flows and use of formal meetings within the companies. They also, more interestingly, confirm the importance of informal channels of information stressed by Aguilar (1967) in this study. Clearly, the sample companies had not allowed their informal channels of information to decay on introduction of formal planning, as Aguilar (1967) found to have occurred in one company in the U.S.A.

Items of Relevant Information Used

Finally, the interviewees were asked about information received, used to signal the need for a review of strategy, and used in the review itself. They

TABLE 19.4. *Means of obtaining information relevant to decisions on strategy*

Means	No. of companies	Ranked importance
1. Written communication within the company (including computer output)	19	2
2. Formal, scheduled meetings within the company	15	4 =
3. Market research and other information gathering by external agencies	6	8
4. Informal, unscheduled meetings—with colleagues	20	1
5. Informal, unscheduled meetings—with subordinates	18	3
6. Informal, unscheduled meetings—with customers	15	4 =
7. Informal, unscheduled meetings—with competitors	8	7
8. Scanning daily and technical press and other media	14	6

also indicated items they thought should be received. Table 19.5 shows if, and how, the companies used the items of information, where they were received. Ranked orders are shown in brackets.

A number of points emerge from scrutiny of Table 19.5. First, there is a fairly high wastage of much information. Although 12 companies agreed, for example, that they received information on financial contribution, no more than eight used this to signal the need for a review and the number using it in the review fell to five. The situation with respect to some types of information on the companies environment was even worse. For example, 13 companies received information on economic trends and prospects, but only five used this to signal need to change strategy, and only one company paid attention to it when choosing between strategies (i.e. in the review). The extent to which information received was thought inappropriate for use is indicated by the simple statistics in Table 19.6. Differences in the medians in particular, suggest how the average company wasted information. These figures are consistent with the complaints, heard frequently during the fieldwork, that information received was over-elaborate. One point to note, though, is that when asked to indicate the "ideal" information for use as a signal for review or in the review, the executives produced a list which agreed closely with that actually used, there being no significant differences in the ranked order of importance.[11] Moreover, though the median for "ideal" items as signals for review fell to 5, the median number of items agreed with companies for use in the review rose from an "actual" of five to an "ideal" of seven. Executives wanted to use more information to reach decisions.

The relative importance of individual items of information is also evident from Table 19.5. To simplify presentation, the items were grouped

[11] Details of the calculations are to be found in D. Norburn (1972).

TABLE 19.5. *Relative importance of items of information*

	No. of companies where:		
Information Item	(a) Received	(b) Used to signal need for review	(c) Used in review
Profit	20	12 (8 =)	17 (1)
Turnover	21	17 (1 =)	11 (4)
Costs	20	11 (11)	10 (5)
Contribution	12	8 (12 =)	5 (12 =)
Volume	19	17 (1 =)	12 (3)
Market share	8	5 (17 =)	4 (15)
Total market	7	4 (19 =)	3 (16)
Capacity utilization	13	8 (12 =)	8 (7)
Product mix	15	6 (16)	1 (17 =)
Obsolescence	3	0 (23)	0 (22 =)
New products	14	12 (8 =)	5 (12 =)
Manpower skills	2	1 (22)	0 (22 =)
Competitive actions	18	15 (5 =)	9 (6)
Government actions	15	7 (14 =)	1 (17 =)
Technological change	19	15 (5 =)	5 (12 =)
Patents	12	7 (14 =)	0 (22 =)
Buyer/supplier risk	7	4 (19 =)	1 (17 =)
Social change	6	4 (19 =)	1 (17 =)
Economic environment	13	5 (17 =)	1 (17 =)
Quality	19	17 (1 =)	7 (9 =)
Price	21	17 (1 =)	14 (2)
Availability	17	12 (8 =)	7 (9 =)
Applicability	14	13 (7)	6 (11)

Notes (1) Ranked order is shown in brackets.
(2) The number of companies are those where the consensus test showed that the agreement of the objectives had less than 5% probability of being due to chance.

TABLE 19.6. *Basic statistics on items of information received by the 21 companies*

	Median	Range
No. of items received	15	6−21
No. used to signal need for review	10	3−17
No. used in review	5	1−16
"Ideal" number for use to signal need for review	7	6−14
"Ideal" number for use in review	7	2−10

N.B. The answers are based on "consensus" answers within the companies (i.e. answers which had less than 5% chance of being due to chance).

into categories, the average utilization by the companies of items in each category was calculated, and the results placed in ranked order.[11] Table 19.7 shows the results. Financial information and that on customers reactions are seen to be the most frequently used.

TABLE 19.7. *Relative importance of categories of information as measured by average utilization over all 21 companies*

Category	Percentage utilization			Ranked importance		
	Received	Used to signal review	Used in review	Received	Used to signal review	Used in review
Finance	87	57	51	1	2	1
Marketing	54	41	30	4	3	3
Production	45	26	13	5	5	4
External	61	39	12	3	4	5
Customer reaction	85	70	40	2	1	2

These scores are based on "consensus" answers and hence relate to agreed use by the companies.

Longer term influences relating to the environment seem to be given surprisingly little weight in the review of alternative strategies. The evidence suggests that many companies are myopic.

The General Situation

A general picture emerges from the above. The chief executive tends to dominate both objective setting and strategic decisions but is strongly influenced by the marketing function. Formal planning processes are widely used but informal means of obtaining information remain very important. Despite this formality, there is confusion over objectives, and most companies agree only on profitability. Similarly there is widespread disagreement on decision making roles. The numbers of items of information received and used vary widely between companies, but the representative company uses a fairly low number, and places emphasis particularly on customer reactions and financial information. Importance is attached to marketing information but very little to production or general environmental trends.

There are, though, considerable differences between individual companies, which may well be related to their financial performance.

Relationships with Financial Performance

As already indicated, the literature suggests that formal planning; explicit statement of and clear recognition of objectives; clear definition of responsibility for strategic decisions; and extensive scanning of the environment pay. To test these assumptions, extensive statistical analysis was undertaken, relating the survey data with respect to each to company financial performance.[12]

Formality

No relationship could be found between formality and financial performance. Since 17 of the 21 claimed to plan formally, and a further two were found to do so by a study of data flows within them, no relationship could be expected to emerge from any analysis of the way the interviewees classified their planning processes. The two companies which claimed to use only informal, unscheduled approaches to planning both obtained a rate of return below the mean for their trading segment, but then so did 13 of the 19 companies which seemed to use formal planning.

Moreover, it was recognized that executives might have wrongly classified their planning process, because of the emotive content of words such as "formal" and "regular" used. Consequently, the number of formal channels of communication, or sources of information, used by each company was taken as a measure of formality. Analysis showed no relationship between this measure and financial performance.[13]

Thus our survey produced no evidence to suggest that formal planning pays.

Objectives

No relationship was found between financial performance and either numbers of objectives agreed among top executives or the extent of their disagreement over objectives. Confusion over objectives seemed to affect companies with good and poor financial performance alike.

However, the analysis strongly suggested[14] two relationships, between objectives and financial performance. Executives in companies with higher financial performance tended to state more objectives though they failed to agree on more. They also displayed more disagreement about objectives which ought to be adopted.

It is difficult to interpret these relationships and one can only hazard a guess. Perhaps the executives in higher performing companies display their greater ability by individually defining the corporate purpose in greater detail even although they cannot agree on it! Alternatively, the explanation may just be that top executives in financially successful companies can afford non-financial objectives, whilst those which are struggling to

---

[12] See Norburn (1972) for a longer account of non-parametric analysis and Grinyer and Norburn (1973) for one of scaling and use of parametric tests.

[13] See Grinyer's parametric analysis in Grinyer and Norburn (1973).

[14] These were almost significant at the 5% level. See Grinyer and Norburn (1973).

survive relative financial failure cannot, but are unable to agree on what these should be.

Perception of Decision Making Roles

Both commonsense and the literature suggest that agreement on responsibility for strategic decisions should improve performance.

No relationships were found between financial performance and the numbers of long term, short term, or all decisions for which companies achieved consensus on decision making roles.[15] But when roles were broken down into decision making and decision influencing a difference emerged. Companies with a the financial performance above the mean for their respective competitive segments exhibited more agreement on responsibility for long term decisions than those below the mean.

Channels of Information Used

When the number of sources of information used was analysed there was a strong suggestion that the companies with better financial performance use more as may be seen from Fig. 19.1.

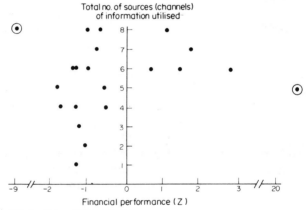

Results of correlation analysis

Sample	Coefficient	Value	Probability apparent relationship due to chance (P_a)
1. 19 Companies (excluding circled extremes)	Product moment	0.4012	$10\% > P_a > 5\%$
2. 6 Top performers	Spearmans rank	-0.5579	$20\% > P_a > 10\%$

FIG. 19.1

[15] This was all the more surprising because of the consistency between numbers of each of long and short term decisions for which companies agreed. Indeed clarity of role perception emerged from the statistical analysis (Factor Analysis) as one of the major dimensions of the planning process (see Grinyer and Norburn (1973)).

The total number of channels used by each company was then broken down into those which were formal and those which were informal. In addition, the number of channels that conveyed information directly from the external environment was established for each firm. Numbers of formal, informal and external channels used were then analysed for relationships with financial performance.

No relationships were found between either the number of formal[19] or "external" channels and financial performance. There was, though, a strong suggestion that use of more *informal* sources of information was associated with better financial performance.[18] As may be seen from Fig. 19.2 though, the number used was widely scattered especially at low levels financial performance.

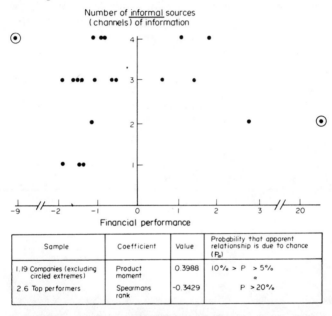

Sample	Coefficient	Value	Probability that apparent relationship is due to chance (Pₐ)
1. 19 Companies (excluding circled extremes)	Product moment	0.3988	10% > P > 5% α
2. 6 Top performers	Spearmans rank	-0.3429	P > 20%

FIG. 19.2

Items of Information Received and Used

Analysis showed no relationship between the number of items of information received and company performance. Nor was there any

---

[16] This is consistent with the findings of Burns and Stalker (1961) that "organic" organizations, with poor definition of decision making roles, are the most successful in some, dynamic environments.

[17] There is less than 10% probability that the apparent relationship is due to luck.

[18] There is less than a 10% probability that this is due purely to chance.

[19] As mentioned under "Formality".

difference in the specific types of information received and used by companies with low and high financial performance. However, there was a tendency for companies with better financial performance to use more items of information.[20] This tendency is apparent visually from Figs. 19.3 and 19.4. There figures show, though, that some companies with comparatively poor financial performance use a lot of information, and some of those with the highest use relatively little (especially in the review itself). There are obviously many other factors which affect financial performance, too!

Because companies with better financial performance tended to use more information, but did not receive more, they obviously made more use of what they got. The way in which use of information received rises with financial performance is evident visually from Fig. 19.5. The relationship is strong. There is a probability of less than 5% that it could have occurred by chance. Again, though, it will be noted from Fig. 19.5 that the company with the spectacularly high financial performance of 20.5 wasted most of the information received.

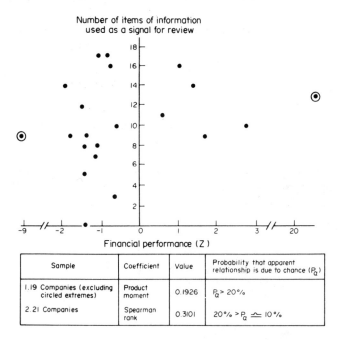

Sample	Coefficient	Value	Probability that apparent relationship is due to chance (P_Q)
1. 19 Companies (excluding circled extremes)	Product moment	0.1926	$P_Q > 20\%$
2. 21 Companies	Spearman rank	0.3101	$20\% > P_Q \simeq 10\%$

FIG. 19.3

[20] For information used in the review the probability that the apparent relationship was due to chance was less than 10% but greater than 5%. The figure for information used as a signal was, however, above 20%

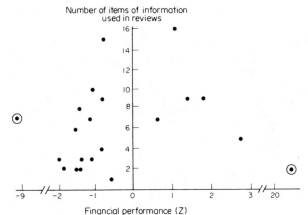

Results of correlation analysis

Sample	Coefficient	Value	Probability that apparent relationship is due to chance (P_a)
1.19 Companies (excluding circled extremes)	Product moment	0.4112	$10\% > P_a > 5\%$
2.6 Top performers	Spearmans rank	-0.6143	$25\% > P_a > 10\%$

FIG. 19.4

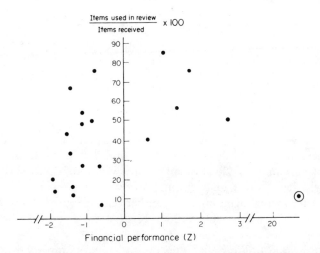

Sample	Coefficient	Value	Probability that apparent relationship is due to chance (P_a)
1.19 Companies (excluding circled extremes)	Product moment	0.51523	$5\% > P_a$

FIG. 19.5

Desire for Change

By comparison of what executives interviewed said was desirable and what they said existed, scales showing desire to change various aspects of the strategy planning process were derived, and relationships with financial performance were sought. Though individually only one of these was shown to be statistically significant, i.e. having a probability of less than 5 % of being due to chance, there was a consistent suggestion of satisfaction among companies with higher performance and desire to change among those with a low financial performance.[21] This was, perhaps, to be expected. After all, why should companies which were doing well financially wish to change their planning process? It was those which were performing badly which had a strong incentive to change.

Practical Implications

To summarize the main findings of the study, nearly all companies claimed to plan strategy on a formal scheduled basis, and were found to use formal flows of information. Yet there was considerable confusion about both objectives and responsibility for making strategic decisions. Moreover, no evidence could be found that use of more formal means of communication was associated with higher financial performance. What seemed to be associated was a greater use of information received to both signal the need for a review of strategy and in the review itself. High performing companies seemed to display more agreement among directors on responsibility for long term decisions.

We cannot necessarily infer from these results that formal, systematic planning does not pay. To establish this, it would be necessary to determine the manner in which formal planning was introduced and implemented in each company, the performance over time before and after implementation, and the way that other factors, too, affected performance. The study reported here could not, because of time and resource limits, collect evidence of this nature. Consequently, we were unable to show, for instance, whether there had been an improvement in performance of companies after formal planning had been seriously adopted, even though their performance still remained poor relative to that of comparable companies.

Again, only one holding and one multinational company had been included in the sample, and it is possible that in such organizations formal planning is desirable as a co-ordinating device. In a study of corporate planning in the electronics industry, which is at present being undertaken, we have been particularly impressed by the similarity of formal planning

---

[21] Details of the scales and the analysis can be found in Grinyer and Norburn (1973).

systems in two multi-national companies, and the way in which they allow the American head offices to exert control over their empires. This is, though, a quite different function to finding the best strategy for the individual operating company in its specific trading environment.

However, even though we cannot conclude from the evidence that formal planning does not pay, it is obvious that it failed in certain respects. Advocates of formal planning stress the benefits of agreement among top managers on explicitly set objectives and clear perception of decision making responsibilities. Yet, despite the fact that all but a few of the companies appear to plan formally there was widespread confusion about both objectives and decision making roles.

By contrast to the lack of evidence that formal planning is associated with success, the strong suggestion that financially more successful companies tended to use more *in*formal channels of communication underscores the importance of *in*formal decision making processes. Those involved in the real process of strategic decision taking recognize that it is ultimately a political process in which power and influence of individuals change with the nature of the challenges to the company, with changing personal relationships, and with other factors like the health of top managers. Within such a process decision making roles may sometimes be blurred, or may be masked by reference to group responsibility (e.g. to Board responsibility). Similarly, objectives may change with relative influence of individuals, as well as with the circumstances of the company. They may also remain largely implicit as a means of holding together political alliances[22] between individuals whose personal value systems differ. Hence lack of agreement about both decision making responsibility and objectives is consistent with the belief that such informal political processes constitute the system by which decisions are really made.

This picture of a political process is reminiscent in some respects of the "organic" organization found by Burns and Stalker (1961) to be most successful in dynamic situations. By contrast, formal planning processes exhibit characteristics of what they called "mechanistic" organizations. They found that these were best suited to stable environments. We were not able to test these findings directly because no attempt was made to classify the technologies and environment of the sample companies. However, our results suggest that high performing companies exhibit some but not all of the characteristics of organic organizations. They use more informal, personal channels of communication, but they also display more agreement among directors on responsibility for taking long term decisions.

Although our findings suggest that the real decision making system is informal and often ill defined, they also highlight the need for top managers

[22] See Cyert and March (1965) for a similar view of decision making.

to be well informed, and to use more information. Financial performance, as has already been suggested, tends to be associated with the use of more items of relevant information to indicate the need for a review of strategy and in the review itself.

If this interpretation of the significance of our findings is correct a number of warning notes should be sounded to those concerned with strategic planning and decision making:

(1) The important decision making process is informal and political. Performance is more likely to be improved by fostering more informal communication and a better use of information than by expending a lot of effort on designing and operating formal procedures enshrined in planning manuals.

(2) Formal planning systems can do no more than provide a framework for the real, political decision making system. If they define responsibilities, or objectives, too rigidly they may be made obsolete by the changing political process. They will then be ignored.

(3) Strategic planners will influence decisions only by becoming embedded in the political process. Since they carry no line decision making authority, they cannot make decisions, they can only influence them. This influence is likely to depend on the planners' understanding of the company and its trading environment, on his role as an informal channel of danger signals to key decision takers, and his ability to collect, analyse, and present data on specific strategic alternatives in a way which decision takers can easily understand and use.

(4) Too much information is wasted because it is thought inappropriate and over-elaborate by decision takers. Yet financial performance is related to use of more relevant information. Clearly, the relevance of information received by decision takers in many companies should be reviewed and presentation of relevant items improved.

(5) Thus, in general, there should be a greater emphasis on facilitating operation of the real, political decision taking system, and provision of appropriate information to participants within it, and less on formal procedures and beautifully documented plans. The latter may have a useful co-ordinating function but are too often either overtaken by unforeseen events or just ignored by those with real decision making power.

Acknowledgement

The authors wish to acknowledge the advice and help of Susan Birley.

References

Ansoff, H. I. (1965) *Corporate Strategy,* McGraw Hill.

Ansoff, H. I., Avner, J., Brandenburg R. G., Portner, F. E. and Radosevich (1970) Does planning pay? The effect of planning on success of acquisitions in American Firms, *Long Range Planning,* **3** (2), Dec.

Aguilar, J. (1963) *Scanning the Business Environment,* Macmillan, New York.

Burns, T. and Stalker, G. M. (1961) *The Management of Innovation,* Tavistock Publications, London.

Cyert, R. M. and March, R. G. (1963) *A Behavioural Theory of the Firm,* Prentice-Hall.

Denning, B. W. and Lehr, M. E. (1971) The extent and nature of corporate long range planning in the U.K., *Journal of Management Studies,* vol. **8**, No. 2, May.

Emery, J. C. (1969) *Organisational Planning and Control Systems,* Macmillan.

Gilmore, F. G. and Brandenburg, R. G. (1962) Anatomy of corporate planning, *Harvard Business Review,* **40** (6), Nov.=Dec.

Grinyer, P.H. (1971) The anatomy of business strategic planning reconsidered, *Journal of Management Studies,* **8** (2), May.

Grinyer, P. H. (1972) Dangerous axioms of corporate planning, *Journal of Business Policy,* **3** (1), Autumn.

Grinyer, P. H. and Norburn, D. (1973) An Empirical Investigation of Some Aspects of Strategic Planning, currently in manuscript and available from Dr. P. H. Grinyer at the Graduate Business Centre, The City University, London.

Hewkin, J. M. and Kempner, T. (1968) *Is Corporate Planning Necessary?*, British Institute of Management publication.

Herold, D. M. (1972) Long range planning and organizational performance: A cross validation study, *Academy of Management Journal,* **15** (1), March.

Irving, P. (1970) Corporate Planning in Practice: A study of the Development of Organized Planning in Major U.K. Companies, M.Sc. thesis, Bradford University.

Norburn, D. (1972) Ph.D. Thesis. The Graduate Business Centre, The City University, London.

Ringbakk, K. A. (1969) *Organized Planning in Major U.S. Companies—A Survey,* Stamford Research Institute.

Ringbakk, K. A. (1972) The corporate planning life cycle—An international point of view, *Long Range Planning,* **5** (3), Sept.

Schollhammer, H. (1970) Corporate planning in France, *Journal of Management Studies,* **7** (1).

Selznick, P. (1948) Foundations of the theory of organizations, *American Sociological Review,* **13**, 25-35.

Simmons, W. W. (1968) Corporate planning: the keystone of the management system, *Long Range Planning,* **1** (3), Dec.

Simon, H. A. (1960) *The New Science of Management Decision,* Harper & Row.

Strigel, W. H. (1970) Planning in West German industry, *Long Range Planning,* **3** (1), Sept.

Thune, S. and House, R. (1970) Where long range planning pays off, *Business Horizons,* Aug.

Wagle, B. V and Jenkins, P. M. (1971) The Development of a General Computer System to aid the Corporate Planning Process, U.K.S.C.—0024, Oct., I.B.M.

20

Pitfalls in Multi-national
Long Range Planning

G. A. STEINER AND H. SCHÖLLHAMMER

Corporate long range planning is increasingly practised throughout the world. It is our belief, however, that too many companies are not getting the benefits which should be produced by their long range planning systems.

There are many explanations for this. First, the planning system may not be designed correctly for the company. Second, what a long range planning system can do for a company may be misunderstood and, therefore, expectations of results may be unrealistic. Third, the planning system may be blamed for what actually is poor management. Fourth, unexpected environmental changes may adversely affect company operations and the planning system may get the blame for it. Finally, a company may fall into one or more of the major pitfalls which should be avoided if good results are to be achieved from its planning system.

This paper deals with the last factor. We present here the results of a survey of planning pitfalls among corporations in six industrialized countries.

The Pitfalls Survey

Over a period of years one of the authors accumulated a list of 50 pitfalls considered to be most important to avoid in starting, understanding, and doing long range planning, and in using the results. This list is shown in Appendix A and was the basis for a questionnaire sent to companies in six countries. As noted above, a complete list of pitfalls would include traps to be avoided in the entire process of management. Also, many pitfalls in doing planning are not included in the list. For instance, it is obviously a mistake to forecast sales on the basis of a simple extrapolation of current

---

This article was originally published in *Long Range Planning*, Volume 8, No. 2, April 1975.

trends. Nevertheless, tests of the list lead us to conclude that it covers the major traps to be avoided.[1]

Respondents were asked to indicate whether their company had fallen into a specific pitfall completely, partly, or not at all. In addition, each was asked to specify the extent to which a pitfall that his company did not avoid had affected its planning effectiveness. Respondents were asked to rank order the most important, and the least important, pitfalls to be avoided. The questionnaire requested further information about the company's organizational structure, the degree of formality of the planning system, the degree of documentation in the planning system, and how satisfied or dissatisfied each company was with its planning system.

There are biases in this survey which should be recognized. To begin with, the questionnaire contained few definitions of terms so the responses reflected definitions of the respondents. The data, therefore, are not precisely comparable. Also, the mix of respondents among executives and staffs varied from country to country. In addition, the proportion of responses to the total number of questionnaires sent and to the total received varies among countries. Despite these biases we believe the data reveal accurately certain selected and important aspects of the state-of-the art of corporate planning around the world.

Table 20.1 shows the distribution among six countries of the 460 usable questionnaires which were returned to us.

TABLE 20.1. *Number of Responses by Country*

Country	Number of responses	
U.S.A.	215	47%
Japan	118	26%
Canada	42	9%
England	32	7%
Italy	31	6%
Australia	22	4%
Total	460	100%

The differences in the size of the sample by country are obvious. However, an analysis of thirty randomly selected responses from among the U.S. and the Japanese replies revealed that the results are essentially the same on the basis of the limited sample as on the much larger number of actual responses from these two countries. For this reason, we feel confident that the responses from Canadian, English, Italian and Australian companies are reasonably representative and reflect an accurate cross-section of the planning situation in the countries surveyed.

Table 20.2 shows the responses distributed by sales volume. Since about 40 per cent of all respondents in each of the surveyed countries had annual

TABLE 20.2. *Distribution of Respondents by Volume of Sales (in per cent of total respondents per country)*

Sales Volume (mill. $)	U.S.A.[a] (N = 202)	Canada[b] (N = 39)	England[c] (N = 28)	Italy (N = 31)	Australia[d] (N = 20)	Japan[e] (N = 109)
Under $50	7.4	12.8	7.1	38.7	35.0	17.4
$50-$99	5.0	7.7	25.0	22.6	30.0	15.6
$100-$250	20.3	28.2	29.3	19.3	25.0	28.5
$251-$500	21.3	20.5	10.7	12.9	10.0	18.3
$501-$750	8.9	12.9	14.3	—	—	5.5
$751-$999	3.9	5.1	3.6	6.5	—	5.5
Over $1,000	33.2	12.8	—	—	—	9.2

[a] 13 firms did not show sales volume.
[b] 3 firms did not show sales volume.
[c] 4 firms did not show sales volume.
[d] 2 firms did not show sales volume.
[e] 9 firms did not show sales volume.

TABLE 20.3. Organizational Characteristics of Responding Firms
(in per cent of total number of responses per country)

Organization forms	U.S.A. N	%	Canada N	%	England N	%	Italy N	%	Australia N	%	Japan N	%
Centralized	87	53	15	45	11	41	13	62	10	48	68	62
Decentralized	78	47	18	55	16	59	8	38	11	52	42	38
	165	100	33	100	27	100	21	100	21	100	110	100
Not reporting	50		9		5		10		1		8	
Total sample	215		42		32		31		22		118	
Divisionalized	173	92	38	97	27	93	20	74	21	95	45	41
Not divisionalized	15	8	1	3	2	7	7	26	1	5	65	59
	188	100	39	100	29	100	27	100	22	100	110	100
Not reporting	27		3		3		4		0		8	
Total sample	215		42		32		31		22		118	

sales between $100 and $500 m, there is less disparity than might appear at first glance.

The responding firms were also asked to provide information about their organizational characteristics. Table 20.3 shows how firms were distributed in terms of centralized or decentralized, and divisionalized or nondivisionalized. Among the U.S., Canadian and Australian respondents centralized and decentralized firms are represented in about equal proportions. As far as the Japanese and Italian firms are concerned, centralized organizational structures are much more prevalent than decentralized organizations. In the case of the English firms the situation is reversed. Table 20.3 also shows that with the exception of the Japanese firms most responding firms are divisionalized. These differences in organizational characteristics are well in line with other empirical research studies[2] and are an indication of the samples' representativeness.

The Most Important Pitfalls to Avoid

Respondents were asked to identify, in rank order, the most important pitfalls which they felt should be avoided. The results are shown in Table 20.4. The pitfall which led the list is "Top management's assumption that it can delegate the planning function to a planner". Canadian, English and Italian executives ranked this pitfall as being the most important. U.S. executives ranked it second, for Japanese respondents this factor was fourth in importance and only Australians considered seven other pitfalls as being more aggravating. This result suggests that a very large percentage of firms in various industrial countries have not yet learned to do justice to a major planning principle which states that: "There can and will be no effective comprehensive corporate planning in any organization where the chief executive does not give it firm support and make sure that others in the organization understand his depth of commitment."[3] Without top management's support and active involvement in the development of company plans, the planning effort is largely unproductive and may be discredited without valid reason. It seems to be difficult to make many top executives really planning-conscious.

The second most important pitfall—on the basis of the total responses—is a direct consequence of the first one: "Top management becomes so engrossed in current problems that it spends insufficient time on long range planning, and the process becomes discredited among other managers and staff." For a majority of the U.S., Japanese and Australian respondents this pitfall is the most important one. Only English executives gave this pitfall a relatively low eighth rank. In England, other planning pitfalls are even more serious. The relative lack of planning consciousness among English top managers has been widely documented. David Granick, for example, characterized the typical English enterprise as "the home of the amateur"

TABLE 20.4. Some of the Most Important Pitfalls to be Avoided as Ranked by Respondents

Pitfall number (see Appendix A)	Description of pitfall	Total sample	U.S.A.	Canada	England	Italy	Australia	Japan
1	Top managements assumption that it can delegate the planning function to a planner.	1	2	1	1	1	8	4
24	Top management becomes so engrossed in current problems that it spends insufficient time on long-range planning, and the process becomes discredited among other managers and staff.	2	1	2	8	2	1	1
28	Failure to develop company goals suitable as a basis for formulating long-range plans.	3	3	3	2	6	3	3
11	Failure to create a climate in the company which is congenial and not resistant to planning.	4	4		3	5	9	7
42	Failure of top management to review with departmental and divisional heads the long-range plans which they have developed.	5	8				2	2
26	Failure to assure the necessary involvement in the planning process of major line personnel.	6	5	10	9	10	7	9
15	Assuming that corporate comprehensive planning is something separate from the entire management process.	7	6	4	10	4		

No.	Pitfall						
16	Failure to make sure that top management and major line officers really understand the nature of long-range planning and what it will accomplish for them and the company.	8		5			6	10
12	Failing to locate the corporate planner at a high enough level in the managerial hierachy.	9	10		6	7		
47	Failure to use plans as standards for measuring managerial performance.	10	9		6			
27	Too much centralization of long-range planning in the central headquarters so that divisions feel little responsibility for developing effective plans.		7	6	4			
43	Forgetting that the fundamental purpose of planning is to make better current decisions.	7						5
13	Failure to make sure that the planning staff has the necessary qualities of leadership, technical expertise, and personality to discharge properly its responsibilities in making the planning system effective.	8					5	8
14	Forgetting that planning is a political, a social, and an organizational, as well as a rational process.	9						
10	Failure to develop a clear understanding of the long-range planning procedure before the process is actually undertaken.	10			5		5	
18	Assuming that plans can be made by staff planners for line managers to implement.					7		
31	Failure to make realistic plans (e.g., due to overoptimism and/or over-cautiousness).				7			

TABLE 20.4 (cont.)

Pitfall number (see Appendix A)	Description of pitfall	Total sample	U.S.A.	Canada	England	Italy	Australia	Japan
45	Top management's consistently rejecting the formal planning mechanism by making intuitive decisions which conflict with the formal plans.					3		
8	Assuming that a formal system can be introduced into a company without a careful and perhaps "agonizing appraisal" of current managerial practices and decision-making processes.					8	4	
37	Doing long-range planning periodically and forgetting it in-between cycles.					9	10	
39	Failure of top management, and/or the planning staff, to give departments and divisions sufficient information and guidance (e.g., top management interests, environmental projections, etc.)							6

and concluded his chapter on this issue by pointing out that

> a common theme runs through all these examples: rejection of professionalism in management and of the enormous attention to planning and control which has accompanied professionalization in the United States. British executives are far more concerned with a straightforward "getting on with the job". Theirs are the advantages and disadvantages of simplicity. [4]

"Failure to develop company goals suitable as a basis for formulating long range plans" was ranked as the third most important pitfall. With the exception of the Italian respondents, the majority of all others ranked this condition among the top three pitfalls. For Italian managers the third most important planning pitfall to avoid is No. 45, "Top management consistently rejecting the formal planning mechanism by making intuitive decisions which conflict with formal plans."

These three pitfalls seem to be universally the most important since a majority of all the respondents of the various countries ranked them among the top 10 pitfalls. These three pitfalls must thus be considered as inherent planning weaknesses with which managers and staff planners everywhere are faced, in which they get very frequently entrapped, and which are very difficult to overcome.

Space does not permit detailed comments on other top pitfalls [5] but a few highlights of Table 20.4 may be noted. A number of pitfalls in the top 10 reveal a lack of understanding of the way in which long range planning is related to management. For instance the ranking of Nos. 11, 42, 26, and 15 seem to say that too many managers do not realize that planning is inextricably interrelated in the entire process of management. To get best results there must be a climate congenial to doing planning; managers up and down the line, especially top managers, must become involved; and top managers must review plans of lower-level managers.

It is noteworthy that generally speaking the top 10 important pitfalls are identified by most managers in the countries surveyed. To be sure, there are exceptions as Table 20.4 shows since a total of 21 pitfalls were identifed as being in the top 10. It seems clear that in Italian companies entrepreneural decisions very frequently override the planning system. In Japanese companies top management does not give much guidance to lower-level line and staff in doing planning. but, fundamentally Table 20.4 shows that there are remarkable similarities to those planning pitfalls considered to be highly important among managers in different countries of the world.

The Most Important Planning Pitfalls Classified by Organizational Size

This study also attempted to find out which pitfalls are the most common and important in firms of different size (as measured by their volume of sales). Table 20.5 shows the findings. This table shows a somewhat surprising finding: regardless of their size, firms identify as being most important to avoid the same planning pitfalls. For instance, on the basis of all responses, pitfall No. 1 ("Top management's assumption that it can delegate the planning function to a planner") has been consistently ranked among the five most important pitfalls, regardless of the size of the responding firm. The same result was found with regard to pitfall No. 24 ("Top management becomes so engrossed in current problems that it spends insufficient time on long range planning"). Pitfall No. 28 ("Failure to develop company goals suitable as a basis for formulating long range plans") was also ranked among the five most important planning problems by the responding companies in each of the three size categories. In addition, pitfall No. 11 ("Failure to create a planning climate in the company which is congenial to planning") was ranked among the five most important weaknesses by firms with annual sales under $100 m as well as those with a sales volume over $1 billion.

Among the five most important pitfalls there is thus only one which was ranked exclusively in one size category. For the large firms with sales over a billion dollars it is pitfall No. 9 ("Ignoring the power structure of a company in organizing the planning process"). For the small firms it is pitfall No. 42 ("Failure of top management to review with departmental or divisional heads the plans which they have developed"). For the medium size firms the unique pitfall is No. 41 ("Failure to secure that minimum of system and information to make the planning process and its results creditable and useful").

A country-by-country analysis of the ranking of the most important pitfalls according to the size of the firm yields essentially the same results. Firms of different size come essentially to the same assessment about their difficulties in avoiding common planning pitfalls. There are, as Table 20.5 shows, variations in the ranking of the significance of individual pitfalls; however, the similarities tend to outweight the differences.

The Least Important Planning Pitfalls

The rational for a special focus on the least important pitfalls is two-fold: (a) they indicate potential planning difficulties which companies find relatively easy to avoid, and (b) their negative impact on planning effectiveness is rather limited. Table 20.6 gives the results of this part of the analysis. It shows that the pitfalls least likely to create problems are: No. 21 ("Assuming that planning is hard"), No. 20 ("Assuming that planning is easy"), and No. 35 ("Assuming that new quantitative techniques are not as useful as advertised). Besides these three least important pitfalls the ranking of others which are considered low in significance does not reflect marked

TABLE 20.5. *Ranking of Most Important Pitfalls to Avoid by Size of Firm (Dollar Sales) Total Samples (Responses of Six Countries)*

Rank order	Under $100 million		$100 million to $1 billion		over $1 billion	
	Responses	Pitfall	Responses	Pitfall	Responses	Pitfall
1st	37	24	82	24	28	1
2nd	36	28	70	1	22	28
3rd	34	1	66	28	19	11
4th	24	11	48	41	16	24
5th	22	42	45	14	15	9
U.S.A.						
1st	15	24	34	1	22	1
2nd	13	28	33	28	28	18
3rd	10	44	24	46	17	11
4th	9	1	25	15_	14	26
5th	7	16	23	26	12	24
Canada						
1st	3	15	11	1	4	1
2nd	3	26	11	24	2	11
3rd	2	7	8	28	2	15
4th	2	27	6	16	2	28
5th	2	37	5	15	2	43
England						
1st	7	1	8	1		
2nd	5	26	6	27		
3rd	4	10	5	10		
4th	4	28	5	11		
5th	4	42	5	25		
Italy						
1st	5	1	6	45		
2nd	4	11	4	1		
3rd	4	15	4	24		
4th	4	28	3	11		
5th	3	24	3	12		
Australia						
1st	5	8	4	29		
2nd	5	24	4	26		
3rd	4	10	3	42		
4th	4	28	2	12		
5th	4	42	2	28		
Japan						
1st	10	24	19	24	4	42
2nd	10	25	18	42	3	9
3rd	10	39	15	28	3	23
4th	9	1	14	1	3	30
5th	8	26	11	43	3	37

TABLE 20.6. *The Least Important Pitfalls in Planning as Ranked by Respondents*
(Ranks 1—10)

Pitfall no.	Total sample	U.S.A.	Canada	England	Italy	Australia	Japan
1							
2							
3							
4	4	5	7			8	4
5							
6							3
7	10	7			8		7
8			10				
9				3			
10							
11							
12							
13							
14				9		9	
15							
16							
17			9				
18							
19				7	9		
20	2	2	3	2	2	5	1
21	1	1	1	4	1	1	2
22	6	8		5		7	8
23							
24							
25	5	6	4	8	4		9
26							
27							
28							
29	9	9	5		6	2	
30							
31							
32							
33		10			10		
34	7					6	6
35	8	3	6		5	10	
36	3	4	2	6	3	4	5
37							
38							
39							
40			10	10		3	
41							
42							
43							
44							
45							

TABLE 20.6 (*cont.*)

Pitfall no.	Total sample	U.S.A.	Canada	England	Italy	Australia	Japan
46							
47							
48				I	7		
49						10	
50							

The least important pitfalls
1:21—Assuming that planning is hard.
2:20—Assuming that planning is easy.
3:36—Assuming that new quantitative techniques are not as useful as advertised.
4:25—Long-range planning becomes unpopular because top management spends so much time on long-range problems that it ignores short-range problems.
5:29—Assuming that equal weight should be given to all elements of planning (i.e., that the same emphasis should be placed on strategic as on tactical planning, or that the same emphasis should be accorded to major function plans).
6:35—Assuming that older methods to choose from among alternatives should be discarded in favour of newer techniques.
7: 4—Assuming that the present body of knowledge about planning is insufficient to guide fruitful comprehensive planning.
8:22—Assuming that long-range planning can get a company out of a current crisis.
9: 7—Thinking that a successful corporate plan can be moved from one company to another without change and with equal success.
10:40—Attempting to do too much in too short a time.

differences from one country to the other. However, the responses from English executives show a somewhat greater variation in this regard. For example, pitfall No. 9 ("Ignoring the power structure of the company in organizing the planning process") and No. 49 ("Failing to encourage managers to do good long range planning by basing reward solely on short range performance measures") were ranked among the three least important pitfalls. Indeed, the frequently observed emphasis on the use of personal criteria for evaluating executives in English firms[6] makes it unlikely that they would get entrapped by such pitfalls as Nos. 9 and 49.

In general, the results of Table 20.6 show less disparity than the results on the most important pitfalls. This means that there is an even greater unanimity among the respondents concerning the less significant pitfalls as compared with the assessment of the most important pitfalls to be avoided.

The Impact of Specific Pitfalls on Planning Effectiveness

Every planning situation creates its own pitfalls in which companies get entrapped. Not every pitfall has the same negative impact on planning effectiveness, however, even though it may be considered an important one to avoid. Table 20.8 shows how the respondents ranked the five most important pitfalls to be avoided and the degree to which these pitfalls reduced effectiveness.

The interesting result of this part of the survey is that pitfall No. 24 (:'Top management becomes so engrossed in current problems that it spends insufficient time on long range planning, and the process becomes discredited among other managers and staff") is shown as having the greatest negative impact on planning effectiveness. This is followed by pitfall No. 28 ("Failure to develop company goals suitable as a basis for formulating long range plans"). Pitfall No. 11 ("Failure to create a climate in the company that is congenial to planning") was ranked third in its negative impact on planning effectiveness.

In contrast, pitfall No. 1 ("Top managements assumption that it can delegate the planning function to a planner") has been pointed out as the most common planning error, yet its negative effect on planning effectiveness is reported to be less severe than pitfalls Nos. 24, 28 and 11. Pitfall No. 42 ("Failure of top management to review with subordinates the long range plans they have developed") was viewed as the fifth most common planning error and the assessment of its negative impact on planning effectiveness corresponds precisely with this rank.

This essential lesson to be learned from the results presented in Table 20.7 is that the greater is top management's awareness of the importance of planning, and the more attention it pays to a clear delineation of organizational objectives, the higher will be the effectiveness of the company's planning effort. A company's planning effectiveness can be reduced more significantly by falling into these two traps than by any other planning pitfalls.

The Degree of Satisfaction with Planning Systems

A quick glance at Table 20.8 shows there is somewhat more satisfaction than dissatisfaction with planning systems in all the nations surveyed except Japan. In Japan not one correspondent felt highly satisfied with his company's planning system. This is probably due to the fact that most of the respondents were managers who did not get what they considered to be sufficient association with and feedback from top management.

The results of Table 20.8 do not support the asserted widespread dissatisfaction which some observers have seen.[7] On the other hand, the dissatisfaction shown is significant. The level of dissatisfaction is not at all surprising, however, in light of the numerous violations of standard planning principles which this survey has revealed.

In the U.S. survey cited earlier, degrees of dissatisfaction were related to

TABLE 20.7. *Incidence of Entrapment and Affect on Planning System of Five Pitfalls Ranked "Most Important to Avoid" (Total Responses from Six Countries)*

Pitfall number	Rank order	Entrapment Has your company at this time fallen into this pitfall?			Affect If you have fallen into the pitfall, has it affected the effectiveness of your long-range planning system?		
		(1) No	(2) Partly	(3) Completely	(1) Not at all	(2) Some	(3) Much
1	1	247	175	31	10	128	68
24	2	106	251	88	12	189	138
28	3	179	193	76	9	153	107
11	4	189	215	43	8	179	71
42	5	235	143	52	4	108	83

Incident of Entrapment of "Most Important Planning Pitfalls to Avoid"

Rank order	U.S.A. Pitfall no.	Canada Pitfall no.	England Pitfall no.	Italy Pitfall no.	Australia Pitfall no.	Japan Pitfall no.
1	24	1	1	1	24	24
2	1	24	28	11	42	42
3	28	28	11	15	28	8
1	11	15	27	24	1	28
5	26	16	10	45	39	13

TABLE 20.8.   *Degree of Satisfaction with the Reported Planning System (In Percentage of Total Number of Responses per Country)*

Degree of satisfaction	U.S.A. (N = 211[a])	Canada (N = 41[a])	England (N = 30[a])	Italy (N = 27[a])	Australia (N = 21[a])	Japan (N = 116[a])
1. Highly satisfied	10.0	19.5	6.7	11.1	4.8	0
2. Above average satisfaction	34.1	34.1	26.7	22.2	38.1	10.3
3. Average satisfaction	32.2	22.0	50.0	40.7	33.3	38.8
4. Some dissatisfaction	15.2	17.1	13.3	18.5	19.0	44.0
5. Highly dissatisfied	8.5	7.3	3.3	7.4	4.8	6.9

[a] Remaining firms (see total sample size) did not answer this question.

whether or not a company had fallen into one of the major pitfalls. It was concluded that: "Without exception, those companies which said they had fallen completely into one of the top 10 most important pitfalls to avoid were more dissatisfied than satisfied with their planning programs."[8] It is our guess that when similar comparisons are made for the data in the worldwide survey that much the same results will appear.

The conclusion to be drawn from these results is that corporate planning is still too often poorly done and misunderstood. At too many companies one does not yet find the attitudes and clear insights that would be conducive to an avoidance of the most important planning pitfalls. As a consequence, satisfactions with current planning systems are not as high as they ought to be.

Planning Satisfaction Related to Organization Structure

Table 20.9 shows that companies with a decentralized organizational structure tend to be somewhat more satisfied with their current planning systems than those that are centralized. A country-by-country analysis, however, does not confirm the universality of this conclusion. In the case of Canadian and Italian firms, for example, the centralized ones expressed greater satisfaction than others. Divisionalized firms expressed consistently a higher degree of satisfaction than nondivisionalized ones.

Dates that Present Planning Systems were Created

Table 20.10 shows that the planning system of most of the responding companies in the various countries is of very recent origin. For a majority of the firms, comprehensive and systematic long range planning is still in an

TABLE   20.9.   *Satisfaction.—With   Planning   System   Versus   Organization
Structure—Total Sample (Six Countries)*

Structural characteristics	Degree of satisfaction (in % of total sample)			
	Very high to high	Average	Low to Very low	Total sample
Centralized	28.5	34.0	37.5	200
Decentralized	38.1	32.4	29.5	170
Divisionalized	40.4	32.8	69.8	317
Non-divisionalized	8.9	44.4	46.7	90
U.S.A.				
Centralized	39.2	28.7	32.1	87
Decentralized	47.5	34.6	17.9	78
Divisionalized	45.0	31.0	24.0	171
Non-divisionalized	13.3	60.0	26.7	15
Canada				
Centralized	60.0	13.3	26.7	15
Decentralized	58.8	11.8	29.4	17
Divisionalized	54.0	21.6	24.3	37
Non-divisionalized	100.0	—	—	1
England				
Centralized	20.0	60.0	20.0	10
Decentralized	37.6	43.7	18.7	16
Divisionalized	34.6	50.0	15.4	26
Non-divisionalized	0	50.0	50.0	2
Italy				
Centralized	38.9	44.4	16.7	18
Decentralized	0	42.9	57.1	7
Divisionalized	38.9	44.4	16.7	18
Non-divisionalized	0	42.9	57.1	7
Australia				
Centralized	40.0	50.0	10.0	10
Decentralized	50.0	20.0	30.0	10
Divisionalized	45.0	30.0	25.0	20
Non-divisionalized	0	100.0	0	1
Japan				
Centralized	6.0	40.2	53.8	67
Decentralized	16.6	31.0	52.4	42
Divisionalized	13.3	35.6	51.1	45
Non-divisionalized	7.8	40.6	51.6	64

evolutionary phase. In more than half of the responding Australian firms, for example, the currently used planning system originated only in 1970 or later and approximately one third of the responding companies from Canada, England and Italy fall into the same category. Only about one-

TABLE 20.10. Distribution of Respondents by Origination of Planning System (in Percentage of Total Respondents per Country)

Origination of Planning system	U.S.A.[a] (N = 190)	Canada[b] (N = 38)	England[c] (N = 28)	Italy[d] (N = 29)	Australia[c] (N = 21)	Japan[f] (N = 109)
Before 1950	1.6	—	—	—	—	3.7
1950–1954	2.6	—	—	—	—	1.8
1955–1959	5.3	5.3	3.4	6.9	4.8	7.3
1960–1964	23.7	15.8	10.4	17.2	23.8	31.2
1965–1969	48.8	39.4	45.2	44.9	19.0	37.7
1970 to date	17.0	39.5	31.0	31.0	52.4	18.3

Number of companies that did not answer the question about the year the planning system was introduced: [a] —25; [b] —4; [c] —4; [d] —2; [e] —1; [f] —9.

fourth of the U.S., and Japanese firms have a relatively mature planning system with more than 10 years of experience with it.

Degree of Formality among Planning Systems

Table 20.11 reveals that there is a rather uniform distribution of degrees of formality in planning systems. The highest incidence of formal systems is found in the United States and the least is in Japan. The most informal are found in Italy and the least in England.

Degrees of Documentation among Planning Systems

The degrees of documentation among planning systems are shown in Table 20.12. The heaviest documentation appears to be in planning systems in Australia, Canada, U.S. and England. Systems having the least documentation appear to be in Italy.

Positive Correlations between Satisfactions, Formality, Documentation and Birthdate of Planning Systems

Correlations were computed, but not presented here, which showed that there is a high and significant relationship between the degree of satisfaction of planning systems and the degree of formality of the systems. About the same level of correlation exists between satisfaction and the extent of written documentation in plans. There was a lower level of correlation but a positive one between the date the planning system was begun and satisfaction. The earlier the year started the higher the satisfaction. This probably supports the thesis that experience with planning really does improve the system and the product.

Major Conclusions

This survey identified the pitfalls which companies around the world feel are the most important ones to avoid if the best results are to be achieved from their planning system. The study also showed that satisfactions with planning systems are higher than dissatisfactions. Those companies having higher formality and greater documentation are also more satisfied with their planning systems. Divisionalized companies are generally more satisfied with their planning systems than nondivisionalized ones. Finally, companies having the most experience with planning, as indicated by the birthday of their planning system, tend to be the most satisfied.

TABLE 20.11. *Degrees of Formality Reported in Planning System*
(in Percentage of Total Number of Responses per Country)

Degree of formality	U.S.A. (N = 210[a])	Canada (N = 42)	England (N = 31[a])	Italy (N = 29[a])	Australia (N = 22)	Japan (N = 117[a])
1. Highly formal	16.7	11.9	16.1	10.3	13.4	6.8
2. Formal	31.9	31.0	25.8	13.8	36.4	15.4
3. Medium	25.2	31.0	38.7	34.5	27.3	41.9
4. Somewhat informal	16.2	16.6	9.7	27.6	18.2	21.4
5. Very loose and flexible	10.0	9.5	9.7	13.8	4.5	14.5

[a] Remaining firms (see total sample size) did not provide an answer to this question.

TABLE 20.12 *Extent of Documentation in Planning*
(in Percentage of Total Number of Responses per Country)

Extent of documentation	U.S.A. (N = 210[a])	Canada (N = 42)	England (N = 31[a])	Italy (N = 29[a])	Australia (N = 21[a])	Japan (N = 116[a])
1. Substantial written documentation	33.8	35.7	25.8	10.3	28.6	5.2
2. Above average documentation	25.7	26.2	32.3	13.8	38.0	22.4
3. Average documentation	26.2	16.7	35.5	34.5	28.6	45.7
4. Below average documentation	8.6	14.3	3.2	27.6	4.8	19.0
5. Short, rough notations	5.7	7.1	3.2	13.8	0	7.8

[a] Remaining firms (see total sample size) did not answer this question.

Appendix A

A. Pitfalls in getting started:

1. Top management's assumption that it can delegate the planning function to a planner.
2. Rejecting planning because there has been success without it.
3. Rejecting formal planning because the system failed in the past to foresee a critical problem and/or did not result in substantive decisions that satisfied top management.
4. Assuming that the present body of knowledge about planning is insufficient to guide fruitful comprehensive planning.
5. Assuming that a company cannot develop effective long-range planning in a way appropriate to its resources and needs.
6. Assuming that comprehensive corporate planning can be introduced into a company and overnight miraculous results will appear.
7. Thinking that a successful corporate plan can be moved from one company to another without change and with equal success.
8. Assuming that a formal system can be introduced into a company without careful and perhaps "agonizing reappraisal" of current managerial practices and decision-making processes.
9. Ignoring the power structure of a company in organizing the planning process.
10. Failure to develop a clear understanding of the long-range planning procedure before the process is actually undertaken.
11. Failure to create a climate in the company which is congenial and not resistant to planning.
12. Failing to locate the corporate planner at a high enough level in the managerial hierarchy.
13. Failure to make sure that the planning staff has the necessary qualities of leadership, technical expertise, and personality to discharge properly its responsibilities in making the planning system effective.

B. Pitfalls related to a misunderstanding of the nature of long-range planning:

14. Forgetting that planning is a political, a social, and an organizational, as well as a rational process.
15. Assuming that corporate comprehensive planning is something separate from the entire management process.
16. Failure to make sure that top management and major line officers really understand the nature of long-range planning and what it will accomplish for them and the company.
17. Failing to understand that systematic formal planning and intuitive (opportunistic, or entrepreneurial) planning are complementary.
18. Assuming that plans can be made by staff planners for line managers to implement.
19. Ignoring the fact that planning is and should be a learning process.
20. Assuming that planning is easy.
21. Assuming that planning is hard.
22. Assuming that long-range planning can get a company out of a current crisis.
23. Assuming that long-range planning is only strategic planning, or just planning for a major product, or simply looking ahead at likely development of present product. (In other words, failing to see that comprehensive planning is an integrated managerial system.)

C. Pitfalls in doing long-range planning:

I. Managerial involvement

24. Top management becomes so engrossed in current problems that it spends insufficient time on long-range planning, and the process becomes discredited among other managers and staff.
25. Long-range planning becomes unpopular because top management spends so much time on long-range problems that it ignores short-range problems.
26. Failure to assume the necessary involvement in the planning process of major line personnel.
27. Too much centralization of long-range planning in the central headquarters so that divisions feel little responsibility for developing effective plans.

II. The process of planning

28. Failure to develop company goals suitable as a basis for formulating long-range plans.
29. Assuming that equal weight should be given to all elements of planning (i.e., that the same emphasis should be placed on strategic as on tactical planning, or that the same emphasis should be accorded to major functional plans).
30. Injecting so much formality into the system that it lacks flexibility, looseness, and simplicity, and restrains creativity.
31. Failure to make realistic plans (e.g., due to over-optimism and/or overcautiousness.)
32. Extrapolating rather than rethinking the entire process in each cycle (i.e., if plans are made for 1971 through 1975, adding 1976 in the 1972 cycle rather than redoing all plans from 1972 to 1975).
33. Developing such a reverence for numbers that irreverence for intuition and value judgments predominates the thinking going into planning.
34. Seeking precision of numbers throughout the planning horizon.
35. Assuming that older methods to choose from among alternatives should be discarded in favor of newer techniques.
36. Assuming that new quantitative techniques are not as useful as advertised.
37. Doing long-range planning periodically and forgetting it in between cycles.

III. Creditability of results

38. Failure to develop planning capabilities in major operating units.
39. Failure of top management, and/or the planning staff, to give departments and divisions sufficient information and guidance (e.g., top management interests, environmental projections, etc.).
40. Attempting to do too much in too short a time.
41. Failure to secure that minimum of system and information to make the process and its results creditable and useful.

D. Pitfalls in using long-range plans:

42. Failure of top management to review with departmental and divisional heads the long-range plans which they have developed.
43. Forgetting that the fundamental purpose of the exercise is to make better current decisions.

44. Assuming that plans once made are in the nature of blueprints and should be followed rigorously until changed in the next planning cycle.
45. Top management's consistently rejecting the formal planning mechanism by making intuitive decisions which conflict with the formal plans.
46. Assuming that, because plans must result in current decisions, it is the short-run that counts and planning efforts as well as evaluations of results concentrate on the short-run.
47. Failing to use plans as standards for measuring managerial performance.
48. Forgetting to apply a cost-benefit analysis to the system to make sure advantages are greater than costs.
49. Failing to encourage managers to do good long-range planning by basing reward solely on short-range performance measures.
50. Failing to exploit the fact that formal planning is a managerial process which can be used to improve managerial capabilities throughout a company.

References

1. Very few of the U.S. respondents and practically none of the foreign respondents listed additional pitfalls. Those that were suggested, such as "developing a planning cycle which is much too long," or "failure to develop an adequate system to monitor those long-range plans," were invariably modifications of one or more of those pitfalls already listed in the questionnaire.
2. See, e.g. Serge Grosset, *Management: European and American Styles*, Wadsworth, Belmont (1970); Michael Y. Yoshino, *The Japanese Managerial System*, MIT Press, Cambridge (1940); Paul J. Gordon, Organizational strategies—The case of foreign operations by non-U.S. companies, *Journal of Comparative Administration* (May 1970); Hans Schöllhammer, Organization structures of multi-national corporations, *Academy of Management Journal* (September 1971).
3. George A. Steiner, *Top Management Planning*, Macmillan, New York (1968), p. 88.
4. David Granick, *The European Executive*, Doubleday & Company, New York (1964), p. 250; see also Robert Dubin, Management in Britain—Impressions of a visiting professor, *Journal of Management Studies.* **7** (2), (May 1970) pp. 183 ff.
5. Fuller descriptions are contained in George A. Steiner, *Pitfalls in Comprehensive Long Range Planning*, The Planning Executives Institute, Oxford, Ohio, U.S.A. (1972).
6. *Op. cit.*, Dubin, pp. 195 f.
7. Patrick H. Irwin, Why aren't companies doing a better job of planning?, *Management Review* (November 1971, pp. 11−16); Merritt L. Kastens, Who does the planning?, *Managerial Planning* (January/February 1972), pp. 1−3; Malcolm W. Pennington, Why has planning failed?, *Long Range Planning* (March 1972), pp. 2−9; Kjell A. Ringbakk, Why planning fails, *European Business* (Spring 1971), pp. 15−27.
8. *Op. cit.*, Steiner, p. 25.

21

Formal Planning in Major
U.S. Corporations

H. W. HENRY*

As the world about us changes, managers in all types of institutions try to cope in a variety of ways. In the early 1960s, many corporate managers realized they could not make sound decisions about future business activities in an expedient, reactive manner because their firms were growing very large and complex with new technologies, products, markets and competition to deal with. As a result, formal planning techniques which had been used in narrow functional applications were introduced on a much broader scale and formal long-range planning became popular. New corporate planning functions appeared in many companies, as well as new staff planning specialists and planning executives. I conducted a field study on the design of these systems in the mid-1960s and that showed great promise for improved management.[1]

With this history in mind, we might ask why such subjects as "planning techniques" and "problems of implementation" are still topics of concern. It would seem that such techniques would be well known and established in most firms after 10–15 years. However, this is not the case, for during a second field study of corporate planning systems which was completed in 1976 I found that many corporations, including some of the largest ones, had redesigned their planning systems in the early 1970s, essentially making a fresh start at formal long-range planning.

This finding was quite surprising and might be explained in various ways:

(1) Perhaps the original planning systems were not properly designed or implemented.
(2) Perhaps stable conditions and satisfactory performance in the 1960s

This article was originally published in *Long Range Planning*, Volume 10, No. 5, October 1977.

* The author is Professor of Industrial Management, University of Tennessee, Knoxville, U.S.A.

caused managers to become complacent and let the planning systems stagnate.

(3) Perhaps changes occurred in the external environment of firms which were so complex or unusual that the existing planning systems could not deal with them effectively.

Each of these general explanations has some validity, based on the specific factors cited by planners and executives in these companies.

However, the most obvious conclusions from my recent field study was that all corporations experience problems in implementing and using a formal planning system. The nature of these *problems* and some possible *remedies* are the subjects I will focus on in this article.

After identifying and listing several problems which were reported, I examined them for similarities and found they could be grouped into three broad categories:

(1) Problems related to *management attitudes and values* (philosophy of management),
(2) Problems related to the *design* of the formal planning system, and
(3) Problems related to the *method of introducing and administering* the system.

I will discuss the problems in each area in the order listed.

Management Attitudes and Values

Since formal planning systems were first introduced in business corporations, the attitude of top managers has been the most criticial factor in attaining effective planning and improved performance. This finding was very evident in the study of several early planning systems I completed in the mid-1960s. At that time, I concluded that "the success of long-range planning efforts in each business corporation seemed to be directly related to the extent of active interest and leadership of the President and other top executives." [2] Many other studies of planning systems have reached the same conclusion.

In my most recent study, the vital role of the top executive was again evident. For example, two contrasting executive views were reflected in these comments I received:

Company A—"The President does not want much formality."
Company B—"The President sends each division head a letter stating acceptance (of the division's plan) and giving guides on how to correct deficiencies and a pep talk on what he thinks should be emphasized."

TABLE 21.1. *Formal planning in major U.S. corporations—year of introduction and/or renewal*

Corporation	Date-formal planning 1st started	Date-formal planning renewed
Electric equipment or electronic cos.		
A	late 1950s	1972
B	early 1960s	continual improvement
C	late 1950s	continual improvement
D	early 1960s	1970
E	1963	1972
F	1964	1970
Chemical cos.		
A	1964	1972
B	mid-1960s	1973
C	1971–1972	—
D	1961	1972
Drug cos.		
A	1963	continual improvement
B	1968	continual improvement
C	1964	1970
D	1968	1973
Paper cos.		
A	1973	—
B	1972	—
C	1968	1973
Machinery cos.		
A	1967–68	1972
B	1971	—
C	1966	1970
D	1964	1973
E	1969	1973
Food and beverage cos.		
A	1973	—
B	1967	—
C	1964	1972
D	1964	1968
E	1961	1973
Automobile cos.		
A	early 1960s	—
B	1969	1973

You can imagine that these two Presidents get different results from their division heads. The problem illustrated may be stated as follows: *When top management views systematic, future-oriented planning as unimportant, the thought and effort exerted by lower level managers will be minimal.*

Another evidence of the way top management views formal planning is the weight assigned to this activity in performance evaluations and reward systems. If compensation and promotions are based strictly on short-term profit performance, that area will receive the most attention. This is an age-old problem and may be stated as follows: *If top management does not reward systematic planning efforts and results, this activity will not receive adequate attention.*

Another problem reported which reflected the philosophy of management of top executives was *lack of direction from top management in the form of corporation goals, statements of mission, or corporation strategies.* Perhaps some managers believed in decentralization so strongly that they did not want to channel or restrict division managers. Perhaps it was the easiest thing to do and was really an abdication of responsibility. In any case, division managers in several companies felt the need for more guidance to avoid random, wasteful searches for new business activities and the effort to develop plans which had to be redrawn or discarded due to unknown constraints.

In some companies, even when goals were formulated and stated, one problem was the *lack of commitment to the objectives by key executives, operating managers and staff specialists.* If goals were stated merely because they were required, without a firm belief that they were desirable and attainable, they did not serve as effective focal points for creating and implementing action plans. One vice-president summed it up when he said—"Planning without commitment to objectives doesn't accomplish much."

Finally, *if top management views the planning process as more important than the thinking and action it is supposed to stimulate, results are often disappointing.* For example, a new planning director was hired in one corporation and he, along with the president, prepared a planning manual and insisted that everybody follow it precisely. Thus, the planning effort was more form than substance. Division heads could get by if they followed the procedures and the value to them for improving the way they managed was missed. Again, the attitude of top management toward formal planning and its role was the root of the problem.

System Design

The largest group of problems found seemed to fall in the category of improper system design. Of course, the design often reflected top management philosophy and the way a system was implemented could reflect on the design, so it is impossible to clearly separate the three classes of problems I have identified.

A basic problem of many companies is that *the planning system is too informal*. Without clearcut responsibility assignments for who does what in planning for the future, effective planning is left to chance, and the most likely results are many gaps in performing vital planning activities and some duplication of effort. In the broadest sense, the problem is the lack of organization. Also, if some guidelines, premises, and schedules are not established, the results are likely to be imcompatible and the efforts will be very inefficient.

On the other hand, some *planning systems are too formal*, with thick planning manuals, excessive required documentation, and extensive number exercises. In such systems, rigid compliance to the formal procedures is usually required. Such a design may not lead to better management, as stated above under the problem of "process orientation" of top management. This problem seems to be one of the primary reasons why many planning systems became ineffective and gradually disintegrated in the 1960s. For example, one executive reported that "a comprehensive planning system was developed in 1967 or 1968 for the operating units, but much documentation was required and it got burdensome". This result, coupled with the autonomy of division managers in this company and the indifference of the top manager toward formal planning, caused the formal planning system to "fizzle out". A similar pattern was cited in other companies which had renewed their planning efforts in the 1970s.

Another design problem is that the *planning staff can be too large and dominant*. For example, one company had nearly 80 persons assigned to a planning unit at one time. The fact that this system is now defunct may tell us something (of value). Such a system often places much reliance on staff efforts, so operating managers who have important experience and technical knowledge to contribute to the planning process may become indifferent or resentful. In either case, their essential inputs are lost.

A structural flaw which affects planning systems as well as other functions in business corporations is that of *excessive centralization*. This usually reflects the philosophy of top management and may be related to the scope of the product lines or required activities in the company. In addition to the dominant role assigned to planning staffs, top executives may feel compelled to make all major decisions, with very little delegation of authority. If this situation exists, the experience, ideas, and values of other managers are not utilized fully and the stimulus to thinking which results from interactions between managers is never realized.

However, the pendulum may swing too far in the opposite direction, so that the problem becomes *excessive decentralization*. If division heads or local managers have too much authority, their actions may not be in the best interest of the corporation and their plans may reflect narrow interests or self-serving ventures. Even divisional planners may become very independent and resent any guidance or intrusion by corporate planning specialists or executives. In such a situation, resources may be wasted due to investments which are inconsistent with a corporation strategy and inefficiencies will result from the lack of cooperative effort.

A problem which is believed to be widespread and very serious is the *failure to forge a link between strategic planning and operational planning*. Again, the system design is critical, but top management attitudes and implementation methods also influence the way managers perceive the relation between strategic and operational planning. There are sound reasons for separating the process of preparing each of these plans, and some companies made a deliberate effort to do so. First, it is only logical to determine major objectives and strategies before operational plans can be developed, for the strategic plan "drives" or determines the type of operations to be performed. Therefore, a strategic planning cycle precedes an operational planning cycle in many firms. Other firms believe it is essential to separate these two types of planning in order to get any strategic planning done at all. Thus, they designate their long-range planning effort as strategic planning in order to get managers to view the business in a broader manner and to avoid any number exercises (to project sales and budgets) which are part of operational planning. Thus, these reasons for separation may be summarized as (1) to concentrate on strategy formulation and (2) to avoid budget projections (which are usually based on the current strategy and prevent any consideration of alternatives).

The problem arises when the results of the strategic planning process are ignored when operational plans are developed. In some cases, different people may be involved in the two processes. Also, the strategies developed may be stated in very broad, general terms which are not understandable or very difficult to translate into operational plans. Finally, inertia tends to keep managers following familiar paths, so they may incorporate too much of current activities and policies in their plans for the future.

In companies which include strategic and operational plans in one set of plans, this last reason for ineffective integration of new strategies into operational plans may cause strategy formulation efforts to be very weak and perfunctory. In other firms, strategic planning may be given very little emphasis in the planning process. Thus, the overall problem which exists in many different types of planning systems is the failure to formulate sound strategies and to reflect them in operational plans. System design can have an important impact both in causing and overcoming this problem.

The final design problem I will discuss is the *imbalance in planning activities* which sometimes exists. For example, a great amount of time and effort may be spent in developing forecasting models, while social, political and technological changes in the external environment are not monitored or evaluated. In other companies, long-range planning efforts may be dominated by financial analysis or by product planning or by marketing considerations. In fact, formal planning systems have evolved in many companies from one specialized function such as long-range financial or product planning or economic analysis. Ideally, a comprehensive planning system should involve every major functional, product, and territorial area within a corporation as well as the major segments of the external environment—social, political, economic, physical, and technological.

Planning System Implementation

When a decision is made *to introduce a formal planning system* in a corporation, it is sometimes made *without consulting or involving many other executives or lower level managers.* Formal planning may be recommended by a consulting firm or a major competitor may start or revive formal planning, so the decision to do it seems logical and everyone is expected to agree. However, it is one thing to get reluctant acquiescence and another to get eager involvement. One vice-president said "if you have to give a directive, it is usually not too successful" and thus implied that imposed systems don't work. If managers do not understand the reasons for formal planning and are not involved in discussions or exercises or conferences where the need is recognized, they may be unwilling or indifferent planners and may actively resist and hinder planning efforts. At best, their motivation will be weaker than if they are involved in the initial decision to plan formally.

Another very serious problem in implementing formal planning systems is the *lack of training of managers* to use such a system. Most managers are strongly oriented toward day-to-day operational problems and achieving short-term results they are responsible for. When they are suddenly asked to become future oriented and think about what the world might be like in the distant future, they face a difficult transition. Also, when they are asked to formulate strategies which will lead to the achievement of important and hard-to-reach goals, they wonder where the bolt of lightning came from. To illustrate this problem—the corporate planner in one large firm would talk to operating managers to learn their broad plan of attack for achieving major goals. Then he would write out the strategy he perceived and send it to them to see if he stated their strategy correctly. This little game was triggered by the inability of the operating managers to write sensible strategy statements in their formal plans.

Also, when managers are asked to look for various types of external changes and trends which may become threats or opportunities, they wonder where to start. In addition, their entire process of thinking must shift from tangibles to intangibles, from actuals to possibilities, from the present to the future, to scenarios, probabilities, priorities, and desirable future goals for the corporation instead of how to get results tomorrow. I think it is too much to expect the average operating manager and many experienced executives to become instant long-range strategic planners. I have heard different planners and executives say that a few years are required to develop an effective planning system in which managers become thinkers and not merely extrapolators. For example, a recent *Business Week* article (Nov. 10, 1975) about Potlatch Corporation stated that a new president set out to reeducate managers to become strategic planners and within about four years, performance was vastly improved.

When formal planning is introduced, the *additional work load on managers* is a significant implementation problem. The number of forms to fill out, the options to evaluate, and the calculations to make require much time and effort and the initial shock may be great. Some managers learn to cope with the increasing paperwork burden (from corporation staffs, governmental units, and universities) by filling out forms faster and faster and providing less and less meaningful data. In other cases, the work is delegated to a subordinate who does not have the knowledge or experience to provide the best inputs. In either situation, the quality of the plans developed and the future performance of the corporation are the things which suffer.

One of the most critical parts of formal planning and one of the most difficult ones to implement is that of capital allocation. Funds are limited in the biggest and best corporations (and even in the U.S. Government) and many managers in each firm are competing to get part of the limited resources. If the *planning process does not include an understandable, logical, consistent and fair way of allocating capital funds*, managers will lose confidence in it and their planning efforts will decline rapidly. If the allocation system is slow, arbitrary and unpredictable, managers will engage in "gamesmanship" to get their part. In addition to seriously undermining the planning system, desirable ventures may be delayed, cancelled, or restructured and corporation performance may decline. In one large chemical corporation, a new formal planning system is struggling to "wean" key managers from making "emergency" capital requests at any time for any purpose.

Remedies for Planning System Problems

In this section, I will outline some possible actions to overcome the problems discussed thus far. At least some of these and perhaps all have been tried in various corporations.

(1) Encourage top executives who practice informal planning to attend conferences on planning, to read articles and books on formal planning, and to discuss with executives in other companies various management techniques and results. I know of no other way to get executives enthused about formal planning except through awareness of what others are doing, and a personal evaluation and decision to try new ways of management.

(2) To motivate managers to plan beyond the current accounting year, it seems that a specific incentive must be provided in the evaluation and reward system. A factor such as "effectiveness in strategic planning" should be specified as one performance evaluation factor and a definite, significant weight should be assigned to it. To measure performance, "effort" may have to be measured at first by determination of time spent in planning alone, time spent in training sessions, or time spent in actual planning activities with other persons. The "quality" of strategies and plans submitted can also be evaluated by line and staff teams. Finally, actual "results" which may be attributed to each manager's planning efforts can be measured as time goes on. Plans submitted each year should be filed and reviewed in later years to find relationships between plans and subsequent results. Also, each manager can be asked to identify such links.

(3) To get more guidance from top executives in the form of corporation goals and strategies, division heads can exert pressure on them to say what is expected. This has happened in some companies, for the division heads have said in effect—we have the resources and capabilities to do many different things; what do you want us to do? Another development which has caused top executives in other companies to give more attention to corporation goals and strategies has been the realization that fragmented, overlapping or incompatible divisional activities resulted from the lack of corporation direction.

(4) Special programs on "commitment" for managers or for all employees can be conducted in a company in an effort to motivate people to commit themselves to goal fulfilment. A "Management by Objectives" program may also be effective for this purpose. In any case, the emphasis on commitment must come through the authority hierarchy from top to bottom, perhaps starting with the board of directors. At the same time it should be stressed that goals must be desirable or worthwhile, realistic or attainable, and also challenging.

(5) To shift the thinking of top management and lower level managers away from the planning process and the completion of forms, a review session in which each key manager has to give an oral summary of his goals, premises, strategies, and action plans before a group of fellow managers should be beneficial. Of course, open discussion should follow each presentation and staff assistance and "crutch" charts should be minimized. This requirement to tell others should stimulate the thinking of managers,

just as required presentations in the classroom or in graduate-faculty seminars motivate the speaker to prepare more thoroughly.

(6) To attain the optimal level of formality in a planning system, especially in regard to the plan required from key managers, it seems better to start in a simple way and increase the complexity rather than starting with a voluminous set of instructions and forms. In the simple approach, managers are not "shellshocked" by the size of the undertaking, they do not have a large increase in work load, and they can understand the reasons for their efforts if the requirements are smaller in scope. As a result, acceptance should be better and efforts should be more conscientious. Also, the learning process and attitudinal changes will advance with increasing planning system sophistication. As managers understand and become more proficient in planning, they will see the need for additional types of analysis. In fact, I think a great deal of flexibility should be permitted in plans so that managers can add parts they consider important. Many companies permit such flexibility.

To illustrate the basic elements of a simple strategic plan, I have listed the section headings from a sample Division Strategic Plan sent to key managers in one large U.S. corporation when top management introduced a redesigned planning system in the early 1970s. They were:

    (i) Business Review
   (ii) Environment for Growth
  (iii) Key Strategic Goals
  (iv) Strategies
   (v) Key Strategic Programs
 (vi) Financial Implications and Support Data.

(7) Planning staffs should be kept small at both the corporate and divisional levels. In some companies, a person with only a part-time assignment to coordinate the planning process is very effective in getting line managers and functional staff specialists to develop strategic long-range plans. Sometimes, functional staffs are located in close proximity and one or more persons from each staff has a key role in reviewing plans or in making inputs to the planning process. In other cases, various types of staff specialists are pulled together in one unit under a Director of Planning or Vice-President Planning.

In contrast to these arrangements where staff personnel have some operational assignments and some strategic planning assignments, some companies designate a planning staff or executive staff to be strictly a strategic planning unit whose job is to identify and evaluate alternative corporate strategies. In this situation, the staff could play a dominant role unless corporate executives were effective in challenging, evaluating, and modifying strategies proposed by the staff unit. Thus, various staff arrangements can be effective as long as both line managers and staff specialists recognize their respective roles and contribute fully to the planning process.

(8) The degree of decentralization of authority which exists in a company is usually a direct reflection of the management philosophy of the chief executive officer and the basic type of organization structure employed. For example, subsidiaries, product divisions, and geographical divisions will be more independent than functional operating units in a corporation. Some managers want to make all major decisions while others believe that much autonomy should be granted to division managers. As a general guideline, divisions should not get so independent in planning and action that they fail to act in the best interest of the corporation. On the other hand, decisions should not be so centralized that division managers are prevented from using their knowledge and experience fully, for they will lose incentive to be innovative and the company will not develop promotable managers very fast.

If an existing organization structure is not suitable for strategic planning by groups, divisions, or departments because one unit does not contain all critical activities related to one business or because it contains two or more businesses, a structure for planning purposes can be superimposed on the existing structure. This has been done successfully in some corporations and such units are called Strategic Business Units.

(9) To ensure that strategic planning receives adequate attention, I think it is best to design a formal planning procedure with a two-stage cycle, the first one for strategic planning and the subsequent one for operational planning. To link the two stages, the approved strategic plan should be summarized at the beginning of operational plans and specific proposed programs or activities should be related directly to the strategies indicated.

Independent reviews of submitted plans by line managers and staff groups or by specially-designated evaluation committees should look for direct linkages between operational and strategic plans. If inconsistencies are found, plans should be returned for revision.

(10) Planning activities can be balanced by first involving every line and staff unit in the planning process. Then to prevent imbalance between functional plans or other elements of a plan, independent reviews by internal managers and/or external consultants could be made periodically.

(11) When introducing a formal planning system, several different approaches may be used. I will review briefly two of these. In the first one, the top manager meets with the vice-presidents to discuss problems, needs, goals, and issues in the company. Ideas from all should be sought and then a list of major needs and ways to attain them can be compiled. This process is continued by each vice-president with his own subordinates (division heads) and by each division head with his respective subordinates. Then the ideas flow upward and are discussed and integrated at each level. When the top executive level is reached, some concrete ideas on desirable goals and

ways to achieve them should emerge. This is the beginning of formal planning and all key managers have been involved in the process.

A second method is to schedule a management conference at a remote location of 100 or more key managers, with a schedule of activities to include outside speakers from other companies or universities or consulting firms who discuss the changing world and how corporations can cope with changes in the future. Informal buzz group sessions to get ideas from all participants should be included with reports from each group and a master compilation of needs, goals, proposed strategies and action plans. This also provides a foundation for formal planning which includes much involvement by many managers.

(12) To provide training for managers on how to plan, some companies have extensive in-house programs, often at remote training centers, and involve corporate executives as well as outsiders in leading the training programs. In some companies, participants in such programs return to their units and train their own subordinates, using visual aids, reading materials, sample plans, and guidebooks provided by the planning staff.

Additional training opportunities exist at strategic planning conferences in other institutions.

(13) Managers can avoid excessive work loads and still do effective planning by using the conventional remedies of hiring more support personnel and by delegating more duties and authority to line and staff subordinates.

(14) To allocate capital in a consistent, fair manner, proposed capital spending plans should be classified in various ways so that priorities can be determined in relation to the major goals to be sought and the strategies to be employed. For example, some spending plans may be for new ventures, others to expand and improve existing facilities, and others to develop new products. The degree of importance can be indicated, as well as the time period when funds will be needed and the likely impacts if implementation is delayed.

In conclusion, if formal planning systems are to be effective, problems should be identified as soon as possible in each corporation and remedies used by other firms or new ones designed internally should be employed to solve each problem. If one solution doesn't work, others should be tried. There is no cook-book formula which can be applied in every firm, but the most important ingredient is to find or develop managers who want to do a better job of managing.

References

1. Harold W. Henry, *Long Range Planning Practices In 45 Industrial Companies*, Englewood Cliffs, N.J.: Prentice-Hall, Inc. (1967).
2. *Ibid.*, p. 28.

22
Business Planning:
The Gap Between Theory
and Practice

J. MARTIN

Introduction

As a member of the Society and someone who has been involved in planning at a governmental and private level, I am diffident to argue through this Journal that the gap between corporate planning theory and practice is alarming and growing. However, I am encouraged by a groundswell against irrelevant and inadequate theory in politics and economics: we must after all live by the courage of conviction—preferably, our own.

Over the past 7 years my company, Planning Research + Systems Limited (PRS), has set out in the context of a research programme to identify "best planning practice" in British industry. The results of this research were made available to clients upon subscription in a Programme entitled the Creative Corporate Planning Programme. More recently I have made some of the findings available in book form.*

The approach adopted in the research was to establish the structured approaches to business problems which work; and in doing so to identify the approaches which fail. The research covered all the major planning areas which concern management, from complete systems to a checklist approach to specific problems (a concern established by research).

The results of the Creative Corporate Planning Programme are essentially practical: some of the best solutions to complex problems are simple; conversely, some complex solutions are useless. In British industry

This article was originally published in *Long Range Planning*, Volume 12, No. 6, December 1979.

The author is a Director of John Martin Publishing Ltd., 33 Cork Street, London W1X 1HB.

* *The Best Practice of Business*, Volumes 1–6 (1978), John Martin Publishing, 33 Cork Street, London W1X 1 HB.

it can be stated with some authority that *among policy makers and senior advisers* the many erudite contributions are little known; and when they are known they rarely do more than decorate the bookshelf.

Contributors to this Journal have argued in recent editions that there is a greater awareness among British companies of the need to plan and some evidence has been given that more companies are planning. It is essentially my contention that "things are rarely what they seem". I know it to be true that many leading British companies have excellent theoretical planning systems developed internally and with the assistance of competent consultants. It is sad to discover that they are rarely perceived (often conceived) as having real relationship to the way a company actually plans its business.

The main responsibility for this sad state of affairs is our own: that is, the readers of this Journal, all those involved in the evolution and teaching of business theory and in consultancy practice. Business planning in Britain (and I suspect in the U.S.A.) is the victim of punditry. We need not be too harsh on ourselves in recognizing this: any discipline or body of practice attracts punditry, and it is flattering and reassuring for the senior executive to arm himself with some measure of it. However, the function of planning is to assist a company to improve its performance and in business we must be judged by results. All too often bad planning impedes or imperils a business: and gifted entrepreneurs who are at the heart of all successful businesses—and hence the generation of real wealth—know it.

In this article I limit myself to one single question—"What planning systems are currently used?" In posing the question I am aware that confusions in definitions can arise and subjective judgments are inevitable. I ask for the application of common (good) sense on behalf of readers.

Method

During the period 1973–1975 PRS carried out a major research programme with the purpose of discovering the actual planning systems used by leading British companies. For this purpose, attention was directed to *The Times* Top 1000 companies by size. While use was made of published data, the main research effort was a comprehensive personal and telephone interview programme with just under 10 per cent of these companies selected entirely at random. It can be claimed, therefore, that the results are strongly indicative of the planning of these companies in general.

These findings are reviewed regularly and PRS has no reason to believe, 3 years later, that planning practices have changed in any material manner.

Current Planning Methods Used

All the companies contacted during the research claimed to plan. In so much as all business activity is undertaken to produce an intended result, this is the only possible conclusion. However, the extent to which these leading companies lacked formal planning methods might be thought surprising. Table 22.1 shows the type of planning existing in these companies:

TABLE 22.1. *Activities claimed to be "planning"*[a]

	Percentage (rounded)
"Informal" planning:	
annual budgets only	10
annual budgets plus formal capital investment appraisal	40
"Formal" planning	40
"Comprehensive" planning	10
	100

[a] The definitions are those claimed by the company. In PRS' consulting experience, companies exaggere the extent to which they plan.

Formal Planning

The majority of those companies which claimed to plan "formally" but not "comprehensively", had in fact developed extended budget forecasts. The only practical separation of these companies from those producing annual budgets and having systems of formal capital investment appraisal shown in Table 22.1, was that the reasons were to some extent written. Extended budget forecasting was carried out by projecting the annual budget over a stated (usually 5-year) period. The sales volume ahead was always considered and production capacity to meet the expected sales was usually, but not always, considered. Only a minority (about one-fifth) considered possible new developments, research and development, or personnel.

Those companies claiming to undertake comprehensive planning considered all the above factors.

Of the companies contacted about half had a "planning" department or a full-time "planner".

One-quarter of the companies contacted had written objectives. Usually these were quantitative targets stated in terms of future sales, profits, and return on investment. Some had written targets for growth in earnings per share. Few companies had qualitative objectives (8 per cent), and most of these were generalizations ("We will provide a good environment for our staff to work in").

One in 12 companies were practising some form of management by objectives. Interestingly these were in the main, not the same companies which were planning comprehensively.

Informal Planning

The reasons for not planning formally were all of one type. There was a widespread belief that "planning" would restrict future action and would leave the company in an inflexible position.

The stated reason confuses planning with forecasting: but even within its own terms it is clearly incorrect. Events tend to favour a company more often if it leads, rather than if it follows, trends. Thus a company which is leading.

- Reduces its need for flexibility.
- Attunes its organization for change.
- Makes it more adaptable and in a better state of preparedness to meet change.

The confusion (amongst planners and non-planners alike) that planning and forecasting are virtually the same, is developed later. The important aspect of this point is that while non-planners "defended" themselves by referring to the inflexibility of target-setting, they did not in most cases show any evidence of entrepreneurial action themselves.

Types of Plans

It is interesting and useful to look at some of the more "successful" claimed planning systems. Six of them located in the programme are described in Table 22.2.

There is no question that an able business man can successfully run a company, even a large one, without a forward plan. An important finding of this part of the research was that the adoption of a particular planning method conditions the business outcome to a large degree. This is so, even in companies where line management planning is emphasized. However, most companies which were planning comprehensively had not thought of this when introducing their planning system. This reveals a planning paradox: there are probably a great many companies, comprehensively and conscientiously, planning on the basis of systems which do not suit their operations. For this reason, it should not be assumed that companies planning informally are worse off than many of those planning formally. A conclusion which will agonize the pundit.

A planning system should not, in the early stages, place too much emphasis on the physical counting of people, resources and end targets. Although such activities are necessary to the task of scheduling, they can

TABLE 22.2. *Examples of types of planning systems in use*

	(1) No formal planning	(2) Simple general operations planning system

Key features	Annual budgeting
	Detailed monthly controls
	
	Current operations only
		Company and competitor analysis:
		    strengths
		    weaknesses
		Forecasts:
		    opportunities
		    threats
		Several strategies demanded
		Current operations only

Advantages	No assumptions made No bias from planning system It is realized that continuous thought is needed Those operating the controls develop a facility for locating trouble	System set out for line manager use System encourages thinking of alternatives The planning documents are not stereotyped for all divisions Method is simple and used
Disadvantages	Needs first-class senior managers Absence of those who operate the system (e.g. illness, causes collapse of the system No conscious effort is applied to the longer term, operationally or strategically	No build-up to the sales volume forecast Concentrates on marketing and finance only No strategic plan

	(3) Dealer/distributor planning system	(4) Distribution company planning system

Key features	Detailed build-up of possible future sales from capacity and projected past trends—converted to financial data and actions
	
	Current operations only
		Uses seminars as part of planning system
		Provides line managers with:
		    objectives
		    inter-company comparisons
		    environment
		    strengths and weaknesses
		    alternatives
		    actions
		Current operations only
		Planning is twice per year

TABLE 22.2. (cont.)

	(3) Dealer/distributor planning system	(4) Distribution company planning system
Advantages	Where all factors needed are known, it allows very detailed consideration to be given to each System set out for line manager use	Is used and taken seriously by line managers Is simple Is particularly useful where a large number of divisions or units exist Is operated without planning department Includes management by objectives
Disadvantages	No alternatives Too detailed—becomes an exercise in itself	Provides no mechanism to improve the best. The method is designed to bring the average up to the best No strategic plan

	(5) Manufacturing operations planning system	(6) Manufacturing strategic planning system
Key features	Provides line managers with: objectives environmental forecast inflation rates Line managers conduct detailed sales analysis Gap analysis and actions Long and short range plans Current operations only	Is a comprehensive plan: strategic operational Demands operating alternatives Demands strategic thought both inside and outside the present operation Provides a simple mechanism for generating strategic thought
Advantages	Is carried out world-wide to same format Does not consume excessive time Is sales detail-orientated System set out for line manager use	Is comprehensive Provides for company development Is considered by the company to be highly effective
Disadvantages	No strategic plan	Is complex—a planning department is essential Sub-systems would be needed for line manager use

too easily become confused with the total act of planning, with a consequent over-emphasis on forecasting to the detriment of creativity. Planners should not shrink from indentifying good opportunities which cannot be fully quantified.

One point is especially important when using planning systems. Naturally such systems consist of a series of connected steps. Each step may itself involve many important questions. There is therefore a danger of planning becoming similar to the comprehensive filling-in of a question-naire, with equal importance being given to each step. While all aspects should be considered, the major portion of time should be spent in identifying and examining those factors which are crucial for success. Emphasis should then be placed on these factors.

Simplicity in Planning

Several major planning problems (see Table 22.3), revolve around the important need for line managers at all levels to undertake their own planning. In one-half of the cases analysed, the line manager was not as cooperative as the planner would wish. Further, in many instances a specific line manager's experiences and training had not equipped him to plan ahead in any other way than continuing as he was and trying to do better. These men were often not numerate and found difficulty in thinking of genuine alternatives. This had led directly to the development of complex step-by-step planning methods. These methods have two serious deficiencies:

TABLE 22.3. *Major problems in planning formally*

	Percentage
(1) Getting line managers to plan	50
(2) Support from top management	40
(3) Inadequate thinking about future	40
(4) Poor business understanding by managers (e.g. what makes for profit)	40
(5) Lack of realism	40
(6) Need for better forecasting	40

- The forms are not filled in with real thought, but merely as "fast as possible"; the detail of the step-by-step approach facilitates this.
- The planning system itself, in leading the line manager's thinking, may introduce serious bias in the results.

The most successful company encountered in the research stated that a large part of its success was attributable to good planning. It emphasized simplicity in the system combined with "planning seminars" for line managers. These seminars are part lecture, part discussion, and part workshop. They are timed to fit specific parts of the planning cycle.

Familiarity with Planning Terms

A number of planning failures were found to be caused by unfamiliarity with planning terms. It was emphasized by planners who felt themselves successful, that the words, meanings and tasks involved in planning should be those of the job, company and industry concerned. "This", commented one planner, "often demands more work than it would seem".

Planning Problems

Those contacted during the project were probed as to their major difficulties and to the causes of partial or total failures. Over half of the companies contacted which claimed to plan formally had had major difficulties. These are shown in Table 22.3.

It can be seen that all the major planning difficulties arose from human problems. Planning is in many cases either resisted by line managers, or the results of planning are apparently ignored by top management when taking decisions. Or again, when line managers do plan, they are found to be ignorant of basic business premises. It is in these circumstances that planning becomes an "ivory-tower" exercise, or the planner himself is thought to be seeking personal power. Respondents who had been at least partially successful in combating these problems, emphasized the need to maintain the principle that line managers do their own planning, while they help, guide, and to some extent educate them from the centre. One successful company had made it a principle to eliminate by divestment all genuine profit centres that were not large enough to employ a manager of sufficiently high calibre, to ensure that basic "planning understanding" problems do not arise.

Table 22.4 lists the 16 common problems that were located.

A Planning Omission: Corporate Development

One major area of business planning was found to be missing from practically all the companies studied. While systematic analysis and planning of current operations was being undertaken, no structural thought was given to planning for change. Most current planning systems are variations of projecting the present operations to all practical purposes "as is". This has been found valuable in pointing our emerging problems and giving managers the added impetus of targets ahead and a feeling of

TABLE 22.4. *Planning problems*

Establishing planning in the company	Developing the planning method	Planning
(1) Weak top management support	(1) Using planning to delay decision-making rather than making the effort to decide on actions	(1) Lack of line manager support
(2) Top managers are seen not to make decisions based on the plan	(2) Not planning the plan	(2) Line managers do not understand business principles
(3) Planning is conducted once per year and then forgotten	(3) Developing inflexible targets in the first place and not reviewing plans in the second	(3) Plans and reasons are not put in writing
(4) The belief that planning is a new addition rather than being an integral part of managing	(4) Abandoning the plan at the first problem or unexpected event	(4) Planner's report too low down in the organization structure
	(5) Confusion of planning success with volume of paper produced	(5) Lack of planning staff at divisional level
		(6) Poor planning system and lack of support, help and information from planner
		(7) Lack of method of implementing plans (management by objectives)

direction in corporate development. It does not, however, organize the company to chart its own future so, with these methods dependent on scheduling within forecast targets, inflexibility is built into the plan. Companies which do plan for "change", tend to view "change" in terms of diversification and acquisitions. It is rare for a company to consciously plan any alteration in the present business and its environment, so that its profit making potential is enhanced.

Current business literature is unhelpful on this point. The difference between operations planning, strategic planning, and development planning (plus a host of other names) is alternately described in terms of:

- Time periods (for example, one company used the following)
  —strategic: 5 − 10 years out
  —development: 3 − 5 years out
  —operations: 1 − 2 years out

- Business function (for example, another company)
  —strategic: the Board
  —development: new products, acquisitions, diversifications
  —operations: all line operations.

Of course, any clear-cut separation of planning terms is open to misuse because the functions are interwoven. Persons interviewed, however, who could not be described as entrepreneurs (many of whom did not believe in formal planning, although they did budget), stressed the need to realize that above-average profit arises from being *usefully different to the competition in a manner which you can protect* * *within a growth market.* Many of these entrepreneurs felt that what they called planning (extended budget forecasts) committed the company not to change and resulted, therefore, in lower profits over time.†

It is clear that many companies do not recognize two distinctive aspects to planning for the current business. These are:

- Operating planning: with the emphasis on targeting, internal co-ordination, and scheduling of needed facilities, persons, and so on; resulting in budgets.
- Development planning: with the emphasis on organizing for change so as to enhance the profit potential of the current operations. This is not necessarily to do with the future. Alternatives to present methods exist now.

If this distinction is recognized, it will be accepted that strategic planning

---

* For example, patents or other forms of proprietary position.
† And, of course, more often than not they would be right.

will cover basic resource allocation: determining choices between current operation, and between current and new business areas.

Although it is recognized by many companies that alternatives need to be considered, and some planning systems allow for this, many line managers find the task of developing them almost impossible. The main reasons for this common shortcoming are:

Tunnel Vision

The operation has been performed in such and such a way for so long that alternatives just cannot be imagined—by anyone.

Fault-finding

People automatically think of reasons why a new solution would not work before the solution has been thought through—very common.

NIH(*Not Invented Here*)

Other departments' (or just other persons') thoughts and experience are often needed to think through a new solution. These persons may not be prepared to be helpful; the larger the company, the greater the problem.

Product Orientation

Over-concentration on cost-cutting, efficiency, existing technical performance improvement, and so on, at the expense of value considerations to the user.

The lack of creative thought‡ in planning leads directly to over-emphasis in forecasting. Since planning is meant to enable a company to determine its own future and since the creative avenue for doing this is not realized, a frustration with forecasting develops. Line managers become exasperated with "planning" when their projected targets do not materialize. This frustration was mentioned by several respondents. Others who had attempted to improve their forecasting pointed out that this was primarily due to a deficiency in accounting data. Accounting data, in its custodian function, is only concerned with facts. But they stated it is often not realized that last year's actual profit was only one point in a range of possibilities. Several other profit outcomes were possible, probably even up to the last week of the year. It is quite wrong, but all too common, to

‡ Creativity, and its importance in planning, is of vital importance and largely ignored in textbook expositions.

project a trend line which consists of factual but nevertheless partially random points, and expect the future points to come true. Even if no changes occurred in the business or its environment, this would be unlikely. Data used for business forecasts must show a range of possibilities. It is unrealistic ever to expect greater forecasting accuracy. For example, in Fig. 22.1 a profit record and forecast is shown. It can be seen that although the profit moves up and down, it does so only within a range of possibilities. It is not the function of planning to reduce the range of probabilities and therefore generate a more accurate forecast. On the contrary, a good plan will attempt to widen the range by raising the upper level while still holding the lower level. Thus in a good plan it may be very difficult to forecast the outcome. Entrepreneurs, many of whom were against "rigid planning" as they understood it, mentioned this form of thinking several times; corporate planners, however, did not generally recognize it.

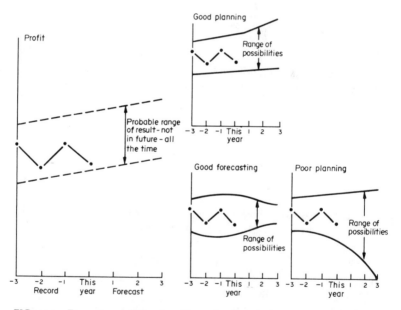

FIG. 22.1. *Forecasting and Planning. Forecasting from single point accounting data is misleadingly "accurate"—ranges should be used.*

A company, therefore, while needing a creative or development plan in addition to operations planning (or extended budgeting), will not be capable of producing it unless the "planner" is capable of the creative ability more commonly associated with entrepreneurs.

A Planning Ommission: Management by Objectives

Most of the companies which were planning formally did not complete the loop and ensure compliance with the plan through some form of management by objectives. Plans commonly ended with specific action statements. These were explicitly or implicitly allocated to individuals. There are many ways of closing the loop, and doing so is highly desirable. One company was found to take this linking very seriously. It stated that once employees knew that they would be judged personally on the achievements of their objectives, the quality and implementation of planning within the company had improved out of all recognition.

A Comparison: Entrepreneurs Compared with a Formal Plan

Since it may be thought to be strange that an entrepreneurial system of control may be preferable to a formal plan a comparison is provided. It should be appreciated that most examples of formal planning are exceptions: drawn from large, capital-intensive, and often multinational companies. Fortunately, it is still true that most economic activity, and the overwhelming majority of enterprises, do not fit this categorization.

Example 1: No Formal Planning System

The Company

The company is medium-sized (£30m sales), distributing consumer durables. It is organized into three divisions each operating a number of branches. Each division is run by a divisional manager. Growth has been good, averaging 10—15 per cent per annum over the last 5 years.

The Planning System—No Formal Planning

This company operates a control system which relies on those operating it to be forward-thinking and alert. The purpose of the system is to provide the divisional managers with as much detail about the company's current operations as possible. These divisional managers develop a facility for reviewing this data speedily, and identifying areas where the business is going astray, or where problems are developing. The senior managers then discuss these with line managers at monthly meetings.

Where the senior managers are competent, the method appears to work well. It has the advantage of flexibility. Its problems are twofold:

- Experienced men are needed to work it. Illness, for example, causes the system to collapse.

- No conscious effort is applied to the longer term. The company is, at best, in a well-managed drift.

The advantage of the system is very powerful. Since no assumptions are made about the future, the planning system itself cannot introduce its own bias, and since thought is demanded, it tends to be reliable. Its efficiency is impressive and, while it has enormous drawbacks, it is felt that it would be perilous for a company to move from this to another planning system that was not fully thought out.

The Method

Each branch provides an estimate of the sales over the next year. These are based on "doing a little better than last year". The total is added and a *pro forma* profit and loss account and balance sheet is prepared. This is discussed and budgets formulated. The agreed budgets are then broken down into branches and departments, and from these, targets are set for the year.

The secret, however, is in the monthly reporting. A monthly report is assembled consisting of operating details for each branch, viz:

- Sales: units; volume; gross profit.
- Stocks.
- Debtors.
- Capital expenditure.
- Operating statement.
- Monthly variance from budget.
- Divisional totals.

As the year progresses, the monthly figures and the cumulative totals are added to the monthly report. The report becomes voluminous, daunting, and without any system for highlighting key factors. The agility of the three divisional managers in using the book is impressive.

This system has limited but important possibilities of development in that there is no reason why the reporting system should not incorporate the key lead indicators for the business, so that "management by exception" become the rule.

Example 2: A Simple General Operations Planning System

This example illustrates a simple operations planning system that is known to work well in practice. The form sets are designed for line managers use and force a consideration of the alternatives facing that part of the business. Its deficiencies are the lack of a build-up of the sales volume forecast and the lack of input from departments other than marketing and finance. The ultimate success of this form of plan depends on the ability of marketing line managers to generate meaningful objectives and alternatives.

The Company

The company is a substantial international durables manufacturer, producing a small number of products sold to a number of geographical markets. In each of the last 5 years it has had a sales growth rate in excess of 15 per cent per annum.

Planning Department

A single planner at head office operates the system, in addition to much *ad hoc* work. He provides advice on the thinking needed to fill in the forms. Through time, the planner knows the line managers' differing thoughts on, and ability to think of, the future and tries to stimulate what he calls "the right ideas". The system has been in operation for 3 years and has been improved each year

Component Parts of the System

The system consists of the following three parts:

(1) An outline of the plan (shown in Fig. 22.2).
(2) Forms for self-analysis (not reproduced here).
(3) Recommended headings for the written plan.

1. *Outline plan.* The outline plan shows clearly how the planning process proceeds from the analysis stage, through the consideration of alternatives, to evaluation and choice—and then to the written plan.
2. *Forms for self-analysis.* The forms for Self-Analysis cover the various aspects illustrated in the outline plan. They cover the following subjects:

(1) Competitive analysis.
(2) Market forecast.
(3) Opportunities.
(4) Threats.
(5) Actions, costs and benefits.
(6/7) Possible strategies.
(8) Evaluation criteria.
(9) Summary.

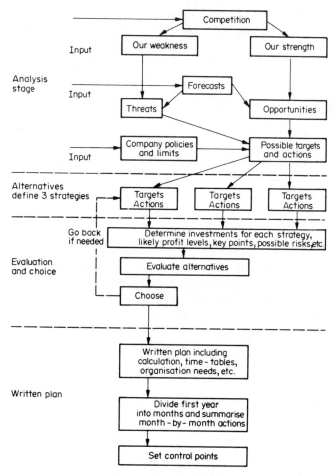

FIG. 22.2. *Outline of planning system.*

A seminar is held before product managers are asked to complete these forms. Each product manager is asked to return a complete set of forms for each product/market to the planning department for collection into the first draft of the corporate plan.

An explanation is given to each manager of the ways in which the planning department will analyse the forms and translate them into recommended headings for the written plan. These headings are set out in full below.

3. *Recommended headings for a written plan.* (Note: the forms are an aid to thinking. In the written report expand on the important aspects and keep the unimportant to a minimum.)

(1) Strengths and weaknesses in present position.
(2) Future opportunities and threats.
(3) Actions to capitalize on opportunities and avert threats.
(4) Strategy 1:
   ● Objectives and targets.
   ● Actions.
   ● Investments.
   ● Profits.
   ● Crucial factors for success.
   ● Risks.
(5) Strategy 2, 3, etc., repeat of 4.
(6) Evaluation criteria used and reasons.
(7) Reasoning for chosen strategy.
(8) Details of chosen strategy presented in depth to show:
   ● Forecasts of sales levels, profits, investment (add chosen strategy from 7 to Form 2. Firm up on figures.)
   ● Time-tables.
   ● Manpower and organization.
   ● Effect on other parts of company.
(9) Detail actions to put strategy into effect:
   ● Who?
   ● What?
   ● When?
   ● How?

Some Conclusions

It can be stated with some confidence that while many leading British firms use excellant planning systems which undoubtedly assist them to profitable growth, corporate planning as advocated by theorists, and as apparently adopted by large corporations, is generally not greatly developed. Nor does it seem that all the formal planning claimed to take place does in fact do so.

The management of large complex businesses necessitates good planning, and it is difficult not to conclude that shortcomings in this area materially affect industrial performance.

The research carried out by PRS shows that there are three major areas of weakness in current business planning systems:

(1) They are rarely a co-ordinated system: that is, parts of a plan are unrelated or overlapping.
(2) They are either too complex or obscure. Systems must be simple and clear if they are to gain consent and achieve results.

(3) The planning process must be familiar to all those persons intimately concerned with making it a success, and clearly related to corporate development objectives. Corporate development objectives must themselves be rational and consistent.

Planning systems provide an essential order of approach to developing a complete understanding of a company's likely results, alternatives and opportunities. To enable one unified assessment to be made of the potential for the company in each business area, the planning system needs to:

(1) Provide a logical base for thinking.
(2) Ensure that comprehensive consideration is given to each alternative.
(3) Keep the necessary re-cycling of the parts of the plan to a minimum.
(4) Be practical, workable, and allow business planning to grow naturally as a function within the company.

Few planning systems possess all these characteristics, and most companies, whether they claim to be "planning" or not, utilize very few in the operation and direction of their businesses.

23
Strategic Management for Competitive Advantage

F. W. GLUCK, S. P. KAUFMAN AND A. S. WALLECK

For the better part of a decade, strategy has been a business buzzword. Top executives ponder strategic objectives and missions. Managers down the line rough out product/market strategies. Functional chiefs lay out "strategies" for everything from R&D to raw-materials sourcing and distributor relations. Mere planning has lost its glamor; the planners have all turned into strategists.

All this may have blurred the concept of strategy, but it has also helped to shift the attention of managers from the technicalities of the planning process to substantive issues affecting the long-term wellbeing of their enterprises. Signs that a real change has been taking place in business's planning focus have been visible for some time in the performance of some large, complex multinational corporations—General Electric, Northern Telecom, Mitsubishi Heavy Industries, and Siemens A.G., to name four.

Instead of behaving like large unwieldy bureaucracies, they have been nimbly leap-frogging smaller competitors with technical or market innovations, in the true entrepreneurial style. They have been executing what appear to be well thought-out business strategies coherently, consistently, and often with surprising speed. Repeatedly, they have been winning market shares away from more traditionally managed competitors.

What is the source of these giant companies' remarkable entrepreneurial vigor? Is it the result of their substantial investments in strategic planning, which appear to have produced something like a quantum jump in the sophistication of their strategic planning processes? If so, what lessons can be drawn from the steps they have taken and the experience they have gained?

To explore these questions, we embarked on a systematic examination of

441

the relation between formal planning and strategic performance across a broad spectrum of companies (see the ruled insert). We looked for common patterns in the development of planning systems over time. In particular, we examined their evolution in those giant companies where formal planning and strategic decision making appeared to be most closely and effectively interwoven.

Our findings indicate that formal strategic planning does indeed evolve along similar lines in different companies, albeit at varying rates of progress. This progression can be segmented into four sequential phases, each marked by clear advances over its predecessor in terms of explicit formulation of issues and alternatives, quality of preparatory staff work, readiness of top management to participate in and guide the strategic decision process, and effectiveness of implementation (see Fig. 23.1).

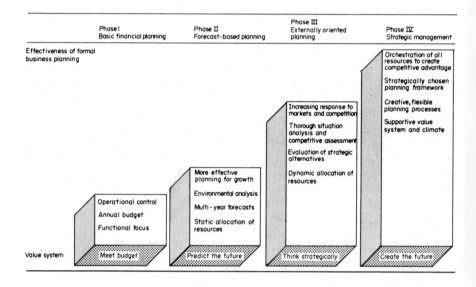

FIG. 23.1. *Four phases in the evolution of formal strategic planning*

The four-phase model evolution we shall be describing has already proved useful in evaluating corporate planning systems and processes and for indicating ways of improving their effectiveness.

In this article, we describe each of the four phases, with special emphasis on Phase IV, the stage we have chosen to call strategic management. In order to highlight the differences between the four stages, each will be sketched in somewhat bold strokes. Obviously, not all the companies in our sample fit the pattern precisely, but the generalizations are broadly applicable to all.

Phase I: Basic Financial Planning

Most companies trace the origins of a formal planning system to the annual budgeting process where everything is reduced to a financial problem. Procedures develop to forecast revenue, costs, and capital needs and to identify limits for expense budgets on an annual basis. Information systems report on functional performance as compared with budgetary targets.

Companies in Phase I often display powerful business strategies, but they are rarely formalized. Instead, they exist. The only concrete indication that a business strategy exists may be a projected earnings growth rate, occasionally qualified by certain debt/equity targets or other explicit financial objectives.

The quality of Phase I strategy depends largely on the CEO and the top team. Do they really know their company's products and markets and have a good sense of what major competitors will do next? Based on their knowledge of their own cost structure, can they estimate what the impact of a product or marketing change will be on their plants, their distribution system, or their sales force? If so, and if they do not plan for the business to grow beyond traditional limits, they may not need to set up an expensive planning apparatus.

Phase II: Forecast-based Planning

The complexities of most large enterprises, however, demand more explicit documentation of the implicitly understood strategies of Phase I. The number of products and markets served, the degree of technological sophistication required, and the complex economic systems involved far exceed the intellectual grasp of any one manager.

The shoe usually pinches first in financial planning. As treasurers struggle to estimate capital needs and trade off alternative financing plans, they and their staffs extrapolate past trends and try to foresee the future impact of political, economic, and social forces. Thus begins a second phase, forecast-based planning. Most long-range or strategic planning today is a Phase II system.

At first, this planning differs from annual budgeting only in the length of its time frame. Very soon, however, the real world frustrates planners by perversely varying from their forecasts.

In response, planners typically reach for more advanced forecasting tools, including trend analysis and regression models and, eventually, computer simulation models. They achieve some improvement, but not enough. Sooner or later plans based on predictive models fail to signal major environmental shifts that not only appear obvious after the fact, but also have a great and usually negative impact on corporate fortunes.

Nevertheless, Phase II improves the effectiveness of strategic decision making. It forces management to confront the long-term implications of decisions and to give thought to the potential business impact of discernible current trends, well before the effects are visible in current income statements. The issues that forecast-based plans address—e.g., the impact of inflation on future capital needs or the inroads foreign manufacturers may make in domestic markets—often lead to timely business decisions that strengthen the company's long-term competitive position.

A quest for common patterns

For two years, we and our colleagues studied the development of formal planning systems in 120 companies, mainly industrial goods manufacturers (client and nonclient) in seven countries. To determine how, and to what extent, formal planning actually influenced the major decisions shaping those companies' business strategies, we sifted material ranging from case histories and interview notes to detailed financial analyses. The four-phase evolutionary model emerging from this work was further explored by indepth analysis of 16 representative companies, each with over $500 million in sales, in which the relationship between planning and strategically important action was especially well documented.

For the purposes of the study, "business strategy" was defined as a set of objectives and integrated set of actions aimed at securing a sustainable competitive advantage. The concept of strategic management described in this article differs somewhat from that of H. Igor Ansoff, who invented and popularized the term.* We define it as a system of corporate values, planning capabilities, or organizational responsibilities that couple strategic thinking with operational decision making at all levels and across all functional lines of authority in a corporation.

* See *From Strategic Planning to Strategic Management*, edited by H. Igor Ansoff, Roger P. Declerch, and Robert L. Hayes (New York: John Wiley & Sons, 1976).

One of the most fruitful by-products of Phase II is effective resource allocation. Under the pressure of long-term resource constraints, planners learn how to set up a circulatory flow of capital and other resources among business units. A principal tool is portfolio analysis, a device for graphically arranging a diversified company's businesses along two dimensions: competitive strength and market attractiveness.

As practiced by Phase II companies, however, portfolio analysis tends to be static and focused on current capabilities, rather than on the search for options. Moreover, it is deterministic—i.e., the position of a business on the matrix is used to determine the appropriate strategy, according to a generalized formula. And Phase II companies typically regard portfolio positioning as the end product of strategic planning, rather than as a starting point.

Phase II systems also do a good job of analyzing long-term trends and setting objectives (for example, productivity improvement or better capital utilization). But instead of bringing key business issues to the surface, they often bury them under masses of data. Moreover, Phase II systems can motivate managers in the wrong direction; both the incentive compensation program and informal rewards and values are usually focused on short-or medium-term operating performance at the expense of long-term goals. In sum, Phase II planning all too easily becomes a mechanical routine, as managers simply copy last year's plan, make some performance shortfall adjustments, and extend trend lines another 12 months into the future.

Phase III: Externally Oriented Planning

In an environment of rapid change, events can render market forecasts obsolete almost overnight. Having repeatedly experiencced such frustrations, planners begin to lose their faith in forecasting and instead try to understand the basic marketplace phenomena driving change. The result is often a new grasp of the key determinants of business success and a new level of planning effectiveness, Phase III.

In this phase, resource allocation is both dynamic and creative. The Phase III planners now look for opportunities to "shift the dot" of a business on a portfolio matrix into a more attractive sector, either by developing new business capabilities or by redefining the market to better fit their companies' strengths. A Japanese conglomerate with an underutilized steel-fabricating capacity in its shipyard and a faltering high-rise concrete smokestack business combined them into a successful pollution control venture.

In the search for new ways to define and satisfy customer needs, Phase III strategists try to look at their companies' product offerings and those of their competitors from the viewpoint of an objective outsider. For example, one heavy equipment manufacturer assigned a strategy team to reverse-engineer the competitor's product, reconstruct its manufacturing facilities on paper, and estimate the manufacturing cost for the competitor's product in the competitor's plant. The team members discovered that design improvements had given the competitor such a commanding advantage in production cost that there was no point in trying to compete on price. But they also found that their own product's lower maintenance and fuel costs offered customers clear savings on a life-cycle cost basis. Accordingly, the sales force was trained to sell life-cycle cost advantages.

Over the next three years, the company increased its market share by 30 % and doubled its net profit.

Another strategy, derived from an external perspective, was devised by a U.S. industrial commodity manufacturer. When sales in one of its major product lines declined swiftly following the introduction of a new, cheaper competitive product, it decided to find out the reason. Through field interviewing with customers, it discovered that the sales slide was nearly over, something competitors had not realized. Since sales of the product had dropped off to a few core markets where no cost-effective alternative was available, it decided to put more support behind this product line, just as the competition was closing its plants.

The manufacturer trained the sales force to service those distributors who continued to carry the line and revised prices to pick up competitive distribution through master distributor arrangements. It even resisted the move of the trade association to reduce government-mandated safety requirements for handling the newer products. By the time its strategy was obvious to competitors, the manufacturer had firmly established a distributor lead in a small but attractive product/market segment.

The SBU Concept

A distinguishing characteristic of Phase III planning in diversified companies is the formal grouping of related businesses into strategic business units (SBUs) or organizational entities large and homogeneous enough to exercise effective control over most factors affecting their businesses. The SBU concept recognizes two distinct strategic levels: corporate decisions that affect the shape and direction of the enterprise as a whole, and business-unit decisions that affect only the individual SBU operating in its own environment. Strategic planning is thus packaged in pieces relevant to individual decision makers, and strategy development is linked to strategy implementation as the explicit responsibility of operating management.

There are limitations to the SBU concept. Many enterprises, such as vertically integrated companies in process-oriented industries, cannot be neatly sorted out into discrete business units because their business share important corporate resources—sales, manufacturing, and/or R&D. In other situations, strategy may dictate a concerted thrust by several business units to meet the needs of a shared customer group, such as selling to the automotive industry or building a corporate position in Brazil. In still other cases, the combined purchasing power of several SBUs or the freedom to transfer technologies from one business to another can be more valuable than the opportunity to make profit-oriented decisions in discrete business units. For example:

A major chemical company found that several of its competitors, who had grown large enough to integrate backward into feedstock production, were beginning to gnaw at its historic competitive edge as a fully integrated producer. Part of the reason was that by licensing certain technology to the competition, the company had given away a raw-material cost advantage that it could not match with its own, older plants. The basic problem, however, was that its product managers were preoccupied with competitive threats in only a handful of the many product/market segments they served. Decisions that seemed to make sense at the individual business-unit level were adding up to deep trouble for the company as a whole.

A major supplier of industrial equipment divided its electric utility business into two SBUs, a power generation business and a power transmission business. Much too late, top management discovered that neither SBU had considered pollution control equipment to be part of its legitimate character. As a result, the company found itself unable to bid on that business—which accounted for a full quarter of electric utility capital spending.

The most significant way in which Phase III differs from Phase II is that corporate planners are expected to offer a number of alternatives to top management. Each choice is usually characterized by a different risk/reward profile or gives priority to a different objective (for example, greater employment security at some cost to ROI). This change is quite pervasive; in fact, one simple way of determining whether a company has advanced to Phase III is to ask managers whether their boss would regard presenting strategy alternatives as a sign of indecisiveness.

The "alternate strategies" approach becomes both the strength and the weakness of Phase III planning, for it begins to impose a heavy—sometimes unacceptable—burden on top management. As the organizational capability for detailed product/market and business-unit planning spreads through the organization, the number of issue raised, alternatives surfaced, and opportunities developed expands alarmingly. Top managers soon recognize that explicit choices are being made by planners and managers deep down in the organization without top-level participation—and that these decisions could significantly affect their company's long-term competitive strength and well-being. This knowledge unsettles top management and pushes it to a heavier involvement in the planning process, Phase IV.

Phase IV: Strategic Management

Phase IV joins strategic planning and management in a single process. Only a few companies that we studied are clearly managed strategically, and all of them are multinational, diversified manufacturing corporations. The challenge of planning for the needs of hundreds of different and rapidly evolving businesses, serving thousands of product/markets in dozens of distinct national environments, has pushed them to generate sophisticated, uniquely effective planning techniques. However, it is not so much planning technique that sets these organizations apart, but rather the thoroughness with which management links strategic planning to operational decision making. This is largely accomplished by three mechanisms:

1. A *planning framework* that cuts across organizational boundaries and facilitates strategic decision making about customer groups and resources.
2. A *planning process* that stimulates entrepreneurial thinking.
3. A *corporate values system* that reinforces managers' commitment to the company's strategy.

Planning Framework

As noted previously, many Phase III companies rely on the SBU concept to provide a planning framework—often with disappointing results. However, there are frequently more levels at which strategically important decisions must be made than the two implicit in SBU theory. Moreover, today's organization structure may not be the ideal framework in which to plan for tomorrow's business, and a strategically managed company may arrange its planning process on as many as five distinct planning levels:

1. *Product/market planning*—The lowest level at which strategic planning takes place is the product/market unit, where typically product, price, sales, and service are planned, and competitors identified. Product/market planners often have no control over different sets of manufacturing facilities and so must accept a predetermined set of business economics.
2. *Business-unit planning*—The bulk of the planning effort in most diversified make-and-sell companies is done at a level where largely self-contained businesses control their own market position and cost structure. These individual business-unit plans become the building blocks of the corporate strategic plan.
3. *Shared resource planning*—To achieve economies of scale or to avoid the problem of subcritical mass (e.g., in R&D facilities), resources are shared. In some cases, the assignment of resource priorities to different business units or the development of a plan to manage a corporate resource as a whole is strategically important. In resource-based or process-oriented industries, strategies for shared resource units often determine or constrain business-unit strategy.

4. *Shared concern planning*—In some large companies, a distinct level of planning responsibility is required to devise strategies that meet the unique needs of certain industry or geographic customer groups or to plan for technologies (e.g., microprocessors, fiber optics) used by a number of business units.

5. *Corporate-level planning*—Identifying world-wide technical and market trends not picked up by business-unit planners, setting corporate objectives, and marshaling the financial and human resources to meet those objectives are finally the responsibility of corporate headquarters.

For corporations involved in only a few, closely related product/markets, a two- or three-level planning framework may be entirely adequate. Even when additional planning levels are required, these companies need not insert another level of organizational hierarchy in order to plan shared resources or customer sector problems. Experience suggests, however, that it is important to recognize such issues where they exist and to assign explicit planning responsibility to an appropriate individual or group in the organization.

Otherwise, critical business decisions can slip between the cracks, and the corporation as a whole may find itself unable to capitalize on its strategic opportunities. Because the selection of a framework for planning will tend to influence the range of alternatives proposed, few strategic planning choices are more important. The definition of a strategic planning framework is, therefore, a pivotal responsibility of top management, supported by the corporate planning staff.

Planning Process

While planning as comprehensively and thoroughly as possible, Phase IV companies also try to keep their planning process flexible and creative.

A principal weakness of Phase II and III strategic planning processes is their inescapable entanglement in the formal corporate calendar. Strategic planning easily degenerates into a mind-numbing bureaucratic exercise, punctuated by ritualistic formal planning meetings that neither inform top management nor help business managers to get their jobs done. Division managers have been known to attempt to escape from the burden of "useless" annual planning by proposing that they fold their businesses into other SBUs, at least for planning purposes.

To avoid such problems, one European conglomerate has ordained that each of its SBUs initially study its business thoroughly, lay out a detailed strategy, and then replan as necessary. It has found that well-managed businesses in relatively stable industries can often exist quite comfortably with routine monitoring against strategic goals every quarter and an intensive strategic review every three to five years. The time saved from detailed annual planning sessions for every business is devoted to businesses in fast-changing environments or those not performing according to the corporate blueprint.

Because it is hard to institutionalize a process that can reliably produce creative plans, strategically managed companies challenge and stimulate their managers' thinking by:

Stressing competitiveness—The requirement for thorough understanding of competitors' strategies recently has been the planning keynote of a U.S. electrical products company well known for its commitment to planning. Top management comes to the planning meetings prepared by its staff to bore in on a few key issues or events. "If, as you say, our competitors are only three years away from introducing microprocessors in their control units, why are they already talking about it in their annual reports?" the president might ask. "What cost savings could our customers achieve with microprocessor-controlled equipment?" or "Who are our competitors' leading engineers?" It takes only one such grilling session to make division managers aware of gaps in their competitive information.

Focusing on a theme—Several major companies periodically reinvigorate their planning processes by asking their managers to key annual plans to a specified theme. International business, new manufacturing process technology, the value of our products to customers, and alternative channels of distribution have all been used successfully. This approach has obvious limitations: it doesn't work with business units in trouble, and it should be avoided until the value of formal planning is well established.

Negotiating objectives—Several companies are trying to negotiate strategically consistent objectives between corporate headquarters and business-unit general management. "We want two years and $35 million in additional investment to prove to you we can make this into a 35% gross margin business," said the new general manager of a division in trouble. "During that time we will make zero profit, but we'll strengthen our market share by three points and reduce material waste at our Atlanta plant from 10% to 3%. Alternatively, you can have $4 million per year at the bottom line next year and $6 million the year after that. No investment, and only minimal share loss. But be prepared to sell out the whole division, because after that it's all downhill." Faced with clear options, corporate management could suggest ideas and concessions that would promise them most of their share growth and some profitability for much less cash commitment up front.

Demanding strategic insights—Avoiding competition by an indirect approach is the essence of creative and innovative strategy: a reformulation of a product's function, the development of new manufacturing methods or distribution channels, or the discovery of dimensions of competition to which traditional competitors are blind. One way to generate this kind of thinking is to ask each business manager to describe the specific business advantage he or she intends to achieve. Top management reviews each business plan skeptically. As one CEO tells division heads: "If you can't tell me something about your business I don't already know, you probably aren't going to surprise our competitors either." This technique relies heavily on the corporate planning staff, who are charged with demonstrating to uncreative business-unit planners that there are new ways of looking at old businesses.

Corporate Value System

The value system shared by the company's top and middle managers provides a third, less visible linkage between planning and action. Although the leadership styles and organizational climates of companies that can be called strategically managed vary considerably, and in even one company a great deal of diversity can be found, four common themes emerge from interviews with personnel at all levels in strategically managed companies:

1. The value of teamwork, which leads to task-oriented organizational flexibility.

2. Entrepreneurial drive, or the commitment to making things happen.

3. Open communication, rather than the preservation of confidentiality.

4. A shared belief that the enterprise can largely create its own future, rather than be buffeted into a predetermined corner by the winds of environmental change.

Teamwork on task force projects is the rule rather than the exception in strategically managed companies. Instead of fearing these uniquely dangerous expeditions beyond the security of the organizational thrust, managers learn to live with the ambiguity that teams create in return for the excitement and variety of new challenges.

The resulting continual reorganization can appear bizarre from outside the organization. For example:

Observers trying to make sense of top management personnel changes in one highly successful telecommunications company were left scratching their heads, as first the chairman stepped down to become president and then he was further demoted to become CEO of a major subsidiary. Who was running the company, observers asked. Which individual was responsible for their brilliantly executed strategy? No one. The whole team at the top was so strong that no single manager deserved sole credit. The changes in title visible to the public were more an indication of the successful execution of phases of the company's strategy than they were signals of the rise or fall of a single individual's career.

Entrepreneurial drive among managers and technical personnel at all levels is a valued form of behaviour in strategically managed companies. One organization's top management was eager to get in on the ground floor of a synthetic fuel equipment business. Six levels down from top management, an applications engineer in the speciality metals division was faced with a notice of a substantial cost overrun on an expensive piece of test equipment.

Instead of cancelling the order to source the equipment from a less costly supplier and thereby incur a six-month delay, the engineer went to the boss, and eventually to the boss's boss, to find out whether the delay to execution of the company's strategy was worth the cost savings. As a result, the engineer did overrun the project budget, but the test equipment was available when needed.

Confidentiality about the company's strategy is one of the hardest things for top management to give up. And yet it is impossible for a company to be strategically managed without the involvement of wide niches of relatively junior people in many aspects of the company's strategic plans. It is not necessary for top managers to divulge everything, but as a minimum, junior managers should know the strategic purposes their actions serve.

In retrospect, one chairman confined that he had overestimated the value of confidentiality. "We had a good idea for a strategy for our speciality business. But we couldn't implement it without letting everyone in the company know about it. We took the chance; now I suspect everyone in the industry knows what we're doing. But they can't get their act together to overtake us. We're moving too fast."

A shared commitment to creating their own future is the underlying ethic of strategically managed companies. Instead of marginal improvements—a few more shares of market or a few percentage points of cost reduction—managers set for themselves ambitious goals that if accomplished will lead to a sustainable competitive advantage for their company. For example:

> A Japanese television manufacturer, faced with rising material and labor costs, ordered its engineers to reduce the number of component parts in its color TV sets by 30%. Innovative design approaches have

since enabled the manufacturer to increase volume substantially while halving the number of workers in its assembly plant.

A machine tool manufacturer has undertaken to change the way a whole industry buys its machinery. Into a sales environment where close personal relations on the plant floor and with the process engineers was formerly the key to success, it is systematically injecting a top-management-oriented, technically and financially argued sales approach.

At the same time, it is radically upgrading its research and development capabilities, adding computer-aided engineering, software development, and systems engineering support. "Very little of our product advantage has patent protection," concedes the CEO. "But if we can persuade the industry to buy on productivity rather than on cost and delivery, the premium we can charge for engineering value will fund enough research to keep us three to four years ahead." Using this approach the manufacturer has already built one of the five largest machine tool companies in the world.

As the economic system becomes more complex and the integration of single business units into multinational, diverse organizations continues, ways must be found to restore the entrepreneurial vigor of a simpler, more individually oriented company structure. Strategic management, linking the rigor of formal planning to vigorous operational execution, may prove to be the answer.

PART 4

Particular Aspects of Planning

Introduction to Part 4

I should like to have been able to include a selection from that very important body of research conducted by Harvard Business School on the relationships of strategy and structure. This began with Chandler,[1] and includes major contributions by Scott,[2] Rumelt,[3] Channon[4] and others. The difficulty is partly the length of many of the works, and partly the fact that the major contributions arose from a series of researches undertaken from Harvard. To do justice to the issue one needs to include the whole body of work. The best service I can do readers of this book is to draw attention to this extremely important series of researches, and to refer them to a book by Galbraith and Nathanson[5] which does an excellent job of synthesising this body of research with other studies of organisational structure.

Channon's[4] study is also a good analysis of the strategic errors of British enterprise. One of the errors was the failure to make an appropriate response to a dramatically changing business environment: the loss of the British Empire; the changing role of the U.K. in the world; the change of marketing conditions from the seller's market of the immediate post-war years: the rise of new competition.

The strategy/structure research is still important and is continuing. Readers might be interested in a study by Kono,[6] which makes comparisons between Japan and the U.S.A. For this book I have included a study by Grinyer, Yasai-Ardekani and Al-Bazzaz, which tests twenty-two hypotheses relating to the linkages of strategy, structure, the environment and financial performance. This survey of forty-eight U.K. companies builds on the work of the Harvard researches, and is an important contribution to the development of understanding of this aspect of planning.

The failure of many organisations with planning systems to relate to the business environment effectively has emerged from some of the earlier chapters in this book. The Society for Long Range Planning survey (Chapter 5) showed some deficiencies. Grinyer and Norborn (Chapter 19) found surprisingly little integration of larger term environmental tendencies into strategic decision-making. In a study (not included in this collection) Gotcher[7] found many deficiencies in the way in which major European companies were reacting to known environmental trends. He

457

also found that "Too few organisations seem to recognise environmental changes as opportunities as well as threats". He also noted an unwillingness (or inability) of major companies to take action to change the environment in which they are operating.

Lahey, King and Narayanan (Chapter 25) review the state of the art (1981) of environmental scanning and forecasting in strategic planning. They find a general recognition of the importance of this issue, accompanied by a failure to develop sophisticated systems or to integrate their output into the strategic planning process. Environmental scanning and forecasting is not currently seen as being important enough to justify a major deployment of resources.

These findings are particularly significant when one remembers that environmental change was a frequently stated reason for introducing planning (see Part 1) and in view of the observed trend towards "strategic management" (Chapter 23).

Do major environmental trauma find their way quickly into strategic readjustment? The evidence of Channon[4] suggests that they do not. Support for this view is provided in Chapter 26 (Voss) which studied management response in the U.K. to the rapidly accelerating inflation rate at the end of 1973. Few had taken any strategic action.

O'Conner[8] found in 1978 that few companies were using multiple scenario planning or contingency planning as a means of coping with environmental uncertainty, but did detect attempts in many companies to improve their forecasting techniques.

It appears to me that the evidence suggests that companies have a great deal to do if they are really to develop the full potential of planning and to relate their strategies to a changing world. This must be one of the greatest areas of challenge.

There are many aspects of corporate planning which benefit from the use of computers. Forecasting and information, one context of which is the environmental issue discussed above, are obvious applications. Corporate models are another. Grinyer and Wooller (Chapter 27) call these ". . . sets of conventional, logical and mathematical expressions that represent the key operations of the company, and in virtually all cases include the items entering the normal profit and loss account and balance sheet . . . much of their value lies in the fact that the speed and storage capacity of the computer has been harnessed".

Grinyer and Wooller (1975) studied corporate modelling in sixty-five U.K. companies. This provides interesting insight into the growing importance of corporate modelling and the use of models in the respondent companies. Naylor and Schauland (1976) (Chapter 28) undertook a wider study of corporate simulation models, achieving an effective sample of 346 corporations in Europe and North America. They found that only 12%

had no plans to develop a model; 73 % were already using or developing a model and 15 % were planning to do so. Sample bias here is the probability that those respondents who did not respond to the questionnaire are likely to include a higher proportion of disinterested companies. The study provides useful information on the nature and use of simulation models.

Naylor and Schauland also explore the politics of corporate model building. The obvious needs, such as for top management support, are documented. Less obvious is the finding that the corporate model has been perceived as an important source of political power. Serious conflicts and rivalries were observed among various departments competing for control of the corporate model.

One strand of thought, relating to the papers on environmental appraisal, is the conclusion that a number of firms have begun to experiment with models of the external environment. Naylor and Schauland believe that this will become much more important over the next few years.

The reader should note one new factor which emerged after the two studies were carried out. This is the development of technology, and in particular the availability of the micro-computer. This makes computer assistance, for some types of problems, even more available to planners.

Channon[4] dealt with some aspects of the strategic failings of U.K. business. Another aspect of strategy has been extensively researched by Kitching. He carried out a major study[8] of the results of acquisition in twenty-two U.S. companies, and was able to draw a number of significant conclusions on the causes of success or failure.

Kitching[9] undertook a significant study of the causes of success and failure in acquisition of Europe. This, a summary of which appears as Chapter 29, showed that only 53 % of mergers were successful. The study is of value to planners because it shows that success or failure is frequently determined by the choice of acquisition target, and the soundness of the underlying corporate strategy. (There is support for the planned strategy in the article by Ansoff *et al.* (Chapter 15).) Contrary to most textbook theories, Kitching shows that synergy is often not achieved in acquisitions. Frequently only financial synergy is realised: marketing, production and research and development synergies often elude the purchaser.

Other aspects of this work have been published in the *Harvard Business Review*.[10]

Other have turned their attention to the issue of diversification, of which acquisition is often a part. Bucker (Chapter 30) studied "new sources of earnings" in 200 U.K. growth companies, a term which he defines as an alternative to "diversification". The only companies which had grown in *real* terms were those which had made substantial moves to find new sources of earnings. He found a 30 % failure rate in new moves and, like

Kitching, noted that moves unrelated to the present business carried a much higher risk of failure.

The studies by Kitching and Buckner should be compulsory reading for all corporate strategists.

References

1. A. D. Chandler (1962) *Strategy and Structure*, M.I.T. Press.
2. B. R. Scott (1971) *Stages of Corporate Development*, Harvard Business School.
3. R. Rumelt (1974) *Structure, Strategy and Economic Performance*, Division of Research, Harvard Business School.
4. D. C. Channon (1973) *The Strategy and Structure of British Enterprise*, MacMillan.
5. J. R. Galbraith and D. A. Nathanson (1978) *Strategy Implementation: The Role of Structure and Process*, West.
6. T. Kono (1978) Comparative study of strategy, structure and long range planning in Japan and the U.S.A., *Angewandte Planning*, Band 2, pp. 6–21, Physica-Verlag, Wien (Kono's article is in English).
7. J. W. Gotcher (1977) Strategy planning in European multinationals, *Long Range Planning*, October 1977.
8. J. Kitching (1967) Why do mergers miscarry? *Harvard Business Review*, November–December 1967.
9. J. Kitching (1973) *Acquisitions in Europe: Causes of Corporate Successes and Failures*, Business International, Geneva.
10. J. Kitching (1974) Winning and losing with European acquisitions, *Harvard Business Review*, March/April 1974.

24

Strategy, Structure, the Environment and Financial Performance in 48 U.K. Companies

P. H. GRINYER, M. YASAI-ARDEKANI AND S. AL-BAZZAZ

A growing and familiar body of literature has explored the relationships between strategy and structure (Chandler, 1962; Stopford, 1968; Fouraker and Stopford, 1968; Wrigley, 1970; Dyas, 1972; Pavan, 1972; Thanheiser, 1972; Channon, 1973, 1975; Rumelt, 1974), the environment (Franko, 1974; Galbraith and Nathanson, 1978), and financial performance (Rumelt, 1974; Channon, 1975). Hypotheses intended to extend this earlier research were tested statistically using data collected during interviews with senior managers within 48 large United Kingdom companies. These hypotheses relate to the correlates of strategy and structure; relationships among strategy, structure, and environmental hostility; and relationships among strategy and structure, their match, and measures of performance.

Data for subsequent analysis were collected in a cross-sectional survey of 48 UK companies with head offices in the southeast of England. These were drawn from 18 different industries. Of the companies, 25 percent were in service industries, 43 percent in manufacturing, and 32 percent in both. All the companies were large ($£200$ million average sales), 77 percent were owned in the United Kingdom, 12 percent in the United States, 4 percent in the European Economic Community (EEC) outside the United Kingdom, and 4 percent jointly by UK and non–UK residents. The distribution of members among Wrigley's (1970) strategic categories and among points on an ordinal scale for degree of divisionalization of structure is shown in Table 24.1.

Data were obtained during structured interviews with the director or most senior manager responsible for corporate planning. Organization

---

This article was originally published in the *Academy of Management Journal*, Volume 23, No. 2, 1980.

TABLE 24.1. *Classification of Sample by Strategy and Structure*[a]

Strategy/Structure	Functional	Geographical divisions	Product divisions	Product and geographical divisions
Single product	5	2	1	—
Dominant product	5	1	4	1
Related product	8	1	9	8
Unrelated product	—	—	2	1
Total	18	4	16	10

[a] These scales are derived from Wrigley (1970).

charts and financial reports were collected to add information on structure, size, and financial performance.

Ordinal and ratio scales, as appropriate, were developed from responses on strategy, structure, other company characteristics, perceived environmental factors, and financial performance (see Grinyer, Al-Bazzaz, and Yasai-Ardekani, 1978; and Al-Bazzaz, 1977). Because a large proportion of the most important scales, like those for strategy and structure, are ordinal, nonparametric analysis was preferred, for reasons advanced persuasively by Siegel (1956), although Pearson's product moment coefficients were used at certain points in the analysis to permit first order partial correlations. To allow further for control of some of the main variables, the sample was subdivided on the basis of specific variables, and nonparametric correlation was undertaken in each subsample for the remaining variables.

Hypotheses

An assumption often is made in the literature that product divisional structures involve greater vertical and lateral spans of control. A greater vertical span of control, defined as the number of levels within the core workflow hierarchy, is implied by interposing an additional, divisional, level between the chief executive and the peripheral business units. Similarly, it often is assumed that a greater number of specialist staff officers report to the chief executive at the head office, thus increasing his lateral span of control. These linkages between divisionalization of organizational structure and the more traditional measures of height and width of the hierarchical pyramid have not, to the present authors' knowledge, been tested statistically and certainly not in the United Kingdom. Table 24.2 shows the hypotheses, H.1.1 and H.1.2, advanced in consequence.

Second, Chandler (1962) hypothesized a positive relationship between

TABLE 24.2. *Hypotheses*

H.1.1	Vertical span of control (number of levels in the core work flow hierarchy) and degree of divisionalization are positively correlated.
H.1.2	The chief executive's lateral span of control and degree of divisionalization are positively correlated.
H.2.1	Degree of diversification (strategy) and degree of divisionalization (structure) are positively correlated.
H.2.2	This positive correlation (H.2.1) remains significant when allowance is made for other correlates of structure and a variety of environmental conditions.
H.2.3	The correlation (H.2.1) remains significant for service companies, manufacturing companies, and those combining both manufacturing and service activities.
H.3.1	Size of companies is positively correlated with their degree of diversification.
H.3.2	Size of companies is positively correlated with their degree of divisionalization.
H.4.1	The number of sites and the degree of divisionalization are positively correlated.
H.4.2	The geographical dispersion of major sites and the degree of divisionalization are positively correlated.
H.5.1	Among companies with "related" or "unrelated" product strategies (Wrigley, 1970) perceived environmental pressures and degree of divisionalization are negatively correlated.
H.5.2	Among companies with "single" or "dominant" product strategies (Wrigley, 1970), perceived environmental pressures and degree of divisionalization are positively correlated.
H.5.3	The better the "fit" or "match" between strategy and structure, as suggested by Chandler (1962) and Galbraith and Nathanson (1978), the lower perceived environmental pressures will tend to be.
H.6.1	Return on capital employed (ROI) and measures of growth are positively correlated with degree of diversification.
H.6.2	Variability of ROI and the degree of diversification are negatively correlated.
H.6.3	ROI and measures of growth are greater and variability in ROI is less for divisionally than for functionally organized companies.
H.6.4	Related product companies will, on average, have higher ROI, higher rates of growth, and lower variability of ROI than other categories.
H.6.5	Divisionalized related product firms outperform those that are functionally organized.
H.7.1	Among functionally organized companies average ROI and growth are inversely related to degree of diversification.
H.7.2	Among product divisionally organized companies average ROI and growth are positively correlated with degree of diversification.
H.7.3	Among single or dominant product companies average ROI and growth are negatively correlated with degree of divisionalization.
H.7.4	Among companies with related and unrelated product strategies, average ROI and growth are positively correlated with the degree of divisionalization.
H.8.1	Where the rate of technological change is high, the market is turbulent, or there are indications of strong competitive pressures, average ROI and growth are positively correlated and variability of ROI is negatively correlated with the degree of diversification.
H.8.2	Under conditions described in H.8.1, average ROI and growth are positively and variability in ROI is negatively correlated with the degree of divisionalization.

strategy and structure, since tested statistically by Rumelt (1974) in the United States and by Channon (1975) among UK service companies. There seems to be value, if little originality, in testing the relationship statistically using a multi-industry sample of UK companies. The basic hypothesis may be extended, however, once one establishes other factors that impinge upon structure. One can argue that the relationship is sufficiently independent of other factors that affect structure to remain significant when one controls for the latter. Again, it can be argued that the relationship remains significant no matter whether the companies involved are service, manufacturing, or both (as with IBM). The second set of hypotheses, then, is H.2.1 through H.2.3 in Table 24.2.

Third, one must recognize the wealth of other evidence suggesting that strategy is but one determinant of structure. For instance, Pugh, Hickson, Hinings and Turner (1968, 1969) and Child (1972) showed that size and measures of organization structuring are strongly positively correlated. Divisional organizations tend to be more "structured," in some respects than do nondivisional ones, because of the introduction of corporate planning and financial control systems to coordinate and control the lower hierarchical levels from the head office (Berg, 1971; Channon, 1973). If these earlier studies are an appropriate guide, then size and divisionalization of structure may well be positively correlated. To this should be added a further argument that goes to the roots of the strategy/structure debate. Chandler (1962) perceived that corporations expand geographically, diversify, then move to divisional structures as they grow. Thus, for this reason alone, one might find a positive correlation between size and divisionalization of structure. Similarly, one would expect to find size positively correlated with strategy itself. These arguments suggest the third set of hypotheses, H.3.1 and H.3.2, in Table 24.2.

Fourth, the number of separate sites operated by a company and their geographical dispersion may be related to both size and structure. For some types of business, the number of sites may be expected to be strongly positively correlated with size of the company, especially in service industries such as banking, restaurants, and retailing. This need not necessarily be the case, however, when the sample contains as many diverse organizations as does that of the present study. However, the linkage between the number of sites and divisionalization is likely to remain, even if other measures of size are not strongly correlated with the former, because a multiplicity of sites can create a complexity and difficulty of coordination and control of its own kind, as does wide geographical separation of major site locations (Chandler, 1962; Stopford, 1968; Fouraker and Stopford, 1968). In each case the appropriate organizational response may be a geographically based divisional structure. This suggests Hypotheses H.4.1 and H.4.2.

Fifth, a theme on which Galbraith and Nathanson (1978) concentrate is that a good fit of structure to strategy promotes better coping with the environment. Franko (1974) observed that increased competition and hence a more hostile environment was necessary to force European companies to adopt structures to fit their strategies. This is consonant with the causal argument of Chandler himself (1962). Structure follows strategy because of pressures generated by a poor fit. In each case, either external or internal pressure is seen to force the change to an appropriate structure. *Perceived* rather than some other objective levels of external pressure are of concern here. Internal pressures stemming from an inappropriate structure are more difficult to gauge but could be expected, with external pressures, to contribute to deterioration of financial performance. Hypotheses H.5.1–H.5.3, which have not been tested to date, follow (see Table 24.2).

To date there are no published results of a United Kingdom study to parallel Rumelt's (1974) analysis of strategy, structure, and financial performance among the *Fortune* 500 companies. Because Wrigley's (1970) scale for structure was used here rather than Rumelt's extension, and the financial data are different, a complete replication of the American study is not possible using data in the present study. However, some of the hypotheses Rumelt developed may be tested using the present data, and these are advanced in H.6.1–H.6.5.

Finally, good match or fit between structure and strategy might be expected to lead to good performance and vice versa. This suggests further hypotheses, H.7.1–H.7.4. Because of the greater spread of business interests and the greater adaptability claimed for divisionally structured companies in meeting environmental perturbations, it may be argued that even if no other relationships with financial performance are found, such companies should perform better in adverse conditions (see Hypotheses H.8.1 and H.8.2 in Table 24.2).

Testing of Hypotheses

Wrigley's Structural Scale, Vertical and Lateral Spans of Control

Lateral and vertical spans of control were correlated with scores obtained using an ordinal scale for structure. Kendall's tau was .25 and .27 for each respectively. Both coefficients are significant at the .05 level. No significant correlation between vertical and lateral spans of control was found. The null form of Hypotheses H.1.1 and H.1.2 can be rejected. Both lateral and vertical spans of control are significantly and positively correlated with the ordinal scale for structure ranging from low for functional, through geographically divisional, then product divisional, to highest for product and geographically based divisional structures. The fact that the coefficients were not higher clearly indicates, however, that other factors too are strongly related to lateral and vertical spans of control.

Strategy, Structure, and Size

Hypotheses H.2.1-H.4.2 all relate to strategy, structure, and aspects of size. For this reason, and for analytical convenience, they are treated together. Table 24.3 shows nonparametric correlation coefficients. The highly significant, positive correlation between *strategy* and *structure* found by Rumelt (1974), and more recently by Channon (1975) in his study of United Kingdom service industries, is found here too. For the sample as a whole, strategy is completely uncorrelated with charter, number of sites, the geographical dispersion of major operations, or with measures of size. The latter can be explained in part by the inclusion in the sample of giants in mature industries, such as coal mining and steel. As in the United States, such single product or dominant product companies have not shown a marked propensity to diversify. Indeed, in the United Kingdom these two industries are dominated by nationalized concerns whose very statutory origins preclude it.

TABLE 24.3. *Nonparametric Correlation Coefficients (Kendall's tau) for Strategy, Structure, Sites, Dispersion, and Size*

	Strategy	Structure	Charter	Number sites	Dispersion	Capital employed	Sales	Number employed
Strategy	1.00	.36^c	NS	NS	NS	NS	NS	NS
Structure		1.00	−.36^c	.35^c	..24^b	.19^a	.29^b	.33^c
Charter			1.00	−.20^a	NS	NS	NS	NS
Number sites				1.00	.24^b	.37^c	.36^c	.42^c
Dispersion					1.00	NS	.18^a	NS
Capital employed						1.00	.82^c	.48^c
Sales							1.00	.50^c
Number employed								

NS: Not statistically significant. ^{b} Significant at the .01 level.
^{a} Significant at the .05 level. ^{c} Significant at the .001 level.

The very uniqueness of the strategy/structure correlation suggests that it is unlikely to be attributed to any third variable in the analysis to which structure is strongly positively correlated. This was confirmed by calculating the Pearson's product moment coefficients, which were consistent with the non parametric ones of Table 24.3, and by deriving the appropriate first order correlation coefficients shown in Table 24.4. Strategy and structure remain significantly, positively correlated, and this relationship seems to be independent of other influences on structure such as charter and size. Thus Hypotheses H.2.1, H.2.2 and H.2.3 were found valid.

Other Correlates of Structure

Table 24.3 shows that, although strategy is significantly correlated with structure, it accounts for a small proportion of the total variance. Charter, geographical dispersion and number of sites, number of employees, annual sales, and capital employed are all significantly correlated with *structure*. As would be expected, the number of sites is positively correlated at a high level of significance with each of the three measures of size, which are themselves strongly intercorrelated. The number of sites is also negatively correlated with charter, suggesting that service companies tend to have more operating sites than do manufacturing ones, as is to be expected from the inclusion of several banks and an insurance company in the sample of 48.

Existence of such strong correlations between other variables and structure, although expected from the research of organizational behavioralists quoted earlier, clearly puts the strategy-structure link into perspective. These other linkages with structure remained statistically significant when the main sample was subdivided on the basis of categories of strategy, charter and high or low levels of environmental pressure (to be discussed later). However, because the correlates of structure other than strategy are intercorrelated, some of the first order partial coefficients are insignificant (see Table 24.4).

The null forms of Hypotheses H.3.2, H.4.1, and H.4.2 may therefore be rejected. Structure is closely related to sales and charter and, via these, to the number of operating sites, their geographical dispersion, capital employed, and number of employees. The analysis provides no support, however, for Hypothesis H.3.1 to the effect that size and degree of diversification are positively correlated.

Fit and Environmental Pressures

The fifth set of hypotheses stems from two related assumptions made by the strategy/structure school. The first is that certain kinds of combinations of structure and strategy, e.g., product divisional structures and related or unrelated strategies, permit companies to cope better with both external pressures and complexity generated internal pressures. The second is that external pressures force diversified companies to move to· the more "appropriate" divisional structures. This argument remains strong despite the fact that Rumelt (1974) found no statistically significant difference in performance between product divisional and nondivisional related product companies.

Five scales were developed for environmental pressure of hostility perceived by interviewees. NSTP, the number of sources of important adverse impacts on the market for the companies' three most important

TABLE 24.4. Strategy and Structure Related First Order Partial Correlation Coefficients

			Controlling for:			
	Strategy	Charter	Number sites	Geographical dispersion	Number employees	Annual sales
Strategy/structure	NA	.41[b]	.49[c]	.45[b]	.43[b]	.43[b]
Structure/charter	−.39[b]	NA	−.31[a]	−.37[b]	−.39[b]	−.39[b]
Structure/number sites	.44[b]	.29[s]	NA	.31[a]	.28[s]	NS
Structure/geographical dispersion	.30[a]	NS	NS	NA	NS	NS
Structure/number employees	.28[a]	.25[s]	NS	.25[s]	NA	NS
Structure/sales	.40[b]	.39[b]	.27[s]	.36[a]	.31[a]	NA
Structure/capital employed	.35[a]	.28[a]	NS	.31[a]	.22[s]	NS
Structure/difficulty of supply	−.33[a]	NS	NS	−.31[s]	−.41[b]	.35[a]

			Controlling for:			
	Capital employed	Difficulty of supply	Number sources of past turbulence	Number sources of expected turbulence	Need for new product innovation	Rate of technological change
Strategy/structure	.44[b]	.43[b]	.43[b]	.42[b]	.43[b]	.42[b]
Structure/charter	−.36[a]	−.39[b]	−.39[b]	−.39[b]	−.38[b]	−.39[b]
Structure/number sites	NS	.30[a]	.35[b]	.34[b]	.34[a]	.34[b]
Structure/geographical dispersion	NS	NS	NS	NS	NS	NS
Structure/number employees	NS	.36[a]	.24[s]	.25[s]	.24[s]	.24[s]
Structure/sales	NS	.41[b]	.38[b]	.38[b]	.39[b]	.39[b]
Structure/capital employed	NA	.33[a]	.31[a]	.31[a]	.32[a]	.33[a]
Structure/difficulty of supply	.32[a]	NA	−.31[s]	−.31[s]	−.22[s]	−.32[a]

Controlling for:

Strategy/structure	% Sales to wholesalers*	% Sales to industry & government	% Sales to general public	% Sales to retailers	% Sales to 5 largest customers	Dependence on largest 10 customers	Market share (1st market)	Market rank (1st market)	Zero order coefficient (Kendall's)
Strategy/ structure	.41[a]	.45[a]	.46[a]	.44[a]	.49[a]	.46[a]	.45[a]	.45[a]	.36[c]
Structure/ charter	NS	NS	NS	NS	NS	NS	NS	NS	−.36[c]
Structure/ number sites	.36[s]	.36[s]	.34[s]	NS	NS	.35[s]	.35[s]	.35[s]	.35[c]
Structure/ geographical dispersion	NS	NS	NS	NS	NS	NS	NS	NS	.24[b]
Structure/ number employees	.34[s]	.33[s]	.35[s]	.39[s]	NS	.35[s]	.34[s]	.35[s]	.33[c]
Structure/sales	.38[s]	.37[s]	.38[s]	.39[s]	NS	.40[s]	.39[s]	.38[s]	.24[b]
Structure/ capital employed	.47[a]	.44[a]	.43[a]	.42[a]	.39[s]	.44[a]	.42[a]	.43[a]	.19[a]
Structure/ difficulty of supply	−.33[s]	−.33[s]	NS	NS	−.35[s]	NS	NS	NS	−.22[a]

* Percent of sales to wholesalers is correlated significantly at the .01 level with structure ($r < 4160$) and not quite significantly .05 $<p>$ .1 with strategy ($r = .2199$).

NA: Not applicable.

NS: Not statistically significant.

[s] Strongly suggested at the .10 level.

[a] Significant at the .05 level.

[b] Significant at the .01 level.

[c] Significant at the .001 level.

TABLE 24.5 Non Parametric Correlations

	Difficulty of alternative supplies	Rate of Technological change	Number of sources of past market turbulence (NSTP)	Number of sources of expected market turbulence (NSTE)	Need for product Innovation	Share of most Important market
Strategy	NS	NS	.14[s]	.14[s]	NS	NS
Structure	−.22[a]	NS	NS	NS	NS	NS
Charter	NS	NS	NS	−.16[s]	.18[a]	NS
Number of sites	NS	NS	NS	NS	NS	NS
Dispersion of sites	NS	NS	NS	NS	NS	NS
Net capital employed in 1973	NS	.14[s]	NS	NS	NS	NS
Sales in 1973	NS	NS	NS	NS	NS	NS
Number employed in 1973	19[a]	NS	−.17[s]	NS	NS	NS
Difficulty of alternative supplies	NA	NS	NS	NS	NS	NS
Rate of technological change		NA	NS	NS	.25[b]	NS
NSTP			NA	.69[a]	.17[s]	−.39[c]
NSTE				NA	NS	−.35[a]
Need for new product innovation					NA	NS
Share of most important market						NA
Rank in most important market						
% sales to 5 most important customers						
Dependence on 10 largest customers						
% sales to wholesalers						
% sales to government and industry						
% sales to general public						
% sales to retailers						

NS: Not significant.	[a] Significant at the .05 level.
NA: Not applicable.	[b] Significant at the .01 level.
[s] Strongly suggested at the .10 level.	[c] Significant at the .001 level.

product lines in the previous three years, measures past market turbulence. Highly correlated with this (see Table 24.5) is the number of expected sources of such adverse market turbulence in the next three years, NSTE. Expectations were obviously conditioned by perceptions on past experience. NSTP was also positively correlated, although not significantly,

TABLE 24.5 (*cont.*)

Rank in most important market	% Sales to 5 largest customers	Dependence on 10 largest customers	% Sales to wholesalers	% Sales to government and industry	% Sales to general public	% Sales to retailers
.20ᵃ	NS	.19ᵃ	.18ˢ	NS	NS	−.15ˢ
NS	−.20ˢ	NS	.26ᵇ	NS	NS	−.25ᵃ
NS	.20ˢ	NS	NS	NS	NS	.35ᵇ
NS	−.32ᵃ	NS	NS	NS	NS	NS
NS	NS	NS	NS	NS	NS	NS
NS	−.28ˢ	NS	NS	−.21ᵃ	.23ᵃ	NS
NS	−.40ᵃ	NS	NS	−.16ˢ	.22ᵃ	NS
NS	NS	NS	NS	NS	NS	NS
NS	NS	NS	NS	NS	NS	NS
.17ˢ	NS	NS	NS	.17ˢ	−.26ᵇ	NS
NS	NS	NS	NS	NS	.23ᵃ	NS
NS	NS	NS	NS	−.17ˢ	.24ᵃ	NS
NS	NS	NS	NS	NS	−.23ᵃ	NS
−.66ᵃ	NS	.41ᶜ	NS	.32ᵃ	−.40ᵇ	NS
NA	NS	−.36ᶜ	NS	NS	NS	NS
	NA	.41ᵇ	NS	NS	NS	NS
		NA	NS	NS	−.41ᵇ	NS
			NA	−.81ᶜ	NS	.24ˢ
				NA	−.46ᶜ	−.61ᶜ
					NA	NS
						NA

with the perceived NEED for new product innovation. This 5-point ordinal scale ranges from not worthwhile to essential for survival and may be taken as a rough proxy for the degree of new product competition in the company's major markets. NEED is highly significantly and positively correlated with a Likert-type scale measuring the perceived rate of technological change in the industry. The final ordinal scale measuring environmental pressures is based on interviewees' perceptions of the difficulty of obtaining alternative supplies of raw materials and brought-in components. This is uncorrelated with any of the others. There is no reason to have expected that it would be.

Competitive pressure, measured by NEED for new product innovation and the market turbulence (NSTP and NSTE), is likely to be inversely related to the market dominance of the company. Similarly, heavy dependence on a few major customers, while implying a potential threat, also may provide security against market and other environmental threats. Such dependence may be mutual when the company is a major supplier. Major customers may then seek to promote the company's stability, and new products emerge more from discussions with them than as a response to competitive pressures. Such mutual dependence may be expected to be related to both the market share of the company and its pattern of distribution. In particular, in companies where sales are mainly to government and major industrial users, and market share is high, mutual dependence is likely to be greater and competitive pressures less.

With these arguments in mind, other considerations—market share, market rank, percent sales to the 5 largest customers, perceived dependence on the 10 largest customers, and percent of sales to each of wholesalers, government, and industry, the general public, and retailers—were introduced into the analysis. Correlation coefficients are shown in Table 24.5. Perceived dependence on the 10 largest customers is positively correlated with market share and negatively with market rank. This suggests that market share, rank (inversely), and dependence on largest customers might be treated together as a cluster of variables expected to reduce the hostility of environmental pressures. Dependence is itself related to the type of distribution pattern adopted, this being almost necessarily so. Percentage of total sales to government and industry was, in turn, positively and percent sales to the general public negatively correlated with market share. As hypothesized, market share was negatively correlated with both measures of perceived market turbulence, NSTP and NSTE, but neither market rank nor dependence on major customers was. Moreover, none of the variables for market power and dependence was significantly correlated with perceived NEED for new product introductions. The positive correlations between percent of sales to the general public and NSTP and NSTE could well be attributed to their common relationships with market share and might disappear when one controls for the latter. This is not so with the weak but statistically significant negative correlation between NEED and percent sales to the general public. This suggests that one strategy for reducing new product competition is to engage in direct selling to the ultimate customer. Larger companies, in terms of net capital employed and sales, tended to sell direct to the general public to a greater extent. By contrast, it was the smaller (but still large) companies in the sample that concentrated their sales on government and industry, and they tended to have a higher percentage of sales to their five largest customers. Percentage of sales to government and industry or to the general public seemed to be unrelated to charter, however. Although, as expected, a higher percentage of sales of manufacturing companies tended to be to retailers.

Structure is significantly correlated with only three environmental variables. First, the negative coefficient suggests that greater difficulty of finding alternative supplies is perceived in functional than in divisionally structured organizations. Divisionally structured companies may indeed be less reliant on existing sources of supplies. Alternatively, within a divisional structure, the corporate management might well fail to perceive such potential difficulties because of greater hierarchical separation from production. However, difficulties of finding alternative supplies were also perceived to be greater as the number of employees rose, and it is well established that vertical span and company size are positively correlated (Pugh *et al.*, 1968, 1969; Child, 1972; Reimann, 1973). Second, the percentage of sales to retailers was significantly, negatively correlated with structure. However, partial correlation, controlling for charter, reduces the coefficient to a statistically insignificant level, suggesting that the apparent relationship could be due to a common dependence on this third variable. The positive correlation between percentage of sales to wholesalers and structure is less easily explained.

From Table 24.5 it may be seen that, of the environmental variables, only the rank of the company in its most important market and perceived dependence on its 10 largest customers are significantly correlated with strategy. The coefficients are consistent with the argument that for some, diversification may be a means of obtaining growth not possible by continued concentration on the major line of business and for others, it is a means of reducing dependence on external trading partners.

Even the significant correlations between the environmental variables and each of structure and strategy were too weak to account for much of the variance. Had they been strong, however, the validity of the fifth set of hypotheses would have been in doubt, for monotonic relationships over the entire range of these variables would have been inferred, which would have been unlikely if a match between the variables rather than their individual values is the dominant factor. Tests of the relationship between match between strategy and structure and environmental variables proceeded in two directions. First the total sample of 48 companies was divided into subsamples on the basis of strategy, structure, and high and low values of each of the eleven most general measures of perceived environmental pressure, market strength, and distribution.

TABLE 24.6. Correlations with Environmental Variables for Different Subsamples

Basis of sample	Correlate	Difficulty of supply	Rate of technological change	NSTP	NSTE	Need for new products	Market share in 1st market
Strategy (single and dominant products)	Structure	NS	NS	.34[a]	.31[a]	NS	NS
Strategy (related and unrelated products)	Structure	-.32[a]	NS	-.26[a]	-.18[s]	-.24[a]	NS
Structure:							
Functional	Strategy	NS	NS	.56[c]	.52[b]	.41[b]	NS
Functional or geographic		NS	NS	.47[b]	.45[b]	.33[b]	NS
Product divisional		NS	NS	Negative but NS	Negative but NS	NS	NS
Product and geographical		NS	NS	Negative but NS	Negative but NS	-.58[c]	.56[a]

Basis of sample	Market rank in 1st market	% Sales to 5 largest customers	Dependence on 10 largest customers	% Sales to wholesalers	% Sales to government and industry	% Sales to general public	% Sales to retailers
Strategy (single and dominant products)	NS	$-.63^b$	$-.34^s$	NS	$-.46^a$	NS	NS
Strategy (related and unrelated products)	NS	NS	NS	$.24^a$	NS	NS	$-.34^b$
Structure:							
Functional	NS	NS	NS	NS	NS	NS	NS
Functional or geographic	NS	NS	NS	$.23^s$	$-.30^a$	NS	NS
Product divisional	NS	$.57^b$	$.30^s$	$-.47^s$	NS	$-.35^a$	NS
Product and geographical	NS	NS	$.56^a$	NS	NS	NS	NS

[a] Significant at the .05 level.
[b] Significant at the .01 level.
[c] Significant at the .001 level.

NS: Not significant.
[s] Strongly suggested at .10 level.

Results of nonparametric correlation analysis undertaken for each are shown in Tables 24.6 and 24.7. These show clearly that match between strategy and structure is related to perceived environmental pressure. Single and dominant product companies perceive less past and expected sources of adverse impacts on their major markets when functionally or geographically organized than when product divisionalized. Similarly, companies with related or unrelated product strategies perceive *less* sources of such past and expected market turbulence and less need for new product innovation when they have a product divisional rather than a functional or purely geographical divisional structure. Also, for functionally and geographically structured companies, strategy and NSTP, NSTE, and NEED for new product innovation are positively correlated, but for NEED the relationship becomes negative for product and geographically organized companies.

In view of the relationships already established among market share, NSTP, and NSTE, it was anticipated that similar results would be obtained when market strength was included in the analysis. However, market share was correlated significantly with degree of diversification only among companies with a product and geographical divisional structure (Table 24.6). This suggests that a stronger market share was associated with a better fit between strategy and structure for this subsample, a relationship consistent with the lower need for new products they then tended to perceive, but it is disappointing that significant correlations were not found for other subcategories of structure and strategy.

Significant correlations for the variables for dependence and distribution channels cast further light on the possible sources of environmental pressures. Among undiversified companies, those functionally structured tend to be mutually dependent on their major industrial customers, with the resulting market stability but potential threat; but divisionally structured ones are not. Adoption of divisional structures among such undiversified companies may possibly be related to efforts to break such dependence. On the other hand the coefficients for companies with product or product and geographical divisions suggest that diversification had not tended to reduce such dependence.

Again from Table 24.7 it may be seen that the correlation between strategy and structure ceased to be statistically significant for companies with high perceived numbers of sources of past (NSTP) and expected (NSTE) market turbulence and high need for new product innovation (NEED). This is consistent with Table 24.6 in suggesting that a match between strategy and structure scales is associated with a perception of a less hostile external world. Correlations between strategy and structure remained statistically significant, however, when the total sample was subdivided on the basis of market share, market rank, and dependence on

TABLE 24.7. *Effects of Division into Environmentally Based Subsamples on the Correlation between Strategy and Structure*

Basic of sample division		Correlation between strategy and structure	Significance level
Number of sources of past market turbulence (NSTP)	High	.26	.208
	Low	.43	.001
Number of sources of expected market turbulence (NSTE)	High	.41	.159[a]
	Low	.38	.001
NEED for new product innovation	High	.03	.428
	Low	.53	.001
Rate of technological change	High	.41	.011
	Low	.38	.002
Share of most important market[b]	Low ($\leq$ 30%)	.44	.013
	High (> 30%)	.47	.014
Rank of most important market[b]	(> 1)	.58	.010
	(= 1)	.37	.037
% sales to 5 most important customers	(> 30%)	.76	.015
	($\leq$ 30%)	.39	.006
Dependence on 10 largest customers	High	.51	.016
	Low	.44	.009
Sales to wholesalers	(< 30%)	.42	.010
	(20% < sales $\leq$ 40%)	.65	.030
	(> 40%)	.00	.500
Sales to industry and government	($\leq$ 20%)	.37	.070
	(20% < sales $\leq$ 60%)	.34	.228
	(> 60%)	.59	.002
Sales direct to public	(= 0)	.46	.009
	(10% < sales $\leq$ 20%)	.30	.233
	(sales > 30%)	.50	.124

[a] This correlation is insignificant because of the relatively small sample size.
[b] The analysis for second and third markets was no different in results.

major customers. Moreover, the insignificant correlations for some subcategories of distribution channels were due largely to the small subsample sizes.

Direct comparison of successive points on the strategy and structure scales show, however, that these tests are still relatively crude for they rest on an assumption that a perfect correlation between the two scales would mean a perfect match. This assumption is not strictly valid. For instance, a functional organizational structure may be just as appropriate to a dominant as to a single product strategy. For this reason a new subjectively determined scale of "match" or FIT between the strategy and structure scales was devised which incorporates the assumptions implicit in the strategy/structure school (see Galbraith and Nathanson, 1978). Details may be found in Grinyer *et al.* (1978).

A negative correlation (Kendall's tau) was found between FIT and each of the numbers of past ($\tau = -.38$, $p < .001$) and expected ($\tau = -.31$, $p < .01$) sources of market turbulence, and the need for new product development ($\tau = -.20$, $p < .05$). Companies with a better match between strategy and structure do, then, perceive their environment as less hostile. Consistent with correlations found earlier between environmental scales, companies with a better FIT also tended to have a higher share of their most important market ($\tau = .19$, $p < .05$), higher percentage of sales to government and industry ($\tau = .21$, $p < .05$), and greater dependence on their major customers ($\tau = .29$, $p < .05$). These further correlations may, indeed, explain in part why they experienced less market turbulence, although the coefficients are not as strong as those with NSTP and NSTE. It is suspected that the relationships are due largely to the observed tendency for companies heavily dependent on major governmental and industrial customers to be both single or dominant product and functionally organized.

These results could be interpreted as providing support for the hypothesis promoted by Galbraith and Nathanson (1978) that a match between structure and strategy facilitates coping with environmental pressures. Better coping might be expected to lead to a more sanguine view of the environment. However, the low values of the coefficients give grounds for caution. Even the most highly significant correlation explains no more than 14 percent of the variance. Other factors clearly bear upon perception of environmental turbulence and fit between strategy and structure too. Moreover, the full meaning of the ordinal scales for environmental pressure is still in doubt. The scales may measure, as intended, the impact of real environmental or other forces that affect performance. But they may also reflect type of business, remoteness of interviewee from the market place or technology because of structural type, and personal loquacity, perceptiveness, or natural optimism or pessimism. These personal factors might be safely assumed with a sample of 48 to generate merely "noise," but for small subsamples the effect of such noise could be important.

To test for the extent to which the "environmental" variables reflect forces that do indeed impact on companies' performance, they were correlated with average return on capital employed (ROI), growth in profits and ROI, and growth in capital employed, sales, and numbers employed. Perceived rate of technological change was significantly, negatively correlated with the four year average ROI, standard deviation for ROI, and four year growth of capital employed and sales. This was particularly so for manufacturing companies and for companies with a related or unrelated strategy; the former but not the latter was to be expected. Somewhat inconsistently, however, growth in ROI over the last two years tended to be higher where a high rate of technological change was perceived, perhaps suggesting that recognition was leading to better coping.

Difficulty of finding alternative sources of supply also was negatively, significantly correlated with growth of net profit, capital employed, sales, and number employed. Among companies combining manufacturing and service operations the adverse effects were extended to average and standard deviation of ROI, too, but effects on growth of ROI were favourable. If one were to place a single interpretation on the "difficulty of supply" variable, therefore, it would be that it measures a constraint on growth. The meaning to be attached to NEED for new products innovation is less clear. It was not statistically significantly related to any measure of performance for the sample as a whole but was negatively correlated with at least one of the measures of growth for most of the subcategories of companies. Yet, like the rate of technological change and difficulty of alternative supplies, it was positively correlated with the growth in ROI between 1972 and 1973 in three subsamples, especially functionally organized companies for which NEED was also negatively correlated with the standard deviation of ROI. This apparent inconsistency with respect to measures of growth possibly could be due to effects of recent actions reflecting perception of the need to introduce more new products if earlier performance is to be improved. Finally, the number of sources of past and expected market turbulence, NSTP and NSTE, respectively, can be given no clear interpretation. Significant results relating to them are inconsistent and category specific.

The analysis suggests, therefore, that the ordinal scales for perception of environmental pressures do, indeed, at least in part, reflect either forces that impact on performance or, alternatively, performance itself. Nonetheless, the very size of the coefficients, and the occasional inconsistencies between categories of companies, suggested that much of the variance in the scales must be explained by other factors.

The general weight of evidence suggests, then, but most certainly does not prove conclusively, that the null forms of the fifth set of hypotheses may be rejected. Companies with a mismatch of strategy and structure tend to perceive a greater environmental turbulence, which may in part reflect forces that have affected performance adversely. However, this is far from proving that environmental forces drive functionally organized but diversified companies into a product divisional structure.

Strategy, Structure, and Financial Performance

Strategy and structure were each correlated with the measures of performance to test the sixth set of hypotheses. To allow for possible differences between subsamples, this was done for both the full and all relevant subsamples, as may be seen from Tables 24.8 and 24.9. Further, to allow for differences that would be obscured by such analysis, pairwise comparisons of performance between strategy and structure related categories of companies also was undertaken.

Table 8 provides little support for the hypotheses that ROI and growth are positively correlated with degree of diversification (H.6.1) or that variability of ROI is negatively correlated with the latter (H.6.2). Indeed, diversification and growth are negatively correlated in most circumstances. Although only growth in net profit between 1969 and 1973 was significantly correlated with diversification (strategy) for the full sample, in all there are 18 statistically significant, negative correlations with measures of growth for the subsamples, and the nonsignificant correlations are virtually all negative. Pairwise comparison provided further support for this finding. The mean growth in net profits between 1969 and 1973 was 75 percent greater for single product than for dominant product, 49 per cent greater than for related and 122 percent greater than for unrelated product companies. Although only the last difference is statistically significant, there is a probability of less than 1 in 10 that the first and second are due to chance. These figures provide no support for Hypothesis H.6.4. Related product firms tended to outperform dominant and unrelated ones, but not significantly, and were inferior to single product ones.

Nor is there evidence to support any hypothesis that companies with a divisional structure tend to outperform others in general (H.6.3). Indeed Table 9 shows that 4-year growth in both ROI and net profits is significantly, negatively correlated with the degree of divisionalization for both the full sample and many of the subsamples. However, in some of the subsamples, divisionalization is positively correlated with growth in capital employed, sales, and number of persons employed. For example, among dominant product companies, those which were not market leaders, and those with a low perceived dependence on major customers, divisionalization was positively correlated with growth in either capital employed or sales and in number of employees, but even this seems to have been achieved at the expense of 4-year growth in ROI. Only among companies with between 20 percent and 60 percent of total sales to government and industry was divisionalization associated with growth in sales and in ROI over four years.

Financial Performance and Match

Results bearing on the relationship between performance and the fit between strategy and structure are mixed. There is partial support for Hypothesis H.7.1 that among functionally organized companies the degree of diversification (STRATEGY) and performance are negatively correlated. Table 24.8 shows significant, negative coefficients for growth in sales and number employed, but those for profitability are too small to be significant. In contrast, Hypothesis H.7.2 that degree of diversification and performance are positively correlated for companies with product divisions must be rejected. Indeed, growth in return on capital employed (ROI) and net profit are negatively correlated with diversification under most circumstances.

From Table 24.9 it may be seen that Hypothesis H.7.3 fares no better. None of the coefficients for single product companies is significant. For dominant product companies, mean ROI, variability of ROI, growth in sales, and growth in capital employed all tend to be significantly better the higher the degree of divisionalization, although growth in ROI tends to be significantly lower. It could well be that adoption of product divisional structures among dominant product companies marks efforts to move increasingly into related or even unrelated products and markets to escape the constraints imposed by maturity of original businesses. If this is so, it is a case of strategy following structure. This would explain the association with high growth in sales and capital employed, higher average ROI associated with dominance in mature industries, yet lower growth in ROI. Whatever the explanation, Hypothesis H.7.3 is clearly unproven for single product companies and rejected in important respects for dominant product companies.

Nor do the results support Hypothesis H.7.4 to the effect that performance and the degree of divisionalization are positively correlated among companies with "related" and "unrelated" strategies. Only growth in the number employed is significantly, positively correlated with degree of divisionalization for these subsamples, and there is a strong suggestion that growth in ROI is negatively correlated. Most of the other coefficients, including that for variability of ROI, are close to zero.

Not surprisingly, in view of the paucity of significant findings from this category related analysis, analysis of correlation between the general measure of match, FIT, and measures of performance revealed no significant results. Most coefficients, although positive, were close to zero.

TABLE 24.8. Correlation Coefficients for Strategy and Financial Performance (Kendall's tau)*

Measure:	Standard deviation of ROI	Growth in ROI over last year	Growth in ROI over last 4 years	Growth in capital employed over last 4 years	Growth in sales over last 4 years	Growth in net profits over last 4 years	Growth in number employed over last 4 years
Sample							
1. All 48 companies	NS	NS	NS	NS	NS	$-.22^a$	NS
2. Functional structures	$-.34^\dagger$	NS	NS	NS	$-.39^a$	NS	$-.51^b$
3. Product and geographical structures	NS	NS	NS	$-.72^b$	NS	$-.60^a$	NS
4. All product divisional structures	NS	NS	NS	$-.34^a$	NS	NS	NS
5. Service companies only	NS	NS	NS	$-.70^a$	NS	NS	NS
6. Manufacturing companies only	NS	NS	$-.38^a$	NS	$.23^\dagger$	$-.38^a$	NS
7. Manufacturing and service companies	NS	$.43^\dagger$	NS	NS	NS	NS	NS
8. Low technological change	NS	NS	$-.21^\dagger$	NS	NS	$-.21^\dagger$	NS
9. High expected source of turbulence	NS	NS	$-.39^a$	NS	NS	$-.28^\dagger$	NS
10. Low NEED for new products	NS	NS	$-.38^b$	NS	NS	$-.35^b$	NS
11. Up to 30% share of most important market	NS	NS	NS	NS	NS	NS	NS
12. Over 30% share of most important market	NS	$-.25^\dagger$	NS	NS	NS	NS	$.25^\dagger$
13. Not leader (rank > 1) in most important market	NS	NS	NS	NS	NS	$-.30^\dagger$	$-.31^\dagger$
14. No more than 30% sales to 5 largest customers	NS	NS	NS	$-.17^\dagger$	NS	$.45^\dagger$	NS

15. Perceived dependence on 10 largest customers (high)	NS	NS	$-.38^a$	NS	NS	$-.39^a$
16. Perceived dependence on 10 largest customers (low)	NS	NS	$.22^†$	NS	$-.22^†$	$.35^a$
17. Sales to wholesalers between 20% of total and 40% of total	NS	NS	NS	$.53^†$	NS	NS
18. Sales to wholesalers greater than 40% of total	NS	NS	NS	$-.59^a$	$-.46^†$	NS
19. Sales to industry and government less than 20% of total	NS	NS	NS	$-.54^a$	$.37^†$	$\times\mathbf{.65}^b$
20. Sales to industry and government between 20% and 60% of total	NS	NS	NS	$.60^a$	NS	NS
21. Sales to industry and government more than 60% of total	NS	NS	NS	$-.23^†$	NS	$-.29^a$
22. No direct sales to general public	NS	NS	NS	NS	$-.30^a$	NS
23. Between 10% and 20% of sales direct to general public	NS	$-.60^†$	NS	NS	NS	NS

* Because the structural scale is ordinal and there are many tied values, Kendall's tau was used. The sample of 48 companies was subdivided successively on the basis of structure, charter (service, manufacturing and service, and manufacturing), high or low rates of technological change, number of sources of past and expected market turbulence, and need for new product innovation. Only samples for which at least one correlation coefficient was statistically significant were included. Similarly, the analysis covered all measures of performance, but they are shown in the table only where at least one coefficient was statistically significant.

NS: Not significant.
† Strongly suggested at the .10 level.
a Significant at the .05 level.
b Significant at the .01 level.

TABLE 24.9. Correlation Coefficients for Structure and Financial Performance (Kendall's tau)*

Measure:	4 Year average ROI	Standard deviation of ROI	Growth in ROI over last 4 years	Growth in capital employed over last 4 years	Growth in sales over last 4 years	Growth in net profits over last 4 years	Growth in number employed over last 4 years
Sample							
1. All 48 companies	NS	NS	$-.30^b$	NS	$.16†$	$-.20^a$	$.21†$
2. Single product strategy	NS	$.54†$	$.60†$	NS	$-.54†$	NS	NS
3. Dominant product strategy	$.57^a$	$-.39†$	$-.48^a$	$.74^a$	$.48^a$	NS	NS
4. Related product strategy	NS	NS	NS	NS	NS	$.37^a$	$.34^a$
5. Related and unrelated product strategy	NS	NS	$-.26†$	NS	NS	NS	NS
6. Low technological change	NS	NS	$-.27^a$	NS	NS	NS	$.39^a$
7. High past sources of turbulence	NS	NS	$-.50^b$	$.29†$	$.44^b$	$-.27^b$	$.28$
8. High expect sources of turbulence	NS	NS	$-.39^a$	$.30†$	NS	$-.28†$	$.35$
9. High NEED for new products	$.41^a$	NS	NS	NS	$.53^b$	NS	NS
10. Low NEED for new products	NS	NS	$-.32^a$	NS	NS	$-.30^a$	NS
11. Up to 30% share of most important market	NS	NS	$-.35^a$	NS	NS	NS	$.42^a$
12. Over 30% share of most important market	NS	NS	$-.36^a$	NS	NS	$-.28†$	$.31†$
13. Not market leader (rank > 1) in most important market	NS	NS	$-.31†$	$.40^a$	NS	$-.37^a$	$.40†$
14. Market leader (rank = 1) in most important market	NS	NS	$-.26†$	NS	NS	NS	$.42^b$

15. More than 30% of sales to five largest customers (dependent)†	.71‡	.71†	-.71†	.71‡	NS	-.63‡	NS
16. No more than 30% of sales of five largest customers (relatively independent)	NS	NS	-.26[a]	NS	.26[a]	NS	.43[b]
17. Perceived dependence on 10 largest customers (high)	NS	NS	NS	NS	NS	NS	.30†
18. Perceived dependence on 10 largest customers (low)	NS	NS	-.45	NS	.41[b]	-.22†	.41[a]
19. Sales to wholesalers between 20% and 40% of total	NS	NS	-.91[a]	NS	NS	NS	.67[a]
20. Sales to wholesalers more than 40% of total	NS	NS	-.60[a]	NS	NS	-.47‡	.71‡
21. Sales to industry and government between 20% and 60% of total	64*	NS	.58[a]	NS	.58[a]	NS	NS
22. Between 10% and 20% of total sales direct to general public	.63†	-.63†	-.63†	NS	NS	-.55†	.91[a]

* Because the structural scale is ordinal and there are many tied values, Kendall's tau was used. The sample of 48 companies was subdivided successively on the basis of strategy, charter, high and low levels of technological change, sources of past and expected market turbulence, and need for new product innovation. Only samples for which at least one coefficient was statistically significant are included. Similarly, the analysis covered all measures of performance but they are shown only where statistically significant results were found.

† The sample size was here very low and not much significance can be attached to the suggested relationship.

NS: Not significant

‡ Strongly suggested at the .10 level.

[a] Significant at the .05 level.

[b] Significant at the .01 level.

Match between divisional structures and diversified businesses seems to have little effect on financial performance.

Environmental Pressures, Strategy, Structure, and Financial Performance

Perhaps diversification has advantages in particularly difficult environments. This view is implicit in Hypothesis H.8.1. However, no significant correlations between diversification (STRATEGY) and any measure of performance were found among subsamples experiencing either high or low rates of technological change, and the only strongly suggested correlations were negative (see Table 24.8). The same is largely true of subsamples based on perceived numbers of both past and future sources of market turbulence, although diversification and growth in ROI were significantly, negatively correlated for companies expecting a turbulent market. Companies with a high perception of need for new product innovation, one proxy for competition in terms of new products in the market, again displayed no significant relationships between strategy and performance. Nor is the position in the company's most important market related to any relationship between strategy and performance. However, although growth in sales and number employed are significantly, negatively correlated with diversification among companies highly dependent on major customers, there are strong indications that the relationship is positive where dependence is low. As suggested earlier, this may well imply a greater exposure to competitive market forces and so provide some support for Hypothesis H.8.1.

In general, though, there is very little evidence that diversification is associated with, let alone causes, high performance in conditions of high technological change and market turbulence. Thus the negative correlation between diversification and growth in net profits, found for the sample of 48 companies as a whole, is largely unaffected by environmental conditions. Nor, indeed, are the directions of relationships affected by the charter of companies, although the relationships are stronger and more statistically significant for manufacturing companies. Hypothesis H.8.1 cannot be supported.

A consistent pattern emerges from the significant and highly suggestive coefficients relating to structure (Table 24.9). More highly divisionalized companies seem to outperform others in terms of growth in sales, growth in capital employed, and number of persons employed where high market turbulence is perceived but continue to do significantly worse in terms of growth in ROI. Worse growth in net profit also is highly suggested. Growth in number employed, as well as capital employed or sales in some cases, also was found to be positively correlated with divisionalization among market leaders and those with a low dependence on major customers, less sales to wholesalers, and relatively low sales to the general public. Again this seems to have been associated with lower growth in ROI. Whether because of entry into new projects with low initial returns on investment at early stages of their life cycle, or expansion of sales at the expense of profit margins, the profit to sales ratio must have been dropping substantially in the divisionalized companies as they grew. Hypothesis H.8.2, clearly, is valid with respect to growth of the size of the business but not profitability.

Discussion

Results of the study of strategy and structure in 48 large UK companies, summarized in Table 24.10, strongly support much of the earlier literature. Like Rumelt (1974) and Channon (1975), they reveal a highly statistically significant positive correlation between strategy and structure. Moreover, the relationship now has been shown to be independent of other correlates of structure including number of sites, geographic dispersion of sites, and size in terms of sales, capital employed, and number of employees, as well as a variety of environmental factors. In addition, the study confirms Channon's (1975) conclusion that the linkage between strategy and structure is as strong among service as among manufacturing companies, but for reasons possibly peculiar to the sample of 48 UK companies was not significant among those combining manufacturing and service operations. The association between strategy and structure is put in perspective, however, by the equally strong correlations between the latter and charter (type of operation), size, number of sites and their geographic dispersion, variables that are not themselves correlated with strategy. This explains the small amount of total variance in structure attributable to its correlation with strategy.

The positive correlation found between each of vertical and lateral spans of control of the chief executive and an ordinal scale measuring divisionalization of organization structure is the first strut in a bridge between the strategy structure school and the organizational behavioralists. Pugh et al. (1968) and Child (1972) in the Aston studies and their extension had already shown vertical span and measures of bureaucracy to be positively correlated. Moreover, Grinyer and Yasai-Ardekani (1978) have recently shown that vertical and lateral span, formalization, functional specialization, and decentralization are not only intercorrelated but are all positively, significantly correlated with an ordinal scale of organizational structure similar to that used in the study reported here. Given the correlation between strategy and the ordinal scale for structure, strategy and measures of bureaucracy are likely to be positively correlated, too. This

TABLE 24.10. *Summary of Tests on Hypotheses*

Number	Hypothesis	Result	Significance level
H.1.1.	Vertical span is positively correlated with degree of divisionalization	Supported	.05
H.1.2	Lateral span is positively correlated with degree of divisionalization	Supported	.05
H.2.1	Diversification is positively correlated with degree of divisionalization	Supported	.001
H.2.2	H.2.1 is independent of other correlates of structure	Supported	.05 to .001
H.2.3	H.2.1 is independent of type of business or "charter"	Holds of manufacturing companies and service companies but not for those combinating both	.001 for first two but rejected at .05 for last
H.3.1	Size of company is positively correlated with degree of diversification	Rejected	.05
H.3.2	Size of company is positively correlated with degree of divisionalization	Supported. Significance level varies between measures	.05 to .001
H.4.1	Number of sites is positively correlated with degree of divisionalization	Supported	.001
H.4.2	Geographic dispersion is positively correlated with degree of divisionalization	Supported	.01
H.5.1	For "related" and "unrelated" product companies perceived environmental pressure is negatively correlated with degree of divisionalization	Supported	.05
H.5.2	For "single" and "dominant" product companies perceived environmental pressure is positively correlated with degree of divisionalization	Supported	.05
H.5.3	"Fit" between strategy and structure is negatively correlated with perceived environmental pressure	Supported	.05 to .01
H.6.1	ROI and growth are positively correlated with diversification	On contrary growth and diversification often found to be negatively correlated	.05 to .01
H.6.2	Variability of ROI negatively correlated with diversification	Not supported	.05

TABLE 24.10 (*cont.*)

Number	Hypothesis	Result	Significance level
H.6.3	ROI and growth are greater for divisionally structured companies	Growth in ROI and net profits *negatively* correlated with divisionalization	.05 to .001
	Variability of ROI is less for divisionally organized companies	Not supported	.05
H.6.4	Related business companies have higher ROI and growth than other categories	Not supported	.05
H.6.5	Divisionalized related product companies have higher ROI and growth than other categories	Not supported	.05
H.7.1	For functionally organized companies, ROI and growth are negatively correlated with diversification	No significant results for average ROI. Confirmed for *growth* in sales and number employed.	.05 to .01
H.7.2	For product divisionally organized companies, ROI and growth are positively correlated with diversification	No significant results for ROI. Rejected for growth. Growth in each of capital employed and net profits *negatively* correlated with diversification.	.05 to .01
H.7.3	For "single" or "dominant" product companies, ROI and growth are negatively correlated with divisionalization	Not supported for single product companies. Rejected for ROI and growth in sales and capital employed among dominant product companies where positive correlations found although negative correlation of *growth* in ROI	.05
H.7.4	For related and unrelated product companies, ROI and growth are positively correlated with divisionalization	Unsupported except for growth in number employed	.05
H.8.1	In unstable environments, ROI and growth are positively and variability of ROI is negatively correlated with diversification	Nor supported	.05

TABLE 24.10 (cont.)

Number	Hypothesis	Result	Significance level
H.8.2	In unstable environments, ROI and growth are positively and variability of ROI is negatively correlated with divisionalization	Confirmed for growth in sales, capital employed, and number employed. Rejected for growth in ROI where correlation is negative	.05 to .01

would be consistent with Chandler's (1962) argument. Decentralization of operational decision making and creation of a general office as a means of addressing the administrative problems inherent in diverse business operations perhaps inevitably involve constraining sets of procedures, role definitions, and the use of technically qualified staff. An extension of the organizational study by Grinyer and Yasai-Ardekani (1978) is being made to test for the existence of a direct link between strategy (diversification) and bureaucracy.

The study also bears upon the hypothesis advanced by Franko (1974) and Galbraith and Nathanson (1978) that a match between strategy and structure is forced by hostile environmental pressure and that an appropriate match facilitates coping. Earlier studies on strategy and structure, to which reference is made in the first section, were largely unable to explore this aspect because of their methodology. Using publicly available data, they were able to use large sample sizes, but were denied the information on perceptions of management that interviews or, less adequately, mailed questionnaires can yield. The study reported here benefits from access to management's perceptions on its environment at the cost of a smaller, but still relatively large, sample. In this respect it may be seen to be complementary to the earlier studies.

Analysis reported in earlier sections shows clearly that there is less perception of environmental hostility (as well as higher market share and greater reliance, mutual dependence, on major customers, which could reduce the likelihood of competitive market pressures) in companies where strategy and structure are matched. Moreover, the variables on environmental hostility were found to be correlated negatively with measures of performance, suggesting that they reflect real rather than imagined forces. Perception of these pressures, and their financial impact, could well induce companies with a poor match between strategy and structure to move to a better one. Consequently, the results are consistent with the proposition advanced by Franko (1974) and Galbraith and Nathanson (1978).

The results on performance may be compared usefully with those of Rumelt (1974). Because Wrigley's (1970) less detailed scale was adopted, the study cannot parallel Rumelt's analysis of the differences between, for example, dominant constrained and dominant-linked strategies. Also, the structural categories and financial variables, although similar, are different. Nevertheless, the similarities are sufficient to permit direct comparison with Rumelt's analysis of major "strategic" and "structural" categories. The results reported in the present study differ substantially. Degree of diversification and growth, particularly in net profits, were negatively correlated. In addition, diversified companies displayed no better than average return on capital employed. Moreover, single product companies had significantly higher rates of growth in net profits. It is possible, however, that the difference between the results of this UK study and Rumelt's study is due to a different distribution of related product companies between the "related-constrained" category which he found to be the best performing and "related-linked" which was average or below. This might have been revealed had a finer analysis of strategic postures been possible in the UK sample, along the lines introduced by Rumelt.

On structure, results of the present UK study are only partially consistent with Rumelt's (1974). Some categories of companies with product divisions tended to grow faster than others in terms of sales, capital employed, and number of employees, but their net profit and return on capital employed grew significantly more slowly. This is consistent with Rumelt's finding that "among product divisional firms sales growth is less closely associated with profitability than among firms with functional structures" (1974, p. 114).

Rumelt (1974) followed a pairwise analysis of strategy, structure, and performance that largely precluded him from examining the relationship between match and performance. Only in his analysis of divisionally and functionally organized related business did he touch upon the issue, and then he found that the only significant difference was in growth in sales. The study of match and performance in the present paper therefore breaks new ground. On the whole, the results are disappointing for there is little relationship between match and financial performance. Moreover, this seems to be true no matter which environmental variable is used to subdivide the sample. There is some doubt, then, on the proposition that a good match or fit between strategy and structure promotes more effective coping with environmental pressures. It may possibly reduce the awareness of environmental turbulence without affecting performance.

Nonetheless, Galbraith and Nathanson's (1978) proposition that better match promotes coping with the environment cannot be rejected. As already seen, better match did reduce perception of environmental hostility, which in turn was related to financial performance. Moreover, the analysis of financial performance is not as strong as was wished, and it certainly is weaker than Rumelt's (1974). It was difficult to obtain measures of performance for the members of the sample that were owned subsidiaries or divisions of other companies. Consequently, a large number of values for some variables are missing, such as average ROI, the highest number being 19 for the 4-year averages. Only nine were missing for the 2-year averages of ROI. Given the sample size of 48, this reduced the number of cases for which the 4-year average and standard deviation of ROI could be analyzed to merely 29, although the number was in the region of 40 or above for other measures. Subsequent subdivision between categories of structure, strategy, charter, and other contextual variables inevitably meant that some subsamples for the average and standard deviation of ROI in particular were very small. In such subsamples the size of coefficient required for results to be statistically significant was often high with a resultant loss of results. Nevertheless, where correlations appear consistently and significantly in different subsamples (as in the case of the main relationships reported) and in the full sample, the findings are likely to be strongly indicative of real associations. Consequently, where the results on performance are contrary to those of Rumelt (1974), they should be interpreted as raising serious questions and underlining the need for further research, rather than contradicting. The basis for the analysis is still sufficiently strong to make these questions important and to suggest possible differences between the United Kingdom and the United States, although Channon (1975) obtained results for the UK service industries very similar to Rumelt's (1974).

Such reservations do not apply to the main contributions of the research: the relationship between spans of control and divisionalization; the independence of the strategy/structure linkage from other correlates of structure; and the relationship between the fit between strategy and structure and perceived environmental hostility.

References

Al-Bazzaz, S. J. (1977) Contextual Variables and Corporate Planning in 48 UK Companies. Ph.D. thesis, The City University Business School, London.

Berg, N. (1973) Corporate role in diversified companies. Working Paper HBS 71–2, Graduate School of Business Administration, Harvard University, 1971. Reprinted in B. Taylor and K. MacMillan (eds.), *Business Policy: Teaching and Research*. London: Bradford University Press and Crosby Lockwood.

Chandler, A. D. (1962) Strategy and Structure. Boston: MIT Press.

Channon, D. F. (1973) The Strategy and Structure of British Enterprise. New York: Macmillan.

Channon, D. F. (1975) Strategy, Structure and Financial Performance in the Service Industries. London: Report HR2098, The SSRC, May.

Child, J. (1972) Organization structure and strategies of control: A replication of the Aston study. Administrative Science Quarterly, **17**, 163−176.

Dyas, G. D. (1972) The Strategy and Structure of French Industrial Enterprise. Unpublished doctoral dissertation, Graduate School of Business Administration, Harvard University, Cambridge, Mass.

Fouraker, L. E. and Stopford, J. M. (1968) Organizational structure and multinational strategy. Administrative Science Quarterly, **13**, 47−64.

Franko, L. G. (1974) The move toward a multidivisional structure in European organizations. Administrative Science Quarterly, **19**, 493−506.

Galbraith, J. R. and Nathanson, D. A. (1978) Strategy Implementation: The Role of Structure and Process. New York: West Publishing Company.

Grinyer, P. H. and Yasai-Ardekani, M. (1978) Dimensions of Organizational Structure: A Critical Replication. Working Paper, The City University Business School, London, July.

Grinyer, P. H., Al-Bazzaz, S. J. and Yasai-Ardekani, M. (1978) Strategy, Structure, the Environment and Financial Performance in 48 UK Companies. Working paper. The City University Business School, London, June.

Pavan, R. J. (1972) The Strategy and Structure of Italian Industrial Enterprise. Unpublished doctoral dissertation, Graduate School of Business Administration, Harvard University, Cambridge, Mass.

Pugh, D. S., Hickson, D. J., Hinings, C. R., and Turner, C. (1968) Dimensions of organization structure. Administrative Science Quarterly, **13**, 65−105.

Pugh, D. S., Hickson, D. J., Hinings, C. R., and Turner, C. (1969) The context of organization structures. Administrative Science Quarterly, **14**, 91−114.

Reimann, B. C. (1973) On the dimensions of bureaucratic structure: An empirical reappraisal. Administrative Science Quarterly, **18**, 462−476.

Rumelt, R. P. (1974) Strategy, Structure and Economic Performance. Cambridge, Mass.: Harvard University Press.

Siegel, S. (1956) Non parametric Statistics. New York: McGraw Hill.

Stopford, J. M. (1965) Growth and Organizational Change in the Multinational Firm. Unpublished doctoral dissertation. Graduate School of Business Administration, Harvard University, Cambridge, Mass.

Thanheiser, H. T. (1972) Strategy and Structure of German Industrial Enterprise. Unpublished doctoral dissertation, Graduate School of Business Administration, Harvard University, Cambridge, Mass.

Wrigley, L. (1970) Divisional Autonomy and Diversification. Unpublished doctoral dissertation, Graduate School of Business Administration, Harvard University, Cambridge, Mass.

25

Environmental Scanning and Forecasting in Strategic Planning—The State of the Art

L. FAHEY, W. R. KING AND V. K. NARAYANAN

The importance of strategic planning as a major activity of organizational management is being increasingly accepted by both academicians and professional managers. Many who have considered the future needs of organizations have argued that a lack of adequate long range and strategic planning would be disastrous for organizations and for society.

As strategic planning moves towards maturity, the viewpoint which is increasingly being applied is that of the organization as an "open system". Simplistically, this notion holds that an organization's growth and survival is dependent on the nature of the environment that it faces. It therefore behooves every organization to be aware of the nature of the environment that it currently faces and those which it may face in the future.

Given this view, it is not surprising that both practitioners and scholars in the field of strategic planning have been devoting attention to "environmental scanning and forecasting" as an important element of planning. A number of environmental scanning and forecasting approaches have been developed—varying from short-term forecasting to "futuristic" planning. Many industrial and governmental organizations have adopted various of these practices.

These various environmental scanning and forecasting practices vary widely in concept, scope, and operational detail. Also, various practices have had different degrees of success in assessing the environment. However, few research studies have systematically assessed the state of environmental scanning and forecasting art and its impact on planning. This paucity of empirical evidence restricts our ability to assess the impact

This article was originally published in *Long Range Planning*, Volume 14, No. 1, February 1981.

The authors are at the Graduate School of Business, University of Pittsburg, PA 15200.

of current practice and to prescribe directions for the future development of this potentially important area.

An objective of this paper is to shed some light on the practical state of the art of the environmental scanning and forecasting function in organizations. This objective is addressed through a multi-faceted survey of planning practitioners. These practitioners were queried to permit a realistic assessment to be made of:

(a) The "most sophisticated level" of environmental scanning and forecasting that is in widespread current practice in various types of organizations;
(b) the "average" level of environmental scanning and forecasting that is in current practice;
(c) future directions in which practice in the field should develop as viewed from various organizational perspectives.

Conceptual Evaluative Model

To guide the data collection and analysis for the study, a conceptual typology of environmental scanning and forecasting systems (ESFS) was developed as shown in Table 25.1. The typology is an extension of an earlier model developed by two of the authors. The typology characterizes scanning and forecasting as either Irregular, Periodic, or Continuous in increasing order of sophistication and complexity. Some of the selected dimensions which are operationally useful in distinguishing among the three categories are defined in the row labels in the table.

Irregular systems are characterized by the reactive nature of planning as well as environmental scanning. These systems respond to environmentally generated crises. Such systems are not really systematic. Their focus is on specific problems which tend to be short term in nature. Methodologically these systems rely on simplistic tools which primarily utilize information from the past. At the extreme, they may focus on the near-term budgetary impact of the events which they monitor. The organizations which use these systems generally have not created a "strategic planning culture". More importantly, however, these systems attempt to reduce uncertainty in the current and near-term future environment and in doing so, they generally fail to detect opportunities to facilitate the creation of radically new solutions to problems.

Periodic systems, on the other hand, are more sophisticated and complex. While the focus of these systems is still problem solving, they exhibit greater proactive characteristics. These systems look more toward the future, but they emphasize near-term environmental changes. As a result, while they are forecasting oriented, the forecasts that they produce are limited in their scope and methodologies: they emphasize economic

TABLE 25.1. *A typology of environmental scanning and forecasting systems*

	Irregular	Periodic	Continuous
Impetus for scanning	Crisis-initiated	Problem-solving decision/issue oriented	Opportunity finding and problem avoidance
Scope of scanning	Specific events	Selected events	Broad range of environmental systems
Temporal nature	Reactive	Proactive	Proactive
(a) Timeframe for data	Retrospective	Current and retrospective	Current and prospective
(b) Timeframe for decision impact	Current and near term future	Near term	Long term
Types of forecasts	Budget-oriented	Economic and sales oriented	Marketing, social, legal, regulatory, culture, etc.
Media for scanning and forecasting	*Ad hoc* studies	Periodically updated studies	Structured data collection and processing systems
Organization structure	(1) *Ad hoc* teams (2) Focus on reduction of perceived certainty	Various staff agencies	Scanning unit, focus on enhancing uncertainty handling capability
Resource allocation to activity	Not specific; (perhaps periodic as "fads" arise)	Specific and continuous but relatively low	Specific continuous and relatively substantial
Methodological sophistication	Simplistic data analyses and budgetary projections	Statistical forecasting oriented	Many 'futuristic' forecasting methodologies
"Cultural" orientation	Not integrated into mainstream of activity	Partially integrated as a "step-child"	Fully integrated as crucial for long-range growth

and sales projections using simple statistical methodologies. There is often a partial integration of the activity into the mainstream of the organization as evidenced by a specific and continuous, resource allocation to the activity. In general, organizations which have systems of this genre tend to treat them as necessary evil.

Continuous systems, as delineated in Table 25.1, are the ideal portrayed in planning literature. Here the focus shifts from mere problem-solving to opportunity-finding and the realization that planning systems contribute to the growth and survival of the organizations in a proactive way. As a result, these systems draw on expertise varying from marketing to cultural analysis, and information gathering becomes a structured activity. In other words, *these systems attempt to enhance the organization's capability to handle environmental uncertainty rather than to reduce perceived uncertainty.* The time horizons which are treated are considerably longer—varying from "long" to "futuristic"—and there is a substantial continuing resource allocation to these activities in the organization.

The typology of systems and operational measures in Table 25.1 forms the framework which was used in structuring the evaluative survey to be reported on here.

Study Methodology

The study involved two phases of data collection from two distinct sub-populations of professional planners and managers involved in environmental scanning and planning.

(1) The first segment of the population—termed "aware professionals"—refers to those in industry, government consulting or academic institutions who, by their membership in a futuristic professional association, were treated as individuals who should be aware of the most sophisticated thinking in environmental scanning and planning.

(2) The second segment of the population—termed "practitioners"—were analysts and managers who are identified as involved in planning activities in a variety of organizations. No attempt was made to select organizations known to be sophisticated planners, because the objectives of the study were to assess the most sophisticated and average levels of environmental forecasting and planning that are in widespread usage.

The two segments, while not necessarily mutually exclusive, are conceptually separable. The study utilized different modes of data collection for each of the segments.

The aware professional segment was surveyed utilizing a mail questionnaire. The questionnaire was structured to ask the respondents to give their perception on a seven-point Likert scale. The questions focused on the nature of environmental scanning practices, the degree to which they were utilized in their own organizations and an assessment of their potential utility to the organization.

The questionnaire was mailed to a random sample of 100 aware professionals selected from the membership roster of World Future Society—a professional group whose interest areas and activities are deemed to reflect the modern point of view of the continuous scanning model of Table 25.1. A total of 36 respondents returned the questionnaire out of which 11 were consultants, 8 were from government and 17 were affiliated with business.

Practitioner responses were obtained by means of personal interviews. The interviewees were primarily vice-presidents of planning, managers of corporate planning or individuals with responsibility for environmental scanning, forecasting and/or analysis.

Personal interviews were conducted for this subgroup because a pilot test revealed the problems of an interpretation involved in an area which involves technical jargon and individuals who may be familiar with the jargon, but not with the substantive meaning of many terms. This mode of study also permitted a level of follow-through which could not be obtained with other data collection approaches.

The interviewer was guided by a structured survey instrument which was developed to reflect current thinking on how environmental scanning and forecasting "should" be performed. As expected, the interviewer found it necessary to ask a number of rephrased questions before a satisfactory answer to each item was obtained.

A total of 12 firms were interviewed. Defined in terms of flexibility of resource utilization over time, 7 firms were defined as capital-intensive and 5 firms were non-capital intensive. Among the 5 non-capital intensive firms, 1 was a large hospital and 2 were large banks. Five of the 7 capital intensive firms served both consumers and industrial markets, while the other 2 served industrial markets exclusively.

Table 25.2 shows the two respondent groups and the two varieties of inquiry which were used in the study. It demonstrates the manner in which the study objectives were addressed. The most sophisticated level of current practice was assessed by querying aware professionals concerning the state of the art in their own organizations. This involves many implicit assumptions, but it avoids assessment problems caused by heresay evidence and the exaggerations to which these professionals may be subjected from colleagues in other organizations.

The assessment of the average level of current practice is shown in

TABLE 25.2. *Study objectives and methodology*

Sample group		Nature of inquiry	
		Current status	Potential utility
Sample group	Aware professionals	Most sophisticated level of widespread practice	Future directions— primary
	Practitioner	Average level of practice	Future directions— secondary

Table 25.2 to involve similar kinds of queries addressed to practitioners. Of course the term "average" is used in a representative sense, since no statistical sampling process was used.

Assessment of fruitful areas for future development was made through questions posed to both sample groups concerning the potential utility of various techniques and approaches. However, as Table 25.2 indicates, the written nature of the responses from the aware professionals subgroup and their greater familiarity with the area meant that this subgroup was primarily relied on in this regard.

Insofar as is feasible and meaningful, all data were separated and analyzed by organization type to permit these assessments to be made on a differential basis for various kinds of organizations.

Study Findings

Because the study objectives are complex and multidimensional, we shall initially organize the study results in more limited form. Subsequently, the broad study objectives will be directly addressed. The study results are here presented in terms of the types of futuristic practices most often employed, the types of expertise deemed necessary, the time horizon considered and the nature of the organization structure which is viewed as most amenable to the application of futuristic forecasting methodologies.

Utility Planning/Forecasting Methodologies

Table 25.3 shows the aware professional's ratings of the *potential* usefulness and *actual* usage of various scanning/forecasting methodologies. Scenario writing emerges as the single most important technique across all three groups studied. Simulation, input/output analysis, and other forecasting techniques were all rated highly in terms of potential utility, although simulation (especially by government and corporate respondents) and

TABLE 25.3. *Aware professional's perceived potential utility and actual usage of planning/forecasting methods* [a]

	Consultants		Government		Corporations	
	Utility	Usage	Utility	Usage	Utility	Usage
Scenario-writing	5.8	5.2	6.1	4.7	6.1	4.2
Simulation	6.1	5.2	4.1	2	4.0	2
Morphological analysis	4.1	3.1	2	2	4.2	2.1
PPBS	3.9	2	4.1	5.1	2	2
Game theory	2.1	2	2.9	2.5	2	2
Cross impact analysis	4.8	2.8	3.6	2.1	3.9	2
Input–output analysis	5.9	3.0	4.8	3.7	4.8	2.9
Field anamolyrelation	3.7	2	3.1	2.9	2	2
Multi echelon coordination	3.8	2	3.1	2.0	2	2
Other forecasting techniques	5.0	4.8	4.7	4.2	6.1	5.1

[a] Measured on a 7-point scale.

input/output analysis were identified as not receiving application commensurate with their potential. Not surprisingly, it is forecasting techniques that corporations most widely use, while in government PPBS receives the greatest application.

The personal interviews corroborated the mail survey findings that organizations in their efforts to forecast the critical elements in their future environment(s) primarily rely on a small subset of the potential range of environmental forecasting methodologies—principally, the Delphi method and to a lesser extent, scenario-writing.

Appropriate Time Horizon

As shown in Table 25.4, a substantial difference appears to exist within and among the various aware-professional respondent groups with regard to both the *ideal* and *actual* time horizon for futuristic practice. Not unexpectedly, both the actual time horizon in corporate efforts to forecast the future and the time horizon considered to be ideal is shorter in the corporate milieu than for consultants and government. *In all three subgroups, however, the actual time horizon in futures forecasting is considerably less than that which is considered appropriate.*

The interviews with practitioners made clear that corporations tend to utilize a short-term horizon in their forecasting efforts and that they do so in a rather haphazard way. Some interviewees admitted they pay very little attention to the time dimension in environmental forecasting. However, in terms of a forecasting timeframe, a significant distinction does arise between capital and noncapital firms (see Table 25.5). Capital intensive

TABLE 25.4. *Planning time horizons—aware professional sample*

Percentage of respondents

Type of organizations

Time horizon (years)	Consulting		Government		Corporate	
	Ideal	Actual	Ideal	Actual	Ideal	Actual
1—5	—	—	—	—	18	70
5—10	—	33	25	63	70	18
10—20	28	50	63	37	12	12
More than 20	72	17	12	—	—	—
h	(11)	(6)	(8)		(17)	

TABLE 25.5. *Firms' forecasting timeframe: practitioner sample*

	Firm	Area	Timeframe
Capital intensive	A, B	Capital/financial requirements	10 years +
		Energy supplies	10 years +
		Regulatory	Not predictable
	C	Economic (basis of capital commitments)	10 years +
		Social	Less than 1 year
		Regulatory	Respond to rather than predict
	D	Economic (the primary area)	5—10 years
	E	Economic (subsumes all other areas)	1—5 years
	F	Economic Energy	Nothing longer than 5 years
	H	All areas	Short-term (less than 1 year)
	J	All areas	Generally short term (related to planning cycle—3 year periods)
Non-capital intensive	K	Where forecasting is possible	Very short—6 months
	L	All areas	Less than 1 year
	M	Where we do forecast	Nothing longer than 3 years

firms generally use a timeframe of 5 years or more and their forecasting efforts are restricted to economic/financial considerations and a long-range assessment of the world energy situation. The noncapital intensive firms adhere to a much shorter range timeframe, generally not more than 3 years.

Required Expertise for Planning/Forecasting

A much greater degree of homogeneity was reflected in the aware professional's perceptions of the types of expertise required for planning/forecasting (see Table 25.6). Expertise in systems, social sciences, planning and environmental issues was generally considered essential for any long-range forecasting efforts though many also mentioned economic and data processing capabilities.

TABLE 25.6. *Type of expertise used in planning/forecasting**

Type of expectation	Type of organizations		
	Consulting (*n* = 11)	Government (*n* = 8)	Corporation (*n* = 17)
Systems	100	63	48
Social sciences[a]	100	75	54
Planning	73	75	100
Environmental[b]	100	100	94
OR/data processing	55	63	48
Other[c]			

[a] Entries are percentage indicating each area. Columns sum to more than 100/ because of multiple responses.
[b] Includes economics. Includes technological.
[c] All others less than 15 per cent.

Organizational Requisites

No clear agreement exists among aware professionals as to what is the appropriate organizational form for the conduct of scanning and futuristic studies. Consultants and government agencies generally preferred that a separate unit or department be charged with conducting futuristic forecasts whereas corporate-based respondents strongly preferred that such forecasts be conducted by, and be a part of, the ongoing corporate planning function.

Only 2 of the 12 firms in which practitioners were surveyed considered futures forecasting of sufficient importance to establish a separate environmental scanning unit to monitor, evaluate and predict environmental changes. Both of these firms emphasized in the strongest terms that change in their environment was occurring at such a rapid rate that those who formulate plans and/or managers who must implement a set of plans could no longer be charged with responsibility for predicting and assessing potential change in a range of environments as diffuse as the political, economic, technological and social arenas. Although constant interaction is maintained between strategic planning personnel, line management and environmental analysts, in an effort to ensure that such systematic and comprehensive environmental analysis is relevant to managements' needs, both firms were quick to point out that environmental scanning and forecasting was not yet fully integrated into their strategic planning processes.

A major organization structure question with regard to environmental forecasting and scanning is the appropriate division of such activities between corporate headquarter staff and divisional management. Because of the generally perceived importance of the economic and regulatory environments, these sphere are most often monitored and assessed by the head office corporate planning staff, with heavy reliance upon input from such units as the economic and legal departments, economic consulting groups and the firm's "Washington office".

Integration of Forecasting and Planning

Table 25.7 indicates the perceived potential applicability and the actual environmental scanning/forecasting usage of practices at various stages of the planning process by the three aware-professional segments. Establishing environmental premises and data gathering for forecasting are generally regarded as the areas where scanning/forecasting practices possess the most applicability. Most of the consultants mentioned an educational role for the field of futures forecasting while government agencies also reported its importance in technology assessment and its impact on the social policy formulation process. The corporate aware-professionals

TABLE 25.7. *Applicability of scanning/forecasting at various states of planning*

	Consultants		Government		Corporations	
	Potential	Actual	Potential	Actual	Potential	Actual
Establishing corporate goals	6.2	4.0	NA	NA	5.3	4.8
Setting environmental premises	6.8	5.4	5.0	4.75	6.1	5.0
Collecting information and forecasting	6.2	5.2	6.25	5.5	6.1	5.0
Establishing divisional goals	2	2	NA	NA	4.0	3.8
Developing divisional plans	2	2	NA	NA	3.1	2
Revising objectives and plans if objectives are not met	2	2			2.1	2

indicated strong potential for and actual usage of futuristic scanning and forecasting practices in the corporate objective-setting process and to a lesser extent at the divisional level, but such practices are apparently little-used in the process of developing divisional plans and revising plans when objectives are not realized.

The in-person practitioner interviews allowed greater probing of the utility and perceived limitations of futurism in corporate strategic planning. This segment of our total sample was much less enthusiastic about the potential usefulness of environmental scanning and forecasting in the strategic planning process. In only one firm were environmental assumptions clearly delineated as inputs to the corporate planning process. Hence, systematic approaches to forecasting the future are little utilized in corporate efforts to establish environmental premises. Only 4 firms stated that they were moving toward a more complete statement of their environmental assumptions; perhaps, significantly both firms which have established scanning units saw this task as one of their major objectives and indicated a major role for futuristic methodologies in explicating a firm's environmental premises.

The need for the use of futures forecasting to help explicate and test managements' assumptions about the future is well illustrated by the reflection of more than half the corporate interviewees that management will generally know what its assumptions are but that they will be the consequence of an implicit and informal process; the remainder were of the opinion that management probably would not even have a "mental conception" or implicit notion of its environmental assumptions given that every plan is premised on a set of assumptions and expectations about current and future environmental developments (whether or not they are explicitly stated). The need for a set of alternative futures, however tentative and speculative, becomes almost imperative if managements' preconceptions and assumptions about environmental changes (and, hence, its plans) are not to be constantly upstaged by unexpected events.

A contingency approach to strategic planning has been widely represented as a feasible method of dealing with an increasingly uncertain future. An integral input into the development of a set of contingent plans is a range of forecasts of alternative states of the environment. However, there was little evidence of such use of futuristic forecasting since only 2 of the 12 firms interviewed had adopted contingency planning as a formal, ongoing aspect of their overall strategic planning process at the corporate level, and even in these 2 firms, the focal point of the array of futures forecasts was the economic/financial milieu. Contingency planning is not used in any systematic manner by any of the firms personally interviewed as a means to assess environmental assumptions and/or to develop alternative sets of assumptions. In short, the integration between contingency approaches to corporate strategic planning and environmental forecasting methodologies would seem to be minimal, at best.

The basic purpose of employing any mode of futuristic forecasting is the identification of those trends, events and discontinuities which may exert significant impact on the firm's long-range plans. All of the practitioners admitted they presently do a highly inadequate job in this regard. Most were involved in, or preoccupied with, the short-term implications of events which have already come to pass.

A number of problems and inhibitions to improving corporate performance in the identification of discontinuities or major changes (i.e. events or trends which are qualitatively different and thus, apt to be missed in any narrow search process) were pointed out: the overly dependence of management on quantitative data, thus missing the underlying qualitative factors; the pressure of day-to-day operating activities; the undeveloped state of the social sciences; and the scarcity of appropriately trained people ("interdisciplinarians") to sift through data both of a qualitative and quantitative nature. One quarter of practitioners went so far as to suggest that it was impossible and/or unnecessary to attempt to identify discontinuities within the environment since "one could adapt to changes as they manifest themselves".

Summary and Conclusions

The study may be summarized in terms of the three broad objectives stated earlier. The "most sophisticated" level of environmental scanning and forecasting that is practised involves a variety of methodologies, the most important of which is scenario writing, with other forecasting methods, such as Delphi, also widely used. In specific sectors, techniques such as PPBS (government), and simulation (consultants) are also extensively used. Generally the corporate sector has not adopted any of these approaches to the extent of the other two sectors. With respect to the time horizon used, government and consultants focus on longer horizons than do corporations. Thus, two sectors also utilize more systems and social science expertise and less "planning" expertise than do corporations in their planning efforts.

The "most sophisticated" organizational approach to scanning and forecasting appears to be the establishment of a separate unit that is to some degree outside of the line manager's purview.

With respect to the "average" level of sophistication in scanning/forecasting, we conclude on the basis of this limited study that it is quite low relative to the viewpoint presented in most sophisticated planning journals and texts. Most of the practitioners interviewed gave descriptions that placed them and their companies only at the doorstep of current planning thought.

The future directions of scanning/forecasting is evaluated somewhat more positively. The potential utility of a variety of techniques such as simulation and input—output analysis was rated highly, while some techniques were not so regarded. There was clear evidence of usage of many of the techniques that were not highly regarded as to potential as well as those that were highly regarded. This suggests that some have failed to live up to their promise. There was also a general recognition of the need to consider longer planning horizons and to consider new organizational forms to facilitate planning.

However, there is no clear agreement as to whether a separate organizational unit should, on will, be employed in the future to conduct scanning and forecasting. Why a separate organization unit is preferred by some government agencies and not by others raises fundamental questions about the problems involved in integrating the output (forecasts) of an autonomous forecasting unit into the organization's ongoing planning efforts. It is, perhaps, for this reason that corporations strongly preferred that futures forecasting be conducted by, and be a part of, the ongoing corporate planning function.

This observation is of critical importance for the *organizational* success of any scanning forecasting effort. Other studies have identified many cases where formal technology forecasting techniques or models have been introduced only to be later discarded or to continue in use in an ineffective manner. (As was pointed out by many of the corporate practitioners, it is not sufficient that scanning/forecasting techniques be adopted, but in order to be used effectively, they must be integrated into the ongoing routine of a firm's strategic planning processes.)

One way of ensuring such integration which some corporations seem to have found very beneficial is the establishment of an "environmental scanning unit" *within* the strategic planning group *or* have line management themselves be part of teams or committees to conduct environmental analysis. Management is thus, integrally involved in the process of environmental and futures forecasting; hence, the likelihood of the successful integration of forecasting efforts into strategic planning decision-making is considerably enhanced.

Table 25.8 shows that, in terms of the conceptual framework developed earlier, there is not a wide difference between the most sophisticated variety of scanning/forecasting and the average level that is in widespread use. The practitioners sample depicts an "average" that is very much like the "irregular" model in Table 25.1. The aware professional sample depicts a system that is, at best, periodic (in terms of Table 25.1). Neither show

TABLE 25.8. *Summary of scanning models*

	Practitioner sample	Aware professional sample
Impetus for scanning	Mostly crisis-initiated	
Scope of scanning	Mostly specific/selected events	Mostly consideration of specific issues
Type of expertise	Móstly disciplinary	Environmental, social sciences and systems
Media for scanning	*Ad hoc* studies	
Organization structure	Mostly line/planning	Part of corporate planning department
Methodological sophistication	Extra polation/economic analysis	Scenarios of forecasting techniques
Resource allocation	Limited	Hardly any
Timeframe for data	Retrospective/current	
Timeframe for decision	1−10 years	5−10 years

significant achievement of the continuous model, although continued movement in that direction is predicted.

These findings support the conclusion that, while there is a general recognition of the importance of environmental scanning/forecasting in government agencies, consulting firms and industrial corporations, these organizations have not yet widely developed sophisticated systems and integrated their outputs into the strategic planning process. More specifically:

(1) The field has had an impact on the thinking and policy making of various social entities and on broadening their perspective, though it has not necessarily resulted in enlarging the timeframe of reference.
(2) The methodologies employed are restricted to those that facilitate adaptive behavior of systems rather than innovative behavior. The latter have not yet been integrated into practitioners' tool kit.
(3) Despite its perceived utility, environmental scanning/forecasting is not regarded currently as so overwhelmingly important as to necessitate a major deployment of resources.

Background Bibliography

Francis J. Aguilar, *Scanning the Business Environment*, Macmillan, New York (1967).

K. R. Andrews, *The Concept of Corporate Strategy*, Dow-Jones—Irwin, Homewood (1971).

James R. Bright, Evaluating of technical change, *Harvard Business Review*, pp. 62−70, January−February (1970).

James R. Bright and Milton E. F. Schoeman (Eds.), *A Guide to Practical Technological Forecasting*, Prentice-Hall, Englewood Cliffs, New Jersey.

Robert Hayes and Raymond Radosevich, Designing information systems for strategic decisions, *Long Range Planning*, **7** (4), 45−48 (1974).

R. W. Kashyak, Managerial information systems or corporate planning and control, *Long Range Planning*, **5** (2), 25–31, June (1972).

A. G. Kefalas, Environmental management systems (ENVMIS): A reconceptualization, *Journal of Business Review*, **3**, 253–266 (1975).

William R. King and David L. Cleland, *Strategic Planning and Policy*, New York, Nostrand Reinhold Publishing Company (1978).

William M. Lindsay and Leslie W. Rue, Impact of the business environment on the long range planning process, a contingency view, *Academy of Management Proceedings*, pp. 116–120 (1978).

H. A. Linstone and M. Turnoff (Eds.), *The Delphi Method: Technique and Applications*, Addison-Wesley (1975).

J. Alex Murray, Intelligence systems of MNCs, *Columbia Journal of World Business*, **11** (5), 63–71, October (1972).

T. H. Naylor, Integrating models into the planning process, *Long Range Planning*, **10** (6), 11–15, December (1977).

Michael Palmer and Gregory Schmid, Planning with scenarios: banking world of 1985, *Futures*, December (1976).

James E. Post and Marc J. Epstein, Information systems for social reporting, *The Academy of Management Review*, **2** (2), 81–87, January (1977).

K. J. Radford, Some initial specifications for strategic information system, *Omega*, **6** (2), 139–144 (1978).

William E. Rothschild, *Putting it all Together: A Guide to Strategic Thinking*, AMACOM (1976).

George C. Sawyer, Social issues and social change: impact on strategic decision, *MSU Business Topics*, pp. 15–20, Summer (1973).

Allan D. Shocker and S. Prakash Sethi, An approach to incorporating societal preferences in developing corporate action strategies, *California Management Review*, **XV** (4) 97–105, Summer (1973).

Philip S. Thomas, Environmental analysis for corporate planning, *Business Horizons*, pp. 27–38, October (1974).

Ian H. Wilson, Socio-political forecasting: a new dimension to strategic planning, *Michigan Business Review*, pp. 15–25, July (1974).

Trend Analysis Reports, issued by Institute of Life Insurance, 277 Park Avenue, New York, NY 10017.

26
Inflation and Management Action—A Survey

C. A. VOSS

Executive Summary

The purpose of the survey was to investigate the impact of inflation on the operation of companies and to determine what management action was being taken to overcome the problems caused by inflation. Forty-seven organisations contributed to the survey, covering a wide range of industries and size.

·A. Impact of Inflation on the Operation of Companies

Seven areas of potential impact were selected. The response of the companies surveyed is shown in Table 26.1 below.

TABLE 26.1

Impact of inflation	% of companies with GREAT IMPACT	% companies AFFECTED
Increasing UNCERTAINTY	60	94
Squeezing COSTS and PRICES	41	100
Difficulty PLANNING	37	96
Squeezing LIQUIDITY	35	76
Raising COST of FINANCE	26	74
Changes in MARKET PLACE	24	81
Difficulty MEASURING PERFORMANCE	24	80

A breakdown of the results by size of organisations showed that in every case there was a greater impact on large organisations than small organisations.

This survey was originally published by Harbridge House Europe in 1975. The author is now with the London Business School.

B. Management Action

Organisations were asked to comment on the impact of each area and to state the steps that they were taking to meet any problems. The replies indicated that firm action was being taken by most firms in the area of asset management, selling and price increases, but very little action was being taken to overcome the problems of uncertainty, measurement of performance and planning. In addition, less than half the firms surveyed were taking positive action to increase productivity.

Table 26.2 summarises the main areas where action is being undertaken and Table 26.3 summarises the main areas where relatively little action is being taken.

TABLE 26.2. *Main areas where action is being taken to meet problems of inflation*

Action	% of companies taking action
Reducing stock levels	88
Increasing prices	87
Reducing sundry debtors	75
Efforts to increase volume to spread fixed costs	69
Reviewing and reducing future capital expenditure plans	69
Reducing overhead costs	63
Reducing discretionary expenditure	62
Delaying payment of bills	62

TABLE 26.3. *Key areas where little management action is being taken to meet the problems of inflation*

Action	% of companies taking action
Reducing labour costs (increasing productivity)	37
Reducing direct costs	31
Pruning product lines	25
Preparing contingency plans	25
Using CPP inflation accounting	19
Incorporating inflation adjusted figures into cost accounts	19
Diverting production to more profitable export markets	19
Using replacement costing	13
Borrowing risk capital	12

Inflation and Management Action—A Survey

A. Introduction

The survey was carried out by Harbridge House Europe using a postal questionnaire covering a sample of forty-seven organisations in the U.K. The sample covered a wide range of industries and sizes of organisations. The objectives of the survey were:

— To investigate the impact of inflation on the operation of companies.
— To determine what management action was being taken to overcome the problems caused by inflation.

B. Survey Results

(a) Impact of inflation on the operation of companies

From prior analysis seven areas were identified where inflation impacted on the operation of companies. These are indicated in Table 26.4.

TABLE 26.4

Impact of inflation	Example of effect
1. Inflation causing increased *uncertainty*	Inflation causing increased uncertainty in forecasts of sales, costs, profits, etc.
2. Inflation squeezing *costs and prices*	Costs inflating faster than prices can react and hence squeezing profits
3. New approaches needed to *plan for inflation*	Difficulty in determining what rates of inflation to incorporate in budgets, plans, pricing and investment proposals
4. Inflation squeezing *liquidity*	Purchasing stocks at inflated prices causing strain on short-term liquidity
5. Inflation raising the *cost of finance*	Inflation making finance of all kinds more expensive
6. Inflation causing changes in the *market place*	Customers' buying behaviour changing as a direct result of inflation
7. Inflation making *measurement of performance difficult*	Inflation distorting conventional accounting figures making it difficult to measure profit in real terms

Organisations were asked to state whether any of these were affecting their operations and if the impact was great. Their responses are shown in Exhibit 1. The breakdown by size shows significant differences by size of organisations. In all areas there was a higher percentage of organisations indicating greater impact in large organisations than in small ones. Whether this is due to large organisations facing more serious problems or

Exhibit 1

Impact of inflation	All companies		Companies broken down by size					
			% of companies with great impact			% companies effected		
	% of companies with GREAT IMPACT	% companies AFFECTED	Large	Medium	Small	Large	Medium	Small
Increasing UNCERTAINTY	60	94	65	60	62	100	93	87
Squeezing COSTS and PRICES	41	100	47	54	25	100	100	100
Difficulty PLANNING	37	96	50	47	13	94	100	93
Squeezing LIQUIDITY	35	76	35	54	19	70	77	81
Raising COST of FINANCE	26	74	44	21	13	81	71	69
Changes in MARKET PLACE	24	81	35	15	19	88	85	69
Difficulty MEASURING PERFORMANCE	24	80	50	23	0	81	69	88

to small organisations failing to realise the seriousness of the situation is impossible to determine.

(b) Working parties

Organisations were asked if they had set up any special working parties or action groups to tackle specific problems caused by inflation; 35 % of the organisations in the survey had done so. There was, however, a great difference between large and other organisations.

Size of organisation	% setting up working parties
Large	65
Medium	21
Small	0
All organisations	35

(c) Management action

Organisations were asked to comment on the impact and to state the steps that they were taking to meet the problems in each area. The following section gives their responses and an overall comment area by area.

1. Inflation Increasing Uncertainty

Great impact in 60 % of organisations surveyed.
Some impact in 94 % of organisations surveyed.

(a) Typical responses

— The suspension of the expansion programme due to this uncertainty in future projections.
— We currently flex our budgets three times a year, but we never know what real level to use for the next few months.
— Political uncertainty more important than inflation.
— Impossible to forecast cash flow without knowing rate of inflation.
— Forecasting out-turns likely to be subject to increased margin of error if predicted inflation rates prove wrong.
— The main difficulty is if and when the rate of inflation forces customers to reduce or stop spending.

Some organisations saw few problems.

— No problems—demand is well known.
— Not a major problem—inflation and forecasts updated quarterly.
— We are very reluctant to accept any fixed price contracts.

(b) Management action to respond to problems

% of organisations taking action	Action (and comments)
50	—REDUCING THE TIME HORIZON OF PLANS AND REPLANNING MORE FREQUENTLY —More emphasis on frequent *ad-hoc* forecasting —Focus on short-term quarterly action plans
44	—DEVELOPING MORE CONTINGENCY PLANS
38	—AVOIDING LONG CONTRACTUAL COMMITMENTS —No long-term commitments
37	—ADOPTING LESS RISKY STRATEGIES
25	—DOING SENSITIVITY ANALYSIS
6	—SUBCONTRACTING RATHER THAN COMMITTING EXTRA RESOURCES WITHIN THE COMPANY
OTHER:	—Need for more careful budgeting and forecasting and up to date cost accounting

(c) Commentary

Uncertainty is having greater impact on organisations than any other factor, although its impact may not be as serious as, say, liquidity pressures. Many respondents found it difficult to separate uncertainty caused by inflation from uncertainty caused by the current political environment. Despite the widespread impact, little positive action is being taken by companies; for example, less than half the respondents are developing contingency plans and only a quarter are performing sensitivity analysis on their budgets. Obviously a lot must be done by the government to reduce external uncertainties, but in the meantime many companies can take more positive steps internally to cope with the present uncertainties.

2. *Inflation Squeezing Costs and Prices*

Great impact in 41% of organisations surveyed.
Some impact in 100% of organisations surveyed.

(a) Typical responses

—Fixed retail prices over which we have little control allied to control over gross margins has greatly magnified the cost price squeeze on profits.
—Reduction in profit margins.
—Increased manufacturing cost % to sales.

—Impossible to control expenditure within budgets, and to adjust prices rapidly enough to take account of increased costs.
—Some reduction in margins.
—Costs up quicker than prices, squeezing margins.
—Combination of counter-inflation legislation and customer resistance is an added factor.
—Will probably come right soon as selling prices start to rise.
—Prices more easily raised because they are expected to rise.

(b) Management action to respond to problems

% of organisations taking action	Action (and comments)
87	—INCREASING PRICES —Unavoidable —Very active with price commission
69	—EFFORTS TO INCREASE VOLUME TO SPREAD FIXED COSTS
63	—REDUCING OVERHEAD COSTS
62	—REDUCING DISCRETIONARY EXPENDITURE (of which 80% specifically stated that advertising would be cut)
50	—REDUCING MANPOWER LEVELS —Main areas being reduced are female labour indirect staff and salesmen
37	—REDUCING LABOUR COSTS (productivity increases, etc.)
31	—REDUCING DIRECT COSTS —20% increase in productivity —Value engineering —Reduction in variety of parts —Value and production engineering
31	—CUTTING DISCOUNTS
25	—PRODUCT LINE PRUNING
19	—DIVERTING PRODUCTION TO MORE PROFITABLE EXPORT MARKETS —High export percentage, home market becoming unprofitable due to productivity deduction
OTHER:	—Bringing subcontracted work in-house —Early warning system to assess effect of cost increases on prices as soon as increases are notified

(c) Commentary

The most widely felt impact was the squeezing of costs and prices causing reductions in profits. Every organisation surveyed felt this in some degree and 46 % of them seriously. Not surprisingly the main response has been raising of prices (though not always sufficiently to raise margins). This is followed by efforts to increase volume to spread fixed costs. Action to cut costs come third and it is noticeable that far more effort is being put into reducing discretionary and overhead costs than is being put into reducing direct costs and increasing productivity. In the area of discretionary costs, advertising budgets seem likely to be hit hardest. It is a little disappointing to see how few companies are taking advantage of higher prices in overseas markets. Half the organisations surveyed are making manpower reductions, but apart from female labour only one respondent was cutting direct labour.

3. New Approaches Needed to Plan for Inflation

Great impact in 37 % of organisations surveyed.
Some impact in 96 % of organisations surveyed.

(a) Typical responses

— Difficult to make plans that mean anything.
— After 1974's experience there seems to be reasonable consistency in the economists' predictions for 1975.
— Need for educating management on impact of *prolonged* inflation on their businesses. Programme now under way.
— Difficulty in determining what rates of inflation to incorporate in budgets, plans, pricing and capital investment proposals.
— Difficulty gaining consensus on approach.
— Difficult to predict trends when quoting for long-term contracts.
— Can we have a realistic approach without a genuine concordant between government, industry and commerce?
— In some areas we have been very wrong.
— No solution yet.

(b) Management action to respond to problems

% of organisations taking action	Action (and comments)
75	— INCORPORATING CENTRALISED ASSUMPTIONS ABOUT RATES OF INFLATION — All expenditure forecasts increased by 20 % — Central guidelines laid down – currently 15–20 %
38	— CONDUCT SENSITIVITY ANALYSIS On plans under different rates of inflation

(b) Management action to respond to problems (cont.)

% of organisations taking action	Action (and comments)
25	—PREPARE FORMAL CONTINGENCY PLANS For major changes in inflation
OTHER:	—Educate management on long-term effects —Adjusting financial forecasts to allow for the rate of inflation —Present pounds always used for future projections —Update budgets on a monthly basis to incorporate all known factors which affect the profit plan —Indices have always been used, they are now more difficult to forecast

(c) Commentary

The problems of planning for inflation were felt in almost all of the organisations surveyed, which is hardly surprising in the light of the uncertainties. This is a difficult area and few organisations are taking many of the steps necessary to plan properly in an inflationary environment. Developing central assumptions on future inflation rates was the only widespread action.

4. Inflation-Squeezing Liquidity

Great impact in 35% of organisations surveyed.
Some impact in 76% of organisations surveyed.

(a) Typical responses

— The most disastrous effect of inflation is that it is impossible to generate sufficient profits to counter-balance the cash out-flow for materials and labour and the hugely increasing debtor balances. For example, we made £55,000 profit last year but ended up owing the bank £90,000 more than we owed them at the beginning of the year. I do not know how to deal with this situation.
— Inflation superimposed on an ambitious expansion programme very quickly turned an "in fund" situation into a position of borrowing.
— Increase in stock depreciation. Reduction in available cash resources, reduction in interest receivable, occasional inability to take suppliers early settlement discounts.
— Cash flow slowed down.
— The overdraft rises at a frightening rate.

— Increased inventory cost. Reduced credit from suppliers.

— Absorbing cash in higher cost of stocks and work in progress.

— May worsen considerably as volume reductions cease to compensate for price increases.

— Suppliers are demanding quick settlement and customers are taking extended credit.

Some organisations are not being squeezed

— No effect due to our providing a service not a product.

— Much worse in good conditions when land prices rise (building business).

— We are capital intensive and liquidity is increased by higher revenues, but our longer-term liquidity is threatened.

(b) Management action to respond to problems

% of organisations taking action	Action (and comments)
88	— REDUCING STOCK LEVELS
75	— REDUCING SUNDRY DEBTORS — Targets related to credit terms — Pro forma invoices for orders value £25 or less — No deliveries to delinquent debtors — Main area of action
69	— REVIEWING AND REDUCING FUTURE CAPITAL EXPENDITURE PLANS — Plant and equipment purchases deferred — Cancelling joint venture — Increasing DCF criteria — General stops on capital expenditure — Expansion capital reduced — Expenditure plans reviewed and classified according to priority
62	— REDUCING VOLUME OF PURCHASES — Agressive adjustment of purchasing requirements — Ordering smaller quantities — Only purchasing exact requirements — Cut back manufacturing activities — Controlling purchase orders and rescheduling deliveries
62	— DELAYING PAYMENT OF BILLS — Maximum delay, but tactical importance of supplier taken into account — Really forced on us — Negotiating longer payment terms
31	— TRY TO INCREASE AVAILABLE SHORT-TERM CREDIT — Extremely difficult

(c) Commentary

Although less widespread than the previous problems liquidity problems when met were extremely serious. More positive action was being taken in this area than in any other in the survey. Strong efforts were being made by companies to reduce working capital with action in all areas. A high proportion (two-thirds) of organisations were delaying payment of bills. The majority of companies were also being forced to review and reduce capital expenditure plans, a trend which if maintained could have serious implications for the economy. There is evidence of companies not facing up to today's realities. Divisions of a number of large companies known to be facing liquidity problems responded that they felt no squeeze on liquidity.

5. Inflation Raising the Cost of Finance

Great impact in 26 % of organisations surveyed.
Some impact in 74 % of organisations surveyed.

(a) Typical responses

— Cost of finance is more expensive thus further eroding profits.
— None (no overdraft). This may be a problem shortly as we are expanding, but anticipate bank will cover.
— This is the real problem. I foresee that if inflation continues at the rate it did last year, we shall become bankrupt, even though our assets (the bulk of which are non-liquid) exceed our indebtedness by a ratio of 2:1.
— No overdraft yet, though obviously the cost of finance is crippling.
— Borrowing to cover liquidity shortages is very expensive; low profits cannot cover borrowing costs.
— Perhaps the most serious consequence of inflation as medium-term finance is not available on acceptable terms.
— It is especially more difficult—would you lend under conditions of uncertain inflation?

(b) Management action to respond to problems

% of organisations taking action	Action (and comments)
50	— TAKING STEPS TO INCREASE LIQUIDITY — Interest rates will remain too high for any borrowings that are related to risk operations
50	— RAISING PRICES TO REFLECT INCREASED COST OF BORROWING

(b) Management action to respond to problems (cont.)

% of organisations taking action	Action (and comments)
38	— RAISING FINANCE COST ON INTERNAL CALCULATIONS AND IN-COMPANY LENDING — Finance cost levy applied to each activity on the basis of working capital in use
12	— BORROWING MORE RISK CAPITAL — Probably not feasible — This is the major problem area as it is almost impossible to fund any substantial growth. After the bull market of the early seventies, rights issues in the foreseeable future will involve unacceptable dilution of equity: the only cure for this appears to be a reduction in the rate of corporation tax and relaxation of dividend limitation
OTHER:	— Considering restructuring long term debt to exploit situation created by fear of inflation — Adjusting asset values in published accounts permits a proper view of the level of gearing

(c) Commentary

The high cost of finance was only felt to be a serious problem in a quarter of the companies surveyed, but in these companies it elicited by far the most alarming responses. This was an area where companies found that there was little positive action they could take to mitigate the effects of expensive money other than to improve liquidity and to motivate managers to improve liquidity by raising the internal cost of funds. Until the government and economic conditions allow either suitable levels of profit to enable the borrowing of risk capital or to provide for adequate cheap short and medium-term borrowing facilities this problem is likely to become more widespread and serious. One respondent gave a long and thoughtful reply which is reproduced in Appendix 1 at the end of this survey.

6. Inflation Causing Changes in the Market-place

Great impact in 24% of organisations surveyed.
Some impact in 81% of organisations surveyed.

(a) Typical responses

— Increased awareness of prices by customers.
— Reduction in customers' inventories.

— Effect not noticeable except capital equipment demand is already way down.
— Postponements of customers' investment decisions.
— Customers buy cheaper quality.
— Volume reductions.
— No changes, but expected.
— More and more credit.
— In leisure field wage inflation is a stimulus.
— Particularly noticeable in catering.
— Essentially good for us.
— Enormous increase in price consciousness.

(b) Management action to respond to problems

% of organisations taking action	Action (and comments)
50	— INCREASED SELLING EFFORT — Concentrate on product lines with a stable market — Focus marketing effort on most productive areas in the short term
38	— DECREASED MARKETING EXPENDITURE
31	— CHANGES IN PRODUCT LINE OR MIX — Addition of cheaper qualities — Dropping certain products
19	— SPECIAL MARKET RESEARCH EFFORT — Selectively employed
OTHER:	— Need to negotiate escalation clauses and sometimes replacement cost formulas

(c) Commentary

The changes in the market place due to inflation are varied and are not all unfavourable. Many companies have found that consumer spending has been stimulated by wage inflation. The principal response to these changes has been more, and in particular, more selective selling effort but often with decreased marketing expenditure.

7. Inflation Making Measurement of Performance Difficult

Great impact in 24 % of organisations surveyed.
Some impact in 80 % of organisations surveyed.

(a) Typical responses

— Impossible to relate government's cost of living index with rate of inflation of prices of goods and materials the company buys.
— Increased work to follow accounting more closely.
— Profit in real terms can only be measured in cash flow. We make a profit on conventional accountancy lines, but our cash-flow situation deteriorates daily.
— Cash flow is now the critical measure of performance and this is not distorted by inflation—only made harder to control.
— Provision for replacement expenditure under consideration.
— Obscures causes of variances on budgets. Valuation of stock an obvious problem.
— Inflation distorting conventional accounting figures making it difficult to measure profit in real terms.

Some companies are coping:

— Not really a problem. Changes from year to year can be conventionally interpreted for inflation.
— Adequate financial tools exist.

(b) Management action to respond to problems

% of organisations taking action	Action (and comments)
	INCORPORATING INFLATION ADJUSTED FIGURES INTO:
56	— INVESTMENT PROPOSALS
44	— PRICING CALCULATIONS
19	— COST ACCOUNTS
19	SHOWING VARIANCES SPECIFICALLY DUE TO INFLATION
19	PRESENTING CPP ADJUSTED SUPPLEMENTARY ACCOUNTS
13	USING REPLACEMENT COST INFLATION ACCOUNTING
	— We account internally and externally using replacement cost principles
6	USING CPP INFLATION ACCOUNTING ONLY INTERNALLY

(c) Commentary

Although not always serious, difficulty in measuring performance in an inflationary environment is a very widespread problem. Many companies are finding cash flow a better and more valid measure of performance than historical profit and cost accounts. With the exception of investment proposals few companies are using any measure of performance adjusted for inflation. Less than half the companies surveyed used inflation-adjusted figures in pricing calculations and less than one-fifth used them in cost accounts. Very few companies are using techniques such as inflation accounting, replacement costing and indexing. There seems to be considerable scope for improvement.

8. General Comments by Respondents

— Making new investments at greatly inflated costs difficult to justify at today's price levels.
— The main problem is earning sufficient on existing capital to provide for their replacement.
— Difficult to maintain differentials between management and labour.
— Profit margins must be higher to finance inflated working capital.

Appendix 1 Detailed Response on Problems of Raising Finance

1. It is not suggested that the following points add anything to what is known already, but they do set out the reasons why it is difficult to undertake new investment in the present U.K. financial situation, despite the fact that expenditure now might well prove to be a first class investment in five years time.

2. U.K. Government actions over the past years have been intervention in economic development rather than involvement. This latter does not mean nationalisation but implies the adoption of term policies which take as many factors as possible into account and strives to avoid *non-sequita*. The result of this intervention is that industry at large is now faced with price controls, high taxation, and the generally uneconomic use of labour (the responsibility of both employers and unions) which make it virtually impossible to generate adequate cash flows in the face of a high rate of inflation. The immediate effect of this, coupled with dividend restriction, is that insufficient return can be offered on risk capital. Inevitably this has led to a seriously depressed equity market which in turn makes it impossible to obtain new risk capital through the market without unacceptable dilution of existing equity.

3. If a business cannot get new finance through equity participation, the only alternative is through borrowing but here there is a different series of very real problems.

   (a) First, the lenders themselves are in difficulty because their own deposits are mainly short term. It is right that the conventional banking practice of a balanced portfolio should prevail unless government is prepared to underwrite the risk of imbalance between short- and long-term funds. No prudent person would recommend an open-ended type of arrangement but it is suggested that only with government support can the handling and recycling of oil money be effective. And it is the distortion which this money has caused which is one of the main problems of the present difficulties.

(b) Second, and again for a mixture of reasons, it remains possible in any period of high inflation to obtain a high yield in "safe" areas. Admittedly such yields are unlikely to discount the effect of inflation but as much of such lending is short term there is a retained flexibility.

(c) Third, the lenders have to view industrial investment as a risk even with adequate security and this dictates a high interest rate. While much lip service is given to planning new industrial investment only when a return of 20 % is assured, in the event this can usually only be the target and few genuinely competitive industries reach this in the initial stages. It may be achievable in the fullness of time, and certainly possible in the future on historic cost if inflation continues at more than a modest rate. But, looking at it from the borrower's point of view, and knowing that the control of inflation is both a prime objective and desirable, currently quoted interest rates cannot be easily justified. Geared rates may be an option but these leave the borrower in the same position: index-linked rates suffer from the same disadvantages unless the opening rate is much discounted from current levels. Summarising, the only hope for the future which a borrower can see if he accepts today's rates is that inflation will continue, and, the greater this is, the more certainty there would be in satisfactorily meeting the commitment.

(d) Fourth, despite the problems of interest rates, there are very few lenders willing to discuss medium- to long-term funding, and in some areas there is no willingness at all.

4. The overall result is that a company cannot raise new money by equity issued, which is the proper source of risk capital, and has virtually no access to medium/long-term borrowings. Over and above this, there is a very real need to preserve a reasonable gearing of capital employed as otherwise the shareholders are in danger of remaining in an inferior position indefinitely. It is argued that only a centrally conceived and supported strategy can break this impasse.

27
Computer Models for
Corporate Planning

P. H. GRINYER AND J. WOOLLER

There are a priori reasons for expecting use of corporate planning to be associated with development of new quantitative tools for evaluation of alternatives explored. Staffs are appointed with responsibility for proper evaluation. In addition, systematic decision making processes focus attention on selection between alternatives.[1-3]

It is not surprising, therefore, that available evidence suggests a close link between development of corporate models and corporate planning, particularly since such models are evaluative tools designed specifically for use in corporate decision taking. In his study of 323 companies in the U.S.A. in 1968, almost 20 per cent of which had or were constructing corporate models, Gershefski[4] found that development of corporate models in companies tended to follow introduction of corporate planning by about 4 years. Grinyer and Batt,[5] in their analysis of experience within three companies, suggested that a major problem is availability of data for input to corporate models and that this tends to be less acute where there is a well established corporate planning process. In a study of 65 U.K. companies with corporate models,[6,7] to be reported more fully later, we found that the proposal to develop a corporate model had been initiated by the corporate planner in 23 per cent of cases and by a director in 35 per cent. Many of the directors who sponsored the exercise had ultimate responsibility for some aspect of corporate planning in their companies. Evidence presented later on the range of applications and the types of planning for which they are used suggests strongly that, in the U.K., corporate models were usually conceived and employed as part of a regular planning exercise.

Recent research has suggested a rapid growth of corporate planning in the U.K. since 1970; whilst research[8-10] in the late 1960s showed that

This article was originally published in *Long Range Planning*, Volume 8, No. 1, February 1975.

Peter Grinyer and Jeff Wooller were at the City University, Graduate Business Centre. (Prof. Grinyer is now at the University of St. Andrews.)

formal planning at corporate level was not widespread, recent work indicates the contrary.[11, 12] Consequently, we would expect a rapid growth of corporate modelling in the U.K.

In the first survey of corporate modelling in the U.K. Neild found in 1972 that 28 companies were developing models, although not all of these satisfy our own more restrictive definition. We ourselves found that in 1973, in a random survey of 100 of the "Times 1000", 9 per cent of the largest U.K. companies had or were developing corporate models.[6, 7] In a second survey we obtained details from 65 U.K. companies with corporate models.[7] These companies were in widely different industries, as may be seen from Table 27.1, and some had started to develop corporate models as early as 1963. However, as Fig. 27.1 shows, the annual rate at which corporate modelling was started did not quicken much until 1970.

TABLE 27.1. *Classification of Modellers included in the survey*

Industry	No. of companies
Banking and Finance	3
Beers, Spirits and Tobacco	2
Building and Construction	5
Chemicals	8
Cinemas, Theatres and TV	2
Coal, Nuclear Energy and Steel	3
Computer Bureaux	2
Electrical and Radio	4
Engineering and Metal	9
Food, Catering, etc.	6
Insurance	3
Motor	4
Newspapers, publishers	2
Oils	4
Paper and Printing	3
Transport	5
Total = 65	

Corporate models are, then, widely used already and the pace of introduction continues to be rapid. It is important that corporate management should recognize what corporate models are, how they may be acquired, how they are used, what they cost, and the payback that may be expected from investment in them. These issues are addressed in following sections in which some of the salient points to emerge from our survey of 65 U.K. companies[7] will be presented. All figures quoted refer to this sample of companies unless otherwise mentioned.

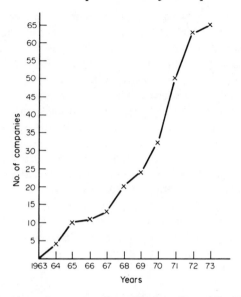

FIG. 27.1. *Cumulative chart on year of start. The figure for 1973 should not be taken as suggesting a fall in the rate of development, since this is the year in which the survey was conducted and only two companies has models which were sufficiently developed to be included.*

What Corporate Models Are

Corporate models have already been introduced as quantitative tools to aid evaluation of corporate alternatives. Like all models they are representations of reality. Ordinance survey maps, architects models, engineers' formulae and the entire accounting system are all models. For instance, accounting conventions represent flows of physical resources in purely monetary terms. Their value lies in the fact that they permit us to understand, plan and control financial aspects of these operations better.

Similarly, corporate models are sets of conventional, logical and mathematical expressions that represent the key operations of the company, and in virtually all cases include the items entering the normal profit and loss account and balance sheet. Whilst these models could be operated with pencil and paper in most cases, this would be slow and tedious, and they are normally programmed for use on a computer. Indeed, much of their value lies in the fact that the speed and storage capacity of the computer have been harnessed.

Most corporate models contain familiar, accounting routines, for instance for calculating depreciation and producing profit and loss accounts and balance sheets. Indeed, many models are purely financial and some are largely computerized versions of existing manual, accounting routines, as at the Anglia Building Society and the London Transport Executive (one of the largest models we encountered). Even where corporate models incorporate relationships based on statistical analysis, as in the case of the ill-fated Sun Oil model[15, 16] or the Van den Bergh and Jurgen's model,[17] they tend to produce the main financial reports among their output. Profit and loss accounts and balance sheets are conventional, and legally required, bases for judging corporate performance. Boards of companies are, therefore, interested in prospective performance as measured in terms of the main items of these reports and resulting financial ratios.

Early models, particularly in the U.S.A. tended to extend down the organizational structure to embrace physical operations, too. Boulden and Buffa[18] give some good examples. In the U.K. the Van den Berghs and Jurgens model,[17] one of those of the British Steel Corporation[19] and the large linear programming model of British Petroleum[20] probably come nearest to this approach. For instance, the Van den Bergh and Jurgen's model can be used for optimizing the mix of materials for various grades of margarine, yet can also produce profit and loss accounts. Such all embracing models are not typical of those developed in the U.K. though. Eighty per cent of companies had adopted a modular approach in which different models are developed for different purposes. At Unilever, for instance, there has been a movement towards development of simple financial models of the company as a whole and quite separate ones of its production and marketing activities.[21]

Although separate, models may be interlinked, normally via use of intermediate files of data (on disc). Output from one model is placed on file and then used as input to another. Forty-six per cent of companies with at least two models were able to interlink at least some of their models in this way. This permitted the companies to gain many of the advantages of large fully integrated models whilst retaining those of separate models. For instance, individual, separate models in the suite are available for use earlier, are easier to program, and consequently cost less. They can also be updated more easily and are more intelligible to top management.

Activities below corporate level are represented in most corporate suites (of one or more models). For instance, 70 per cent of companies had models of divisional operations and 43 per cent had modelled the activities of their operating units, too. Fuller details are given in Table 27.2 which also shows the nature of the relationships represented within the corporate suites. Whilst all suites had models representing accounting relationships, and hence financial flows, 57 per cent also had at least one model in which physical operations of the company were represented. The figures for divisional and operating unit levels suggests that a higher proportion of models representing activities of companies at these levels mapped physical

TABLE 27.2. *Levels to Which Corporate Models Extend in the 65 Survey Companies*

Level	Percentage of companies	
	Physical flows represented	Financial flows represented
Corporate level	57	100
Subsidiary level	51	83
Divisional level	45	71
Operating unit level	31	43

flows. For instance, 71 per cent of companies with models of operating units had represented physical as well as financial flows.

Experience in the companies suggested, though, that with some major exceptions top management use mainly financial models. Tactical decisions on plant shutdowns, material mix, and so on are separable from strategic ones, and moreover use information that is largely irrelevant to strategy. Perhaps for this reason, many of the modellers said that, if they were to start again from scratch, they would build, in the first instance, more simple, financial models for use purely at corporate level.

Experience also suggested that use of simulation is preferable to that of optimization in corporate models. Simulation models merely show the result that will be obtained in the event of certain conditions obtaining. They are passive; they don't give management the best answer; they merely aid the decision taker to explore the possibilities. The decision taker decides what alternatives to test and which would yield the best results. In contrast, optimization models use mathematical routines like linear and integer programming to give the solution which is "best" given the accuracy of the input data and the validity of the model.

Ninety-eight per cent of the companies had simulation but only 22 per cent had optimization models. Thus only one company (2 per cent) relied exclusively on an optimization model. With the notable exception of the oil companies, users were not generally happy with their optimization models, and made fuller use of their simulation models. Quite apart from difficulties of specifying strategic objectives precisely, which all corporate planners will recognize, optimizing models suffer from two additional drawbacks in strategic planning applications. Senior management in most companies finds it difficult to understand them and is, consequently, rightly loathe to accept their output. There is, too, some question about the value of reaching an optimum solution on the basis of estimates which, because they relate to future periods which may sometimes be distant, have high inherent errors.

Ninety-seven per cent of the companies had deterministic simulation models. Deterministic models assume that the figures input to them are known with certainty; consequently each factor is represented on a model run by a single figure. This is, of course, just the way that accountants and managers normally calculate, and often use little more than basic arithmetic. By contrast, probabilistic models use mathematical functions to generate input in such a way that the relative frequencies with which values occur reflect those with which they are expected to occur in real life, and by repeated operation of the model a profile showing the probability with which each outcome may be expected can be obtained. Such probabilistic models give much more information to the decision taken, but are more difficult for him to understand, and cost more to develop and run.

For these reasons, only one company used a probabilistic simulation model solely; although a further 15 (23 per cent) had both deterministic and probabilistic corporate models. However, only one of this 15 used its probabilistic model for more than half of all model runs, the others preferring their deterministic models. Indeed, 13 of the 15 used their probabilistic models for 10 per cent or less of all runs. In three of the companies the probabilistic models were available but not in use. Quite a lot of the modellers spoke of early, abortive efforts with probabilistic models, before they switched to deterministic ones.

Overall, therefore, a picture emerges which should hearten corporate management without a strong mathematical bent. As used in the U.K. in 1973, and especially at the corporate level, corporate models tend to be mathematically simple, they use accounting routines, are deterministic, and simulate rather than optimize. Most of them use little more than basic arithmetic with which all managers should be completely at home. An example of the logic of a very simple model of this kind is shown in Fig. 27.2.

How Companies Obtained Their Corporate Models

Corporate models can be acquired in two main ways. A company may obtain a model "ready-made" or it may have one developed specifically for it. For convenience we will call the latter "tailor-made" models.

Ready-made models are suites of computer programs which may be bought or rented. Their main characteristic is that they require absolutely no programming by the user. Because most can be used via computer terminals, the user requires no prior knowledge of computing whatsoever to make use of a ready-made model.

Some of the suites have cost a great deal to develop, one of the most expensive being reputed to have cost £160,000, and this development cost can be spread between a number of users. Again, they are available almost

Section (a) Accounting Data and Logic (in £000s)

Sales for 1974	=	2000
Sales	=	Sales for 1974 × Growth Factor of 10%
Materials	=	Sales × 30%
Wages	=	Sales × 20%
Other Charges	=	200 + (Sales × 5%)
Depreciation	=	100
Loan Interest	=	10
Net Profit Before Tax	=	Sales − Expenses
Tax	=	Net Profit × 50%
Net Profit After Tax	=	Net Profit − Tax

Section (b) Computer Print Out of Results

Forecast Profit and Loss Accounts
Date 4-DC-73   Time 17:04

	1975	1976	1977	1978	1979
Sales	2200	2420	2662	2928	3221
Materials	660	726	799	878	966
Wages	440	484	532	586	644
Other Chgs.	310	321	333	346	361
Depreciation	100	100	100	100	100
Loan Int.	10	10	10	10	10
P/Tax Profit	680	779	888	1008	1139
Tax	340	390	444	504	570
A/Tax Profit	340	390	444	504	570

FIG. 27.2. *Examples of the logic of a simple corporate financial model.*

immediately, which can be a considerable asset if, say, a takeover battle is looming.

Their very strengths contain the seeds of their weaknesses, though. Because they are designed for all and sundry, they normally contain only the most general accounting routines, and are inappropriate if the companies financial structure or accounting rules vary much from the possibly somewhat arbitrary structure built into the model. However, in many cases the owner of the model will make appropriate changes to it if paid an appropriate fee for doing so, but the user may find that he is the prisoner of the owner in this respect. This problem has been overcome to a large extent in one of the most sophisticated ready-made models, which already has over 60 users, by incorporating a large number of alternative routines for, say, depreciation. On installation of the system, the owner's consultants study the accounting procedures of the client, and choose the most appropriate combination of routines. By feeding "control data" to the computer at the start of each computer run this combination is selected for use by the client. What this amounts to is that the ready-made model is being made to approximate more closely to a tailor-made one.

For the same reasons that flexibility of logic is more restricted in ready-made models, that of content and format of both input and output is too. Consequently, with many ready-made models data not normally collected at corporate level may be required, and output reports will be in an unfamiliar sequence and format. Sometimes these restrictions may not matter. Moreover a few of the more sophisticated ready-made models do allow a degree of flexibility in these respects, in one a high degree. Nonetheless, inflexibility is an important deterrent. Only two of the 65 companies had elected to acquire a ready-made model. One of these also had a tailor-made model; the ready-made model was used for a specific purpose whilst the more flexible, tailor-made one was used more generally. When the remaining 63 were asked to distribute 100 points between reasons for not using ready-made models 21, 12 and 14 points respectively were given, on average, to each of inflexibility of logic, input and output. So almost half of the total points were attributed to inflexibility (see Table 27.3).

Thus 98 per cent of the companies chose to build tailor-made models which more faithfully mapped their own company's logic. In all, 93 tailor-made models were developed within the 64 companies, and of these, 12 per cent were built entirely by consultants, 18 per cent by consultants and the firms own staff jointly, and 70 per cent entirely by the companies' own staff. Most companies avoided use of consultants on the grounds that their charges "were extortionate". However, all but one of the companies which had used them thought that the consultants had given reasonable value for money.

Companies using their own staff gave the modelling, in many cases, to their data processing and operational research specialists. Table 27.4 shows that 34 per cent of all corporate model builders were operational researchers, mathematicians, or statisticians. A further 16 per cent were from data processing departments. The fascinating feature of the data we collected on backgrounds of model builders in the 65 companies was, though, the high number of accountants (17 per cent), planners (6 per cent) and other non-data processing specialists who had turned their hands to developing corporate models. At the London Transport Executive a large corporate model for financial planning had been built entirely by accountants. The same was true of Lansing Bagnall. At Yorkshire Imperial Plastics the Finance Director had built his own initial models, without previous experience of modelling. We noticed a strong trend towards construction of models by potential users which was associated with the increased availability of special computer packages, called modelling systems, from the computer bureaux.

TABLE 27.3. *Aspects Deterring Modellers from use of Bureaux Packages*

	Ready-made model	Modelling system
Inflexibility of		
(i) Logic	21	9
(ii) Inputs	12	3
(iii) Outputs	14	4
	47	16
Costs	10	21
No knowledge of suitable model	8	9
Size restriction	7	8
Not available when job started	5	4
Appropriate models not on market	4	4
Not considered	3	9
Model intended as research tool	3	7
Insecurity of data	3	4
Contrary to company policy	2	4
Discontinuity of service	2	3
Difficulties of data transfer	2	2
Extra time learning system	2	2
Advantages not so great as to outweigh		
Time spent on package evaluation	2	0
Presence of own programmers	0	7
Experienced in a general purpose		
Language		
Total	100%	100%

TABLE 27.4. *Functional Backgrounds of Model Builders*

Type	Frequency	Percentage
Operational Researchers	78	30
Accountants	44	17
Data Processors	42	16
Analysts	23	9
Planners	19	7
Actuaries (insurance companies)	11	4
Mathematicians/Statisticians	10	4
Economists	8	3
Others	27	10
Total	262	100

During the 1960s, until ICL developed PROSPER, the only way to develop a tailor-made model was to produce the logic and then program it in a general purpose language. Seventy-five per cent of the companies had models of this kind. Most of them used a widely known language called FORTRAN.

During the late 1960s and early 1970s a trickle then stream of special programs to aid corporate modelling became available in the U.K. In 1971 and 1972 there was a marked increase in the number available. These packages have been sold aggressively by computer bureaux and seem now to be increasingly replacing the more traditional modelling approach. A full analysis of available modelling systems is available elsewhere, Grinyer and Wooller,[7, 22, 23] but some of their most important features may be summarized. The modelling systems provide special programming languages to facilitate computer programming. These are called "high level planning languages" because they are directed specifically at planning applications and use terms which are close to everyday English. They can be learnt in a few days by most managers and hence provide an entry to modelling for those without prior experience of programming. Moreover, they have special routines for handling input, files, and output. This can be a considerable advantage. Production of such routines using, say, FORTRAN can call for experience and skill on the part of the programmer. In addition, most modelling systems provide routines for calculating net present value, for consolidation and for forecasting.

As a result, the time taken to program a model using a modelling system may be as low as 1/5th of that required with FORTRAN, and programming can be done by non-specialists. Moreover, once constructed, models may be modified more easily because of the easier programming, and the costs of model updating are reduced.

A number of disadvantages may be set against these advantages. Operating costs may be higher because a computer bureau must normally be used to run the model and/or a royalty must be paid. In addition, to some extent the company becomes a hostage of the bureau it has selected. At one time there were fears, too, about security of confidential data, but these have now been largely relieved by information about checks on access to files held by bureaux.

The attractions of modelling systems appear to have been strong enough, though, to outweigh these disadvantages for 54 per cent of the companies. These had used modelling systems. Moreover, data collected suggested a clear trend towards greater relative use of modelling systems as opposed to languages like FORTRAN.

Table 27.5 summarizes the general approach to getting a corporate model taken by the 65 companies. The greater weight apparently given to general purpose language models reflects in large measure the fact that

TABLE 27.5. *Category of Corporate Model*

Category of model	No. of companies with ready-made model	No. of companies with different types of tailor-made models			
Approach to acquisition	No. of companies with ready-made model	General purpose language	Modelling system	Optimization code	Total
Bought-in	2	—	—	—	2
Built by own staff only	—	37	24	4	65
Built by consultants only	—	6	2	3	11
Built by own staff and consultants	—	6	9	2	17
Total	2	49	35	9	95

many were built before modelling systems became widely available. The number of models shown in Table 27.5 exceeds the number of companies in the sample because some companies had models in more than one category. The extent to which companies had used more than one approach is Illustrated in Fig. 27.3.

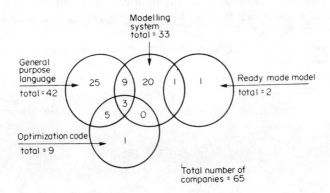

FIG. 27.3. *Category of corporate models.*

Our survey findings lead us to believe that by 1976, if not before, most companies building corporate models for the first time will do so with their own staff, selected on the basis of their knowledge of the accounting routines or operations of the company rather than of data processing, and will use modelling systems.

How Corporate Models Are Used

A link between corporate planning and the advent of corporate models has already been suggested. This would lead us to expect that corporate models would be found to be used in the regular planning process. As may be seen from Table 27.6, they were indeed used this way in 90 per cent of the companies, and in 46 per cent of these were also used as an aid to *ad hoc* strategic decisions. Since corporate models were used only for the latter in 8 per cent of companies, they were used for *ad hoc* decisions in 54 per cent.

TABLE 27.6. *Type of Planning in Which Models are Used*

	No. of companies	Percentage
(a) As *ad hoc* devices (e.g. for merger proposals) only	5	8
(b) In regular corporate and divisional planning only	29	44
(c) Both (a) and (b)	30	46
(d) As a research tool	1	2
Total	65	100

In line with these findings, we found that most models were said to be used by planners or accountants, who in quite a lot of the companies were responsible for financial aspects of corporate planning. Table 27.7 shows that this was true of 63 per cent of the companies. Where operational researchers or computer specialist used the model, they normally processed results for planners, accountants and senior management. Moreover, in such cases the models were often optimization or probabilistic, and called for specialist knowledge. Where planners or accountants had built their own models with modelling systems they were invariably the users.

TABLE 27.7. *Model Users*

	No. of companies	Percentage
Planners	21	32
Accountants	20	31
Operational researchers	9	14
Actuaries	2	3
Computer specialists	4	6
Others	9	14
Total	65	100

As corporate models were used by planners and accountants themselves in a high proportion of the companies to aid regular planning it is scarcely surprising that many of them are used as a matter of course within the planning process. Thus in 60 per cent of the companies, the corporate models were said by respondents to be fully integrated into the planning process. Indeed, in 6 per cent they were so central to the planning process that they were said to constitute the planning system. Table 27.8 shows that models were only partly integrated, that is used sometimes but not as a matter of course, or rarely used (not-integrated) in the planning system in only 22 and 18 per cent respectively of the companies. Reasons for this failure to make routine use of the models varied. In $7\frac{1}{2}$ per cent of companies it was intended to integrate the corporate model into the planning system but the model was still regarded as experimental. In another $7\frac{1}{2}$ per cent, management involved in planning seemed to be unwilling to use the model, and in yet another 3 per cent of companies the models were designed as *ad hoc* devices never intended for regular use in planning.

TABLE 27.8. *How Well the Models were Integrated into the Planning System*

	No. of companies	Percentage
Models constituted planning system	4	6
Fully integrated	35	54
Partly integrated	14	22
Not integrated	12	18
Total	65	100

Nonetheless, even allowing for the possible bias towards reporting success, the data collected suggest that, on the whole, companies with corporate models use them as standard planning tools.

Specific uses to which the corporate models were put in the 65 companies are given by Tables 27.9 and 27.10. Table 27.9 shows what the corporate models were designed to do and Table 27.10 the outputs they produced. From both it is apparent that financial planning and cash flow analysis are the most important uses but that marketing and production applications are widespread, too. Use in production decisions is consistent, of course, with the high number of corporate suites with models of physical flows (see Table 27.2). As may be seen from Table 27.10, these applications are almost as frequent at the divisional level as at the corporate one, and indeed in practice the reports used at corporate level are often based directly on inputs at the lower organizational level (at which the detailed

TABLE 27.9. *Major Uses of Models*

Application	No. of companies	Percentage of companies
Financial planning (up to 1 year)	25	38
Financial planning (1 to 5 years)	51	78
Financial planning (over 5 years)	29	45
Cash flow analysis	49	75
Aid marketing decisions	42	65
Air production decisions	39	60
Project evaluation	29	45
Aid distribution decisions	25	38
Financing	9	14
New venture evaluation	9	14
Acquisition studies	8	12
Manpower	8	12
Aid purchasing decisions	7	11
Market share forecasting	5	8
Computer evaluation (purchase or rent)	3	5

TABLE 27.10. *Output Reports Produced by Models*

Report	Total company	Subsidiaries	Divisions	Operating units
Profit and loss	64	28	26	14
Balance sheet	51	24	16	8
Cash flow	50	24	18	10
Financial ratio analysis	44	20	15	12
Source and use of funds statement	36	18	13	7
Marketing operations	22	16	20	15
Project evaluation	22	16	8	10
Production	22	14	18	14
Distribution	19	11	13	11
Purchasing	7	5	5	4
Manpower	6	4	6	4
Financing	5	1	1	1
New venture	2	1	2	1

information on marketing and production exists). Corporate models are also used frequently for project evaluation, new venture evaluation, and the like at both corporate and lower levels.

Tables 27.9 and 27.10 provide no support for one of the early beliefs about corporate models. When they were relatively new in the U.K. in the late 1960s, it was often thought that they would be useful as an aid to financing decisions. It is now clear that they are rarely designed to facilitate these in particular. They involve use of a set of experience—based rules of thumb and judgment on likely trends in the stock market, which tend to make the use of a corporate model somewhat irrelevant. Moreover, most companies do not consider acquisitions frequently enough to warrant design of a corporate model specifically for this purpose, though it was a consideration in 12 per cent of the companies. Nonetheless, most of the corporate financial models could certainly be used for this purpose, and the low number of specific references to acquisitions recorded in Tables 27.9 and 27.10 should not mislead the reader in this respect.

A generally encouraging picture of use of corporate models emerges from our survey, then. Most companies with corporate models used them in regular planning. In almost half they aided *ad hoc* decisions, too. Moreover, they were used in the planning process as a matter of course in a majority of the companies. They were applied by staff like planners and accountants, rather than by operational researchers or mathematicians, to a variety of problems at different organizational levels.

Costs

Management considering acquiring a corporate model will be interested in costs as well as uses. Costs of corporate models fall into two main categories; those of developing the model and those of using it. Major difficulties are involved in accurately calculating figures for each; these are fully explored by us elsewhere.[7] Nonetheless, we have made as objective an estimate as possible of costs for each of the companies for which data were collected, and are confident that the resulting figures will provide at least rough guides.

For a variety of reasons, most of our emphasis during the survey was on costs of developing corporate models, which means building tailor-made models with modelling systems or using general purpose programming languages like FORTRAN. It will be recollected that only two of the companies in the 65 had ready-made models and so we obtained little information of interest in this respect. However, our analysis of modelling systems and ready-made models available from the bureaux[22,23] gives further information on this point. When analysed late in 1973 we found that the most sophisticated ready-made model involved an annual support cost of £500 to £1000. An initial fee to access the system of between £100 and £2000 was also charged. Detailed terms are, though, best obtained direct from bureaux concerned.

Costs of producing tailor-made models ranged, among the 64 companies with them, from a few hundred pounds to over £200,000. Five of the companies had incurred costs of over £50,000 before they had produced a first model capable of producing useful results. A further three found that their costs had escalated to this level before their present model was obtained. These figures are far from typical, though. When the extreme values are excluded, as distorting the results, the average costs for developing the first working model were £3952 and those for the present model were £6591. The way in which these were distributed between different cost categories are shown in Table 27.11.

TABLE 27.11. *Total Development Costs of the Average Corporate Model*

	First working model		Present model	
	£	%	£	%
Feasibility study	1000	25	1400	21
Programming	1100	28	1800	27
Implementation	500	13	1100	17
Manpower costs	2600	66	4300	65
Consultancy costs	471	12	622	10
Computer costs	881	22	1669	25
Total	3952	100%	6591	100%

A more detailed analysis may be found in our chapter on costs in Ref. 7. We show there that the cost of developing a corporate model is related to a number of factors. Most important of these are the size of the model and the approach to programming. Not surprisingly, the larger the model, the more it tends to cost (though the detailed relationship is not quite so simple). Again, for any given size, it is likely to be much cheaper to develop a model with a modelling system than with a general purpose language like FORTRAN.

However, savings in development costs by using a modelling system may be eroded quickly by higher operating costs in some cases. Nineteen companies told us how much it cost them annually to use a modelling systems accessed via terminals (which are rather like typewriters connected to the computer by means of GPO lines). These costs ranged from £100 to £13,500 with a mean of £2400. Obviously, the precise point at which a company's bill lies within the range depends on a variety of factors like the frequency with which it uses its corporate suite, the size of the models, the way in which they are used (thinking time at the terminal is expensive), and the bureau used. It is fair to report, though, that there was a clustering of costs around the mean.

However, not all modelling systems are used via a computer terminal, some like PROSPER being available either for use in batch mode on an in-house ICL computer or in conversational mode on the bureau computer, at the client's convenience. For instance, both the London Transport Executive and Mambre and Garton have models developed with modelling systems run on their own computer. The modelling system models should, in these cases, share the lower operating costs normally thought to be associated with batch run general purpose language models. The assumption is that the company saves the additional costs incurred by use of an external bureau. Unfortunately, we were unable to collect objective evidence on this score, although details of the basis on which charges were allocated to jobs were available in many companies. The true cost of using the in-house computer for the corporate model is the resulting increment in total costs of the company. Where there is idle capacity on the computer, this may amount to little more than the cost of paper and electricity consumed, but where other work is made to queue the cost of disruption may be high.

Costs given above for developing and using corporate models may seem relatively high. However, the cost of staff employed in planning, who are liberated by the models from the drudgery of routine calculations, is also considerable. Moreover, if the models really do what is claimed for them by many of their advocates, and allow a much wider, fuller exploration of alternatives, the ultimate pay off can be very great.

Pay Off

No matter what the potential uses or costs of a corporate model, and its apparent attractions, the key question of interest to corporate management and model builders alike is whether the exercise is worthwhile. Ideally, one would like to measure benefits, and compare these with costs. This is impossible. It is out of the question to determine to what extent precisely output from a model contributes to a decision. Moreover, even if we could, it would rarely help much. Strategic decisions are, singly, only points in a continuum of decisions, and who can say how much each contributed to the final outcome.

Consequently, to gain some indication of the extent of success or failure, subjective views were sought on a number of proxy measures of success. We have already dealt with one of these, the extent to which corporate models had become integrated into the planning process, and found that the results were, on the whole, encouraging.

The second proxy measure was the extent to which respondents thought the models had contributed to improved forecasts. This measure was used because of the heavy emphasis placed on this aspect by a number of computer bureaux selling modelling systems. Table 27.12 summarizes the answers. Fifty-five per cent of the companies thought that forecasts had improved significantly or very significantly because of their corporate

TABLE 27.12. *How Much Modellers Consider Use of Models has Improved Forecasts*

	No. of companies	Percentage
Very significantly	6	9
Significantly	30	46
Not very much	16	25
Not at all	6	9
Too early to comment	5	8
No reply	2	3
Total	65	100

models. The main reasons advanced for this were increased accuracy and reduction in time taken to prepare the forecasts. For instance, at London Transport Executive we were told that because the previous manual system took 5 days to prepare a set of forecasts, compared with a few hours with the model, it was expensive and slow to make even minor amendments. Others found that in practice the computer model often reveals inconsistencies in planning assumptions that would not have been revealed by the manual process.

Thirty-two per cent of the answers were non-committal. Only 9 per cent thought that there had been definitely no improvement; in all of these companies difficulties had been encountered in gaining management acceptance.

This difficulty is reflected in the third proxy measure, top management reaction to use of the corporate model, see Table 27.13. Exactly the same number of companies reported a favourable or very favourable attitude on the part of top management as recorded an improvement in forecasts. The number of non-committal responses was, again, about the same, as was the

TABLE 27.13. *Top Management Reaction to Use of Corporate Models*

	No. of companies	Percentage
Very favourable	11	17
Favourable	25	38
Unfavourable	7	11
Undecided	20	31
Other	2	3
Total	65	100

number who registered failure (an unfavourable reaction). Many of the companies which refused to commit themselves had only fairly recently started corporate modelling.

Respondents were asked a related, but different, question about the reliance top management placed on output from the corporate models when making decisions. They were asked to distribute 100 points between computer reports, manual reports, and intuitive judgment in such a way as to indicate the relative importance of each. Table 27.14 shows the results. As expected, the dominant factor in strategic decisions was seen to be intuitive judgment, but on average an equal weight was placed on computer and manual reports. Extreme 2 was due to computer reports being converted manually into typewritten ones before presentation to the board. Extremes 4 and 5 are each, in their different ways, alarming. The former suggests an uncritical acceptance of the computer printout and the latter an excessive propensity to "fly by the seat of the pants".

TABLE 27.14. *Reliance Modellers Perceive Top Management Place on Reports*

	Computer reports percentage	Manual reports percentage	Intuitive judgment percentage	Total percentage
Average	29	28	43	100
Extreme 1	50	50	0	100
Extreme 2	0	50	50	100
Extreme 3	50	0	50	100
Extreme 4	100	0	0	100
Extreme 5	0	0	100	100

Finally, respondents were asked whether their top management thought the modelling exercise a success in terms of benefits derived given the costs. Their answers are recorded in Table 27.15. Again, whilst 55 per cent

TABLE 27.15. *Modeller' Views on Top Management's Assessment of Modelling Exercise (in Terms of Cost/Benefits)*

	No. of companies	Percentage
Successful	36	55
Partly successful	12	18
Not successful	5	8
Too early	9	14
No reply	1	2
Other	2	3
Total	65	100

answered that the board thought the exercise a success, only 8 per cent replied that top management thought it a failure. Clearly, in 18 per cent of the companies the board was thought to regard the corporate model with mixed feelings.

The general picture to emerge from the different proxy measures is both consistent and heartening. Over 50 per cent of the companies using corporate models thought them successful but only 12 per cent regarded them as failures. In the latter cases this was largely because modellers had failed to either gain or retain management involvement and support. A large number of the remaining companies had still to make up their minds on the issue. One should, though, exercise a little caution in interpreting the significance of these results. Whilst we were impressed by the frankness of replies during interviews, the answers are in all cases subjective, and any bias is likely to be in the direction of success. Those interviewed were modellers and might find it difficult to admit failure even to themselves. Consequently, we suspect that some of those who gave non-committal answers, suggesting partial success, for instance, might be better classed as failures.

Concluding Points

Even when this is taken into account an overall picture of success emerges. However, management is well advised to take a balanced view on corporate models. They can make a considerable contribution by allowing rapid calculation of the results of alternatives open to management. However, they are only able to evaluate quantitative aspects, and imponderables may dominate some strategic decisions. Moreover, the estimates input to them have been produced by a human process, explored by Bower[24] for major capital investment decisions, which can create considerable bias. Indeed, as Hall[25] has rightly pointed out, strategic decisions are the result of a political process, in which the corporate model may be used as little more than a device for rationalization. It may be argued, though, that provision of a generally available evaluative tool which draws on a common set of planning assumptions should do much within this political process to clarify issues as well as showing quantitative implications of available alternatives. It can never be a substitute for the political process but it can, by providing a further discipline within it, make it more effective.

References

1. H. Igor Ansoff, *Corporate Strategy*, McGraw Hill (1965).
2. F. G. Gilmore and R. G. Brandenburg, Anatomy of corporate planning, *Harvard Business Review*, **40** (6), (1962).

3. Peter H. Grinyer, The anatomy of strategic planning reconsidered, *Journal of Management Studies*, **8** (2), (1971).

4. G. W. Gershefski, Corporate models—the state of the art, *Managerial Planning*, Nov.–Dec. (1969); also *Management Science*, B303–311 (1970).

5. Peter H. Grinyer and C. Batt, Some tentative findings on corporate financial models, *Operational Research Quarterly*, **25** (1), 148–167, (1974).

6. Peter H. Grinyer and Jeff Wooller, Corporate financial modelling in the U.K. Paper presented at the *Conference on Corporate Financial Models*, at The City University, November (1973).

7. Peter H. Grinyer and Jeff Wooller, *Corporate Models Today* to be published by the Institute of Chartered Accountants, February (1975).

8. J. M. Hewkin and T. Kempner, *Is Corporate Planning Necessary?*, British Institute of Management (1968).

9. B. W. Denning and H. E. Lehr, The extent and nature of corporate long range planning in the United Kingdom.

10. B. Taylor and P. Irving, Organised planning in major U.K. companies, *Long Range Planning*, **3** (4) (1971).

11. Peter H. Grinyer and D. Norburn, Strategic planning in 21 U.K. companies, *Long Range Planning*, **7** (4) (1974).

12. Management Control Project Report No. 2, *Planning and Reporting Systems*, Centre for Business Research, Manchester Business School (1973).

13. P. G. Neild, Financial modelling in U.K. industry, *Report prepared for the European Federation of Financial Analysts Societies, VIIth Congress*, Torremolinos, Spain (1972).

14. P. G. Neild, Financial planning in British industry, *Journal of Business Policy*, **3** (1973).

15. G. W. Gershefski, Building a corporate financial model, *Harvard Business Review*, July–August (1966).

16. G. W. Gershefski, *The Development and Application of a Corporate Financial Model*, The Planning Executives Institute, Oxford, Ohio (1968).

17. J. Cooper and P. Jones, The corporate decision, *Data Processing*, March–April (1972).

18. J. B. Boulden and E. S. Buffa, Corporate models: on-line, real-time systems, *Harvard Business Review*, July–August (1970).

19. Reported in the *Financial Times*, 16 January 1973 and discussed with members of the staff of British Steel by the authors.

20. See chapter in R. Stewart, *How Computers Affect Management*, Macmillan, London (1971).

21. A. Carruthers, Company systems and models. Paper presented at the *Conference on Simulation Models for Financial and Corporate Planning*, The City University, November (1972).

22. Peter H. Grinyer and Jeff Wooller, Financial modelling packages in the U.K. Paper presented at the *Conference on Corporate Financial Models*, at The City University, November (1973).

23. Peter H. Grinyer and Jeff Wooller, A survey of software for corporate simulation modelling, *Computer Management*. Published in 3 parts. First November (1974).

24. J. L. Bowers, *Managing the Resource Allocation Process, A Study of Corporate Planning and Investment*, Harvard Business School (1970).

25. W. K. Hall, Strategic planning models: are top managers really finding them useful?, *Journal of Business Policy*, **3** (2) (1973).

28

Experience with Corporate Simulation Models— A Survey

T. H. NAYLOR AND H. SCHAULAND

Introduction

Through direct personal contact we have identified over 2000 corporations in the United States, Canada, and Europe who are either using, developing, or planning to develop some form of corporate planning model. In September of 1974 we mailed a 47-question questionnaire to 1881 corporations which were thought to be either using, developing, or planning to develop a corporate planning model. Our objectives were to ascertain (1) who is using corporate models, (2) why are they being used, (3) how are they used, (4) which resources are required, (5) which techniques and structures arc being employed, (6) what are the costs and benefits, (7) what enhancements are planned, and (8) what does the future hold for corporate modeling. A total of 346 corporations responded to the survey yielding a response rate of 19 per cent.

In 1969, George W. Gershefski conducted a similar survey of 1900 corporations of which 323 (17 per cent) responded.[1] At that time Gershefski was only able to identify 63 corporations (20 per cent of his sample) who claimed to be using or developing a corporate planning model. The results of our survey are summarized in Table 28.1.

In summary, 73 per cent of the firms in our sample were either using or developing a corporate model. Another 15 per cent were planning to develop such a model and only 12 per cent had no plans whatsoever to develop a planning model.

Of those firms which indicated they are using a corporate simulation model, 39 per cent claimed to have modeled the "total company". We

This article was originally published in *Long Range Planning*, Volume 9, No. 2, April 1976. Copyright Social Systems Inc.

TABLE 28.1. *Number and Percentage of Firms Using Corporate Simulation Models*

	Number of corporations	Percentage
Using a corporate model	213	62
Developing a corporate model	37	11
Planning to develop a corporate model	55	15
No plans to develop a corporate model	41	12
Total	346	100

suspect that this figure overstates the case and may reflect differences in interpretation as to what constitutes the "total company". In actual practice, relatively few firms have managed to integrate the financial, marketing, and production activities of the firm into a truly integrated corporate simulation model. Three notable exceptions to this rule are CIBA-GEIGY, IU International, and Anheuser-Busch. Each of these firms has successfully achieved the development and implementation of a total corporate simulation model. The CIBA-GEIGY model is probably the most sophisticated corporate simulation model in existence today. It is used extensively by corporate and division management to evaluate long range plans.

That 80 per cent of the firms which are using corporate planning models have modeled the financial structure of their business comes as no surprise to anyone. Indeed, the only surprising thing about that percentage is that it was not 100 per cent. Financial models are quite easy to develop, require a minimum amount of data, and can be validated against the firm's existing accounting structure. Some form of marketing model is being used by 41 per cent of the firms which have operational corporate planning models. This percentage reflects the fact that forecasting and econometric modeling techniques are not as well known to corporate planners as the more traditional tools of financial analysis. The production activities of the corporation have been modeled by 39 per cent of the firms which are users of corporate planning models. In most cases these production models are relatively straightforward activity analysis (cost accounting) models which reflect the cost of operating at different rates of output. However, CIBA-GEIGY and Anheuser-Busch make use of linear programming models to determine minimum cost production plans which are in turn linked to corporate financial models. The important point to realize is that while many firms (particularly the petroleum industry) make extensive use of mathematical programming models to run their refineries, relatively few of these mathematical programming models are linked into a corporate model.

Who is Using Corporate Models?

We asked those firms which are using corporate simulation models to indicate who the actual users of the model are. The results are tabulated in Table 28.2. The table shows the percentage of firms in our sample for which a particular person is receiving and using information produced by the corporate model.

TABLE 28.2. *People Receiving and Using Output from the Model*

User	Percentage
Vice-President of Finance	55
President	46
Controller	46
Executive Vice-President	32
Treasurer	30
Other Vice-President	30
Vice-President of Marketing	29
Chairman	23
Board Member	21
Vice-President of Production	21

These results are indeed encouraging for they indicate that in approximately half of the corporations which are using corporate simulation models, the right people are receiving and actually using the output generated by the models. There is abundant evidence available to support the hypothesis that it is crucial to the success of any corporate modeling project to have the active participation of top management in both the problem definition phase of the project and the implementation stage. The fact that the president and senior financial executive of half of the firms using corporate models are among the users of these models bodes well for the future of corporate modeling.

Having established which people are involved in the use of corporate models, we now turn to the industries which are using them. Table 28.3 lists the users by major industrial classification.

Next we examine the relative size of the firms in our sample which are using corporate simulation models. We use total sales as a measure of the size of these corporations.

Although over half of the firms in our sample of corporate modeling users have sales in excess of $500 m., it is interesting to note that 10 per cent of the users of corporate models have sales which are less than $100 m. With the advent of timesharing computer languages which facilitate the

TABLE 28.3. *Firms Using Corporate Models Classified by Industry*

Industry	Number of firms
Manufacturing	64
Banking and Finance	30
Regulated Industries (transportation, communications, utilities)	20
Service	15
Mining	7
Agriculture	5
Other	18
No Response	54
Total	213

development of corporate planning models, corporate modeling is now economically feasible for firms with sales less than $10m.

The geographic distribution of corporations which are employing corporate simulation models may also be of some interest. As can be seen in Table. 28.5, firms using corporate models are spread rather evenly over the Midwest, Northeast, and South. Most of the Canadian firms using corporate models are located in or near Toronto and Montreal. (Table 28.5 only reflects the location of the corporate headquarters of the firms.)

Finally, some descriptive information of the people who filled out the questionnaire may help put the results of this survey in perspective. In response to the question 'What is your relationship to your firm's corporate model?' fifty-two per cent of the respondents were users of the model, 69 per cent were model builders, and 29 per cent were sponsors of the project.

TABLE 28.4. *Sales of Firms Using Corporate Models*

	Percentage
Under $50 m.	7
$50 m. to $100 m.	3
$100 m. to $250 m.	8
$250 m. to $500 m.	16
$500 m. to $1 billion	21
Over $1 billion	38
No response	7
Total	100

TABLE 28.5. *Geographic Location of
Firms Using Corporate Models*

Location	Percentage
United States	
Midwest	18
Northeast	17
South	14
West	7
Canada	12
Europe	5
No Response	27

As for the age distribution of the respondents, 26 per cent were under 30 years old, 49 per cent were between 31 and 40 years old, 17 per cent were between 41 and 50, and 5 per cent were between 51 and 60. None of the respondents were over 60 and 3 per cent chose not to reveal their age. The respondents were found to be members of the following professional organizations—The Institute of Management Science (TIMS) 31 per cent, Operations Research Society of America (ORSA) 18 per cent, North American Society for Corporate Planning 14 per cent, Planning Executives Institute 9 per cent, Association for Computing Machinery 6 per cent, and Financial Executives Institute 3 per cent.

Why are They Used?

Financial applications dominate the list of reasons why corporations are using corporate planning models these days. Cash flow analysis, financial forecasting, balance sheet projections, financial analysis, pro forma financial reports, and profit planning are among the leading applications of corporate simulation models. Table 28.6 contains a summary list of existing applications of corporate models based on our survey results. The percentages denote the percentage of firms in our sample of users which make use of a particular application.

How are They Used?

Next we shall analyze the results of a series of questions aimed at determining how corporate models are used. Table 28.7 indicates that corporate simulation models are used most often (1) to evaluate alternative policies, (2) to provide financial projections, (3) to facilitate long-term planning, (4) to make decisions, and (5) to facilitate short-term planning.

TABLE 28.6. *Applications of Corporate Models*

Applications	Percentage
Cash flow analysis	65
Financial forecasting	65
Balance sheet projections	64
Financial analysis	60
Pro forma financial reports	55
Profit planning	53
Long-term forecasts	50
Budgeting	47
Sales forecasts	41
Investment analysis	35
Marketing planning	33
Short-term forecasts	33
New venture analysis	30
Risk analysis	27
Cost projections	27
Merger-acquisition analysis	26
Cash management	24
Price projections	23
Financial information system	22
Industry forecasts	20
Market share analysis	17
Supply forecasts	13

TABLE 28.7. *How Corporate Models are Used*

Use	Percentage
Evaluation of policy alternatives	79
Financial projections	75
Long-term planning	73
Decision making	58
Short-term planning	56
Preparation of reports	47
Corporate goal setting	46
Analysis	39
Conformation of other analysis	35

The time frame on which corporate models are based varies widely. Forty-five per cent of the corporate models in our sample are *annual* models, 5 per cent are *quarterly* models, 14 per cent are *monthly* models, and 33 per cent are some combination of the above. The average length of the planning horizon turned out to be 8 years for the firms in our sample. The frequency with which the model is used was found to vary from several times a day to annually. One third of the respondents indicated the model was used "when necessary".

TOTAL   28.8. *Frequency of Use of*
Corporate Model

Frequency of use	Percentage
Several times a day	5
Daily	7
Weekly	9
Monthly	18
Quarterly	17
Yearly	8
When necessary	33
No response	3
	100

Resource Requirements

Most of the existing corporate models (67 per cent) were developed in-house without any outside assistance from consultants, 25 per cent were developed in-house with outside consulting, and 8 per cent were purchased from an outside vendor.

Eighteen man-months was the average amount of effort required to develop models in-house without outside assistance. The average cost of these models was $82,752.

For those models which were developed in-house with the help of outside consultants, the average elapsed time required to complete the model was 10 months. The average cost for those models was $29,225.

In terms of computer hardware, 42 per cent of the models are run on in-house computing equipment, 37 per cent are run on an outside timesharing bureau, and 19 per cent run both in-house and on a timesharing bureau. Of the firms using corporate models in our sample, 62 per cent run their models in conversational mode while 56 per cent utilize the batch mode of computation. In our sample of firms using corporate models, 43 per cent ran these models on IBM computers, 5 per cent on UNIVAC, 4 per cent on Honeywell, 3 per cent on Xerox, 2 per cent on Burroughs, 1 per cent on Digital Equipment Corporation and 1 per cent on NCR.

FORTRAN is by far the most widely used computer language for programming corporate simulation models. Fifty per cent of existing models were programmed in FORTRAN, 8 per cent in COBOL, 5 per cent in PL/1, 4 per cent in APL, 2 per cent in Assembler, and 1 per cent in DYNAMO. Another 26 per cent of the models were programmed in one of over 40 planning and budgeting languages which are available to facilitate the development and programming of corporate planning models. These include languages like PROPHIT II, PSG, SIMPLAN, and ORACLE. These languages tend to be much more user (management) oriented than scientific languages such as FORTRAN, APL, and PL/I. Although firms with sales less than $100 m. typically would not employ scientific programmers, it is possible to teach financial analysts a language like SIMPLAN or ORACLE in a matter of a few hours. With the availability of planning languages on timesharing bureaus, much smaller firms now find it economically feasible to develop and use corporate models.

Although econometric modeling techniques are not used very extensively even by the largest corporations in the United States, Canada, and Europe, we found that 57 per cent of the firms using corporate models subscribed to some national econometric forecasting service. In the United States these services include Wharton, Chase Econometrics, and DRI.

Model Structure

In this section we shall summarize the features which characterize the logical structure of the corporate models which are presently in use. The vast majority (94 per cent) of these models are what management scientists call *deterministic* models. That is, they do not include any random or probabilistic variables. Models which incorporate one or more probability distributions for variables such as sales, costs, etc. are called *risk analysis* models. Only 6 per cent of the corporate models in our sample make use of risk analysis. This result is by no means surprising, since risk analysis models involve a host of statistical and computational complexities which one can avoid by using deterministic models.

Most (76 per cent) of the corporate planning models are *what if* models, i.e., models which simulate the effects of alternative managerial policies and assumptions about the firm's external environment. Only 4 per cent of the models in our sample were optimization models in which the goal was to maximize or minimize a single objective function such as profit or cost, respectively. However, 14 per cent of the models use both approaches. The remainder of the firms in our sample either did not respond to the question or use some other approach.

The average number of equations in the models in our sample was 545. The range varied from 20 equations to several thousand equations. Most of the equations are definitional equations which take the form of accounting identities. The average number of definitional equations was 445. The average number of behavioral (empirical) equations was only 86. Behavioral equations take the form of theories or hypotheses about the behavior of certain economic phenomena. They must be tested empirically and validated before they are incorporated into the model.

Twenty-nine per cent of the respondents described their models as a collection of independent single equations not related to one another. Another 36 per cent of the models were said to consist of a set of causally ordered (recursive) equations linked together over time. Only 16 per cent of these models were jointly determined (simultaneous) linear equation models. And 6 per cent were simultaneous non-linear equation models.

Forecasting Techniques

Many corporate simulation models incorporate some form of short term forecasting techniques particularly for sales and revenue projections. Table 28.9 indicates the extent to which forecasting routines have been utilized in the corporate models in our sample.

The conclusion from Table 28.9 is that the less complex forecasting techniques like simple growth rates, time trends, and moving averages are used more extensively than the more sophisticated techniques such as adaptive forecasting and Box-Jenkins techniques. Although time trends and exponential smoothing are relatively easy techniques to use and interpret, the Box-Jenkins technique is not a technique for amateurs. On the other hand, adaptive forecasting may yield forecasts which are equal to those produced by the Box-Jenkins method, but the technique is much easier to understand than Box-Jenkins.

TABLE 28.9. *Forecasting Techniques Used in Corporate Models*

Forecasting technique	Percentage
Growth rate	50
Linear time trend	40
Moving average	22
Exponential smoothing	20
Non-linear time trend	15
Adaptive forecasting	9
Box-Jenkins	4

Benefits

As can be seen in Table 28.10, the major benefits which current users of corporate models have derived include: (1) ability to explore more alternatives, (2) better quality decision making, (3) more effective planning, (4) better understanding of the business, and (5) faster decision making.

TABLE 28.10. *Benefits of Corporate Models*

Benefits	Percentage
Able to explore more alternatives	78
Better quality decision making	72
More effective planning	65
Better understanding of the business	50
Faster decision making	48
More timely information	44
More accurate forecasts	38
Cost savings	28
No benefits	4

Limitations

Opinions about the limitations of corporate models do not appear to be as intense or as well defined as opinions about the benefits of these models. The three shortcomings mentioned most often were: (1) lack of flexibility, (2) poor documentation, and (3) excessive input data requirements.

Important Features

Also included in our survey was a question about "Which methods and techniques do you need most in your model building efforts?" The answers generated by this question can provide a basis for the design of future

TABLE 28.11. *Shortcomings of Corporate Models*

Shortcomings	Percentage
Is not flexible enough	25
Poorly documented	23
Requires too much input data	23
Output format is inflexible	11
Took too long to develop	11
Running cost is too high	9
No shortcomings	9
Development cost was too high	8
Model users cannot understand model development	8
Analytic process is not understandable	5
Output is not detailed enough	4
Not user-oriented	3
Results are obviously inaccurate	3
Output is too detailed	3
Does not model what is intended	2

TABLE 28.12. *Important Features of Corporate Models*

Features	Percentage
Sensitivity analysis	52
Simple database utilization	50
Flexible report generation	50
Accounting functions	39
Simple commands	37
Risk analysis	36
Least squares estimation	33
Seasonal adjustment	30
Graphics	28
Linear programming	25
Simultaneous system of equations	25
Recursive system of equations	24
Exponential smoothing	22
Frequency distributions, histograms, or bar charts	22
Linear, quadratic, and logarithmic trend lines	19
Security	15
Analysis of variance	12
Box-Jenkins method	11
Adaptive smoothing	10
Non-linear programming and optimization	10
Two stage least squares estimation	9
Non-linear least squares estimation	8
Scatter diagrams	5
Polynomial distributed lag estimation	5

corporate models. Table 28.12 contains a list of the features which were mentioned most often.

The Politics of Corporate Model Building

Crucial to the successful implementation of any corporate simulation model is the political support of top management. Although suitable models and computer software are necessary for the success of corporate modeling, they are by no means sufficient. If the president of the company or at least the vice-president of finance is not fully committed to use of a corporate model, then the results are not likely to be taken seriously and the model will see only limited use.

To get some feeling for the political environment in the firms where corporate modeling is being used, we asked a series of attitudinal questions concerning the interest of management in the corporate modeling activities of their firm. Table 28.13 contains a summary of the attitudes expressed by

TABLE 28.13. *Attitudes of Management Towards Corporate Modeling*

	Very interested (per cent)	Somewhat interested (per cent)	Indifferent (per cent)	Not at all interested (per cent)	No response (per cent)
Top management	30	60	8	1	1
Planning	57	22	4	1	6
Finance	54	37	5	3	1
Marketing	23	39	24	8	6
Production	15	31	31	8	15
Data processing	31	24	26	9	10

the firms in our sample. The findings displayed in Table 28.13 seem to imply that the corporate models included in our survey enjoy a relatively high degree of political support on the part of management. In 60 per cent of the firms which are using corporate models top management is "somewhat interested" in corporate modeling while another 30 per cent are "very interested". On the other hand, the degree of interest in corporate modeling expressed by planning departments and finance is even higher.

Another political consideration which can prove to be important is the question of which department is responsible for the development of a corporate model. Table 28.14 indicates that although the planning department is the department which most often has the responsibility for developing the model, there is a fairly even spread among other companies which have chosen either finance, operations research, or management science as the department responsible for development of the model.

If a company has centralized corporate planning and if the director or vice-president of corporate planning reports to the president, then it is

TABLE 28.14. *Departments Responsible for Corporate Model Development*

Department responsible	Percentage
Corporate planning	27
Finance	16
Operations research	15
Other	13
Management science	12
Data processing	7
Management information systems	7
Marketing	3
	100

difficult to find any compelling reason why development of a corporate planning model should be under the auspices of any other department. It is interesting to note, however, that in a number of corporations, the control of the corporate model has been perceived as an important source of political power. As a result, one frequently finds serious conflicts and rivalries among various departments competing for control of the corporate model.

The Future of Corporate Modeling

As we indicated in the introduction, the number of firms using of developing corporate simulation models has increased from less than 100 in 1969 to over 2000 in 1975. In a field characterized by such dramatic growth in such a short period of time, one can anticipate rapid changes in both the technology and application of corporate models over the next 10 years.

Before speculating about the future of corporate modeling, it may be useful to go beyond the results of our survey and attempt to identify a number of reasons why so many firms are turning to the use of corporate planning models. The reasons people are turning to corporate planning models are almost identical to the reasons for implementing centralized corporate planning. The essence of corporate planning is risk and uncertainty. The degree of risk and uncertainty present in the external environment faced by most corporations is perhaps at an all time high. Nearly every firm in the United States is facing the following problems:

(1) Energy.
(2) Inflation.
(3) Liquidity Crunch.
(4) Shortages.
(5) Declining Productivity.
(6) Economic Uncertainty.

Faced with some combination of all of these problems, corporations are looking for new technologies such as computer simulation models which enable them to evaluate the impact of alternative policies, opportunities, and external events on the performance of the entire corporation.

If corporate simulation models are going to help management meet the challenges and the opportunities generated by the events described above, then some changes must necessarily take place in the theory and application of corporate simulation models.

First, there seems to be a definite need to make corporate simulation models more user-oriented. If top management is going to be motivated to participate in the development of a corporate model and to make use of the model once it has been completed, then both the model and the modeling language must be relatively easy to understand. Corporate models which have been written in scientific programming languages like FORTRAN and APL do not tend to be very user-oriented. A number of the new planning and budgeting languages like PROPHIT II and SIMPLAN are highly user-oriented and greatly facilitate both the conceptualization and the coding of corporate simulation models.

Second, we anticipate that the use of production planning models linked into an overall corporate simulation model will become increasingly important. The energy crisis, shortages, and problems of declining productivity, necessarily imply that greater attention will be given to production modeling than has been the case in the past.

Third, some firms may soon begin experimenting with the use of optimization techniques linked to corporate planning models. This linkage is likely to occur in two important areas. The most obvious area is in production planning where mathematical programming routines can be used to generate the minimum cost production plans associated with given demand forecast. In addition, some firms are beginning to experiment with the use of goal programming and portfolio optimization models to assist in the allocation of resources among alternative divisions or strategic business units in the firm.

Fourth, although relatively few firms have successfully integrated finance, marketing, and production into a single overall corporate simulation model, there is every indication that we will see an increasing number of firms moving in this direction. In the past, these types of linkages were very cumbersome to do in conventional scientific programming languages. It was difficult to build in adaptability and flexibility. Some of the new corporate simulation languages greatly simplify the integration of finance, marketing, and production into a single corporate simulation model.

Fifth, a number of firms such as Xerox and General Electric are now beginning to experiment with models of the external environment as well as internal corporate planning models. We see this type of modeling becoming much more important during the next decade. A series of global, economic, political, social, and environmental problems have given rise to a new breed of corporate futurists.

Sixth, we believe that both model builders and users of corporate simulation models are becoming increasingly aware of the importance of corporate politics in the successful implementation of a corporate planning model. Model builders are finally learning to speak the language of top management. Top management has learned to ask the right questions.

Reference

1. George W. Gershefski, Corporate Models—The State of the Art, *Managerial Planning*, November–December (1969) and reprinted in *Management Science*, February (1970) and *Corporate Simulation Models*, Albert N. Schrieber (ed.), Graduate School of Business, University of Washington, Seattle, Washington (1970).

29

Acquisitions in Europe

J. KITCHING

I. Why They Succeed—or Fail

The B1 survey covers the results of 407 acquisitions in 16 European countries and 32 industrial sectors. The acquiring companies were about evenly divided between U.S., British, French and German firms, and the acquisitions were both domestic and cross-border.

With the benefit of hindsight, top executives of the acquiring companies rated the results of their acquisitions in terms of whether or not they fulfilled the original objectives. Only 53 % were scored as successful, 26 % were outright failures, and the remaining 21 % were deemed "not worth doing".

Against this background of roughly 50/50 odds on a satisfactory result, the interviews zeroed in on *the reasons* some acquisitions turn out happily and others backfire. The fundamental conclusion—which runs counter to much previous thinking on the subject—is that success or failure is primarily determined not by the managerial skill applied to implementing an acquisition decision, but by the decision itself—that is, the choice of a target, and the soundness of the corporate strategy on which that choice is based.

As one chief executive summed it up, "If you've made a fundamental mistake in strategic thinking, nothing the best manager can do afterwards will put it right".

There is, of course, no ready-made strategy that will fit all companies. Each firm must define its own objectives, tailored to its financial structure and other resources (especially managerial) and to the opportunities presented to it by the European environment (market growth, competitive structure, etc.), and then work out a coherent strategy based on these objectives. This strategy should determine the choice of target

---

* *Acquisitions in Europe: Causes of Corporate Successes and Failures*, by John Kitching (price $fr400).

Reproduced with the permission of Business International S.A. 12–14 Chemin Rieu CH1208, Geneva. Issues 1.6, 73, 8.6, 73, 15.6, 73, 22, 6.73, 29, 6.73.

companies—by country, industry, size, market share, etc. And acquisition proposals that do not fit the strategy should be resisted. "The major problem", said one executive, "is always what to say 'no' to."

The key strategic factors that determine success or failure are the following:

- *Choice of country and industry.* Rates of success and failure differ appreciably from one country or industry to another. A number of elements enter into this, but most important is the (future) growth rate of the country/industry in which you are acquiring. As one executive put it, "If I have to row a boat, then put me in the middle of a stream which is moving fast too". Surprisingly few companies subject their acquisition projects to the same rigorous market-research tests that precede a new investment.
- *Degree of diversification.* The strong correlation between diversification and risk is one of the most striking results of the survey. The success rate is highest (59 %) in horizontal acquisitions, where the new parent is familiar with both the market and the technology. It drops to 53 % in vertical acquistions, i.e. of a supplier or customer, and then falls off sharply with increasing degrees of diversification, to a low of 35 % in conglomerate acquisitions (where neither the market nor the technology is familiar). Interestingly, however, the frequency of outright failure is smaller for conglomerate takeovers than for intermediate types of diversification, where either the market or the technology (but not both) are familiar—perhaps because the latter present some points of contact with the acquirer's business that lull him into a false sense of security.
- *Market share purchased.* The market share of the target company is another key to the outcome. The success rate is 73 % where the company has more than half the market, dropping to 43 % where it has less than a 5 % market share (and most of the successes in this latter group were "fill-in" horizontal acquisitions where the parent already had a sizeable market share). The crucial point is to define the target company's "relevant market" correctly: even a small acquisition can sometimes secure a dominant position in a watertight market segment, but underestimating the size of the battlefield is a sure road to defeat.
- *Relative size of the acquisiton, compared to your own company.* In this respect, boldness pays off more frequently than caution. Where the target company's sales were over a quarter of the parent's, the success rate was better than 75 %. But for the small fry with less than 1 % of the parent's sales volume, success dropped to 49 % (again, most of the successes in this group were horizontal fill-ins). The clue to the higher

success rate in large takeovers is provided in one executive's comment: "Once you have them, you *have* to manage them." Too often the smaller acquisitions do not get the necessary attention from the new parent.

● *Profitability of the target company.* Many acquirers prefer to buy unprofitable companies which can be picked up cheap, on the theory that if you've got a good management team you can make anything work. One-third of the acquisitions surveyed were earning less than 5 % before tax on capital employed, or were losing money. But the survey suggests strongly that it's better to look for profitable companies, even if this means paying a premium. The success ratio was 67 % for purchases of "high-flyers" that were earning 20 % or more on capital, but sank to 36 % successes with takeovers of the under-5 %-profit "dogs".

II. Selecting the Right Target

From the overall finding that strategic acquisition considerations are the primary determinants of success or failure it follows that the critical need is to define sharply the criteria by which candidates for acquisition will be assessed—country and industry, size and market share, profitability, etc.

Apart from these, it is essential to consider the "fit" of the target company's financial characteristics (growth patterns, cost and balance-sheet structures), and its product range, with your own. The survey revealed that the financial aspects—especially the impact of the acquisition program on the parent's debt/equity ratio and earnings-per-share growth—too often receive inadequate attention. The acquirer who fails to think through this part of the problem may unwittingly make his own company an attractive takeover target tomorrow.

The survey produced striking evidence of the enormous workload involved in implementing an acquisition strategy. Over and over again, top managers stressed in interviews the high "hidden costs" of making acquisitions, in terms of scarce management time.

Here is the track record of one of the more sophisticated acquirers interviewed:

— 100 proposals initially screened, of which
— 30 selected for desk analysis, of which
— 20 approached directly, of which
— 15 given full-scale analysis (by teams of financial, marketing and manufacturing staff, with cooperation of the seller), of which
— 8 recommended to the board, of which
— 4 finally acquired.
— Total management time expended: *2978 hours.*

These enormous hidden costs are often forgotten when figuring the return on an acquisition investment. And as one executive remarked, "Never forget that the management time required for small acquisitions is the same as for large". But some firms have managed to reduce the problem by creating an appropriate organisation for acquisitions and by developing systems and procedures for screening and evaluation of prospective targets.

Experienced acquirers interviewed made one major recommendation: create a "go/no-go" initial screen. One acquisitions director put it as follows: "The phone rings and it's someone with a suggestion for us. We've spelled out our criteria pretty well. As he talks, I review the proposition in terms of what we want to do. In five minutes I can give a go/no-go answer."

If the proposition passes this "coarse" screen, the next phase is preliminary desk analysis and internal discussion. One U.S. company, Johns-Manville, has developed a sophisticated scoring system (see Table 29.1) that rates prospective targets in terms of their market position, financial characteristics, and fit with J-M operations.

The end result of the screening process should be a clear determination whether the candidate fits with your objectives. And if it does, the screening also provides the basis for developing your negotiating strategy for the next phase.

III. The Negotiating Process

Before actual negotiations begin, would-be acquirers should have worked out the bargaining strategy or "game plan", covering such items as the presumed objectives of the seller, points to stress in wooing the prospective bride (e.g. more financial or marketing muscle to help achieve their growth ambitions), and the final price you are prepared to pay.

Once the talks get under way, the survey suggests that the key points are:

- *Uncovering the seller's wants.* Apart from the desire for a good price, these may include solving personal or inheritance tax problems, future income for the shareholders, and security for the employees. The successful negotiator must have the sensitivity to identify the seller's needs at an early stage, and the tactical shrewdness to relate them to his own objectives—giving way to individual points and pressing for others that are important to the acquirer.
- *Identifying the management's motivation and capabilities.* As negotiations progress, your aims with regard to the former owners and management group should begin to crystallize. The decision on retaining or replacing the existing management requires time, patience, and negotiating skill. But probably no other tactical decision is more critical to the succesful outcome of an acquisition (see Table 29.1).

TABLE 29.1. *J-M's "Global Evaluation"*

	Range of point scores
1. Fit	
—falls within 6 corporate growth areas	0—50
—falls within 4 European growth areas	0—20
—marketing fit	0—20
—manufacturing & mining fit	0—20
—R & D fit	0—20
2. Market position	
—image	0—10
—market growth	%/year × 2
—ratio to top competitor	× 10
	(max. 50 points)
—proprietary activity or other clear advantage	$\frac{1}{2}$ of % of business
—feedback to parent (chances)	0—10
3. Financial	
—sales:	
current	$M × 2
	(max. 40 points)
5-year forecast	$M × 2
	(max. 60 points)
—earnings before taxes:	
current	% × 2
5-year forecast	% × 2
—return on investment:	
current	% × 2
5-year forecast	% × 2
Global evaluation	(Total points)

Tentative scale: 400—500 Excellent
300—400 Good
200—300 Acceptable

● *The pre-purchase investigation.* This is primarily aimed at establishing "grey areas" in asset or liability values, evaluating management, etc. Frequently, standard checklists are used. While such a checklist cannot offset a flawed acquisition strategy, it can prevent costly oversights like that reported in one interview:

"All along we intended to replace the top management group. But we forgot to check their contracts. Would you believe it cost us $300,000 to replace them?"

- *Setting the price.* While various rules of thumb exist (e.g. multiple of earnings, premium on market price), none is really useful—except perhaps in persuading the seller to accept a lower price than you would otherwise have paid. The proper price depends on the particular acquirer's objectives and what he can do with the new subsidiary. The important thing is to work out in advance the maximum price you are prepared to pay—and back off if it's exceeded. Also consider the use of escrow or earn-out formulae as a safeguard against fictitious assets, hidden liabilities, or unrealistic profit forecasts.

- *The importance of an agreed plan.* As the negotiation approaches a conclusion, it is highly desirable to embody some type of plan or forecast in the agreement. They can serve as guidelines for subsequent management teams, and of course as the basis for earnout formulae.

    The survey shows that such a jointly prepared plan improves the chances of successful acquisition, especially if the plan focuses on the key factors for the type of business acquired (e.g. volume output, market share), and not just on generalities like profits or asset growth.

- *Unsolicited vs. agreed bids.* The preceding observation apply to agreed takeovers, where the two managements have time and opportunity to get together and to appraise each other and the business before arriving at a negotiated settlement. About 95 % of the acquisitions surveyed were agreed bids.

But what about the 5 % of unsolicited takeovers? One would expect a lower success ratio in these forcible raids, since the acquirer has less data on the target company, no chance of a pre-purchase investigation or agreed plans, and faces a potentially hostile management group in the new subsidiary.

But the survey belies this expectation. On the contrary, the success ratio was 75 % for unsolicited takeovers, vs. only 53 % for peaceful bids. The explanation apparently is that the acquirer in such cases has spotted exceptional underlying values (to it) in the target company and, once the difficulties inherent in a raid are surmounted, is able to realise the latter's full potential. This violent approach is not recommended by foreign companies acquiring in Europe, however, for evident political reasons.

IV. Solving Post-purchase Problems

The post-acquisition situation was described by one executive as "like kicking the top off an ant's nest. There they are, exposed—and running about in all directions." The new parent company's first task must be to calm the chaos, restore a sense of order, and communicate its intentions.

Apart from the myriad details, there are several key areas that must be dealt with promptly:

- *Setting up communications channels* (in both directions) is essential to reduce anxiety among acquired personnel and uncertainty as to the new parent's intentions. The techniques vary from press releases and mailed statements to customers and suppliers, to formal or informal conferences and meetings between counterparts in the two management groups. And don't forget the workers.
- *Deciding whom to keep or fire among the management group.* As already noted there is no consensus on how to handle this delicate issue, but the crucial need is for *early* decisions. And if you do let some managers go, be sure to bend over backwards to give them fair and tactful treatment. This may be expensive, but it pays off in maintaining the morale of those you keep—and assuring that future acquisition candidates will get good references on your company's past behaviour record.

What to do with the former owners/managers

The survey did not produce definitive recommendations on keeping or firing the existing management. Nevertheless, one firm conclusion can be drawn: successful acquisitions are characterised by early decisions on retaining or replacing managers; the worst possible policy is what one executive termed "ruthless indecision," allowing things to drift in uncertainty.

Most acquirers—especially multinational—normally want to put their own team in. There are two exceptions: (1) when a company is making a substantial diversification and feels incompetent to manage the strange new business itself; and (2) when the parent company does not have sufficient spare management talent to look after the new acquisition.

Though there are no hard and fast rules, acquirers do agree on some common principles with respect to:

- *Owners/managers.* If you are convinced of their motivation, leave them to run the company. Otherwise, get rid of them immediately. Put your own man—often a Finance/Information Systems top manager—in at once.
- *Professional management.* Generally, try to keep. But subject them to review, and replace as necessary. Many times you will find highly competent second-level managers who, with a bit of guidance, can be brought on to become a better management group than the preceding.

● *Minority shareholders.* U.S. acquirers in particular generally favour 100 % ownership as a matter of corporate policy. The problems that local partners create for a multinational group were cited repeatedly in the interviews, as was the desirability of removing members of the former owning family from management positions that were often sinecures.

Surprisingly, however, the survey results did not support this conventional wisdom. For one reason or another, some minority shareholdings remained in almost half the acquisitions. Moreover, the success/failure ratings revealed that full takeovers are riskier than partial ones: for U.S. acquirers, the ratio of successes was only 42 % in full takeovers, compared to 63 % when the former owners (who "know the ropes") were retained as minority shareholders, at least for a time.

● *Setting up reporting relationships.* Two basic patterns emerge from the survey:

(1) Appointment of a "merger manager" from the parent firm's top management or (for smaller acquisitions) one with divisional manager status. Spending most of his time at the acquired company's headquarters, he identifies action areas and is responsible for implementing programs, calling on parent resources for needed help.

(2) Establishment of a merger committee including senior managers of both companies. It deals with implementing the plans agreed in the pre-merger phase, and with sorting out the many post-merger problems. This organisational device is probably more appropriate when two companies are of roughly comparable size and the acquisition is an agreed one.

Smaller acquisitions typically lead to a "span of control" problem. Because the chief executive frequently negotiates the acquisitions, he is often manoeuvered into the position where the new subsidiaries report directly to him. To head off this problem, several companies make it a rule to have the relevant group or divisional head present at the negotiations. After the acquisition, the new sub reports to this level. This approach helps reduce the high failure rate among relatively small acquisitions due to lack of attention.

● *Installing the parent's planning and control systems.* Practices differ widely on how fast to introduce your own systems: some acquirers move in quickly, while others are more tolerant ("What would you rather have—reports or profits?"). The formula for success appears to be: proceed with all deliberate speed, backing off whenever the subsidiary's resistance gets too strong. The survey threw up several examples of personnel in controller's departments, etc., resigning wholesale as a result of excessive demands requiring weekend work for six months.

Where do the Synergies Lie?

Experience in both the U.S. and Europe points to the *finance function* as the most fruitful area for readily releasable synergies in integrating the new acquisition with the parent company's business. Particularly when the acquisition is a relatively large one, it can have a healthy impact on the parent's debt/equity ratio, earnings per share, and borrowing power. The opportunities to explore include: redeployment of cash or near-cash; tightening up on receivables; squeezing the hidden profits out of inventory accounts; sale and lease-back of fixed assets (or outright disposal of unwanted property); and spinning off product groups or whole divisions that do not fit into your business, or are losing money.

Realising these synergies requires specialised skills. Many companies appoint an executive whose sole function is to liquify assets found in acquired companies. Others give early priority to centralizing cash management and capital expenditure controls.

In the *marketing function*, a thorough scrutiny should be given to all potential synergies. Although individual brands may be kept separate for market-segment reasons, almost everything else has the possibility of integration—sales forces, marketing staffs, advertising and promotion efforts, physical distribution channels, and product lines. The survey produced a number of success stories in spreading heavy investments or high-cost support activities over extra sales volume, discontinuing redundant product lines, renegotiating customer trading terms, and the like.

Achieving synergies in the *production function* is generally tougher, and takes time. But there are possibilities, for example, in grouping the manufacture of similar products under one roof, closing down superfluous plants, and reviewing sourcing patterns.

Integration of *research and development* is also a long and difficult task. While the survey revealed a few cases of synergistic payoffs in this area, most companies experienced acute problems in transferring technological capacity either way. The "NIH factor" (Not Invented Here) was mentioned several times as a barrier to technology transfers. Successes seem to come easily where there have been prior licensing agreements and technical collaboration.

V. Problems of U.S. Acquirers

The higher proportion of failures in cross-border acquisitions is readily explainable by such factors as distance and communications problems (including language), conflicting cultural styles and business philosophies, and the acquirer's lack of intimate familiarity with the local market, competition and customers.

These disadvantages apply, to some extent, to European companies acquiring outside their borders, as well as to U.S. companies in Europe. But the latter face additional complicating factors, arising from:

- *National reactions to "dollar imperialism"*, typified by one French executive's complaint: "What I can't stand is American multi-nationals buying under-priced French assets with over-valued dollars." While recent currency changes have altered the calculations drastically—to the extent that the shoe now appears to be on the other foot—the underlying emotions stirred up by the "American challenge" still persist in Europe.

  Many U.S. acquirers have done an outstanding public relations job in their host countries, emphasizing their contributions in terms of jobs, above-average wages, expanded investment and new technology. But the excellent record built by the more responsible firms is tarnished by the actions of some maverick companies, whose ill-conceived and poorly executed acquisition strategies—leading to arbitary firings, closed plants, and broken businesses—have left a residue of bitterness.

  This makes other U.S. firms' task more difficult in negotiating new acquisitions. The implications for U.S. acquirers are clear: (1) the negotiating team must possess diplomatic and political, as well as business skills; (2) management must recognise that negotiations will consume many man-hours per company acquired; and (3) U.S. firms will increasingly be forced to buy low-profit or money-losing "dogs" and turn them around through injections of capital and managerial competence.

- *US accounting and exchange control regulations.* While U.S. acquisitions in Europe hitherto have been mainly for cash, the 1970 revision of U.S. accounting principles governing business combinations imposes heavy tax penalties on cash purchases as opposed to payment in equity shares (which qualifies as a "pooling" transaction). The share-exchange method may thus be dictated for relatively large acquisitions; but this may be less attractive for the seller, particularly if the U.S. firm is not on European exchanges. Exchange controls are another problem area. Because of the U.S.' capital export restrictions (OFDI) and the more recent spread of exchange controls in Europe against incoming capital, U.S. acquirers have often had to finance their acquisitions by borrowing locally—and now face higher repayment burdens as a result of European currency upvaluations.

This is bearable (though hardly welcome) if the repayment can be covered out of the new subsidiary's earnings.

- *Problems of remote management control.* For companies whose centre of decision-making power is in the U.S., the width of the Atlantic creates problems both in the evaluation/negotiation of acquisitions and in subsequently running the acquired businesses. More than one attractive acquisition opportunity has been missed because parent-company HQ was too slow in responding.

   Obviously, companies with a strong regional headquarters in Europe are less prone to this difficulty. But even for them, it is essential to have a well-defined acquisition strategy and criteria, delegating to the local management powers to commit the parent within understood guidelines. These powers can be restricted, e.g. by referring all acquisitions above $10 million for central evaluation, or only allowing the European management group to buy companies inside their own business sector.

- *Strategies developed without reference to European situations* are often at the root of unsuccessful acquisitions. It is too easy to build in assumptions, based on U.S. experience, which do not hold up in practice. As the European director of a U.S. drug company sums it up: "90% of U.S. acquisition failures in Europe are due to the incompetence in handling local problems. They get overconfident about their own abilities. They underestimate the competitors. They irritate their own managements and the labour force. And they don't bother to get to know the legal and institutional structure of the country. . . ."

Despite such perils—and the prospect of further complications in future, for example from the EEC's increasingly rough antitrust policy and its fledgling industrial policy—it's a safe bet that U.S. companies will continue to brave the hazards of acquisitions in Europe, to secure a piece of the action in one of the world's most important, and fastest-growing, markets.

30

Seeking New Sources of Earnings*

H. BUCKNER

This paper is based upon a number of research studies conducted within the Creative Corporate Planning Programme of Planning Research & Systems Limited. This is a subscription service designed to "extend the reach" of planners in industry by providing planning approaches and business data. The specific research referred to in the paper was based on personal interviews with managing directors, financial directors and corporate planners of companies featured in "Management Today's" top 200 growth league. This league table shows the fastest growing companies

---

NEW SOURCES OF EARNINGS

Definition

The term "new sources of earnings" has been used as it represented a more meaningful expression than the term "diversification". Diversification does not mean the same thing to different people. To some it implies that moves are unrelated to the current business, while in this definition, the moves, although separate, may be highly related.

New sources of earnings cover investment in and generation of new lines of business which include:

All forms of acquisition, joint ventures, mergers.

Internal development in new business areas.

Internal developments in existing business areas that effectively form or could form an independent operation (for example, totally new products sold to current customers).

New sources of earnings moves do *not* include greater sales penetration for existing products (unless to a radically different market) and extensions of the range of current products to the current market.

This article was originally published in *The Corporate Planner's Yearbook*, D. E. Hussey (Editor), Pergamon 1974. *Copyright Planning Research and Systems Limited.

over a 10-year period, based on percentage change in share price plus gross dividends issued. Thus it provides a measure, although imperfect, of earnings per share growth. The sample frame—Management Today's top 200 growth companies—provides a wide range of growth rates: the bottom companies are, when corrected for inflation, actually declining.

1. The Need for New Earnings

One startling factor emerged from this study of 200 companies. With a small number of notable exceptions, the only companies which had grown in real terms over the last 10 years were those that had made substantial* moves to develop new sources of earnings. Those that had remained in their existing business had either stood still or declined.

The diversifiers' profits grew by an average of 178% with almost all beating inflation. In contrast the profits of those companies who did not take positive steps to develop new business grew by an average of only 77% in total over the 10 years with only one-quarter of respondent companies beating inflation. To place the sample above in perspective, the average profits of United Kingdom quoted manufacturing companies between 1960 and 1968 actually declined.

It can be seen that the odds are against companies who do not develop new sources of earnings. They do not develop the widespread of "in demand" activities which give security against down-turns in any one sector. Nor can they be opportunistic in exploiting the best sectors, letting the temporarily poor sectors ride, and cutting the worst.

Thus, while many in business continue to hold the view that real growth is achieved by "cobblers sticking to their lasts", the evidence over a large number of companies is the opposite.

2. Management Want

The companies that grew faster than average showed no common industry, technology or market background. They ranged from shipping companies, plant equipment distribution companies, electronics firms and builders to hotel operators. In many instances other companies in the same industry had not grown. However, all had one factor in common. Their managements *wanted* to grow. Few companies started a new earnings programme because their current business area was declining. For most the reasons were to exploit skills, balance interests or simply grow aggressively as is shown in Table 30.1.

---

* Defined as over 30% of profits in 1970 being derived from businesses in which the company did not participate in 1960.

TABLE 30.1. *Reasons for Seeking New Sources of Earnings*
(Substantial diversifiers only)

	Percent of respondent companies
To utilise and exploit skills	27
To achieve balanced interests	25
To achieve aggressive growth	23
Offset current business decline	10
Utilise capacity	10
Correct deficiency in product/market range	5
	100

Source: New Sources of Earnings, Report 4, Creative Corporate Planning Programme. Planning Research & Systems Limited.

3. Number of Moves Made

The substantial diversifier companies studied made on average a total of sixteen moves during the period 1960–70. However, one or two large moves accounted for a substantial proportion of the total contribution made by new earnings. On average, over 60% of the total new earnings profit came from the largest move, and over 80% from the two largest moves. Thus one or two large moves were responsible for the new earnings growth in the companies interviewed. This is shown in Table 30.2.

The majority of companies stated that they recognised the potential success of these large moves in advance and had deliberately set out to exploit the real potential which they saw as being open to them. In retrospect many regretted making the, on average, fourteen other moves that accounted for under 20% of profit.

TABLE 30.2. *Average Number of New Moves Made and Profit
Contribution from Large Moves*
(Substantial diversifiers only)

Average number of new moves made per company	Average percentage contribution to new earnings profit from	
	Single largest move	Two largest moves
16	61	83

Source: as for Table 30.1.

The key implication of the above is that a new sources of earnings programme should be planned on a relatively large scale. Unless this is done, time and effort is dissipated on a progressive number of small moves which are unlikely to make a significant impact on profits. Respondents emphasised that there are heavy costs involved in initiating a new earnings programme. Nearly 40 % of the respondents had spent more than £5000 evaluating several alternatives to each move, excluding executive time, and 70 % had reported cost over-runs on internal developments ranging from 20 % to over 200 %. Only large moves or those seen to be potentially large moves are capable of recovering the high costs involved. Additionally, where acquisitions are involved, small moves are unlikely to provide adequate management, and making good the shortage of management skills is often an insuperable problem to the acquirer. It would appear that when large new earnings moves are made that the method used was not crucial: both internal development and acquisition were equally successful. Of the large moves made almost one-half were internal developments and one-half acquisitions. The fact that internal development features so prominently may be thought as surprising since it is often stated that planners are over-concerned with acquisitions and neglect the possibility of major internal developments. There was no correlation between the total number of moves made by a company and the profitability of the new earnings programme.

4. Time to Reach "True" Profitability

Those companies who had achieved significant growth did not do so as a result of new sources of earnings moves made over a short period. All started prior to 1965 and had taken from 5 to 10 years to achieve a major shift in emphasis from their original business. Equally whether a move was an internal development or an acquisition it took time to reach the expected or "true" level of profitability. Typically, internal developments took $3-4$ years or more, versus 2 years for acquisition. The profitability of new moves is shown in Table 30.3.

TABLE 30.3. *Emergence of True Profitability of New Moves*
(Substantial diversifiers only)

	Percentage of total respondents				
	1 year	2 years	3 years	4 years	Total
Internal development	9	25	33	33	100
Acquisition	15	55	7	23	100

Source: as for Table 30.1.

It can be seen in Table 30.3 that acquisitions reached "true" profitability in the second or fourth year. This was found to depend upon the time taken to assume control of the acquisition. Many companies initially left their acquisitions to develop on their own only to find that they had to step in and ensure that management action was taking place correctly. Thus the peak after 4 years is due to a number of parent companies taking a deeper management interest in their acquisitions after an initial period of indifferent results. Many acquirers found that the acquired company's profits declined in the first year of acquisition.

The substantial diversifier companies where new earnings represented 30% of 1970 sales appear to have made new moves faster than other companies. On average, it took 14 months between the initiation of an idea and final accomplishment, compared to 20 months for the remainder. In addition, they appear to react more quickly in closing a move, taking an average of 5 months between the first action and final accomplishment compared with 10 months for all others.

5. Divestment of New Earnings Moves

Some 80% of the total moves made by respondent companies were in business fields related to the existing business. The relationship was most frequently seen as market, technology and management skill. However, where moves were made in an unrelated business field (for example, a dairy respondent made moves into ice-cream, motor businesses, tyres and agricultural implements), over half the moves were subsequently sold after being held for an average of some 2 to 3 years. The figures for the number of moves sold excluded, in the case of acquisitions, divestments which were planned in advance of actual purchase. In contrast, where moves were made in a related business field, only 20% of moves were subsequently sold. Overall, nearly 30% of total moves made over the 10-year period were subsequently sold (Table 30.4).

An analysis of total moves made showed that 62% were by acquisition and 38% by internal development, but of those that were sold, nearly 90%

TABLE 30.4. *Direction of New Moves*

	Percentage of moves		
	Related	Unrelated	
Total moves	80	20	100
Percentage subsequently sold	20	53	30

Source: as for Table 30.1.

were acquisitions. The most frequently mentioned reasons for selling were low profitability, changes in policy or market strategy, or incompatibility with the company's field or skills (Table 30.5).

TABLE 30.5. *Reasons for Disposal of New Moves*

	Ranking
Low profitability	23
Change of company policy	17
Incompatibility with company's business field/skills	12
Change in market strategy	12
Rationalisation	12
Government decree	6
Release management resources for main business	6
Customer antagonism	6
Insufficient size to warrant further effort	6

Source: as for Table 30.1.

The data strengthens the conviction that planners should show a willingness to cut off unprofitable moves and redirect resources and efforts to the more profitable areas. The critical decision time is 2–3 years after a move has been made. It has already been reported that it takes 2 years before the true profitability emerges.

6. Relationship of New Moves to Existing Business

Research was undertaken to investigate the common themes used by successful companies in their new earnings programmes, and to relate the types of skill/resource match made to difficulty of attainment. The most common type of match sought was common marketing, followed by R. & D. and raw materials or products. Management and production skills featured less prominently.

It emerged clearly that the chances of success are much greater when the move is related to the existing business since obviously it trades on the company's strengths, skills and knowledge. As noted above, if moves are made in an unrelated business field, at least half are likely to be sold subsequently, and it would appear that if it is an acquisition in an unrelated field, the chances of divestment are even greater.

7. Problems with Acquisitions

The broad conclusions from the findings of this study concerning both fast and slow growth companies raise serious doubts on the validity of the vast majority of all acquisition activity encountered in the research. The major conclusion which clearly emerges from the research findings is that most companies using acquisition in their search for growth have failed and that company managements need to give priority to a reassessment of their acquisition policies.

The research showed that most acquisitions were poorly conceived in terms of earnings per share growth, and could only be considered successful in terms of sheer size agglomeration. It was concluded that there was no difference between acquisition and internal growth as a method of generating earnings per share growth, but that acquisition failure was due more to weaknesses in companies' acquisition policies, than a fundamental weakness in the method itself.

The study shows clearly that companies should consider acquisitions as only one of a number of alternatives for achieving their growth objectives, and that a formal planned approach is a necessary prerequisite for success.

The following summarises the more detailed major conclusions drawn from the research findings:*

1. Taken over a wide range of companies, acquisitions do not produce growth rates in earnings per share which exceed those achieved by companies who are growing internally.
2. Many companies had paid an unrealistically high price for their acquisitions. This particularly relates to contested bids or those which attracted a rival bidder. In these situations managements often became involved in an auction-bidding situation where emotional considerations took precedence over financial considerations.
3. The majority of acquisitions made have slowed the earnings per share growth rates of fast-growth companies, and accelerated those of slow-growth companies. That is, because they are poorly conceived, most acquisitions move their parent company towards average performance.
4. Acquisitions have an emotional effect on the stock market. In contrast to 3 above, the stock market improves the rating of fast-growth companies even further when acquisitions are made. This emotional effect tends to magnify the "share price collapse" of these companies when the true effect of their policies emerges.
5. Size for its own sake appears to be the most frequent single motivation for acquisitions.

A life-cycle of acquisition activity could be seen in some respondents companies. Starting as a small growth company, an organisation can through acquisition increase its growth in earnings per share. However, after a time a number of factors (such as size, increasing complexity,

* *Success Factors in Acquisitions*, Report 8, Creative Corporate Planning Programme. Planning Research & Systems Limited.

of new earnings development: but also in many cases this was highly successful. The success of some internal developments clearly caused problems, in that difficulty was experienced in maintaining a balance in the claims on scarce resources between the new earnings and existing products. For example, greater than anticipated growth caused severe production bottle-necks. The time taken for internal developments to come to profitable fruition was, in many instances, underestimated. This miscalculation placed a strain on financial resources, which was often severe: some cost over-runs of up to 200 % were recorded in the research. The important implications of this finding for planners is not necessarily the question "can it be done internally?" but "is there time?".

Internal development is clearly very successful when the opportunity is closely related to the present business, and sufficient time and financial resources are available for development. Alternatively licencing can be an effective and more speedy alternative; providing it is combined with a high degree of product development to reduce over-dependence on the originator in future years. Interestingly, many of the less successful companies had acquired competitors when they could probably have increased their market share as or more effectively by internal development.

The comments made by respondents involved in acquisition programmes reflected the findings of the research already reported. They centred around the need to make a more detailed company evaluation, either in the search for likely candidates, or when they present themselves; on the importance of ensuring the right skill/strength match is made; and the weighting that should be given to a direct exploitable link with the current business. All respondents in one form or another mentioned management as a problem once an acquisition had been made. The important implication for planners is that in many cases the top-priority candidates in any good business area will be very few. They are likely to be expensive, and these companies would have already received many approaches. As a result, it is necessary in some instances to resort to second-choice candidates, which usually have some weakness. The need for the acquiring company to take a direct operational part to correct the weakness is often under-estimated, and as a result the main business can be endangered. However, acquisitions do represent a speedy form of market entry, make an immediate contribution to profits and by acquiring an on-going business effectively reduce the risks on entering a new business.

10. Recommended Approach

There are only two ways of identifying new earnings opportunities. The method most often used by industry is to solicit *ad hoc* ideas from all sources including internal committees and external advisors. The success record of this method is low for the following reasons:

1. No one agrees unless the move is small.
2. The alternatives are not measured.
3. The method is not comprehensive and, therefore, there is a tendency to wait and see what other alternatives occur.

A fully comprehensive approach overcomes these problems by allowing ideas to be generated and measured one against the other so that selection can be undertaken with a clear idea of the alternatives.

Comprehensive and ordered approaches are usually based on three methods:

1. The skills and strengths of a company can be used to lead it into new areas.
2. A broad definition of a field is chosen which looks particularly attractive (or fashionable): for example, the recent "crazes" for hotels, computer service bureaux and so forth.
3. A research and development programme, in which some original new idea with a large market potential is developed: for example, Xerox.

The first of the comprehensive methods emerged from the research as being the best. Thus, the recommended approach to seeking new sources of earnings is to use corporate capabilities and skills to systematically point out new business fields and opportunities and also help to ensure that the right skill/strength match is obtained.

Growth companies systematically examined all possible growth businesses to see where relationships with their present operations existed. The steps followed are set out below:

1. Identify business areas.
2. Develop information on market size and growth.
3. Eliminate obvious misfits.
4. Eliminate small low growth businesses.
5. Develop detailed information on the remainder.
6. Place a priority order on the resulting areas.

acquisitions for their own sake, more opportunities than the capacity of management to develop them and lack of suitable or sizeable acquisition candidates) all combine to reduce the rate of growth and the company's growth performance plateaus out. These findings clearly show that explosive growth through acquisition alone is unlikely to be maintained over a period of years. Thus, unless companies clearly see what business advantage is being derived from their acquisitions, they are likely to follow this "S"-shaped growth curve.

Table 30.6 shows that the pre- and post-acquisition percentage change in median performance for key operating variables for the alternative planning methods.

TABLE 30.6. *Method of Search and Growth Performance*

| | Method of planning | |
Performance variables	Informal	Formal
Sales growth	− 3.7	+ 2.6
Earnings per share	+ 3.1	+ 15.0
Earnings on total capital	− 7.6	+ 11.8
Share price growth	− 1.0	+ 0.3

Source: H. Igor Ansoff, *20 Years of Acquisition Behaviour.*

These findings demonstrate that companies who formally planned their acquisition programmes out-performed informal planners, whatever yardstick of performance is taken. The difference in performance was most marked in the critical test of growth in earnings per share. The reasons why formal planning methods are more successful than informal methods can be summarised as follows:

Comprehensive search in directed industries or types of technology ensures that the best opportunities are identified.

Measured evaluation of alternatives is more likely to obtain commitment to action.

Formal methods ensure that the right skill/resource match is made and that the acquisition is both compatible and recognisably related to the present business.

A formal approach ensures that the acquisition programme is integrated with the company's strategic objectives.

9. Major Post-entry Problems and Lessons Learnt

The comments made by respondents where the new moves took the forms of internal development, re-enforced that this was the slowest form